ERPA International Congresses on Education (ERPA 2018)

SHS Web of Conferences Volume 48 (2018)

Istanbul, Turkey
28 June - 1 July 2018

Editors:

Ercan Masal
Ismail Onder
Huseyin Caliskan
Senol Besoluk

ISBN: 978-1-5108-7064-2

Printed from e-media with permission by:

Curran Associates, Inc.
57 Morehouse Lane
Red Hook, NY 12571

proceedings.com

Some format issues inherent in the e-media version may also appear in this print version.

Printed by Curran Associates, Inc. (2018)

For additional information, please contact EDP Sciences – Web of Conferences at the address below.

EDP Sciences – Web of Conferences
17, Avenue du Hoggar
Parc d'Activité de Courtabœuf
BP 112
F-91944 Les Ulis Cedex A
France

Phone: +33 (0) 1 69 18 75 75
Fax: +33 (0) 1 69 28 84 91

contact-edps@webofconferences.org

Additional copies of this publication are available from:

Curran Associates, Inc.
57 Morehouse Lane
Red Hook, NY 12571 USA
Phone: 845-758-0400
Fax: 845-758-2633
Email: curran@proceedings.com
Web: www.proceedings.com

TABLE OF CONTENTS

 https://doi.org/10.1051/shsconf/20184800001

Preface

It is the great honor for us to edit this special issue of SHS Web of Conferences for the selected proceedings presented in the ERPA International Congresses on Education 2018 which was held in İstanbul/Turkey from 28 June to 1 July 2018. Each paper submitted to the conference has been peer reviewed by the reviewers and at the end of the review process, a total of 72 high quality papers were selected and accepted for this publication. Special thanks are given to all the reviewers, the members of the Scientific Committee and Organizing committee.

We hope that you enjoy reading the papers of this issue.

Yours faithfully,

Editors
Dr. Ercan Masal
Dr. İsmail Önder
Dr. Hüseyin Çalışkan
Dr. Şenol Beşoluk

 https://doi.org/10.1051/shsconf/20184801001

Teaching a Second Foreign Language in the Russian School

Alfia Gazizova[1,*], *Nailya* Mingazova[2], and *Vitaly* Subich[2]

[1] Kazan National Research Technical University named after A.N. Tupolev - KAI, Russia, 420111, Kazan, K.Marx St., 10
[2] Kazan Federal University, Russia, 420008, *Kazan,* Kremlevskaya str., 18

Abstract. Development of international cooperation which led to the inclusion of the second foreign language into the compulsory discipline list, according to the Federal Standards of Basic Education of the Russian Federation, raises the questions of radical changes, directions and conditions of teaching foreign languages which influence the formation of multilingual personality. The paper is aimed at looking into the peculiarities and problems of teaching a second foreign language in the Russian school in terms of goal-setting and the organization of educational process. The study is based on the experience of 22 schools in the Republic of Tatarstan, having been realized through investigating academic papers, official documents, contemplation of the educational process, etc. The results of the study reflect the organizational and methodological issues of foreign language teaching in the Republic (starting time of studying, duration of learning a foreign language, teaching staff, means of teaching, methodological basis, etc.) as well as the demand for learning European and oriental languages. The authors point out the relevance of better conditions for teaching a second foreign language (creating of organizational models, definition of the course length, etc.) and defining the objectives, connected with the contents of the academic discipline, efficiency of teaching a foreign language and the professional qualities of the teacher, his competence.

1 Introduction

1.1 The problem of teaching a second foreign language in the Russian school

Development of international cooperation and communication in the modern world leads to the necessity of a good command of a few foreign languages, basing on international requirements of the language competences, which logically actualizes the issues of qualitative transformations of the directions, approaches and conditions in foreign language teaching.

* Corresponding author: Alfgazva@mail.ru

The growing interest to the problem in the Russian education system is caused by the definitions of what the second foreign language's status is (SFL). According to articles 11.1, 18.3.1. of the Federal State Educational Standard of Basic Education (FSESBE), SFL has been included in the list of subjects under the title "Philology" along with "Foreign Language". Dealing with its school curriculum, an educational body may include SFL into the plan as a compulsory subject starting from the 5th grade in the event of the parents' request and the school's ability to provide necessary conditions. In general, it reflects real progress in the direction of polycultural education and formation of multilingual personality; the students develop linguistic faculties, verbal intellect, language reflexion, analytical thinking, memory, language intuition, other cognitive faculties. Bilingual competence is transformed into megalinguistic competence, which is characterized by the higher level of abstraction [1].

1.2 Objectives and organization of SFL school teaching

Analysis of official documents reveals that formulation of aims and objectives stated by the FSESBE of the second generation is of little difference from the first generation FSESBE. According to it, the main aim of the modern foreign language class is communicative competence which combines linguistic and sociocultural competences, giving birth to the personal active approach to the organization of the teaching process.

The English language, being the means of intercultural communication and the language of the community which has a significant economic and political influence in the world, is taught as the first foreign language (FFL). As for SFL, the students may choose between a Roman language (Spanish, French) and German, sometimes an oriental language such as Arabic, Turkic or Chinese, etc.

These relations between languages in favour of English exist in many world countries. At the same time there is a growing tendency to learn SFL. This tendency in the modern world is important since it reflects the real need in knowing foreign languages, other social cultures and types of political systems, that is why it develops the competences connected with intercultural communication. In such conditions, the problem of SFL teaching associated with the awareness of language material and linguistic peculiarities is gaining specific relevance, introducing significant changes to the language educational policy.

Introduction of SFL into the school should mean that the education is becoming multilingual: mother tongue, first foreign language and second foreign language combine to form the unique linguistic phenomenon, which is called artificial triglossia. According to N.V.Baryshnikov, [2], triglossia is characterized by imperfect command of two foreign languages with the communicative nature of triglossia being changed throughout FFL and SFL acquisition. Triglossia, the part of modern reality, compels to deal with the question of SFL teaching objectives not in isolation, but being aware of the existing trilingualism, which is, in fact, a daunting task as it is the objectives which influence the manner of all major components of the teaching process.

National pedagogical literature is represented by a relatively significant number of works in which attempts are made to state the aims and objectives of SFL school teaching (N.V. Baryshnikov, I.L. Bim, N.D. Galskova, L.G. Denisova, S.F. Shatilov, etc.). The definitions, offered by the scholars, reflect pragmatic, pedagogical aspects of teaching a foreign language and their sociocultural orientation as well as certain requirements to the level of students' competence within a wide variety of communicative activities. They are justified since they bear in mind the factor of linguistic experience adopted prior to the given stage, however they are not fully adequate owing to the fact that the experts do not pay attention to the difference in teaching the basic levels of FFL and SFL (in a variety of aspects), which, in fact, means that SFL should have its own basic level of communicative and other competences.

Another issue of paramount importance in teaching SFL is connected with the organization of the educational process. Taking in account the introduction and realization of FSESBE, this task is by no means an easy one; it is connected with a series of organizational and methodological problems, located both on theoretical and practical (even more relevant) levels alike, which are in need of being settled. To these may relate: which exactly SFL should be chosen for learning, what are the conditions of its instruction (availability of teaching staff, equipped classes, various means of teaching, etc.), the primary (and secondary) objectives and the core parameters for the course. The answers to these questions determine the design of the appropriate organizational models and methods of teaching.

2 Purpose and methods

The paper is aimed at looking into the peculiarities and problems of teaching a second foreign language in the Russian school in terms of goal-setting and the organization of educational process on the basis of works on the problems of SFL introduction into the Russian schools (V.A.Lapidus, N.V. Baryshnikov, N.D. Galskova, N.I. Ghez, L.N.Yakovleva, E.N.Solovtsova, L.B.Cheptsova and others), statistics, legal documents authorized by the Ministries of Science and Education of the Russian Federation and the Republic of Tatarstan, direct scrutiny over the educational process. The analysis of the organization peculiarities of teaching SFL has been conducted in 22 Tatarstan schools which are realizing the project comprising 2500 students: 6 schools with German as SFL, 6 schools with Turkic, 5 Chinese schools, 5 French schools, 2 English schools (FFL is either French or German), and 3 schools where the students are provided with Spanish, Arabic or Hebrew.

3 Results

The results of the investigation show that the conditions of SFL learning in the schools considered are by all means different. Starting points of learning SFL and course duration vary in relation to the type of school. Some of the schools start SFL teaching from the 6th or 7th grade (for the syllabi where FFL is learned from the 5th grade) while other schools introduce SFL only in the senior school (10th-11th grades); there are as well cases when SFL is introduced in the 2nd or 3rd grade as part of the extension group. More extended learning of SFL (7th – 11th grades) is realized mainly in the 5 boarding lyceums (with the Turkic language) and one gymnasium which implemented teaching of the German language.

The demand for the second language learning in Tatarstan Republic is of two kinds: on the one hand, a preference for the European languages, and on the other hand, a desire for learning oriental languages, while noting the language parity. The interest in learning the languages of the world's most developed countries is explained by the desire of parents or students to follow their interests for mastering one of the European languages, which is considered to be prestigious. As for referring to the oriental languages in our republic, it is connected to social and economic peculiarities of the region, the priority international relationship with Asiatic countries, educational possibilities, in the sphere of professional education in particular (the existence of particular fields of study in Tatarstan educational institutions). Traditionally, Tatarstan Republic has close relations with Turkey, China, etc. There are a lot of joint enterprises, projects, and investment programmes. All these are reflected in the educational policy: the choice of learning an oriental language.

The educational situation in a particular school is a significant factor while introducing a second language: availability/lack of relevant teaching aids, qualified FL pedagogical staff, their own FL teaching traditions. Moreover, "Foreign languages in the Republic of Tatarstan are mastered in the conditions of the parallel studying of the native languages – Russian and Tatar. This should be taken into account when organizing the educational process to create the whole valuable language personality" [3].

Explaining to parents the preference for learning this or that foreign language in our region and in a particular school plays a major role [4, p.37]. It is obvious that parents should be informed of the educational services in FL teaching provided by the school (FFL or SFL, learning duration, FL learning results, further SFL learning perspectives while continuing studies in higher education, etc.). Informing parents of the achievements of the teachers speaking two FL and having a success in teaching FFL (their students take part in Olympiads and enter universities, etc.), presenting students' achievements in learning a particular FL and displaying students' choice of a language (artistic events) are of great importance and serve as the basis for introducing SFL in a particular school. It would be useful to inform parents that SFL learning process is much easier and more successful on the basis of mastered FFL. Intensive and successful training contributes to improving the educational process and students' motivation. FL 3 is being introduced in many European countries, with children acquiring it easily and parents supporting this idea enthusiastically.

There are certain problems in the republic in this field such as shortage or lack of qualified teaching staff. SFL choice is a difficult task for students because the teachers with two FL skills have changed the qualification or teach only English and do not want to develop SFL course due to some reasons. Issues relating to the teaching organization and conditions for different types of schools (such as the starting point of learning SFL, duration and intensity of training, total course hours, etc.) are not sufficiently developed. Lack of sufficient teaching methodology in secondary schools is among the main problems. There are no special textbooks for the full SFL learning course. Sometimes the textbooks for foreigners published in other countries and compiled according to the students' native language norms are used. Respectively, their FFL knowledge and skills that can be used while learning SFL and make FFL learning process much easier are not taken into consideration, as Titova points out in her research [5].

As Chiknaverova, Gazizova and Trofimova stated, "The first and second foreign language programs are similar in form and content, with the exception of hours allocated. Hence, some aspects under study remain outside curriculum. The differences also concern control and assessment as far as the time needed to complete a task, and the volume of teaching material" [6].

The peculiarities of SFL teaching (such as the later beginning of SFL learning, age factor, more restricted training time, etc.) that determine the setting of objectives, content and structure of the teaching methodology and the principles of students' educational process organization are not mostly taken into consideration. Among the positive results is the program "Arabic for the 5th – 11th grade schoolchildren of secondary schools and gymnasiums" approved by the Republic of Tatarstan Ministry of Education and Science in 2010. On its basis the Arabic textbooks for the 5th, 6th, 7th and 8th grades have been published and introduced in the Republic of Tatarstan schools and in other regions of the Russian Federation [7]. As Subich, Mingazova, Zakirov and Al-foadi R.A. noted, "The improvement of Arabic teaching is achieved by the unification of the educational materials for secondary schools" [8].

4 Discussion

The data of the research reveals the necessity of improving SFL teaching organization conditions (such as defining organization models, learning hours, staff issues, etc.) and priority-setting that defines the selective content and effective methods of SFL teaching. According to the experts, FL teaching has to be based on learners' background linguistic and cultural knowledge and skills such as: implementing language training (individually or in pairs/groups); observing, comparing, contrasting, analyzing, arguing; recognizing linguistic phenomena and meaningful notions (international words, proper names, articles, sentence structure, auxiliary words and expressions, etc.); planning your speech, mastering listening skills, expressing your opinion; using the dictionary, guessing the meaning of new words in relation to word formation and context, extracting information [9].

The basic principles of effective SFL teaching methods in schools take into account the following:

a) positive transfer of knowledge and skills from the native language and FFL and interference prevention;

b) activation of learners' linguistic experience, acquired as a result of native and FFL learning;

c) learners' socio-cultural experience;

d) motivation to learning, contrasting new languages and cultures;

e) bipolar and tripolar comparison of languages and cultures;

f) the reflection of integration processes currently occurring in the international community in the teaching content;

g) systematic and consistent cross-discipline ties formation.

According to the abovementioned, SFL acquisition brings about two logical conditions – the interference problem and the possibility of positive transition. Interference, which occurs as the negative impact of the mother tongue and FFL on SFL, penetrates all the linguistic levels (phonetic, lexical, grammatical) but in a different way and cannot but influence the speech activity in SFL and non-verbal behavior [10].

Positive impact of the mother tongue on FFL and SFL is called positive transition or transference. "The transition in which the influencing language does not cause any norm violations in the language which is studied, but rather stimulates its features"[11] can take place on different levels:

– on the level of verbal cognitive activity: the more languages a person speaks, the more developed are his verbal cognitive skills: short-term memory, visual and audial perception, strategies of choosing language means, their combining, and production in speaking and writing;

– on language level: similar linguistic phenomena in the mother tongue and FFL are transferred by the learners into SFL and contribute to its acquisition;

– on the level of educational skills, which are developed when studying FFL;

– on sociocultural level: sociocultural knowledge, behavioral skills may be the objects of transference, especially in the case of similar European cultures.

As M.V. Shcherbakova stated [10], familiarization of learners with the language means of SFL requires contrastive approach, which assists in understanding similarities among languages (native, FFL, SFL) as well as discrepancies. Thus, it is of paramount importance to encourage learners to compare/contrast the language means of the languages in contact in all the cases when it will help prevent interference and initiate positive transition.

The effective usage of these approaches in SFL teaching is connected with teachers' professionalism, expertise, and qualification, including the ability to prepare for lessons, choose appropriate activities and materials basing on the planned result, analyze mistakes and shortcomings of the work done, communicate and interact with students, provide the educational support aimed at developing learners' independence, self-confidence and desire to be a success. Respectively, the key skill for FL teachers is the desire for self-development and self-improvement in the sphere of their subject activity and educational process organization [12; 4].

Teachers' mega linguistic competence, including foreign language professional and communicative competence [13], that help them solve the existing tasks more effectively is of particular importance. Among the tasks are the following: to achieve the connection between extra linguistic content and formal structures of the language studied, foresee the interference, find the final ways of overcoming it and provide with the positive transfer of background knowledge and skills.

5 Conclusion

Currently, the introduction of SFL is a multiaspect and complex task which is connected with the definition of priority objectives of teaching SFL at a comprehensive school on the basis of which appropriate selection of practical syllabus, methods of teaching, and the organization of education (organizational models, duration of courses, teaching staff matters, etc.) are established.

Not all Russian schools, including our republic's, are ready to introduce second language teaching at the appropriate level and develop the basis for a step-by-step approach to the teaching process. So, further research and discussions of the problem analyzed at the round-table meetings, scientific-methodological and learning seminars are still up to date and in demand at the current stage of the education development.

References

1. L.V. Opolonetc. Nekotoryey osobennosti obucheniya vtoromu inostrannomu yazyku, Nauchno-metodicheskiy elecronniy zhurnal «Kontcept», V. 5, pp. 172–176. (2016). URL: http://e-koncept.ru/2016/56185.htm [Accessed 29 January 2018]
2. N.V. Baryshnikov Metodika obucheniya vtoromu inostrannomu yazyku v shkole, M.: Prosvescheniye, 159 p.(2003)
3. N.G. Mingazova, V.G. Subich, R.R. Zakirov Mastering English as a second language via the parallels with the native language (using project work), Journal of Language and Literature, ISSN: 2078-0303, V. 7 (1), February, pp. 176-180. (2016)
4. Obucheniye angliyskomu yazyku v rossiyskikh shkolakh; Materialy IV vserosiyskogo seminara, Doklady I vystupleniya, Obninsk; Titul, 192 p. (2001).
5. O.A. Titova. Problemy obucheniya nemetckomu yazyku kak vtoromu inostrannomu v usloviyakh sovremennogo pedagogicheskogo vuza, Izvestiya Tulskogo gosudarstvennogo universiteta. Gumanitarniye nauki, V. 1, P. 172-176. (2008)
6. K. Chiknaverova, A. Gazizova, G.Trofimova G. The system of foreign language teaching at the master`s level in Russia, New Trends and Issues Proceedings on Humanities and Social Sciences. [Online], 4(1), pp. 639-647. (2017). Available at: www.prosoc.eu
7. R.R. Zakirov, N.G. Mingazova. Mezhtcivilizatcionniy dialog v Respublike Tatarstan (na primere prepodavaniya arabskogo yazyka), Evraziyskiy juridicheskiy zhurnal, Vol. 2 (105), pp. 284-286. (2017)
8. V.G. Subich, N.G. Mingazova, R.R. Zakirov, R.A. Al-foadi. Improvement Strategies of Teaching the Arabic Language in The Tatarstan Schools, Modern Journal of Language Teaching Methods (MJLTM). Iran. (2017)

9. N.S. Ivanova. Kulturovedcheskiy podhod k obucheniyu studentov yazykovogo vuza yaponskomu yazyku kak vtoromu inostrannomu: dissertatciya ... kandidata pedagogichrskikh nauk: 13.00.02 Sankt-Peterburg, 276 p. (2006)
10. M.V. Shcherbakova. Osobennosti obucheniya vtoromu inostrannomu yazyku studentov yazykovyh fakul'tetov, Vestnik VGU, Seriya lingvistika i mezhkul'turnaya kommunikaciya, Vol. 2., pp..84 -87. (2003)
11. L.V. Molchanova. Obuchenie vtoromu inostrannomu yazyku v usloviyah formirovaniya funkcional'nogo mnogoyazychiya v yazykovom vuze: avtoref. diss…kandidata pedagogicheskih nauk: 13.00.02 Ryazan. (2009)
12. N.D. Galskova, N.I. Gez. Teoriya obusheniya inostrannym yazykam. Lingvodidaktika I metodika: uchebnoyeposobiye, 5th edition, M: Izdatelskiy tcentr «Akademiya», 336 p. (2008).
13. V. Panfilova, A. Panfilov, A. Gazizova, N. Samarina. Professional and communicative foreign language competence of future teacher, SHS Web of Conferences [Online]. Vol. 37. International Congresses on Education 2017 (ERPA 2017), Budapest, Hungary, May 18-21, 2017. URL: https://www.shs-conferences.org/articles/shsconf/abs/2017/05/contents/contents.html

Students' Understanding of Quantum Numbers: A Qualitative Study

Senar Temel[1] *and Özgür Özcan*[1,*]

[1]Hacettepe University, Department of Mathematics and Science Education, 06800, Beytepe, Ankara

Abstract. Quantum physics involves counterintuitive abstract concepts and complex mathematical procedures that are difficult to understand by physics and chemistry students at university level. This study employs case study- one of the methods of qualitative study- and it aims to determine the difficulties prospective chemistry and physics teachers encounter in understanding quantum numbers. 17 students in total were included in the study. The data were collected via a test of three open-ended questions developed by the researchers. The collected data were then analysed by using the content analysis method. It was found accordingly that both prospective chemistry teachers and prospective physics teachers had difficulties in understanding quantum numbers. The findings obtained in this study were compared with the ones obtained in similar studies and were discussed accordingly.

1 Introduction

Quantum Theory is a theory explaining sub-atomic particles behavior and the laws about the particles successfully. Because of the abstract concepts the theory contains and mathematical basis of it, it has cause educators to encounter many problems in teaching the relevant subjects. The major problem encountered is the understanding difficulties and misconceptions that both prospective chemistry and physics teachers have about the concepts of this theory [1 – 4]. Understanding difficulties related to the important concepts of the theory such as quantum numbers emerge as an important problem in teaching quantum physics/mechanics. The misconceptions and understanding difficulties in relation to basic concepts such as quantum numbers indicate that students cannot learn those concepts very well.

Only a limited number of studies are available in the literature aiming to reduce or eliminate the learning difficulties in quantum numbers [5 – 9]. Even though several materials such as making analogies were developed in those studies, the materials did not work very well in eliminating the learning difficulties. Apart from that, another concept student had difficulty in understanding is the concept of "spin". The concept is magnitude related to quantum numbers, and it has no counterparts in classical physics. It may be considered normal for students not to understand intuitively the concept that has no counterparts in classical physics but the situation is not so simple in reality. The reason for this is that students consider "spin" as a rotation movement [10]. A limited number of

* Corresponding author: ozcano@hacettepe.edu.tr

studies on the difficulties of understanding and misconceptions directly related to this and such quantum numbers constitute the reason for this study.

1.1 Purpose of the study

Understanding difficulties in quantum numbers and in matters directly related to this and misconceptions about it all form the base on which this study is conducted. In other words, this study sets out to determine the understanding difficulties of prospective chemistry and physics teachers have in relation to quantum numbers. In this context, the following research questions will be answered:

- How do the prospective chemistry and physics teachers understand and use the quantum numbers?
- What are the prospective chemistry and physics teachers' difficulties related to the concept of quantum numbers?

2 Method

The current study that was conducted by using case study method was one of the qualitative research methods included 17 pre-service teachers in total [11].

2.1 Participants and the course setting

The participants were chosen in purposeful sampling method. The questions on which the study focused were demonstrated in greater details in this way. All the participants, who were in the 19-23 age range, were included in the research on the basis of volunteering. Eight participants (4 females and 4 male) were prospective chemistry teachers whereas nine (6 females and 3 male) were prospective physics teachers. All of the participants had taken all the courses involving the fundamental concepts about quantum numbers. The courses were mostly teacher-centred and special teaching techniques such as concept maps or demonstration experiments were not employed in those courses.

2.2 Data collection tool and analysis

The data for the study were collected by means of three open-ended questions prepared by the researchers. The participants were allowed 20 minutes to answer the questions. The data were then analysed by using content analysis. The analyses done by the researchers separately were compared and the differences emerging were re-considered. The understanding difficulties prospective teachers had been determined on the basis of the analyses both researchers had done. Then the initial results of the researchers' analysis results compared and discussed. So, the inter coder reliability coefficient was archived to be 0.92 in first time. After discussing the contradictions between the researchers, the full agreement was reached finally.

2.3 Validity and reliability

Validity and reliability are very important especially in qualitative research studies. Data collection tools and the process of data analysis were clearly explained to the participants in this study for the purpose of validity. Thus, the participants' characteristic properties, data collection instruments and the way pursued in analysing the data will be clearly known in case a similar study is conducted. Intercoder reliability was calculated in obtaining the findings for the purpose of reliability [12]. The reliability coefficient was found by comparing the results for data analysis performed by the two researchers. While the reliability coefficient was fond as 0.92 in the first analysis, full agreement was attained between the two researchers in the second analysis.

3 Findings

This section includes the findings obtained through the analysis of the data collected. First, the findings for the first research question are summarised in Table 1. As is clear from Table 1, prospective teachers' levels of understanding are considered in three categories labelled as "complete understanding", "incomplete understanding" and "no understanding" [10]. The way prospective teachers use quantum numbers, on the other hand, was coded as "correct use" and "incorrect use". The participants giving no answers to the questions were labelled as "no answer".

3.1 Students' understanding and usage of quantum numbers

According to Table 1, there is only one prospective teacher using quantum numbers correctly and making correct explanations (coded as P16).

Table 1. Students' understanding of quantum numbers.

Participants (P)	**Quantum Numbers**			
	n	l	m_l	m_s
P1	+, IC	+, IC	+, IC	+, IC
P2	+, IC	+, IC	+, IC	+, IC
P3	+, IC	+, IC	+, IC	+, IC
P4	+, CU	+, CU	+, CU	+, IC
P5	+, IC	+, CU	+, CU	+, NoU
P6	+, IC	-, IC	-, NoU	-, NoU
P7	+, IC	+, IC	-, NoU	NA
P8	+, IC	-, NoU	+, IC	+, IC
P9	+, IC	+, IC	+, IC	+, IC
P10	+, IC	+, IC	+, IC	+, IC
P11	+, IC	-, NoU	-, NoU	+, IC
P12	+, IC	-, NoU	+, IC	+, IC
P13	+, IC	+, IC	+, IC	+, IC
P14	+, IC	-, NoU	NA	+, IC
P15	+, CU	-, NoU	+, CU	+, CU
P16	+, CU	+, CU	+, CU	+, CU
P17	+, CU	+, NoU	+, NoU	+, NoU

+: Correct use, -: incorrect use, CU: Complete Understanding, IC: Incomplete Understanding, NoU: no understanding, NA: No Answer.

Prospective physics teacher coded as P15 both used three quantum numbers correctly (n, m_l, m_s) and had the level of "complete understanding". However, P15 used angular momentum quantum number incorrectly and made incorrect explanations about the quantum number. Besides, six prospective teachers- three of whom were prospective chemistry teachers and three of whom were prospective physics teachers- could not make correct explanations despite using quantum numbers correctly. In other words, they could find the names of quantum numbers correctly but they could not offer scientific explanations on what they are for or what their functions are. Only P7 and P14 could not answer the questions about spin quantum number and angular momentum quantum number respectively. That is to say, these two prospective teachers mentioned only two of the four quantum numbers; and they could not write even the name of the other quantum numbers.

3.2 Students' difficulties related to the quantum numbers

Answers are sought to the second research question in this section. It was found in this context that prospective teachers had difficulty in understanding the situations corresponding to certain values of quantum numbers given in the questions. For instance, three prospective chemistry teachers (P1, P2 and P3) had incorrect answers about angular momentum quantum numbers and spin quantum numbers although they guessed the quantum numbers correctly for the situations given in questions two and three. P1 made operations only for l=2angular momentum quantum number for n=3 principal quantum number. Thus, the prospective teacher did not take other probable values that angular quantum number can take on into consideration. Besides, P3 had difficulty in determining the type of orbital and the spin quantum number and thus determined the two quantum numbers incorrectly. P3's explanation about question three is quoted below:

> *"We can say d-orbital for n=3, and nothing can be said for spin value because spin quantum number is not given"* (P3).

A similar comment was made by P1. The participant (P1) stated that no comments could be made for the spin of electron since the number of spin quantum was not given. P1's explanation was as in the following:

> *"l= can take on values until n-1 for n=3... since m_s value is not given, we cannot make comments about the situation of the electron. It is 3d orbital..."* (P1).

On examining the above quoted statements, it can be said that the three prospective chemistry teachers had problems in the meaning of quantum numbers and that they had difficulty in how to use the numbers on determining the situation of an electron. In other words, they had conceptual difficulties about angular momentum quantum number and orbitals or the way an electron is placed in orbitals.

On analysing the answers prospective physics teachers had given to question two, it was found that only the participants coded as P15 and P16 had given correct answers to the question. The prospective physics teachers coded as P10, P11, P14 and P17 made operations in the question by considering the value l=2 and they determined the values for spin quantum number incorrectly. The statements made by them were as in the following:

"It is determined according to the orbital corresponding to l=2" (P10)
"By *using l=n-1, l=2 for n=3. Thus, m_s = 2n+1, and m_s =7"* (P11)
"l=n-1. m_l=2l+1=5. m_s=1"(P14)

"l=2 (orbital d) for n=3. M_l=-2,-1,0,1,2 (5 value). m_s=2l+1=2.2+1=5 and the number of electrons is 10" (P17)

On analysing the answers prospective physics teachers had given to question three, it was found that they could usually determine the types of orbitals correctly. On the other hand, six of them (P10, P11, P13, P14, P15, P17) could not say the electron value of spin correctly for the situation given in question three. They wrote spin values as +1/2 or -1/2. The prospective physics teachers apart from those six, could give correct answers in relation to the types of orbitals and the probable spin values of electrons. Some of the statements made by prospective teachers who could not answer question three completely are as in the following:

"It takes on the values of -2, -1, 0, 1, 2 and orbital d is - orbital because n=3. Yet, magnetic quantum number is the minimum value due to the value of -2 and nothing can be said about spin." (P109
"We can say two electrons are available in d-orbital; because these values indicate the position of the electron" (P11)
"It is d-orbital. It takes on the values of -2, -1, 0, 1, 2. We have determined the place of the electron in accordance with the values given" (P14)
The electron is in d-orbital and m_s =5 (Spin quantum number)" (P17).

As is clear from the above-mentioned quotes, prospective physics teachers have significant conceptual difficulties about quantum numbers and their meanings. Prospective physics teachers coded as P10, P11, P14 and P17 in particular had incomplete knowledge about the concept of spin and they could not make sense of the concept of spin.

4 Discussion and conclusions

Quantum theory is not easy for students to understand since it involves abstract concepts and difficult mathematical operations. On analysing the findings for the first research question it can be said that prospective physics and chemistry teachers both have incomplete knowledge and understanding in relation to quantum numbers. Almost all of the prospective teachers used quantum numbers correctly but only a limited number of them could explain the meaning of those numbers. A close examination of Table 1 makes it clear that the number of prospective chemistry teachers who could use quantum numbers correctly and who could explain them correctly is six whereas the number of prospective physics teachers who could do them is seven. Many students cannot explain these two quantum numbers correctly and they have difficulty especially in explaining angular momentum quantum numbers and spin quantum numbers and have misconceptions or alternative concepts for quantum numbers due to the abstract structure of sub-atomic world [2, 3]. Ways of thinking especially about spin quantum numbers cannot go beyond the thinking style of classical physics. That is to say, prospective teachers try to explain quantum numbers by using the laws of classical physics. The reason for this is that the presentation of the concept of spin in general chemistry, organic chemistry and physico-chemistry course books is contradictory and misleading for students [13, 14]. Such course materials cause students to develop misconceptions or alternative concepts and lecturers' false analogies also cause misunderstanding.

The prospective physics and chemistry teachers were asked to make operations representing a quantum situation given by using quantum numbers within the scope of the second research question. The prospective teachers were expected to offer solutions by analysing the given quantum situation both mathematically and conceptually. As is clear from the participants' statements quoted in the findings section, prospective physics and chemistry teachers have incorrect conceptual understanding and mathematical difficulties. For instance, relation 2l+1, used for magnetic quantum number, was also used as it was for spin quantum number. Moreover, the prospective teachers interpreted the results (numbers) they had obtained in their calculation in the two ways of usage and they explained their finding as the total number of electrons in the relevant quantum situation. The numbers (the results obtained by using the relation 2l+1) do not mean the number of electrons but they mean space quantization. In other words, m_l has different angular momentum components for each value it has. Therefore, these two quantum numbers are not used to find the number of electrons. Thus, prospective teachers have important misunderstanding and conceptual difficulties especially about the use of magnetic quantum numbers and spin quantum numbers. On comparing the findings obtained in this study with those obtained in other relevant studies, we see that the results are similar [2, 3]. According to [15], the main difficulty for students to understand quantum numbers is that the concepts are abstract and incomprehensible. Additionally, difficult mathematical operations also cause students and teachers to display negative attitudes towards quantum physics [16]. Niaz and Fernandez (2008) also state that most of the students face significant difficulties in understanding quantum mechanics and quantum numbers.

5 Implications for Teaching

Concepts related to quantum mechanics are the concepts that we cannot experience in daily life. That is to say, it is quite difficult to picture them in mind. In this context, it is also difficult to teach them. It would be beneficial to prepare rich in-class activities and course books in a manner to support their complete learning of such abstract concepts as orbitals and quantum numbers. In addition to that, visuals can also be used heavily during in-class activities. Concepts difficult to understand intuitively can be made visible by using computer software. Activities that are probable to lead to misunderstanding on the part of students or to develop false models in students' mind should be avoided in doing this. Arrangements or activities of this kind that are to enrich the lessons can help students to make sense of the knowledge and they can also increase retention in learning; and thus meaningful learning can occur.

Appendix: Questions about Quantum Numbers

1. What does the quantum numbers (n, l, m_l, m_s) mean? What do you think about it? Explain your reasoning?
2. For n=3 quantum state, please write down the possible values of l, m_l, and m_s? Explain your reasoning?
3. What could be say about an electron's spin and orbital quantum numbers when it is found at the quantum state such as n=3 and m_l=-2?

References

1. N. Didiş, Ö. Özcan, M. Abak, H.U. J. of Edu. **34**, 86 (2008)
2. G. Papaphotis, G. Tsaparlis, Chem. Edu. Res. and Prac. **9**, 332 (2008)
3. S. Sunyonu, L. Tania, A. Saputra, J. of Bal. Sci. Edu., **15** 452 (2016)
4. Ö. Özcan, N. Didiş, M.F. Taşar, H.U. J. of Edu. **36**, 169 (2009)
5. W. C. Chung, J. of Chem. Edu. **90**, 1090 (2013)

6. E. Harvey, C. Gingold, *Haptic representation of the atom* (EEE International Conference on, 2000)
7. A. S. Lang, D. Kobilnyk, J. Vir. W. Res., **2**, 1 (2009)
8. J. Trindade, C. Fiolhais, *Students'visualization and conceptual understanding of atomic orbitals using a virtual environment* (The 3rd IEEE International Conference on, 2003)
9. B. Stewart, D.J. Hylton, N. Ravi, *Using maple to visualize atomic orbitals* (The National Conference On Undergraduate Research, University of Wisconsin La Crosse, 2013)
10. Ö. Özcan, Eur. J. Edu. Res. **52**, 21 (2013)
11. M.Q. Patton, *Qualitative Research & Evaluation Methods* (Thousand Oaks, CA, 2002)
12. M.B. Miles, A.M. Huberman, *Qualitative Data Analysis: An Expanded Sourcebook* (Sage Publications, London, 1994)
13. T.P. Charles, D.L. Peterson, J. Chem. Edu. **66** (1989)
14. Ö. Özcan, Eur. J. Phys **36**, 065042 (2015)
15. R.J Gillespie, J.N. Spencer, R.S. Moog, J. Chem. Edu. **73** 617 (1996)
16. P. Garik, P. Kelley, A. Crosby, D. Dill, A. Golger, M.Z. Hoffman, *Modernizing General Chemistry for the Year 2050: Why Are General Chemistry Instructors Hesitant to Teach Quantum Concepts? (*NARST, 2005)
17. M. Niaz, R.Fernández, Int. J. Sci. Educ. **30**, 869 (2008)

Teachers of secondary school as Democracy Coaches: Study of their conceptions during their initial formation

Mario Ferreras-Listán[1,*], *José Antonio* Pineda-Alfonso[1], and *Elena* Guichot-Muñoz[2]

[1]University of Seville, Didactics of Experimental and Social Sciences Department, Calle Pirotecnia, s/n. 41013-Sevilla. España.
[2]University of Seville, Didactics of Language and Literature and Integrated Philologies Department, Calle Pirotecnia, s/n. 41013-Sevilla. España.

Abstract. This study has been developed within the framework of a European Erasmus + project called ELEF†. The aim of this project is to develop, implement, evaluate and replicate innovative democratic learning environments. With this purpose, the Democracy Coaches are trained as agents of citizen participation and generators of democracy, both in educational centres and in informal educational settings. In this context, and during various training sessions, the Democracy Coaches work with the knowledge and skills they need to acquire. This paper focuses on the study and analysis carried out on the concepts expressed by these teachers of secondary education during their training. In order for them to become democracy coaches in the formal educational field, we address concepts such as democracy, citizenship and the most appropriate teaching-learning methodology for illustrating these concepts and competences, bearing in mind that they should educate citizens with full awareness of their rights and duties.

1 Introduction

The European countries, following the recommendations of the Council of Europe, have faced the responsibility of transmitting to young people the civic, democratic and pluralistic values shared by the European society. The public education (of any democratic community) has the obligation to enable its citizens to participate actively in civil and political society without the risk of exclusion. Therefore, being a citizen requires an adequate training in the structuring of a participatory democracy, autonomously and in accordance with the society and culture in which we are situated. No democracy is possible without the active participation of citizens. Democracy is the political system that recognizes and respects human and social rights and demands political and legal duties.

---

* Corresponding author: mferreras@us.es

† ELEF: European Learning Environment Formats for Citizenship and Democracy, Reference number 580426.

From the European Erasmus + project called ELEF (European Learning Environment Formats for Citizenship and Democracy), three different formats of innovative democratic learning environments will be implemented, developed, evaluated and replicated. These three formats have been piloted by the University of Bremen as project coordinator.

One of the three forms of innovative democratic learning environment is limited to the formal education field. In this field, students of the University Master's degree in Teaching in Compulsory Secondary Education and Baccalaureate, Vocational Training and Language Teaching (MAES, from University of Seville, Spain) are trained to be Democracy Coaches, a figure that promotes the development of democratic competence in schools. Especially, this format addresses the need to support teachers and educators in conflict resolution and student diversity. It therefore focuses on the training of future teachers to improve democratic competence and conflict resolution of teachers and pupils in secondary schools. The didactic approach is based on introducing and implementing research and exploration learning approaches in the curriculum (and in the context of didactic projects). The purpose of this action is to encourage students and teachers to develop a learning approach based on reflection, practice, participation, autonomy and criticism, to develop a better understanding and reflection on society. This provides an innovative learning approach for students and an innovative teaching methodology for future teachers who will soon join the education system. After a comprehensive training, these future teachers are expected to take these methods to their professional practices in secondary schools, high schools and vocational trainings, where they will work as Democracy Coaches directly with the students.

Democracy must be based on the laws that regulate the coexistence of people, as well as on a political culture that makes it possible. To this end, this democracy must be promoted through education. Therefore, the understanding of democracy depends not only on the laws, but also on the democratic competencies, attitudes and values shared by its citizens.

According to Bolívar[1], civic virtues, which make it possible to live in common in a democracy, are transferred through education. If we want to preserve democracy alive, the first challenge is to educate for active citizenship. Therefore, exercising citizenship requires an adequate level of education, which is necessary to implement a real democracy and to participate in it autonomously and coherently.

Democratic education must promote the active participation of citizens in all areas of their personal development, especially in school, since it is in this context (together with the family) that individuals are trained as individuals and as citizens. That is why we understand democracy, in the broad sense, as a way of life, rather than merely a procedure for electing representatives to take political decisions, to govern our existence. Democratic education has an educational value and should encourage participation in all the school areas: school and classroom management, coexistence, etc. It must be present in the basic decisions that determine the very nature of the school and the curriculum.

In this paper the conceptions on democracy and democracy perception of forty students of the MAES (from Spain) are collected and analysed. Among other issues, students have been asked on how democracy in schools can be studied, by creating a more democratic environment, or what relationship is established between democracy and education for citizenship. Of course, all these students took a BA prior to the MA.

In order to know the believes of these future teachers, we have sent them a questionnaire of ten questions, in which each one has exposed his/her personal opinion. Subsequently, a Focus Group has been set up to discuss the responses obtained.

2 Methodology

2.1 Design and procedure

As mentioned above, one of the objectives of this research is to learn about the conceptions that future secondary school teachers have of the teaching and learning active democracy in education, through a questionnaire.

To this end, we can indicate that the design of the research corresponds to a non-experimental, systematic and empirical design in which the independent variables are not manipulated because they have already happened, conceived to capture respondents' perceptions. According to Hernández, Fernández and Baptista[2] the inferences about the relationships between variables are made without direct intervention or influence. It is also a cross-sectional, descriptive design by analyzing the status of various variables at a given time, when the instrument was applied, and the data collected. The purpose is to describe variables and analyze their incidence and interrelation at the time of the study. The phenomenon under study is worked on in its natural context (training classes in the MAES). The research has a quantitative approach because the data from the surveys were quantified.

2.2 The sample

The sample of the study was made up of 40 students belonging to the University Master's Degree in Teachers of Compulsory Secondary Education and Baccalaureate, Vocational Training and Language Teaching (MAES). These students have been selected because they have taken the subject of "Education for Citizenship" which is an optional subject with a total duration of 40 hours. The heterogeneity of the degree of the students, is very diverse such as History and Geography, English and French Philology, Architecture, Journalism, Biology, etc.

2.3 Instruments

In this research, the instrument used to collect the information was an eight-question questionnaire, which was developed within the project by the researchers. The procedure to determine the validity of the research instruments consisted of handing over the questionnaire and the system of categories to three professionals from the University of Seville, experts in the field. An expert in methodology, design and construction also validated the questionnaire. The experts made the necessary and relevant corrections to the ambiguities of form or content they found in the instruments. These eight questions attempt to answer three different dimensions or categories: the first category is the conceptualization of democracy (questions 1, 2 and 3), the second is how democracy is perceived in schools (questions 4, 5 and 6) and the last is how democracy relates to education for citizenship (questions 7 and 8). The questions are as follows:

1. What does democracy mean to you?
2. Do you consider yourself an active democrat? Why?
3. How is this reflected in your daily life? Think about everyday situations
4. Do you think the school is a democratic environment?
5. Did you experience as a student (primary/secondary) that democratic school environment? where and how did you experience it?
6. What are your personal expectations and possible challenges regarding the idea of generating "more democracy in schools"?
7. Do you think that democracy and education for citizenship are related?

8. How is democracy and capitalism related?

Table 1. Category system for information analysis.

1. Conceptualization of democracy			
Subcat.	Variable	Descriptor	Level
1.1. What is democracy	*Simple/ ambiguous vision*	*It is not clearly defined as a democracy, or different perspectives are mixed.*	I
	Theoretical/ restrictive vision	*It provides an institutional vision or definition of democracy, defining some kind of democracy, linking it to purely political issues (direct, liberal, Christian-Democratic, representative, popular, etc.).*	II
	Integrated/ Participatory vision	*In addition to the institutional aspects, the definition of democracy also includes the full participation of people in their context in an active and direct way (political, social, environmental, etc.).*	III
1.2. How to live in democracy	*No active participation*	*Democracy is not involved in people's daily lives*	I
	Indirect participation	*Democracy is identified and exercised in specific actions or moments (political elections, etc.) (representative democracy)*	II
	tive participation	*Democracy as a fundamental principle for people's decision-making in any aspect of their lives (active and participatory democracy)*	III
2. Democracy and School			
2.1. The School as a democratic environment	*Non-democratic*	*The school is not a democratic context, so no truly democratic actions are carried out.*	I
	Democratic Guardianship	*It appears to be a democratic context but not all people have the same real decision-making capacity. The actions are apparently democratic but ultimately must be supervised by the management of the centre.*	II
	Fully democratic environment	*It is a fully democratic environment. In general, the people involved in decision-making (teachers, students, parents, etc.), they have the same capacity. There are governing and management bodies that promote and ensure democratic participation in the centre.*	III
2.2. Democratic experiences	*No democratic experiences*	*They have not perceived, as a student, any democratic experience*	I
	Punctual Experiences	*Democratic experiences take place at specific times (election of delegates, etc.).*	II
	Democratic experiences	*There is a great diversity of experiences in different moments that demonstrate the regularity in time of this type of actions.*	III
2.3. Expectations for generating democracy in schools	*Low expectations*	*Democracy cannot be generated in schools, because management, organisational and decision-making issues are imposed by teachers or regulations.*	I
	Intermediate expectations	*Despite the impositions of the regulations and management of the centre, shared decision-making may be included in some governing bodies of the centre and in specific activities.*	II
	High expectations	*The school must function as a true democratic community (and "open the doors to society") allowing the democratic intervention of all the agents that make up the educational centre (teachers, students, PAS, family, etc.). The decisions taken in the classroom must be shared (choice of subjects/contents, coexistence, etc.).*	III
3. Democracy and Citizenship Education			
Subcat.	Variable	Descriptor	Level
3.1. Democracy and Citizenship Education	*Unrelated or ambiguous*	*Democracy is a political issue with some relation to education for citizenship, but not a determinant one in relation to the other.*	I
	Simple relationships	*Democracy and its implementation is related to education for citizenship as it sets certain standards of behaviour for citizens when it comes to living in society.*	II
	Complex relationships	*Democracy and education for citizenship are closely related and influence each other, as the type of citizen marks and dictates the type of democracy and vice versa.*	III
1.2. Democracy and	*Unrelated*	*No relations are established since one is a political system and the other is an economic system.*	I
	Linear relationships	*A linear relationship is established between the two, identifying democracy with the current system of liberal capitalism.*	II
	Critical Relationships	*Complex relations are established between the two, even considering that capitalism can be an obstacle to the development of an advanced democracy.*	III

Regarding the analysis of the information obtained through the questionnaires, a system of categories has been designed, consisting of three main categories which in turn contain a series of subcategories. In other words, each of these variables has three possible variables that are organized hierarchically through three levels of complexity, from the simplest view to the most complex or developed. In this way, the category system is organised as a progression hypothesis [3]. This system is constituted not only as a reference point for research and for understanding the construction of knowledge in schools but also to guide the teaching-learning processes that take place in this context in a substantiated manner[4],[5],[6]. The category system is presented below (Table 1.)

3 Results

To present the results obtained from the analysis of the questionnaires, we focus mainly on the three dimensions proposed by our study. In this way, a series of graphs are presented with the answers inferred from the questionnaires.

3.1 Conceptualization of democracy

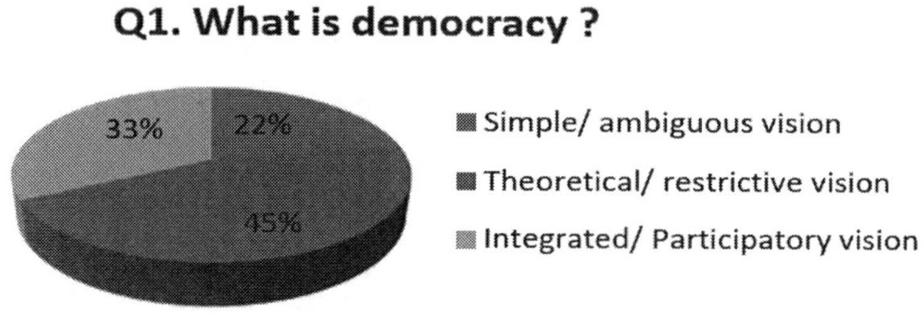

Fig. 1. What is democracy

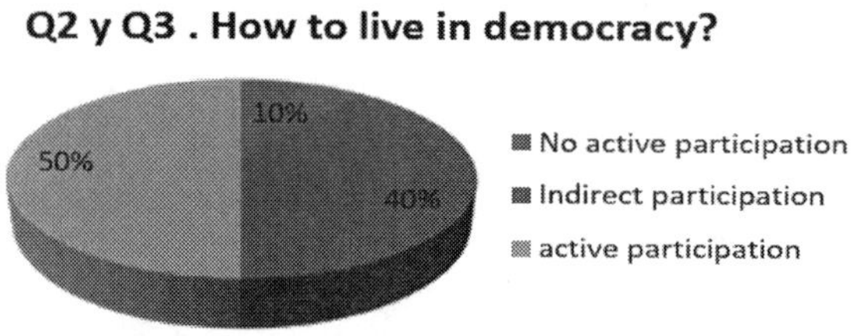

Fig. 2. How to live in democracy

Regarding the conceptualization of democracy, as can be seen in Figure 1, the most chosen option is the "theoretical/restrictive view" (level II) of the concept of democracy. Forty-five percent of respondents define democracy from an institutional perspective, linking it to purely political issues. As an example, subject no. 24, in this perspective, writes the following:

"Democracy means to me the government of the people as well as its etymological meaning in classical Greek. Today we could continue to link it to the same meaning, that is to say, to leave it to the citizens to choose their representatives and the form of government".

However, about the variable how to live in a democracy, the most frequently chosen option is "full and active participation" (level III), where 50% of those surveyed consider themselves to be active democrats, as they consider this to be a fundamental principle for decision-making in any aspect of their lives. This way, subject 27 indicates the following:

"I consider myself a democrat because I am tolerant, and I fight for the rights and duties of those around me, accepting all opinions even if they are contradictory to mine.... In work we reach a consensus, by majority, every time we want to decide something. With my friends and family, we discussed different topics when we met, showing first interest and respect"

3.2 Democracy and school

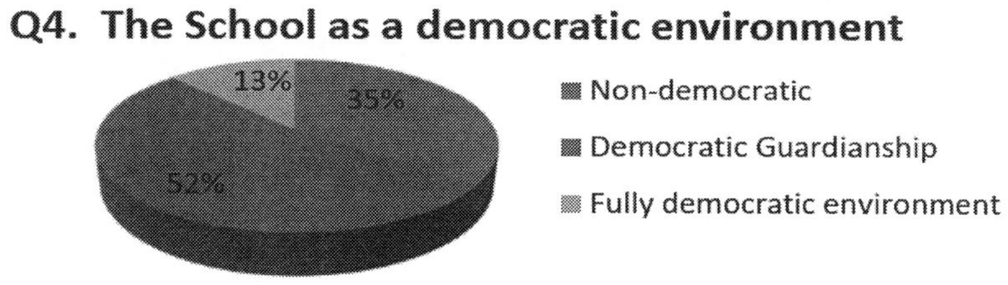

Fig. 3. The School as a democratic environment

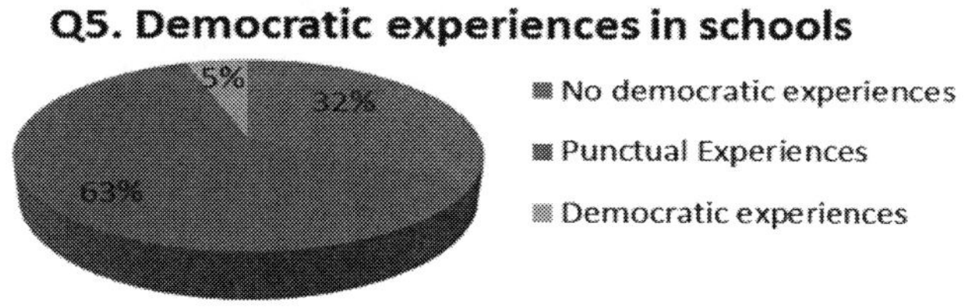

Fig. 4. Democratic experiences in schools

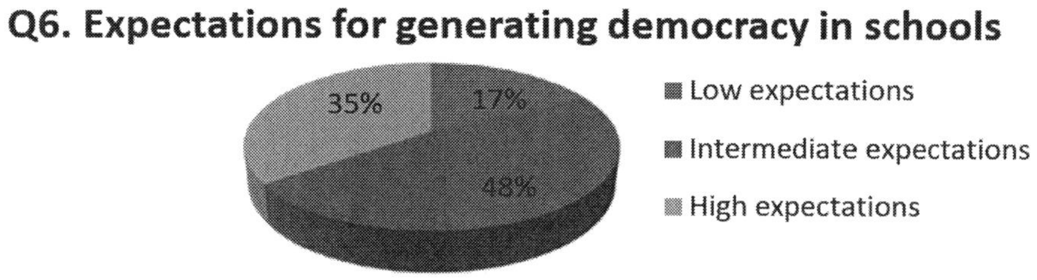

Fig. 5. Expectations for generating democracy in schools

With respect to the relationship between democracy and school, we see how the three variables analysed (graphs 3, 4 and 5) stand out in the intermediate or level two of the category system. This is because, in general, the students surveyed characterise the school as a context with a "supervised democracy" (with an allocation of 52%). This happens because although the school context is apparently democratic, ultimately the decision making is supervised by the teacher or the school management. In addition, they are usually "one-off experiences", as 63% of the students surveyed indicate, either through the election of a delegate (once per year) or where to go on a field trip, etc. It is also significant that 48% of students have intermediate expectations regarding the generation of democracy in schools, since they recognize that although there are regulations governing classroom and/or school management, it is possible to include actions that promote greater democratization in the processes of management, coexistence and socialization in schools, with certain limits. We can exemplify these questions with the answers of subject no. 9:

"The school is not always a democratic environment, but it must be, because the school is made up of the entire educational community. The whole group must be listened to because the form and the decisions are made by everyone.... I experienced this democratic

environment in some subjects, especially in the Integrated Project subjects, where we all chose what we were going to do in the subject... the way of giving the subject and the activities should not be chosen by the teacher, but should be decided by the whole class..."

3.2 Democracy and citizenship education

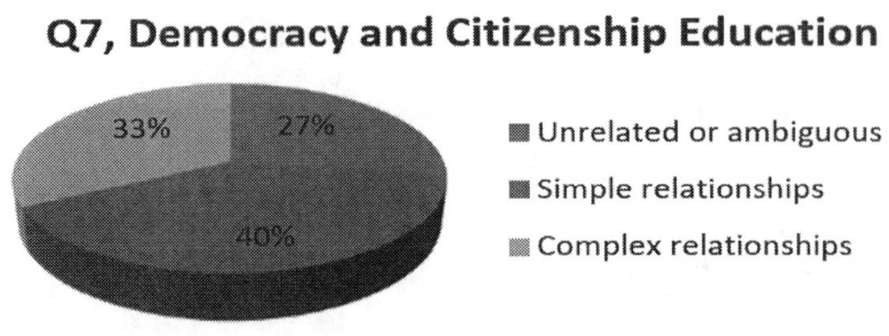

Fig. 6. Democracy and Citizenship Education

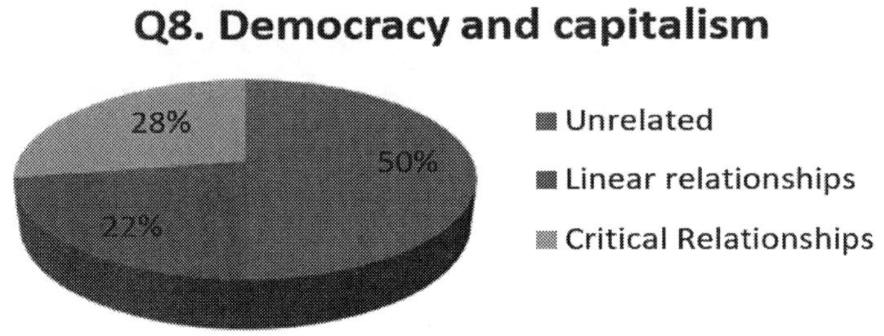

Fig. 7. Democracy and capitalism

Finally, concerning the relationship established between democracy and citizen education, as well as with capitalism, certain discrepancies can be observed. In category 7, although the most popular option, with 40%, is again the intermediate option (level II) "Simple Relationships", the other two options are closely followed. Therefore, there is one group (33%) with responses at level III or higher, "Complex Relationships", and another group (27%) with responses at level I, "Unrelated". This indicates a certain heterogeneity in answering this question, as it is a question that had not been asked before (in their own words) in a rigorous manner. Regarding the question how democracy relates to capitalism, we see for the first and only time that level I (50%), "No Relationship", predominates over the others. This is because half of those surveyed feel that relationships are not established, as one is a political system and the other is an economic system. For example, subject 35 answers the eighth question with the following statement:

"No, I don't see any connection. They seem different to me."

4 Conclusions

It is worth noting that throughout the entire research process, students have shown a great deal of interest in the issues raised, even though they indicate that the issue of education for democracy has never been explicitly addressed during their compulsory training. They point out that they have studied what democracy is, or what its historical origin is, or how it appears and is implanted in certain countries, etc., but always from a theoretical perspective and never from a practical one.

It is also noted that the concept of democracy they have is not shared. Some students identify democracy with social welfare and the benefits of the state, beyond political or economic issues, while others are practically confined to these two issues.

Some of them have not experienced any democratic situation in the school as students, or do not remember it, which is equally significant. While others do remember in a pleasant way, the election of a delegate or the vote to carry out a specific activity, etc. It is noteworthy that only 5% of those surveyed remember having carried out regular democratic activities or actions at school. This has a clear relationship with a traditional teaching methodology, where the relations between teachers and students are unidirectional and clearly hierarchical. The teacher is the one who has all the decision-making power in the classroom and shares it with the children or the parents on specific occasions. This issue is of great importance, since it is assumed that schools should provide "in-depth" training for citizenship and democracy, both practical and theoretical.

Finally, regarding the relationship between education for citizenship and democracy, we find a wide variety of answers. There are contributions that indicate that no relationship is established. However, other contributions indicate that education for citizenship and democracy are closely linked, since education for global citizenship must start from a democratic situation for decision-making linked to the constitutional principles of freedom and equality of all people.

References

1. A. Bolívar, RIEJS, **5** (1), 69-87 (2016).
2. R. Hernández, C. Fernández M.P Baptista. *Metodología de la Investigación*. (2010).
3. F. Rodríguez-Marín, J. Fernández Arroyo, J.E. García, Enseñanza de las ciencias, **32**(3), 303-318. (2014)
4. R. Porlán, R. Martín Del Pozo, A. Rivero, J.Harres, P. Azcárate, and M. PIZZATO, Enseñanza de las Ciencias, **28**(1), 31-46. (2010).
5. R. Porlán, R. Martín Del Pozo, A. Rivero, J.Harres, P. Azcárate, and M. PIZZATO, Enseñanza de las Ciencias, **29** (3), 413-426. (2011).
6. C. Martínez, and V.G. Martínez, Nodos y nudos. **32**, 50-64. (2012).

Digital competences of parents in the matter of electronic threats

Łukasz Tomczyk[1, *]

[1] Pedagogical University of Cracow, Ingardena 4 street, 30-060 Kraków, Poland

Abstract. Digital competences have become one of basic skills in XXI century. Due to the ability to digitally access data and manage information and use electronic services, the quality of life has improved, and there has been an improvement in many activities connected with communication, shopping, ticket booking and a range of other repetitive activities. However, there is an additional layer overlapping the technical skills, which layer is connected with understanding the threats deriving from common availability of ICT. The aim of this paper is a diagnosis of digital competences level of parents in the matter of safe use of electronic media. To do this, quantitative research have been prepared, which measure six crucial areas of internet threats: ability to evaluate reliability of information on Internet, safety in the matter of contact with other users, image protection on Internet, knowledge concerning copyrights, knowledge concerning cyber-bullying mechanisms, proper performance of financial operations. The weakest areas of digital literacy seem to be: copyright protection and issues concerning contact with other users. The research was realized with the use of a competence test. The analysis was carried out on 260 parents of students attending secondary schools in the second half of 2016.

1 Introduction

Today's generation of young Internet users are mainly digital natives who do not know life without new technologies. For them, using mobiles, Internet, game consoles or digital television is as normal as using "old media" (radio, television) for their parents. Both generations are going through similar processes that are taking place in information society, have educational impact on one another and mutually model values, according to M. Mead's concept. This happens also through and with the support new media.

Parents see that new technologies bring not only positive changes associated with quick access to information, data sharing or various forms of entertainment, but they also generate many threats, [11,13]. Ability to participate intentionally in new media space requires taking advantage of the positive aspects of digital media, and protection against both, popular and less visible e-threats, such as: cyberbullying, [3]. Internet addiction and various forms of pathologic use of it, [15], sexting [7], self-control and self-evaluation in terms of using electronic media [1], protection of online image [4] or legal consequences of Internet abuse, [21]. These threats are only typical and the most common, negative results of

* Corresponding author: tomczyk_lukasz@prokonto.pl

omnipresence of electronic media. Once in a while, the group of typical and well known risky behaviours grows by new media-related situations that refer, for example, to promoting destructive behaviours like patostreaming or fake news.

With the growing number of online threats, it becomes necessary to develop new skills that would allow to improve digital safety in families. Individuals who do not properly understand how new media works and how to secure their electronic devices, are the most prone to different limit situations. Therefore, central government administration units, NGOs and schools more and more often take responsibility for raising the level of digital safety Following one's intuition, searching for support in Internet portals dedicated to solving educational issues, family counselling or consultations with other parents may prove to be insufficient in the age of increasing electronic threats, [2,20].

2 Definition of digital literacy in the aspect of e-threats

There is a reason why digital literacy, or wider, IT literacy, is considered one of the key skills, along with: literacy and languages; basic skills in maths, science and engineering; personal, social and learning competencies; civic competence; entrepreneurship, and cultural awareness and expression. This set has been agreed by the European Parliament and European Commission as a set of necessary, basic competencies that enable full family and professional functioning, [5]. Digital literacy (DL) is an ability to use of new media fluently, usually in the technical context of obtaining, processing, presenting, sending and archiving data, by means of applications and websites However, it is worth to add that DL is also an ability to understand changes caused by new media. Thus, it is the ability to interpret processes associated with positive and negative influence on children, self, family and society, [6]. Holistic view of DL involves connecting knowledge and technical skills with reflection on the influence of electronic media on individuals and groups.

DL are also connected with ability to create, and securing access to the Internet, digital etiquette and digital safety, [19,14]. Development of Internet-based technologies also forces parents to know not only typical digital threats, but also those hidden in other networked devices, for example toys that collect and process data about activity in family environment or spyware, [7]. We need to point out that without adequate and proven educational methods, having advanced DL is insufficient to strengthen digital safety, [12]. Therefore, the subject matter literature mentions a subcategory of digital literacy, described as "family digital literacy" [10], meaning DL extended by skills regarding education to safe use of digital media and also ability of parents to self-educate [17] and extend media socialisation onto other family members [18], including older generations who have been increasingly better in using digital media [9].

Save for traditional offline threats, modern parents are forced to develop their awareness and educational strategies related to online reality. Offline and online threats are very often intertwined, and effective minimising means development of knowledge and skills that are useful in both of these environments, creating a set of factors protecting from risky behaviours.

3 Methodology

3.1 Research objectives

The objective of the study was to diagnose level of digital literacy of parents, in the area of secure use of new media. This is to improve cognition and application, by diagnosing the weakest DL components and strengthening them through engaging parents in informal education process. The research was commissioned by the Polish Ministry of National Education and conducted by Cities on the Internet Association from Tarnow, within the program Bezpieczna+ (Safety+). Data was collected during realisation of the project Cyfrowo Bepieczni (Digitally Safe).

3.2 Sampling and research procedure

Schools that participated in the Digitally Safe project were responsible for diagnosing DL level of their students, parents and teachers. This text presents results of a competency test, in six priority DL areas, such as: protection of image in the Internet, sexting and data privacy, copyright, credibility of information, cyberbullying and financial operations. For each area 3 indicators were designed and obtained based on answers to questions checking knowledge and skills. The whole test consisted of 18 questions rated with points (positive points for every correct answer, for partially correct answers, e.g. selection of only some correct answers — some positive points, and negative points for wrong answers). Then, the total number of points for each area was calculated and finally, a percentage result (100% meant correct answers to all the questions) was drawn.

The research was anonymous and conducted according to pedagogical research ethics. Data was collected by a private research-educational agency NAVIGO, led by dr Łukasz Srokowski. The tool and methodology were consulted with dr Arkadiusz Wąsiński from the University of Lodz.

3.3 Sample characteristics

The survey was conducted among parents of students learning in secondary schools in Poland, in the second half of 2016. The sample consisted of 183 women (70.66%) and 76 men (29.34%). Education of parents was: vocational (15.83%), secondary (41.70%), higher (30.89%), post-secondary (5.79%), lower-secondary (2.32%), primary (3.47%). Respondents stated their families lived modestly (11.97%), had financial means adequate to their needs (65.25%), were well-off (22.78%). The graph below presents how did parents evaluate their knowledge and skills related to electronic threats.

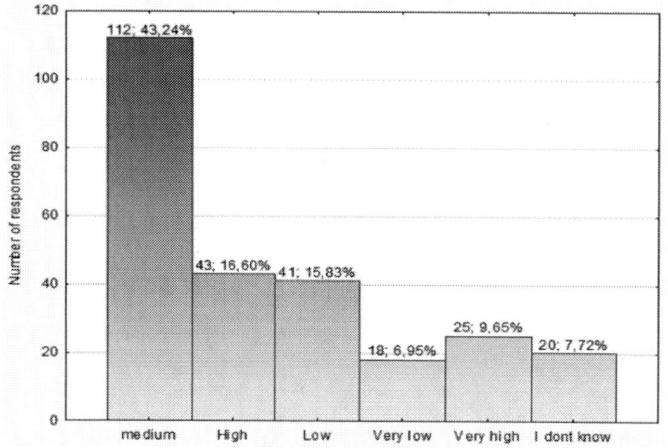

Figure 1. How do you evaluate your level of literacy and knowledge related to securing against e-threats?

4 Results

Parents obtain relatively satisfactory results as for protection of online image and cyberbullying prevention. These two areas are also strongly related. Unsatisfactory results refer mainly to copyright, that is information about downloading and sharing copyrighted files in the Internet, and safe interactions with other Internet users (including sexting).

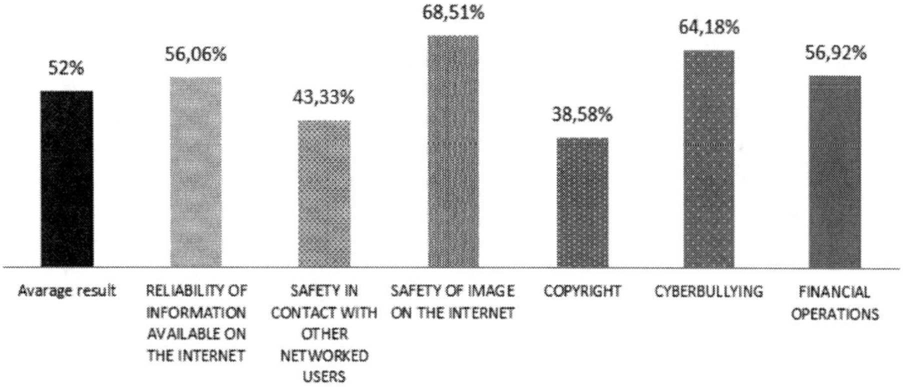

Figure 2. Average results in competency test, Source: (Tomczyk, Srokowski, Wąsiński, 2016).

Presented percentage distribution of correct answers indicates a necessity to improve DL in the analysed group, as level of knowledge and skills of parents determines digital safety in the family.

Parents who regularly use e-services like e-administration, had much better test results than the rest of the group F(3, 255)=4.4631, p=.00448. In schools where a serious incident of breaching digital safety had taken place, parents obtain slightly better results F(2, 256)=6.2733, p=.00219. Regardless if there are special, comprehensive programs introduced in a school or if there are no DL development procedures in terms of digital safety, parents obtain similar results F(2, 256)=2.0752, p=.12764. Thus, we can develop a working hypothesis that it is more individual conditions that facilitate parents' knowledge and competencies rather than school programs within the so called non-formal education. Controlling the ways the youngest family members use new technologies is not related to test results F(4, 254)=1.6990, p=.15069. Similarly, there are no correlations for talking with children about electronic threats F(5, 253)=1.4823, p=.19602. At the same time, we should point out that parents who highly evaluate their literacy and knowledge about e-threats, obtained high results in the competency test F(5, 253)=7.1716, p=.00000. Parents who think their competencies in using digital devices like computer and Internet are high or very high, get good or very good results. It means parents evaluate themselves adequately. This refers also to parents who stated their DL are at a low level F(5, 253)=6.5660, p=.00001.

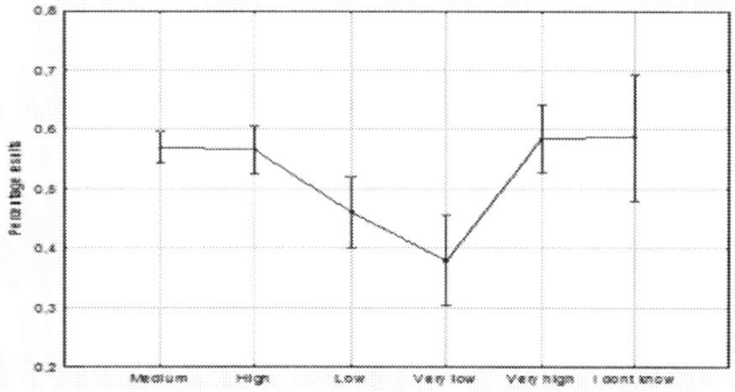

Figure 3. How do you evaluate your level of literacy and knowledge related to use of digital devices (computer, Internet)?

Similar strong relation can be found for results regarding self-evaluation of ability to use portable devices like tablet or smartphone $F(5, 253)=5.7995$, $p=.00004$. Place of residence does not affect the discussed DL aspect in any way $F(4, 254)=1.2786$, $p=.27885$. DL is not influenced by gender $F(1, 257)=4.6867$, $p=.03132$ (very small statistical difference between test results), education $F(5, 253)=1.9192$, $p=.09159$, or declared financial standing $F(2, 256)=1.2168$, $p=.29789$.

For each DL component, an average value was calculated based on points received in the test. Each variable (DL component) turned into arithmetic value out of three answers, was compared to other variables using Pearson correlation coefficient. We can notice that all results have high level of confidence – p is less than 0.001. A general conclusion is that advanced knowledge and skills in one area of DL translates into w high or average level in other DL areas. This correlation is the strongest for the area of financial operations. This may result from the fact that technical knowledge regarding access to one's account, ability to recognise different types of attacks on bank accounts or other confidential data needed for processing financial information, requires parents to be aware of other areas, like evaluating credibility of information or mechanisms that strengthen online privacy. Linear correlation is visible, but we should point out that there are many mediating factors to DL.

Table 1. Relation between certain DL components in the area of security

	Image on Internet	Sexting and privacy	Intellectual law	Information trust	Cyberbullying
Sexting and privacy	,2689***	1,0000			
Intellectual law	,1779**	,3008***	1,0000		
Information trust	,2808***	,3439***	,3750***	1,0000	
Cyberbullying	,2394***	,3250***	,2888***	,4030***	1,0000
Financial operations	,2607***	,3409***	,3821***	,4393***	,4470***

*p<0.01; ** p<0.05, *** p<0.001

5 Discussion

Considering diagnostic of digital literacy, we should emphasize that proposed methodology, basing on six selected competencies in the area of digital safety, does not exhaust the scope of factors assigned to different variables. Due to volume limitations of competency tests, our methodology was designed to measure safety issues related to the most popular networked services, accompanying skills and knowledge. Authors of the tool are aware that changing reality of the information society generates many new problems, thus factors and variables that define digital safety are fluent and transform over time.

It is worth to point out that many of the six selected DL components intertwine. This is confirmed, for example, by r2 test coefficients, as well as percentage distribution of answers to questions about cyberbullying and protection of online image. We also need to emphasize that cyberbullying and relatively advanced knowledge parents have about online image are connected with years of prevention of risky behaviours in this area, carried out by NGOs like Empowering Children Foundation or activities of Ministry of Education, Educational Supervising Authorities and Police. These initiatives are strengthened with media messages about causes and consequences of long-term or serious cyberbullying, for example sexual abuse. Some forms of cyberbullying are not just" excesses" of adolescence, but they can be classified as stalking or infringement of personality rights. Probably, because these preventive activities have been carried out a long time, the respondents obtained high results in the area of cyberbullying.

Dynamics of changes happening in the information society forces us to modify our view on DL. Therefore, we postulate that future competency tests addressed to parents, teachers and students should include the following issues: fake news, problematic use of Internet (including FOMO and Internet addiction) or patostreaming. They are phenomena that also require an in-depth analysis.

6 Conclusion

DL is definitely one of the key competencies in today's world. When DL is analysed in the context of family functioning, they receive a completely new meaning. There are many DL factors related to: technical use of media, reflection regarding influence, preventive skills or response to electronic threats. Usually, parents update their DL through self-education. This may not be apparent, but DL is a complex hybrid of knowledge, skills and attitudes connected with new media, that transform along with the development of digital services. The research results presented in this test indicate that some DL components are significantly related with one another.

Awareness of the necessity to develop DL in Poland grows, also in the context of lifelong learning. This is proved, among others, by ministerial projects dedicated to the development of DL not only among students and teachers, but also parents. At the same time, parents responsible for digital safety, begin to recognise the necessity of improving their own knowledge in a non-formal or informal way. We also need to point out that the research results show a relatively high level of self-awareness regarding DL. Unfortunately, despite the above mentioned positive conditions, the results in the selected areas of the competency test should be treated as an argument to design further systemic and one-time solutions facilitating development of DL.

Acknowledge

Research was realized in the frame of CyfrowoBezpiecznie project, realized by Stowarzyszenie Miasta w Internecie (Tarnów) in the frame of Bezpieczna+ ministry programme. The author would like to thank the research team eg. dr. Łukasz Srokowski (NAVIGO), for administrative part of this project.

References

1. Bayraktar, F. Online Risks and Parental Mediation Strategies Comparison of Turkish Children/Adolescents Who Live In Turkey and Europe. TED EĞİTİM VE BİLİM. doi:10.15390/eb.2017.6323, (2017).
2. Davis, V. Interconnected But Underprotected? Parents' Methods and Motivations for Information Seeking on Digital Safety Issues. Cyberpsychology, Behavior & Social Networking, 15(12), 669-674. doi:10.1089/cyber.2012.0179, (2012).
3. Del Rey, R., Casas, J. A., Ortega-Ruiz, R., Schultze-Krumbholz, A., Scheithauer, H., Smith, P., … Plichta, P. Structural validation and cross-cultural robustness of the European Cyberbullying Intervention Project Questionnaire. Computers in Human Behavior, 50, 141–147. doi:10.1016/j.chb.2015.03.065, (2015).

4. Frania, M. Selected aspects of media literacy and new technologies in education as a challenge of Polish reality. Perspectives of Innovations, Economics and Business, 14(2), 109–112. doi:10.15208/pieb.2014.13, (2014).
5. García-Lozano, C., Las-Heras-Casas, J., Fraile-García, E., & Ferreiro-Cabello, J. DIDACTIC STRATEGIES TO DEVELOP KEY COMPETENCIES. INTED2016 Proceedings. doi:10.21125/inted.2016.0958, (2016).
6. Hannaford, J., & Beavis, C. When will the Internet be connected? Digital worlds and belonging in the lives of globally mobile children. Literacy, 52(1), 47-54. doi:10.1111/lit.12123, (2018).
7. Harrison, E., & McTavish, M. 'i'Babies: Infants' and toddlers' emergent language and literacy in a digital culture of iDevices. Journal Of Early Childhood Literacy, 18(2), 163-188. doi:10.1177/1468798416653175, (2018).
8. Kopecký, K. Sexting Among Slovak Pubescents and Adolescent Children. Procedia - Social and Behavioral Sciences, 203, 244–250. doi:10.1016/j.sbspro.2015.08.289, (2015).
9. Mackowicz, J., & Wnek-Gozdek, J. "It's never too late to learn"–How does the Polish U3A change the quality of life for seniors? Educational Gerontology, 42(3), 186–197. doi:10.1080/03601277.2015.1085789, (2015).
10. Marsh, J., Hannon, P., Lewis, M., & Ritchie, L. Young Children's Initiation into Family Literacy Practices in the Digital Age. Journal Of Early Childhood Research, 15(1), 47-60, (2017).
11. Plichta, P., & Pyżalski, J. Narażenie uczniów ze specjalnymi potrzebami edukacyjnymi na hazard tradycyjny i internetowy oraz inne zachowania ryzykowne. Niepełnosprawność. doi:10.4467/25439561.np.16.015.6841, (2016).
12. Rodríguez-de-Dios, I., van Oosten, J. M., & Igartua, J. A study of the relationship between parental mediation and adolescents' digital skills, online risks and online opportunities. Computers In Human Behavior, 82186-198. doi:10.1016/j.chb.2018.01.012, (2018).
13. Siegle, D. Cyberbullying and Sexting: Technology Abuses of the 21st Century. Gifted Child Today, 33(2), 14-16, (2010).
14. Szotkowski, R. Dangerous behavior of children and youth in the internet and possibility of their protection. Journal of Technology and Information, 2(1), 110–114. doi:10.5507/jtie.2010.024, (2010).
15. Tomczyk, Ł., & Selmanagic-Lizde, E. Fear of Missing Out (FOMO) among youth in Bosnia and Herzegovina — Scale and selected mechanisms. Children and Youth Services Review, 88, 541–549. doi:10.1016/j.childyouth.2018.03.048, (2018).
16. Tomczyk, Ł., Srokowski, Ł., Wąsiński, A. Kompetencje w zakresie bezpieczeństwa cyfrowego w polskiej szkole. Tarnów: Stowarzyszenie Miasta w Internecie, (2016).
17. Veteska, J. Uvod do teorie zdelavani dospelych a andragogiky. Usti nad Labeb: Univerzita J. Purkyne, (2017).
18. Walotek-Ściańska, K. Persuasion strategies in Polish advertisements addressed to young people. Zeszyty Naukowe Wyższej Szkoły Humanitas Zarządzanie, 18(1), 0–0. doi:10.5604/01.3001.0010.2886, (2017).
19. Wang, X., & Xing, W. Exploring the Influence of Parental Involvement and Socioeconomic Status on Teen Digital Citizenship: A Path Modeling Approach. Educational Technology & Society, 21(1), 186-199, (2018).

20. Wurtele, S. K., & Kenny, M. C. Technology-Related Sexual Solicitation of Adolescents: A Review of Prevention Efforts. Child Abuse Review, 25(5), 332-344. doi:10.1002/car.2445, (2016).
21. Ziemba, E. Factors Affecting the Adoption and Usage of ICTs within Polish Households. Proceedings of the 2016 InSITE Conference. doi:10.28945/3508, (2016).

Development of student's initiative in future profession: the lecturer's option of interaction based training forms approach

Dmitry Luchaninov[1, a], *Ruslan* Bazhenov[1], *Natalia* Bazhenova[1], *Tatiana* Gorbunova[2] and *Sergey* Bogatenkov[3]

[1]Sholom-Aleichem Priamursky State University, 679016, Birobidzhan, Russian Federation
[2]Moscow State University of Civil Engineering, 129337, Moscow, Russian Federation
[3]South Ural State University, 454080, Chelyabinsk, Russian Federation

Abstract. In the article, the option of pedagogical interaction based training forms for student's initiative in future profession development is analyzed. The concepts of student's initiative, process of pedagogical interaction, pedagogical interaction based training forms are described. Sholom-Aleichem Priamursky State University, Moscow State University of Civil Engineering and South Ural State University served as an experimental base. The purpose of the experiment was to analyze effect of using pedagogical interaction based training forms for the student's initiative in future profession development. Two groups were selected for research: experimental (212 students) and control (219 students). Quantitative indicators of the dynamics testify the effectiveness of the experimental work: control group shows 16 percent progress while the experimental have 31 percent.
Keywords. Student's initiative in future profession, pedagogical interaction, pedagogical interaction based training forms, university informational-educational environment, social network community.

1 Introduction

The specific feature of contemporary higher education is considered to be a great number of networking tools to offer interaction opportunities. It is reflected in the development of Ubiquitous learning idea (U-learning) [1], mobile learning [2], e-learning system of interactive computer-based training settled through various educational settings [3], and promoting comprehensive partnership among all participants of the educational process to work together [4]. Using elements of learning environments [5], in addition to adaptation of current systems for a common use such as social networks, blogs, etc. are success criteria for teaching [6] at the moment. In this situation, a lecturer creates an educational space for students' training, consults them, and provides research direction [7].

Blended learning technologies are largely used in training health and care professionals [8], psychologists [9], and engineers [10]. Numerous studies have been carried out to strengthen efficiency of education using various educational tools: monitoring training

[a] Corresponding author: dvluchano@mail.ru

systems by data mining technologies is conducted [11], methods for constructing the effective personal student learning environment are explored [12] and educator professional training [13].

Considering the situation, it is necessary to understand that these days an educator has to work in fairly strict accordance with modern information systems used at university, the curriculum and the number of classes. For that reason, a trainer has to look for all available means to improve the effectiveness of student learning. One of the ways to achieve that can be the choice, adaptation and provision of participatory training while using advanced learning tools as a part of all-pervading learning.

Moreover, the successful development of students' initiative, especially among freshman students, can make it much easier for the arrangement of such classes, removing various obstacles: communicative (fear of communication with a lecturer outside the class, in social networks), psychological (fear of failure), motivational [14]. The development of initiative in the professional field for senior students will help them to work more successfully, cooperate with colleagues and encourage a successful career in future.

The purpose of this article is to review the impact of a lecturer's choice of interactive learning methods on the development of student initiative in further career.

2 Methods

In the context of an evolving higher education, the review of studies indicates the focus on the description of a structure, types, systems, different options for the competencies of student professional training for mastering their competence in future career by the competence approach. Thus, there can be formed sets of information competence, social competence, and ethical and speech competence of students as a part of professional and general competence.

Besides, the research is being conducted on the relationship between academic subjects of educational programs and a part they take for the competencies that are being formed:

– the identification of correlation between academic subjects with the same set of competencies;

– the definition of specific subjects of one format with a different set of competences;

– the influence of a subject set on a single competence;

– the selection of the content of subjects according to competences mastered.

At the same time, the labor market significantly increases the demand for initiative and leading professionals who are able to work out practical problems using innovative approach. When applying for jobs, similar recommendations occur more often. Some scientists emphasize that at present employers start paying attention not only to professional skills of university graduates, but also to their personal qualities: social and communicative and general cultural competences, creative thinking, and the ability to respond quickly to challenges in the situation and find non-standard, innovative solutions.

Reviewed studies make it possible to identify interactive teaching methods that are recommended to a lecturer to use for developing students' leadership:

1. Conversation. Lecture in a conversational form involves a direct contact of a lecturer with the audience. While having a talk, the audience is constantly attracted to information, as an educator often turns to learners for feedback.

2. News conference. When arranging the news conference, an instructor gives the assignment to make up questions on the topic of the lecture. The lecturer plans a lecture according to students' questions, and comment on especially those matters that are the most interesting for students.

3. The project-based learning method means students' creating small information products, either individually or in small groups. Using this form, one can apply role plays. In other words, students are offered a part of a project manager, performers, an advertising

manager, etc. After completing a student's individual or group work, they usually organize the project protection, where it is also possible to use the key features of the interview.

4. Learning management system. When training the subject, an electronic course is used, which proceeds in parallel. As part of the e-course, students perform assignments; consult with educators through indirect pedagogical interaction. In addition, webinars for all-pervading learning can be organized in the system.

5. Case method. During these classes, students are presented a particular actual task, which needs to be solved. As a rule, the task requires them to search and review some available information on the issue related to the topic given.

6. Disputation. Using this method is relevant if there is some information that can be submitted implicitly and divides the participants into two or more opposite groups. It is necessary to provide learners with data sufficient to prove the opinion on this issue, the ability to gather scientific facts or quotes which they can refer to.

7. Debate. It is used in case there are several methods for solving the problem, and each of them has advantages and disadvantages. In this particular case, they arrange a group of experts. They must be convinced that they have chosen a proper method. Debate can be also used in project-based learning methods to decide who wins.

8. Edutainment methods. Using simulation programs allow students to get real data during the research, generate their own suppositions, and assess their validity. This form can be used in preparation for discussions to obtain visual data on the topic observed.

9. Public presentation of the project means developing presentation materials available for public discussion, as well as possible protection of the project. It allows students to analyze the information they study, use infographics, multimedia devices. As part of using games, one can define roles of opponents, defenders, etc. in advance.

10. Brainstorming. Using this form, students are encouraged to generate ideas in order to solve the problems offered, develop projects so that accomplish these goals. It is possible for students to generate issues by themselves. For this purpose, news conference is held first.

All interactive learning methods mentioned above can be applied both for direct and indirect pedagogical interaction. Interactive learning methods are used in indirect pedagogical interaction through interactive means of educational environment.

The authors are observing the methodology for developing students' leadership illustrated by the students' elective course "Development of web-sites for educational purposes". The peculiarity of this subject is a quite small number of classes. It forced the educator to organize a great amount of indirect interaction.

The methodology for developing students' initiative is achieved by means of organizing educational process in accordance with the curricula developed by lecturers. Lecturers' work in dealing with the e-course consists of the development of electronic versions of materials applied to distance educational technologies.

While developing the e-course in Moodle, a zero module for support was designed. Now it includes interacting means of connection with a lecturer, monitoring students' current academic achievements, and software links used in the course. In addition, recommendations on the design and attachment of electronic reports in the system were made in the module of the e-course. To arrange indirect interaction, the developers design a consultation forum where students can ask questions on topics they are interested in.

The main work out on pedagogical interaction is carried out in the Russian online social media and networking service VKontakte (meaning In Contact). There is also a shift to other components of information and educational setting of the university.

A rating system is used to record the students' academic achievements and to manage with counting and reporting information on points scored by students for the course they study. A link to a score page is also inserted into the zero module of the subject considered.

In the first module of the course "Basic Website Development" the lecture materials, lab works are presented. There are more detailed components of the course below.

Lecture (LC) #1. Web-sites for educational purposes. Since this lecture was the first (introductory) class of the course, it took place in the form of a conversation. During the lecture, the educator addressed to students' experience in working with web-sites, including educational ones. Also, the lecturer focused on the concept of an educational website and observed types of educational sites. The participants of the lecture determined criteria of the educational site quality, and commented on the principle to navigate a site map. Materials on this lecture, as well as all lectures of the course, were downloaded in Moodle in a similar way.

The lecture is presented in the Moodle system by means of an appropriate course element and ends with questions and assignments for testing. The system assessed the correctness of questions, but the instructor checked the assignments.

LC#2. Installing Joomla CMS on the local server. This lecture was held in the format of news conference. Students prepared questions on the material installed in Moodle. The lecturer covered the questions that students asked more fully. Then the lecturer concluded to general statements, taking into account those notices that were not reported on by students for one reason or another. In this lecture, the concept of a local server was touched upon, its position in web-sites development, the local Open Server was concerned, the Joomla content management system (CMS) location on this server.

Lab#1. Joomla installation and configuration. This lab was held in a combined format. First, students worked in groups to find a common solution according to the elements that would be applied in their educational web-sites. Then they worked on their own mastering their skills of using the local Open Server, its installation and configuration for Joomla. They studied the basics of administering the Joomla content management system, the hierarchical structure of the objects of this system.

Lab#2. Designing a blog in Joomla. In this lab, students developed the content of the educational website: theoretical doctrines, images. They considered various settings of text and graphic information in the system, displaying the created materials on the site. All labs were taken from the authors' book. During the lab, a disputation was arranged on designing materials using CMS Joomla. Students were willing to offer options of using various interactive elements when submitting the material.

The next module of the subject is devoted to designing the external interface of the website. Students were given lectures, labs and a seminar during this course.

LC #3. Site templates and design. In this lecture, learners examined menu types on websites, the designing standards of the web sites menu, and the algorithms for developing an order of links in the context menu. As a result of the lecture, students put the selected templates for the sites and worked together to refine them matching a particular project. Finally, they used brainstorming through the debriefing method taken from Workshop #1.

Workshop #1. Template analysis for Joomla. This assignment was done in a discussion workshop, transferred to Moodle. The seminar was conducted by means of the distance communication system "Forum". "Debriefing" technique was used in this assignment. Students chose templates to design the educational website on their topics and assessed them according to selected criteria. They posted information on each study at a separate thread of the Forum where students evaluated each other's work.

Workshop #2. Websites analysis in Joomla. In this seminar-disputation students chose websites on topics similar to their project and studied those websites according to the criteria they had developed independently. The proceedings were the same as in Workshop #1.

Lab #3. Template installation and configuration for Joomla. In this lab, students installed the template chosen for the site for educational purposes in Workshop #2 and designed by Joomla. Then they set up that template, i.e. they changed a template logo, a color scheme of the design.

Lab #4. The website menu design. During this lab, students designed the left, top and right menu of the site, decided the hierarchy of menu objects, and submenus.

The next module of the subject "Website administration" is dedicated to the processes of adding some extra functions to the educational website, as well as indexing and publishing it. During the study, students studied lectures and labs.

LC #4. Website management. In this lecture, news conference was held, similar to Lecture #2. The lecture observed the principles of defining user roles, distribution of rights for user groups in Joomla CMS.

Lab #5. Installation of additional modules on the website. While working, students mastered the algorithms for installing additional modules for the educational website. Students installed and configured the CAPTCHA service, RSS news feed, text processing modules on the site, inserting tools for playing sound and video on the site. Before doing the lab, the work in a social network was arranged.

Lab #6. Working with users on the website. While working using a case method, students organized registration for users on the site, defined rights for standard roles of user groups, and started new user groups.

Lab #7. A website hosting. During that work, students were indexing their educational website, finding hosting for the site, and registering it in search systems.

As a result of performing all labs, a student received a fully functional educational website, which he/she represented at the seminar-conference. Students prepared reports and presentations of their website, discussed guests and peers' comments at the conference.

During the training, students were given an opportunity to write papers on the proposed topics. The students selected the topics from the "The headlines of the course articles for writing" designed in Moodle.

A follow-up phase of the subject was also conducted in Moodle. The control test was being open for doing on the date of the credit test. So the students had an access to it for two hours, and each student was given one attempt.

The main recommendations for a lecturer on choosing interactive learning methods for a particular academic subject are the following:

1. The effectiveness of using interactive educational methods directly depends on the quantity of participants and membership in the educational process. Using verbal activities while working with two or more student groups has more difficulties in socialization. In addition, there cannot be many participants for forms such as debate, brainstorming, etc. The optimal number is 6-8 learners. It will ensure the activity of all students when using this form. If a group of students is more numerous, it is possible to divide it according to different topics within a distance pedagogical interaction, for example, to make up different topics in a social network service.

2. It is necessary to make each student's maximum use, give everyone an opportunity to speak out, and moderate communication. If some students are too active, it is necessary to stop them by means of prearranged regulations of the class. In addition, it is necessary to prepare students for classes using short warm-up activities. Such tasks (time spent) must be taken into account when drawing up the format of the class.

3. The software and hardware that are going to be used must be prepared for the class. To do this, one should gather all the students first, connect the required equipment, enable and authorize in required software systems.

4. A clear schedule of the class is established while giving out the assignments. In such interactive training methods as news conference, presentation of the project, etc., one should inform students about the rules of the class, distribution of roles and functions of participants on the spot. All the materials referring to the class are recommended to download in the e-course of the subject and a social network service.

5. There is no need to form voluntary groups in case of group work is supposed. It is better to use random number generators and divide students into equal groups.

3 Results and discussion

The main task of studying students' information competence was to observe and record the dynamics of indicators. The object of the research is the process of developing the student information competence, and the subject is the dynamics of changing the level of the student information competence which helps to overcome obstacles in the usage of information technologies.

The surveys to assess the effectiveness of student initiative development by interactive learning methods used by a lecturer were conducted in the academic year 2107/18 at three universities located in different Russian regions. They are Sholom-Aleichem Priamursky State University, Moscow State University of Civil Engineering and South Ural State University. There were 212 students in a pilot (experimental) group and 219 ones in a control group who participated in the project.

The purpose of the studies is to assess the level of initiative development in a student future career before training. It also includes monitoring changes during the training course, and giving a check test at the end of training. These findings are presented as the ranking in Table 1.

Table 1. Levels of students' initiative

Students' Initiative Level	**Level Characteristics**
Low	While working, a student reproduces and applies algorithms of a learned basis for work accomplished on his/her own
Middle	While working, a student produces new information subjectively when synthesizing a known basis by himself/herself
High	While working in each new situation or task, a student sets up new rational ways, i.e. fairly new information

Two groups of students were selected for the study. The first control group was trained according to the system of blended learning. LMS Moodle was employed as the site which contained materials and assignments to carry out. The most part of classes was conducted in the classroom. The second experimental group was trained using a special system of interactive learning methods provided by an instructor.

Test measurements showed quantitative changes in the levels of students' initiative in the control and experimental groups.

Table 2. Students' initiative levels dynamics in control group

Groups	**Number of students**	**Students' initiative levels**					
		Low		***Middle***		***High***	
		No.	*%*	*No.*	*%*	*No.*	*%*
Before	219	154	70.3	53	24.2	12	5.5
After	219	102	46.6	70	32.0	47	21.4

Table 3. Students' initiative levels dynamics in experimental group

Groups	**Number of students**	**Students' initiative levels**					
		Low		**Middle**		**High**	
		No.	**%**	**No.**	**%**	**No.**	**%**
Before	212	136	64.2	41	28.8	15	7.0

After	212	88	41.5	63	20.3	81	38.2

The data analysis culled from those studies proved that it is more effective to use a system of prepared interactive training methods in a subject for students' initiative development in their future career than a standard methodology of blended learning. The fulfillment confirms that pedagogical interaction regarding a lecturer's choice of interactive training methods for students' initiative development contributes to identify and solve problems, and masters their professional skills development.

The results of the experimental evaluation demonstrate students' growing initiative. The number of students with high-level initiative has increased by 16% in the control group, while that in the experimental group has risen by 31%. This is the evidence that the methodology used encourages students moving to the next high level of initiative, while the standard methodology does not provide this development, but lets students achieve only the middle one.

4 Conclusion

Positive changes, in their development over time, testify to the effectiveness of the experiment, that is, using the system of prepared interactive training methods in an academic subject is efficient for students' initiative development in their future career. At the same time, using pedagogical interaction ensures goal-centered, regular, systematic and effective educational process. The data analysis culled from those studies showed that the authors have achieved the scientifically sound and tested goal.

Further research can be related to continuing enhancement of this methodology, as well as its adaptation to develop other students' competences.

Acknowledgements

The study was conducted with the financial support of the Ministry of Education and Science of the Russian Federation, grant no. 2.8720.2017/8.9.

References

1. G. A. M. Lopez, A. J. B. Jovani, and C. B. V. Sindey, "Overview of u-learning. Concepts, characteristics, uses, application scenarios and topics for research." IEEE Latin America Transactions 14.12 (2016): pp. 4792-4798.
2. K. MacCallum, S. Day, D. Skelton, and M. Verhaart, "Mobile Affordances and Learning Theories in Supporting and Enhancing Learning," International Journal of Mobile and Blended Learning (IJMBL), vol. 9, no. 2 (2016). pp. 61-73.
3. F. Albertos-Marco, V.M. Penichet, and J.A. Gallud, "Distributing Web Interaction Capabilities: The Web Interaction Hub." In Proceedings of the XVII International Conference on Human Computer Interaction (2016). pp. 37.
4. M.M.M. Adnan, "Effective learning through moodle management, social media, and peer-guided learning". Preparing the Next Generation of Teachers for 21st Century Education (2018). pp. 89-108.
5. L. Umek, D. Keržič, A. Aristovnik, and N. Tomaževič, "An assessment of the effectiveness of Moodle e-learning system for undergraduate public administration education." International Journal of Innovation and Learning 21(2) (2017): pp. 165-177.

6. Al-Azawei, P. Parslow, and K. Lundqvist, “Investigating the effect of learning styles in a blended e-learning system: An extension of the technology acceptance model (TAM).” Australasian Journal of Educational Technology, 33(2) (2017).
7. N. Chafiq, and M. Talbi, “Tutoring Functions in a Blended Learning System: Case of Specialized French Teaching,” International journal of advanced computer science and applications, vol. 8, no. 2 (2017). pp. 24-28.
8. S. M. Karen, L. Baur, and J. Barrett, "Evidence-Based Principles for Using Technology-Enhanced Learning in the Continuing Professional Development of Health Professionals." Journal of Continuing Education in the Health Professions, vol. 37, no. 1 (2017). pp. 61-66.
9. N. Popovic, T. Popovic, I.R. Dragovic, and O. Cmiljanic, “A Moodle-based blended learning solution for physiology education in Montenegro: A case study.” Advances in Physiology Education, 42(1) (2018). pp. 111-117.
10. X. Maldague, M. Kuimova, D. Burleigh, and S. Skvortsova, “Information and Communication Technologies in Engineering Education.” MATEC Web of Conferences 79 (2016): pp. 01044.
11. W. Villegas-Ch, S. Lujan-Mora, D. Buenano-Fernandez, and M. Roman-Canizares, “Analysis of web-based learning systems by data mining.” IEEE 2nd Ecuador Technical Chapters Meeting, ETCM 2017 (2017). pp. 1-5.
12. A.C. Lagman, and D.M. Mansul, “Extracting personalized learning path in adaptive e-learning environment using rule based assessment.” ACM International Conference Proceeding Series, Part F135375 (2017). pp. 335-340.
13. K.S. Sharifzyanova, J.N. Shtreter, and R.N. Nauryzbayeva, "Structural-Functional Model of Designing Individual Educational Path of Teacher's Professional Development in Conditions of Information Educational Environment," International Journal of Environmental and Science Education, vol. 10, no.4. (2015). pp. 523-532.
14. H. N. Cheng, Z. Liu, J. Sun, S. Liu, and Z. Yang, “Unfolding online learning behavioral patterns and their temporal changes of college students in SPOCs,” Interactive Learning Environments, vol. 25, no. 2. (2017). pp. 176-188.

Cigarette smoking and school culture: An analysis of smoking at a high school according to different variables

Cem Gercek[1,a]

[1]Faculty of Education, Department of Mathematics and Science Education, Hacettepe University, Ankara, Turkey

Abstract. This research aims to analyse the smoking status of students and teachers at a high school and their mental images in relation to cigarette smoking according to different variables. In this way, it will be possible to be informed of school culture formed about smoking. This is a descriptive research using the survey model. The research group was composed of 537 students attending a high school and 41 teachers. The research data were collected with a form. Data collected were analysed by means of descriptive statistics and Chi-square test. The findings obtained demonstrated that smoking had increased according to grade levels. Accordingly, boys smoked more than girls. 27% of the teachers were smokers. It was found that teachers as well as students had positive metaphors about smoking. Based on these conclusions, it may be stated that smoking has become a school culture in that school.

Keywords: Cigarette smoking, mental image, high school students, teacher, school culture, health education.

1 Introduction

Smoking is at the top of harmful habits which are increasing day by day [1, 2]. Cigarette smoking, threatening non-smokers as well as smokers, is one of the considerable factors in millions of people's loss of their life in the world each year. According to World Health Organisation, a person dies of smoking every 13 seconds in the world [3]. Research has shown that passive smoking is as dangerous as smoking [4, 5]. To exemplify, several diseases such as cardiac diseases, stomach ulcer, COPD (chronic obstructive pulmonary disease), emphysema and cancer can develop in individuals who are exposed to cigarette smoke for 30 minutes.

Tobacco product humans consume the most is cigarette [6]. Studies report that smoking and alcohol drinking is common among young people [7, 8]. Young people's inclination to substance addiction forms prepares the ground for starting smoking, drinking alcohol or using drug. The period when young people try smoking and when they are most biased towards tobacco addiction is adolescence [7]. Adolescence is an important period for

[a] Corresponding author: cgercek@hacettepe.edu.tr

physical and cognitive development. Individuals are also psychologically and socially influenced by each other in that period. According to Erikson's Psycho-social Development Theory, individuals experience identity crisis in the period of adolescence [9]. Adolescents are occupied with completing their social roles, status, professional preparation and sexual identity in that period. Individuals experiencing identity crisis have more inclination to substance addiction and smoking is at the leading position in this respect. Young people start smoking at early ages with desire to prove themselves at school or in the circle of friends or in order not to be isolated by their peers. This situation increases the importance of prevention from harmful habits at school [10, 11]. National approaches are important in struggling with smoking.

According to data coming from the Ministry of Health, approximately one out of ten secondary school students and one out of five high school students smoke [12]. It was found that training at school against smoking (primary prevention training) was effective in refusing smoking and in developing the behaviour of struggling with smoking [13, 14]. Research shows that more than half of the individuals in Turkey smoke at 11 or at an earlier age for the first time [12, 15]. A study conducted in Turkey found that the number of high male high school students was more than two times as many as female students [16]. Another study found that 64% of students had smoked at least once in their life [17]. More than half of young people smoked even in provinces having the lowest percentages [12]. This high rate of smoking in young population indicates the necessity for taking precautions. A study performed in the USA with the participation of students reports that the rate of using tobacco products is 6.5% for secondary school students and 22,9% for high school students [18].

The risk factors for the youth can be listed as peers, family, stress, misbeliefs and advertisements. An examination of the factor of peers shows that adolescents' need to be accepted by their friends makes them smoke. Friends are as important as families for individuals in adolescence. And friends are sometimes even more important for them [19, 20]. Young people can start smoking because their friends smoke or for such reasons as gaining popularity at school, fear of being isolated from their group of friends, socialising and peer pressure.

As to the factor of family, having parents who are smokers is a factor in starting smoking [21]. Young people can accept their family members as role models in childhood and they can start smoking at very young ages in order to imitate their parents. This is undesirable. Even if young people do not want to try smoking their bias to smoking can increase due to being passive smokers in consequence of having smoking parents. Besides, having smokers in their family reduces young people's age of starting smoking. Apart from that, the rate of smoking also increases as the socio-economic and educational levels of families fall. Parents' inadequate knowledge about child development and their attitudes can also cause their children to have unbalanced and undesired behaviours [9].

Advertisements have undeniable effect on young people in starting smoking. Multinational cigarette companies choose the youth as their audience so as to increase cigarette consumption. The packets of cigarettes are important tools of marketing in increasing cigarette consumption. Incentive advertisements on cigarette packets attract especially young people's attention and encourage them to smoke. The ads on cigarette packets mask the real identity of cigarettes. This puts the youth into great danger. There are scientific studies showing that smoking in movies encourages young people to smoke and thus causes an increase in rates of smoking. Moreover, cigarette producing companies also sponsor events that young people participate in (festivals, concerts, etc.), they focus on the properties of young people's development periods and they aim to give them the impression that smoking provides them with such feelings as excitement, adrenalin, independence, freedom, entertainment and socialising.

This research is important in that it analyses students' and teachers' smoking at a high school and their mental images about smoking as a whole according to different variables. By determining teachers' and students' mental images about smoking, it will also be possible to be informed of school culture in terms of smoking. Thus, it is thought that important knowledge will be offered in primary prevention activities within this research.

1.1 Aim of the Research

This research aims to analyse the smoking status of students and teachers at a high school and their mental images in relation to cigarette smoking according to different variables. In line with this purpose, the research seeks answers to the following questions:

1. 1. What is the smoking status of students according to gender and grade levels?
2. 2. What is the smoking status of teachers?
3. 3. What are the students' and teachers' positive and negative metaphors for smoking and what ae the reasons for this?

2 Methodology

This is a descriptive research in survey model. Descriptive studies try to describe actions, groups and institutions in a period of time in terms of "what happens" and "how it happens" [22].

2.1 Research group

The research group was composed of 537 students attending a high school in Ankara in 2015-2016 academic year and 41 teachers. Of the students, 307 (57%) were girls while 230 (43%) were boys. 144 of them (26%) were the prep class students while 142 (26%) were 9th graders, 128 (24%) were 10th graders, 81 (15%) were 11th graders and 42 (9%) were 12th graders. Of the teachers, on the other hand, 26 (65%) were female while 15 (35%) were male.

The data were collected with a form having received the necessary permission. The form consisted of 3 parts. Part 1 contained demographic properties (age, gender, grade level); Part 2 contained smoking status, where they first started smoking, the number of cigarettes smoked a day; and Part 3 contained metaphors about smoking and questions about the reasons.

A meeting was held with the researcher and the teachers during the applications. A 20-minute presentation entitled "Smoking and Life" was made in the meeting. 25 slides and 2 videos were presented during the 20-minute presentation, and then a 10-minute discussion was held with teachers on "teachers as models" and "smoking prohibition at schools".

2.2 Data Analysis

The data were analysed in percentages, frequencies and in Chi-square. The topics discussed in the meeting with teachers were noted down. The notes taken were presented to teachers' confirmation for reliability.

3 Findings

Whether or not there were any significant differences between students' smoking status according to grade levels was tested with chi square analysis.

Because the data for smoking status and grade levels did not have normal distribution, Chi Square test, which was a non-parametric test, was administered. Accordingly, smoking status differed significantly according to grade levels [X2=83.894; sd:16; p<0.01]. Thus, smoking increased as the grade level increased (Table1).

Table 1. The distribution of students' smoking status in percentages

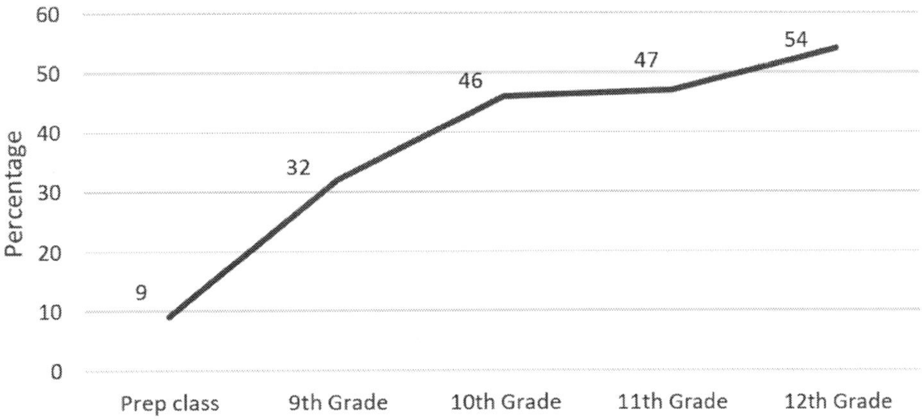

Students' smoking status on the basis of gender was examined in accordance with the first research problem. The issue was analysed with Chi square test- a nonparametric test- since the data did not have normal distribution. Accordingly, smoking status differed significantly according to gender. It was found that boys smoked more than girls [X2=22.010; sd:4; p<0.01].

Detailed examination of students' smoking status according to gender showed that 165 (54%) of the girls and 109 (49%) of the boys did not smoke. On the other hand, 64 (22%) of the girls and 59 (26%) of the boys said that they smoked. 25 (8%) of the girls and 29 (13%) of the boys said that they used to smoke but that they no longer smoked. 528 students in total-305 of whom were girls and 223 of whom were boys- answered this question. In relation to the question about the place where they first smoked, 95 (18%) of the students said that they first smoked at a meeting with friends, 61 (11%) said they first smoked at school, 55 (10%) said they first smoked somewhere else (in the dormitory room, in a relative's house, in the street, on the car) and 35 (6%) said they first smoked at home. In relation to the number of cigarettes they smoked a day, 82 students said that they smoked 12 cigarettes a day on average while 12 students said that they smoked 25 cigarettes a week.

In line with the second research problem, teachers' smoking status was analysed. Accordingly, it was found that 13 teachers (32%) said that they had never smoked so far, 8 (19%) said they had tried smoking once in their life, 7 (17%) said they had smoked occasionally but then gave up smoking, 4 (10%) said they sometimes smoked but fewer than one a day on average, and 7 (17%) said that he/she was a regular smoker- which meant at least one cigarette a day. 2 teachers (5%) did not answer the question. 6 teachers smoked 14 cigarettes a day on average whereas 4 teachers smoked 6 cigarettes a week on average.

In line with the third research problem, teachers' and students' metaphors about smoking were analysed, and the reasons for those metaphors were also examined. Table 2 shows the metaphors teachers and students created about smoking. Accordingly, teachers created 5 positive and 19 negative metaphors and one neutral metaphor. Students created 70 positive metaphors, 84 negative metaphors and 8 neutral metaphors.

Table 2. Metaphors created by teachers and students

Metaphors	Positive	Negative	Neutral
Teachers	Friend, hobby, coffee, food, fruit	Instrument of addiction, hell, illness, disgusting, hypocrite people, escape, murderer, joy, rotten food, heroin, an object with bad smell, smoke, ash, ash tray, wood, death, shackle, satan, drug, poison	Nothing
Students	A habit, anti-depressant, antibiotic, friend, love, fire, way for escape, organ, relaxing, dream, gap, tea, flower, chocolate, change, child of depression, a break while studying, confidant, cure to problems, medicine, pal, entertainment, eating bread with salt, bread, adolescents' addiction, personal belonging, opportunist, football, passing fancy, real friend, the sky, a source for showing off, fertiliser, smell of a rose, nice, stylish, life, drink, need, medicine, human, different, escape, woman, a break to empty your mind, coffee and chocolate, killer dog, reading a book, mineral water, happiness, something great, nargile, game, toy, relaxing, soothing, insincere friend, art, something that needs respect, love, darling, stress ball, water, music you listen to on your mobile phone, hopelessness, sleep, loneliness, tranquiliser, controlling time, joy	Bitter, alcohol, foolishness, asphalt, smoke of fire, angel of death, addiction, bacteria, simple and aimless, meaningless, scaffold, error, human, suicide, poison, dirt, glass, spare time, harm filling a gap, too deep pool, monster, lung, tool of murder, sexual intercourse, mud, desperation, bank with high interest rates, garbage, dustbin, stick crackers, rotten fruit, drum, excrement, exhaust gas, mouse poison, unnecessary tool, prison, damaged lung, illness, mistake, exhaust gas polluting the air, thief, disgusting, bad habit, instrument for committing suicide, lack of willpower, waste, paper, sewage, cancer, black hole, murderer, a deceiving friend, shroud, handcuffs, polluted air, polecat, bad, king, gambling, water well, ash tray, expenditure, stomachache, germ, hatred, oxygen, school, ocean, deadly, being penniless, a deodorant with bad smell, nonsense, chewing gum, enemy, slot machine, steroid, telephone, cliff, drug, virus, snake, eggs, harm, poison	Chimney, excuse, I don't know, grass, pipe, willpower, carstic shape, soap

The following are some examples for teachers' reasons for their positive, negative and neutral metaphors:

Positive	*Having changes sometimes relaxes me.* *It relaxes me, it shares my loneliness.* *It makes me move away by keeping me busy.*
Negative	*Its smell disturbs me most* *It influences an individual while smoking, but then everything is the same.* *When I do not smoke, I feel physical deprivation.* *I feel addicted to and captured by cigarettes* *Its smell makes me sick.* *I cannot breathe*
Neutral	*It means nothing to me.*

The following are some examples for students' reasons for their positive, negative and neutral metaphors:

Positive	*The only thing that has not left me alone for 5 years.* *You suffer but you keep loving.* *It occasionally moves you away.* *I sometimes feel like smoking.* *It soothes me.* *The thing that likes burning and killing, the only thing that considers me valuable.* *It is a need.* *Something I use in my spare time.* *It makes me forget everything when I am depressed.* *You smoke when you like, so it is not complete addiction.* *It is beside you when you are bored or when you feel like smoking.* *When you inhale, you see its smoke and the smoke takes you to your dreams.* *It is very nice.* *I like it very much.* *It is sweet; it removes stress and helps to focus on something.* *You are heated when you approach.* *You smoke when are depressed.* *It takes away all my problems and ir relaxes me, it also hinders me from putting on weight.* *It has worldwide value.* *It is the most beautiful and most relaxing thing in the World.* *It is unnecessary, people smoke to gain popularity.* *It is always beside me whenever I am bored, whenever I wake up in the middle of a night, before and after a meal.* *It is an excuse for any problem.* *Everybody smokes in the circle of friends to show off.* *Everybody wants to try smoking, and they think it is stylish.* *I enjoy it.* *I lose my vital functions unless I smoke.* *When you do not have what you feel you need, it replaces them.* *You imitate others and you smoke.* *People feel as if they were different while smoking.* *You like it to be beside you when you want it or need it.* *It is something disturbing for those who do not want it but it is something relaxing for those who want it.* *It empties your mind. ıt takes away all your problems and sorrows.* *It is the thing that is beside you when you feel empty and it is the thing that makes you feel numb.* *I cannot do without smoking.*
Negative	*It causes addiction and you cannot quit even if you want to.* *It reminds me of the treachery of life.* *It is simple but enjoyable death.* *Most people start smoking to be accepted by their friends or with their encouragement, and they cannot say "no".* *First it relaxes you, it seems as if it eliminated all your problems. But then causes*

	waste of large amounts of money and health problems. *Some foolish children spend their spare time smoking because they have nothing to do.* *Nobody entering into this darkness can reach the daylight.* *I sometimes smoked when I was bored, but I saw no benefits of smoking.* *There is a cure but you sometimes cannot get rid of it.* *I know it is poisonous and I know what illness it causes.* *I had a violent cough when I tried smoking, it also tastes bad.* *Smoking is the most dangerous weapon in the world.* *Most of the adolescents' smoke just to show off.* *It separates one from his/her beloved ones around him/her.* *It affects my physical activities.* *It is unnecessary and harmful addiction.* *It is clearly one's attempt at killing oneself.* *It gives harm to individuals financially and medically.* *It is harmful in every respect; even trying once can make one feel guilty.* *It is the starting point of every bad habit (of addiction)* *You lose something at every inhaling* *It kills hundreds of people every year.*
Neutral	*It does not make much sense to me. It is meaningless.* *It has no contributions to me.* *You cannot compare it to something else.* *It is both nice and harmful.*

4 Conclusion and discussion

Smoking is the behaviour which is believed at childhood and youth that it will make individuals appear more mature and adult. The risky developmental period to start using substances is adolescence and young adult period [23]. Students' smoking status on the basis of gender and grade levels was evaluated in this research in accordance with the first research problem. The results indicated that boys smoked more than girls. Global Youth Tobacco research found that smoking prevalence was higher among male participants than among female participants [12]. Thus, the findings are similar. It may be stated that the rate of smoking rises in parallel to the rise in grade levels. The places where students smoked for the first time were the meeting place with friends, school and other (namely- dormitory, room, relatives' house, streets and car) mostly according to the participants' statements. It was found that students smoked at least 3 cigarettes a day. Having smokers in a family or in the immediate neighbourhood, psycho-social factors, imitation and social pressure play important roles in one's starting smoking [9, 24, 25]. Young people identify their feelings of freedom and independence in particular with smoking.

Gender, age, whether or not family members smoke, family income and circle of friends are important factors in starting smoking [8]. Hence, children learn smoking habit from their parents, peers and social environment [26]. The most important factor in causing addiction to smoking is the social environment and circle of friends in early youth [27]. In addition to that, taking one as a role model, imitation and curiosity also encourage adolescents to smoke. Peer education in activities of struggling with smoking in schools is important for this reason [11, 28].

On evaluating teachers' smoking status, it was found that the rate of those who had started smoking and had still been smoking was 3 times as high as the rate of those who had never smoked. It was found that those teachers smoked 14 cigarettes a day on average.

Research has shown that teaching is a profession in which burnout level is high [29]. This finding makes us think that this is an important factor in starting smoking and in continuing smoking. Teachers stated in meetings with them that they obeyed smoking prohibition in school and in the school garden. However, they said that they smoked during breaks a few metres away outside the school gate. They said that students would not take them as role models even if they saw them smoking. Yet, would it be right to think that students will not take their teachers- who teach that smoking is harmful and forbidden at school- as role models [30, 31] after seeing them smoking? Or can we think that what they have learnt will be turned into gains? It should not be forgotten that students are biased to take teachers as role models and that they internalise the behaviours which are displayed rather than the behaviours which are taught. Such factors are important in the formation of school culture in relation to smoking.

It was found that teachers and students had positive and negative metaphors about smoking that students' positive metaphors were fewer than the negative ones but that they were more than they should be. Teachers' reasons for their positive metaphors were as in the following: relaxing in a different way, sharing their loneliness and moving them away by keeping them busy. Students' reasons included the following: soothing, eliminating stress, making happy, being an instrument of focusing and controlling, removing the problems/sorrows, hindering putting on weight, being a life style and confidant. Students' statements such as "it has worldwide value", "ıt is the most beautiful and relaxing thing in the world", when I do not have what I feel I need, it replaces them", "it is the thing which is beside me when I feel empty and it is the thing that makes me feel numb", "it is a therapy at hard times" were important. Teachers' and students' negative statements such as "its smell disturbs me most", "I feel addicted to and captured by it", "we cannot breathe", you cannot give up once you start smoking", "it is simple and enjoyable death", "first it relaxes you, it seems as if it eliminated your problems. But then causes waste of large amounts of money and health problems", "I sometimes smoked when I was bored but I saw no benefits of smoking" there is a cure but you sometimes cannot get rid of I", "it gives harm without making you feel", and "although smoking has no benefits, young people smoke because they imitate others and smoking is deceptive" show that they have adequate knowledge about the issue. Studies conducted also demonstrated that smokers and non-smokers were knowledgeable about smoking [32, 33, 34].

References

1. H.-W. Huang, C.-C. Lu, Y.-H. Yang, C.-L. Huang, Smoking Behaviours of adolescents, influenced by smoking of teachers, family and friends. Int. Nursing Review, 61, 220–227 (2014).
2. M. O. Raji, H. Muhammad, A. M. Usman, U. Muwafaq, R. A. Oladigbolu, A. U. Kaoje, Cigarette smoking among out-of-school adolescents in sokoto metropolis, North-West Nigeria. Health Science Jounal, 11(3), 1-10 (2017)
3. World Health Organization [WHO], Health for the World's adolescents: a second chance in the second decade. Geneva, Switzerland: WHO Document Production Services (2014).
4. R.R. Kipping, R.M. Campbell, G. J. MacArthur, D.J. Gunnell, M. Hickman, Multiple risk behaviour in adolescence. J. of Public Health, 34(S1) (2012).
5. C.Y. Lovato, C. Zeisser, H. S. Campbell, A. W. Watts, P. Halpin, ... K. S. Brown, Adolescent smoking: effect of school and community characteristics. American Journal of Preventive Medicine, 39(6), 507–514 (2010).

6. T. Ortabag, S.Ozdemir, B. Bakir, N.Tosun, Health promotion and risk behaviors among adolescents in Turkey. J. School Nursing, 27(4), 304-31 (2011).
7. B. Challier, N. Chau, R. Prédine, M.Choquet, B. Legras, Associations of family environment and individual factors with tobacco, alcohol, and illicit drug use in adolescents. Eur. Journal Epidemiology, 16, 33-42 (2000).
8. O. S. Icmeli, H.Turker, B. Gundogus, M. Ciftci, U. Aka Akturk, Behaviours and opinions of adolescent students on smoking. Tuberculosis and Thorax, 64(3), 217-222 (2016).
9. S. A. McLeod, E. Erikson. Retrieved 24 April 2016 from www.simplypsychology.org/Erik-Erikson.html (2013).
10. O. O. Adeyeye, Cigarette smoking habits among senior secondary students in Lagos, Southwest Nigeria. Int. J. Medicine Research, 2, 1047-1050. (2011).
11. H. J. Paek, T. Hove, H. J. Oh, Multilevel analysis of the impact of school-level tobacco policies on adolescent smoking: the case of Michigan. J. of School Health, 83(10), 679–689 (2013).
12. Ministry of Health, Küresel yetişkin tütün araştırması türkiye raporu. [Global adult tobacco survey: Turkey report], (Report No: 943). Retrieved April 15, 2016 from http://www.halksagligiens.hacettepe.edu.tr/KY-TA_TR.pdf (2012).
13. H. Beckmann, S.Mechnich, Kinder vor dem Rauchen schützen [Protect children from smoking]. Frankfurt: Fischer Taschenbuch Verlag GmbH (2001).
14. A. Beelmann, B. Thomas, Wirksamkeit von Präventionsmaßnahmen bei Kindern und Jugendlichen [Effectiveness of preventive measures in children and adolescents]. Zeitschrift für Klinische Psychologie und Psychotherapie, 35(2), 151-162 (2006).
15. G. Emekdar, R. Çıtıl, Y. Önder, Y. E. Bulut, Ö. Yaşayancan, N., Ö Kazancı, E. Sönmezgöz, M. Eğri, Smoking prevalence and related factors among secondary and high school students in tokat province. J. of Contempporary Medicine, 7(1), 58-56 (2017).
16. D. Dogan Gumuş, B. Ulukol, Factors contributing to smoking and efficiency of two different education models among adolescents. J. of Inonu University School of Medicine, 17(3), 179-185 (2010).
17. M. Bektas, C. Ozturk, Development of smoking prevention program and evaluation of the program effectiveness. Buca Faculty of Education Journal, 34, 1-21 (2012).
18. S. R. Dube, R. A. Arrazola, J. Lee, M. Engstrom, A. Malarcher, Pro-Tobacco Influences and susceptibility to smoking cigarettes among middle and high school students-United States, 2011. J. of Adolescent Health, 52(S5), 45-51 (2013).
19. H. Darling, A. I. Reeder, S. Williams, R. McGee, Is there a relation between school smoking policies and youth cigarette smoking knowledge and behaviors? Health Ed. Res., 21(1), 108-115 (2006).
20. M. Kleinjan, R. Engels, J. van Leeuwe, J. Brug, R. van Zundert, R. van den Eijnden, Mechanisms of adolescent smoking cessation: roles of readiness to quit, nicotine dependence, and smoking of parents and peers. Drug & Alcohol Dependence, 99(1–3), 204–214 (2009).
21. A.B. Albers, L. Biener, M. Siegel, D. M. Cheng, N. Rigotti, Household smoking bans and adolescent antismoking attitudes and smoking initiation: findings from a longitudinal study of a Massachusetts youth cohort. American J. of Public Health, 98(10), 1886–1893 (2008).

22. J. W. Creswell, Araştırma deseni. [Research Design] (Ed. Selçuk Beşir Demir) Ankara: Egiten Kitap (2013).
23. J. L. Johnson, P. A. Ratner, R. S. Tucker, J. L. Bottorff, B. Zumbo, K. M. Prkachin, J. Shoveller, Development of a multidimensional measure of tobacco dependence in adolescence. Addictive Behaviors, 30(3), 501–515 (2005).
24. L. M. O'Brien, M. Polacsek, P. B. MacDonald, J. Ellis, S. Berry, M. Martin, Impact of a school health coordinator intervention on health-related school policies and student behavior. J. of School Health, 80(4), 176-185 (2010).
25. C. M. Sabiston, C. Y.Lovato, R.Ahmed, A. W.Pullman, V. Hadd, H. S. Campbell, C. Nykiforuk, K. S. Brown, School smoking policy characteristics and individual perceptions of the school tobacco context: are they linked to students' smoking status? J. of Youth Adolescence, 38(10), 1374-1387 (2009).
26. D. Piontek, A.Buehler, U. Rudolph, K. Metz, C. Kroeger, S. Gradl, S. Floeter, C. Donath, Social contexts in adolescent smoking: does school policy matter? Health Edu. Res., 23(6), 1029–1038 (2008).
27. M. Virtanen, M. Pietikainen, M. Kivimaki, J. Luopa, J. Jokela, M. Elovainio, J.Vahtera, Contribution of parental and school personnel smoking to health risk behaviours among Finnish adolescents. BMC Pub. Health, 9, 382–390 (2009).
28. T. A. Barnett, L.Gauvin, M. Lambert, J. O'Loughlin, G.Paradis, J. J. McGrath, The influence of school smoking policies on student tobacco use. Archives Pediatrics & Adolescent Medicine, 161(9), 842-848 (2007).
29. B. Byrne, The Nomological Network of Teacher Burnout: A Literature Review and Empirically Validated Model. In R. Vandenberghe and A. Huberman (Eds.), Understanding and Preventing Teacher Burnout: A Sourcebook of International Research and Practice (The Jacobs Foundation Series on Adolescence, pp. 15-37). Cambridge: Cambridge University Press (1999).
30. D. Jourdan, J. Pommier, F. Quidu, Practices and Representations of Health Education among Primary School Teachers. Scandinavian J. of Public Health, 38, 86-94 (2010).
31. S. A. Myers-Clark, S. E. Christopher, Effectiveness of a health course at ınfluencing preservice teachers' attitudes toward teaching health. J. of School Health, 71(9). 462-466 (2001).
32. P. L. Chen, W. G. Huang, K. Y. Chao, Susceptibility to initiate smoking among junior and senior high school nonsmokers in Taiwan. Preventive Medicine, 49(1), 58–61 (2009).
33. M. Dobbins, K. DeCorby, S. Manske, E. Goldblatt, Effective practices for school-based tobacco use prevention. Preventive Medicine, 46(4), 289-297 (2008).
34. B. R. Flay, The promise of long-term effectiveness of school-based smoking prevention programs: a critical review of reviews. Tobacco Induced Diseases, 5(1), 7 (2009).

An analysis of university students who are smokers according to their levels of addiction

Cem Gercek[1 a]

[1]Faculty of Education, Department of Mathematics and Science Education, Hacettepe University, Ankara, Turkey

Abstract. Young people constitute one fifth of world population. Youth's reasons for smoking include looking for excitement, getting away from problems and meeting emotional and social needs. Smoking addiction is the most common addiction among young people especially due to the fact that cigarettes are sold legally, and it is known that one out of two young people who try smoking become addicted. Being knowledgeable about youth's smoking addiction will also raise the effects of health education activities. This study aims to evaluate the smoking addiction levels of university students who smoke. Thus, it uses survey model- which is one of quantitative research methods. The study group was composed of 93 volunteering university students chosen randomly. The research data were collected with Fagerström Nicotine Addiction Test. The data collected were put to descriptive analysis (percentages, frequencies, etc.). Accordingly, it was found that the majority of the participants had low or very low levels of smoking addiction, and that male students were more addicted than female students. The reason most commonly mentioned by the participants for taking up smoking was the circle of friends, while the reason for why they were smoking was their feeling of relaxation.

Keywords: Students, smoking, addiction, health education

1 Introduction

Smoking is an important problem of public health. According to the data coming from World Health Organisation, smoking has been increasingly continuing even though its negative effects are known to all [1]. It is predicted that the rate of smokers will increase at least by 50% until the year 2025. Smoking has risks not only for smokers but also for non-smokers. If smoking continues at this pace, it is certain that smoking-related deaths will increase.

Young people constitute one fifth of world population. Young population in the 10-19 age range is above one billion. 80% of them are in developing countries. Youth's reasons for smoking include looking for excitement, getting away from their problems and meeting their emotional and social needs. Especially because it is legal to sell cigarettes, smoking

[a] Corresponding author: cgercek@hacettepe.edu.tr

addiction is the most common addiction type among young people; and it is known that on out of two young people who try smoking become addicted [2].

The ratio of smokers in men aged 15 or above is 63% in Turkey whereas the rate is 24% for women. 20% of smokers start smoking at ages 11-14, 39% at ages 15-18 and 49% start smoking after age 18. Research conducted by Turkish Statistical Institute (TUIK) found that 31% of individuals aged 15 and above smoke tobacco every day or occasionally [3]. Despite efforts to make them quit smoking or hindering their smoking, individuals could not be prevented from starting smoking or they could not be made to quit smoking. Therefore, investigating the reasons especially for youth to start smoking is important in that it sheds light on precautions that can be taken in this respect.

Smoking is an important health problem among university students [4, 5]. Individuals' social life and life in their circle in earlier ages shape their perspectives and beliefs in relation to smoking (see Figure 1). Individuals with positive attitudes towards smoking have more tendency than non-smokers to smoke [4]. Besides, positive attitudes also cause supporting and arguing for smoking. Research conducted with 3101 first year university students demonstrated that the rate of students who had tried smoking only once was 58% while the rate of those who were still smoking was 22% [2]. To illustrate the case with examples from the world, the rate of smokers among university students in Syria is 23% [6], it is 29% in Jordan [7], 14% in Saudi Arabia [8], 17-32% in African countries [9] and 22% in European countries [10]. Another study found that smoking young people were less knowledgeable about the harmful effects of smoking than those who had never smoked or who had given up smoking [11]. In parallel to this, another study conducted with university students found that individuals who had been smoking for longer had reduction in self-efficacy beliefs [12]. Türkoğlu (2007) demonstrated that there were positive correlations between addicted people and nicotine addiction [13].

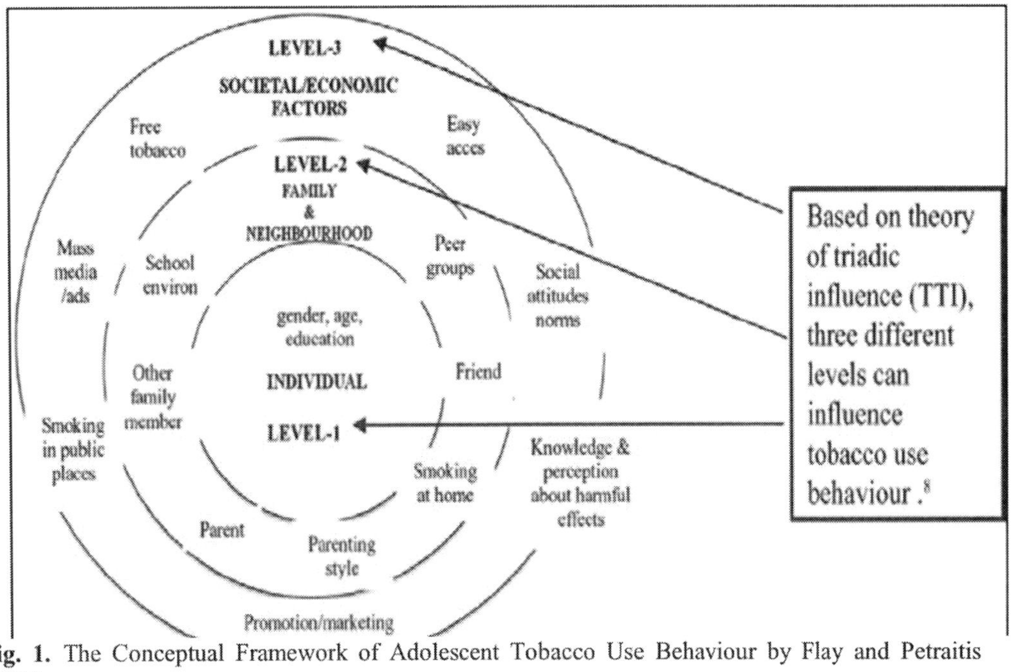

Fig. 1. The Conceptual Framework of Adolescent Tobacco Use Behaviour by Flay and Petraitis (1994).

One of the reasons why young people are inclined to smoking is that they ignore health problems that can emerge. The fact that smoking-related health problems do not arise immediately or that they are not noticed very soon is also an important factor in addiction. However, starting smoking or becoming addicted to smoking will cause negative effects on those individuals' life in the following years. More than 150 million young people smoke all over the world, and it is estimated that they will die of a smoking-related disease [2].

The number of cigarettes smoked a day was found to be directly proportional to age. Accordingly, the number of cigarettes smoked a day increases in parallel to the increase in age. This is important in quitting smoking and in the emergence of serious health problems. The findings obtained demonstrate that there should be struggle against starting smoking at earlier ages [15]. In this context, becoming knowledgeable about young people's smoking addiction will increase the effects of health education activities.

1.1 Aim of the Study

This study aims to analyse the smoking addiction levels of university students who smoke. In accordance with this purpose, the study seeks answers to the following questions:

1. 1. What are the smoking addiction levels of students who smoke, and what is the distribution of the levels according to gender?
2. 2. What are the students' reasons for starting smoking?
3. 3. What do students feel while smoking?

2 Method

This is a study conducted in survey model- which is one of quantitative research methods.

2.1 Study Group

The study group was composed of 93 students 44 of whom were female and 49 of whom were male students attending various faculties of the universities chosen randomly in 2017-2018 academic year. Having informed the students of the study, they were asked to participate on the basis of volunteering. The average age of the students attending Science, Architecture, Engineering, Medical, Law, Educational and Economic and Administrative Sciences faculties was 23. The age of starting smoking was 17 on average; and the length of time they had been smoking was approximately 6 years.

2.2 Data Collection Tools

Fagerström Nicotine Addiction Test was used as the tool of data collection [16]. The test was translated into Turkish by Uysal et al in 2004 [17], and validity and reliability analyses were done. Fagerström Nicotine Addiction Test (FNAT) contained 6 questions in total. The test evaluates smokers' levels of addiction in 5 categories. Accordingly, scores of 0-2 points are labelled as low level addiction, 5 points as medium level addiction and 6-7 points as high level addiction. After the study group was given this test, they were asked two more questions about their reasons for starting smoking and what they felt while smoking.

2.3 Data Analysis

The data collected with FNAT were put to descriptive statistical analyses (frequencies, frequencies, etc.) and thus evaluated.

3 Findings

The findings are evaluated in this section in line with the purpose of this study. Accordingly, addiction levels and the distribution of the levels according to gender were analysed in the context of the first research question. In consequence, it was found that 34% of the students had very low level of smoking addiction whereas 30% had low level and 8% had medium or high level of addiction. The distribution of the levels according to gender is shown in Table 1. Of female students, 34% had very low level of addiction, 41% had low level of addiction, 11% had medium level of addiction, 10% had high level of addiction and 4% had very high level of addiction to smoking. Of male students, on the other hand, 35% had very low level, 21% had low level, 16% had medium level, 18% had high level and 10% had very high level of cigarette addiction.

Table 1. The distribution of addiction levels according to gender

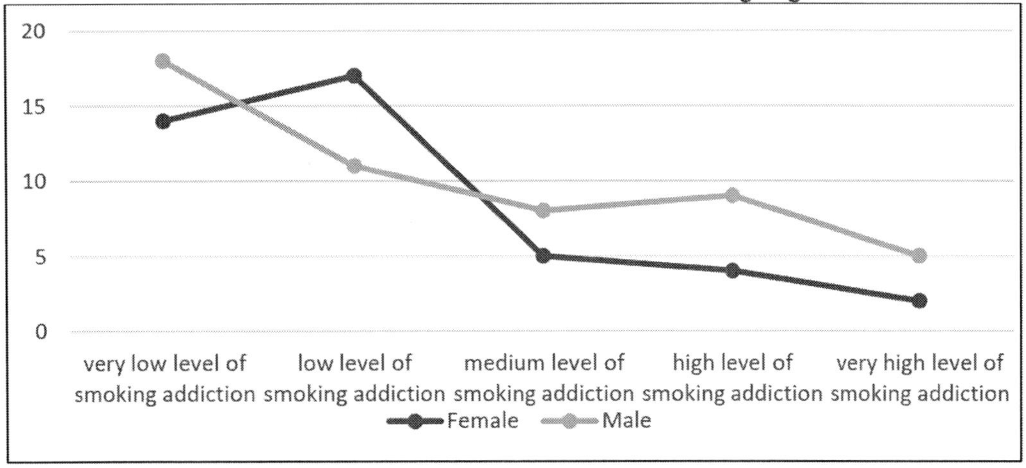

The reasons for starting smoking were determined based on the second research question. Accordingly, the reasons found included such elements as circle of friends (46%), stress (17%), curiosity (16%), pleasure (9%), emulation (8%) and proving oneself to others (3%). The participants mentioned separating from a friend, school, sorrow and boredom as stress; they talked of entertainment, attracting attention as pleasure; and they talked about being influenced by their father, friends, elder brothers and other elderly people as emulation. A student said "I don't know" (1%).

In accordance with the third research question, the feelings they had while smoking were determined. They listed such feelings as relaxation (36), happiness (10), pleasure (9) enjoyment (4), different (3), good (3), confidence (2), bad (2), obligation (3), clearance in lungs (1), pride (1), need to quit (1) and liking. 11 of the smokers said they felt nothing while smoking whereas 3 did not want to answer the question.

4 Conclusion and Discussion

This study determined the addiction levels of university students attending different faculties. Accordingly, the addiction levels were found to be low and very low. On analysing smoking addiction according to gender, it was found that most of the female students had low levels of addiction and that male students had very low levels of addiction. Yet, it was observed that male students had higher levels of smoking addiction than female students. Research conducted in Turkey in relation to smoking has shown that male students had higher levels of smoking addiction than female students [1, 2, 3].

The reason for starting smoking participants mentioned most frequently was the circle of friends. According to Özcebe (2008), having a friend who is a smoker increases the risk for the young to start smoking 3-4 times. Apart from that, the participants also mentioned such reasons as stress, curiosity, pleasure, emulation and proving oneself to others, respectively. The students talked about separating from their boyfriend/girlfriend, school environment, sorrow, examinations and boredom as the sources of stress as the cause for starting smoking. They talked about entertainment, attracting interest and enjoyment as the source of pleasure; and they talked about their father, friends and elder brothers as the source of emulation. Having a smoker father and mother increases the probability of the young to smoke twice [2]. In addition to that, such factors as insufficient relations with their family and copying others also facilitate young people to start smoking. Several studies conducted emphasise that taking others as a model, immediate surrounding and friends are influential in starting to smoke.

Students who smoke said that they mostly felt positive things such as relaxation, happiness, pleasure, good, pride, good and liking while smoking. Those who felt relaxation made such descriptions as having a rest, calming down, fulfilling their responsibility and like tea. Yet, some of the students also mentioned negative feelings such as something lacking, different, bad, obligation and need to quit. In addition to that the students who said that they felt enjoyment while they were smoking made statements such as "although I know it is harmful", "as a feeling of obligation" and "fulfilling the responsibility"; on the other hand, the students who felt bad made statements such as hopelessness, regret, and feeling good even though knowing that it is bad. Smokers stated that they felt relaxed, they solved their problems, they organised their thoughts and that they had better social communication [12]. Some research report that cigarettes smoked so as to reduce stress increase the levels of concern and stress as the number of cigarettes increases and that it diminishes self-efficacy beliefs. Addiction develops in this context. More physiological and psychological problems will emerge in addicted people.

The findings obtained in this study are considered important in organising activities about education on smoking. However, this study is restricted to university students and to FNAT. Therefore, conducting further studies is important for primary prevention for young people's starting to smoke.

References

1. WHO MPOWER package. WHO report on the global tobacco epidemic. Denmark: Publications WHO regional office for Europ. (2008).
2. H. Özcebe, Gençler ve Sigara [Adolecents and Smoke]: Ministry of Health (Report No: 731) Retrieved October 3, 2017 from https://sbu.saglik.gov.tr/Ekutuphane/kitaplar/t18.pdf (2008, February).
3. TUIK, Global adult tobacco survey, publication number: 3324, Turkey: Turkish Statistical Institute, Printing Division, Ankara (2008).
4. M. R. Gillmore, E. A. Wells, E. E. Simpson, D. M. Morrison, M. J. Hoppe, A. A. Wilsdon, E. Murowchick, Children's beliefs about smoking, Nicotine & Tabocco Research, 4(2), 177-183 (2002).
5. W. G. Shadel, R. Niaura, D. B. Abrams, How do adolescents process smoking and antismoking advertisements? a social cognitive analysis with ımplications for understanding smoking ınitiation, Rev. of General Psychol., 5, 429-444 (2001).

6. W. Maziak, S. Rastam, T. Eissenberg, T. Asfar, F. Hammal, M. Bachir, Gender and smoking status based analysis of views regarding waterpipe and cigarette smoking in Aleppo, Syria. Preventive Medicine, 38(4), 479–484 (2004).
7. L. G. Haddad, M. Z. Malak, Smoking habits and attitudes towards smoking among university student in Jordan. Int. J. of Nursing Studies, 39(8), 793-802 (2002).
8. A. Mandil, M. A. BinSaeed, R. Dabbagh, S. A. Shaikh, M. AlSaadi, M. Khan, Smoking among Saudi university students: consumption patterns and risk factors. Eastern Mediterranean Health J., 17(4), 309-316 (2011).
9. L. Mpabulungi, A. S. Muula, Tobacco use among high school student in Kampala, Uganda. Croatian Medical J., 45(1), 80-83. (2004).
10. T. Baska, W. C. Warren, M. Baskova, N. R. Jones, Prevalence of youth cigarette smoking and selected social factors in 25 European countries. Int. J. of Public Health, 54(6), 439-445 (2009).
11. M. A. Freeman, E. V. Hannessy, D. M. Marzullo, Defensive evaluation of smoking messages among college-age smokers: The role of possible selves. Health Psychology, 20, 424-433 (2001).
12. H. Yazıcı, Y. Özbay, Examining the relationship between smoking behavior and self-efficacy beliefs of university students, Sakarya Üniversity Journal of Education Faculty, 7, 91-107 (2004).
13. M. Türkoğlu, Adnan Menderes Üniversitesi öğrencilerinin sigara içme ve bırakma davranışlarının değerlendirilmesi. Basılmamış uzmanlık tezi. Adnan Menderes Üniversitesi Tıp Fakültesi Aile Hekimliği Anabilim Dalı, Aydın (2007).
14. B. R. Flay, J. Petraitis, The theory of triadic influence: A new theory of health behaviour with implications for preventive interventions. Advences in Medical Sociology, 4, 19-44 (1994).
15. A. Yıldırım Kaptanoğlu, G. Polat, M. Soyer, The relation between smoking habit among the students and faculty members in Marmara university and steady cost of smoking. Journal of Higher Education and Science, 2(2), 119-125 (2012).
16. T. F. Heatherton, L. T. Kozlowski, R. C. Frecker, K. O. Fagerström, The Fagerström Test for nicotine dependence: a revision of the fagerström tolerance questionnaire. British J. of Addiction, 86, 1119–1127 (1991).
17. M. A. Uysal, F., Kadakal, C., Karşıdağ, G., Bayram, O., Uysal, V. Yılmaz, Fagerström test for nicotine dependence: Reliability in a Turkish sample and factor analysis. Tuberculosis and Thorax, 52(2), 115-121 (2004).

The Importance of Foreign Language Instruction in the Current Multicultural World

Alena Josefova[1,*]

[1]Univerzita Hradec Kralove, Rokitanskeho 62, 50003 Hradec Kralove, Czech Republic

Abstract. The current multicultural world is characterized, on the one hand, by the intense encounter of people from different cultures, and of various races and nationalities, and on the other hand, by a high degree of technological modernization in all aspects of our lives. The area of education plays, undoubtedly, an irreplaceable and crucial role nowadays. Language is not only about the mutual cooperation of people coming from different parts of the world, but especially in Europe, it is connected with the increase of problems connected with the integration of newcomers into the majority society of the new country. Foreign languages instruction and, in particular, its intensive support by individual countries becomes a necessity in today's diverse world. The author's research at universities in 2 countries confirms the importance of foreign language teaching promotion in the current globalized world.

1 Variability of languages

In today's multicultural world, only few people think about the emergence of languages. How did the language ever come into our world? There was no language at the time of the universe, it appeared gradually. The ancestors of human apes communicated with their hands and legs. The issue of language development and its variety, including foreign language learning, has been addressed by many authors around the world [1, 2, 3, 5, 6], from a variety of perspectives. Today, a bit of evolution is experienced by the smallest children - toddlers, who begin to communicate with the environment using sloppy words, and then combine them into sentences. This is a very individual process, depending on whether parents are bilingual, etc. It is advisable that foreign language learning starts from a very early age when children perceive much more information. And those who, in addition, grow up with more languages, learn to switch between different language systems [4].

There are currently around 6,000-8,000 languages in the world, and there is a huge variety of criteria according to which languages and dialects are divided. These are differences in phonology, vocabulary and grammar. Languages belong to different language groups, e.g. Finnish is completely different from Swedish. English as a mother tongue and a 1st foreign language is spoken by about 1 billion people in the world. The

[*] Corresponding author: alena.josefova@uhk.cz

absence of a common language is the language boundary between the German and the English languages or between the French and Italian languages. The similarity of the Czech language with Slovak and Polish is not accidental, as these are the so-called West Slavonic languages. Speakers of these languages are particularly close to East Slavic languages, such as Russian or Ukrainian, although they have a different Cyrillic written language that one has to learn. Among the South Slavic languages of Croatian, Serbian, Bulgarian, Slovenian or Macedonian, the Slavs are also somewhat understandable, i.e. their speakers are able to communicate with one another.

What causes Europeans troubles is learning distant languages such as Arabic or Chinese. E.g. the Chinese language sounds very musically but we can confirm from our own experience that although it is surprisingly simple in terms of grammar, the written form (existence of more than 50,000 Chinese characters) and especially intonation are a very difficult tasks for foreigners. Nowadays, the expansion of Chinese language around the world can be observed. Most recently China has invested tremendous sums of money in Chinese language teaching in Africa, where a new generation of Chinese-speaking young people is emerging opposed to the English-speaking ones.

It is clear that Czech or German are significantly different from Chinese, because these languages are not historically connected. Within the summer school program at the University of Hradec Kralove, we teach German for beginner students from Taiwan, Hong Kong, China, Malaysia and Japan. German language is very distant, especially in terms of grammatical phenomena and also pronunciations. In 1870 when trying to learn German language the American writer Mark Twain become almost mad. "My philological studies have satisfied me that a gifted person has to learn English in 30 hours, French in 30 days, and German in 30 years."[7]. However, the German language is difficult not only for foreigners, but also the Germans have tried to overcome their own difficulties in language learning through a new reform of the written form of German [8]. Many adult Germans aged 18-64 are unable to read and write correctly. Of course, when it comes to our native language - the Czech language, it is a great challenge for most foreigners in terms of both morphology and phonetics.

1.1 Dialects

A specific group is made up of local dialects, for example, Bavarian is not any specific language, even though the German speakers claim it. Here we can talk about great patriotism, they are not just proud Germans, they are proud Bavarians. The German formal language covers all local dialects in Germany and allows communication beyond the dialects. E.g. the distinctive Saxon dialect, which may sound funny for the listener, is unrepeatable and is closely related to life and culture in Saxony. The local dialect, for example in Valencia, makes it difficult for foreigners to understand Spanish. The so-called valenciano is referred to as a spoken variation of the Catalan language used in the autonomous region of Valencia (3).

2 Universal language

Every language includes the mentality of the society. Once, Latin was a common language, but in the Middle Ages it was more or less differentiated in every country. As a consequence, the Spaniard does not understand what the French say, while the Spaniard and Italian can still understand each other because their languages are more conservative and have changed much less in the past centuries.

2.1 Johan Amos Comenius

Johann Amos Comenius was a Czech theologian, philosopher, teacher and writer of Latin, language teacher and social reformer. Comenius was thinking of life and the world in two levels: level religious-educational and the level of systematic thinking about the whole world, about its organization and knowledge. The image of the world is taken as an image of the school. Comenius longs to turn the 17th-century society into a community of people who will cooperate in peace. His philosophical work, "De rerum humanarum emendatione consultatio catholica" (in English, "The General Advise on the Correction of Human Issues"), proposed a renewal of philosophy, politics and religion.

It was a correction of the relationship not only to individuals but also to others, to the world and to God. Comenius wanted to give people a goal and show them the possible outcomes of the difficult personal and social labyrinths. His work should give not only individuals, but also the whole society and the Church a new hope, how to achieve better coexistence under certain conditions. He wanted people to realize everyone can be satisfied and prosperous if the whole society is satisfied and prosperous. Comenius felt the need to spread Latin as a tool of scientific work and means of versatile communication. During his latest work Comenius wished to introduce artificial language without any irregularities and without any learning difficulties. His efforts culminated in the idea of "PANGLOTTIE" ("General Classification of Languages").

Here he presents a demonstration of a common world language [9]. The multitude and confusion of languages in the world has been a barrier to versatile contact among the peoples. Comenius was characterized by efforts to understand and make the language easy to learn by removing irregularities and ambiguities, which eventually had a rather schematic effect. The word is to express itself as accurately as possible so as to impress an idea or an image of the same thing as quickly as possible in the mind of whoever hears the word. The attempt to create a universal language at the time of Comenius was nothing special, as great thinkers such as F. Bacon, R. Descartes, G. Leibnitz and others also dealt with this problem. Only Comenius, however, has made his reflections on the new universal language part of his corrective project of all human society.

3 Research

People with different cultural identities meet within the intercultural communication in today's globalized world. Ignorance of the foreign language as well as cultural differences is often the source of many misunderstandings and conflicts [10]. Research carried out at universities in the Czech Republic and Germany involved a total of 239 respondents. The questionnaire survey was completed by university students aged 18-29. Germany was chosen as an example of a modern multicultural state, which has been linked to the issue of immigration through its rich historical past. As part of its foreign policy, Germany has had to face the problems associated with the integration of newcomers into the majority society for decades. Here, education is an important factor, including the promotion of language education across cultures and age groups.

It should be noted that this is only a local research in the academic environment of selected universities, the results of which cannot be taken as being quite general, however, they support the diversity of language offerings and teaching methods used in the countries concerned, which differ both in the number of inhabitants and in their national composition. See Fig 1.

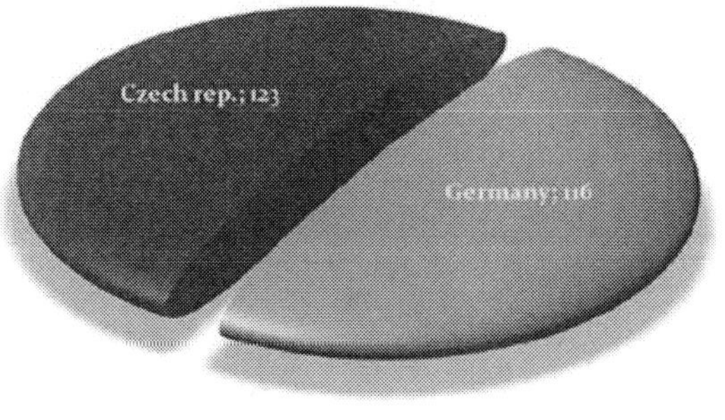

Fig. 1. Total number of respondents (students from the Czech Republic and Germany)

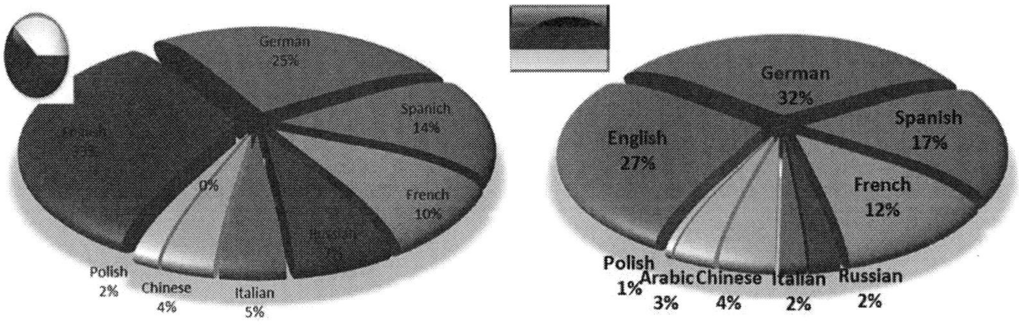

Fig. 2. Whish foreign languages do you speak? (Students from the Czech Republic and Germany)

From Fig.2 is clearly seen that the respondents' answers from the two countries differ to a certain extent, which is undoubtedly influenced by different ethnic composition of the country's population. The most students speak English and German, followed by Spanish, French and other languages.

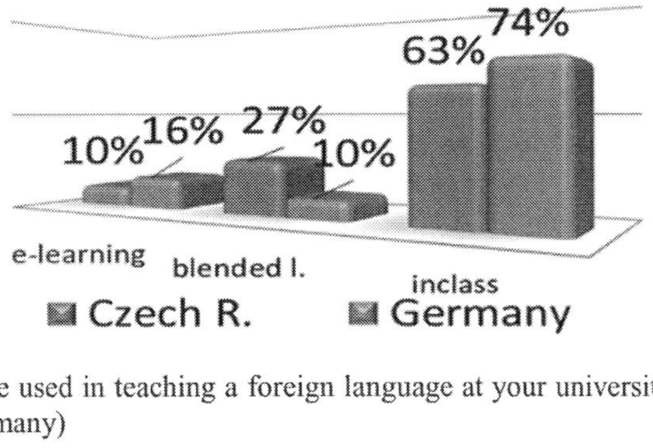

Fig. 3. What methods are used in teaching a foreign language at your university? (Students from the Czech Republic and Germany)

According to the respondents the most often used teaching method is the direct contact with the teacher (in class method), followed by the blended learning method. The least used method is e-learning.

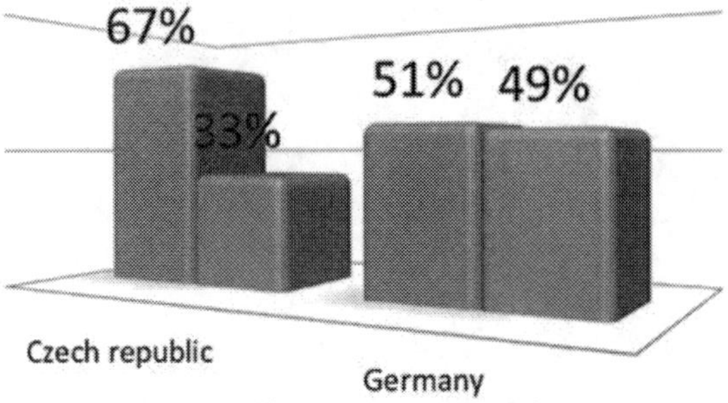

Fig. 4. Is foreign language instruction sufficiently supported in your country? (Students from the Czech Republic and Germany)

In both countries, foreign language learning is largely supported, but more in the Czech Republic than in Germany. At present, there are problems with the integration of newcomers into the majority society, often linked to the lack of qualified professionals.

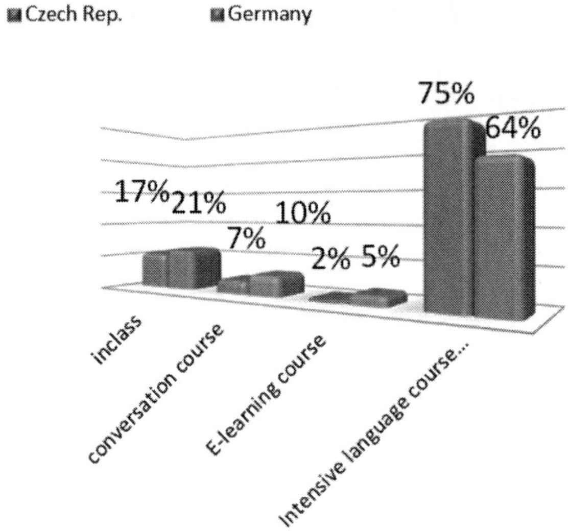

Fig. 5. What do you think are the most efficient methods of foreign language instruction? (Students from the Czech Republic and Germany)

Out of the traditional teaching methods (in-class, conversational language course, e-learning language course, intensive language courses abroad), as the most attractive appeared to surveyed group of student's language courses abroad, however, they are very costly for many parents and not everyone can afford them. In class instruction and the conversational language course are also popular, the least effective seem to be an e-learning course.

4 Summary

There has always been a high regard for speech and writing, which extend the possibilities of human understanding and working enrichment not only to the present but also to past generations and to the generations that will be born after us. Given the world global developments and the enormous cultural diversity in Europe, we will certainly not see the emergence of a single European culture or a common universal language in the near future.

The research conducted in the Czech Republic and Germany confirms the importance of teaching foreign languages in today's globalized world. Above all, frequent language inaccuracy and lack of information on the cultural diversity of newcomers into the majority society makes it difficult both for initial and for overall integration and this situation leads to the creation of parallel society and feared ghettos. Therefore, it is necessary to cultivate and support the diverse teaching of mother tongues and national languages by individual states. According to the local research, the combination of in-class instruction, e-learning and blended methods to the level B1 (according to the European Framework Program) are the most effective ways of teaching foreign languages, at higher levels of language competence intensive foreign language courses are recommended. The problem of intercultural communication, however, lies not only in the reliable knowledge of a foreign language, but also in the mutual knowledge of the participating cultures, including the elimination of all prejudices and stereotypes.

The acknowledgements: This research was conducted thanks to the project IGA 1903/2018 at the Faculty of informatics and management, University of Hradec Kralove.

References

1. H. Haarmann „Weltgeschichte der Sprache“, Verlag C. H. Beck (2006)
2. T. Steinfeld, Der Sprachverfuhrer“, Schriftenreihe Bd.112 (2012)
3. H. Bussmann, Lexikon der Sprachwissenschaft, Aufl.Stuttgart (1990)
4. P. Schroter, Visuelle Worterkennung bei Billingualen Kindern im Deutschen, Berlin (2016)
5. W. Butzkamm, Psycholinguistik des Fremdsprachenunterrichts, Tubingen, Francke Verlag (1993)
6. K.R. Bausch, H. Christ, W. Hullen, H. J. Krumm, Handtuch Fremdsprachenunterricht, Tubingen. Francle Verlag (1989)
7. M. Twain. The Awful German Language. s. 11, (Fluter, Nr. 39)
8. R. von Bredow, V. Hackenbroch. Die neue Schlechtschreibung. p. 96-104.(Der Spiegel 25/2013)
9. J. A. Komenský, Obecná porada o nápravě věcí lidských, Svoboda, Praha (1992) J. A. Comenius, De rerum humanarum emendatione consultatio catholica, (1992)
10. A. Josefová, Language education in an intercultural society. Lifelong learning: continuous education for sustainable development, SPbGu, Sankt Petersburg, s. 139-140 (2013)

Resolving the conundrum of superior performers in organizations with the utilization of competency profiling

Nornazira Suhairom[1,*], *Nur Husna* Abd Wahid[1], *Rafeizah* Zulkifli[1] and *Ahmad Nabil* Md Nasir[1]

[1]School of Education, Faculty of Social Science & Humanities, Universiti Teknologi Malaysia, 81310 Johor, Malaysia

Abstract. Studies have shown that superior performers provide increased productivity, profit and revenue especially for service and business-driven organizations. Undeniably, good people are great for business; however, previous studies provide limited indication on how to identify superior performers from average performers. In this study, the Star-Chef Competency Profile Assessment test was developed to help organizations identify and differentiate superior performers. The instrument helps in identifying and articulating the distinguishing characteristics of people who perform exceptionally well compared to those that do not. The Star-Chef Competency Profile Assessment analyses a person's fit with six pillars of competency that encompass important competencies required for culinary profession: technical (culinary-specific), non-technical (generic), self-concept, personal quality, physical state and motives. Further, the competency profiling technique utilized the Rasch Measurement Model in identifying the superior performers. Competency profiling assessment was conducted among culinary professionals in Malaysian hotels sector. This is a practical, unique approach in improving organizational talent management practices for employee training and development. Identifying and keeping the superior performers is important in enhancing work performance outcome which eventually will contribute to the organizational effectiveness. This information hones the organization ability to nail down the best employees that could be polished for higher level.

1 Introduction

Since 2008, Malaysian government has embarked on important missions to increase the number of high-skilled workers in the industry. As in 2010, there are 6638 recognized and accredited institutions which are responsible for MSOQ (Malaysia Occupational Skills Qualifications) training programmes. Data from Table 1 shows the certification status for MOSQ according to each level since 1994, the year where the qualification systems started being introduced until 2009. The numbers of certifications are progressing from years to

* Corresponding author: p-nazira@utm.my

years though it fluctuates a bit. However, there is a huge gap in the number of certification according to each level which is 87 percent for Low Levels (Level 1 and 2) and only 13 percent for High Levels (Level 3 to 5) (Department of Skills Development, 2013). To date, any regulatory approaches to continuing competence as well as professional licensure for chef's profession in Malaysia are not available.

Table 1. Statistic of Malaysia occupational skills qualification (1994-2009)

YEAR	NUMBER OF CERTIFICATIONS					
	Low Level		High Level			TOTAL
	1	2	3	4	5	
1994	556	42	0	0	0	598
1995	1550	278	0	0	0	1828
1996	2864	1291	7	0	0	4162
1997	7390	2362	207	0	0	9959
1998	8140	4169	537	1	1	12848
1999	13751	8771	1844	1	0	24367
2000	19642	21603	4883	0	0	46128
2001	18185	22504	7441	2	2	48134
2002	26495	19583	2857	2	0	48937
2003	53526	50649	9550	0	0	113725
2004	36998	41508	12939	985	0	92430
2005	43190	39819	16259	1469	5	100742
2006	40108	33652	8932	2322	11	85026
2007	42203	33402	10049	2942	16	88612
2008	49091	40905	11776	2440	32	104244
2009	42262	35098	12722	1376	68	104244
TOTAL	405951	355636	100003	11540	135	91526
	761587 **(87%)**		111678 **(13%)**			873265 **(100%)**

(Source: Ministry of Human Resource, 2010)

In Malaysian context, culinary profession is observed as one profession that is labor-intensive and dynamic in the diversified career market. Views related to the importance of culinary as one of the most demanding professions in the Malaysian hospitality and tourism were shared by Hamed, Wahab, Zakaria, & Jasmi [44]. Culinary tourism creates vast job opportunities for young generations and thus, reducing the rate of unemployment. Furthermore, a study by Mokhtar, Poo & Salleh [30] revealed that employment demand for 2015 manpower from sub-sectors hotels and restaurants in Malaysian tourism sector shows a significant impressive improvement. This clearly shows that the industry provides promising future career undertakings as positive employment prospects in these sub-sectors are expected in the near future.

The broader discourse of competency issues was immensely discussed in the realm of culinary world. Although culinary professionals' role in the emergence of food tourism is considered greatly significant and approached in literature [45], there is ambiguity that has yet to be conferred. Current changes in the Malaysian hospitality and food tourism market have impacted the requirements and the tasks to be performed by workforce in the industry [37]. Culinary cadres are required to master wide range of competencies in order to remain relevant in the industry. Research in the area of culinary profession is scarce, and so as the research in identifying competencies required for the culinary professionals' superior work performance. Several studies related to chef's competencies were conducted in other countries such as in Cyprus [45], Costa Rica [1], Hong Kong (Hu, 2010; 26], United Kingdom (Bisset, Cheng & Brannan, 2010) and United States [10,11] which provides a preliminary views on what is expected from the culinary professions globally.

Identification of superior performers through competency profiling is useful where the organization will be able to map the worker's competency in identifying potential superior performers. Nevertheless, currently there is a limited indication on a specific mechanism in identifying the competencies possessed by existing professionals in the industry. Thus, this study provides insights that using a well-developed competency measurement instrument, employees' competency could be measured. Eventually, a competency profiling which emphasized on the mastery level of culinary professionals could be developed. The findings will contributes in generating relevant data that could be used to guide improvement interventions in the industry. In line with the recommendations by Orr, Sneltjes and Dai [32], competency profiling is one of the best practices for selecting, developing and deploying talents. The results from the competency measurement using the Star-Chef Competency Profile Assessment test, where applicable, could help the human resource management in identifying areas of professional development that necessitates for attentions. The current study seeks to answer the following research question:

To develop a competency profile for culinary professionals based on the SC-SAT Competency Measurement Scale.

2 Literature Review

2.1 Competency Model as Guidance of Individual Behavior at Workplace

Organizational quality is much dependent on the quality of the workforce [28] as well as the identification of critical needs and resources for the changing workplace (Society of Human Resource Management, 2008). These two aspects are important for todays' contemporary hospitality and tourism industry. The industry are labor intensive, employing a wide variety of individuals, each having a unique experience, skills sets, and motivational pattern. Thus, the challenge for the human resource management is to manage the human capital in effective manner so that individual performance can be well-managed [18]. According to Koopmans [27] and Viswesvaran [39], individual performance is determined by the person's skills and capabilities. Research which emphasizes into individual performance in organizations is important in order to provide better understanding of the managerial and economic proficiency among individuals in the profession.

Theory and research note the prominence of competencies for individual work performance. For an individual to perform the best at workplace, they need to have a synergy of competencies along with experience in delivering job task on any given day, even on any given circumstances [42]. Competencies can be gathered through education, training or experience. Experience is the duration of life within work. Nevertheless, to learn a lesson from experience gained at the workplace also requires certain amount of competency [3,4]. In line with these ways of competency acquisition is the behavior (understanding of the consequences of the action taken and having the right attitude towards work performance).

Several researchers [29, 40] agree that competency model is a model that provides a list of competency statement that is necessary for effective job performance. Specifically, competency model consists of a combination of individual competencies that represents competency required for employees' superior performance and success in the profession. In the realm of culinary, competency frameworks and models has been developed and applied in various hospitality settings especially in the hotels and restaurants. Studies show that competency model has been used widely in the hospitality, tourism and culinary industry [23, 24, Cheng, 2012). For instance, several competency models have been developed in hospitality management that focuses on the leadership and management competencies of hotel and restaurant managers [14, 25]. In more specific culinary research area, there are a number of studies that present chef's competency studies [11, 12, 45].

2.2 Competency Profiling for Culinary Professionals

Workers in the industry need to stay relevant with the latest trends and progress in the industry, or else their knowledge and skills might become obsolete. For instance, retraining and skills upgrading is one way which of paramount importance to enhance the quality of workforce so that it is versatile and adaptable to the changing technological and business environment (Human Resources Development Fund Malaysia, 2013). Recently, there have been growing interests of research studies aiming at distinguishing the characteristics of exemplary employees in the industry. High performer is an employee who is a key contributor, demonstrates high performance, is capable of a lateral move, may be qualified for a broader role within the same profession and has reached the potential to move "upward" in a management capacity [15].

According to Azrilah, et al., [6], competency profiling refers to a model which comprises competency attributes required by the employees. Competency profiling is the process of finding out the skills that are needed to do the job effectively. In organizations, the competency profiling provides an opportunity for the upper level management executives to identify competencies that are important for professional training and development. Researchers has agreed that the development of competency profiles will benefit organizations in efficaciously define and identified employees' competencies that can then utilized as performance benchmarking [31]. It is important to build competency profiles in order to assist the human resource management of organizations in the recruitment process. Furthermore, for personal utilization, the competency profiles may benefits individual worker in identifying their own strengths and weaknesses. With adequate and sufficient resources, employees will be able to perform their job well.

3 Methodology

3.1 Design

A cross-sectional survey was conducted among culinary professionals. Two-stage of instrument development testing was carried out among culinary professionals working at 4- and 5-starred hotels in Malaysia.

3.2 Sample

The instrument was tested on two groups of culinary professionals, representing two Instrument Testing stages (Instrument Testing I, n=35 and Instrument Testing II, n=42). The study involved culinary professionals in 4-star and 5-star hotels in Peninsular Malaysia.

3.3 Instrument

The Star-Chef Competency Profile Assessment test was used to gather information about competency. The first instrument testing was conducted among 35 culinary professionals in 4-star and 5-star hotels which involved an analysis of 203 items measuring six constructs (technical, Non-technical, Personal Qualities, Self-concept ad Motives).

3.4 Data Analysis

The collected data were analyzed using SPSS 24.0 and Winstep software. The first stage of data analysis mainly focused on the psychometric analysis of the SCSAT Competency Scale. In this study, Rasch measurement model is the basis of analysis in identifying the reliability and validity of the instrument. The purpose of each instrument testing is to examine the reliability and generate empirical evidence to support the validity of the instrument in eight areas of Rasch diagnoses: (i) item and person separation and reliability coefficients (ii) item polarity (iii) item fit (iv) person abilities fit (v) value of standardized residual variance (vi) scale category function (vii) unidimensionality of the constructs and (viii) level of items difficulties and person response. Consequently, the data which analyzed using Rasch analysis were utilized to develop the competency profile of the culinary professionals based on the SC-SAT instrument. The item strata were utilized in the study. To construct strata in identifying the performance level of the culinary professionals, the formula used is

$$\text{Number of Person or Item Strata, } H = \frac{4G + 1}{3}$$

where G is the separation index of item or person

The strata are defined as statistically distinct measures as suggested by Fisher [17] and Wright & Masters [43]. By this means, the level of competencies among culinary professionals could be classified into several categories based on their responses in the SC-SAT instrument.

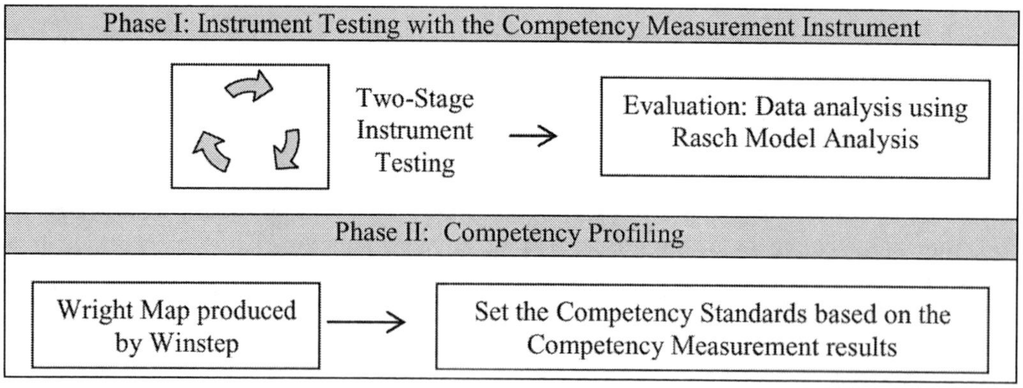

Fig. 1. Operational research framework

4 Findings

The aim of this competency profiling is to describe the useful information related to the culinary professionals whom involved in the study (n=35) in Instrument Testing I and (n=42) in Instrument Testing II.

4.1 Instrument Testing 1

The performance of the respondents in answering the SC-SAT items was examined. The SC-SAT yield an item reliability of 0.80, item separation of 2.01 and person reliability of 0.99, person separation of 9.97. In this study, the performance of the culinary professionals is based on their ability to perform task in SC-SAT instrument. Thus, the item strata were utilized. To construct the strata in identifying the performance level of the culinary professionals, the formula used is

$$\text{Number of Person/ Item Strata, } H = \frac{4G + 1}{3} \quad \text{where G is the separation index}$$

The item strata is [4(2.01) + 1] /3 = 3.01. This means the performance towards SC-SAT instrument can be separated into 3 levels, which are High, Mediocre and Low (Omar, Rodzo'an, Saidfudin, Zaharim & Basri, 2010). Previously, the competencies were categorized into threshold (T) and differentiating (D) competency by the subject-matter experts during the Content Validity Procedure (CVR) process. The experts identified 36 sub constructs as differentiating and 8 sub constructs as threshold. Based on these categories, there are 156 differentiating items. Experts also agree that 90% mastery of the differentiating competency is required for a superior work performance in culinary profession. With an expectation of 90% mastery of the differentiating competencies, there are 140 items to be put into attention. The 156 differentiating items were divided into 3 performance levels, resulting 52 differentiating items in each performance levels. As shown in Table 2, the item measure is summed up and divided by the number of items in each group, thus establishing the mean of item measure as cutscore for the respective performance levels.

Table 2. Indicators of performance levels: Instrument testing I

Group	Item Measure (logit)	No of items	Mean (logit)	Standard Error (SE)
Group 1 (High)	COGN3 (+0.44) to SCI3 (+1.21)	54	+0.72	0.23
Group 2 (Mediocre)	CAR15 (-0.15) to ENTR6 (+0.44)	70	+0.10	0.25
Group 3 (Low)	SOCI6 (-1.82) to CAR18 (-0.15)	79	-0.60	0.27
Total items		203		

Table 3(Appendix) demonstrates the Item Measure for the first instrument testing. Based on the list, the cut-scores for performance levels were identified. The expected 90% of competency mastery level of 140 items is identified and bookmarked at item CRE4 (Ability to make products with vitality) with measure of +0.86 logit. Rasch analysis has indeed made the evaluation more objectively and produce the demarcation line in a very clear graphical presentation which is easy to read and easier to understand. This enable thorough analysis of the grading pattern according to performance level.

The established demarcation lines is superimposed on the Person Measure Order Table as shown in Figure 2 (Appendix). The expected 'mastery' level of 90% agreed at 0.86 logit located at the High Performance level. Previously, there are three performance levels that were identified. However, upon reviewing the findings, the High Performance level could be divided into one more group, which is the Superior Performance level. Thus, it can be identified that 20% of these 35 culinary professionals are superior performers (seven culinary professionals). From the figure, it can be seen that there are two person from the High Performance group level who perform below the 90% of mastery which are person S11 and A30. There are 46% culinary professionals categorized in the High Performance level, 23% in Mediocre Performance and 11% in Low Performance level. These findings show that superior, high, mediocre and low performers can be observed in the actual assessment process.

4.2 Instrument Testing 2

For the second instrument testing, the profiling was developed based on the data from the performance of 42 culinary professionals towards the SC-SAT instrument. The SC-SAT instrument yield item reliability is 0.91 with separation index of 3.21 and person reliability 0.98 with separation index of 8.01. The calculated item strata is [4(3.21)+1] / 3 = 4.61. Thus, the performance towards SC-SAT instrument in Instrument Testing II can be separated into 5 levels, which are Very High, High, Mediocre, Low and Very Low. Again, the experts evaluation on threshold and differentiating competencies were referred. Based on the identified 36 differentiating competency and 8 threshold competency, there are 130 differentiating items and 34 threshold items. With an expectation of 90% mastery of differentiating competencies, there are 117 items that need to be put into attention. The 130 differentiating items were divided into 5 performance levels, resulting 26 differentiating items in each performance levels. In each level, the item measure is summed up and divided by the number of items in each group to establish the mean of item measure (in logits) and cutscore for the respective performance levels. Table 3 showed the details regarding the indicators of performance levels.

Table 3. Indicators of performance levels: Instrument testing II

Group	Item Measure (logit)	No of items	Mean (logit)	Standard Error (SE)
Group 1 (Very High)	CRE4 (+0.88) to SCI2 (+2.59)	26	1.34	0.23
Group 2 (High)	EST3 (+0.30) to RES1 (+0.88)	31	0.58	0.23
Group 3 (Mediocre)	SAF4 (-0.23) to FIN3 (+0.30)	38	0.04	0.23
Group 4 (Low)	LEA2 (-0.62) to CAR14 (-0.23)	30	-0.12	0.24
Group 5 (Very Low)	OPS7 (-1.79) to CAR6 (-0.62)	39	-1.06	0.25
Total items		164		

Table 5 (Appendix) demonstrates the Item Measure for the first instrument testing. Based on the list, the cut-scores for performance levels were identified. The expected 90% of competency mastery level of 117 items is identified and bookmarked at item SCI4 (I know the purpose of using food additives in foods preparation) with measure of +1.23 logit. With this Rasch analysis, the demarcation lines were produced and thus, enabled a thorough analysis of the grading pattern according to performance level. The established demarcation lines are superimposed on the Person Measure Order Table as shown in Figure 3 (Appendix). The expected 'mastery' level of 90% was agreed at +1.23 logit located at the High Performance level. Previously, there are five performance levels that were identified. Upon reviewing the findings, there is no culinary professionals who falls within the Very Low performance level. There is only one person in the Low performance level (3%), six person in Mediocre performance level (14%) and eight person in High performance level (20%). Majority of the culinary professionals are classified into the Very High performance level (46%). However it can be identified from the figure that there are seven

Superior performers, those who perform beyond one Standard Deviation above the Mean (exceeding logit +2.70).

5 Discussions

In this section, the researcher discusses on the competency profiling among culinary professionals, which were generated from the Rasch analysis. One advantage of item response theory analysis is that both estimates can be arranged on the same scale and easily compared. The item-person-map for each model visualizes the item difficulties on the right, by ordering them from more difficult (top) to less difficult (bottom), and the latent trait levels on the left (grouping persons with the same values together). Ideally, the item difficulties should be well dispersed around the mean, having the most items in the medium difficulty range, but also providing items with high and low difficulties. Additionally, the latent traits are separated by dimension. The current study examines the high performer's competency profiles of culinary professionals in Malaysian hotels setting. Two-stage of instrument testing were conducted to yield data on workforce competencies. Thirty-five responses from Instrument Testing I and forty-two responses from Instrument Testing II to the SCSAT Competency Scale were used to profile the competencies. There are six competency elements, which are technical, non-technical, personal quality, self-concept, physical state, and motives of culinary professionals who work in the 4- and 5-starred rated hotels. The competency profiling from each instrument testing shows that majority of the culinary professionals have a high mastery level of competencies in culinary. This study indicates that our Malaysian culinary industry is indeed having a substantial numbers of superior culinary talents. It can be observed that 20 percent of superior performers were identified in Instrument Testing I and 17 percent of superior performers in Instrument Testing II.

5.1 Competency Profiling based on data from Instrument Testing I

In the first instrument testing, there are three persons were identified as having a very good performance with a profile of culinary professionals who have knowledge of high degree of scientific cooking, possess entrepreneurial talents with characteristics as a daring person who are outspoken and a risk-taker. It was found that there are five items which are considered as the most difficult items. The first three items; "marketing for product promotion", "foresee new market", and "willingness to take risk in promoting new products" were categorized under entrepreneurial competency with a specific sub themes, which are the business acumen and opportunity alertness.

In line with these findings, Balasz [7] mentioned about the role of the chefs in France's great restaurant as creators, entrepreneurs and businessman. The chefs are being referred as rare species of individual [8]. The chefs involved in the business-related fragments of the operations and investment decisions, particularly in creating new products and services while at the same time working towards the creation of outstanding dining experiences. Furthermore, it was found that majority of the respondents easy to endorse an agreement towards their teamwork as the easiest item is "ability to work in teams". Working in the commercial hotels" kitchen requires the participations of all kitchen crews. Most of the times, teamwork approach is transferred into daily work, therefore, working in teams has become their way of working, the culture of work [19].

The next difficult item for the respondents to endorse their agreement is "outspoken", which measure the personal quality in the aspect of extraversion. The finding is contradicted to the personality of those in the chefs" job which often associated with vocal, loud and flamboyant. Extravert chefs often associated with the celebrity chefs who involved working with the medias [16, 21] This might be due to the nature of working in the commercial kitchen, where the senior positions such as Head Chefs and Executive Chefs are the one who dominated the culinary cadre. Commonly, the extravert quality exhibits especially when the culinary professionals had reached the highest rank of chef's job. Their role as leaders contributes to the development of their personal quality [7, 13].

Accordingly, Rothmann and Coetzer [34, 35] mentioned that extraversion includes traits such as sociability, assertiveness, boldness. These qualities often displayed by those involved with jobs characterized by social interactions such as leaders and managers. Another difficult item is "knowledge of molecular cuisines", which measure science in culinary. Several authors [20, 38] highlighted on the importance of understanding meal sciences among todays' culinary professionals. Traditionally, emphasis was given only on the artistic element of the cuisines. Nowadays, culinary profession is considered as one profession that combine the arts and sciences of cooking where the concoction of arts and sciences is valuable and highly demanded for the current culinary world. With the current emergence of haute cuisine, the innovation processes of high level cooking brings new paradigm for science explorations in the cooking process [22].

Additionally, the highest logit value was demonstrated by a person who is an Executive Sous Chef in a 4-star hotel, aged between 36 to 45 years old whom has been working in culinary industry for more than 20 years. There are two people at lowest position in the scale. One of the person is a Chef de Partie who works in the culinary industry between 11-15 years while another person is a Commis who have 6 to 10 years working experience. The findings are unexpected because lowest logit means that it is difficult for the person to endorse an agreement that reflects his or her ability to perform the competencies. It is expected that person with such period of working experience could demonstrate high level of competencies. Several authors shared their views regarding this matter. Although years of experience are required for culinary professionals, Baum [9] stipulated that experiential intelligence is one of the capabilities that are hardly possessed by individuals. Similarly, Ruokonen & Saarenketo [36] asserted that the way workers capitalize the information gathered through their years of working will be determined by their experiential intelligence. Thus, the ability in manipulating experiences robustly for professional development is the key for successful career.

5.2 Profiling based on data from Instrument Testing II

There are two items which are considered as the most difficult items; SCI2 (know how to prepare molecular cuisine) and SCI1 (knowledge in cooking chemistry). Both items measure the technical competency from the aspect of culinary science. Culinary professionals are found to have difficulty in assenting that this statement reflects their competencies in culinary science. As mentioned earlier by Gustaffson [20], the acquiescent towards scientific culinary is important in understanding the meal sciences. Behind the cooking process, there are various chemical excitations that drive the transformation from raw ingredients into cooked meals. On the other hand, the easiest item is OPS7 (able to organize ingredients and equipment in readiness for food preparation – mise en place). This item is measuring technical competency in the kitchen operations. The finding is supported by the previous study by Zopiatis [45] which showed that technical culinary-specific competency is ranked as the highest level in competency acquisition and development.

The person who demonstrates the highest logit value is a male Executive Chef aged between 36 to 45 years old, with more than 20 years of experience. The person also has experience working in foreign country. Nevertheless, the person does not have MOSQ certification. It was found that the lowest logit position is a female Commis aged between

18 to 25 years old. Her working experience is approximately five years and below. The finding is quite unanticipated because she has a MOSQ certification. For our local culinary professionals, the opportunity of working abroad is an added value because there is plentiful knowledge to be learned from foreign culture. International job relocation provides learning cosmoses where they learn new techniques and dishes. There is always a connection between travel and foods. Sullivan & Arthur (2006) conceptualized on boundary less career as physical mobility (movement between jobs, institutions and countries) and psychological mobility (the perceptions of the capacity to make transitions).

There are careers which require both types of mobility where the authors put chef's profession as an example. The growing complexity in the career landscape requires chefs to work in several diverse restaurants where each new job contributes to a larger body of expertise and self-confidence. Within evaluation field, the issues of competency credentialing, licensure, certification is communal, with various implications came along with the process [2]. Additionally, Woolcock [41] and Audant [5] emphasized on the hands-on skills validation for culinary students through formal culinary education to advance their college completion. In the context of Malaysia, MOSQ certification for students, named as Malaysia Skills Certificate is offered by the culinary schools and institutions appointed as Accredited Centre for the Department of Skills Development (DSD), Ministry of Human Resources Malaysia. Some of the courses offered are food preparation/ chef training, bakery, pastry and food and beverages services (Department of Skills Development, 2015). However, normally the MOSQ certification for industrial workers is on voluntarily-basis. The connotations of certification among culinary professionals in Malaysia have yet to be achieved as efforts many efforts need to be done in order to improve the awareness of people in the industry regarding the MOSQ certification.

6 Conclusion

In designing 21st century culinary competencies, competency profiles help organizations in providing directions for future requirements in the forthcoming decades. Implications derived are the need for more robust training schemes which equipped culinary professionals with relevant competencies to encounter complex high performance work settings in the modern contemporary culinary tourism.

The research is funded by Research University Grants (Potential Academic Staff Grant) of Universiti Teknologi Malaysia PY/2016/08211 (Q.J130000.2731.03K10)

References

1. Aguirre, J., & Andrade, L. Students perception of the 21st Century Chefs. *Revista de Turismo Y Patrimonio Cultural, 11*(2), 417–425, (2013).
2. Altschuld, J. W. Ceritification, Credentialing, Licensure, Competencies, And The Like: Issues Confronting The Field Of Evaluation. *The Canadian Journal of Program Evaluation*, *20*(2), 157, (2005).
3. Anders Ericsson, K., Roring, R. W., & Nandagopal, K. Giftedness and evidence for reproducibly superior performance: an account based on the expert performance framework. *High Ability Studies*, *18*(1), 3–56, (2007).
4. Anders Ericsson, K., & Towne, T. J. Expertise. *Wiley Interdisciplinary Reviews: Cognitive Science*, *1*(3), 404-416, (2010).
5. Audant, A. B. Stackable credentials and career/college pathways in culinary arts at Kingsborough Community College, CUNY. *Community College Journal of Research and Practice*, *40*(4), 299-309, (2016).

6. Azrilah, A. A., Azlinah, M., Noor Habibah, A., Sohaimi, Z., Hamza, A. G., & Mohd Saidfudin, M. Development of Rasch-based descriptive scale in profiling information professionals' competency. *2008 ISIT*, 1–8, (2008).
7. Balazs, K. Some Like It Haute : Leadership Lessons From France ' s Great Chefs, *30*(2), 134–148, (2001).
8. Balazs, K. Take One Entrepreneur : The Recipe for Success of France ' s Great Chefs, *20*(3), 247–259, (2002).
9. Baum, T. Implications of hospitality and tourism labor marets for talent management strategies. *International Journal of Contemporary Hospitality Management, 20*(7), 720-729, (2008).
10. Birdir, K. Identified competencies of research chefs, (1998).
11. Birdir, K., & Pearson, T. E. Research chefs ' competencies : a Delphi approach Research in brief Research chefs ' competencies : a Delphi approach. *International Journal of Contemporary Hospitality Management Emerald Article*, *12*(3), 205–209, (2000).
12. Bissett, R. L., Cheng, M. S. H., & Brannan, R. G. A Qualitative Assessment of Culinary Science Competencies Defined by the Research Chefs Association. *Journal of Culinary Science & Technology*, *7*(4), 285–293, (2010a).
13. Bloisi, W. *Bullying and negative behaviour in commercial kitchens* (Doctoral dissertation, The University of Manchester (United Kingdom), (2012).
14. Chung-Herrera, B. G., Enz, C. A., & Lankau, M. J. A competencies model: Grooming future hospitality leaders. *Cornell Hotel and Restaurant Administration Quarterly*, *44*(3), 17-25, (2003).
15. Deloitte, H. Global Human Resource. SHRM (9), (2013).
16. Ehrmann, T., Meiseberg, B., & Ritz, C. Superstar effects in deluxe gastronomy–An empirical analysis of value creation in German quality restaurants. *Kyklos*, *62*(4), 526-541, (2009).
17. Fisher, W., Jr. Reliability, Separation, Strata Statistics. *Rasch Measurement Transactions, 6*(3), 238, (1992).
18. George, G. Philosophical foundations of workplace spirituality: A critical approach. *Journal of business ethics*, *78*(4), 575-600, (2008).
19. Gröschl, S. Presumed incapable: Exploring the validity of negative judgments about persons with disabilities and their employability in hotel operations. *Cornell Hospitality Quarterly*, *54*(2), 114-123.Gog and Joo, 2011), (2013).
20. Gustafsson, I. -B. Clinary arts and meal science – a new scientific research discipline. Food Service Technology, 4 (1), 9-20, (2004).
21. Henderson, J. C. Celebrity chefs: expanding empires. *British Food Journal*, *113*(5), 613-624, (2011).
22. Hervas-oliver, J. L., de Miguel-Molina, B., & Albors, J. How much important is the cluster effect? making sens of the firm's internal and meso (relational) resources to explain innovation. In *DRUID Paper to presented at the Summer Conference, page 26p*, (2009).
23. Hu, M. L. Developing a core competency model of innovative culinary development. *International Journal of Hospitality Management*, *29*(4), 582–590.
24. Hu, M. L. (2010b). Discovering culinary competency: An innovative approach. *The Journal of Hospitality Leisure Sport and Tourism*, *9*(1), 65–72, (2010a).
25. Huang, Y.-L., & Lin, C.-T. Management Trainee Core Competencies in the Hospitality Industry: Differences Between Managers and Scholars. *Journal of Human Resources in Hospitality & Tourism*, *10*(1), 1–13, (2010).

26. Ko, W.-H. To evaluate the professional culinary competence of hospitality students. *Journal of Culinary Science and Technology*, 8(2-3), 136-146, (2010).
27. Koopmans, L., Coffeng, J. K., Bernaards, C. M., Boot, C. R. L., Hildebrandt, V. H., de Vet, H. C. W., & van der Beek, A. J. Responsiveness of the individual work performance questionnaire. *BMC Public Health*, *14*, 513, (2014).
28. Malhi, R. S. The hard truth about graduate employability and soft skills. *ADEPT: Higher Education Leadership Research Bulletin*, *3*, 45-56, (2001).
29. Marrelli, A. F., Tondora, J., & Hoge, M. A. Strategies for developing competency models. *Administration and Policy in Mental Health and Mental Health Services Research*, *32*(5-6), 533-561, (2005).
30. Mokhtar, N. A., Poo, B. T., & Salleh, N. H. M. Analisis keperluan tenaga manusia dalam industri pelancongan di Malaysia. *PERKEM Proceedings*, *7*, 4-6, (2012).
31. Moustroufas, E., Stamelos, I., & Angelis, L. Competency profiling for software engineers: literature review and a new model. In *Proceedings of the 19th Panhellenic Conference on Informatics* (pp. 235-240). ACM, (2015, October).
32. Orr, J. E., Sneltjes, C., & Dai, G. The art and science of competency modeling. *The Korn/Ferry Institute*, 1–16, (2010).
33. Sanghi, S. The Handbook of Competency Mapping: Understanding, Designing and Implementing Competency Models in Organizations, 2nd Edition. SAGE Publications Pvt. Ltd., (2007).
34. Rothman, S., & Coetzer, E. P. The relationship between personality dimensions and job satisfaction. *Management Dynamics: Journal of the Southern African Institute for Management Scientists*, *11*(1), 29-42, (2002).
35. Rothmann, I., & Cooper, C. Organizational and Work Psychology. *Hodder Education* (303), (2008).
36. Ruokonen, M., & Saarenketo, S. The strategic orientations of rapidly internationalizing software companies. *European Business Review*, *21*(1), 17-41, (2009).
37. Suhairom, N., Musta'amal, A. H., Ismail, S., Wahid, N. H. A., Hamid, M. Z. A., Ali, D. F., & Jambari, H. A Qualitative Study of School-to-Work Transition Experience of New Culinary Graduates Towards a Sustainable Growth in the Profession. *Advanced Science Letters*, *23*(8), 7407-7411, (2017).
38. Tittl, M. (2008). Careers in Food Science: Undergraduate to Professional, 267–275.
39. Viswesvaran, C., & Ones, D. S. Perspectives on models of job performance. *International Journal of Selection and Assessment*, *8*(4), 216-226, (2000).
40. Wang, W., Gao, J., & Xie, X. A study to develop a competency model for Chinese EHS managers. *Frontiers of Business Research in China*, *5*(4), 580-596, (2011).
41. Woolcock, C., & Ferguson, P. Paper code: 2265, 1–11, (2006).
42. Workitect, I. Competencies and Competitiveness. *Www.workitect.com*, 1–6, (2006).
43. Wright, B. D., & Masters, G. N. Number of person or item strata. *Rasch Measurement Transactions*, *16*(3), 888, (2002).
44. Zakaria, M. A., Wahab, S. H. A., & Jasmi, M. A. Culinary art education: A demanding profession in culinary tourism for Malaysian's New Economy Niche. In *Proceeding of the 1st UPI International Conference on Technical and Vocational Education and Training*, (2010, November).
45. Zopiatis, A. Is it art or science? Chef's competencies for success. *International Journal of Hospitality Management*, *29*(3), 459–467, (2010).

Adaptation algorithms of mathematical educational content in e-learning courses

Yulia Vainshteina[1,*], *Victoria* Shershneva[1], *Roman* Esin[1], *Gennady* Tsibulsky[1], and *Konstantin* Safonov[2]

[1]Siberian Federal University, Kirenskogo st., 26, Krasnoyarsk, 660074, Russia
[2]Reshetnev University, Krasnoyarskii Rabochii av., 31, Krasnoyarsk, 660037, Russia

Abstract. This article is devoted to the development of algorithms for the adaptation of mathematical educational content and their implementation in the e-learning system. The adaptation of a mathematical content consists in the selection of an optimal edition of the material that best suits the individual characteristics of the student. The novelty of the work is the organization of the adaptation algorithms of the educational content in a three-level system: "introductory content adaptation" (an adaptation of the content of introductory materials of the discipline based on the initial level of students) - "current adaptation of the content" (an adaptation of the mathematical content based on current effective actions of students in the electronic course) - "appraisal-correcting adaptation" (an adaptation of normative parameters of the level of assimilation of materials, taking into account the results achieved by students). The introduction of the proposed three-stage system makes it possible to implement in individual educational trajectories and to form for each student a personal space of mathematical educational content that adapts to its level of mastering the material, which helps to improve the quality of instruction in mathematical disciplines. An approbation of the proposed algorithms was carried out in the adaptive e-course in discrete mathematics, implemented at Siberian Federal University in Russia.
Keywords: Adaptive e-learning cource, teaching mathematics, adaptation of mathematical content, adaptive E-Learning, personalized education, individual educational trajectory, LMS Moodle

1 Introduction

New educational technologies are developing in the world education system, including the individualization of the educational process in an electronic environment is becoming increasingly widespread. Contemporary trends in the development of training in the electronic environment determine the need to use adaptive electronic educational courses, the experience of development and implementation of which in higher education is currently very limited. Adaptive learning courses in the electronic environment are

* Corresponding author: YWeinstein@sfu-kras.ru

understood as electronic learning courses that provide the student with a personal educational space filled with mathematical content that adapts to his individual characteristics, providing the necessary information [1]. As individual characteristics of a student, the level of mastering the material in the discipline and the activity in the e-course are considered.

The range of functional tasks solved with the help of adaptive educational courses implemented in e-learning systems is extremely wide, ranging from the organization of independent work of students and distance learning to the development of professional competencies in the conditions of the modern trend "Life Long Learning".

The key tasks in the development of adaptive learning courses in mathematical disciplines are: structuring of educational mathematical content, building the normative model of a learner, and elaboration of algorithms and methods of an automatic navigation for the participants of the educational process in the e-learning system.

The review of research directions in the development and implementation of adaptive educational courses and environments has made it possible to single out the following main directions: designing individual educational trajectories [2-4], searching for approaches to modeling subject areas of disciplines [5-7], the formation of models of learners behaviors [8-11] and the development of adaptation algorithms in learning systems and environments [12-17]. Of course, to elaborate adaptive learning courses in mathematical disciplines with a wide range of functionalities, it is advisable to integrate the results of research in all these directions.

The article is devoted to the development of algorithms for the adaptation of mathematical educational content and their implementation in the e-learning system. A feature of the proposed algorithms is the possibility of its application in an adaptive e-learning course (AELC), implemented in learning management systems, including on the platform Learning Management System (LMS) Moodle.

The novelty of the work is that algorithms for adaptation of the educational content are developed within a three-level system: «introductory adaptation of content» (adaptation of the content of the introductory material of discipline on the basis of entry-level students) - «the current adaptation of content» (adaptation of mathematical content based on current productive activities students in adaptive e-course) - «appraisal-correcting adaptation» (adaptation of the normative parameters of the level of assimilation of materials, taking into account the student's learning outcomes).

2 Adaptation algorithms of educational content

The proposed algorithms for adaptation of mathematical educational content in adaptive e-courses have been tested in the development of AELC in the virtual learning environment LMS Moodle. The wide opportunities for the management of educational activity in the electronic environment LMS Moodle make it one of the most common in the development of AELC in Russian and foreign higher education institution [18]. The general structure of the three-level system of adaptation of educational content in the AELC and the implementation of individual educational trajectories by forming a personal space for study materials for each student is shown in Fig. 1.

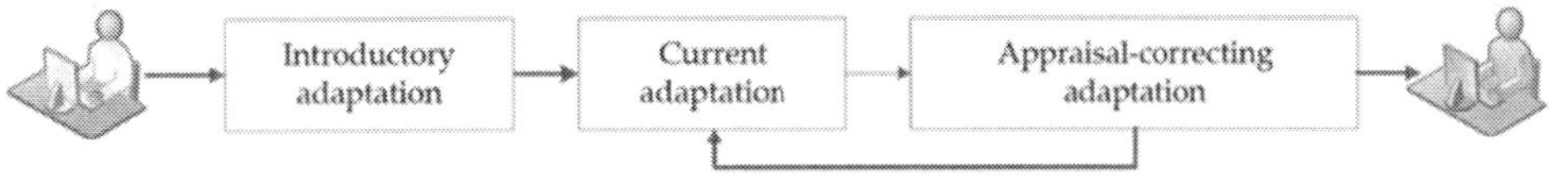

Fig. 1. The system of the educational content adaptation in AELC.

At the initial stage of the training the introductory adaptation of the content to the individual characteristics of a student is carried out; the enlarged algorithm for this adaptation is shown in Fig. 2.

The algorithm at the introductory adaptation stage includes an assessment of the initial level of a student preparation, identification of gaps in the necessary (basic) mathematical knowledge that interferes with the assimilation of new material in the mathematical discipline. Based on the assessment of the level of initial training, it is recommended to conditionally divide all students into three groups: "low", "medium" and "high" level of training. Students of groups with "low" and "medium" levels are individually recommended additional corrective materials that allow them to fill the missing mathematical knowledge and in the future to quickly learn the material. Thus, at this stage, an individual educational trajectory begins to be built for each student, and by the beginning of the study of the basic material in the adaptive e-course in mathematics everyone reaches a level of preparation that is sufficient for further development of the course.

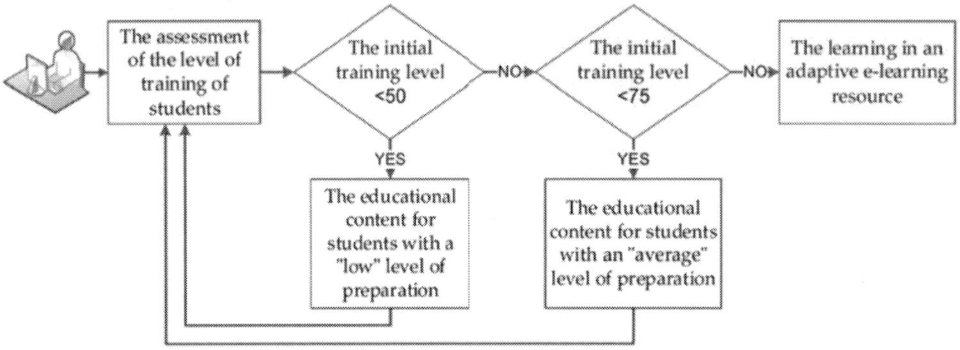

Fig. 2. The algorithm of introductory adaptation in AELC.

A feature of the current adaptation stage is the opportunity to increase the level of mastering of the material by providing the student with the content of the discipline in the edition corresponding to the current level of mastering of the material (the level of mathematical competence formation).

A structuring of the educational content of AELC in mathematical disciplines is proposed to be done by singling out the minimal theoretical units representing the semantically complete microportions of the educational material called terms, and determining the sequence of their study. Principles of the allocation of terms based on the logical and epistemological analysis, proposed by E.K. Voishvillo, are detailed in the work [19].

Based on educational practice, when presenting material in AELC, it often becomes necessary to present it in various editions. This is especially actually for mathematical content in connection with the high level of abstraction and the complexity of the perception of mathematical disciplines. So, it is proposed to use at least three editions of the presentation for each term of mathematical content. In our opinion, the editions of the terms of educational content must be based on the levels of mathematics competence. We have highlighted the following three levels: the level of reproduction, the level of establishing links and dependencies, and the level of reasoning.

The presentation of the term of mathematical content in the first level (reproduction) edition is constructed in such a way that it gives an idea of the application of facts and standard methods in a familiar situation, acquaints with mathematical objects and their properties, standard expressions and formulas, demonstrates the implementation of standard procedures and known algorithms, and also the direct execution of calculations and transformations.

The presentation of the term of mathematical content in the edition of the next level (establishment of links and dependencies) contains, along with the material of the first-level term, material demonstrating examples of establishing relationships and dependencies between data in the condition of a task, as well as approaches to analyzing the conditions of tasks and methods of integrating mathematical methods and knowledge in their solution, as well as examples of solving mathematical problems that, although not quite typical, are still familiar to students or to a small extent go beyond the known.

The presentation of the term of mathematical content in the third level (reasoning) edition includes materials aimed at developing skills of independence and initiative, including a problem approach to the presentation of material, encourages students to independently formulate problem solving algorithms, integrate knowledge of the entire course, substantiate and interpret the results.

The proposed features of editions of educational content reflect the specifics of the formation of mathematical competence.

The students get an opportunity to better understand complex theoretical material due to the variable representation of the content of the mathematical term corresponding to different editions. A fragment of the enlarged algorithm of the current adaptation of an educational content, allowing one to switch between its editions E1.1., E1.2, E1.3, depending on the level of mastering the material of the current term 1, then choose one of the versions E2.1., E2.2, E2.3 of the next term 2, and if necessary switch between them, is shown in Fig. 3.

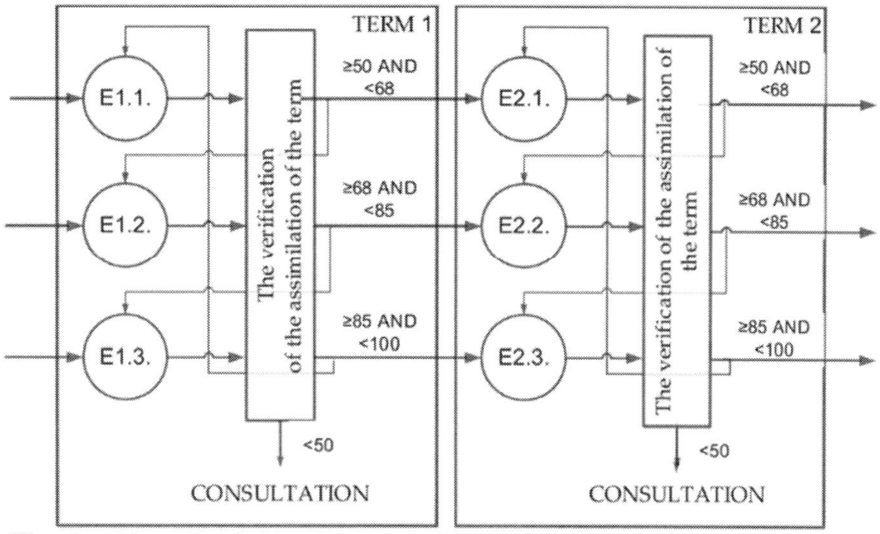

Fig. 3. The algorithm of switching between editions of the term in the process of the current adaptation.

This algorithm allows one to build multiple trajectories with the possibility of re-learning the material in various editorial versions of the presentation. The rules for the selection of educational content, included in the model of management of the learning process, allow students to provide optimal editions of the studied terms on the basis of individual characteristics of students. Effective actions of students initiate an automated transition to the study of the materials of the next term or the repetition of materials of the current term in the wording corresponding to the achieved level.

The process of verifying the assimilation of educational material for each term is realized in the triad of "knowledge-skill-possession." Complex monitoring of the presented triad makes it possible to assess the level of mathematics competence formation expressed in the ability to apply knowledge of mathematical disciplines in professional activity [20].

The purpose of the appraisal-correcting adaptation is the assessment and adjustment of the normative values of the level of assimilation of AELC training materials, which are the parameters of the transition between the editions of materials and the terms of educational content. Initially, the normative values are established on the basis of expert teaching evaluation. Further, based on the results of AELC assimilation by students, the initial normative values are adjusted, based on the average values for the group of students, Fig. 4.

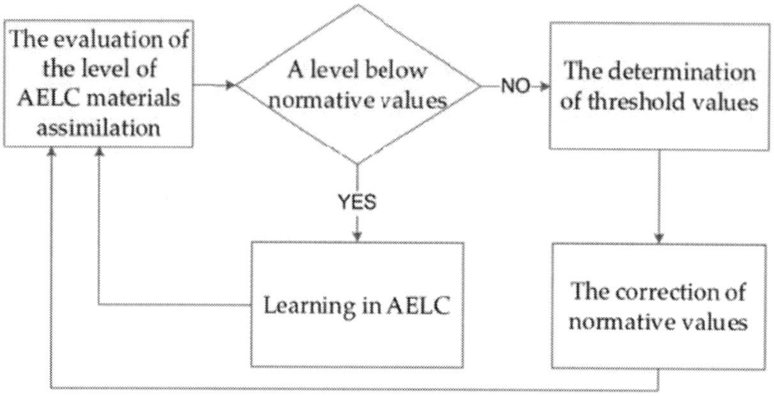

Fig. 4. The algorithm of appraisal-correcting adaptation.

The software implementation of the proposed adaptation scheme was carried out in LMS Moodle by imposing restrictions on the training elements of the electronic course: tracking the execution of the element - studying a determined edition of the term or passing through a checkpoint and monitoring the level of assimilation of the term. The adjustment of AELC elements on the basis of the proposed algorithms makes it possible to realize the variability of the presentation of educational information within the framework of a single e-course, forming an individual profile for the representation of mathematical content for each student.

3 Results

An approbation of the algorithms proposed in this report was carried out in AELC in the discipline "Discrete Mathematics" at the Siberian Federal University in Russia. 121 students of the experimental group and 119 students of the control group participated in the experiment. As a result of the final control over the assimilation of the materials of AELC in discrete mathematics, the results of which are shown in Fig. 5, the effectiveness of the experimental group was on average 14% higher than in the control group.

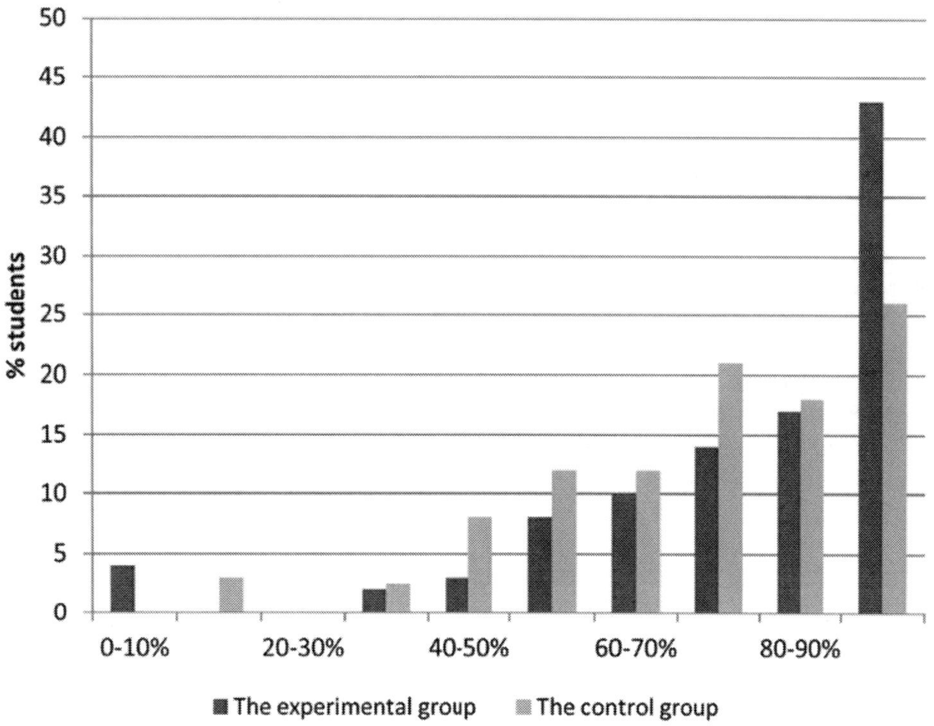

Fig. 5. The final control over the assimilation of AELC materials.

In addition, to assess the effectiveness of the proposed algorithms, a questionnaire was carried out for the students of the experimental group and demonstrated the positive reaction of the students to the introduction of AELC in the study of discrete mathematics.

Thus, when assessing adaptability to the level of assimilation of the material, 67.4% of respondents noted the option "high level of adaptability", 28.3% considered "the level of adaptability is rather high" and only 4.3% chose the option "I do not know".

The majority of respondents (86.1%) noted an increase in motivation to study the discipline in AELC conditions, 13.8% abstained from an answer and the adaptation of the content seemed rather uninteresting only for 1.1% of respondents; no one spoke for the total lack of interest in the methods of adapting the educational content.

67% of students noted that studying the discipline in AELC provides better mastery of the subject as compared to traditional teaching, 15% noted the importance of the proposed approach and 18% found it difficult to answer this question.

Thus, the approbation of the adaptation algorithms proposed in this work within the framework of AELC in discrete mathematics showed their effectiveness in the educational process.

4 Conclusions

The adaptation algorithms of a mathematical educational content in the electronic environment are presented in the paper. A novelty of the proposed algorithms is to implement the content of the educational content in the three-level system: "introductory content adaptation" - "current content adaptation" - "appraisal-corrective adaptation." The proposed three-level system of adaptation of the mathematical educational content fulfills the functions of the student's "a conductor" from the beginning to the end of the training in the discipline, adapting the teaching materials taking into account the considered specificity of the formation of mathematical competence.

The implementation of the proposed adaptation algorithms to the mathematical content in AELC makes it possible to create individual educational trajectories for students within the framework of a flexible personalized educational schedule with multiple control of the process of self-education. When using the system presented in the work, for each student an optimal personal space of mathematical educational content is formed, which corresponds to its individual characteristics as much as possible.

The pedagogical experiment confirmed that the organization of the adaptation of the mathematical educational content allows the teacher to provide an individual approach to teaching students in the electronic environment, regardless of the number of students in the group, ensuring the simplicity of building a personal educational scenario for a student.

The results can also be used to develop AELC for other disciplines. Further development of the proposed adaptation algorithms of the educational content in a three-level system is assumed by developing a formal model that includes control rules which correct the normative values of the content assimilation estimation based on the methods of expert assessments and fuzzy sets theory.

The reported study was funded by RFBR according to the research project №18-013-00654

References

1. Yu.V. Vainshtein, R.V. Esin, G.M. Tsibulsky, Education and Informatics, *Adaptive model of developing individual educational trajectories for blended learning*, **2**, 86 (2017)
2. B. Lazarov, Information Models and Analyses, *Application of some cybernetic models in building individual educational trajectory*, **2**, 90 (2013)
3. D.H. Clements, J. Sarama, Mathematical Thinking and Learning, *Learning Trajectories in Mathematics Education*, **6**, 81 (2004)
4. V.V. Kureychik, V.V. Bova, Open Education, *Modeling of Process Knowledge Representation in Intellectual Instructional Systems Based on Competence Approach*, **3**, 42 (2014)
5. G.A. Atanov, Educational Technology & Society, *The modeling of an educational subject domain or the subject model of a learner*, **1**, 111 (2001)
6. T. Murray, S. Blessing, S. Ainsworth, Interactive and Intelligent Educational Software, *Springer: Netherlands*, *Authoring Tools for Advanced Technology Learning Environments: Toward Cost Effective Adaptive*, 557 (2003)
7. O. Shabalina, S. Chickerur, Recent Patents on Computer Science, *Technology - centered higher education: best approaches and practices in technology integration*, **9**, 104 (2016)
8. E. Davidova, A. Sergushicheva, Open Education, *Models of a student and a teacher for the multi-agent training system*, **5**, 25 (2015)
9. L. Zaytseva, E .Bul', Educational Technology & Society, *An adaptation in computer systems based on the structuring of learning objects*, **9**, 422 (2006)
10. M. Kolyada, Artificial Intelligence, *The kinds of models trained in automated learning systems*, **2**, 28 (2008)
11. L. Rastrigin, Riga: Zinatne, *An adaptive learning a the model of a learner*, 160 (1988)
12. V. Wade, Digital Libraries and Archives: 13th Italian Research Conference on Digital Libraries, IRCDL 2017, Modena, Italy. *An Adaptive Cross-Site User Modelling Platform for Cultural Heritage Websites*, **733** (2017)

13. E. O'Donnell, S. Lawless, M. Sharp, V. Wade, International Journal of Distance Education Technologies, *A Review of Personalised E-Learning: Towards Supporting Learner Diversity*, **13**, 22 (2015)
14. O. Conlan, A. Staikopouslos, C. Hampson, S. Lawless, I. O'Keeffe, New Review of Hypermedia and Multimedia, *The narrative approach to personalisation*, **19**, 132 (2013)
15. P. Brusilovsky, A. Kobas, W. Nejdl, Verlag Berlin Heidelberg. Springer, *The adaptive web, methods and strategies of web personalisation* (2007)
16. P. Brusilovsky, International Journal of Artificial Intelligence in Education, *Adaptive and Intelligent Web-based Educational Systems*, **13**, 156 (2003)
17. W.J. Van der Linden, Springer Science, Business Media, LLC Statistical for social and behavioral sciences, *Elements of adaptive testing*, 437 (2010)
18. K. Hicks, Understanding The Top Learning Management Systems, URL: http://www.edudemic.com/the-20-best-learning-management-systems/ (2016)
19. Yu.V. Vainshtein, R.V. Esin, G.M. Tsibulsky, Bulletin of Krasnoyarsk State Pedagogical University, *Adaptive e-learning resources for the advanced training of teaching staff*, **2**, 52 (2017)
20. V.A. Shershneva, L.V. Shkerina, V.N Sidorov, T.V. Sidorova, K.V. Safonov, European Journal of Contemporary Education, *Contemporary Didactics in Higher Education in Russia*, **17**, 357 (2016)

Good Practices in School to Educate Critical Citizens. The Youth Parliament programme from the perspective of secondary school teachers in training*

Olga Moreno-Fernández[1,†], *María* Puig-Gutiérrez[1] , and *José* González-Monteagudo[1]

[1]Faculty of Education Sciences, University of Seville, Spain

Abstract. This paper refers to the European project Erasmus + ELEF (European Learning Environment Formats for Citizenship and Democracy, Reference number 580426). The aim of this project is to develop, implement, evaluate and replicate democratic and innovative learning environments (good practices) in both educational institutions and informal and community learning environments. In this context, over the course of a year, a number of experiences considered relevant have been selected, which constitute the sample of this research on good practices. This contribution presents the educational programme "Youth Parliament". This is a project with a long history and whose main objective is to train responsible citizens, with the collaboration of various educational agents. The evaluation carried out by the Secondary Education teachers in training on the potentialities and limitations of the programme is shown, based on the experiences carried out in the participating educational centres during the academic year 2016-2017.

1 Introduction

In Spain, due to the various changes in educational matters in recent years, education for citizenship has been contemplated in different ways according to current educational laws. Thus, with the advent of the LOE (Organic Law of Education) in 2006, education for citizenship became a compulsory and evaluable subject within the school curriculum, at the same time that it was considered a cross-cutting issue and was considered as one of the so-called basic competencies (social and citizenship competence), introduced in this law. The political changes that took place brought about reforms in the educational field and so in 2012 there was a change in the name of the subject and the contents dealt with in it.

Subsequently, with the entry into force of the LOMCE (Organic Law for the Improvement of Educational Quality) in 2013, the subject of Citizenship Education is eliminated as a compulsory subject in the curriculum, being relegated to an optional

* This paper refers to the European project Erasmus + ELEF (European Learning Environment Formats for Citizenship and Democracy, Reference number 580426).

† Corresponding author: omoreno@us.es

subject, alternative to religion, called Social and Civic Values. It is thus maintained as a cross-cutting theme and the name of basic social and civic competence is also changed. The competences are now referred to as key competences and what we are dealing with is called social and civic competences.

In short, we have experienced a process of loss of value in education for citizenship, a fact that comes into conflict with what is happening in Europe. We must not lose sight of the fact that education for citizenship is a concern at European level and this is reflected in the various reports drawn up in recent years by the European Commission [1], [2], [3]. In its conclusion, it states that "citizenship education is one of the main means by which European countries help young people acquire the social and citizenship skills they will need in their future lives" ([2]), all of this by focusing on four specific fronts: the presence of citizenship education in school curricula; democratic culture in schools; leadership of management teams and teacher training; and assessment of learning and monitoring by the authorities.

Since the European project Erasmus + ELEF (European Learning Environment Formats for Citizenship and Democracy), which aims to implement, develop, evaluate and replicate different formats of innovative democratic learning environments (good practices), various experiences have been selected over more than a year as a sample of this research on good practices.

In this regard, we present the experience gained with the educational programme Youth Parliament, a project that has a long history and aims to train responsible citizens with the collaboration of various educational agents. To this end, we have worked with students who are doing the Master's Degree in Secondary Education (MAES) at the University of Seville (Spain), in this academic year 2017/2018.

2 Method

Forty-three students participated in this experience. In the experimentation carried out, the Youth Parliament Programme was presented, later analysing in small groups the formative actions carried out by the different municipalities participating in the 2016/17 academic year. These training actions were analyzed on the basis of the information contained in the worksheets that each center sends to the coordinating administration of the program, once the course is over. For the analysis, a script of questions was designed to allow future teachers to reflect on various elements that appeared in the cards.

Questions such as: What relevance does democratic citizenship have to work?, What possibilities and limitations do you consider the experience to have?, What problems have been worked on?, What kind of activities have been carried out?, Which are the bodies involved?, Do you think that this programme really favours the development of participatory and democratic citizenship in schools?, Why?

In this way, four discussion groups were organized, from the analysis of which it can be deduced that the Youth Parliament program, despite being considered an educational program that favors good citizenship education practices, presents limitations such as the number of school-age participants that can be part of it or that the themes can sometimes deviate from relevant socio-environmental issues focused on what citizen education should respond to.

3 Results

The results obtained in the discussion groups show us that most of the participants consider the Youth Parliament programme to be a useful programme, of great relevance for working on democratic citizenship, since it favours the participation of young people in the exercise of citizenship and brings them closer to making decisions on real problems in their environment. Therefore, we take as examples the following phrases:

> "We believe that this is a project of great importance since it will introduce young people to citizen political participation, which should be one of the objectives of citizenship training, creating citizens with a vocation for citizen participation" (subject 6)
> "Very relevant because it puts into practice the exercise of citizenship at an early age, introducing adolescents to the real functioning of public institutions" (subject 12)

Among the main possibilities that the participants highlight in the program, are to give voice to young people who, due to their minority, are not usually heard in the political arena and therefore offer them the opportunity to intervene in the life of their municipality. It also emphasizes learning to exercise citizenship and participation. Let us look at some examples:

> "I believe that this is a programme with great development possibilities, since it encourages young people to participate in the life of their municipality, which is the most immediate and can be a good stimulus to awaken interest in participation" (subject 10)
> "It facilitates the teaching of education for citizenship in a practical way" (subject 4)

In spite of the possibilities attributed, the participants also pointed out various limitations of the programme, among which the following stand out: "the scarce training of teachers to carry out this type of initiative, the complex network of relations between the agents involved, the scarce number of students directly involved, the dependence on the police will of the mayors and the maintenance of the current parliamentary democratic model, in which direct participation is limited to only a few".

When asked about the problems that had been worked on in the various projects analyzed, they were mentioned: lack of knowledge of the culture and customs of the local environment, help and solidarity among neighbors, healthy lifestyle habits, reading habits, creation of leisure spaces for young people, among others. Having explained the problems, the participants on several occasions showed their rejection of the idea that some of them were not directly related to relevant socio-environmental issues that responded to what education for citizenship really is. Thus, one of the subjects stated:

> "There are issues that are not related to education for citizenship and that we should not consider relevant socio-environmental problems" (subject 3)

The next issue addressed concerns the type of activities carried out, including gymkhana-type activities, games, sports activities and workshops. For the development of these activities and the proper functioning of the project, various actors are involved. Thus, when the participants were consulted by the agents involved in the different projects, in almost all of them, together with the educational centre and the families, local businesses and associations and the town councils were involved. In addition, on some occasions, other larger-scale entities such as La Caixa took part in the development of the projects.

The participants are asked whether they really consider that the projects they have analysed favour the development of participatory and democratic citizenship in schools. The answers are mostly negative, since despite having initially highlighted the possibilities of the youth parliament programme, they believe that the concrete projects they have analysed are somewhat far removed from the socio-environmental problems relevant to the development of a critical citizenship.

Finally, each working group was asked to draw or draw a diagram on a piece of cardboard on what characteristics a program should have in order to be considered a good educational practice that favors democratic and citizen values. A work that was put in common and in which there were many coincidences. The words that represented it were: social values, equality, participation, critical reflection, freedom of expression, dialogue...Some examples of the works presented by thc participants are presented below (Figures 1and 2).

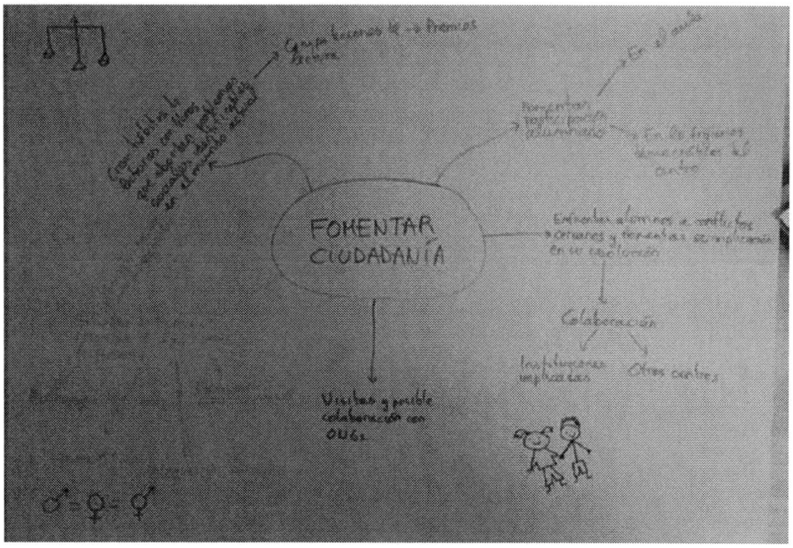

Fig. 1. Mural "Promoting citizenship". Authors: Students participating in the IDA format of the Erasmus+ ELEF programme (Reference number 580426).

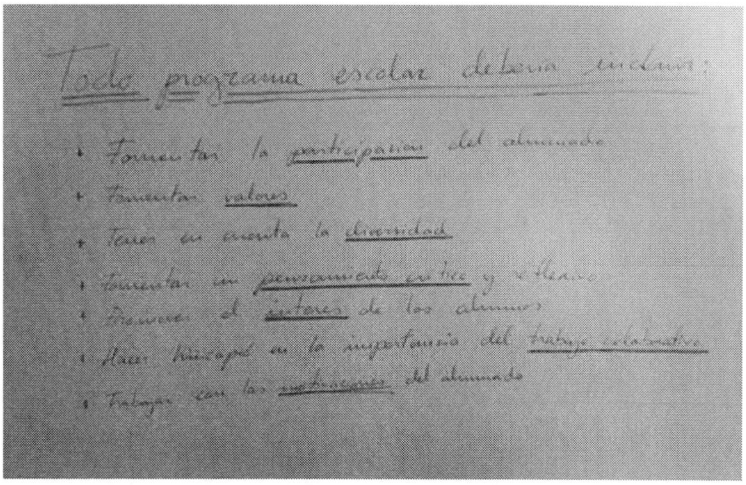

Fig. 2. Mural "Good practices". Authors: Students participating in the IDA format of the Erasmus+ ELEF programme (Reference number 580426).

https://doi.org/10.1051/shsconf/20184801011

4 Conclusion

Analyzing the data, it is observed that the teachers in participating training value positively the need to educate responsible and critical citizens in the classroom, as well as to approach good practices that are being carried out in schools. With this experience, the future teachers of Secondary Education have been given the opportunity to approach the reality of the centers and programmes that are being carried out successfully. This first contact made it possible for them to reflect on the importance of having good educational practices for civic education in the classroom.

References

1. Eurydice Report, Education for citizenship in the European school context (Brussels, European Commission, 2005)
2. Eurydice Report, Education for citizenship in Europe (Brussels, European Commission, 2012)
3. Eurydice Report, Citizenship education at school in Europe (Brussels, European Commission, 2017)

University Students in Southwestern Spain Digital Competences

Olga Moreno-Fernández[1,*], *Pilar* Moreno-Crespo[2], and *Coral I.* Hunt-Gómez[1]

[1]Faculty of Education Sciences, University of Seville, Spain.
[2]Faculty of Education Sciences, University of Huelva, Spain.

Abstract. The European Higher Education Area has marked a milestone in Higher Education. Consequently, teaching methodologies have experienced several transformations and their focus has turned to the incorporation of ICT in socio-educational environments. Thus, it can be stated that digital competences development is a paramount element for university students' training, as they need to be digitally competent. This study explores the degree of knowledge and training about digital competences that students pursuing undergraduate or postgraduate studies in Educational Sciences have. The questionnaire "University Student' Basic Digital Competences 2.0" (COBADI/ Trademark 2970648) was applied to students of Early Years Education, Primary Education, Social Education and postgraduates of the Master's Degree in Secondary Education from the Universities of Seville and Huelva (Southwestern Spain). Results show that digital competence in university students needs to be improved. There is, therefore, a definite need for transversal and organized training allowing students to master digital contexts efficiently.

1 Introduction

The European Higher Education Area (EHEA) has marked a milestone in Higher Education. Consequently, teaching methodologies have experienced several transformations and, in many cases, their focus has turned to the incorporation of ICT (Information and Communication Technologies) in socio-educational environments. If ICT is to be incorporated into Higher Education, several digital competences allowing students, as well as their educational institutions, to manage software and hardware and other digital resources are needed ([1], [2], [3], [4]). Thus, it can be stated that digital competences development is a paramount element for university students' training, as they need to be digitally competent.

2 Method

This study explores the degree of knowledge and training about digital competences that students pursuing undergraduate or postgraduate studies in Educational Sciences have. To

* Corresponding author: omoreno@us.es

do so, an exploratory, quantitative, transversal and non-probabilistic study has been carried out ([5], [6]). Subjects were undergraduate students of Early Years Education, Primary Education, Social Education and postgraduate students of the Master's Degree in Secondary Education from the Universities of Seville and Huelva (Southwestern Spain). The questionnaire "University Student' Basic Digital Competences 2.0" (COBADI/ Trademark 2970648) was applied and data were analysed using Statistical Package for the Social Sciences (version 24, IBM SPSS).

3 Results

90.09% of the participants in the study were women and 9.91% men. The ages of the participants are varied, however the vast majority of them were aged 22-26 (53.60%) and 17-21 (36.94%) (Figure 1).

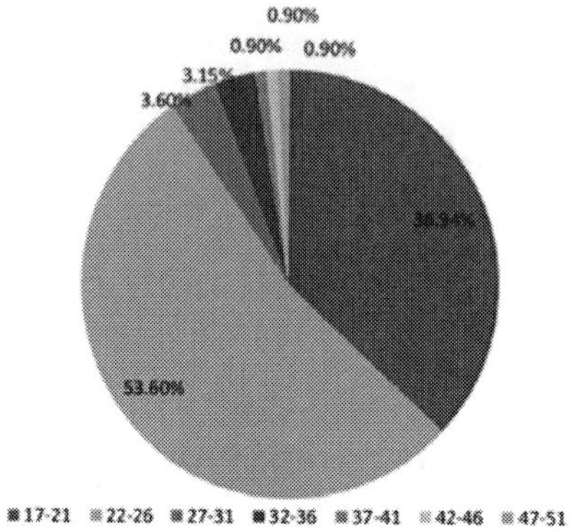

Fig. 1. Age of the participants.

Regarding the studies of the participants, 43.24% were students of the Degree in Social Education, 34.23% were students of the Degree in Early Years Education, 13.51% were students of the el Master's Degree in Secondary Education, and 9.01% were students of the Degree in Primary Education (Figure 2). 68.02 of the subjects were students of the University of Huelva and 31.98% of the University of Seville.

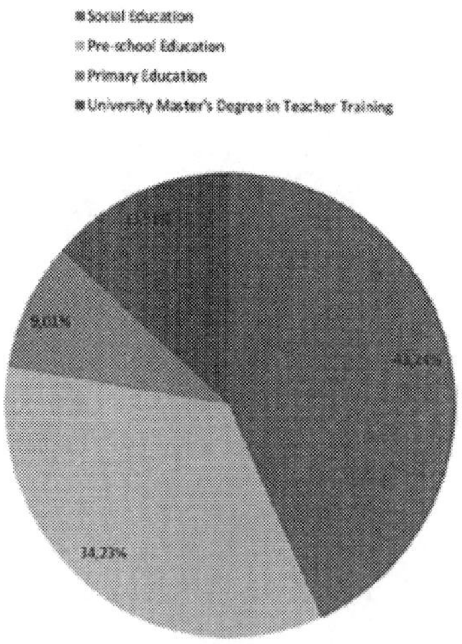

Fig. 2. Studies of the participants.

Regarding the use of ICT, the two most used electronic devices were the following: mobile phone (94.1%) and laptop y (92.3%). Other devices appeared with lower percentages tablet (21.2%), desktop computer (7.7%), e-book (1%), television (0.5%) or printer (0.5%) (Figure 3). Subjects were able to mark all the options they considered appropriated.

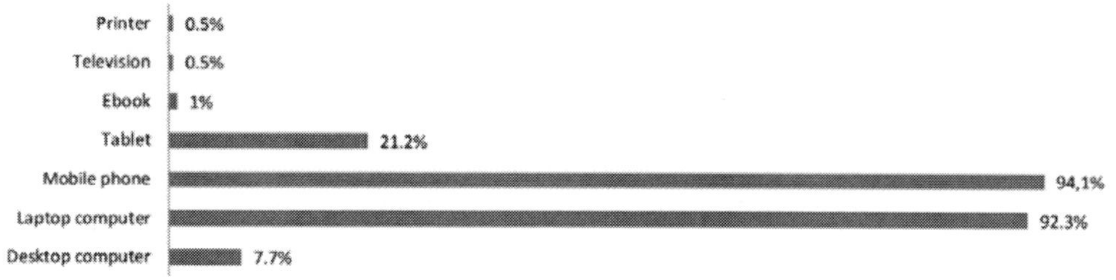

Fig. 3. Most used electronic devices by university students.

Regarding their Internet connection, 98.2% of the subjects state that they have connection on their mobile phone, 96.8% in the lap-top, 34.7% in the Tablet, 22.1% in the computer, and 1% in their television (Figure 4). E-book and printers do not appear in this list. Subjects were able to mark all the options they considered appropriated.

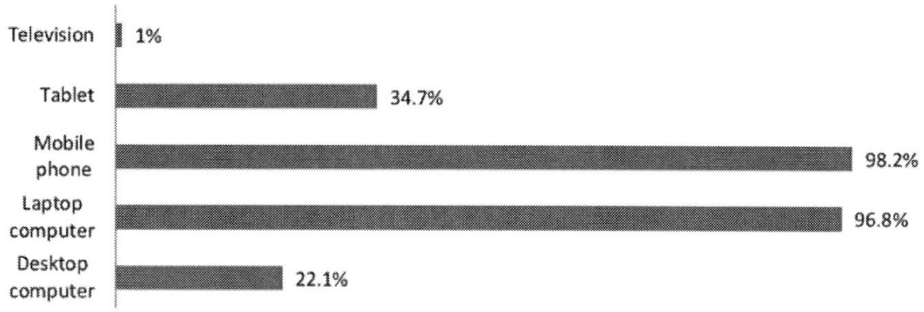

Fig. 4. Most used electronic devices with internet connection by university students.

Regarding the amount of time they have availability of internet connected electronic devices, 86% of the subjects stated that they are connected all day long, 24.3% of the students also get connected in public spaces which offer free Wi-Fi (Figure 5). Subjects were able to mark all the options they considered appropriated.

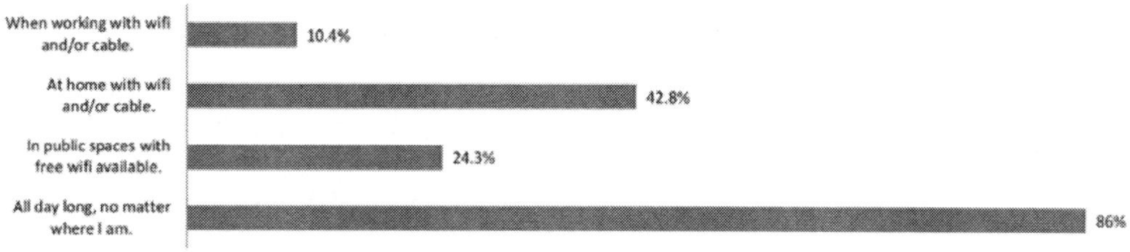

Fig. 5. Most ranked places were university students get connected.

The resources most frequently used by students when connected to the Internet is chatting using the App WhatsApp (88.7%), followed by using search engines like Google (77%), using social networks like Facebook (77%) and consulting the e-mail (71.6%), and using platforms like YouTube (64.4%) (Figure 6). Subjects were able to mark all the options they considered appropriated.

Fig. 6. Most frequently used resources by the university students.

When describing the academic use of electronic devices made by university students, 93.2% of subjects stated to use mainly the laptop, 32% of the mobile phone and, only 9.9% use the tablet and 4.1% the desktop computer (Figure 7).

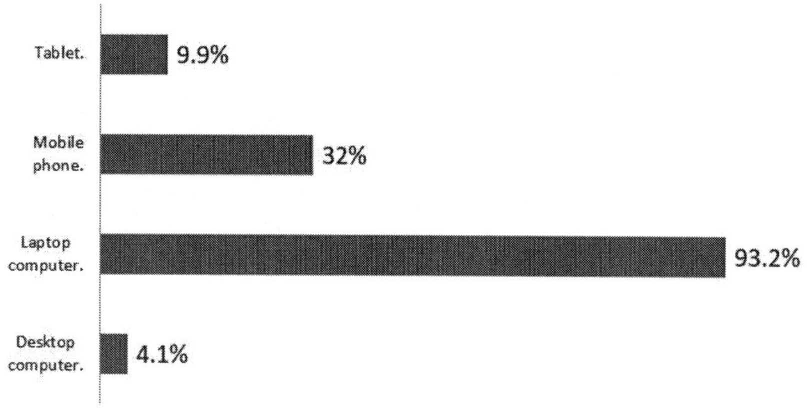

Fig. 7. Most used electronic devices by university students for academic purposes.

The use made by university students with academic purposes of these electronic devices can be ranked as follows: 91.9% using to the virtual platform of the subjects, 87.8% using search engines like, 69.4% using the e-mail, 27.5% communicating apps such as WhatsApp, 11.7% using platforms like YouTube, 5% using social networks such as Facebook (Figure 8). Subjects were able to mark all the options they considered appropriated.

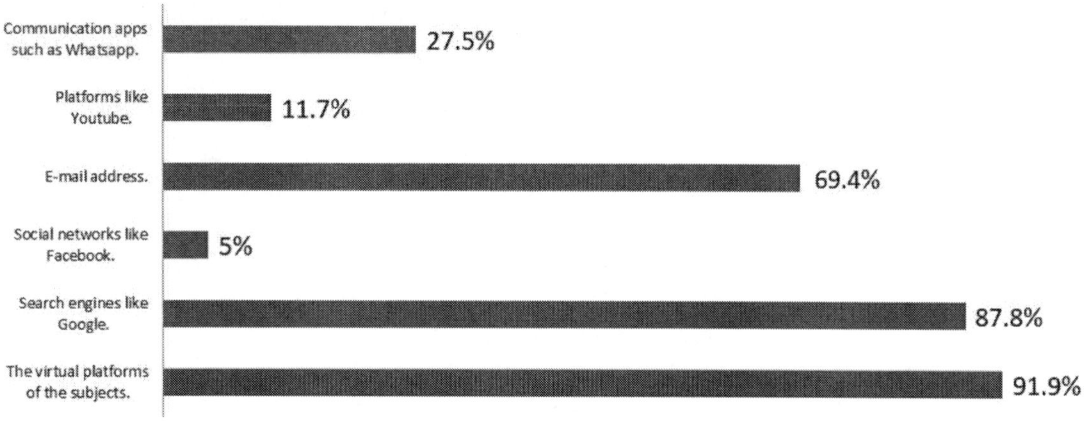

Fig. 8. Most used devices for academic purposes by university students.

When describing the COBADI items, it must be highlighted that 60.4% strongly agree and 32.9% showed some agreement with the statement 'I can communicate with other via email'. 5% showed some disagreement and 1.8% strongly disagree. Another tool considered important to connect people were instant massaging apps. 74.8% of the subject completely agreed with the statement, 16.2% showed some agreement, 5.9% somehow disagreed and 3.2% strongly disagreed. 63.1% considered social networks (Twitter, Facebook, Ning among others) as a mean of communication, 27.5% somehow agreed with that statement, 6.8% somehow disagreed and 2.7% strongly disagreed. Students were asked to state their degree of agreement to the use of professional networks like Linked-in or Xing . Only 11.3 % of students showed strong agreement. 38.3% showed some agreement, 27.5% showed some disagreement and 23 % strongly disagreed (Figure 9).

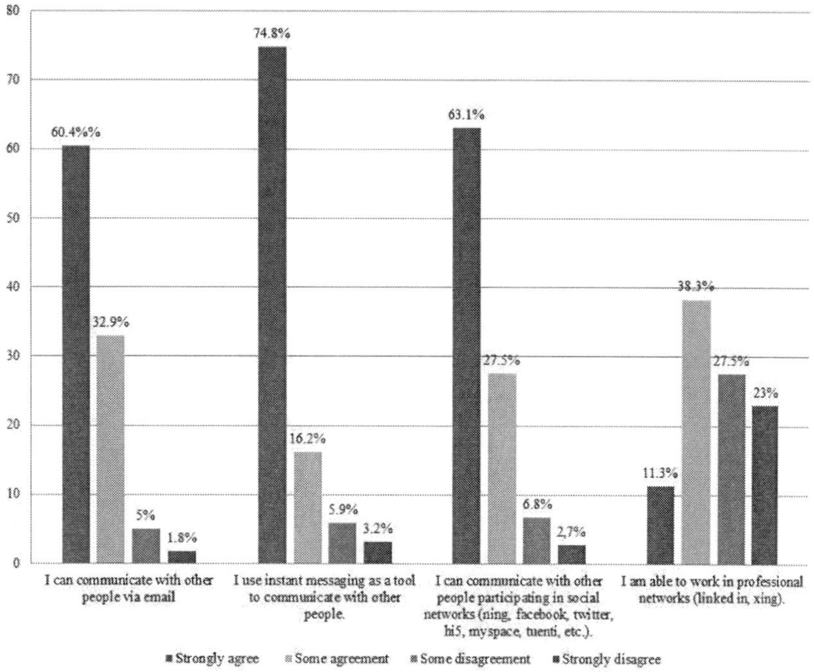

Fig. 9. Digital Communication Competences.

In regard to the item 'I know how to use wikis' like Wikipedia or aulawiki21", 27.9% of the subjects strongly agreed, 50.9%showed some agreement, 17.6% showed some disagreement and 3.6% strongly disagreed. As to the item 'working with documents in the web (google drive, skydrive)' 55.9% of the subjects strongly agreed, 28.8 % showed some agreement, 12.2 % showed some disagreement and 3.2% strongly disagreed. Thus, it can be stated that 84.7% of the university students use this king of tools to have their tasks updated. Regarding the item 'I am able to organize, analyse and synthetize information through concept maps using some social software tools (cmaptool, mindomo, text2mindmap...)' 28.8% of the subjects strongly agreed, 27.9% showed some agreement, 26.1 % showed some disagreement and 17.1% strongly disagreed. Participants were asked about their degree of agreement to the statement 'I feel competent to work with social software tools to help me to analyse and/or navigate through content included in blogs (wordle, Tagxedo...)". 39.6 % of the subjects showed some disagreement and 31.1% strongly disagreed (Figure 10)

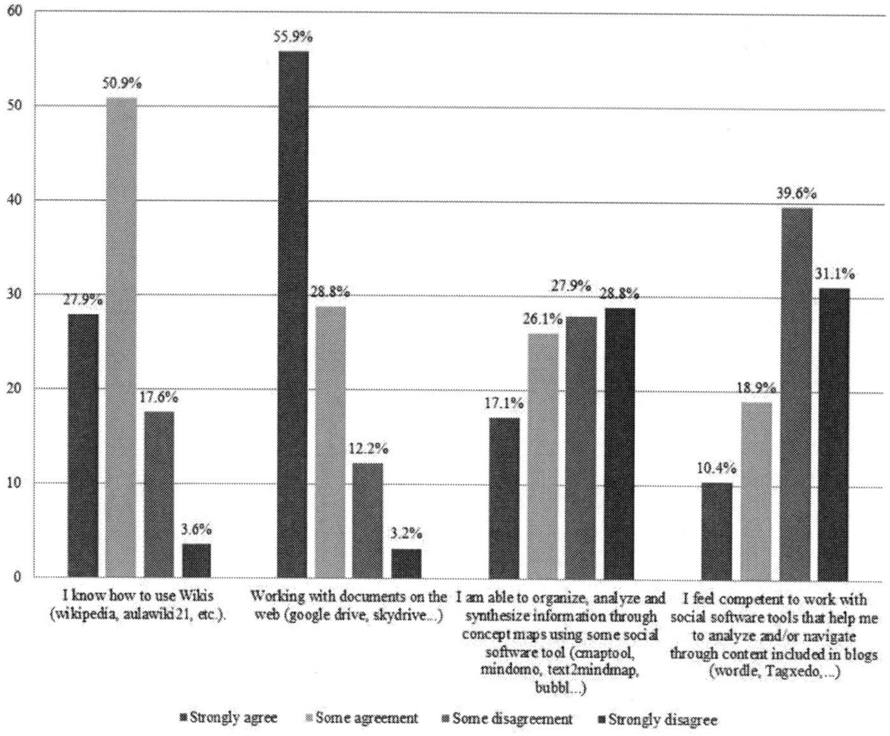

Fig. 10. Digital Use Competences.

4 Conclusion

Results indicate that a high percentage of university students use e-mail and instant massaging as a way of communication with others. The use or social networks as a mean of communication is also significant. Subjects regard themselves as competent in the use of Internet search engines and highly competent when working with documents on line. However, participants acknowledged their lack of competences regarding information organization, analysis and synthesis when working with conceptual maps included in social software tools.

Results show that digital competence in university students needs to be improved. There is, therefore, a definite need for transversal and organized training allowing students to master digital contexts efficiently. If the requisites of the European Higher Education Area are to be fulfilled, digital competences need to be in the centre of the educational agenda.

References

1. UNESCO, Enfoque estratégico sobre TIC en educación en América Latina y el Caribe. Oficina Regional de Educación para América Latina y el Caribe (OREALC/ Unesco Santiago) (2013)
2. E. Vázquez-Cano, E. López-Meneses, E. Fernández-Márquez, Concept Mapping for Developing Competencies in European Higher Education Area, Inter. Journal of Humanities and Social Sci., **3 (15)** (2013)
3. L. Johnson, S. Adams Becker, M. Cummins, V. Estrada, A. Freeman, C. Hall, *NMC Horizon* Report: 2016 (Higher Education Edition, 2016)
4. E. Vázquez-Cano, V. Marín-Díaz, G.A. Maldonado-Berea, E. García-Garzón, E., La competencia digital del alumnado universitario de Ciencias Sociales desde una perspectiva de género, Prisma Social. Revista de Investigación Social, **19**, (2017)
5. M. Canales, M, *Metodologías de investigación social* (Santiago, Lom Edicione, 2006)
6. R. Hernández, C. Fernández, P. Baptista, *Metodología de la investigación,* (México, McGraw-Hill, 2006)

Study regarding the use of movement games in order to improve coordination abilities in primary school pupils

Talaghir Laurentiu-Gabriel[1, a] and *Cherepov* Evgeny[2]

[1]University „Dunarea de Jos",Domneasca Street, no. 46, 800008, Galati, Romania
[2] South Ural State University, Lenin's Street no. 76, Chelyabinsk, 454080, Russian

Abstract. The purpose of the research, performed during the school year 2015 – 2016, was to observe the role of movement games during the PE class, carried out with primary school pupils. The aim of the present paper is to present the way in which we influenced the coordination skill manifestation indicators so that they are suited to the pupils' age possibilities. The games were combined and we used two games during each practical PE class. In order to achieve this, we changed the working method at the structure level of the lesson. Thus, in the second part of the lesson, which includes types of walking and running in order to engage the body in the effort, we used movement games. As an assessment test, we used the trial "Throw at a vertical target". This trial tests the coordination skill (the dexterity) within the school assessment system. The results obtained in the trials were statistically processed by means of the SPSS 23.0 program. The results indicated a significant progress for the group of girls and an insignificant progress for the groups of boys.

1 Introduction

The education system represents the coherent ensemble of the school institutions of all levels, specialisations and forms, which is designed, organized and functions on the basis of a number of general educational principles, with an organisational character, and some of them with a legal character, as well as of some educational standards [1].

Physical Education is a school subject, component of the education and teaching process, together with other subjects within the compulsory school curriculum. The importance of PE was and is permanently emphasized by specialists in the domain. The physical and emotional development of the young generation strongly relies on a healthy body. The methodology of organising and conducting PE classes in pre-university education [13] includes Physical Education and Sport among the global education components, their content having a strong influence on the health, development and growth of the body, as it helps in developing motor skills and emotional processes and in socializing.

[a] Corresponding author: gtalaghir@ugal.ro

Physical Education is present in the educational and teaching process from very early ages (6 years old) until university studies, when the individual has already become an adult (≥ 20 years old). This very long period of time during which PE follows the transformation process of the child into an adult speaks for itself in point of the beneficial effects it has on the body [21].

The evolution of PE as a school subject has been permanently achieved with the help of the curriculum. In Romania, beginning with the school year 2015-2016, a new curriculum for primary school was introduced [22, 23]. This curriculum is trying to shift focus from objective-centred learning to competence-centred learning. This is one of the directions which are considered a priority for Romanian education. The new curriculum intends, at least at a conceptual level, to orient students' skills towards the pleasure of practising physical exercises as a means of preserving health. The aspects regarding the performance achieved within the school physical education process are outweighed by the new curricular guidelines [20].

Concerns regarding curricular evolution are also topical at an international level. Specialists in the domain around the world agree with the idea of adapting curricula to the reality and evolution of society [3; 9, 15, 18, 26]. Also, some authors highlight the importance of the behavioural component and the role that PE has in shaping it [5, 6, 17].

The specificity of PE classes is different from the other school subjects regarding the content, the structure of the lesson, the activity organisation methodology, the location, the dynamics or the learning particularities [8].

In addition to shaping some skills and competences referring to health and personal hygiene, the school PE classes are fundamentally oriented towards shaping some motor skills, on the one hand, and improving the motor skill manifestation indicators, on the other hand. These two components condition each other. Most often than not, a low level of motor skill index manifestation determines a delay in learning a skill or even the impossibility to learn it.

By taking into consideration this truth, the specialists from the domain are permanently searching for new and attractive solutions, which could more easily lead to the development of motor skills [4, 19].

From this perspective, a great number of specialists agree that movement games, or games in general, as a form and means of education, can have an extremely positive effect on young age pupils [2, 14,16, 25, 27].

The improvement of the coordination skill indicators (dexterity) is closely correlated with psychomotricity and the spatial and temporal orientation. In order to achieve this, the games used during primary school education are beneficial. The activities proposed to pupils will be accessible. The concern for increasing the variety of such programs, which focus on this skill, can also be found in the domain-specific literature [7, 10, 11, 12].

In theory, in the physical education school curriculum from Romania, the improvement of the coordination skills in primary school pupils is reflected as a permanent concern through the entire school year. Also, the other motor skills, together with the skills specific to certain sport branches are to be found in the annual planning document drawn up by teachers. In practice, at the level of the lesson plans, the subjects that contain exercises or activities which contribute to the increase of the coordination skill indicators are not found very often.

Accordingly, in the present research, we proposed a number of movement games, which could be used in practice during PE classes in order to improve coordination skills (dexterity). The present paper is the result of the equal contribution of all authors.

2 Procedures

The research activity was performed in Secondary School no. 18, Galați, during school year 2015-2016. The subjects with whom we worked within the experiment were pupils in the 3rd grade. There was a total number of 59 pupils involved in the research, out of which there were 29 boys and 30 girls. Within the experiment we used movement games, whose aim was to improve the motor skills manifestation indicators.

In the present paper we shall present the results and discussions connected with the development of coordination skills. The results recorded for the other motor skills were presented in different papers.

The data was collected separately for each motor skill, for which we used a combination of motor games, specific to the skill for which they were proposed.

The results recorded for each motor skill were analysed an interpreted with the help of the statistical program SPSS 23.0. This led to a more accurate reflection of the influence the games proposed within the experiment had on the respective motor skill.

A number of 12 movement games were selected in order to increase the coordination skill indicators (the dexterity). They were used during the entire school year. The implementation method was different. We used one or two movement games in order to develop dexterity within each lesson from the curriculum. They were used at the beginning of the lesson, during the first part of the lesson. For this, the structure of the lesson was changed, that is the second moment of the lesson "preparing the body for effort" was replaced by the proposed games used to improve dexterity.

The control group performed the activities from the planning documents approved by the school management at the beginning of the school year.

The assessment trial used was called *"Throw at a vertical target"*. The trial took place behind a line drawn on the ground and consisted in throwing an oina ball, with one hand above the shoulder, at a vertical target having the width of 0.5 m and height of 2 m and being situated at a distance of 2m. Five executions were performed and the results were recorded. The assessment trial was performed at the beginning and at the end of the school year.

Here are some movement games used to develop coordination skills, as part of the working procedure used. These games were coded and combined among them in view of creating diversity during the entire school year.

Games for developing the coordination skill (dexterity)

Game no. 1 "THE DEXTEROUS PUPILS" (I.1)

Description: The pupils are scattered on the field, with their hands behind their backs, holding a handkerchief (a piece of string). At the first whistle, they will run on the field as they please, having their hands behind their backs all the time. At the second whistle, they will stop and they will tie around their knees the string and they will run to a pre-established place. The pupil who arrives first at the pre-established place, with the string tied under his/her knee is the winner of the game. The most dexterous pupils are those who have been ranked most times among the first four.

Game no. 2 „THE BUILDERS" (I.2)

Description: The pupils are scattered on the field. Following the indication "Let's build a square quickly", they must gather and make a square with right sides. At the teacher's whistle, they scatter again on the field. Then, they are asked to build a tram track as quickly as they can (they must form two rows), then a tractor wheel etc. The pupils who organised faster, proved to be good builders. In order to stimulate them more, they can be divided into groups, each group having the name of one building yard. In this case, the result will focus on one group.

Game no. 3 "THE TRAIN CROSSES THE BRIDGE" (I.3)

Description: The pupils are arranged on two rows in front of the gymnastics bench. They will go one after the other on the gymnastics bench and, then, they will come back to their places. The action is repeated twice. The same exercise is afterwards repeated twice or three times, but with the arms held raised sideways and with a book or a notebook on the head. The same exercise is repeated two or three times by amply rotating the arms. The same exercise is repeated by using the narrow part of the gymnastics bench.

Game no. 4 "THE GOALKEEPERS' GAME" (I.4)

Description: From a sitting position, the children, in pairs, will throw the ball to each other, trying not to drop it. The one that succeeds in performing well, will be declared the best goalkeeper. From a sitting position, the same game will be repeated, by insisting on the throwing position (from the chest). When the throwing and the catching become more accurate, the exercise is performed under the form of a contest. The pairs that manage to catch and throw the ball for 10-15 times without dropping it will be declared champion.

Game no. 5 "THE PAIR RACE" (I.5)

Description: The pupils are arranged on two rows, in pairs, behind the start line. At the teacher's whistle, they throw the ball to each other, in movement (they will have to throw the ball as soon as they catch it) until the pre-established place, from where they come back in the same manner. The game ends when all the pairs execute the required action, i.e. throwing and catching the ball while in movement. During a second repetition, the same action is performed while jogging.

Game no. 6 "THE TRAVELLING BALL" (I.6)

Description: The pupils are divided into 6-8 pupils and they are arranged behind a line. The teams are at a distance of 3-4 steps. The distance between the players has an arm length when the ball is offered. The first player from each team receives one, preferably bigger, ball. The game consists in transmitting the ball from player to player, from the first one to the last. When the ball reaches the last player, he runs with the ball in front of the row; the game continues in this way until the first player comes again in front of the row. Offering procedures: with arms stretched forward, with the arms stretched out in the back, with the legs apart, between the legs, by means of a lateral twist.

Game no. 7 "THE BALL ON THE BRIDGE" (I.7)

Description: The pupils are divided into teams of 6-8 pupils and they are aligned behind a line. The teams are at a distance of 3-4 steps and the distance between the players has an arm length. The first player from each team has a ball which, at the beginning whistle, will pass over the head to the pupil behind him who, in its turn, will pass it forward. When the ball reaches the last player, he comes in front and the game continues until the first pupil will be in front again. The team that finishes first is the winning team.

Game no. 8 "HARVESTING THE CROP" (I.8)

Description: The pupils are divided into 4-6 teams. Each team will have two baskets, one at the start line, in which there are 3-4 small balls and the other, put in front of each row at a distance of 20-25 m. At the teacher's whistle, the first pupil from each row runs with the ball basket to the other empty basket. He loads the balls in the basket and brings it to the next pupil. The game repeats until all the pupils manage to perform the same action.

Game no. 9 "THE DOG AND THE CAT" (I.9)

Description: The pupils are placed in a circle, facing inward (they are allowed to stay with their feet crossed). Two balls of two different colours (or two small objects) represent one, "the cat" and the other one, the coloured one, "the dog". "The cat" is passed around the circle, from hand to hand, without omitting any player. After 6 children, the dog" comes into the play, which is passed from hand to hand in the same direction, with the aim of catching "the cat". The player in whose hand "the dog" catches "the cat" is eliminated from the game. The ones that manage to remain in the circle without any mistake are the winners of the game.

Game no. 10 „THE DWARFS THROUGH THE TUNNEL" (I.10)

Description: The children are divided into teams of eight. Four of them stand in a row, the other ones in front of them keep the circles in a vertical position on the ground, at the distance of 1 m, making up a tunnel. At the teacher's whistle, the children from each team go crouched (like little dwarfs) through the tunnel, trying to reach the place where they started from as soon as possible. While moving through the tunnel, they must keep a one-arm distance, not being allowed to push one another. The game is repeated several times, the children keeping the circles being changed every time.

Game no. 11 "THE BALL THROUGH THE TUNNEL" (I.11)

Description: The players are lined up in rows, with their feet apart, 3-4 teams making up a tunnel. The first pupil from each team has a ball. At the teacher's whistle, the players with the ball roll it between their legs, the others are careful they help each other by pushing the ball with their hands to the last player from the team. This player catches the ball and runs with it to the right of his row, stands in front of his team with his feet apart and they roll the ball again between the legs. The game continues in this way until the first player from each team comes in front of the row. The team whose first player came to his place the first is the winner. If any player throws the ball out of the tunnel, he must bring it back to the same place and continue. The game can also be played with a medicine ball or with an old stuffed ball.

Game no. 12 "THE SMALL GATE" (I.12)

Description: Two pupils, standing face-to-face, at a distance of 5-6 metres, one of them standing with his feet apart (like a small gate) opens and closes the "gate" by jumping, the other pupil tries to send the ball through the "gate" with his hand or foot. After more repetitions, the roles are changed. The pupil who managed to pass the ball through the "gate" most often will be the winner. The pupils will keep the score by themselves, fact which educates their honesty and fair play.

3 Results and discussions

The trial "throw at a vertical target" is the only trial within the assessment system by means of which you can test the level of the coordination skill manifestation indicator (dexterity). The analysis of the results recorded in the initial and final tests of the groups involved in the pilot experiment were statistically processed with the help of the SPSS 23.0 program. This was necessary in order to ensure the objective character of the assessment of the proposed program, represented by movement games, which could influence the improvement of the coordination skill manifestation indicators (dexterity).

The statistical data processing followed two directions: a statistical analysis within the groups (the control and the test group) and a statistical interpretation referring to the comparison of the results obtained in the final trials between groups.

The results obtained in the initial and the final tests by the group of girls are analytically presented in table no. 1.

In the data presented in table no. 1, we may notice the statistical results within the groups of girls. Thus, the results obtained by both groups in the initial tests had close values. The control group achieved an average of successful throws of 1.53, whereas the test group obtained an average value of successful throws of 1.60. We may notice that the two values are close, fact which indicates a relatively unitary level of the coordination skill indicators.

In the final tests, the control group obtained an average value of successful throws of 2.40 throws, whereas the test group obtained an average value of successful throws of 3.80

throws. The results obtained in the final tests by the group of girls indicate a positive evolution of the dexterity motor skill manifestation level.

Table 1. The statistical analysis between the initial and the final tests for the groups of girls

Groups / Trials	Girls							
	The control group (n=15)				The test group (n=15)			
	T.I. $\bar{x} \pm m$	T.F. $\bar{x} \pm m$	t	p	T.I. $\bar{x} \pm m$	T.F. $\bar{x} \pm m$	t	p
Throw at a vertical target (no. of successful throws)	1.53 ± 0.99	2.40 ± 1.05	-4.51	.000	1.60 ± 0.98	3.80 ± 1.08	-12.60	.000

Both groups recorded significant progress, within the group, because the significance level was, in both cases, extremely significant (p<0,000).
Further on, we performed an analysis of the centralised data obtained by the two groups of girls in the final tests. These results are presented in table no. 2.

Table 2. The statistical analysis of the final results obtained by the two groups of girls

TRIALS	GIRLS – Final trial			
	TF $\bar{x} \pm m$	TF $\bar{x} \pm m$	t	p
Throw ata vertical target (no. of successful throws)	2.40 ± 1.05	3.80 ± 1.08	-3.58	.001*

*p<0.001;

The results presented in the table above clearly indicate that the average value of successful throws recorded by the test group is higher than the average value of the successful throws recorded by the control group. By performing a statistical analysis between the groups and by taking into consideration only the results obtained in the final tests, we may notice that the progress recorded by the test group is strongly significant as compared to the control group (p<0.001).
Further on, we shall present the results obtained by the groups of boys participating in our study. The level of the performance obtained by them is presented in table no. 3.

Table 3. The statistical analysis of the final results obtained by the two groups of boys

Groups / Trials	Boys							
	Control group (n=14)				Test group (n=15)			
	T.I. $\bar{x} \pm m$	T.F. $\bar{x} \pm m$	t	p	T.I. $\bar{x} \pm m$	T.F. $\bar{x} \pm m$	t	p
Throw at a vertical target (no. of successful throws)	2.00 ± 1.03	2.92 ± 1.14	-4.75	.000	1.86 ± 1.06	3.40 ± 1.18	-11.50	.000

In the initial tests, the average values of successful throws were close. The control group obtained an average value of successful throws of 2, whereas the test group obtained an average value of successful throws of 1.86. We may notice that the level of the coordination skill indicator was slightly better than that of the control group, even if very close to it. In the final tests, the control group obtained an average value of successful throws of 2.92, whereas the test group obtained an average value of successful throws of 3.40. In the statistical analysis performed within the groups, presented in table 3, we may notice that both groups recorded significant progress in the final tests as compared to the initial tests. Thus, we may state that the influence recorded at the level of the coordination skill manifestation indicators were significant ($p<0,000$) both in the case of the traditional training means and in the case of using movement games specific to this motor skill.

As in the case of the groups of girls, the statistical analysis was performed on the results recorded in the final test by the two groups of boys. The summary of this statistical analysis is presented in table no.4.

Table 4. The statistical analysis of the final results obtained by the two groups of boys

TRIALS	Boys – Final test			
	TF $\overline{x} \pm m$	TF $\overline{x} \pm m$	t	p
Throw at a vertical target (no. of successful throws)	2.92 ± 1.14	3.40 ± 1.18	-1.09	.587**

**p>0.05

In the table above we may notice that the average value of successful throws is higher for the test group as compared to the control group.

Nevertheless, by taking into account the fact that the value of p is > 0.05, we may state that the difference is not significant from a statistical point of view. Thus, the influence exerted by means of movement games can be considered similar to the influence exerted by other means used in the teaching process. We consider that it is possible for this fact to become manifest at this age group for the group of boys.

4 Conclusions

After analysing all the data obtained in the initial and final tests conducted within our pilot experiment, we may draw more categories of conclusions, some of them referring to the means of action, others referring to the structure of the PE lesson and, why not, some others referring to the correlation between the objectives of Physical Education, the learning content and the existing assessment system.

From the point of view of the means of action, we consider that they were efficient because the average values obtained by the group of girls (3,80 successful throws) and by the group of boys (3.40 successful throws) were superior to the results obtained by the control groups. As we have shown above, these results were strongly significant for the groups of girls ($p<0.001$) and not significant enough for the group of boys ($p>.05$). This aspect of the low significance level for the groups of boys could be due to their age and to the tested motor skill. It is well-known that the coordination skills (dexterity) are closely connected to the emotional aspects, which are not sufficiently developed at this age.

As far as the structure of the PE class is concerned, which is traditionally accepted and promoted in the Romanian school system, it couldn't be applied in its present form. We altered this structure and we replaced the second moment of the lesson, "preparing the body for effort", with movement games, specific to developing coordination skills.

We did this because we couldn't find a possibility to implement these action methods in another moment of the lesson so that we could observe the planning documents approved by the school management for the respective grades. On the other hand, the use of these games, which presuppose attention and focus, were used at the beginning of the lesson, when pupils were rested. Thus, the learning was performed in accordance with the psycho-pedagogical principles.

As far as the assessment system is concerned, the trial used is the only one that can assess the development of the coordination skill indicators [24]. The performance aspects are not relevant for the PE activity [20]. Also, the performance assessment is not in accordance with the aims of physical education as a school subject [22, 23].

We consider that the game, as a means of organising teaching activities and as a working method is suitable for this age segment, represented by primary school pupils.

Movement games proved to be attractive and they generated an active participation from the part of the pupils. Group participation and problem-solving in groups or in pairs can represent the premises for achieving the general competences proposed in the curriculum for PE as a school subject.

References

1. ***, 2011, *The Law of National Education*, The Official Monitor of Romania, no. 18
2. E. Bota, *Contribution of the game in the development of motor skills during the physical education class*, Timisoara Physical Education and Rehabilitation Journal, vol. 6, no. 11, pp. 59-63, (2016)
3. N. Carse, Primary teachers as physical education curriculum change agents, *European Physical Education Review,* Vol. 21, no. 3, pp.309-324, (2015)
4. W. Chen, S. Mason, A. Hypnar, A. Bennett, *Assessing Motor Skill Competency in Elementary School Students: A Three-Year Study*, Journal of Sport Science & Medicine, vol. 15, no. 1, pp. 102–110, (2016)
5. J.L. Currie, *Teaching Physical Education in Primary School - An integrated health perspective,* Publisher: ACER Press, 112-118, (2013)
6. Griggs G., (Ed.), *An Introduction to Primary Physical education,* Publisher: Routdlege, 151-161, (2012)
7. L.L. Hardy, B.J. O'Hara, K. Rogers, A. St. George, A. Bauman, *Contribution of Organized and Nonorganized Activity to Children's Motor Skills and Fitness*, Journal of School Health, vol. 84, no. 11, pp. 690-696, (2014)
8. T.M. Iconomescu, *Didactics of Physical Education and Sport / Course notes*, Publisher: Zigotto, Galati, (2013)
9. M. Jess, N. Carse, J. Keay, The primary physical education curriculum process: more complex than you might think!, *Education 3-13 International Journal of Primary, Elementary and Early Years Education*, Vol. 44, no. 5, 502-512, (2016)
10. H. Koç, A. Tekin, E. Aykora, *Impact of Physical Education Classes on Selected Motor Skills of Children*, Middle-East Journal of ScientificResearch, vol. 11, no. 3, pp. 386-390, (2012)
11. C. Lämmle, S. Kobel, O. Wartha, T. Wirt, J.M. Steinacker, *Intervention effects of a school-based health promotion program on children's motor skills*, J Public Health, vol. 24, pp. 185–192, (2016)
12. V. Lyakh, J. Sadowski, Z. Witkowski, *Development of coordination motor abilities (CMA) in the system of long-term preparation of athletes*, Pol. J. Sport Turism, vol. 18, pp. 187-191, (2011)
13. The Ministry of Education, Research, Youth and Sports, Order 3462 regarding the approval of *The organisation and conducting methodology of physical education activities and sport in pre-university education*, The Official Monitor of Romania, (2012)
14. G.C. Nobre, P.F.R. Bandeira, N.C. Valentini, The relationship between general perceived motor competence, perceived competence relative to motor skill and actual motor competence in children, *J. Phys. Educ.* [online]. 2016, vol. 27, pp. 1-12, (2016)

15. M. O'Sullivan, *New directions, new questions: relationships between curriculum, pedagogy, and assessment in physical education*, Sport Education and Society, Vol. 18, no.1, pp 1-5, (2013)
16. L. Raudsepp, P .Päll, *The relationship between fundamental motor skills and outside-school physical activity of elementary school children*, PediatrExerc Sci., vol. 18, no. 4, pp. 426–435, (2006)
17. C.M. Rus, *Communication characteristics during teaching physical education and sport*, Sport Science 6 (2), 82-84, (2013)
18. S. Şahin, *Education supervisors' views on the new curriculum and its implementation in primary schools*, EgitimArastirmalari-Eurasian Journal of Educational Research, Vol. 53, pp. 1-20, (2013)
19. L.G. Talaghir, V. Mîndrescu, M. Ion-Ene, *Study regarding the use of movement games and relays in order to improve primary students' strength qualities,* SHS Web Conference, ERPA International Congresses on Education, vol. 37, pp. 1-7, (2017)
20. L-G. Talaghir, T.M. Iconomescu, *Study regarding the evolution of the primary school curriculum for physical education in Romania in accordance with the assessment system application,* INTED2017 Proceeding, 11th International Technology, Education and Development Conference Valencia, Spain, pp 2542-2551, (2017)
21. L-G. Talaghir, *Gimnastica acrobatic şcolară,* Zigotto Publishing House, pp 6-7, (2015)
22. The Ministry of National Education, *Curriculum for Physical Education*, The preparatory grade, the first grade and the second grade, Bucureşti, (2013)
23. The Ministry of National Education, *Curriculum for Physical Education*, The third grade and the fourth grade, Bucureşti, (2014)
24. The Ministry of National Education, Research and Innovation, *Curriculum for Physical Education*, V – VIII grade, Bucureşt, (2009)
25. N. Wattie, M. Tietjens, J. Schorer, M.C. Ghanbari, B. Strauss, I. Seidel, J. Baker, *Does relative age influence motor test performance of fourth grade pupils?*, European Physical Education Review, vol. 20, no. 3, pp. 398 – 406, (2014)
26. J. You, *A self-study of a national curriculum maker in physical education: challenges to curriculum change*, Journal of Curriculum Studies, Vol. 43, no. 1, pp. 87-108, (2011)
27. A. Ungureanu-Dobre, C.M. Rus, L. Mihailescu, Bocoş Muşata, *The development of motor capabilities of pupils in the 4th grade through movement games*, Literature, Discourse and Multicultural Dialogue, vol. 2, pp. 88-95, (2014).

Study regarding the use of gymnastics - related alternative methods during the physical education class

Talaghir Laurentiu-Gabriel[1, a], *Stoica* Leonard[1], and *Ocak* Yucel[2]

[1]University Dunarea de Jos, Domneasca Street, no. 46, 800008, Galati, Romania
[2] Afyon Kocatepe University, Erenler Mahallesi, Afyonkarahisar, 03200, Turkiye

Abstract. The improvement of motor qualities and skills represents the main concern of the Physical Education lesson. In the present paper we present a general motor exercise training routine, designed as an alternative to the traditional approach of the PE lessons. The routine was divided into three components, namely a cross fit exercise routine, an aerobics routine and an acrosport routine. This routine was implemented in the 5th grade syllabus. The test group was represented by 207 pupils, out of which 114 girls (55.07%) and 93 boys (44.93%). Most participants came from rural areas (66.18%) and 33.82% came from urban areas. The routine was implemented during the first semester of the current school year (2017-2018) in one of the two compulsory lessons. The topics from the traditional PE lesson were replaced by the proposed routines and used alternatively. The assessment consisted of 4 tests from the national assessment system. The results showed significant progress obtained in the final tests for all the 4 trials used ($p < 0,001$).

1 Introduction

The Physical Education system from Romania goes through a reformation period from a conceptual and structural point of view. Thus, in the last few years, new curricular documents have been designed for this school subject. These documents intend to offer a modern vision regarding the competences that pupils must acquire. Also, in obtaining these competences, the focus has been laid on the unitary component of the educational process, thus the syllabus was designed on a long-term basis. As a consequence, at present, new curricula for primary school [25, 26] and for secondary school [28] are implemented. These curricula brought about new conceptual elements.

The physical education system in our country relies on the methodology of the lessons organised on 7 moments [12, 20]. This system has responded to educational requirements for a long time. In the last decade, due to technological progress, to social evolution and the emergence of various forms of physical exercise, the lesson organised in the traditional

[a] Corresponding author: gtalaghir@ugal.ro

seven-moment manner seems to no longer meet the demands of the educational teaching process.

Domain-specialists from Romania [4, 21] and from abroad [6, 14, 24] created and proposed different ways of practising physical exercise, which could engage student groups in practical activities. The content of these exercises is oriented towards general physical development, towards the formation and maintenance of an optimal state of health, towards the integration into group activities, towards the pleasure of practising exercise independently as a means of maintaining health [19, 22, 29].

The technical and performance content of the previous school curricula [27] focuses on pupils with special skills for practising sport. This content is not accessible to most students and, as a result, students avoid attending activities they cannot perform, not feeling comfortable and successful. The idea of adapting the content of practical activities from the physical education lesson to social realities is based on European studies on the use of effective ways of exercising [10, 13].

The possibilities to change the way in which practical activities take place led to the idea of implementing changes at the structure level of the lesson as well as at its content level. In the present paper, we intend to present a general motor exercise training routine, designed as an alternative to the traditional approach of the PE lessons. The routine was divided into three components, namely a cross fit exercise routine, an aerobics routine and an acrosport routine

There are many advantages to practising aerobic routines [2, 31]. Their positive influences are emphasized and studied at a global level because they can be varied, used with different age groups, and their use does not imply aprevious level of fitness. Also, aerobic exercises are preferred due to their direct influence on the well-being and health of people who practise them [1, 7, 18, 30].

The crossfit exercise routines are used for different age groups, especially for recreational physical activities. Crossfit defines fitness as an increase in working capacity over time and in various fields [11] which, in fact, means the ability to perform varied movements of any kind (cardio, strength, power) for any length of time (short, middle or long duration) [23]. The good effects of these exercises on the health status [9] were not recognized so that they could be transferred to activities in physical education school lessons. Crossfit activities do not require highly developed pieces of equipment and the level of previous physical training should not be high either. These aspects constitute a good premise for the use of this type of exercise in school physical education lessons. Effort intensity adjustment can be achieved by adapting the number and structure of the proposed exercises to the possibilities of the students who practise them as compared to the possibilities of adults [23].

Acrosport is an activity that provides students with a quick motivation and gives pupils the opportunity to be interpreters and choreographers at the same time, thus allowing direct involvement in the activity [15]. This is an alternative to the curriculum when the skills that physical education wants to develop are cooperation, creativity [16], self-confidence [17] and task distribution [5]. The mission of acrosport gymnastics is to provide a safe, and enjoyable educational environment in which participants gain and enhance self-esteem, self-confidence and an "I can" attitude. There are studies that show that the practice of acrosport exercises could improve students' attitude towards physical education, which would contribute to the adoption of a more active lifestyle [3].

The physical requirements that a student must have are agility, mobility, balance, synchronization, harmony and artistic expression. Unlike the other sports disciplines, acrosport does not require any other equipment except for the human body [8].

According to IFSA, the International Federation of Acrobatic Sports, acrosport is defined as an acrobatic sport performed with a partner or as a group, through the creation of human pyramids, acrobatic jumps and choreographic elements, in which the participant fulfils two clearly-defined functions, portor and agile [16].

The methods used by gymnastics are varied and their direction of manifestation comprises both the motor skills and the specific skills that are trained in students. The use of such a training program (A.C.A. - Training Program) is a prerequisite for a more effective engagement of groups of students in school activities and constitutes an alternative to the content of sports games that prevail in planning documents. The paper represents the equal contribution of all the authors.

2 Procedures

As far as the procedure is concerned, the subjects involved in our study were represented by pupils from urban areas (33.82%) and from rural areas (66.18%). The total number of students was 207, out of which 93 boys (44.93%) and 114 girls (55.07%). The research was carried out during the first semester of school year 2017 – 2018. The semester had 17 weeks and 34 practical lessons. The proposed routine was used in one of the two weekly lessons, i.e. it was implemented in 15 lessons. The implementation was made alternatively, namely one cross fit lesson, an aerobics lesson and an acrosport lesson and so on and so forth.

The aerobics routine was performed on a musical background and lasted 20 minutes, being made up of 20 -22 exercises adapted to the pupils' age possibilities. The exercises had simple structures and were performed in a continuous manner so that the pupils move all the time.

For the cross fit exercises, we proposed 6 exercises. They were carried out for 30 seconds with a 30-second break. The exercises were repeated three times. The break was of 1 minute after each exercise. The cross-fit routine lasted 20 minutes. The cross fit exercises were selected in such a way that they influence all muscle groups.

The acrosport exercises were used in view of developing the pupils' teamwork abilities. These structures are not new, but they are totally unused by the domain specialists. The acrosport structures involve the performance and maintenance of a number of acrobatic postures. Thus, they also involve focus, the cooperation with a partner, strength and balance. We proposed acrosport exercises that can be performed in pairs or in groups of three. The acrosport exercises can also be performed in larger groups, but a larger number of participants also involve a high level of motor training. There were three exercises to be performed in pairs, which were repeated for four times, and two exercises to be performed in groups of three, which were repeated for four times. The break after each exercise was of 30 seconds. Thus, the exercises lasted 18 – 20 minutes, depending on the need for further explanations from the part of the teacher.

The assessment process was made by means of 4 tests from the National Assessment System for this age group. The assessment tests were the following: relays 10X5 m., endurance running, throwing the oina ball at a distance and crunches. These trials presuppose the assessment of the basic motor skills.

The tests were carried out according to the following procedure:

The "10x5m relays" test – we drew two parallel lines, at a distance of 5 m from each other; on the lines we place two cones at a distance of 5 m from each other. The student is positioned in front of one of the lines / one of the cones, with one leg touching the line and the other back. At the teacher's signal, he must run as quickly as possible to the other line, touching it with both feet and running back to the start line. One such run is considered a cycle, 5 cycles being needed for this test.

The "long run" test - takes place on a flat ground, individually or in a platoon, each student adopting the personal tempo so as to run continuously, without stopping for four minutes. We measured and recorded the distance covered by each pupil in the four-minute continuous run.

The "Throwing the oina ball" test – we drew a line on the ground; the pupil who was behind the line threw the oina ball as far as possible. We measured the distance from the line drawn on the ground and the point where the ball first touched the ground.

The "crunches" test – was performed by raising the torso vertically for 30 seconds. We recorded the number of repetitions the pupil managed to perform in the given period of time.

3 Results and discussions

The results recorded in the initial and final tests were centralised and statistically interpreted. They are presented in table 1 for the group of boys and in table 2 for the group of girls.

In the case of the group of boys from table 1, we may notice the fact that the results obtained in the final tests were favourable, superior to all the initial tests. This is highlighted by the fact that, for all the tests, the statistical indicator had a highly significant value, $p<0.000$.

Table 1. Result of tests – boys' group

Groups / Tests	TI(n=93) $\bar{x} \pm m$	TF(n=93) $\bar{x} \pm m$	t	p
The 10x5m (sec) relays	21.93±0.14	20.15±0.08	18.43	.000
The long run 4 min (m.)	566.66±6.34	644.62±5.29	-24.40	.000
Throwing the oina ball (m)	22.04±0.20	24.24±0.14	-16.69	.000
Crunches (30 sec.) (No. of reps)	20.04±0.17	22.30±0.05	-18.47	.000

$p<0.000$

In the case of the group of girls, too, the value of the significance limit between the results recorded in the final test as compared to the initial test was of $p<0.000$, fact which demonstrates that in the case of the group of girls the tests proposed within the experiment contributed to increasing general motor skills and their manifestation indices.

Table 2. Result of tests – girls' group

Groups / Tests	TI (n=114) $\bar{x} \pm m$	TF (n=114) $\bar{x} \pm m$	t	p
The 10x5 (sec) relays	21.92±0.12	20.51±0.08	19.22	.000
The long run 4 min (m)	499.12±10.64	566.84±9.13	-20.69	.000
Throwing the oina ball (m)	18.09±0.19	20.50±0.18	-29.24	.000
Crunches 30 sec. (No. of reps)	19.35±0.18	21.71±0.18	-21.50	.000

$p<0.000$

In order to synthetically express the obtained results in the final tests by those involved in the experiment, we represented them graphically.

The results of the test are presented in figure 1, in which we may notice that, in the initial test, the groups recorded similar values, the group of girls 21.93 sec and the group of boys, 21.92 sec. These results showed a normal level of growth and development for this age group.

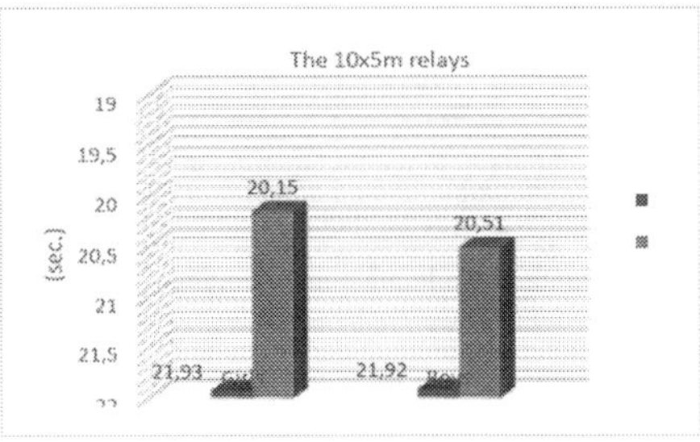

Fig. 1. Results of the "10x5 m. relays" test

In the final tests, the results of the group of girls had an average of 20.15 seconds for the group of girls and 20.51 seconds for the group of boys. We could notice that by means of the activities proposed in the experiment, the motor speed significantly improved, p <0.000. The girls, who record an advance in mental development as compared to boys at this age, obtained an average performance better than the boys.

Figure 2 shows the results recorded in the "long run" test. The average values of the initial tests were of 499.12m for the group of girls and 566.6m for the group of boys. Even from the initial test, we noticed a large difference between these results that showed a better effort adaptation of the boys' group.

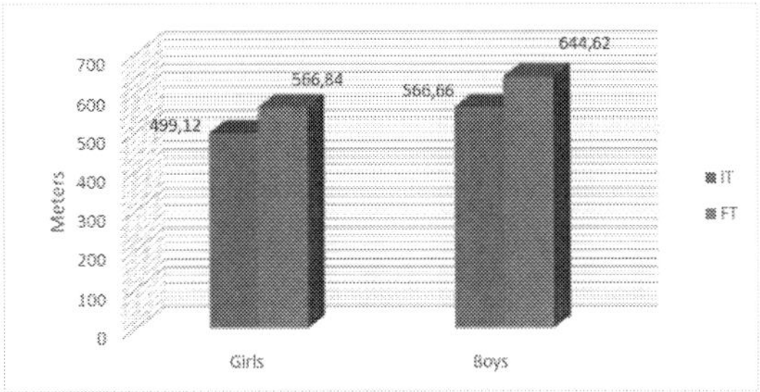

Fig. 2. Results of the "long run" test (m)

The results obtained in the final "long run" test were of 566.84m for the group of girls and of 644.62m for the groupof boys. The distance measured during the 4 minutes of running significantly increased so that the progress of the final tests was highly significant, p <0.000.

The results obtained in the "Throwing the oina ball" test are highlighted in figure 3. In figure 3 we may notice that, in the initial test, the group of girls recorded an average performance value of 183.09m, whereas the average performance value recorded by the group of boys was of 22.04m.The major difference recorded by the group of boys can be explained by a better throwing technique and not by the level of motor development of the upper limbs.

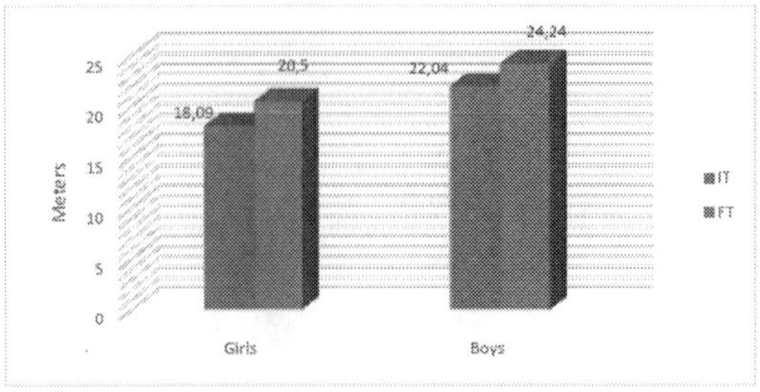

Fig. 3. Results of the "Throwing the oina ball" test (m)

In the final test, the group of girls obtained an average performance value of 20.5 m., significantly better than that recorded in the initial test, p<0.000. Also, the result obtained by the group of boys was superior to that obtained in the initial test, recording an average performance value of 24.24 m (fig. 3). In this case, too, the progress achieved was significant, p<0.000.

The last test within the assessment system we proposed was "crunches". In figure 4, we present the results of this test. As we may notice, in the initial test, the group of girls obtained an average performance value of 19.35 repetitions. In the final test, the average performance value for the group of girls was of 21.71 repetitions. This fact indicated significant progress, p<0.000.

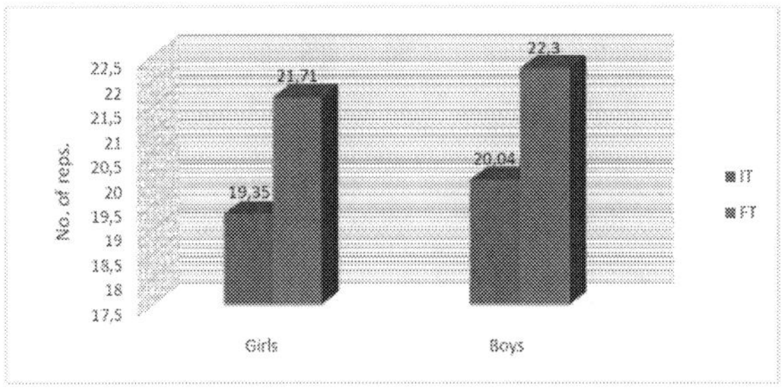

Fig. 4. Results of the "crunches" test 30 sec.

In figure 4, we can also notice that, in the initial test, the average value of the obtained performance by the group of boys was of 20.04 repetitions, whereas, in the final test, the average performance value was of 22.3 repetitions.

We can also assert that the result obtained by the group of boys is a good one and that the recorded progress in this case, too, was a significant one, p<0.000.

The good results recorded in all the final tests can be explained by more factors, which directly or indirectly influence the results. These factors are related to the level of growth and development, to the level of participation in the PE class and in these practical activities.

4 Conclusions

The conclusion of our study was that PE lessons during which alternative methods are used represent a good and efficient alternative for the practical activities. The accessible exercises engaged all the pupils in the effort. The technical aspects that create discomfort during traditional PE classes were removed.

The use of aerobic exercises led to pupils' involvement in effort for longer periods of time because the exercises proposed were accessible. The musical background probably contributed significantly to increasing the attractiveness of the lessons in which it was used. CrossFit exercises, which use natural movements that are encountered in everyday life, were also well assimilated by the groups of pupils we worked with. Higher levels of intensity made these exercises highly attractive. Even doing the joint tasks led to the possibility of their realization because the students were ambitious to carry out the proposed activities at an upper level, seeing that they had the opportunity to perform such actions.

The acrosport exercises created a high emulation effect among students who were asked to work in groups or teams and to support each other in conducting such actions. Involvement in the activity has led to superior results in the final test.

The results obtained in the final tests showed that the progress recorded by pupils was a significant one for all the trials ($p < 0,001$). We didn't use a specific test in order to measure the development level of the behavioural component.

After the implementation of the "Aerobic CrossFit Acrosport - Training program" at the pilot experimental level, we consider that it can be proposed as an alternative to the physical education lessons in secondary school. We strongly believe that this type of exercise leads to a better involvement of the groups of students in the activity and determines a higher degree of actual participation. The technical-content classes, which also presuppose skills that are not found in pupils' everyday activity, currently, represent a limiting factor in school physical education lessons.

We also believe that this type of exercise routine "A.C.A. - Training program" can represent the content of an optional subject that may exist in the educational offer of schools. Applying it to optional subjects would also contribute to increasing the number of Physical Education classes, which, at the moment, is only maintained at a declarative level in the Romanian education system.

References

1. E. Aadland, O.M. Kvalheim, T. Rajalahti, et al., *Aerobic fitness and metabolic health in children: A clinical validation of directly measured maximal oxygen consumption versus performance measures as markers of health,* Preventive Medicine Reports, vol. 7, pp. 74-76, (2017)
2. E. Aadland, L.B. Andersen, O. Lerum, , G. K. Resaland, *The Andersen aerobic fitness test: New peak oxygen consumption prediction equations in 10 and 16-year olds,* Scandinavian Journal of Medicine & Science in Sports, 28 (3), 862-872, (2018)
3. Á. Abós, J.S. Serrano, J.A. Julian, , *Improving students' predisposition towards physical education by optimizing their motivational processes in an acrosport unit,* European Physical Education Review 23(4):444-460, (2016)
4. D. Badau, *The Educational Impact of Implementing the Education through Adventure Subject in the Physical Education and Sports Academic Curriculum,* Physical Education of Students, Vol. 21, no.3 pp. 108–115, (2016)
5. J.J. Barba, *Diferencias entre el aprendizaje cooperativo y la asignación de tareas en la Escuela Rural,* Comparación de dos estudios de caso en una unidad didáctica de acrosport en segundo ciclo de primaria, https://www.researchgate.net/publication/46253994, (2010)
6. M. Betti, J. Knijnik, L. Venancio, L.S. Neto, *In search of the autonomous and critical individual: a philosophical and pedagogical analysis of the physical education curriculum of Sao Paulo (Brazil)*, Physical Education and Sport Pedagogy, Vol. 20, no. 4, pp. 427-441, (2015)

7. R.D. Burns, J.C. Hannon, T.A. Brusseau, et al, *Cross-Validation of Aerobic Capacity Prediction Models in Adolescents,* PEDIATRIC EXERCISE SCIENCE, vol. 27 (3) pp. 404-411, (2015)
8. L. Dina, *Methodological aspects of learning the static structures in acrobatic gymnastic*, Procedia - Social and Behavioral Sciences 117 (2014) 374 – 377, (2013)
9. N. Eather, P. Morgan, D. Lubans, *Improving health-related fitness in adolescents: The CrossFit Teens randomized controlled trial*, Journal of Science and Medicine in Sport, vol. 19, supplement, pp. e11-e32, (2015)
10. European Commission / EACEA / Eurydice, Physical Education and Sport at School in Europe. *Eurydice Report. Luxembourg: Publications Office of the European Union*, pp 7-20, (2013)
11. G. Glassman , CrossFit level 1 training guide, *CrossFit Journal*, from http://journal.crossfit.com/2010/05/crossfit-level-1-training-guide.tpl, (2011)
12. T.M. Iconomescu, *Didactics of Physical Education and Sport / Course notes*, Publisher: Zigotto, Galati, (2013)
13. T.M. Iconomescu, D.I. Alexe, Differences and similarities in curriculum and assessment in physical education in Eastern European states, *The Annals of Ovidius University,* Constanţa, *Series Physical Education and Sport - Science, Movement and Health*, Volume XV, Issue1, pp.41- 46, (2015)
14. M. Jess, N. Carse, J. Keay, T*he primary physical education curriculum process: more complex that you might think!!,* Education 3-13 International Journal of Primary, Elementary and Early Years Education, Vol. 44, no. 5, pp. 502-512, (2016)
15. J.M.V. Martínez, *Unidades didácticas para Secundaria: Juegos y Deportes: Acrosport, Unidades Didacticas Secundaria*, EDITORIAL WANCEULEN, S.L., P 118, (2005)
16. J. A. León-Prados, *Seguridad e higiene en la práctica saludable del acrosport*, Revista Internacional de Medicina y Ciencias de la Actividad Física y el Deporte. vol. 4 (16) pp. 276-285, (2004)
17. L. Llamas, G. Hellín, J.A. Moreno, *La enseñanza de habilidades gimnásticas y acrobáticas em la etapa escolar*, Revista Internacional de Medicina y Ciencias de la Actividad Física y el Deporte vol. 4 (14) pp. 82-105, (2004)
18. M.T. Mahar, A.M. Guerieri, M.S. Hanna, et al., *Estimation of Aerobic Fitness from 20-m Multistage Shuttle Run Test Performance,* AMERICAN JOURNAL OF PREVENTIVE MEDICINE, 41 (4) supp 2, pp. S117-S123, (2011)
19. V. Mîndrescu, *The Formative Role of Dance Sport in the Extracurricular Activities in Gymnasium*, New Approaches in Social and Humanistic Sciences, Iasi, Romania, LUMEN Proceedings, pp. 283-293, (2018)
20. G.D. Mocanu, *The Didactics of Physical Education and Sport*, The "Dunărea de Jos" University Foundation Galaţi, (2015)
21. C.M. Rus, L.E. Radu, *The Implications of Physical Education and Sport in the Moral Education of High School Students*, The Research and Social Intervention Magazine, pp. 45-55, (2014)
22. C.M. Rus, *Communication characteristics during teaching physical education and sport*, Sport Science 6 (2), 82-84, (2013)
23. B.A. Sibley, *Using sport education to implement a CrossFit unit*, Journal of Physical Education, Recreation & Dance, vol. 83 (8) pp. 42-48, (2012)
24. G. Starc, J. Strel, *Influence of the quality implementation of a physical education curriculum on the physical development and physical fitness of children*, BMC Public Health, pp. 2-7, (2012)
25. The Ministry of National Education, *Curriculum for Physical Education*, The preparatory grade, the first grade and the second grade, Bucureşti (2013)

26. The Ministry of National Education, *Curriculum for Physical Education*, The third grade and the fourth grade, Bucureşti, (2014)
27. The Ministry of National Education, Research and Innovation, *Curriculum for Physical Education*, V – VIII grade, Bucureşt, (2009)
28. The Ministry of National Education, School Curricula for Physical Education and Sport, 5th to 8th grades, Bucureşti, (2017)
29. A. Ungureanu-Dobre, C.M. Rus, L. Mihailescu, Bocoş Muşata, , *The development of motor capabilities of pupils in the 4th grade through movement games*, Literature, Discourse and Multicultural Dialogue, vol. 2, pp. 88-95, (2014)
30. L.D. Wyndham, R. Doug, P. Comper, MG. Hutchison, *Earlier time to aerobic exercise is associated with faster recovery following acute sport concussion*, PLOS ONE, 13 (4), (2018)
31. F. Zurita-Ortega, F. Salvador-Perez, E. Knox, VM. Gamiz-Sanchez, R. Chacon-Cuberos, S. Rodriguez-Fernandez, JJ. Muros, *Physical activity and health-related quality of life in schoolchildren: structural equations analysis*, Anales de Psicologia, Volume: 34 (2), pp 385-390, (2018).

Determinants of unemployment in less developed countries

Asma Riaz[1,*], and *Fareeha* Zafar[2]

[1]M.Phill Scholar , School of Management sciences , National college of business and e-Commerce, DHA Campus, Lahore, Pakistan
[2]University Of Derby, United Kingdom

Abstract. Unemployment is a major issue all over the world in both developed and under developed countries. This study analyzes those factors which determine unemployment in Pakistan. The data is taken from1990-2015 to see the empirical relationship between GDP, Population, Technical & Vocational education, degree colleges and universities enrollment. ARDL (Auto Regressive Distributed Lag) approach is used to check the determinants of unemployment in Pakistan. Long run results show that there is a negative relationship between GDP and unemployment. Population has positive and significant relation and technical & vocational education has positive and insignificant relation with unemployment in Pakistan. The results of Short run ECM-1(Error correction model) show that the negative and significant relationship with unemployment. The CUSUM and CUSUMQ (Graph) are represent that model is structurally stable within critical bound at 5% level of significance.

Keywords: Unemployment (UNE), Gross Domestic Product (GDP), Population (POP), Technical and Vocational Education (T&V), Degree colleges enrollment 16 years of qualification (Degr coll), Universities enrollment 16 years of qualification(UNI ENR)

1 Introduction

Unemployment is the major problem of every country. Unemployment is an ever rising in Pakistan as determined by Ahmed at.al [1]. The variables are used in this paper, Population growth rate, inflation rate, Foreign Direct Investment and Gross Domestic Product growth rate in framework of Pakistan economy. also. The time series data from 1973 to 2010 was taken to analyze using the ARDL test. The results show that unemployment has significant positive relationship with output gap, Productivity and Economic Uncertainty while it has statistically significant negative relationships with Gross Fixed Investment and Trade .The data was taken from Hand Book of State Bank of Pakistan 2010, This study applies augmented dicky fuller and Philips perron Unit Root tests to confirm the stationary of the

* Corresponding author: asmariaz316@gmail.com

data series. The results show that in the long run or short run there is positive relationship between unemployment and the output gap.

Muhammad Arslan et al., [8] This paper describe that unemployment is the common factor in all over the world. The variables are used in this paper, Population growth rate, inflation rate, Foreign Direct Investment and Gross Domestic Product growth rate in framework of Pakistan economy. In this foreign direct investment, gross domestic product rate, CPI based inflation rate and population growth rate is taken as explanatory variables. The methodology used in this paper is Ordinary Least Square Model. According to the results of our foreign direct investment, gross domestic product rate and CPI based inflation rate there is there is negative relationship on unemployment between the variables. And there is positive relation between unemployment and Population growth rate. The dependent variable is unemployment and independent variables are foreign direct investment, Gross domestic product growth rate, Inflation rate. According to results FDI has inversely relationship with unemployment.

Muhammad Shafiur Rehman et al. [2] unemployment is the crucial issue in all the countries. Economic growth is also an important factor for unemployment. The data is taken from 2000-2011 and Simple Single Equation Linear Regression Model is used for this paper. The variables are used for this study are Unemployment rate, GDP growth rate, Exchange rate and Inflation rate. The result of Simple Regression Model shows that all variables are significant. Inflation rate positively impact on unemployment and while GDP growth rate and Exchange rate has negatively affected on unemployment.

Dr Aurangzeb et al. [3] examined the economic study of unemployment used for India, China and Pakistan. Data was collected from year for the period 1980 to 2009. The methodology was used integration, granger causality and regression analysis. The variables select for the study are unemployment, inflation, gross domestic product, exchange rate and the increasing rate of population. The result shows the significant impact on three countries. GDP of Pakistan represent the positive relation with unemployment. The granger causality not exists in any variable in all of three countries. Co integration results shows that long term relationship exist between the variables for all the countries.

The meaning of the unemployment is people want to do work but they have not many opportunity. One of the main causes is Population. Approximately the total population of the Pakistan is 195,194,877 [11] Pakistan population ranked no 6 in the world. And now the population literacy rate is 60% while in 2014 58 %(survey 2015).another most important key factor is technical education. Now a day's people not got technical education and the reason is that they have not good job. Our nation does not neglect educated persons. Our youth graduate can change our nation. Government should introduce new training centers and technical education or entrepreneurship which is much benefitted for our society. There are many factors which determine the unemployment in less develop countries but here we use these variables are GDP, population, crude activity rate, employment labor force, industrialization, technical education.

According to (Pakistan Higher Education Commission 2013-2014) 3 million students enrolled in graduates 13, through in Pakistan 1,086 degree colleges and 161 universities. Pakistan qualified age group from 18 to 24 years 3 million people enrolled is 15% of 20 million. In technical and vocational institutes 255,000 Pakistani students are enrolled (TEVTA).In Pakistan we need 1 million skilled people for industry whereas only 100,000 skilled people are obtainable.90% labor are unskilled. Over half a million graduates are producing in Pakistani universities. Graduates universities are increased now in our country 380,773 in 2005-2006 to 493,993 in 2008-2009.In the (2003-2008) 400,000 student are enrolled in universities. Now in 2014, the number of universities is 161 and 1.5 million students are enrolled.

34 million people are unemployed in all around the world. According to the Labor Force Survey 2013-14, the total labor force is 60.09 million in the country. Out of this, 3.58 million people are unemployed and 56.52 million people are employed. [4,5] *"According to IPR's factsheet, 2012-13 and 2014-15 the number of jobs created was 1.4 million. Accordingly, the decrease in the number of unemployed workers was 100,000. As such, by the end of 2014-15, the number of unemployed workers was 3.6 million. However, the total number of unemployed currently in Pakistan 5.3 million"* The latest Labor Force Survey of 2014-15 released by the Pakistan Bureau of Statistics [10].

2 Data and methodology

In the determinants of unemployment we take the data from Economic Survey of Pakistan [2,4,5,6,7] and from "The World Bank" [12]. Data is collected from 1990 to 2015. The dependent variable is unemployment and the Independent variable is GDP, Population, Technical & Vocational Education and Universities enrollment.

For this purpose we use Econometrics model

Unemployment=f (GDP, POP, T & V, DEG COLL, UNI NUM).

GDP= All finale goods and services produce in the market in a given year. There is inverse relationship between GDP and unemployment.

POP= the number of persons are in a country called population. And if the population are increased then unemployment also raise. Population data in million.

T&V=technical and vocational data in thousands.

DEG COLL=no of enrollment in degree colleges data 16 years of qualification (In numbers).

UNI=universities enrollment data in numbers (16 years of qualification

2.1 Model

$$\Delta UNE_t = \alpha_0 + \sum_{j=1}^{n} \alpha_j \Delta GDP_{t-j} + \sum_{j=1}^{n} \mu_j POP_{t-j} + \sum_{j=1}^{n} \delta_j T\&V_{t-j} + \sum_{j=1}^{n} \theta_j \, Deg\ coll_{t-j}$$
$$+ \sum_{j=1}^{n} \pi_j UNIt-j + d_1 GDP_{t-j} + d_2 POP_{t-j} + d_3 T\&V_{t-j}$$
$$+ d_4 Deg\ coll_{t-j} + d_5 UNI_{t-j} \ + \epsilon_t$$

In the model of the paper where unemployment is the dependent variable and GDP, Population, Technical and Vocational education, Degree college's enrollment and Universities enrollment are independent variables.

2 Findings

Table 1. Augmented Dicky-Fuller (ADF) test of stationarity of time series data

NO	Description	Variables	Lags	T-statistics	P-value
1.	Unemployment	Une	I(0)	-3.561	0.0066
2.	Gross Domestic Products	GDP	I(0)	-3.452	0.0093
3.	Population	POP	I(1)	-4.328	0.0004
4.	Technical & Vocational Education(16 years)	T&V	I(1)	-4.353	0.0004
5.	Degree Colleges Enrollment	Deg Coll	I(1)	-4.172	0.0007
6.	Universities Enrollment(16 years)	Uni Enr	I(1)	-9.022	0.0000

In the Table 1 Augmented Dicky Fuller test are apply to see the stationarity of all the variables

Table 2. Autoregressive Distributed Lag Estimates ARDL (1,0,0,0,0,0) selected based on Schwarz Bayesian Criterion

Regressor	Coefficient	Standard Error	T-Ratio[prob]
Une(-1)	.66252	.21785	3.0412[.007]
GDP	-.062933	.034892	-1.8036[.087]
POP	.011976	.010173	1.1772[.254]
T&V	.0013848	.0022128	.62584[.539]
DEG	.3037E-5	.1301E-5	2.3341[.031]
UNI	-.1458E-5	.6191E-6	-2.3546[.029]

R-squared=.11252, R-Bar-Squard=-.12103, F-statistics= (5,19) .48178[.785]

Akaik Info Criterion=-5.5035 Schwarz Bayesian Criterion=-9.1601
DW-statistics=1.4987
Diagnostic Tests:

Test statistics	LM Version	F Version
A: Serial Correlation	CHSQ (1)=.0024595[.960]	F(1,18)=.0017710[.967]
B: Functional Form	CHSQ (1)=9.3193[.002]	F(1,18)=10.6977[.004]
C: Normality	CHSQ (2)=17.1100[.000]	Not applicable
D: Hetroscedasticity	CHSQ (1)=5.3955[.020]	F(1,23)=6.3300[.019]

Table 3. Estimated Long Run Coefficients using the ARDL approach ARDL (1,0,0,0,0,0) selected based on Schwarz Bayesian Criterion

Dependent Variable is GDP			
Variables	**Coefficient**	**Standard Error**	**Ratio (Prob)**
GDP	-.18648	.17782	-1.0487[.307]
POP	.035486	.010395	3.4137[.003]
T&V	.0041035	.0079529	.51597[.612]
DEG COLL	.8999E-5	.5566E-5	1.6168[.122]
UNI ENR	-.4319E-5	.2204E-5	-1.9601[.065]

In the Table 3 estimated long run coefficients GDP has negative and insignificant relation with unemployment while population has positive and significant relationship with unemployment, Technical and vocational education and degree colleges has positive and insignificant relation with unemployment.

Table 4. Error Correction Representation for the selected ARDL model ARDL(1,0,0,0,0,0) selected based on Schwarz Bayesian Criterion

Regressor	Coefficient	Standard Error	T-Ratio[prob]
Dgdp	.062933	.034892	-1.8036[.087]
Dpop	.011976	.010173	1.1772[.254]
Dt	.0013848	.0022128	.62584[.539]
Ddegre	.3037E-5	.1301E-5	2.3341[.031]
Duni	-.1458E-5	.6191E-6	-2.3546[.029]
Ecm(-1)	-.33748	.21785	-1.5492[.000]

R-Squared=.30441, R-Bar Squared=.12137,F Stat. F(5,19)=1.6630[.192]
Akaike Info. Criterion=-5.5035 Schwarz Bayesian Criterion=-9.1601

In the Table 4 According to the short run results coefficient of gdp, population, technical and vocational education and universities enrollment are .062933,.011976 and 0013848. The short run coefficient is smaller than long run. ECM (-1) is one period lag value of error term that is come from long run relationship. ECM values represent that the disequilibrium of short run will be fixes long time period.

CUSUM and CUSUMQ sum of squares Graphs

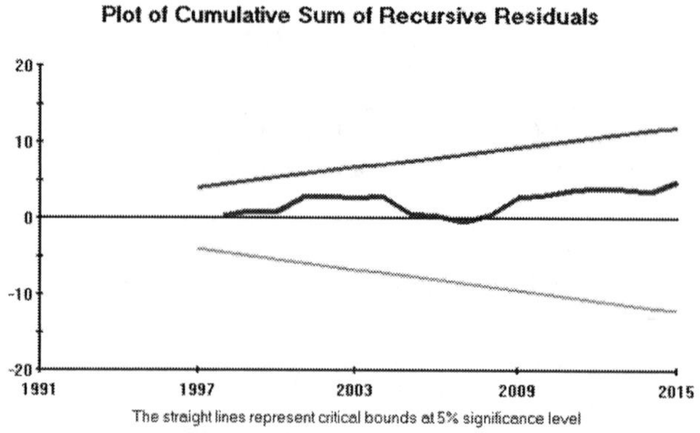

Figure 1.

In CUSUM chart the lines are not crossing each other means that there is no issue of recursive residuals in terms of mean. Similarly, there is no issue of recursive residuals in terms of variance.

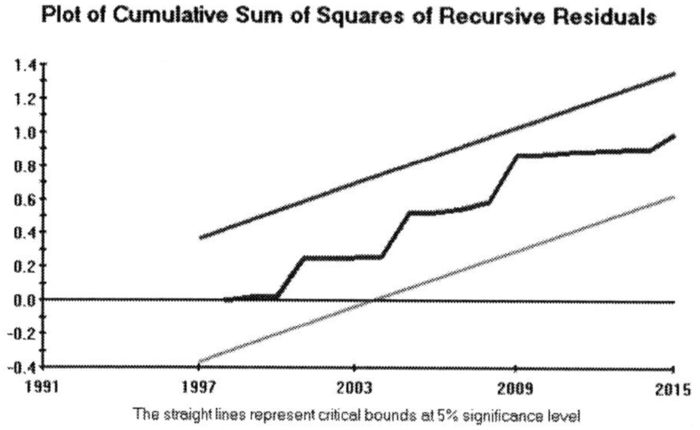

Figure 2.

Figure 1 and 2 represent that cumulative sum of recursive residuals the cumulative sum of square of recursive residuals. Both CUSUM and CUSUMSQ are within critical bound of 5% so this shows that model is structurally stable.

3 Conclusion

The impact of GDP, Population, Technical & Vocational education, Degree college's enrollment and universities was examined on the unemployment rate of Pakistan and the period is 1990-2015.We have used ARDL

(Auto Regressive Distributive Lag) test on it. The Long Run results have shown that there is negative relation between GDP and unemployment. Population has positive relation with unemployment while Technical & Vocational education has positive effects on unemployment. Short Run results explain that Population, Technical and Vocational Education have positive effects. ECM (-1) represents the lag value one period of error term that come from long run relation. ECM (-1) represent disequilibrium of short run. ECM (-1) has statistically significant and negative value. The main focus of our study shows that our education or technical and vocational education system may control the determinants of unemployment in Pakistan.

This study is helpful for the policy makers which are trying to control unemployment in Pakistan. Government should increase the numbers of tech n vocational institutes. These institutions can play a vital role to decrease the unemployment in Pakistan.

References

1. Ahmed Raza Cheema, A. A. Economic Determinants of unemployments in Pakistan. *International Journal of Business and Social Science* , **5** (3), (2014).
2. Chowdhury, M. S., & Hossain, T. M. Determinants of Unemploment in Bangladesh:A case study. Developing Country Studies , **4**, (2014).
3. Dr Aurangzeb, k. A. Facyor Effecting Unemployment:A cross Country Analysis. *International Journal of Academic Research Business and Social Science* , **3** (1). (2013).
4. *Economic survey*. Retrieved from IPR's factsheet. (2012-13 and 2014-15).
5. *Economic survey of Pakistan*. (2013-2014).
6. *Government of Pakistan Ministry of Finance*. Retrieved from Ministry of finance: www.finance.gov.pk (1990-2015).
7. *Government of Pakistan ministry of finance*. Retrieved from Pakistan economic survey: www.finance.gov.pk (2014-2015).
8. Muhammad Arslan, R. Z. Unemployment and Its Determinants:A Study of Pakistan. *Journal of Economics and Sustainable Development*, **5** (13).
9. *PakAlumni World wide*. (n.d.). Retrieved from Pakalumni: www.pakalumni.com
10. *Pakistan Bureau of Statistics government of Pakistan*. (2015-2016). Retrieved from Pakistan Bureau of Statistics: www.pbs.gov.pk
11. *Pakistan world meter*. (2017). Retrieved from worldmeters: www.worldmeters.info.pk
12. *The World Bank*. (1990-2015). Retrieved from World Bank: www.data.worldbank.org

Gaining of common culture perception to students in divided societies and the role of Art course in this context; Northern and Southern Cyprus

Fatma Miralay [1,*]

[1]Near East University Atatürk Faculty of Education, North Cyprus Boulevard, 88138 Nicosia TRNC Mersin 10 – Turkey.

Abstract. Cultural dimension in education bears importance in terms of transferring and sustaining cultural values in addition to creating local and upper intercultural awareness in individuals. Especially in divided societies, gaining cultural values to individuals via education eliminates boundaries between societies, ensures cultural integration and carries local values to a universal point without terminating them. In this paper, effort is paid to identify the importance of preserving common cultural values of Cyprus in the content of art course curricula applied in Northern and Southern Cyprus societies according to teacher opinions. In accordance with this purpose, research data were collected using a semi-structured interview form which is a qualitative research method. The study was conducted on 20 secondary education art teachers in capital Northern and Southern Nicosia regions. Descriptive analysis method was used in the analysis of data. An examination of research results shows that there is no difference between the opinions of Turkish Cypriot and Greek Cypriot teachers, but that Turkish Cypriot teachers give more prominence to the basic needs as regards the course. It has been determined that material needs of Greek Cypriot teachers are supported by the ministry whereas the opportunities of Turkish Cypriot teachers are limited. A majority of the teachers emphasized that the topic should be included in education curricula and the methods should serve to put this into practice. In the study, it has been concluded that the similarity of positive opinions between Turkish Cypriot and Greek Cypriot teachers is high and that there are fewer disagreements.

[*] Corresponding author: fatma.miralay@neu.edu.tr

1 Introduction

Rapid changes in the globalizing world affect human life and bring about changes in education systems. This, in turn, creates the need for renovating and structuring of education; it must also respond to the future-oriented needs of societies. Education, which plays an essential role in the planning of futures of societies and individuals, is determinant on their cultural development [8]. It is known that the dimension of culture in education is included in different education curricula starting from pre-school period [7]. Education curricula which also equip individuals with cultural acquisitions make contribution to provide them with high-level development, reinforcement of values at local dimensions, compromising skills and formation of a sense of belonging [11]. It is also known that in the last decade UNESCO has been organizing several workshops on equipping students with cultural transfer and determining short-term and long-term objectives in the field of education and culture. In these studies, the functionality of art and the harmony between contents in cultural affairs has been displayed. In addition, a call has been made to take immediate action in education so that the lost cultural values could be regained and cultural awareness could be created [15]. Art education, which is an essential part of the cultural entirety in education, attracts attention with the function of gaining individuals local and different intercultural relations and stands out among other disciplines with this feature [6]. Art education, which is the cornerstone of contemporary education process, displays the necessity of art education programs regardless of racial, class and gender differences. Maziere [9] claimed that visual arts course, which was a part of education curricula depending on art education, assumed the role of creating a common language in European countries in addition to aesthetic acquisitions. Cabedo-Mas et al. [5] believed that gaining cultural values to individuals in societies with education could eliminate boundaries between societies, realize economic and cultural integration and create a universal culture without terminating local values. Miralay [10] conducted a similar study and argued that especially in societies which experienced conflicts, comparative arts education studies could create solution-oriented alternative visions to societies. In the light of such information, covering the topic of common cultural values in Northern and Southern Cyprus within the framework of art education curricula and evaluating based on teacher opinions is seen as a topic worth studying. Within this scope, below are the sub-problems of the study:

1. What are the opinions of art teachers in Northern Cyprus concerning the common cultural values of Cyprus?
2. What are the opinions of art teachers in Southern Cyprus concerning the common cultural values of Cyprus?
3. Are there any similarities and differences between the opinions of art teachers working in both societies?

2 Method

The purpose of this study is to evaluate the common cultural values of Cyprus in the content of art course curricula offered in Northern and Southern Cyprus based on teacher opinions. Within this objective, "interview technique" which is a qualitative research method has been used in this study.

2.1 Study Group

The sample of the study consists of secondary school teachers in Northern and Southern Nicosia. Convenience sampling, which is a purposive sampling method, has been used in determining the participants. Two schools (Secondary schools A and B) and 10 art course teachers in Southern Nicosia region and 2 secondary schools (Secondary schools C and D) and 10 art course teachers in Northern Nicosia region constituted the study group of the study. A total of 20 art teachers serving at secondary stage were included in the study and demographic information on the teachers is provided in Table 1.

Table 1. Demographic Variables of Teachers

	Turkish Cypriot Teachers		Greek Cypriot Teachers	
	f	%	f	%
Gender				
Male	3	%30	4	%40
Female	7	%70	6	%60
Age				
31-45	2	%20	4	%40
36-40	3	%30	1	%10
41-45	5	%50	3	%30
Field of undergraduate study				
Fine arts faculty	7	%70	8	%80
Education faculty fine arts	3	%30	2	%20
Education status				
Undergraduate	7	%70	5	%50
Master of Arts	2	%20	4	%40
PhD	1	%10	1	%10
Professional seniority				
1-5 years	-	-	1	%10
6-10 years	4	%40	5	%50
11-15 years	3	%30	3	%30
16-20 years	2	%20	-	
21 years and more	1	%10	1	%10
Participation in artistic activities				
1-2 a year	2	%20	3	%30
2-4	3	%30	5	%50
5 and more	-	-	2	%20
None	5	%50	-	-
Total	10	100	10	100

Table 1 provides information on the art teachers who work at secondary education institutions of both societies. Considering the genders of teachers, it is seen that the number of "female" teachers in both societies is higher. Considering the mean age values of teachers, it has been determined that in the north they are between 41 and 45 ages whereas in the south the age interval is 31 to 45. An examination of the branch of teachers shows that teachers in both societies are graduates of fine arts faculties. Considering the education status of teachers shows that graduate education is widespread in both societies. An examination of professional seniority interval of teachers shows that they have between 6 and 10 years of experience in both north and south. Finally, an examination of the participation of teachers in artistic activities shows that teachers in the north do not participate in such activities whereas teachers in the south show participation for 2 to 4 times a year.

2.2 Data collection tool

In this study, a semi-structured interview form was prepared by the researcher with the purpose of determining the opinions of art course teachers. In order to write the question items, literature search was made first in the creation of question form stage and effort was paid to identify the present situation of curricula in both societies. Then expert opinion, reliability and scope validity stages were followed and the form was thus given its final form.

2.3 Application

In the application of the study, interviews were held with the managers of 4 secondary schools in northern and southern Nicosia regions and permission was obtained which was necessary for the application. Then, interviews were conducted with art teachers who worked at these schools and it was clearly stated that the application was based on voluntarism. Later, discussions were held with teachers who accepted to participate in the study and interviews were held between November 2017 and January 2018. In the application stage of the form, the researcher visited the schools and conducted face-to-face interviews with teachers and the opinions of teachers who permitted voice recording were recorded.

2.4 Analysis of Data

In order to find answer to the research question in the analysis of data, the interview data obtained from the interviews with study group members were analyzed with descriptive analysis method. In accordance with this objective, the basic framework of data analysis of the topic was prepared with the coding's based on interviews, research objectives and research questions. Based on these coding's, meaningful and logical categories and themes were formed. Tables were created based on each question in the interview form and findings were digitalized and the findings were presented in the form of frequencies. In order to distinguish the nationalities of teachers, they were coded as Turkish Cypriot teachers (T.C.T) and Greek Cypriot teachers (G.C.T).

3 Findings

In this section, the findings obtained from the interview form applied to teachers are tabulated and presented below.

3.1 Are there any activities in your school with the purpose of introducing the cultural values of Cyprus?

Table 1. The opinions of Turkish Cypriot teachers concerning school activities aiming at teaching the common cultural values of Cyprus

	Activities	*f*
T.C.T	The need for a curriculum	10
	The need for ministerial and school support	9
	Inadequate class hours	8
	Overcrowded classrooms	5
	Difference of topic	2
	Inadequate awareness as regards the topic	1
Total		**35**

Table 2. The opinions of Greek Cypriot teachers concerning school activities aiming at teaching the common cultural values of Cyprus

	Activities	f
G.C.T	Regular competitions held by the ministry	10
	Increasing activities on the topic of common culture	4
	Financial support opportunities	4
	Regular workshop facilities	3
Total		21

An examination of table 1 shows that a majority of Turkish Cypriot teachers stated that, first and foremost, they did not have a curriculum (f=10). A group of teachers claimed that support from the ministry and the school for extra-school trips was negligible (f=9). In addition, they stated that class hours were short for this kind of trips (f=8), that classrooms were overcrowded (f=5) and that course topics were not consistent with this type of activities (f=2). One of the teachers emphasized that the school management and the ministry was not sensitive towards this topic (f=1). An examination of Table 2 shows that a majority of Greek Cypriot teachers are satisfied with the ministerial support (f=19= but that they complain that common cultural topics are not given adequate place in activities (f=4). A group of teachers expressed that they received financial support from the ministry (f=4) as a result of which they could organize activities at the school (f=3).

3.2 Are there any topics directed towards recognizing the common cultural values of Cyprus in the content of the curriculum that you implemented?

Table 3. Opinions of Turkish Cypriot teachers on the inclusion of common cultural values of Cyprus in the curriculum of art course.

	Program content	*f*
T.C.T	Program deficiency	9
	The importance of improvement and diversification of program	7
	Including extra-curriculum topics as regards cultural values	7
	The need for conducting cultural-based learning outside school	5
	Redesigning the content of program according to teacher opinions	3
	Redesigning the content of program according to student needs	1
Total		**32**

Table 4. Opinions of Greek Cypriot teachers on the inclusion of common cultural values of Cyprus in the curriculum of art course.

	Program content	***f***
G.C.T	The importance of giving more place to Cyprus culture in program content	10
	Supporting cultural topics with extra-school activities	7
	Teachers creating a suitable environment for the topic of culture	3
	The need for on-the-job training concerning the topic	2
	School management being more sensitive towards the topic	1
Total		**23**

An examination of table 3 shows that most of Turkish Cypriot teachers stated that they did not have any program concerning visual arts course (f=9). A group of teachers, on the other hand, displayed that the topic should be included in the curriculum (f=7). It has been stated that extra-curriculum classes should be offered concerning common cultural values (f=7) and, as a result, teachers wanted to cover these topics outside school, too (f=5). Some teachers stated that the curriculum should be designed by specialized people after receiving the opinion of teachers (f=3). One teacher said that the curriculum should be designed after determining the needs of students (f=1). Table 4 shows that a majority of Greek Cypriot teachers displayed the importance of Cypriot common cultural values in the content of curriculum (f=10). In addition, a group of teachers stated that teaching cultural values should be performed based on extra-school activities (f=7). Some teachers claimed that preparing a suitable environment for the topic in the class is the task of the teacher (f=3) whereas some others stated that they needed on-the-job training on the topic (f=2). One teacher argued that school management should be more sensitive towards such topics (f=1).

3.3 Do you organize extra-school trips so that the cultural values in our country can be learned by students?

Table 5. The opinions of Turkish Cypriot teachers concerning extra-school trips in the curriculum process of art course.

	Extra-school trip	***f***
T.C.T	Transportation problems	10
	Inadequate class hours	9
	The necessity to visit historical places	8
	Teaching the folkloric values of Cyprus in class environment	7
	The teacher creating opportunities with his/her own facilities	5
	Academic program-focused school management	4
	Overcrowded classrooms	3
Total		**74**

Table 6. The opinions of Greek Cypriot teachers concerning extra-school trips in the curriculum process of art course.

	Extra-school trip	***f***
G.C.T	Adequate transportation facilities	7
	Introducing to students the history and artists of Cyprus in extra-school environments	7
	Inadequacy of class hours	3
	Intense academic program	1
	Economic limitations	1
Total		**29**

As can be seen in Table 5, a majority of Turkish Cypriot teachers complain that they do not conduct extra-school trips due to transportation problems (f=10) and that the length of class hours prevents organizing such trips (f=9). A group of teachers emphasized the importance of visiting historical places (f=8). Some teachers who cannot perform extra-school trips argued that folkloric values belonging to Cyprus could be transferred to the students in class environment (f=7) whereas some others claimed that academic-oriented curriculum imposed limitations on many topics (f=5). On the other hand, Table 6 shows that most Greek Cypriot teachers are satisfied with transportation opportunities (f=7) and that they have the opportunity of introducing to students the history and artists of Cyprus outside school (f=7). A group of teachers claimed that class hours were inadequate (f=3). Some teachers argued that teaching curricula were academic-oriented (f=1) and that there were economic restraints for extra-school trips (f=1).

3.4 According to you, how important is the inclusion of common cultural values in visual arts course curriculum?

Table 7. The opinions of Turkish Cypriot teachers on the importance of including common cultural values of Cyprus topic in art course curriculum.

	Importance	*f*
T.C.T	Creating a contemporary and democratic student profile	9
	Contributing to the societies in knowing each other more closely	8
	Creating opportunities so that students can cover different topics	8
	Creating a student profile who is humanist and respectable to historical values	7
	Introducing to the society individuals which know cultural awareness	6
Total		**38**

Table 8. The opinions of Greek Cypriot teachers on the importance of including common cultural values of Cyprus topic in art course curriculum.

	Importance	*F*
G.C.T	Individuals who know the culture of both societies	10
	Equipping the student with the awareness of history between both societies	10
	Making contribution to the development of humanist personality	9
	Creating an awareness for preserving cultural values	3
	Establishing affinity between societies	2
Total		**34**

An examination of Table 7 shows that a majority of Turkish Cypriot teachers believed that including this topic in teaching curriculum would create a contemporary and democratic student profile (f=9). A group of teachers stated that it would allow for the societies to know each other more closely (f=8). A different group of teachers argued that it would contribute the students to learn different cultural topics which were not included in course curriculum (f=8). Some teachers, on the other hand, claimed that students would gain a humanist personality and the ability to respect historical values (f=7). Some teachers stated that students with developed cultural awareness could be introduced to the society (f=6). Table 8 provides the opinions of Greek Cypriot teachers such as they would be individuals who knew the culture of both societies (f=10). They also stated that an awareness of the history between two societies would be given to students (f=10). A group of teachers argued that it would contribute to the formation of a humanist culture in students (f=9) whereas another group mentioned the awareness of preserving

 https://doi.org/10.1051/shsconf/20184801016

cultural values in students (f=3) and the opportunity of establishing an affinity between societies (f=2).

3.5 What is the extent of your knowledge about common cultural values in Northern and Southern Cyprus?

Table 9. Opinions of Turkish Cypriot teachers concerning their competencies on common cultural values of Cyprus.

	Teacher competencies	*f*
T.C.T	Thinking that they have adequate knowledge	10
	The will for possessing more information	7
	Not finding necessary	2
	Thinking that it is parallel to course content	1
Total		**20**

Table 10. Opinions of Greek Cypriot teachers concerning their competencies on common cultural values of Cyprus.

	Teacher competencies	*f*
G.C.T	Thinking that they have adequate knowledge	9
	Relating to course curriculum	5
	Having very negligible knowledge	1
	Not finding necessary	1
Total		**16**

An examination of table 9 shows that a majority of Turkish Cypriot teachers think that they are adequately knowledgeable about common cultural values of Cyprus (f=10). A group of teachers, on the other hand, stated that they wanted to be more knowledgeable (f=7). Another group of teachers believe that this knowledge is unnecessary (f=2). With a different viewpoint, another teacher expressed that the topic was not parallel to the course and knowledge was unnecessary at this point (f=1). Table 10 provides the opinions of Greek Cypriot teachers. Most of them think that they have adequate knowledge (f=9). A different group of teachers stated that they could not relate the topic with the course (f=5) and that they were not much knowledgeable (f=1). A teacher displayed a different viewpoint and argued that this knowledge was unnecessary (f=1).

3.6 What kind of a generation will be created in the future if common cultural values of Cyprus are taught to art students?

Table 11. Opinions of Cypriot Turkish teachers concerning the teaching of cultural values of Cyprus in visual arts class and their acquisitions.

	Student profile	*f*
T.C.T	Pacifist individual	10
	Individual who respects cultural values	9
	Constructive individual with developed personality skills who can produce solution to problems	9
	Individual with humanist characteristics	8
	Individual who comprehends the importance of culture	7
	Finding unnecessary	3
Total		**50**

Table 12. Opinions of Greek Cypriot teachers concerning the teaching of cultural values of Cyprus in visual arts class and their acquisitions.

	Student profile	f
G.C.T	Individual with strong sense of belonging	8
	Respectful and democratic individual with an awareness of human rights	8
	Individual who lays claim to his culture	7
	Intellectual individual who knows cultural features	4
	Contemporary individual who gained an awareness for peace	4
	Individual who is able to transfer his cultural heritage	3
Total		**53**

An examination of table 11 shows that a majority of Turkish Cypriot teachers believe that pacifist (f=10), respectful to cultural values (f=9), constructive individuals who can produce solution to problems (f=9) would be raised. Another group of teachers stated that they believed that individuals who haved humanist characteristics (f=8) and comprehended the importance of culture (f=7) would be raised. With a different viewpoint, a group of teachers expressed that they found this topic unnecessary (f=3). Table 12 shows that Greek Cypriot teachers generally believed that students with strong sense of belonging were raised (f=8) and that respectful and democratic individuals with a sense of human rights would be raised (f=8). Another group of teachers stated that they believed that individuals who laid claim to their culture (f=7) and intellectual students who recognized the characteristics of their culture (f=4) would be raised. Another group of teachers stated that they believed that contemporary individuals with a sense of peace (f=4) and able to transfer their cultural heritage would be raised (f=3).

3.7 How sensitive are our students towards Cypriot common culture issues?

Table 13. Opinions of Turkish Cypriot teachers on the sensitiveness of students towards Cypriot common cultural values.

	Student sensitiveness	f
T.C.T	Difference of the area of interest of students	10
	Differences based on family cultural structure of students	9
	Peer and community factor effects	8
	Teacher-based awareness-raising	8
	Low level of student sensitiveness	6
	Students suffering from expression issues	5
	Motivation by teacher	1
Total		**66**

Table 14. Opinions of Greek Cypriot teachers on the sensitiveness of students towards Cypriot common cultural values.

	Student sensitiveness	f
G.C.T	Cultural differences	10
	Technology-based student profile	9
	Course content limitations	8
	Academic liabilities	6
	Importance of family factor	4
	Readiness level of student	4
	Differences in student objectives	3
Total		**45**

An examination of table 13 shows that a majority of Turkish Cypriot teachers mention the differences in the area of interest of students (f=9), peer and community factor effects (f=8) and teacher-based awareness raising (f=8). A different group of teachers emphasized that students suffered from low sensitiveness (f=6) and expression issues (f=1) whereas one teacher claimed that an increase in this sensitiveness depended on motivation by teachers (f=1). Table 14 shows that a majority of Greek Cypriot teachers mentioned cultural differences (f=10), technology-oriented student profile (f=9), course content limitations (f=8) and academic liabilities (f=6). Another group of teachers emphasized the importance of family factor (f=4), student readiness level (f=4) and differences in student objectives (f=3).

4 Discussion and Conclusion

The results obtained from this study have revealed that the content of art course applied in northern and southern Cyprus does not include the topic of common culture. The research compared the opinions of Turkish Cypriot and Greek Cypriot teachers working in both societies and evaluated the content of the curricula in both societies as regards the topic based on teacher opinions. Within the scope of the questions asked to the teachers, it has been found out that there is not huge difference between the opinions of Turkish Cypriot and Greek Cypriot teachers but that the basic needs of Turkish Cypriot teachers concerning the course have more priority. For example, in the opinions of Turkish Cypriot teachers as regards whether any activities are performed concerning the topic, it was expressed that basic needs had priority. On the other hand, Greek Cypriot teachers emphasized that they did not have any problems as regards course-related needs but that the content of the course should be enriched. For example, Bellenge-Morris and Stuhr [3] concluded in their study that school activities were almost compulsory in drawing class which increased motivation in students and ensured permanence in their learning.

The answers given to another question of the study revealed that the content of the curricula applied in both societies lacked common culture topics but that positive opinions as regards the participation of teachers were very similar. Barkhordari et al. [2] studied the popularization of peace culture through art education and stated that including cultural phenomena especially in the contents of course curricula had positive effects on individuals. Teachers were also asked about their opinions on extra-school trips and visits to historical places in the application process of the course. The results obtained here make clear that there are differences in both societies. It has been found out that the material needs Greek Cypriot teachers are supported by the ministry and that Turkish Cypriot teachers have more limited opportunities. In addition, it has been determined that teachers in both societies have problems in terms of the length of lectures, academic curriculum and classroom size and that their opinions at this point are similar. For example, Akhmetov et al. [1] claim that extra-school trips and introduction of historical places to students at art classroom prevents loss of cultural heritage. A similar study by Şahin and Yağcı [14] emphasized the importance of local cultural values in art classroom in the socialization process of individuals and concluded that students enjoyed integrity in knowledge by seeing what they draw. A similar conclusion reached in another question of the study is that teachers working in both societies think that including the topic of common culture in the program content is essential. Teachers especially emphasized the importance of course content in preserving local culture and establishing affinity between societies. Bianchi [4] explained that the formation of cultural identity in societies is intertwined with art education and emphasized that this fact should be related to the course content. In another question, the competency of teachers concerning the topic was examined and it was revealed that the teachers in both societies thought that they did not have adequate knowledge. It has been found out that teachers believed that they should be given more opportunities and that they wanted to transfer their competencies to students in similar patterns. In another question of the study, the manner with which Cypriot cultural values could make contribution to students in the course was searched. In this regard, it was expressed that teacher opinions were similar and that they believed that they would raise humanist and pacifist individuals.

As a result, this study found out that Turkish Cypriot and Greek Cypriot teachers had an optimistic viewpoint towards common cultural values of Cyprus and that they displayed the benefits and uses of including this topic especially in the content of art course. In addition, teachers stated that they did not cover the common cultural values of Cyprus in their classes before but that as a result of the positive developments in the island in the last 10 years they began to mention these topics verbally in the classroom environment. Some teachers emphasized that the topic should be included in the education curricula and that both societies should pay effort to put it into realization. It has been concluded that in relating the topic of common cultural values of Cyprus with art course curricula, there are more similarities between Turkish Cypriot and Greek Cypriot teachers than the disagreements.

References

1. Akhmetov, L. G., Badaev, V. S., Komelina, V. A., and Kuzmin, V. K., National arts and crafts in the content of art education of Russia. Review of European Studies, 7(1), 1, (2014).
2. Barkhordari, M., Nasrabadi, H. B., Heidari, M. H., & Neyestani, M. R., The Importance of Art-Based Curriculum in Peace Education. *Review of European Studies*, ***8*** (4), 220, (2016).
3. Ballengee-Morris, C., & Stuhr, P. L., Multicultural art and visual cultural education in a changing world. *Art Education*, *54*(4), 6-13, (2001).
4. Bianchi, J., Intercultural identities: Addressing the global dimension through art education. *International Journal of Art & Design Education*, ***30***(2), 279-292. (2011).
5. Cabedo-Mas, A., Nethsinghe, R., & Forrest, D., The role of the arts in education for peacebuilding, diversity and intercultural understanding: A comparative study of educational policies in Australia and Spain. *International Journal of Education & the Arts*, ***18***(11), (2017).
6. Duncum, P., *A Critical Review of the Postmodern Implosion of Fine Art and Popular Visual Culture in Art Classrooms*. United Kingdom: Palgrave Macmillan. (2017).

7. Freedman, K., and Stuhr, P., Curriculum change for the 21st century: Visual culture in art education. *Handbook of research and policy in art education*, 815-828, (2004).
8. LeVine, R. A., *Culture, behavior, and personality: An introduction to the comparative study of psychosocial adaptation*. Routledge, (2018).
9. Maziere, C., Artistic education in France: from the state to the classrooms' practices. International Journal of Education and the Arts, 16(23), (2015).
10. Miralay, F., "*Comparison and Evaluation of Visual Arts Course Curricula in Turkish Republic of Northern Cyprus and Republic of Cyprus and a Draft Program proposal* (Unpublished PhD Thesis) Near East University Education Sciences, (2018).
11. Moore, A., *Teaching and learning: Pedagogy, curriculum and culture*. Routledge, (2012).
12. Morley, S., Analytic and holistic approaches to fine art education: A comparative approach. *Journal of Visual Art Practice*, 13(2): 101-113, (2014).
13. Sacco, P., L., Culture 3.0: A new perspective for the EU 2014-2020 structural funds programming. *OMC Working Group on Cultural and Creative Industries*. (2011).
14. Şahin, D., & Yağcı, M. M., The importance of art education in socialization process of individual. *Journal of Life Sciences*, *1*(1), (2012).
15. United Nations Educational, Scientific and Cultural Organization (2009). *Road Map for Arts Education. The World Conference on Arts Education: Building Creative Capacities for the 21st Century*, Lisbon, 6-9 March 2006.

Investigating career guidance needs of middle school students

Süleyman Balcı*

[1] Kırıkkale University, Education Faculty, Guidance and Counseling Department, Yahşihan, Kırıkkale, 71450

Abstract. Purpose of this study is to analyze career guidance needs of middle school students. This study has been carried out in 2017-2018 academic year. Participants of this study are year-seven students of middle schools (n=241). In order to determine the sample, purposeful sampling technique were used. In the study, it was used Guidance Needs Determining Form, which is three-likert-type scale and were developed for primary education students. This scale has three sub-scales as personal/social guidance needs, career guidance needs and educational guidance needs. Sub-scale of career guidance needs were used to collect necessary data. Subsequently, frequencies and percentages concerning data of sub-scale items of career guidance needs were calculated. Moreover, findings related with career guidance needs of middle school students were given as in the table. Results have shown that career guidance needs of middle school students is meaningfully high in terms of some items.

1 Introduction

People need to work for a variety of reasons, especially to earn a living, honor and contribute to their families and communities, achieve self-growth, establish a public identity, and structure their lives. Moreover, there are several more reasons for working such as social and psychological needs like friendship, intimacy, self-esteem and personal growth for need of fulfillment. Because work can enable people to meet basic survival needs and provide the context for fulfilling people's needs for security, social belonging and intimacy by enhancing the material comfort of one's family as well as personal esteem by providing a sense of personal worth and accomplishment. In addition, Super, Savickas & Super claim that work provide personal identity as an expression of self-image and a self-concept. Situations and roles related with work has great importance in people's lives by considering the reasons of why people work [1] .

* Corresponding author: meb.suleyman@gmail.com

1.1 Career development and developmental career theories

Career development is defined as a process that encompasses much of the life span from beginning of childhood to adulthood. In other words, it begins in childhood and includes the formal and informal experiences that give rise to talents, interests, values, and knowledge of the world of work, continues into adulthood via the progression of one's career behavior such as entry into and adjustment to work throughout life span [2]. According to Gysbers career development is self-development over the lifetime through the integration of the roles, settings, and events in a person's life [3]. Several factors such as people's gender, ethnic origin, spirituality, race, sexual orientation, and socioeconomic status may influence one's career development by shaping the life roles, lifesettings and life events of people. Career development also pertains to the interventions used by practitioners to facilitate age and situation appropriate career behaviors across one's lifetime [4].

Career theories provide systems for explaining which factors operate together to determine occupational choice and development over the life periods such as preparation for work with education and training, work entry, adjustment to work and disengagement from work. Developmental career theories explain how the work role relates to other life roles such as parent and leisurite, how contextual factors such as socioeconomic status affect career trajectories and how people partly construct their own career and life stories and experiences. In addition, developmental career theories state the predictable tasks and challenges that accompany career development such as learning about oneself, exploring the world of work, developing a vocational identity, narrowing down career options from a broad range of career alternatives and establishing and maintaining one's career.

Developmental career theory of Super proposes that career choice and development includes a lifelong and developmental process that begins in childhood and proceeds continuously over the life time. Each life period presents particular problems to solve, and these problems may surface and resurface in predictable and unpredictable ways at various times in life. By taking attention to the developmental nature of careers, counselors can help clients understand and deal with developmental tasks to promote effective career planning, career exploration, career decision making at all life periods for designing their careers and navigating successfully through anticipated transitions. In addition, Super's theory contributes counselors for assisting students to arrange their work and other life roles into a livable and satisfying pattern. According to Super, major roles in life constitute the typical life structure in chronological order of child, student, leisurite, citizen, worker, spouse, homemaker, parent, and annuitant [5]. Among these roles, the worker role typically represents a core role, given the cultural, social, and personal imperative to work.

In the developmental theory of occupational choice, Ginzberg, Ginsburg, Axelrad, and Herma argued that children's first career awareness is developed as a fantasy [6]. Children at about age 11 begin to become aware of themselves in relation to the world of work and their interests and choices become more crystallized at about age 18. These life periods are called relatively fantasy stage, tentative stage and realistic stage in this theory.

Another developmental theory is Developmental Theory of Circumscription and Compromise developed by Gottfredson [7]. This theory supposes that circumscription and compromise processes exist for deciding apporiate career in middle and later adolescence. The process of circumscription involves continually narrowing of occupations that person will consider. Compromise process includes eliminating the most preferred career options for less compatible careers. By this way, children and adolescents can reach the fulfillment of their internal unique selves by choosing occupations that they perceive to be more socially acceptable. This process begins in early childhood by identifying segments of the occupational world as unattainable. Moreover, this process continues throughout middle and later adolescence. During this life stage adolescents make vocational preparation decisions that is more likely affect their ability to enter into more prestigious careers [7] [8].

According to Gottfredson's theory, children are influenced by their understanding of prescribed gender and prestige roles within social environment. As a result of this influence, children may have consideration about their own interests, values, competencies, and intelligence. This theory supposes that from ages 3 to 5 children become oriented to size and power. Moreover, children (ages 6 to 8) become aware of socially determined gender roles. Between 9 and 13, they become oriented to these roles which social class and abilities play in their career aspirations and choices in future [8].

According to Gottfredson, socialization plays important roles in children's developing career awareness [7]. Career choices are eventually made through a process of orientation to vocational choice, gathering information and planning, and developing one's self-concept. Assisting children in this process may be necessary to enable them become aware of career possibilities by providing appropriate and timely information [9].

1.2 Career guidance in schools

Career guidance contains the career-orienting activities which are generally provided by school counselors and teachers in order to help students to become aware of possible career alternatives with a variety of services such as guidance, advising, education, placement, coaching, and mentoring in educational settings [10]. Many countries recognise the importance of career guidance programs in terms of enhancing the lives of their citizens and improving their economy [11]. Several type of guidance services are delivered according to the country or location of the service provider [12]. In some countries, such as the United States and Turkey, career guidance is often delivered as a part of the school counselors' responsibilities [13]. Career guidance services were provided by means of several formats, such as individually, group-based, face-to-face, or at a distance including help-lines and web-based services.

Guichard emphisized that career guidance should be lifelong, comprehensive and accessible in a way that is suitable for people in terms of their economic, social, cultural, educational, and personal situation [14]. Likewise, according to Killeen and White [15] career guidance is needed to be lifelong, accessible, and meaningful for all individuals. This can be possible with the collaboration of trainers, practitioners and teachers, school counselors and other personnels to guarantee the integration and evaluation career guidance services and the effectiveness of career guidance [16].

It was determined that career guidance interventions which involve a career counsellor were significantly more effective than those interventions that were without career counselor. Particularly, when computer system and career counseling were used together it may be more effective than allowing individuals to just use a computerised guidance system [17].

As for data collection regarding evaluation of career guidance interventions, Benkofske and Heppner stressed that data collection can be rather straightforward with proper planning and preparation [18]. Before gathering data it is needed what information is necessary and the most appropriate methods for collecting that information. Otherwise, the entire evaluative process may produce negative consequences for the career guidance program suh as insufficient data to support ongoing funding. Prior to actual process, piloting the data collection process may be suitable option to identify possible problems, such as participants' misunderstanding the instructions or survey questions or difficulties in retrieving archival or institutional data concerning graduation rate and employment record of participants.

1.3 Career guidance needs of children and adolescents

School counselors provide career guidance for students in order to help them become aware of possible career alternatives with a variety of services such as guidance, advising, education, placement, coaching, and mentoring in educational settings [19]. Moreover, While practising these career guidance activities, school counselors assist these children and adolescents explore working environment and give information about working conditions and materials used during working [8]. Need for career guidance and counseling in elementary and secondary schools has been getting greater [4]. As a result of this necessity, career guidance and counselling activities is increasingly delivered in elementary and secondary schools in some countries such as Turkey [12].

It is possible to promote career awareness among elementary and secondary children and adolescents by enabling them to visit work places and observing the types and process of jobs that workers do in work places [20]. In addition to visiting work places, mentoring can enable children and adolescents to broaden their awareness about job tasks, attitudes, and supports needed to work successfully in any occupation. By this way, children who live in rural areas with fewer opportunities may gain early awareness concerning certain specialized careers and can prepare themselves in middle school and high school for entry into high school and university department regarding specialized careers [21]. Moreover, computerized career guidance and information systems have been developed to aid the guidance function.

Children and adolescents need to learn sets of skills and develop the types of motivational styles and approaches that will assist them in their efforts to establish satisfying life structures across their lifetime [1]. School counselors help children and adolescents understand their abilities, interests, values, and personality styles; the specifics of current labor market information; and how to make better and more satisfying career decisions in order to establish appropriate career development and manage for the significant challenges they face creatively and proactively [22]. Because children and adolescents experience difficulties and special challenges such as gender related circumscription of vocational aspirations, career decision-making readiness, and school-to-school or school-to-work transitioning during their career development. In addition, Career guidance assistance provided by school counselors for students help them develop career awareness, support career development and develop satisfying, productive, and fulfilling career choices in future.

What knowledge should students acquire, what skills should they develop, and what attitudes should they form as a result of participating in the activities of career guidance and counselling? These are important questions because they presuppose that there are learning outcomes for career guidance and counselling. Replying these questions is important because it is necessary to determine contents of career guidance to meet the needs of students [2]. For this reason, this study is related with career guidance needs of year-seven middle school students. Therefore, purpose of this study is to analyze career guidance needs of year-seven students of middle schools.

2 Method

2.1 Sample

In order to determine the sample of this study, purposeful sampling technique were used. This study has been carried out in 2017-2018 academic year. Students from nine different middle schools in a urban area in a small province in the middle region of Turkey participated in the study (N = 241). All students were in the seventh grade and their ages ranged from 12 to 13 years. Almost half of participants were girls (n = 120), (49,5 %) attending the seventh grade of these schools.

2.2 Data collection and analysis

In the study, Guidance Needs Determining Form was used. This instrument is a three-likert-type scale and were developed by Erkan for primary education students [23]. This scale contains 26 items concerning guidance needs of primary education students and have three sub-scales. These sub-scales are personal/social guidance needs, career guidance needs and educational guidance needs. Items regarding sub-scale of career guidance needs were used to collect necessary data related with career guidance needs of seventh grade students. Participants were asked to rate all items used in this investigation on a 3-point Likert scale (1 = no, 2=undecided, 3 = yes). Subsequently, frequencies and percentages concerning data of sub-scale items of career guidance needs were calculated. Before conducting data gathering instrument, it has been taken official permission by researcher from district educational administration for collecting data with this scale in schools.

3 Results

After collecting necessary data concerning career guidance needs stated by year seven students (n=241) of middle schools by conducting Guidance Needs Determining Form, the frequency and percentage (%) values of each item were calculated. These values are given in the table 1.

Table 1. Career Guidance Needs of Middle School Students (n=241)

Items for career guidance needs	frequency					
	Yes	%	Undecided	%	No	%
11- I need to learn jobs which I will be succesful mostly	119	49	59	25	63	26
12- I need to learn features of several vocations	109	45	52	22	80	33
13- I need to learn how what I learn in school will help me for my vocation in future	129	54	45	19	67	28
14- I need to learn about necessary education for several vocations	121	50	55	23	65	27
15- I need to learn relations of my interest and aptitudes with my vocation in future	139	58	46	19	56	23
16- I need to learn which activities people do in various vocations	86	36	65	27	90	37
17- I need to learn which activities will make me happy	121	50	33	14	87	36

As seen in the table, career guidance need with highest ratio is item 15 with 58 % 'yes'; Item with second highest ratio is item 13 with 54 % 'yes'; next item with highest ratio is item 14 and 17 with 50 % 'yes'; than other items coming is item 11 and 12 with 49 and 45 % 'yes'; item with lowest ratio is item 16 with 36 % 'yes'.

4 Conclusion

Purpose of this study is to analyze career guidance needs of year-seven students of middle schools. According to the finding of data analysis, career guidance needs of year-seven students is meaningfully high in terms of item 15 and 13 with 58 and 54 % 'yes'. Results related with career guidance needs of year-seven students have shown that year-seven students need career guidance so high that it is necessary to practice planned and comprehensive career counseling regularly and periodically. In addition, this result indicates that these students need career guidance activities for their optimum career development and suitable working options in future.

References

1. Super D. E., Savickas, M. L., & Super, C. M. The life-span, life-space approach to careers. In D. Brown & L. Brooks (Eds.), *Career choice and development: Applying contemporary theories to practice* (3rd ed., pp. 121–178). San Francisco, CA: Jossey-Bass. (1996)
2. Gysbers, N. C. Career guidance and counselling In primary and secondary Educational settings. In Athanasou, J.A. & Van Esbroeck, R. (Eds.). *International Handbook of Career Guidance (pp. 249–264).* Springer Science & Business Media B.V. (2008)
3. Gysbers, N. C. Implementing a whole school approach to guidance through a comprehensive guidance system. As. J. Coun., **7**, 5–17. (2000)
4. Herr E. L. Social Contexts for Career Guidance Throughout the World. In Athanasou, J.A. & Van Esbroeck, R. (Eds.) *International Handbook of Career Guidance (pp. 45–69).* Springer Science & Business Media B.V. (2008)
5. Super, D. E. A life-span, life-space approach to career development. In D. Brown & L. Brooks (Eds.), *Career choice and development: Applying contemporary theories to practice* (2nd ed., pp. 197–261). San Francisco, CA: Jossey-Bass (1990)
6. Ginzberg, E., Ginsburg, S., Axelrad, S., & Herma, J., *Occupational choice: An approach to a general theory*. New York, NY: Columbia University Press. . (1951)
7. Gottfredson, L. S. Applying Gottfredson's theory of circumscription and compromise in career guidance and counseling. In S. D. Brown & R. T. Lent (Eds.), *Career development and counseling: Putting theory and research to work* (pp. 71–100). Hoboken, NJ: Wiley. (2005.
8. Turner, S. L. & Lapan, R.T. Development, and school success in children and adolescents. In Brown, S. D.& Lent, R. W. (Eds) *Career development and counseling : putting theory and research to work* (2nd ed.). Hoboken, New Jersey, USA: John Wiley & Sons, Inc. (2013)
9. Patton, W., & McMahon, M. Theoretical and practical perspectives in Australia. I. J. Ed. Voc. Gui., **2**, 39–49. (2002)
10. Savickas, M. L. The theory and practice of career construction. In S. Brown & R. Lent (Eds.), *Career development and counseling: Putting theory and research to work* (pp. 42–70). Hoboken, NJ: Wiley. (2005)
11. Hartung, P. J. Internationalizing career counseling: Emptying our cups and learning from each other. Car. Dev. Qua, **54**, 12–16. (2005)
12. Watts, A. G., & Sultana, R. G. Career guidance in 37 countries: Contrast and common themes. I. J. Ed Voc. Gui.e, **4**, 105–122. (2004)

13. Whiston, S. C., Eder, K., Tai, W. L., & Rahardja, D. *Research supporting schoo lcounseling: Comprehensive findings*. Paper presented at the annual meeting of the American School Counselor Association, Orlando, FL. (2005)
14. Guichard, J. Career counselling for human development: An international perspective. Car. Dev. Qua., 51, 306–321. (2003)
15. Killeen, J., & White, M. *The impact of careers guidance on adult employed people*. DfEE Research Report, Sheffield, UK: Department for Education and Employment. (2000)
16. Balcı, S. Perceptions of teacher candidates concerning ethically suitable behaviours for teaching profession. SHS Web of C. 31, 01020. (2016)
17. Whiston, S.C. & Buck I.M. Evaluation of career guidance programs. In Athanasou, J.A. & Van Esbroeck, R. (Eds.) *International Handbook of Career Guidance (pp. 677–694)*. Springer Science & Business Media B.V. (2008)
18. Benkofske, M., & Heppner, C. C. Program evaluation. In P. P. Heppner, D. M. Kivlighan, & B. E. Wampold (Eds.), *Research design in counseling* (pp. 488–513). Belmont, CA: Wadsworth. (1999)
19. Savickas, M. L. Career construction: A developmental theory of vocational behavior. In D. Brown (Ed.), *Career choice and development* (4th ed., pp. 149–205). San Francisco, CA: Jossey-Bass. (2002)
20. Balcı, S. Analysis of metaphoric perceptions stated by candidate school counselors regarding contribution of the career guidance for students. PESA Int. J. S. S., 3:4, 193-202. (2017)
21. Balcı, S. Investigating metaphoric perceptions stated by candidate science teachers regarding contribution of the guidance services at school for students (fen bilgisi öğretmeni adaylarının okuldaki rehberlik hizmetlerinin öğrencilere katkısına ilişkin metaforik algılarının incelenmesi). S. S. S. J., 4:18, 1859-1864. (2018)
22. Balcı, S. Okul psikolojik danışmanı öz yetkinlik ölçeği'nin Türk kültüründeki psikometrik özellikleri. Ahi Evran Ün. Kırşehir E. F. D. (KEFAD), **18**:2, 633-649. (2017)
23. Erkan, S. İlköğretim öğrencilerinin rehberlik ihtiyaçlarının belirlenmesi üzerine bir araştırma. K. U.yg. Eğ. Yön. 3:333-406. (1997)
24. Blustein, D.L. The Psychology of Working: A New Perspective for a New Era. In Blustein, D.L. (Eds) *The Oxford Handbook of the Psychology of Working*. International Debate Education Association. (2015)
25. Brown, S. D.& Lent, R.W. *Career development and counseling : Putting theory and research to work* (2nd ed.). Canada: John Wiley & Sons, Inc. (2013)
26. Gottfredson, L. S. Gottfredson's theory of circumscription, compromise, and self-creation. In D. Brown (Ed.), *Career choice and development* (4th ed., pp. 85–148). San Francisco, CA: Jossey-Bass. (2002)
27. Gottfredson, L. S. Gottfredson's theory of circumscription, compromise, and self-creation. In D. Brown & Associate (Eds.), *Career choice and development* (4th ed., pp. 85–148). San Francisco, CA: Jossey-Bass. (2002)
28. Guichard, J., & Lenz, J. Career theory from an international perspective. C. Dev. Qua., **54**, 17–28. (2005)
29. Leung, S. A. The Big Five Career Theories. In Athanasou, J.A. & Van Esbroeck, R. (Eds.) *International Handbook of Career Guidance (pp. 115–132)*. Springer Science & Business Media B.V. (2008)

30. McMahon, M., & Patton, M. (Eds.). *Career counselling: Constructivist approaches.* Abingdon, UK: Routledge. (2006)
31. Van Esbroeck, R. & Athanasou, J.A. Introduction: An ınternational handbook of career guidance. In Athanasou, J.A. & Van Esbroeck, R. (Eds.) *International Handbook of Career Guidance (pp. 1–22).* Springer Science & Business Media B.V. (2008)
32. Super, D. E. A life-span, life-space approach to career development. J. Vo. Beh.r, **16**, 282–298. (1980)
33. Watts, T. Career education for young people: Rationale and provision in the UK and other European countries. In. J. Edu. Voc. G., ***1***, 209–222. (2001)

Total quality management applications in sports and an application on Kocaeli amateur sports club federation sports clubs

Ayşe Demir[1,*] and *Kürşad* Sertbaş[2]

[1] Istanbul Aydin University, Faculty of Sport Sciences, 34295 Kucukcekmece-Istanbul, Turkey
[2] Kocaeli University, Faculty of Sport Sciences, 41000 Umuttepe-Kocaeli, Turkey

Abstract. In this study, the quality management systems in sports clubs were handled specifically for amateur sports clubs and the perceptions of sports club managers regarding quality management systems were searched. The aim of the research is to determine whether the applications for total quality management in amateur sports clubs are implemented effectively and efficiently and to determine the precursors which have an impact on total quality management processes simultaneously. The scale developed by Özdemir (2015) was used to determine the perception of Total Quality Management in sports clubs as a measurement tool in the research. The survey sample is composed of 123 managers, including 4 female (3,3%) and 119 male (96,7%) volunteers who act as managers in the clubs operating under the Kocaeli Amateur Sports Clubs Federation and voluntarily respond to the questionnaires. Analyzes of the collected data using the total quality scale (Cronbach's Alpha: 0,970). It is found that amateur sports clubs are positive towards the applicability of total quality management processes, whereas amateur sports clubs are positive about the applicability of total quality management processes, it is predicted that managers have sports history (μ = 4,022> μ = 3,98) The positive attitude towards the applicability of total quality management processes in the clubs was not the result of the managers being trained in sport management and quality system (μ = 3.99> μ = 4,03).
Keywords: Total Quality Management, Amateur Sports Clubs, Quality in Sports[1]

1 Introduction

Quality and total quality management concepts are important concepts which are frequently discussed in today's world. By the effects of globalization the competition conditions are increasing day by day and in today's global markets, these concept which are about quality, process quality and total quality are important for both sustainability and profitability of each organization. Products and services quality is important not only for the organizations operating in the production sector but also for all the organizations regardless of the sector difference. Within this scope, organizational processes are being carried out with total quality understanding today. The main focus of total quality understanding is to make all processes related to knitting, both internal and external customer satisfaction, efficient, efficient and sustainable towards the objectives of the organization and aiming at continuous improvement in this process. In other words, total quality understanding is a

* Corresponding author: aysedemir@aydin.edu.tr

managerial strategy for today's organizations, and the most basic expectation in this process is to produce quality products, services and processes aimed at determined organizational goals and targets in a way that satisfies the demands and needs of the customers at the maximum level. The main focus is on this process. It is not only the organization's customers who are the customers of the products and services but also the employees who work in processes to bring these products, services and processes together with the customers at the same time.

Sports clubs are one of the most important actors in the sport sector. The quality levels of the outputs produced by sports clubs will increase in parallel with the satisfactory satisfaction of the activities carried out by the sports club stakeholders producing the sports service from the processes in the sports club. The concept of quality and quality systems in sports clubs are considered systematically, including the monitoring of sports services, the identification of problems related to the processes and the improvement of quality and feedback processes [1]. Regarding all processes carried out in a sports club; implementation of quality and quality management practices effectively, such as training processes, infrastructure activities, team work processes - will provide value to the sports clubs.

Quality is a concept which has different definitions with the reason that it is a concept that is handled by many different disciplines in the field of writing. In other words, there is not a generally accepted definition of the concept, but there are different definitions that explain the multidimensional nature of the concept. In the most basic sense quality relates to the quality of a product or service or a process, its predefined goals and its suitability for use [2]. According to another definition, the judgments reached for quality, products, services or processes [3]. Quality is the whole systematic process for approaching excellence in products, services or processes [4].

When the history of the concept of quality is examined, it is seen that the history of the concept is as old as the history of humanity. Even though there are considerable differences between the initial definitions of concept and the way the concept is handled and the framework of the present quality concept, quality is basically a concept held equal to aiming to be the best in every period.

The period of important and structural developments related to the concept of quality is the beginning of the twentieth century. At the beginning of the twentieth century, the most important reason for the importance of quality-oriented studies and researches is the spread of statistical thinking in everyday and economic processes.

The total quality management approach is based on the most basic understanding of all the qualitative steps in the historical process - leadership, scientific approach, team work, continuing education, responsibility, authority [5]. Total quality management is, in a sense, systematic for the focus of all organizational employees in order to help increase the efficiency of an organization at all levels and in all its processes [6]. If total quality management is implemented effectively and productively, it results in quality improvements in terms of process improvement, positive employee contribution and goals and targets in terms of all organizations. In this context, it is seen that the processes related to quality and total quality management are important when they are considered from the perspective of success oriented organizations such as sports clubs.

At the point of adopting total quality understanding in sports clubs, it is possible to identify the strengths of the clubs and to identify the weak points in the process. Through the quality management systems carried out in this context, it is seen that there is an increase in the organizational culture and team unity in sports clubs. It is important to integrate certain steps into existing systems at the point of applying qualitative systems in sports clubs [7];

• Strategic planning: identification of the institutional identity of the sports club, plans for the goals and targets and processes related to financial management

• Internal procedures and system: planning external services to ensure the sustainability of the processes in the sports clubs, setting up internal procedures

• External relations: identification of activities and activities of sports clubs related to the public

• Organizational culture: organizing tournaments, organizations and similar activities to increase the team culture and team unity and spread the culture towards clubs

• Management structuring: to be systematized with the board of directors and other working committees to make total quality understanding sustainable as a managerial strategy

• Success: Adoption of total quality understanding, ensuring internal and external customer satisfaction, and continuous improvement approach spread to all processes, achieving success in sportive and economic sense.

Managers working in the management positions of sports clubs [8], at the point of making the implementation and sustainability of total quality management systems in sports clubs;

• Establishing the necessary trust environment in sports clubs to make quality management systems workable

• One of the key factors in the effectiveness of quality management systems is the adoption of team work by all process stakeholders. In this framework, one of the most important tasks of the managers is to strengthen the team working environment.

• To effectively manage processes to increase the motivation of sports club employees and to create internal customer satisfaction, which is the primary necessity of total quality management systems.

Another important aspect of sports total quality management is that, after the establishment of quality management systems, it is often necessary to develop and continually audit in parallel with quality management standards. At the point of development of quality management systems; determination of common goals, openness to innovation, dissemination of team work, determination of continuous improvement approach are important factors.

2 Methodology

2.1 Aim of the Research

The aim of the research is to determine whether the applications for total quality management in amateur sports clubs are implemented effectively and efficiently and to determine the precursors which have an impact on total quality management processes simultaneously.

2.2 Research Method

Quantitative research method is used in in this research and the research design is descriptive survey model. The research has been conducted on the managers of the clubs affiliated to the Kocaeli Amateur Sports Clubs Federation. At the beginning of the implementation period, the necessary permissions were obtained from Kocaeli University and Kocaeli Amateur Sports Club Federation and the application was implemented using face to face interview technique.

2.3 Research Hypothesis

H_1 = the perception towards the practicality of total quality management is favorable in amateur sports clubs.

H_{1a} = the perception towards the practicality of total quality management is not favorable in amateur sports clubs.

H_2 = the managers of the sports club do have sports background is an antecedent on the favorable perception towards the practicality of total quality management in amateur sports clubs.

H_{2a} = the managers of the sports club do have sports background is not an antecedent on the favorable perception towards the practicality of total quality management in amateur sports clubs.

H_3 = the managers of the sports club do have education about quality management is an antecedent on the favorable perception towards the practicality of total quality management in amateur sports clubs.

H_{3a} = the managers of the sports club do have education about quality management is not an antecedent on the favorable perception towards the practicality of total quality management in amateur sports clubs.

2.4 Population and Sample

The population of the research is the amateur sports clubs in Turkey. The sample of the research is composed of 123 managers, including 4 female (3,3%) and 119 male (96,7%) volunteers who act as managers in the clubs operating under the Kocaeli Amateur Sports Clubs Federation and voluntarily respond to the questionnaires.

2.5 Data Collection Tool

There are two data collection tools are used in this research. These are;

- Personal information form, is a form which measures participants' age, gender, occupation, duration of being a sports club manager, educational background, sports background (amateur or professional), education about sports management, education about total quality systems.
- Total quality scale is a scale developed by Özdemir (2015) for designating the perception of total quality management in sports clubs. The Cronbach's Alpha is calculated for the reliability of the scale and the Cronbach's Alpha of the scale is founded 0,970, which shows that the scale do have high reliability.

2.6 Data Analysis Technique

SPSS 22.0 is used for analyzing the data collected via the scales of the research. The reliability is measured by calculating Cronbach's Alpha. The descriptive statistics are calculated and the confidence level % 95, the significance level $p<0.05$ is considered during the analysis conducted for the research hypothesis.

2.7 Premises and Restrictions

The premises of the research are;

- Each question answered by the sample group is assumed to reflect its own individual considerations,
- It is assumed that the resources used for the questions in the questionnaire used as data collection tools are sufficient

The restrictions of the research are;

- Research is limited to data collection tools (scales).
- The findings of the research are limited to the population and sample of the research.

3 Findings and Discussion

3.1 Descriptive Statistics of the Sample

Table 1. Descriptive Statistics

	Frequency	Percentage
Gender		
Female	4	3,3
Male	119	96,7
Total	123	100,0
Age		
<18	-	-
19-30	10	8,1
31-42	46	37,4
43-54	37	30,1
55-66	25	20,3
66<	5	4,1
Total	123	100,0
Occupation		
Coach	30	24,4
Sports Manager	1	0,8
Self-Employment	18	14,6
Educator	3	2,4
Officer	13	10,6
Dormitory Manager	1	0,8
Business Manager	1	0,8
Retired	23	18,7
Quality Manager	2	1,6
Artisan	13	10,6
Accountant	3	2,4
Worker	10	8,1
Operating Manufacturer	3	2,4
Certified Public Accountant	1	0,8
Sailor	1	0,8
Total	123	100,0
Educational Background		
Primary School	8	6,5
Secondary School	27	22,0
High School	55	44,7
Associate Degree	7	5,7
Bachelor's Degree	25	20,3
Master's Degree	1	0,8
Total	123	100,0

3.2 Findings about Scale Questions

The table below showing the responses of the amateur sports club managers to their quality systems.

Table 2. Findings about Scale Questions

Questions	Frequency	Percentage
Implementation of strategic planning and goal setting activities in club activities		
Not at all important	9	7,3
Slightly important	1	0,8
Neutral	11	8,9
Important	37	30,1
Extremely Important	65	52,8

Table 2. (continues)

Full and clear definition of the duties, powers and responsibilities of club employees		
Not at all important	8	6,5
Slightly important	2	1,6
Neutral	8	6,5
Important	39	31,7
Extremely Important	66	53,7
Our club has a working environment that is satisfactory and increases productivity		
Not at all important	7	5,7
Slightly important	4	3,3
Neutral	17	13,8
Important	31	25,2
Extremely Important	64	52,0
Supporting the participation of employees in the decision-making process within the limits that our managers require		
Not at all important	7	5,7
Slightly important	4	3,3
Neutral	10	8,1
Important	51	41,5
Extremely Important	51	41,5
Solidarity, cooperation and team spirit among the staff in our club		
Not at all important	8	6,5
Slightly important	2	1,6
Neutral	5	4,1
Important	45	36,6
Extremely Important	63	51,2
To have a competitive environment to enhance performance among employees in our club		
Not at all important	7	5,7
Slightly important	5	4,1
Neutral	23	18,7
Important	46	37,4
Extremely Important	42	34,1
In-service training activities within the club are adequate		
Not at all important	6	4,9
Slightly important	7	5,7
Neutral	13	10,6
Important	53	43,1
Extremely Important	44	35,8
Making our appreciation and rewarding with our clubs objective criteria		
Not at all important	5	4,1
Slightly important	4	3,3
Neutral	17	13,8
Important	40	32,5
Extremely Important	57	46,3
Considering the domain information of the people to be selected for club management		
Not at all important	9	7,3
Slightly important	4	3,3
Neutral	12	9,8
Important	40	32,5

Table 2. (continues)

Extremely Important	58	47,2
Appraisal of the wishes and complaints of employees and supporters in club management		
Not at all important	7	5,7
Slightly important	5	4,1
Neutral	14	11,4
Important	54	43,9
Extremely Important	43	35,0
Having social facilities in our club		
Not at all important	10	8,1
Slightly important	7	5,7
Neutral	13	10,6
Important	22	17,9
Extremely Important	71	57,7
Having a sports consultation center in our club structured		
Not at all important	9	7,3
Slightly important	6	4,9
Neutral	13	10,6
Important	42	34,1
Extremely Important	53	43,1
The volunteer human resources information bank in our club		
Not at all important	9	7,3
Slightly important	9	7,3
Neutral	27	22,0
Important	38	30,9
Extremely Important	39	31,7
Not at all important	1	0,8
Having official internet site		
Not at all important	5	4,1
Slightly important	7	5,7
Neutral	15	12,2
Important	36	29,3
Extremely Important	60	48,8
The club management system includes sports and social work commissions for members outside the management board		
Not at all important	7	5,7
Slightly important	6	4,9
Neutral	12	9,8
Important	52	42,3
Extremely Important	46	37,4
Involving volunteers in management and organizational committees in sportive competitions organized by our club		
Not at all important	6	4,9
Slightly important	6	4,9
Neutral	19	15,4
Important	48	39,0
Extremely Important	44	35,8
Having a knowledge bank where technical and administrative information in our club		
Not at all important	6	4,9
Slightly important	5	4,1
Neutral	15	12,2
Important	46	37,4

Table 2. (continues)

Extremely Important	51	41,5
Providing coordination between departments regarding club activities		
Not at all important	6	4,9
Slightly important	3	2,4
Neutral	20	16,3
Important	45	36,6
Extremely Important	49	39,8
Our club has library and internet service		
Not at all important	7	5,7
Slightly important	6	4,9
Neutral	15	12,2
Important	43	35,0
Extremely Important	52	42,3
Having a sales center / store in our club which sells licensed products of our club		
Not at all important	14	11,4
Slightly important	11	8,9
Neutral	27	22,0
Important	30	24,4
Extremely Important	41	33,3
Having club publications (newspaper, magazine, etc.)		
Not at all important	14	11,4
Slightly important	7	5,7
Neutral	19	15,4
Important	45	36,6
Extremely Important	38	30,9
Revising and updating employees and departments' targets		
Not at all important	9	7,3
Slightly important	3	2,4
Neutral	16	13,0
Important	51	41,5
Extremely Important	44	35,8

It is seen that amateur club managers have positive perceptions of the factors related to the applicability of quality management systems when the responses given in the context of the question asked to measure the perceptions of the quality management processes of the amateur club managers are evaluated. In particular, managers seem to agree that the adoption of total quality understanding at the managerial level and the handling of the quality management system at the strategic level are very important. In this context,

H_1 = the perception towards the practicality of total quality management is favorable in amateur sports clubs.

H_{1a} = the perception towards the practicality of total quality management is not favorable in amateur sports clubs. The H_1 hypothesis is accepted. One of the other hypotheses established within the scope of the research;

H_2 = the managers of the sports club do have sports background is an antecedent on the favorable perception towards the practicality of total quality management in amateur sports clubs.

H_{2a} = the managers of the sports club do have sports background is not an antecedent on the favorable perception towards the practicality of total quality management in amateur sports clubs.

The following research findings are conducted for research hypotheses established to determine whether amateur sports club managers have individual amateur or professional sports backgrounds and if favorable perceptions for the implementation of quality management systems in sports clubs are antecedents.

Table 3. Sports Background – TQM Perception

	Yes		No	
	Mean	#	Mean	#
TQM_1	4,1942	103	4,25	20
TQM_2	4,233	103	4,3	20
TQM_3	4,1359	103	4,2	20
TQM_4	4,068	103	4,25	20
TQM_5	4,2816	103	4,05	20
TQM_6	3,8932	103	3,95	20
TQM_7	4	103	3,95	20
TQM_8	4,1359	103	4,15	20
TQM_9	4,1456	103	3,8	20
TQM_10	3,9903	103	3,95	20
TQM_11	4,1359	103	4	20
TQM_12	4,0097	103	4	20
TQM_13	3,7184	103	3,7895	19
TQM_14	4,1553	103	4	20
TQM_15	4,0388	103	3,85	20
TQM_16	3,9709	103	3,9	20
TQM_17	4,1068	103	3,85	20
TQM_18	4,0388	103	4,05	20
TQM_19	4,0583	103	3,9	20
TQM_20	3,5534	103	3,8	20
TQM_21	3,6699	103	3,85	20
TQM_22	3,9709	103	3,9	20
Mean	4,0229455		3,9881591	

When the perceptions of the quality management systems of the sports club managers who are amateur or professional sports background are evaluated, it is seen that the level of participation of the 20 managers who were not amateur or professional sports history before had an average of 3.99, while the quality of 103 managers who are amateur or professional sports history it is observed that the level of participation of the management systems in the sports clubs is higher by an average of 4.022. In this context, it is important to say that having a sport history is an influential factor in the variability and H_2 hypothesis is accepted.

The research findings about the third hypothesis of the research are shown in the below table.

Table 4. Sports Management Education / TQM Education – TQM Perception

Sports Management Education					TQM Education – TQM Perception				
	Yes		No			Yes		No	
	Mean	#	Mean	#		Mean	#	Mean	#
TQM_1	4,1923	52	4,2113	71	TQM_1	4,1091	55	4,2794	68
TQM_2	4,0962	52	4,3521	71	TQM_2	4,2	55	4,2794	68
TQM_3	4,1731	52	4,1268	71	TQM_3	4,1273	55	4,1618	68
TQM_4	4,0577	52	4,1268	71	TQM_4	4	55	4,1765	68
TQM_5	4,2115	52	4,2676	71	TQM_5	4,1273	55	4,3382	68
TQM_6	3,9231	52	3,8873	71	TQM_6	3,8909	55	3,9118	68
TQM_7	3,9808	52	4	71	TQM_7	3,8727	55	4,0882	68
TQM_8	4,2115	52	4,0845	71	TQM_8	4,1818	55	4,1029	68
TQM_9	4,0192	52	4,1408	71	TQM_9	4,0364	55	4,1324	68
TQM_10	3,9808	52	3,9859	71	TQM_10	4,0545	55	3,9265	68
TQM_11	4,1154	52	4,1127	71	TQM_11	4,1455	55	4,0882	68
TQM_12	4,1154	52	3,9296	71	TQM_12	4,1091	55	3,9265	68

Table 4. (continues)

TQM_13	3,6731	52	3,7714	70	TQM_13	3,7818	55	3,6866	67
TQM_14	4,0962	52	4,1549	71	TQM_14	4,1818	55	4,0882	68
TQM_15	4,0769	52	3,9577	71	TQM_15	4,0182	55	4	68
TQM_16	3,8654	52	4,0282	71	TQM_16	3,8909	55	4,0147	68
TQM_17	4,0385	52	4,0845	71	TQM_17	4,0364	55	4,0882	68
TQM_18	3,9615	52	4,0986	71	TQM_18	4	55	4,0735	68
TQM_19	4	52	4,0563	71	TQM_19	4	55	4,0588	68
TQM_20	3,6731	52	3,5352	71	TQM_20	3,5818	55	3,6029	68
TQM_21	3,6923	52	3,7042	71	TQM_21	3,6182	55	3,7647	68
TQM_22	4	52	3,9296	71	TQM_22	3,9273	55	3,9853	68
Mean	4,007		4,0248182		Mean	3,9950455		4,0352136	

When the perceptions of the sports club administrators participating in the survey were evaluated in terms of their perception of sport management and quality management systems training, there was no significant difference between the averages and the averages of the responses of the two groups appeared to be parallel to each other. In this context H_3 is accepted.

4 Result

In today's global world, the sport industry is considered as one of the most important industries and according to this consideration, it is important for the sports clubs, one of the most important actors in the sport industry, to protect the sustainability and success levels of this industry in terms of the clubs and the continuity of the industry. It is accepted as an important precondition for integrating quality and quality related processes into all processes of sports clubs at the point where successes such as success, profitability and productivity can be realized in this continuity and sports clubs. In other words, it is a must that every sports club that aims to maintain its sustainability within the sport industry and to ensure its profitability within the scope of sport aim and to maintain its assets should integrate continuous understanding of improvement within the club and total quality understanding into its systems. In this context, both the internal customers of the sports clubs, i.e. the employees, will be included in the maximal efficiency and processes, and the demands, needs and expectations of the target groups of the sports clubs addressing the massive target masses will be satisfied to the maximal level. The main argument in this framework is the need for sports clubs to implement quality management systems. Within the scope of the research carried out from this basic argument, a special evaluation was made on amateur sports clubs. The basic approach to evaluation is that the applicability of the quality management system in a sports club is a managerial decision and in this context the importance of the sports club managers is important. At the point of maintaining the quality management system as a strategic managerial approach, it is necessary for the individuals at the management level to make an effective effort to the applicability of the quality management systems and to establish the organization processes to serve the quality approach. In this context, the positive perceptions of the managers of the amateur sports club managers regarding the quality management systems are in parallel with the effective and efficient sustainability of the sports clubs' quality systems. Within the scope of the research, it has been concluded that amateur sports club managers have a positive perception of the implementation of quality management systems in sports clubs. Therefore, in amateur sports clubs it has become possible to establish quality management systems effectively and efficiently, to be sustainable as a strategic management process within the framework of total quality understanding.

References

[1] M.Z. Seraslan, A. Kepeoğlu. *Spor Örgütlerinde Toplam Kalite Yönetimi: Serkep Spor İşletmesi Modeli* (Morpa Kültür Yayınları, İstanbul, 2005).

[2] M. Tekin. *Kalite Güvence ve Standartlar* (Günay Ofset, Konya, 2007).

[3] S. Parlak. *Toplam Kalite Yönetimi ve Kalite Yönetim Sistemi Standartları* (Ekim Basım Yayın Dağıtım, Bura, 2013).

[4] T. Koçel, T. *İşletme Yöneticiliği* (Beta Yayıncılık, İstanbul, 2010).

[5] M. Çoruh. Sağlık Hizmetlerinde Toplam Kalite Yönetimi ve Performans Ölçümü Sempozyumu (1996).

[6] S. Mehra, S. Ranganathan. Int. J. of Qul. And Relb. Mang. **25 (9)** 913-927. (2008).

[7] P.D. Knop, J.V. Hoecke, D. Bosscher. (2004). Sprt. Mang. **7** 67-71. (2004).

Examination of decision-making skill in the context of critical situations

Fatma Nur Aktaş[1*], *Esra Selcen* Yakıcı-Topbaş[1], and *Yüksel* Dede[1]

[1]Gazi University, Faculty of Education, Departmen of Mathematics Education, Ankara, Turkey

Abstract. A teacher, who has a major role in the formation of class culture, needs to have proficiencies to design effective learning environments. The reflection of these proficiencies on classroom practices takes place via the decisions taken under critical situations. This study aims to find out the components underlying teachers' decision-making. Participants of the study which was designed as a case study were elementary school mathematics teachers. The study was carried out through the individual interviews with participants about the decision making under critical situations after analysing participant teachers' course observations which were video-recorded by the researchers. Data obtained from the interviews were analysed through content-analysis method. Based on the findings, it was found that teachers' professional proficiencies could be presented in the same frame with the variables reflected on decision making.

1 Introduction

Teacher proficiencies are important in designing effective learning environments in the class in which many dependent or independent conditions occur at the same time. In these critical situations, the teacher who has one of the most important roles in the class is notable for his decision making. When we examine the conceptual framework of the components that influence the decision-making process, which can be defined as the sum of the physical and cognitive efforts in the selection and preference of various conditions, it is seen that the variables affecting this process are quite diverse: teaching situations, goals, learning outcomes, experience, awareness, beliefs and values. Students, expressions of the students and their thinking are important elements that should be taken into consideration in classroom practices by the teacher who is an actor in the class. These elements, in which teachers display their skills and proficiencies are crucial situations necessitate important decision making. Therefore, it is important to identify the elements underlying the decision-making mechanisms of the teachers to whom we cast a significant role in designing effective learning environments or the variables reflected on this process.

Classroom environment as the complex structure of historical, social and cultural influences, which are classroom discussions, small group works, problem solving activities, researches and skills of carrying out similar activites of a teacher are limited as explicit or

[*] Corresponding author: fnuraktas@gmail.com

implicit by classroom atmosphere, [5]. All variables occurring during the classroom practices such as socio-cultural interactions affected as socially or personally, grade, gender, ethniticity, teacher-student interactions influence classroom culture. In mathematics as a discipline among those variables reflecting on classroom practices, it is possible to mention about the affective factors of teachers together with the cognitive factors [2,6]. McClain [8] exemplifies the classroom practices and mathematical ideas in mathematics class with activities such as reasoning, discussing and symbolising. In mathematics teaching process, it is possible to mention about classroom practices such as placing different problem solving strategies and discussions, having students work in groups, selecting problem solving method.

The skills that teachers need to own to make decisions so as to respond to the growing needs of their students also increase. Partnership21 (2015) categorized the learner skills as shown in Table 1. Those skills take place as lifesaving skills in 21st century in literature.

Table 1. 21st century skills

Learning and innovation skills	Life and career skills	Information, media and technology skills
critical thinking and problem solving	flexibility & adaptability	information literacy
creativity and innovation	Initiative & self-direction	media literacy
communication and collaboration	social & cross-cultural skills	ICT (information, communications & technology) literacy
	leadership & responsibility	

These skills have importance in terms of teachers' both individual and professional development as educators in addition to being a requisite by the students. When teacher professional proficiencies which were revised by Ministry of National Education are taken into consideration, it is seen that professional knowledge (pedagogical content knowledge, knowledge of legislation) and skills (educational planning, creating learning environments, management of teaching and learning, assessment and evaluation) are associated with attitude and values as in Table 2 below to 21st century skills.

Table 2. Teacher proficiencies and 21st century skills

21st century skills	Teacher proficiencies
creativity	educational planning
critical thinking	educational planning
	management of teaching and learning process
	measurement and evaluation
communication & collaboration	educational planning
	creating learning and teaching environments
	management of teaching and learning process
information, media and technology literacy	knowledge of legislation
	knwoledge of pedagogy
flexibility & adaptability	creating learning and teaching environments
	educational planning
	management of teaching and learning process
social & cross cultural skills	educational planning
	creating learning and teaching environments

Based on this view, it can be said that the educational requirements of modern days, the new meanings of education and teaching attributed to teachers, the differentiating needs of the students, new approaches on the education of the individuals lay new responsibilities on the teachers regarding their professional dimension. In this context, teaching is regarded as a profession that requires high qualifications that can completely bear the responsibility of human life. It is inevitable to say that when the reflection of such skills and proficiencies on classroom practices is examined, the teacher plays the decision-making mechanism role in role in the classroom. Decision-making as a skill and decision-making process need to be evaluated and explained as teacher-centered in the context of classroom practice.

1.1 Teacher and Decision Making

The teacher, like an actor, plays a role for which s/he is expected to make and maintain the necessary arrangements according to the content of the subject. This role of the teacher is to organize the learning environment according to the objectives of the teaching. The situations that the teacher should make a decision can be taken in a broad perspective as all critical situations of classroom practice, culture and interaction.

The Turkish Language Association [16] defines "decision-making" compound word as "finalizing a problem to a decision, determining". However, Kuzgun [7] takes the decision making as a behaviour when there are more than two ways taking to an object, a person, a situation etc. thought to meet the need, or to determine whether these are adequate to satisfy the need intended to reach. In the widest sense, it is the sum of physical and mental efforts related to making a choice and a preference among various situations, [15].

Teachers often have to make decisions in teaching environments to design, implement, maintain, complete, and evaluate classroom practices, and to determine about the probable situations or problems in these processes. Because of this reason, decision making is one of the most fundamental aspects of the teaching process, and the more information about how the teachers make decisions is obtained, the more prediction about how to make their teaching can be done [1]. Thus, it is important that mathematics teachers have the ability to make decisions besides the mathematical knowledge necessary for teaching mathematics in order to enhance mathematical thinking of the students and maintaining this capability. Therefore, decision-making skill is a skill including the pre-inclass interaction, in the moment-course of interaction and post-class interaction. Teacher decisions are not only about inclass behaviors, but they also involve the beginning and the end of the classes.

Simon deals with decision-making process in three basic stages:

• gathering information: identifying situations that need to be decided;
• planning: finding possible styles of action and
• making choice: a choice among the styles of action, [14].

By following these steps and passing through the decision-making filter, the teacher's decisions emerge in classroom practices, and this process is called the teacher's strategy by [1]. Bishop and Whitfield [3] demonstrate the teacher's decision-making filters and interpretations of decision making in the frame of Figure 1.

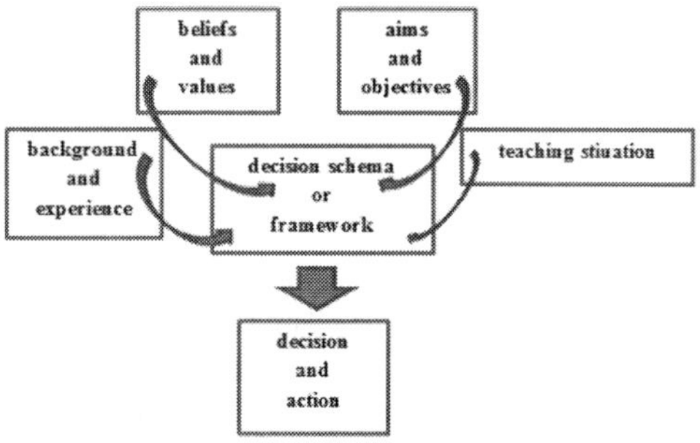

Fig. 1. Bishop and Whitfield, the framework of teacher' decision-making ([3], p.6)

Munby [11], on the other hand, dealt with teacher decisions based on student thinking in the context of teacher decision-making. Here, situations that need to be decided rather than the decision of the teacher is focused. For example, he provided a broad framework covering outputs such as pre-requisites (student information, school environment etc.), personality of teacher (belief etc.), cognitive processes (such as information and goals), planning of teaching and interaction with the student. In other words, Munby [11] presented an overview of the teacher's thinking, decision-making and practice field. As can be seen, there are researches revealing and examining the decision-making ability as well as the variables reflected in the teacher's decision-making process.

In this research, it is aimed to examine and determine the situation of the critical situations in which teacher has to make decision and that occur in the classroom environment, the variables influencing these critical situations and what the decisions taken are. Thus, it will be possible to obtain a broad perspective on teacher decision-making processes. The emphasis on the importance of decision making skill under all possible components when examining teacher proficiencies and indicators of those proficiencies. At the end of our research, it is aimed to establish a framework for effective decision making as a teacher proficiency.

2 Method

The participants of this research, which was designed in a multiple-case study design of the qualitative research designs, were three mathematics teachers with differentiating seniority (years). Participants determined based on volunteer basis with easily accessible sampling of purposeful sampling methods work in two state secondary schools located at the same socioeconomic level. In the literature, it is emphasized that in elementary school classrooms, there are a lot of student-student and student-teacher interaction and that the situations in which the teacher needs to pay much more attention and make decision how to behave is often encountered in comparison to the level of secondary school education [4,12,13]. For this reason, teachers instructing 7th grade mathematics courses that include outcomes of algebraic, analytical, and geometric thinking coexisted, and thus providing opportunities for different student thinking, were included in the research.

Westerman [17] identified significant differences between the decision-making processes of a expert and novice teacher. One of the most notable of them was an experienced teacher gave feedback by taking student needs into consideration while novice teacher ignored those variables or didn't take into account. Considering this framework, participants were chosen by varying in their seniority years, as shown in Table 3.

Table 3. Participant information

Teacher	Gender	Seniority (year)	Graduated faculty
T1	female	1	department of secondary school mathematics teaching
T2	male	14	department of elementary & secondary school mathematics teaching
T3	male	41	institute of mathematics education

Data collection instruments were video recordings taken during classes (4 hours of consecutive lesson), observation notes and semi-structured individual interviews during instruction.

Firstly, the lessons designed by teachers for the outcomes (polygons and transformation geometry) in different sub-learning areas were recorded in video recording. In the video recordings analyzed by the researchers, situations where participants make decisions or require decision making. These specific phenomena were defined as critical situations in our study. In other words, these critical situations in our research were the phenomena that we observed based on specific situations, such as giving a right to speak, feedback, comprehension, or focus on the student, either directly or through a teacher interview. In individual interviews, the critical situations determined for each participant's own lectures were inquired by the participant. The interview sessions lasted about 6 hours in total with each teacher in 3 sessions. The findings obtained from these interviews and the variables reflecting the decision-making process in critical situations were identified. Through the individual interviews, the variables identified by the researchers were both confirmed by the teachers and underlying variables of the decisions were determined. The obtained data were analyzed by content analysis, [9]. The analysis unit of the study were the variables underlying decision making with teacher opinions based on the critical situation and their decision making. Indicators of critical situations and the components underlying decision making were identified by researchers in consensus, [10].

3 Findings and Conclusion

The findings of the teachers' decision-making processes about critical situations, the reasons for the decisions and the variables influencing the decision making and the findings from the course records were presented to describe the analysis process in order to facilitate the interpretation of the results.

A part of T2 from the praticipants for reviewing with the students of the previous lesson is given:

T2: What is polygon? Who will explain it to us?

Only three students raise their fingers. The teacher does not wait the other students to raise their fingers.

T2: Friends! Listen, then we'll go on. Görkem[†]*, can you explain?*

Görkem: The shape that has at least three sides and a corner.

T2: Yes. [...]

The critical situation here is why T2 didn't wait for the others and why he gave the right to speak to Görkem. The reason why T2 chooses Görkem can be indicated as the factor influencing his decision-making process. When T2 had the classroom application watched in the interview, he explained his reasons to make this decision with the following statements.

T2: Görkem is a passive student. But, she is successful and also smart. When I ask her a question or want her to summarize, she both feels self-confident and I take her attention to the class. Görkem is a kid requiring attention. I want every student speak and be active in the class. Sometimes, I try to encourage them to participate in discussions as well.

Here there are two notable reasons of T2's decision making. While, at first, the reason for choosing Görkem openly is to take the student's self-confidence and motivation into account, the emphasis on the importance given to the freedom of expression of students takes place implicitly.

It is observed that the variables influencing the decision making skill of T3 in a noticeable situation in the video recording of the lesson are to provide active participation

[†] Student names used in this chapter are all nicknames

of the students in the class and to give equality of opportunity to the students at different levels.

T3 divides the board into four and have students write different questions at the same time.

When T3's opinion on this situation was taken about this situation, he presented the following explanation.

T3: There is a student who is very fast, that is, the student who makes the question very quickly, I divide the board in order to give time for them to do other questions. [...]

Class culture, the relationship between student and teacher, and school culture are important variables playing role on teacher decisions and classroom practices. One of our participants, T1, is an inclusive class teacher. The interaction of the inclusive student and inclusive student with teacher and other students creates critical situations for the teacher decision-making process. Below, it is seen that the variables reflected in T1's decision to classroom practices are found implicitly in the interviews, even if not in the course video-records.

T1 draws various polygons with the help of GeoGebra. Ekrem (inclusive student) starts to laugh. T1 turns and looks at Ekrem. While T1 was explaining the examples, Ekrem brings his notebook and shows it to his teacher.

T1: Good. Do you want to wash your face?

Ekrem goes out of class.

Ekrem: You've kicked me out of it, have not you? (Crying)

T1: No, I've asked you to wash your face.

Ekrem closes the door. T1 continues to explain the examples. T1 finishes explaining the problem. Then, T1 opens the door and has look at Ekrem. Ekrem and the training coach have been waiting in front of the door.

T1: I wanted him to wash his face.

Ekrem and the training coach go to the lavatory. T1 goes on his class.

In this video recording of the course, that T1 asked Ekrem a question, the question she asked, her focusing preliminary on the problem which she was explaining, and then, opening the door and controlling Ekrem all generate critical situations. Out of those critical situations, T1's focusing on classroom practice and then decision of paying attention to Ekrem emerged in the interview.

T1: The training coach will ask me whether I kicked him out of the class or not. He is asking me if I have taken him out of class. Training coach is always interested in Ekrem. This is very good for us. Because, someone constantly has to take care of him.

Thus, it can be said that T1 has a priority order of the variables focused depending on the situation. Here, training coach is a variable influencing the order of the situatons of the teacher.

It is possible to interpret the results in the light of the findings and to categorize the variables that influencing teacher decision making processes. The most notable result of our research is that the teacher's decisions change depending on the situation. The teacher needs to be interested in many situations at the same time and to decide to respond (or ignore) to these situations. Therefore, it is necessary to put these critical situations in order of priority and to choose important ones.

In this case, there are variables reflected on the teacher's decision. In Figure 2, there are categories from the findings of the decision making of the teachers.

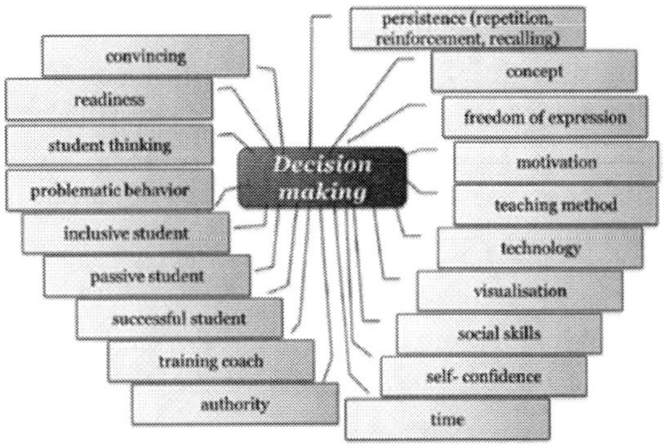

Fig. 2. Variables reflecting on decision making

When the obtained categories were analysed, it is possible to sum all under themes such as student knowledge (student thinking, readiness, passive-active student, inclusive student etc), content knowledge and pedagogical content knowledge (concept and teaching methods etc) creating learning environment (visualisation and freedom of expression etc), planning of education and training as teacher proficiencies. We can say that decision making skill reflects on each dimension of teacher proficiency. In other words, it is a significant result to deal decision-making skills within teacher proficiencies. It is therefore important to develop decision-making skills to train qualified teachers and to develop them as professional teachers. Thus, it may be recommended that the ability to make decision as a teacher professional proficiency is to be included in the literature.

The study finding out the result that novice teachers unlike from the experienced ones teach by not taking the needs of student needs into account differs from the inexperienced teacher of this current study [17]. This complies with the result setting forth that there are many factors playing role on the teacher's decision making. That is to say, interpretation of the decision making skill is not sufficient enough based on only seniority year and experience. With this result, many teacher proficiencies are emphasized together.

This research on critical situations reveals that the teacher's decision making skill can take form based on the specific situation as well as the reflection of the related variables. In short, as the decisions taken may change, underlying reason of the decision may also change. Thus, we can say that decision making is a changing skill depending on the situation. Based on this conclusion, organizing situation-specific activites to have teachers and pre-service teachers gain and develop decision making skill and analysing the videos of their own courses or different course videos having critical situations can be recommended as a proposal for teacher training and in-service teacher training.

It was found that while some of the decisions of teachers in various situations within the classroom environment were clearly observed, in some cases their decisions were implicit. This is why it is useful to support this process of identifying, reasoning or developing decision-making skills with observations of behaviors involving classroom interactions, as well as interviews reinforced by participant confirmation. Additionally, a comprehensive investigation of the variables underlying teacher decision-making skills with teachers with long-term and different qualifications (seniority, school level, class level, etc.) can be presented as a proposal for further studies.

This paper was presented as an oral presentation at ERPA International Congresses on Education 2018 congress.

References

1. Bishop, A. J., Teacher Decision Making. *Critical Issues in Mathematics Education* (Edt.Clarkson, P., Presmeg, N.), Springer, (2008).
2. Bishop, A. J., FitzSimons, G., Seah, W. T. & Clarkson, P., Values in mathematics education: Making values teaching explicit in the mahematics classroom. Paper presented at the combined Annual Meeting of the Australian Association for Research in Education and the New Zealand Association for Research in Education. Melbourne, Australia, (1999, November).
3. Bishop, A. J., & Whitfield, R. C., Situations in teaching. McGraw-Hill, (1972).
4. Chapman, O. (2017). Understanding elementary school teachers of mathematics. Journal of Mathematics Teacher Education, 20(3), 203-205.
5. FitzSimons, G., Seah, W., Bishop, A.J. & Clarkson, P. (2000). Conceptions of values and mathematics education held by Australian primary teachers: Preliminary findings from VAMP. Proceedings of the History and Pedagogy of Mathematics Conference, National Taiwan Normal University, Taipei. http :// www. education. monash. edu. au/ projects / vamp / hpm2000c. pdf (November 2012).
6. Handal, B., Teachers' mathematical beliefs: A review. The Mathematics Educator, 13(2), 47-57, (2003).
7. Kuzgun, Y., Meslek Gelişimi ve Danışmanlığı (2. Baskı). Ankara: Nobel Yayın Dağıtım, (2006).
8. McClain, K., A methodology of classroom teaching experiments. Researching Mathematics Classrooms: A Critical Examination of Methodology. Edt: Googchild, S. ve English, L. USA: Information Age Publishing, (2005).
9. Merriam, S. B., Qualitative Research: Designing, Implementing, and Publishing a Study. In Handbook of Research on Scholarly Publishing and Research Methods (pp. 125-140). IGI Global, (2015).
10. Miles, M. B., Huberman, A. M., Huberman, M. A., & Huberman, M., Qualitative data analysis: An expanded sourcebook. sage. (1994).
11. Munby, H., The place of teachers' beliefs in research on teacher thinking and decision making, and an alternative methodology. Instructional science, 11(3), 201-225, (1982).
12. Öztürk, B., Sınıf içi etkileşim. Kuram ve Uygulamada Egitim Yönetimi Dergisi, 6(4), pp. 621-640, (2000).
13. Rowland, T., Huckstep, P., & Thwaites, A., Elementary teachers' mathematics subject knowledge: The knowledge quartet and the case of Naomi. Journal of Mathematics Teacher Education, 8, 255–281, (2005).
14. Simon, H. A., Yönetimde yeni karar verme bilimi, Amme İdare Dergisi, 7(3). Translate: Mustafa Tosun, (1970).
15. Taşçı, Ö., İlköğretim Öğretmenlerinin Okul Yöneticilerinin Karar Verme Sürecindeki Etkilerine İlişkin Algıları İle Örgütsel Adanmışlıkları Arasındaki İlişki. Master Thesis, Yeditepe University, Institute of Social Science, İstanbul, (2011).
16. Türk Dil Kurumu [TDK]. Türkçe sözlük (9. bs). Ankara, (1998).
17. Westerman, D. A., Expert and novice teacher decision making. Journal of teacher education, 42(4), 292-305, (1991).

Examination of the preservice chemistry teachers' understanding of periodic table concepts

Şenol Şen[1,*]

[1]Hacettepe University, Faculty of Education, 06800, Beytepe, Ankara, Turkey

Abstract. The purpose of this study was to examine the preservice chemistry teachers' understanding of periodic table concepts and some atomic properties. The study group of this study was comprised of 17 preservice chemistry teachers who were undergraduate students at a public University. The preservice teachers' ages are between 19 and 26, and the mean is 21.12 (SD=1.83). In addition, the 14 of the preservice teachers are female and three are male. In the study, concept maps and lotus blossom technique were used as data collection tools in order to determine the understanding of preservice chemistry teachers about the periodic table concepts. Data obtained through these techniques was analysed to figure out the useful of these assessment tools. The results of the analysis indicated that preservice teachers have limited understanding of the periodic table and its properties. In addition, at the end of the study, it was determined that they have many misunderstanding.

1 Introduction

Studies on chemistry education aim to reveal the way students learn and construct the concepts of chemistry, their applications and thinking styles; the difficulties they have in learning processes and the problems they encounter. In addition to that, developing effective approaches of teaching to cope with the difficulties in the learning process is also among the areas of research for chemistry education researchers [1] Most of the research on chemistry education available in the literature focusses on the way students understand the concepts of chemistry [2, 3]. A review of those studies has made it clear that many students have misconceptions in this respect [4, 5, 6]. Periodic table, one of the basic subjects of chemistry, plays important roles in understanding chemical elements [7]. Several studies have emphasized the importance of periodic table [7, 8, 9, 10].

Periodic table is a cornerstone in learning chemistry and it is an instrument helping to organise whole chemistry [11]. It would be more rational to know the typical members of the eight main groups and their properties instead of learning the properties of more than one hundred elements in the periodic table separately. For instance, students who know the properties of noble gases, transition metals and of rare earth elements can make guesses

* Corresponding author: schenolschen@gmail.com

about such physical and chemical properties of the elements in those groups as melting point, freezing point and electron configuration [11].

1.1 Purpose of the study

The main objective of studies concerning science education is to improve science teaching and learning. Chemistry teachers, who are to benefit from research results, can learn about the difficulties students have in understanding the concepts of chemistry. One of the concepts students mostly learn incorrectly and generally try to memorize is periodic table. However, the periodic table has an important and central role in understanding of chemical and physical properties of chemical elements. It was initially a list of elements consisting of increasing atomic masses. However, in time, it became a complex table of many different chemical and physical properties of the elements (such as melting point, boiling point, chemical bonding, atomic radius, ionization energy, intermolecular forces isotopes and allotropes). For this reason, it is expected that there will be difficulties in understanding of these concepts [10]. Some studies available in the literature report that the main problem students trying to learn chemistry have is students' failure to learn the basic concepts [12, 13, 14]. From this point on, the purpose of this study is to examine the preservice chemistry teachers' understanding of periodic table concepts and some atomic properties. Besides, standardized tests are limited in revealing students' understanding due to the complex nature of knowledge structure in chemistry [15]. Therefore, concept maps and lotus blossom technique have been used in determining pre-service teachers' understanding of periodic table.

2 Method

This study uses case study, which is one of qualitative study methods. In a case study, efforts are made to suggest results related to a certain case. Here, a case or several cases are investigated in-depth and factors related to the case (such as the setting, persons, event) are analysed in a holistic approach. Additionally, research on how the factors influence the case and how they are influenced by the case is also performed [16].

2.1 Process

Before the data collection process, preservice teachers were informed about the concept map and lotus blossom technique. The end of the term, preservice chemistry teachers were requested to construct their own concept maps related to these concepts such as periodic table, group, period, elements, atomic numbers, metals, non-metals, noble gases, atomic radius, ionization energy, electron affinity. In this way, the interrelationships among these concepts were determined. At the same time, the preservice teachers prepared their lotus blossoms.

2.2 Study group

The study group of this study was comprised of 17 preservice chemistry teachers who are undergraduate students at the Department of Mathematics and Science Education of a public University in the spring term of 2017-2018 academic year. The preservice teachers' ages are between 19 and 26, and the mean is 21.12 the standard deviation is 1.83. In addition, the 14 of the preservice teachers are female and three are male (Table 1). The study is conducted in a Chemistry course that included the concepts related to periodic table and properties of elements in periodic table.

Table 1. Preservice chemistry teachers' characteristics

Variables	f		
Age	19-26 (Mean= 21.12, SD= 1.83)		
Gender	**Female**		**Male**
	14		3
Grade point average	**Female**		**Male**
	2.66		1.97
	2.54 (SD=.56) (Overall)		
Class	**2nd**	**3rd**	**4th**
	14	2	1

2.3 Data collection tools

In the study, concept maps and lotus blossom technique were used as data collection tools in order to determine the understanding of preservice chemistry teachers about periodic table. Concept maps were developed by Novak et al on the basis of Ausubel's "meaningful learning" [17]. Concept maps are pictures showing how an individual associates the key concepts related to a subject in his mind [18]. They can be used as an effective instrument to uncover learners' conceptual frameworks [19]. In this study, the method of concept mapping from scratch is used. The concept maps can use to as an assessment tool as an instructional tool to support learning [17]. However, in this study they were used to assess the preservice teachers' understanding and misunderstanding. Concept maps are the knowledge representation tools that generate new ideas, organize and represent the knowledge structures. Furthermore, they show that how learners integrate new knowledge into pre-existing knowledge and how relate al concepts in their minds.

The second data collection tool of this study is lotus blossom technique. Lotus Blossom Technique was produced from creative techniques developed in Japan [20]. The technique is based on the use of analytic skills and it helps to generate ideas to offer the best possible solution to the problem, which is considered. In the centre of lotus blossom diagram, there is a main (central) concept that was written by the researcher. There are eight boxes around the main concept, and each eight boxes have further eight different boxes. Firstly, students are asked to fill out the eight boxes around the main concept and then the other eight boxes of the each of eight boxes (Figure 1). After students write down 8 different thoughts or concepts about the central concept, they write down 8 new concepts again associated with those 8 concepts. They can also draw shapes or write down analogies, descriptions, explanations or examples instead of concepts. The central topic (theme) is divided into pieces and new ideas are generated to perform analyses in this technique [21].

a1	a2	a3	b1	b2	b3	c1	c2	c3
a8	A	a4	b8	B	b4	c8	C	c4
a7	a6	a5	b7	b6	b5	c7	c6	c5
h1	h2	h3	A	B	C	d1	d2	d3
h8	H	h4	H	M	D	d8	D	d4
h7	h6	h5	G	F	E	d7	d6	d5
g1	g2	g3	f1	f2	f3	e1	e2	e3
g8	G	g4	f8	F	f4	e8	E	e4
g7	g6	g5	f7	f6	f5	e7	e6	e5

M: Main (central) concept

Fig. 1. The overall sheet of lotus blossom technique.

2.4 Data analysis

The data collected through concepts maps and lotus blossom technique was put to content analysis. The concepts related to periodic table were determined in lotus blossom technique and thus the themes for the concepts were distinguished. The themes and concepts were tabulated. External auditor was consulted for help during the analyses, and the concepts and themes were analysed together.

Concept maps prepared by the pre-service teachers were also evaluated through holistic scoring- one of concept map scoring methods [22]. Then, the incomplete incorrect parts and errors appearing in students' proposals were detected. Member checking was made for the proposals determined by the researcher. Pre-service teachers' incomplete or incorrect concepts were determined in this way, and they were tabulated.

3 Findings

Concept maps and lotus blossom technique were used as the tools of data collection in determining pre-service teachers' understanding of periodic table concepts. The data collected through both instruments were analyzed by the researcher with the help of an external auditor and with exchange of views. While the data collected through lotus blossom technique indicated pre-service teachers' knowledge of periodic table, the data collected through concept maps demonstrated pre-service teachers' misconceptions. Lotus blossoms filled by the pre-service teachers were examined and the concepts most commonly used by the participants were shown in tables. The concepts they had determined for eight categories and the concepts they later used for the eight concepts were determined. As is clear from Table 2, the categories were divided into six subcategories as metals, nonmetals, noble gases, group and period. Six concepts were determined as the cut off point for the first eight concepts around the central concept and five concepts were determined as the cut off point for the concepts around eight concepts. Pre-service teachers wrote down other concepts in addition to such concepts as atom, atomic number, transition elements/ Group B elements, block, alkali metals, acids/bases, electronegativity, halogens, chemistry, chemical bonds, etc. for the eight central concepts as seen in the Table 2.

Table 2. Pre-service teachers' concepts about periodic table according to lotus blossom technique

Central 8 Concepts	f	Other Concepts	f	Central 8 Concepts	f	Other Concepts	f
Metal	16	Alloying	6	Noble Gases	14	8A	6
		Alkali Metal	5			Atomic structure	10
		Basic Oxide	5			Chemical inertness/ inability to form chemical compounds	7
		Conductors of heat and electricity	11			Low boiling and melting points	5
		Cation	6			Gas	6
		Lustrous (shiny)	10			Electron configurations are very difficult to alter	11
		Malleable and ductile	9			Oktet	5
		The Alkaline Earth Metal	5			Nonreactive	8
Nonmetal	15	Anion	6	Group	13	Alkali Metal	8
		Nonconductors of heat and electricity	7			Atomic radius	6
		The most negative electron affinities	7			The number of Valence electron	6
		Ionic Bond	6			Noble Gases	7

		Solid, liquid, or gas,	5			The Alkaline Earth Metal	9
		Brittle	5			Atomic radius	9
		Covalent Bond	11			Atomic number	7
		Not lustrous (dull appearance)	10	**Period**	9	Electron affinity	6
		Molecular structure	6			Ionization energy	5
		Atomic Structure	5			Horizontal rows	5
		Same Type Atom	11			Orbital	5
Element	15	Metal	7				
		Molecular structure	8				
		Pure substance	9				
		Chemical symbol	8				

The proposals available in the concept maps prepared by the pre-service teachers were examined one by one and they are shown in Table 3. Thus, attempts were made to reveal the incomplete or incorrect concepts that the preservice teachers had.

Table 3. Incorrect or incomplete proposals available in pre-service teachers' concept maps

Proposition	f
Of group elements, atomic radius increases from top to bottom.	16
As moving from the left to the right along a period, atomic radius becomes smaller.	17
Ionization energy increases from the left to the right in the same period.	13
Ionization energy diminishes from top to bottom in the same group.	13
Electron affinity increases from the left to the right in the same period.	14
Electron affinity diminishes from top to bottom in the same group.	14
Melting point rises as moving from the left to the right along a period.	12
Electronegativity increases as atomic number increases.	3

4 Conclusion and Discussion

This study aimed to determine pre-service teachers' understanding of periodic table. For this purpose, 17 pre-service chemistry teachers attending a public university in Turkey were included in the research. Concept maps and lotus blossom technique were used as the tools of data collection so as to determine pre-service teachers' understanding of periodic table concepts. Lotus blossom technique was used rather in determining pre-service teachers' concepts about periodic table. Concept maps, on the other hand, were used in member checking in terms of pre-service teachers' incorrect or incomplete concepts.

On examining lotus blossoms prepared by pre-service teachers, it was found that the concepts most frequently written by pre-service teachers for the eight concepts in relation to the central concept were divided into six groups- namely, metals, non-metals, noble gases, group and period. An examination of the pre-service teachers' lotus blossoms demonstrated that pre-service teachers had misunderstandings. Since some of the concepts could be included due to the fact that cut off point was five and above, many incorrect concepts were not included in Table 2. Yet, the majority of the pre-service teachers said that noble gases could not form compounds, as seen in Table 2. However, it is known that some of the noble gases form compounds.

A large portion of the participants stated that atomic radius would increase as moving from top to bottom within a group. Although this knowledge is generally consistent with group members having small atomic numbers, it is not a really consistent proposal for group members having big atomic numbers. Increase in atomic radius is very little in bigger atoms. This is because inner-shell electrons in d and f orbitals in atoms with big atomic numbers are screened less than the outer-shell electrons when compared to d and f orbitals [23].

Another proposal made by the pre-service teachers was that atomic radius became smaller as moving from the left to the right along a period. However, this change in atomic radius is not very correct for transition elements because the radius of transition elements remain constant along a period- apart from a few deviations. In transition elements along a period, each electron added enters inner electron shell and is involved in screening outer-shell electrons against nucleus load [23].

The propositions saying, "ionization energy (IE) increases as moving from the left to the right in the same period" and "ionization energy (IE) diminishes from the top to the bottom in the same group" were detected in the concept maps. However, $IE1 < IE2 < IE3 < IE4 < IE6 < IE5 < IE7 < IE8$ relation is available between A group elements in the same period for the first ionization energies [23, 24]. Some of the pre-service teachers associated electronegativity with atomic number. Accordingly, they believed that electronegativity increased in parallel to the increase in atomic number. Electronegativity can be defined as an atom's ability to attract electrons from other atoms on which it is dependent. Thus, although fluorine's atomic number is not very big, it is the atom with the biggest electronegativity.

The participants did not include the proposals saying "electron affinity increases as moving from the left to the right in the same period" and "electron affinity diminishes as moving from top to bottom in the same group" in their concept maps. Electron affinity can be defined as enthalpy change during electron gain of an atom, which is in gas state. The pre-service teachers did not, for instance, say that some atoms such as noble gases did not tend to gain electrons. Although electron affinity diminishes as moving from top to bottom in the same group, the situation is different for the second period elements (for N, O and F) available in 5A, 6A and 7A groups. The electron affinity of the N, O and F elements which are in the second period is smaller than the one of P, S and Cl elements in the third period [23, 24].

It was found that the pre-service teachers had the knowledge "melting point rises as moving from the left to the right along a period". Although the knowledge seems to be correct, it may not be said to be certainly correct. The pre-service teachers were found not to be aware of the fact that Si element in the third period had the highest melting point [23].

Consequently, in the present study, the concept maps and lotus blossoms technique were used as qualitative assessment tools of preservice teachers' understanding of some of the fundamental concepts of periodic table. Data obtained through these techniques was analysed to figure out the useful of these assessment tools. The results of the analysis indicated that preservice teachers have limited understanding of the periodic table and its properties. In addition, at the end of the study, it was determined that they have many misunderstanding. It was found that the pre-service teachers preferred memorizing the concepts related to periodic table. They said that a property would certainly increase or decrease as moving from top to bottom in a group and as moving from left to right in a period. It was also found in consequence of member checking that the pre-service teachers were not aware of exceptions and that they were not knowledgeable about this. Therefore, learners can probably learn some of the concepts by memorizing. Nevertheless, what is important is to determine whether they have learnt in depth. Thus, it would be beneficial to use differing techniques as instruments of measurement and evaluation. Concept maps and lotus blossom technique can be alternative instruments for measurement and evaluation.

References

1. H. Tümay, Sci. Educ., **25**, 21 (2016).
2. K. C. Trundle, R. K. Atwood, J. E. Christopher, Res. Sci. Teach, **39**, 633 (2002).
3. M. Çalık, A. Ayas, J. Res. Sci. Teach., **42**, 638 (2005).
4. R. Driver, J. Easley, Stud. Sci. Educ., **5**, 61 (1978).
5. P. J. Garnett, D. F. J. Treagust, Res. Sci. Teach., **29**, 121 (1992).
6. M. B. Nakhleh, J. Chem. Educ, **69**, 191, (1992).
7. A. Brito, M.A. Rodríguez, M. Niaz, J. Res. Sci. Teach., **42**, 84 (2005).
8. J. L. Marshall, J. Chem. Educ, **77**, 979 (2000).
9. M. Niaz, M. Luiggi, *Facilitating conceptual change in students' conceptual understanding of the periodic table*. (Dordrecht: Springer, 2014).
10. H. J. Schmidt, T. Baumgärtner, H. J. Eybe, J. Res. Sci. Teach, **40**, 257 (2003).
11. H. Demircioğlu, G. Demircioğlu, M. Çalık, Chem. Educ. Res. Pract, **10**, 241 (2009).
12. M. M. Cooper, N. Grove, S. M. Underwood, M. W. Klymkowsky, J. Chem. Educ., **87**, 869 (2010).
13. N. L. Burrows, S. R. Mooring, Chem. Educ. Res. Pract, **16**, 5 (2015).
14. A. K. Griffiths A. K. A critical analysis and synthesis of research on students' chemistry misconceptions, in Schmidt, H. J. (ed.), *Proceedings of the 1994 international symposium problem solving and misconceptions in chemistry and physics*, ICASE (International Council of Associations for Science Education), 70 (1994).
15. K. S. Taber, *Chemical misconceptions: Prevention, diagnosis and cure* (Vol. I). (London: Royal Society of Chemistry, 2002).
16. A. Yıldırım, H. Şimşek, *Sosyal Bilimlerde Nitel Araştırma Yöntemleri (8. Basım) [Qualitative Research Methods in Social Sciences (8th Ed.)] (Ankara: Seçkin Yayıncılık, 2011).*
17. J. D. Novak, D. B. Gowin, *Learning how to learn*. (New York: Cambridge University Press 1984).
18. M. A. Ruiz-Primo, S. E. Schultz, M. Li, R. J. Shavelson, J. Res. Sci. Teach, **38**, 260 (2001).
19. J. J. Mintzes, J. H. Wandersee, J. D. Novak, *Assessing science understanding: A human constructivist view*. (San Diego, CA: Academic 2000).
20. T. L. Shen, J. C. Lai, EURASIA J. Math., Sci Tech. Ed, **14**, 1509 (2018).
21. Ş. Şen, A. Yılmaz, NFE-EJSME, **7**, 144 (2013).
22. J. R. McClure, B. Sonak, H. K. J. Suen, .J. Res. Sci. Teach.,**36**, 475 (1999).
23. R. H. Petrucci, F. G. Herring, J. D. Madura, C. Bissonnette, *General Chemistry: Principles and Modern Applications* (10th ed.). (Toronto: Pearson Canada Inc, 2011).
24. R. Chang, K. A. Goldsby, *Chemistry* (12th Ed.). (New York, McGraw-Hill Education, 2016).

Prospective chemistry teachers' cognitive structures about the concept of globalization

Şenol Şen[1*], *Sinem* Dinçol Özgür[1], and *Senar* Temel[1]

[1]Hacettepe University, Beytepe, Ankara, 06800, Turkey

Abstract. This study aims to determine prospective chemistry teachers' cognitive structures about the concept of globalization. The study employs case study- one of qualitative research methods. 20 prospective chemistry teachers were included in the research. The participants were chosen in purposeful sampling method. The research data were collected through a test of three open-ended questions developed by the researchers. The prospective teachers were asked questions on what globalization meant, what the environmental consequences of globalization were, and what the effects of globalization on the world were and they were required to answer the questions in writing. The written answers that prospective chemistry teachers gave to the open-ended questions will be put to content analysis. The findings to be obtained through content analysis were divided into themes related to the concept of globalization and categories defined. After the analysis of the themes and categories, prospective chemistry teachers' cognitive structures about the concept of globalization were revealed and then the findings were discussed in details.
Keywords: Case study, cognitive structure, content analysis, globalisation

1 Introduction

Cognitive structures are the schemata through which students organise various concepts and they relate them so that they can understand a subject better [1, 2]. Deficiencies or lacking conceptual links in those schemata result in difficulties in learning new knowledge or adding new concepts into the inconsistent structure of knowledge [3]. Analysing students' cognitive structures informs educators of their knowledge structures, prior knowledge and probable misconceptions, and this also makes it possible to notice their knowledge gaps [4, 5]. This study aims to determine prospective chemistry teachers' cognitive structures about the concept of globalization by setting out from the significance of investigating cognitive structure. Globalization causes nations to face environmental problems that they cannot solve on their own. Those negative effects and harms of globalization especially in terms of environment can only be prevented or reduced through solutions and precautions involving global cooperation, international agreement, solidarity and universal approaches [6]. Thus, this study intends to analyse the cognitive structures of prospective teachers-who will probably have a voice in the future about the environment- about the concept of

* Corresponding author: schenolschen@gmail.com

globalization. A review of literature makes it clear that only a small number of studies analysing students' cognitive structures about various environmental issues [greenhouse effect and global warming- 7, 8; carbon cycle- 9] are available. On reviewing literature of globalization, on the other hand, it was found that studies investigating the process of globalization, the reflections of globalization into education, the globalization of education [10, 11, 12, 13] in general and studies analysing prospective social studies teachers' views on globalization [14], the youth's perceptions of identity in Turkey in the process of globalization [15] and discussions on globalization in Turkey [16] were available. In addition to that, there were also studies on the way globalization influenced education [17] and educational policies [18] throughout the world as well as studies about what globalization meant for changes in education [19]. Yet, the absence of studies analysing the concept of globalization along with students'/prospective teachers' cognitive structures demonstrates the importance of this current study in that it is the first in relevant literature.

1.1 The aim of the study

This study aimed to determine prospective chemistry teachers' cognitive structures about the concept of globalization.

2 Method

Case study, one of qualitative research methods, was employed in this study. Case study was preferred due to the fact that it was a research method which was based on the questions of how and why and which enabled researchers to investigate in depth a phenomenon or event which they could not control [20].

2.1 Study group

The study group was composed of prospective chemistry teachers. All of the participants took a course in Environmental Protection in 2017-2018 academic year. The participants were chosen through purposeful sampling. Purposeful sampling is a method enabling researchers to examine the situations having rich information in depth and thus to illuminate better the questions that a study focuses on [21]. All the participants- who were aged between 21 and 23- were included in the study on the basis of volunteering. Prior to the study, they were informed of the content, evaluation of the data and confidentiality of their names.

2.2 Data collection tool

The research data were collected through a test of three open-ended questions developed by the researchers. The test questions were prepared by reviewing the studies available in the literature. The data were collected in the spring semester of 2017-2018 academic year. The participants were allowed 20 minutes to respond to the questions. They were asked questions about what globalization meant, what the effects of globalization on the world were and what the environmental consequences of globalization were; and they were required to answer the questions in writing.

2.3 Analyses of the data

The written answers given by the prospective teachers to the open-ended questions will be put to content analysis. Content analysis was preferred so as to reach the concepts and relations which would be able to explain the data collected [20]. The findings obtained through content analysis analysed in themes and then categories will be distinguished. Following the analyses, codes were created with themes and categories related to the concept of globalization. Expert opinion was consulted in analysing the qualitative data and thus efforts were made to raise internal validity. "Similarities and differences in coding" between the two encoders were compared and interrater reliability was found to be 91%. Reliability formula suggested by Miles and Huberman [22] was used in calculating the reliability in this study. 70% reliability should be attained at the minimum in qualitative studies [22, 20]. Efforts were made in this way to increase reliability in this study.

3 Findings

The findings obtained through content analysis are shown in Table 1. Whereas nothing was written in the frequency (f) part of the Table for the data which were mentioned only once, the number of statements repeated more than once were shown with a number.

Having analyzed the themes and categories distinguished, efforts were made to reveal prospective chemistry teachers' cognitive structures about the concept of globalization. As is clear from Table 1, prospective chemistry teachers' cognitive structures were considered in three categories- namely, "the definition of the concept of globalization", "environmental consequences of the concept of globalization" and "the effects of globalization on the world (environmental, economic, technological, cultural and political dimensions)"

As evident from the prospective teachers' statements in the category of "the definition of the concept of globalization", two of the prospective teachers mentioned the process of integrating societies and cultures, world's becoming an open market and the process of international integration; six mentioned regional phenomena's becoming global phenomena and five mentioned nation's coming together and searching for solutions to environmental problems.

Prospective teachers' statements in the category of "the environmental consequences of the concept of globalization", on the other hand, demonstrated that three of them mentioned increase in greenhouse gases in consequence of economic development; four mentioned emergence of environmental problems in consequence of increase in competition between countries and companies; three mentioned world countries' search for solutions to environmental problems; four mentioned countries' remaining in contact for the environment; three mentioned environmental problems being the concern for all humans and fourteen mentioned increase in environmental problems.

Table 1. Findings obtained from the content analyses related to the concept of globalization

Theme: The concept of globalization													
Definition of the concept of globalization		**Environmental consequences of the concept of globalisation**		**The effects of the concept of globalization on the World**									
words-phrases (codes)													
	f		**f**	**Environmental**	**f**	**Economic**	**f**	**Technological**	**f**	**Cultural**	**f**	**Political**	**f**
The process of integrating societies and cultures	2	Increase in greenhouse gases in consequence of economic development	3	Use of more energy		Countries' search for markets	2	Rapid access to information	3	Having modern life style	2	National problems becoming international problems	2
The process of countries' international integration		Increase in environmental problems	14	Harming the environment for economic development		Increase in competition between countries	5	Increase in technological pollution		Diverse cultures' influences on each other	6	Searching for global solutions to national problems	4
The state of countries interaction in cultural, social, economic terms	2	Emergence of environmental problems in consequence of increase in competition between companies and countries	4	Increase in environmental pollution	2	Competition between countries to attract capital		Technological development	2	World countries' sociocultural uniting		Developed countries' oppression on undeveloped countries	
A phenomenon's becoming international		Overuse of natural resources	2	Destroying the environment more	5	Recovery in economy	4			Increase in interaction between nations		Integration between nations	
Regional phenomena's becoming global phenomena	6	Protecting the environment with international agreements		Considering environmental problems on international scale	3	Increase in economic imbalance				Mentality of consuming more	5	Removal of borders in the world	
The world's becoming a global village		Unconscious use of sources of energy		Generating joint ideas for the solution of environmental problems internationally	5	World nations' uniting in terms of economy						Countries' search for solutions to problems looking out for their own interests	

The removal of world borders	2	Countries' remaining in contact for the environment	4	Increase in carbon footprint per person		Nations' priority over economic development	2						
The world's becoming an open market	2	World countries' search for solution to environmental problems	3	Increase in air pollution	2								
The process of international integration as a result of exchange of ideas, cultures and world views	2	Negative effects of industrialisation on the environment	3	Increase in water pollution	2								
World nation's having joint attitudes towards environmental problems without thinking of their own interests	2	Environmental problems being the concern for all humans	3	Increase in greenhouse gases	2								
The prevalence of the effects of an event (global climate change) throughout the globe		Countries' making decisions jointly and acting accordingly for the environment	2	Increase in acid rains	2								
Increase in competition between world's nations													
Nations' coming together and searching for solutions to environmental problems	5												

An examination of the prospective teachers' statements in the category of "the effects of the concept of globalization on the world (environmental, economic, technological, cultural and political dimensions)" showed that five of the prospective teachers mentioned destroying the environment more; two mentioned increase in environmental pollution; one mentioned increase in carbon footprint per person; three mentioned considering environmental problems on international scale and five mentioned generating joint ideas for the solution of environmental problems internationally. On economic dimension, two of them mentioned countries' search for markets, five mentioned increase in competition between countries and two mentioned countries' priority over economic development. On technological dimension three mentioned rapid access to information, one mentioned increase in technological pollution and two mentioned development in technology. On cultural dimension two mentioned having modern life style, six mentioned diverse cultures influences over each other and five mentioned mentality of consuming more. On political dimension two participants mentioned national problems becoming international problems, four mentioned searching for global solutions to national problems and one mentioned countries' search for solutions to problems looking out for their own interests.

4 Conclusion And Discussion

The written answers prospective teachers had given to the open-ended questions about the concept of globalization were put to content analysis. Following the analysis, prospective teachers' knowledge of the concept of globalization was analyzed in three categories.

On examining the participants' statements in the category of "the definition of the concept of globalization" it was found that they generally described globalization as the process of integrating societies and cultures; the state of countries' interaction in cultural, social and economic terms; the removal of world's borders and as world's becoming an open market. However, the percentage of the participants making these statements (10%) was low. The percentage of those describing globalization in connection with environmental problems and environmental phenomena was higher. Accordingly, 30% described globalization as regional environmental phenomena's becoming global phenomena and 25% described it as countries' coming together and searching for solutions. These findings demonstrated that prospective teachers had deficiencies in knowledge about the definition of the concept.

An examination of the prospective teachers' statements in the category of "environmental consequences of the concept of globalization" demonstrated that the majority (70%) mentioned increase in environmental problems, 15% mentioned increase in greenhouse gases in consequence of economic development and 15% mentioned negative effects of industrialization on the environment. Although the fact that the participants mentioned world countries' search for solutions to environmental problems (25%), environmental problems being concern for all humans (15%), countries' remaining in contact for the environment (20%) and countries acting together by making joint decisions (10%) demonstrated that approaches such as cooperation between countries and solidarity should be adopted for the solution of environmental problems; low percentages indicated lacks in their knowledge.

The participants' statements in the category of "the effects of the concept of globalization on the world" were analyzed on five dimensions. Accordingly, the participants were found to have mentioned increase in environmental pollution, increase in air pollution, increase in water pollution, increase in greenhouse gases and increase in acid rains; but the rate of those making the statements was very low (10%). The participants also associated environmental effects with the concept of globalization and mentioned such issues as considering environmental problems on international scale (15%) and generating joint ideas internationally (25%). As to the economic effects of globalization, the prospective teachers mentioned countries' search for markets (10%), increase in capital in countries (5%), increase in competition between countries (25%) and increase in economic imbalance (5%) as negative effects while 20% of them mentioned economic recovery as the positive effect. As the technological effects of globalization, they mentioned rapid access to information (15%), technological development (10%) and increase in technological pollution (5%). As the cultural effects, they made limited number of statements about such issues as having modern life style (10%), diverse cultures' influences on one another (30%) and mentality of consuming more (25%). They mentioned national problems' becoming international problems (10%), searching for solutions to national problems globally (20%), developed countries' oppressing undeveloped countries (5%) and removal of the borders in the world (5%) in terms of the political effects of globalization.

On evaluating the results in general, it was seen that the percentage of prospective teachers defining the concept of globalization within the framework of environment was higher although they made general definitions of the concept. In other words, they defined the concept of globalization by associating it with the environment. It was found that the percentage of those stating that globalization caused increase in environmental problems was quite high. The percentage of participants saying that world countries should search for solutions to the problems together and that they should generate solutions together was low. On examining the prospective teachers' statements in the category of the effects of globalization on the world it was found that they had mentioned 5 dimensions of globalization. On comparing the dimensions, it was found that the participants suggested limited number of ideas on economic, technological, cultural and political dimensions but that they put forward more ideas on environmental dimension. In parallel to those statements, this study also reached general ideas that countries would be in interaction in consequence of globalization, that global solutions would be searched to national problems and that diverse cultures would influence each other. Although these results were consistent with the ones obtained by Kaya [16], Fidan [15] and Gürbüz [14]; it may be said that prospective teachers' cognitive structures about the concept of globalization are not rich enough and that therefore they are lacking in knowledge.

References

1. Novak, J. & Cañas, A.J. The theory underlying concept maps and how to construct them. Technical Report IHMC CmapTools 2006-1. Florida Institute for Human and Machine Cognition, Pensacola, (2006).
2. Novak J. D. Learning, creating, and using knowledge: concept maps as facilitative tools in schools and corporations. *Journal of e-Learning and Knowledge Society*, 6(3), 21 – 30, (2010).
3. Taber, K. S., & Coll, R. K. Chemical bonding. In J. K. Gilbert, O. de Jong, R. Justi, D. F. Treagust & J. H. Van Driel (Eds.), Chemical Education: Research-based Practice (pp. 213-234). Dordrecht: Kluwer Academic Publishers BV., (2002).
4. Jonassen, D. H. Assessing cognitive structure: Verifying a method using pattern notes. Journal of Research and Development in Education, 20(3), 1–14, (1987).
5. Ifenthaler D., Masduki I. & Seel N. M., The mystery of cognitive structure and how we can detect it: tracking the development of cognitive structures over time. *Instructional Science*, 39(1), 41-61, (2009).
6. Özdemir, B. Küresel kirlenme, sürdürülebilir ekonomik büyüme ve çevre vergileri. *Maliye Dergisi*, 156, (2009).

7. Chang, C-Y., Yeh, T-K., & Barufaldi, J. P. The positive and negative effects of science concept tests on student conceptual understanding. International Journal of Science Education, 32(2), 265–282, (2010).
8. Oskay, Ö. Ö., Temel, S., Özgür, S. D., & Erdem, E. Determination of preservice chemistry teachers' cognitive structures via flow map method and their knowledge level on "greenhouse gases and their effects" topic. *Eurasian Journal of Physics & Chemistry Education*, 4(1), 30–45, (2012).
9. Selvi, M., & Yakışan, M. Akış haritaları yoluyla öğrencilerin bilişsel yapılarının belirlenmesi: Ekolojik döngüler. *Türk Fen Eğitimi Dergisi*, 2(1), 46–55, (2005).
10. Akkutay, E. A. Yükseköğrenimde küreselleşme ve yansımaları. *Eğitim ve Toplum Araştırmaları Dergisi/JRES*, 4(1), 1-16, (2017).
11. Dağlı, A. Küreselleşme karşısında Türk eğitim sistemi. *D. Ü. Ziya Gökalp Eğitim Fakültesi Dergisi*, 9, 1-13, (2007).
12. Eser, E. Küreselleşme süreci ve eğitime etkisi. *Muş Alparslan Üniversitesi Sosyal Bilimler Dergisi*, 2(2), (2014).
13. Korkmaz, M. Küreselleşen dünyada eğitimin küreselleşmesi. *Ar&Ge Bülten*, Temmuz-Ağustos, (2015).
14. Gürbüz, Z. *Sosyal bilgiler öğretmen adaylarının küreselleşmeye yönelik görüşleri.* Yüksel lisans tezi. Marmara Üniversitesi, Eğitim Bilimleri Enstitüsü, İstanbul, (2015).
15. Fidan, S. (2011). *Küreselleşme Surecinde Türkiye'de Gençliğin Kimlik Algısı (Üniversite Gençliği Üzerine Bir Araştırma).* Doktora Tezi. Sakarya Üniversitesi. Sosyal Bilimler Enstitüsü.
16. Kaya, P. *Türkiye'de Küreselleşme Tartışmaları.* Ankara Üniversitesi. Sosyal Bilimler Enstitüsü. Yüksek Lisans Tezi, (2002).
17. Vulliamy, G. Educational Reform in a Globalised Age: What is globalisation and how is it affecting Education world-wide? *幼兒教保研究期刊, 第5期.* (2010).
18. Burbules, N., & Torres, C. (Eds.). *Globalization and education: Critical perspectives.* New York: Routledge, (2000).
19. Carnoy, M. & Rhoten, D. What does globalization mean for educational change? A comparative approach. *Comparative Education Review*, 46(1), 1-9, (2002).
20. Yıldırım, A. & Şimşek, H. *Sosyal Bilimlerde Nitel Araştırma Yöntemleri* (8. Baskı). Ankara: Seçkin Yayıncılık, (2011).
21. Patton, M. Q. *Qualitative Research & Evaluation Methods* (3rd ed.). Thousand Oaks, CA: Sage, (2002).
22. Miles, B. M., & Huberman, A. M. *Qualitative data analysis: An extended sourcebook.* (2nd edition). Thousand Oaks, CA: Sage, England, (1994).

Learner autonomy in modern higher education

Alexey Danilenko[1*], *Irina* Kosmidis[1], *Victoria* Shershneva[1], and *Yulia* Vainshtein[1]

[1]Siberian Federal University, Kirenskogo st., 26, Krasnoyarsk, 660074, Russia

Abstract. This article deals with the concept of learner autonomy as well as the peculiarities of the use of the learner autonomy-based educational technology in the educational system of Russia. The analysis of the concept of learner autonomy is given basing on the works of both foreign and Russian specialists: the origin of the concept is traced back, different variants of defining the concept are given, and the teacher role in the context of learner autonomy is laid emphasis on. Generalizing the views the authors put forward their own definition of the concept of learner autonomy. The authors also point out the correlation of learner autonomy and the concept of communicative concept proposing their own view of communicative competence structure. Besides, the authors consider the prospect of implementing the learner autonomy-based educational technology into the realm of adaptive learning, which is also topical for modern Russian Education.
Keywords: academic mobility, life-long learning, autonomous learning, learner autonomy, independent learning, self-instruction, learning strategies.

1 Introduction

The pedagogy of the XXth century is marked by the creation of a wide range of educational technologies: The Montessori Method of education, Waldorf education, Dewey's Instrumental pedagogy, and many others. The technology based on the concept of learner autonomy is worth mentioning as a separate point. Though this concept came to be used in Russia a short time ago, it has become the object of interest of homeland specialists due to the topicality of learner autonomy in global education. In this regard, the following questions have to be answered: is learner autonomy a personal characteristic or an educational technology? What are the prospects of learner autonomy being Russian education?

To answer the questions raised, we must first trace the roots of learner autonomy in foreign pedagogy. The word "autonomy" comes from Greek «αὐτονομία» which literally means "setting law for oneself". The idea of a student taking the responsibility over his studying, hailed by learner autonomy ideologists, is not new. Galileo Galilei said: "A person cannot be taught. One can only help a person reveal everything in oneself" [1].

To some extent, Jean-Jacques Rousseau's ideas also anticipated the creation of learner autonomy concept. He realized the importance of student responsibility for his own

* Corresponding author : danilenko.alex.91@mail.ru

learning and the value of the knowledge gained independently. He offered the following strategy of working with students: "arise the students' interest, offer them a problem and leave it for the students to be solved. Everything they know must be gained by them personally, and not be transmitted by you. Do not correct any mistakes as long as they see them. If they cannot do it, help them; only by making mistakes can they learn something" [2].

Kolb model, which was put forward by an American educator David Kolb in the mid-1980s, stands on the same ground. This theory describes stage-by-stage development of mental activities. According to Kolb model, at the stage of learning the main material students are offered a certain range of tasks with the aim to independently gain knowledge and skills; it is gaining knowledge in individual work which plays the main role in the model [3].

2 Learner autonomy – the history of the concept

At the same time, certain economical and social changes, which had taken place in the world, lead to the creation of a language-teaching technique basing on the learner autonomy concept. When speaking of the theoretical prerequisites for learner autonomy, M. Gremmo and P. Riley show the importance of 1960s social progress when social orientation shifted itself from material values to personality development and social interactions [4]. H.Holec states that "language learning education becomes the interlink to global economy, and language skills are transformed into a kind of economic capital", indicating to economic reasons for language learning spreading which results in the creation of a new language teaching concept [5]. Russian researchers Zh. S. Anikina and L. I. Agafonova see the reasons for learner autonomy concept creation in the global informational explosion of the 60's and 70's, the development of Internet technologies, commercialization of education, as well as the development of international tourism [6].

The concept of learner autonomy appeared in Nancy University Language Centre (Centre de Recherches et d'Applications en Langues – CRAPEL) in 1971 with respect to the project of the British Council for Foreign Language Learning. The centre was founded by Yves Chalonne; after his death in 1972 the centre was headed by Henry Holec, who published "Autonomy and Foreign Language Learning" in 1981. In this work autonomy was defined as "the ability to take responsibility for his own learning." The centre activities were aimed at creating such an educational model which would develop personal freedom, independent goal setting and self-assessment skills. The CRAPEL specialists consider the following conditions to be essential for successful learner autonomy development:

1)Unlimited access to a resource centre equipped with authentic materials;

2) Psychological training of student aimed at self-organization, self-control, and self-assessment [6].

It should be noted that the actively developing concept of learning autonomy received no acclaim in Soviet pedagogy. First of all, it can be assigned to the fact that the ideological and collective orientation of the Soviet education did not share the idea of personalization of education which hindered the development of learner autonomy in the USSR. Besides, the political isolation of the country could not promote to the spread of foreign scientific ideas, including the concept of learner autonomy.

Various studies devoted to the phenomenon of learner autonomy have revealed its versatility. We will consider a couple of examples to illustrate how the views on learner autonomy might vary. Thus, Holec sees learner autonomy as the ability acquired during the learning process. Another specialist, L. Dickinson, understands it as a learning model, where all students bear responsibility for all decisions related to their studies, as well as for the outcomes [7].

As the concept of learner autonomy was gaining its theoretical justification, certain attention was paid to the teacher role in the context of this concept. For example, P. Voller marks three stages of teacher-student interaction:

1) the transition of educational process control from the teacher to the student;

2) partnership relations with students;

3) observing applied learning strategies and the ways of interacting with students from the teacher side [8].

Besides, the Chinese specialist S. Yan ascribes the teacher place in the context of learner autonomy to the following roles:

1) Organizer – the teacher takes the responsibility for organizing classroom activities, offering appropriate and effective tasks that will best meet students' needs and expectations. The teacher should be aware of the importance of giving clear instructions to what it is to be done.

2) Facilitator – the teacher lends students psycho-social and technical assistance. Psycho-social assistance implies the ability to motivate students which helps them overcome difficulties. Technical assistance includes helping students plan and carry out learning activities, evaluate progress and acquire knowledge and skills. In a classroom language learning environment, the teacher also acts as the model of a native speaker - in this role the teacher encourages students into using the foreign language and corrects the mistakes that appear in students' speech.

3) Counselor – the teacher must show the example of effective communication with an attempt to mesh speaker intention and hearer interpretation [9].

3 Learner autonomy, capability of learning autonomy, the technology of learner autonomy development

We think it necessary to make our view of learner autonomy more specific in order to avoid confusion in the conceptual framework we use. We put the following meaning into "learner autonomy": the ability of the student to take responsibility over his or her own learning. It is important to note that we see learner autonomy not only as the ability which manifests at various stages of (its development during) the educational process, but also as the readiness to apply this ability in practice in future career. By "capability of learner autonomy" we mean a personality trait of the student which is manifested in an acquired ability to take responsibility for his or her own learning being represented at several levels: 1) setting learning objectives; 2) choosing personal learning strategy; 3) intermediate and overall self-reflection related to learning objectives.

Further, we call the educational technology aimed at forming the abovementioned personality trait "the technology of learner autonomy development". Besides, we are concerned that learner autonomy consideration should not be reduced to a particular subject study – in this case one cannot trace which personal traits are developed after the end of learning process. In our opinion, learner autonomy is to be viewed ambiguously. On the one hand – developing the ability to take the responsibility for learning in the framework of the subject which is studied within the conditions of learner autonomy. On the other hand – developing the competencies that will remain developed after the end of learning process and can be applied in various spheres, e.g. in further self-education, professional and creative activities.

4 Learner autonomy in Russian educational system

We have already mentioned the fact that learner autonomy concept could not be developed under the conditions of the Soviet education. The system, which was famous for teaching exact sciences, had issues with the effectiveness of teaching foreign languages. Thus, if it was possible to shift the teaching methods for mathematics, psychics and other exact sciences from the Soviet educational system to a new Russian one, then there was no point in borrowing the Soviet foreign language teaching method. This circumstance cleared the way for a number of overseas foreign language teaching methods to be implemented in the Russian educational system, including the concept of learner autonomy.

Another reason for learner autonomy to appear in the Russian educational system can be found in the following sociopolitical step. In the 1990s European states signed the Bologna agreement. One of its objectives was to raise academic mobility in higher education which would, in turn, require such personal traits as independence and responsibility for learning. Russia's joining the Bologna agreement in 2003 promoted the spread of the learner autonomy concept in Russian educational system.

The obligatory requirements for education in Russia are presented in the Federal state learning standard of higher education. It contains the list of competencies that a graduate must acquire that also includes "the capability for self-management and self-instruction", that, in our opinion, can be reached by plunging students into learner autonomy environment throughout mastering academic program.

It should be noted that plunging students into learner autonomy conditions can also successfully be used in adaptive e-learning, in which it is possible to adapt educational content to student's individual abilities, knowledge and skills. The created individual educational trajectories are used as the basis for adaptive e-learning courses on foreign language. The obtained theoretical conclusions may be used for developing learning strategies in teaching various subjects [10].

The founders of the concept of learner autonomy thought free access to authentic materials to be one of the factors of its development. Nowadays, the enormous development rates for information and computer technologies (ICT) provide education with a wide range of tools for educational process. It also creates favorable conditions for developing learner autonomy, since the use of ICT in educational process enables orientation on personal achievements.

It is obvious that the objective of language learning is not only studying vocabulary, grammar, cultural peculiarities typical for native speakers. The long-run objective is to develop oral skills, i.e. the readiness to express thoughts verbally, to perceive the utterance of an interlocutor. Due to the orientation of learner autonomy on individual work, teaching oral skills, which demands the combination of pair and group work, requires further development. In our opinion, the use of learner autonomy in teaching foreign language makes sense only in case the learner autonomy skills are used as the certain foundation, which is necessary for forming personal traits that develop responsibility for student's own learning for more effective foreign language mastering. Teaching verbal aspect of a foreign language has to be carried out with the application of pair and group work. In our opinion, the use of learner autonomy technology in teaching foreign languages is essential for developing the certain foundation which contributes to developing such personal traits as responsibility for learning, independence in making decisions, confidence in one's abilities. These traits will help form oral skills in further studying.

Thus, a course on a foreign language (designed for four years) under the conditions of learner autonomy is to consist of three stages. At the first stage the current foreign language proficiency level is to be assessed in order to complete classes and to create individual educational trajectories in e-learning environment. The second stage is devoted to plunging students into learner autonomy with the aim to develop independence in making decisions, to choose an individual trajectory of studying educational content and to evaluate progress. At the third stage the attention is paid to the most important objective of foreign language learning – oral speech, both as monologue and dialogue.

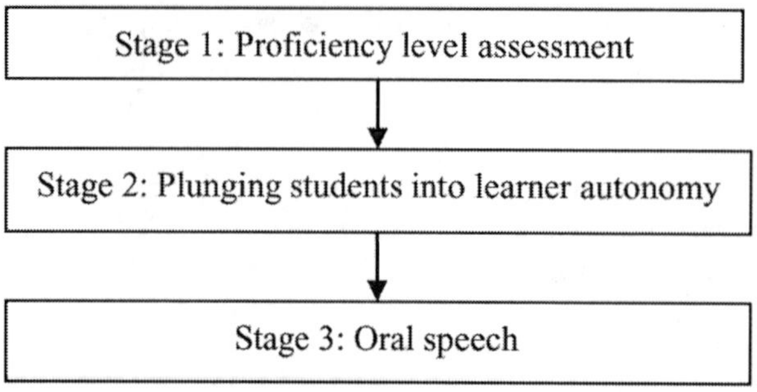

Fig. 1. A foreign language course under the conditions of learner autonomy

Speaking of oral speech training we imply communicative competence development. This notion was coined in 1970s by Dell Hymes to emphasize the dependence of the use of certain lexical items or grammar structure on speech situations [11]. In our opinion, communicative competence is divided into three levels – linguistic, speech and professional ones. The linguistic level, in its turn, consists of three equally important sublevels:

1) Lexical, which includes obtaining certain vocabulary and using lexical items depending on speech context.

2) Grammatical, which implies knowledge of the language grammatical system and an ability to use grammar rules in different types of speech.

3) Phonetic, which unites knowledge of the language phonetic system and prosody and an ability to pronounce words and sentences correctly.

Speech level is divided into the following sublevels:

1) Discursive – an ability to build logically finished utterances and to perceive interlocutor speech adequately.

2) Strategic – an ability to compensate lacking knowledge in case of communication breakdown.

Taking a special place in this structure, professional level of communicative competence includes:

1) an ability to use the foreign language interdisciplinarily,

2) an ability to apply foreign language skills in professional activities.

The hierarchy of communicative competence levels is formed as follows: linguistic level acts as the foundation for developing this competence as to make an utterance it is necessary to obtain certain vocabulary (obtaining vocabulary is included into lexical sublevel of linguistic level of communicative competence) and grammar structures (grammatical sublevel). Speech level, which takes the second step of the hierarchy, is gradually developed basing on the elements of linguistic level – various layers of vocabulary and necessary grammar structures. Speech level is followed by professional level – mastering the professional language is possible only after the development of linguistic and speech levels. The essence of professional level is to develop skills and abilities required for special purpose application of the foreign language in professional activities [12].

Professional level
Speech level (discursive, strategic sublevels)
Linguistic level (lexical, grammatical, phonetic sublevels)

Fig. 2. The structure of communicative competence.

5 Results

The experiment was carried out at Siberian Federal University within a period of four years. To assess efficiency of the educational process implementation of the abovementioned technology, the academic record comparison with the use of Mann – Whitney U-test was made between the control group and the experimental group before the onset of studying, during each stage and after accomplishing each stage. The students were offered to take a placement test and a final test assessed in points at each stage. In doing so hypothesis H0={point distribution in the control group and the experimental group is equal} under the alternative hypothesis H1={point distribution in the experimental group takes a bigger value} was checked. Taking the results of the experiment into account, it is fair to say that with a probability of 95% better academic record in learning foreign language was reached in the experimental group, furthermore, the following personal trait were formed – self-sufficiency, responsibility, confidence in one's abilities. Being applied at Siberian Federal University, the technology of learner autonomy development has shown that the traits acquired at the second stage of the experiment contribute to the future progress in mastering a foreign language.

6 Conclusions

Thus, basing on the analysis of the various views on learner autonomy concept, the authors have proposed their own idea of it underlining the ambiguity of learner autonomy. The correlation between teaching foreign language under the conditions of learner autonomy and communicative competence development has been pointed out. The difference between the notions "learner autonomy", "capability of learner autonomy", and "technology of learner autonomy development" has been shown. The authors have also analyzed the current state of affairs in Russian educational system, paying attention to the fact that Russia's joining the Bologna agreement in 2003 promoted the spread of learner autonomy concept in Russian education. The article also presents the results of the experiment carried out at Siberian Federal University to show the effectiveness of the technology of learner autonomy development in teaching foreign language.

The reported study was funded by RFBR according to the research project №18-013-00654

References

1. P. Benson, *Teaching and Researching: Autonomy in Language Learning (2nd edition),* 272 (2001)
2. D. Thanasoulas, *What is Learner Autonomy and How Can It Be Fostered,* URL: http://iteslj.org/Articles/Thanasoulas-Autonomy.html (2000)
3. D. Kolb, *Experiential learning: experience as the source of learning and development,* 272 (1984)

4. M-J. Gremmo, P. Riley, System, *Autonomy, self-direction and self-access in language teaching and learning: the history of an idea,* **23(2)**, 154 (1995)
5. H. Holec, Foreign language learning: meeting individual needs, Learner *training: meeting needs in self-direct learning,* 36 (1980)
6. Zh. S. Anikina, L.I. Agafonova, Vestnik Tomskogo gosudarstvennogo pedagogicheskogo universiteta, *Learner autonomy in language teaching: history of the concept in foreign pedagogy,* **4 (82)**, 25 (2009)
7. L. Dickinson, *Self-instruction in Language Learning*, 156 (1987)
8. P. Voller, Autonomy and interdependence in language learning, *Does the teacher have a role in autonomous learning,* 105 (1997)
9. S. Yan, Journal of Sociological Research, *Teachers' roles in autonomous learning,* **2**, 559 (2012)
10. Yu.V. Vainshtein, R.V. Esin, G.M. Tsibulsky, Education and Informatics, *Adaptive model of developing individual educational trajectories for blended learning,* **2**, 86 (2017)
11. E.V. Krasilnikova, Pedagogicheskiy vestnik, *Communicative competence in the proceedings of homeland and foreign specialists*, **1(58)**, 188 (2009)
12. A.S. Danilenko, Vestnik Krasnoyarskogo gosudarstvennogo pedagogicheskogo universiteta imeni V.P. Astaf'eva, *The structure of communicative competence,* **1(35)**, 188 (2016)

Environment from a different perspective: Analysing the environmental problem awareness of undergraduates

Sinem Dinçol Özgür[1], *Lütfiye* Varoğlu[2*], and *Ayhan* Yılmaz[1]

[1]Hacettepe University, Beytepe, Ankara, 06800, Turkey
[2]European University of Lefke, Lefke Northern Cyprus TR-10 Mersin, 99728, Turkey

Abstract. The study aims to analyse the awareness levels of university students towards the environmental problems in terms of the variables of faculty and gender. The study was conducted with 149 undergraduate students from the faculty of engineering, health sciences and educational sciences in North Cyprus. The research conducted with survey study and identified the awareness levels of students towards environmental problems through "Environmental Problems Awareness Scale", developed by Güven and Aydoğdu [1] in consideration with the cognitive steps according to the Bloom Taxonomy. In addition to descriptive statistics, t-test, ANOVA and MANOVA analyses were used for the analysis of data. The study concluded that the total students' scores for awareness of environmental problems show statistically significant difference based on gender, and no significant difference based on faculties. Additionally, the factor scores of the scale have statistically significant difference based on faculties, and no significant difference based on gender.

Keywords: awareness for environmental problems, Bloom's taxonomy, environmental education, environmental problems, university students

1 Introduction

The elements such as increasing use of resources in parallel with the increase in population, fast use of natural resources to meet raw material and energy needs, consumption of fossil fuels, industrializing society and increase in the pace of rural depopulation has begun to major problems in terms of environment. Therefore, some ecological and environmental problems such as population increase and problem of settlement, energy problem, agricultural problems, desertification, deforestation, extinction of species and global warming have arisen [2]. Nowadays, environmental problems threaten the whole world [3]. The individuals, who have an impact on the occurrence of environmental problems, can only contribute to the elimination of such problems through an effective environmental education [4, 5]. Vaughan et.al [6] defined the environmental education as a continuous learning process aiming to ensure environmental awareness among individuals and provide knowledge, skills, values, attitude and experience with regard to solve the environmental

* Corresponding author: lvaroglu@eul.edu.tr

problems. Environmental education aims to make individuals be aware of environmental problems, be sensitive to environmental problems through the acquisition of information regarding such problems and make individual contribute on the solution of environmental problems through the positive attitudes about the environment [7]. Literature emphasizes that the interdisciplinary environmental education should be commenced under the pre-school science education programs and should become in various levels of primary, secondary and higher education [8]. The increasing environmental knowledge would change environmental attitudes, and the environmental attitude and environmental knowledge would affect the environmental policies [9]. Environmental problems are not only the issues of individuals but whole mankind; hence primarily the individuals should be aware of environmental problems with regard to their solution. The creation and development of environmental awareness and motivation of all individuals to protect their environment are both important steps in the solution of environmental problems [10]. Consequently, this study aims to analyse the awareness levels of university students for environmental problems in consideration with the cognitive domain process under the Bloom Taxonomy. The cognitive domain taxonomy of Bloom is comprised of six levels that are in a hierarchical structure from simple to complex as the knowledge at the bottom and them comprehension, application, analysis, synthesis and evaluation respectively. Any step is the prerequisite of the successor and in order to gain the behaviour on the one-step ahead, the behaviours of previous levels should be acquired. While knowledge, comprehension and application are considered as the sub-cognitive levels; analysis, synthesis and evaluation are as higher-cognitive levels [11, 12, 13].

In consideration with the literature, the studies conducted on the environment mainly analyse the attitudes of students towards environmental problems [14, 15, 16, 17, 18]. There are a limited number of studies analysing the awareness of various student groups regarding environment and environmental problems [19, 20, 21, 22]. In Northern Cyprus, there are a limited number of studies about environment with respect to the environmental awareness and environmental attitude [23, 24, 25], yet there are not any studies analysing the awareness concerning the environmental problems. This study is important as it would influence the environmental awareness towards environmental problems and potential environmental behaviour, and it would guide the environmental education. Hence, this study works towards assessing the awareness of university students in Northern Cyprus for environmental problems.

2 Method

2.1 Significance and aim of study

Awareness has an impact on the relation of attitude and behaviour, and higher awareness leads individuals to appropriate attitude and behaviour [26]. Consequently, the determination of awareness of students for environmental problems is vital in an effective environmental education regarding the development of positive attitude and behaviours towards the environment. This study is important as it would influence the environmental awareness towards environmental problems and potential environmental behaviour, and it would guide the environmental education. The aim of this study is to analyse the awareness levels of first-year university students in the Northern Cyprus from health, education and engineering faculties for environmental problems as a global subject. Within the framework of this aim, this study pursued to find answers for the following research problems:

1. What are the awareness levels of students for environmental problems?

a. What are the total scores for awareness levels for environmental problems and scores for knowledge, comprehension, application, analysis, synthesis and evaluation factors?
b. What is the distribution among the answers of students concerning the knowledge, comprehension, application, analysis, synthesis and evaluation factors?
c. What is the distribution of the total score of the awareness for environmental problems and factors by faculties?

2. Is there a statistically significant difference between students' total score and factor scores of the awareness for environmental problems according to their faculties?
3. Is there a statistically significant difference between students' total score and factor scores of the awareness for environmental problems according to their gender?

2.2 Research model

The survey study conducted with 149 undergraduate students from the faculty of engineering, health sciences and educational sciences at 2017-2018 spring semester in North Cyprus. The survey studies are conducted with relatively bigger samples than other researches in order to identify the views of participants about a subject or event, or their characteristics such as interest, skills and attitude [27].

2.3 Participants

The study was conducted with 149 undergraduate students from the faculty of engineering, health sciences and educational sciences at a higher education institution in North Cyprus during the spring term of 2017-2018. The ages of students vary between 18 and 27 with an average of 19.97. Table 1 shows the distribution of students with regard to their genders and faculties.

Table 1. Distribution of students with regard to their genders and faculties

Faculty	Female	Male	Total
Faculty of Health Sciences	48	17	65
Faculty of Engineering	7	30	37
Faculty of Education	28	19	47
Total	83	66	149

2.4 Data collection tool

The Awareness Scale for Environmental Problems: The Awareness Scale for Environmental Problems developed by Güven and Aydoğdu [1] was used in order to identify the awareness of students towards the environmental problems. The scale is comprised of 44 items rated as "yes", "no" and "no idea" and six factors. In the development of scale and creation of factors, the researchers considered the cognitive levels under the Bloom Taxonomy. The Cronbach Alpha values of scale are calculated as 0.90 for total; 0.95 for knowledge factor; 0.95 for comprehension factor; 0.91 for application factor; 0.90 for analysis factor; 0.75 for synthesis factor and 0.71 for evaluation factor. Under the scale, the answers as "yes" were rated with "2" points, "no" with "0" points and "no idea" with "1 points". The highest score that is possible to get from the scale is 88 and 0 as the lowest [1].

2. Data analysis

In addition to the descriptive statistics, t-test, ANOVA and MANOVA analyses were also used accordingly for data analysis.

3 Findings and Interpretation

3.1 Findings

The findings generated as a result of this study are presented with respect to the order of research problems. Concerning the first research problem and sub-problems;

1.a. Firstly, in the analysis of awareness levels of students for the environmental problems, the total scores of participant students and their scores from the factors of knowledge, comprehension, analysis, synthesis and evaluation were assessed. The average scores students from the total of scale and factors are given in Table 2.

Table 2. The average scores students from the total of scale and factors

	N	Minimum	Maximum	Mean
Total score	149	49.00	77.00	66.59
Knowledge	149	7.00	16.00	11.70
Comprehension	149	7.00	15.00	11.28
Application	149	4.00	12.00	9.81
Analysis	149	4.00	16.00	12.78
Synthesis	149	2.00	14.00	9.60
Evaluation	149	5.00	14.00	11.40

1.b. Figure 1 reflects the distribution of answers given by the students regarding the factors of scale, as "yes, no idea and no":

While 74.9% of students answered the statements under the application level as "yes" with the highest percentage, 19.1% of them answered as "no" for the statements under the synthesis statement as the highest percentage. Moreover, figure 3 shows that 38.3% of students answered the statements under the knowledge level as "no idea".

1.c. Table 3 shows the total scores of students obtained from the awareness scale for environmental problems and the distribution of scores with regard to the factors by their faculties.

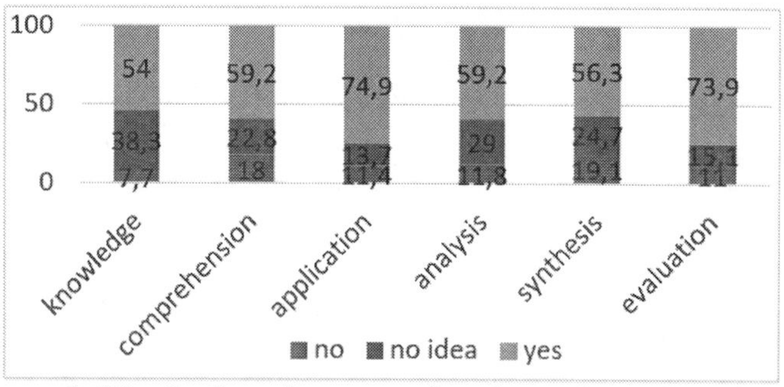

Figure 1. Distribution of answers given by students about factors

Table 3. Distribution of average scores among students in terms of the total scale and factors

	Faculty	N	Mean	Std. Dev.
Total score	Health Sciences	65	67.50	6.00
	Engineering	37	65.91	7.19
	Education	47	65.87	5.61
Knowledge	Health Sciences	65	12.06	2.03
	Engineering	37	11.21	1.88
	Education	47	11.59	1.81
Comprehension	Health Sciences	65	11.60	1.23
	Engineering	37	11.21	1.61
	Education	47	10.91	1.57
Application	Health Sciences	65	10.15	1.59
	Engineering	37	10.00	1.66
	Education	47	9.19	1.80
Analysis	Health Sciences	65	12.83	1.78
	Engineering	37	12.78	2.07
	Education	47	12.72	1.47
Synthesis	Health Sciences	65	9.32	2.42
	Engineering	37	9.45	2.34
	Education	47	10.10	2.22
Evaluation	Health Sciences	65	11.53	1.55
	Engineering	37	11.24	1.93
	Education	47	11.34	2.07

Table 4 delivers the answers concerning the statements selected from each factor in order to analyse the answers of students in terms of factors in detail to the extent of their faculties and genders.

Table 4 indicated that 83.2% of students answered the item on renewable energy as yes with regard to the knowledge factor. In terms of comprehension factor, 97.3% of students answered the item about the generalization of environmental education as yes. With respect to analysis factor, the majority of students noted that they acknowledge the existence of environmental problems causing significant global problems and through the item under the evaluation factor; they consider the prevention of such environmental problems with the contribution of all countries. Similarly under the synthesis factor, 72.5% of students answered the 27th item indicating that environmental problems are global as yes.

The result of single factor ANOVA test conducted for **the 2nd research problem** noted that the total awareness level scores of students for the environmental problems do not vary based on their faculties [$F(2,146) = 1.24$, $p>.05$]. Pursuant to the research problem, the MANOVA results undertaken over the factor scores of knowledge, comprehension, application, analysis, synthesis and evaluation indicated that the students from educational sciences faculty, health sciences faculty and engineering faculty show significant difference in terms of their faculties [Wilks Lambda (Λ) = 0.829, F (12,282) = 2,31, $p<.01$]. This findings shows that the scores generated from the linear component composed of factor scores differ based on the faculties of students. Therefore, the comprehension and application scores of scale show significant difference by faculty [$F(2,146) = 3.12$, $P<.05$; $F(2,146) = 4.78$, $P<.05$], there is not any significant difference between the factor scores of knowledge, analysis, synthesis and evaluation. While the students from faculty of health sciences have the highest scores from comprehension and application, the students from Engineering and Educational Sciences follow up respectively (Table 3).

Table 4. Distribution of answers given to example items selected under factors

Item	Factor	Faculty	Yes					No idea					No				
			f	F	M	Sum	%	f	F	M	Sum	%	f	F	M	Sum	%
1. Air pollution causes crucial global problems such as greenhouse effect, global warming, climate change and thinning ozone layer.	Analysis	1	63	48	15	146	98.0	2	-	2	3	2.0	0	-	-	0	0.0
		2	37	7	30			-	-	-			0	-	-		
		3	46	27	19			1	1	-			0	-	-		
2. The solution of environmental problems is possible with environmental awareness and education.	Comprehension	1	64	48	16	145	97.3	1	-	1	2	1.3	0	-	-	2	1.4
		2	36	7	29			1	-	1			0	-	-		
		3	45	27	18			0	-	-			2	1	1		
4. Biomass energy, hydraulic energy, hydro and wind energies are renewable energy resources.	Knowledge	1	55	45	10	124	83.2	7	2	5	20	13.4	3	1	2	5	3.4
		2	31	5	26			5	2	3			1	-	1		
		3	38	23	15			8	4	4			1	1	-		
7. The contribution of only one country is not enough in the prevention of environmental problems; all countries must struggle.	Evaluation	1	64	48	16	147	98.7	0	-	-	1	0.6	1	-	1	1	0.6
		2	36	7	29			1	-	1			0	-	-		
		3	47	28	19			0	-	-			0	-	-		
14. Uses of natural gas and preference for public transportation significantly reduce the air pollution.	Application	1	57	41	16	126	84.5	4	3	1	12	8.1	4	4	-	11	7.4
		2	32	5	27			4	2	2			1	-	1		
		3	37	20	17			4	3	1			6	5	1		
27. Environmental problems are global.	Synthesis	1	45	34	11	108	72.5	14	10	4	32	21.5	6	4	2	9	6.0
		2	25	4	21			10	2	8			2	1	1		
		3	38	21	17			8	6	2			1	1	-		

1: Health Sciences Faculty, 2: Engineering Faculty and 3: Educational Sciences Faculty. F: Female, M: Male

The result of independent sample t-test conducted regarding **the 3rd research problem** reflected that the total awareness scores of students for the environmental problems show significant difference by their gender t(147) = 2.35, p = .02, p<.05. The total awareness scores of female students for the environmental problems are ($\overline{X}$=67.65) are higher than male students ($\overline{X}$=65.27). Table 5 gives the average factor scores for female and male students.

Table 5. Average factor scores for female and male students

	Average Scores					
	Knowledge	**Comprehension**	**Application**	**Analysis**	**Synthesis**	**Evaluation**
Female	12.04	11.40	9.72	13.00	9.82	11.68
Male	11.28	11.15	9.92	12.51	9.33	11.06

Table 5 indicated that the averages of knowledge, comprehension, analysis, synthesis and evaluation factors are high in favour of female students whereas the average score of application factor is even a little high in favour of male students. Considering the result of MANOVA test, which was conducted in order to analyse whether scores for the factors of knowledge, comprehension, analysis, synthesis and evaluation vary based on the genders of student, the factor scores of students do not show any difference based on their gender [Wilks Lambda (Λ) = 0.917, F(6,142) = 2.13, p = .052 p>.05].

3.2 Conclusion and Discussion

This study was performed to analyse the awareness levels of undergraduates from various faculties of a university located in the Northern Cyprus for environmental problems, and to assess in terms of variables as faculties and gender. In consideration of descriptive analyses, the average awareness scores of students for environmental problems were found as $\overline{X}$ = 66.59 and distributed between 49 and 77. Pursuant to the highest score (88) that is possible to get from the scale, the students have a certain awareness level. With regard to the answers given for the factors under the awareness scale for environmental problems, the students mainly answered as yes for all levels. While 74.9% of students gave the answer of yes to the application level with the highest rate; the lowest rate for the answer of yes and the highest rate for the answer of no idea were given to knowledge level with 54.0% and 38.3% respectively. Such rates indicate that the students have insufficient knowledge with regard to the environmental problems. On the other hand, pursuant to the rates for the answer of yes towards the scale items under Table 4, the students are considered as aware that the environmental problems are global issues of all countries around the world (98.7%) and they believe that environmental education should become more general (97.3%) for the solution of such problems. However, considering that the awareness levels of individuals for the environmental problems would support the positive attitude and behaviours on the environment, the awareness of university students was found as below the desired level. Özdemir et.al. [28] noted that the awareness and sensitivity levels of medical school students are insufficient. In parallel with the study outcome and literature, the awareness levels of individuals for the environment and environmental problems were referred as insufficient [29, 30, 31, 32].

Pursuant to the awareness score averages of students for the environmental problems in terms of their faculties, the students of health sciences faculty have higher awareness scores when compared with the students from engineering and educational sciences faculty. As the field of students from the health sciences faculty is health itself, and considering the relation between health and environmental problems, such higher awareness levels among these students might be expected. Ek et.al. [33] noted that the attitude and sensitivity of students regarding the environmental problems vary based on their on-going academic program. The studies of Köse et.al [34] stated that the environmental attitudes of students from the health sciences faculty are higher than the students from the faculties of engineering and economic and administrative sciences. Yıldırım et.al [35] concluded that although the students of health sciences faculty have more environmental knowledge than the students from other programs, their environmental behaviours do not differ. According to the study of Tekin and Güneş [36] regarding the environmental awareness of first and fourth grade students from various faculties, the education level of parents and hobbies have an impact on the environmental behaviours; and the students from the dentistry faculty have lower level of attitudes although the students from the engineering faculty have higher pro-environmental attitude than the students from the faculty of economics and administrative sciences.

The total awareness scores of students for the environmental problems were found as in favour of female students, yet the factor scores do not show any significant difference by gender. Biswas [37] noted that the environmental awareness of female students is higher than male students and Blocker and Eckberg [38] stated that in relation with the gender identity, the male individuals are in the role of breadwinner and the environmental attitude differ with the gender factor. Moreover, depending on higher awareness levels of female students than the male students with regard to the individual responsibility and environmental problems, the female students have also higher environmental attitudes [39]. The study of Doğan and Purutçuoğlu [20] concluded in their study that the general awareness scores of social service officers do not vary with their genders but in terms of comprehension dimension, women are more aware of environmental problems and more successful in comprehending its reasons. Pursuant to various researches, the female students have higher environmental awareness than male students; bear more environmental concern and are more sensitive in taking measures for the protection of environment [28, 40].

Nowadays, as the environmental problems have the tendency to increase, the most effective way to minimize such problems would be the education of individuals and development of environmental awareness, consciousness and attitude. Education is a long process starting from pre-school to university and further on. As the university students of today would have the duty to raise the future generations, all undergraduate programs should be comprised of effective environmental education curricula aiming to raise conscious and sensitive graduates with higher awareness level. One of the restrictions of this study is that the awareness level for the environmental problems are not associated with the courses of students with regard to the environment. It is recommended to ascertain this relation in the future studies.

References

1. Güven, E., & Aydoğdu, M. (2012). Çevre sorunlarına yönelik farkındalık ölçeğinin geliştirilmesi ve öğretmen adaylarının farkındalık düzeylerinin belirlenmesi. *Öğretmen Eğitimi ve Eğitimcileri Dergisi*, **1**(2), 185-202.
2. Türkmen, L. (2017). Ekolojik konu ve sorunlar. O. Bozkurt (Ed.), *Çevre eğitimi* (153-178). Ankara: Pegem Akademi.
3. Oweini, A., & Houri, A. (2006). Factors affecting environmental knowledge and attitudes among Lebanese college students. *Applied Environmental Education and Communication*, **5**(2), 95-105.
4. Ünal, S., & Dımışlı, E. (1999). UNESCO-UNEP himayesinde çevre eğitiminin gelişimi ve Türkiye'de ortaöğretim çevre eğitimi. *Hacettepe Üniversitesi Eğitim Fakültesi Dergisi*, **17**(17), 142-154.

5. Şahin, N. F., Cerrah, L., Arzu, S. A. K. A., & Şahin, B. (2014). Yüksek öğretimde öğrenci merkezli çevre eğitimi dersine yönelik bir uygulama. *Gazi Üniversitesi Gazi Eğitim Fakültesi Dergisi*, **24**(3), 113-128.
6. Vaughan, C., Gack, J., Solorazano, H., & Ray, R. (2003). The effect on environmental education on schoolchildren, their parents, and community members: a study of intergenerational and intercommunity learning. *The Journal of Environmental Education*, **34**(3), 12-21.
7. İleri, R. (1998). Çevre eğitimi ve katılımın sağlanması. *Ekoloji Çevre Dergisi*, **7**(28), 3-9.
8. Yılmaz, A., Morgil, F. İ., Aktuğ, P., & Göbekli, İ. (2002). Ortaöğretim ve üniversite öğrencilerinin çevre, çevra kavramları, ve sorunları konusundaki bilgileri ve öneriler. *Hacettepe Üniversitesi Eğitim Fakültesi Dergisi*, **22**(22), 156-162.
9. Arcury, T. (1990). Environmental attitude and environmental knowledge. *Human organization*, **49**(4), 300-304.
10. Jinliang, W., Yunyan, H., Ya, L., Xiang, H., Xiafel, W., & Yuanmei, J. (2004). An analysis of environmental awareness and environmental education for primary school and high school students in Kunming. *Chinese Education & Society*, **37**(4), 24-31.
11. Bloom, B. S. (1956). Taxonomy of educational objectives. Vol. 1: Cognitive domain. *New York: McKay*, 20-24.
12. Krathwohl, D. R. (2002). A revision of Bloom's taxonomy: An overview. *Theory into practice*, **41**(4), 212-218.
13. Köğce, D., Aydın, M., & Yıldız, C. (2009). Bloom taksonomisinin revizyonu: Genel bir bakış. *İlköğretim Online*, **8**(3), 1-7.
14. Aksu, Y., & Erduran Avcı, D. (2009). Fen ve teknoloji ile sınıf öğretmenlerinin çevre sorunlarına yönelik tutum ve görüşlerinin belirlenmesi: Burdur ili örneği. *Sakarya Üniversitesi Eğitim Fakültesi Dergisi*, **17**, 59-80.
15. Bradley, J. C., Waliczek, T. M., & Zajicek, J. M. (1999). Relationship between environmental knowledge and environmental attitude of high school students. *The Journal of Environmental Education*, **30**(3), 17-21.
16. Hacıeminoğlu, E., Alp, E., & Ertepınar, H. (2006). Öğretmen adaylarının çevreye ve çevre konularını öğretmeye yönelik tutumları. *VII. Ulusal Fen Bilimleri ve Matematik Eğitimi Kongresi Özetler Kitabı*, 07-09.
17. Özmen, D., Çetinkaya, A. Ç., & Nehir, S. (2005). Üniversite öğrencilerinin çevre sorunlarına yönelik tutumları. *TSK Koruyucu Hekimlik Bülteni*, **4**(6), 330-344.
18. Worsley, A., & Skrzypiec, G. (1998). Environmental attitudes of senior secondary school students in South Australia. *Global Environmental Change*, **8**(3), 209-225.
19. Coertjens, L., Boeve-de Pauw, J., De Maeyer, S., & Van Petegem, P. (2010). Do schools make a difference in their students'environmental attitudes and awareness? Evıdence from pisa 2006. *International Journal of Science and Mathematics Education*, **8**(3), 497-522.
20. Doğan, İ., & Purutçuoğlu, E. (2017). Sosyal hizmet uzmanlarının çevresel farkındalık seviyeleri ile çevreye yönelik tutumlarının belirlenmesi. *Türkiye Sosyal Araştırmalar Dergisi*, **2**, 389-405.
21. Korhonen, K., & Lappalainen, A. (2004). Examining the environmental awareness of children and adolescents in the Ranomafana region, Madagascar. *Environmental Education Research*, 10(2), 195-216.
22. Özdemir, A., & Yapıcı, E. (2010). Öğretmen adaylarının çevre sorunlarına yönelik farkındalık ve ilgi düzeylerinin karşılaştırılması. *Anadolu Doğa Bilimleri Dergisi*, **1**(1), 48-56.
23. Akış, S. (2000). Kuzey Kıbrıs' ta çevre bilinci. *Doğuş Ünivesitesi Dergisi*, 1 (1), 7-17.
24. Özdemir, E. B., Kaşot, N. (2015). *Fen Eğitimi ve Araştırmaları Derneği Fen Bilimleri Öğretimi Dergisi*, **3**(1), 16-39.

25. Varoğlu, L., Temel, S., & Yılmaz, A. (2018). Knowledge, attitudes and behaviours towards the environmental issues: Case of Northern Cyprus. *EURASIA Journal of Mathematics, Science and Technology Education*, **14**(3), 997-1004.
26. Hutton, D. G., & Baumeister, R. F. (1992). Self-awareness and attitude change: Seeing oneself on the central route to persuasion. *Personality and Social Psychology Bulletin*, **18**(1), 68-75.
27. Fraenkel, J. R., Wallen, N. E., & Hyun, H. H. (1993). *How to design and evaluate research in education* (Vol. 7). New York: McGraw-Hill.
28. Özdemir, O., Yıldız, A., Ocaktan, E., Sarışen, Ö. (2004). Tıp fakültesi öğrencilerinin çevre sorunları konusundaki farkındalık ve duyarlılıkları. *Ankara Üniversitesi Tıp Fakültesi Mecmuası*, **57**(03), 117-127.
29. Aminrad, Z., Zakaria, S. Z. & Hadi, A. S. (2011). Influence of age and level of education on environmental awareness and attitude: case study on Iranian students in Malaysian universities. *Medwell Journals*, **6**(1), 15-19.
30. Demirbaş, M., & Pektaş, H. M. (2009). İlköğretim öğrencilerinin çevre sorunu ile ilişkili temel kavramları gerçekleştirme düzeyleri. *Necatibey Eğitim Fakültesi Elektronik Fen ve Matematik Eğitimi Dergisi*, **3**(2), 195-211.
31. Hassan, A., Noordin, T. A. & Sulaiman, S. (2010). The status of the level of environmental awareness in the concept of sustainable development amongst secondary school students. *Procedia - Social and Behavioral Sciences*, **2**(2), 1276-1280.
32. Oğuz, D., Çakcı, I., & Kavas, S. (2011). Yüksek öğretimde öğrencilerin çevre bilinci. *Turkish Journal of Forestry*, **12**(1), 34-39.
33. Ek, H. N., Kilic, N., Ogdum, P., Duzgun, G., & Seker, S. (2009). 1st and 4 th grade students who are taught in different areas at Adnan Menderes University attitudes toward environment problems and sensitiveness to environmental issues. *Kastamonu Journal of Education*, **17**(1), 125-136.
34. Köse, S., Gencer, A. S., Gezer, K., Erol, G. H., & Bilen, K. (2011). Investigation of undergraduate students' environmental attitudes. *International Electronic Journal of environmental education*, **1**(2), 85-96.
35. Yıldırım, F., Yücel Işıldar, G. A., Erkoç, F., Onat, P., & Nazan Alparslan, Z. (2015). Examining impacts of natural sciences education in comparison with health and social sciences for pro-environmental behaviours in Turkey. *Journal of Integrative Environmental Sciences*, **12**(3), 189-204.
36. Tekin, C., & Gunes, G. (2018). Environmental awareness in university students and the affecting factors. *International Journal Of Community Medicine And Public Health*, **5**(2), 422-429.
37. Biswas, M. M. (2017). A study on the environmental awareness of secondary school students in relation to gender, locale of study and medium of instruction. *International Education and Research Journal*, **3**(12), 86-88.
38. Blocker, T. J., & Eckberg, D. L. (1997). Gender and environmentalism: Results from the 1993 general social survey. *Social Science Quarterly*, **78**(4), 841-858.
39. Tuncer, G., Ertepinar, H., Tekkaya, C., & Sungur, S. (2005). Environmental attitudes of young people in Turkey: Effects of school type and gender. *Environmental Education Research*, **11**(2), 215-233.
40. Straughan, R. D., & Roberts, J. A. (1999). Environmental segmentation alternatives: a look at green consumer behavior in the new millennium. *Journal of consumer marketing*, **16**(6), 558-575.

Middle school students' conceptual understanding of earthquakes

Döne Toprak-Dereli[1] *and Funda* Savaşcı-Açıkalın[2,*]

[1]Graduate Student, Istanbul University-Cerrahpasa Graduate School, Istanbul, Turkey
[2]Associate Professor, Istanbul University-Cerrahpasa Hasan Ali Yucel Faculty of Education, Istanbul, Turkey

Abstract. The purpose of the study was to investigate middle school students' conceptual understandings of earthquakes. Data were collected by using Understanding Earthquakes Test [1] and semi-structured interviews. Participants were a total of 1024 middle school students from the fifth to the eighth grade studying at ten different schools in Istanbul. Semi-structured interviews were conducted with thirty six students selected based on their test scores for three levels of understanding as high, middle, and low level. Findings of the current study indicated that students have lack conceptual understanding of earthquakes with many alternative conceptions. Students mostly from all grade levels seemed to have more scientific understanding in terms of protecting ways from earthquakes damage rather than explaining what earthquakes are and how earthquakes happen.

1 Introduction

Earthquakes are one of the destructive natural disasters for many countries all over the world. Turkey is one of the most seismically active regions on the earth due to the complex plate interaction among Arabia, Eurasia and Africa [2]. The most active fault zone in Turkey passes close to Istanbul and other major urban cities [3]. Moreover, more than half of the country falls under the earthquakes zones while almost all of the population lives in hazardous earthquake areas in Turkey [4].

Earthquakes are unavoidable natural disasters but the damage of earthquakes can be reduced by increasing people's knowledge and awareness about earthquakes [5-9]. There are have been many national and international studies investigating students' conceptual understandings of earthquakes in the literature [10-14]. Research indicated that both teachers and students have lack scientific knowledge about earthquakes with many misconceptions [1, 4, 5, 8, 10, 15-20]. A number of misconceptions were identified in the literature and some of them were listed as follows:

- Earthquakes occur in warm cities.
- Cracks that are resulted with heating earth by sun cause earthquakes.

* Corresponding author: fsavasci@istanbul.edu.tr; This study is a partial of the first author's Master thesis.

- Volcanic eruptions create earthquake.
- The source of earthquakes are weather events.
- Sun, thunder, rain, wind, heat, landslide and avalanche cause earthquakes.
- Earthquakes more likely occur near to islands.
- God creates earthquakes as a result of people's crime.
- The reasons of earthquakes are human activities (environmental pollution, soil pollution) [10, 11, 13, 14, 17, 19-22].

It is necessary to study students' conceptual understandings about earthquake in order to teach scientific understanding of earthquakes [19]. If students learn what earthquakes are and how they occur as well as how they protect themselves from the damage of earthquakes, it is possible to build earthquake literate society [5, 19, 23]. Therefore, the purpose of the study was to investigate middle school students' conceptual understandings in terms of not only what earthquakes are, how they occur but also how they protect themselves from the damage of earthquakes. The current study also consisted of a large sample size of middle school students studying at different grade levels in Istanbul and was conducted by a mixed research methodology including quantitative and qualitative data collection. As a result, it is expected to add significant contribution to the literature. The following research questions were designed;

1. How are fifth, sixth, seventh, and eighth grade students' conceptual understandings of earthquakes in terms of what earthquakes are, how they occur, what are their effects, and how people protect themselves from the damage of earthquakes?
2. Is there any significant difference of students' conceptual understanding in terms of grade levels?

2 Methodology

2.1. Data Collection

Mixed research methodology was conducted in order to investigate research questions in the current study. Data were collected by using Understanding Earthquakes Test [1] and semi-structured interviews. The test consisted of 60 questions with three-point Likert scale under four main categories: what earthquakes are (Part A), how earthquakes happen (Part B), how earthquakes affect other things (Part C), and how to protect ourselves from earthquakes (Part D). Thirty-six students selected based on their test scores as three levels as high, middle, and low were invited to semi-structured interviews. Each interview session took 15-20 minutes and students were asked about what earthquake is, how and why earthquake happens, how to protect earthquake damages. All interview records were transcribed before analyzing data.

2.2. Participants

Data were collected from a total of 1024 middle school students from the fifth to the eighth grade studying at ten different schools in Istanbul. School district permission was obtain before collecting data. All students were voluntarily participated in the study.

2.3. Data Analysis

Quantitative data was analyzed by using SPSS. Percentage and frequency of student responses for each question were calculated as descriptive statistics. Middle school students' conceptions of earthquakes were analyzed in terms of four major categories including definition of earthquakes (Part A what earthquakes are), the process of earthquakes (Part B how earthquakes happen), the effects of earthquakes on other things (Part C how earthquakes affect other things), and possible way for protecting people from earthquake damage (Part D how to protect ourselves from earthquakes). In order to analyze if there is any significant difference among students' conceptions in terms of grade level, ANOVA test was calculated. Student responses from semi-structured interviews were coded and categorized by using an inductive approach.

3 Findings

Findings of the current study indicated that middle school students have lack of scientific understanding of earthquakes. Firstly, both test scores and student responses in interviews indicated that middle school students in the current study had difficulty defining what earthquakes are. Figure 1 shows some examples of questions related to what earthquakes are and percentage of student responses to those questions. As seen in Figure 1, most of the students responded questions related to what earthquakes are as undecided. Many of them seemed to be unsure that earthquakes created seismic waves, or they occur on faults.

A7: Earthquakes are a release of energy stored in rocks.

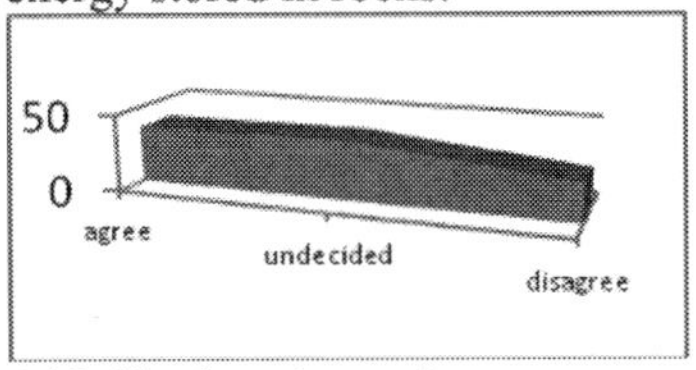

A10: Earthquakes occur on faults.

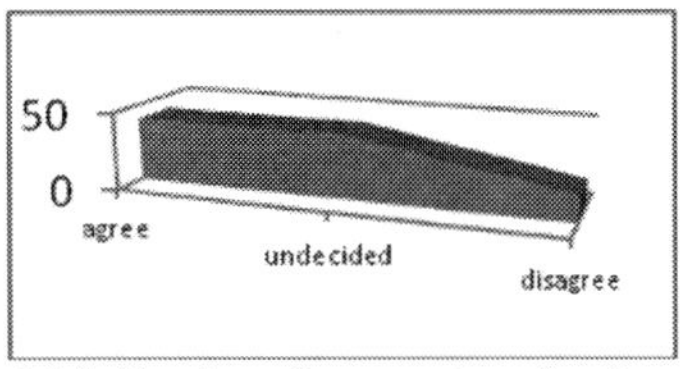

A12: Earthquakes only come to fruition in the world's crust

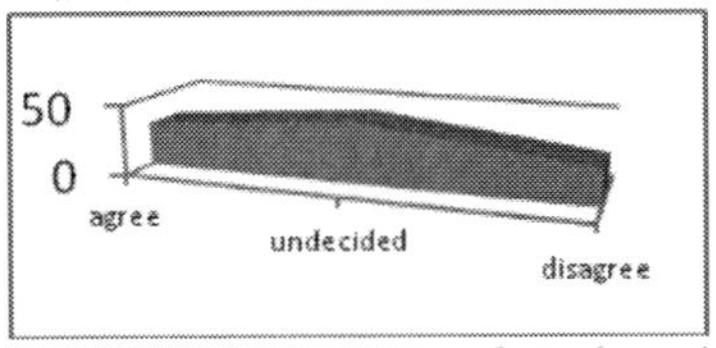

A14: Earthquakes create seismic waves.

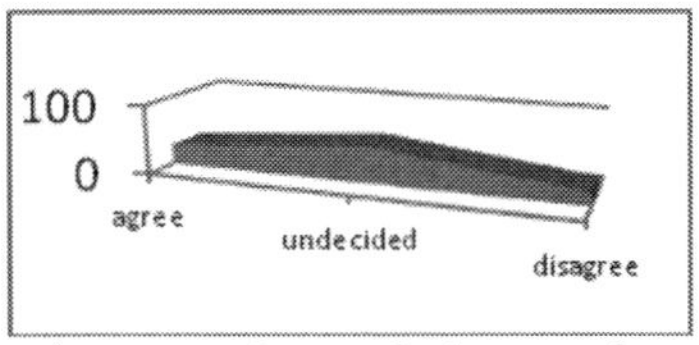

Figure 1 Percentage of students' responses related to questions of what earthquakes are

Figure 2 gives some examples of questions related to how earthquakes happen and percentage of student responses. As seen in Figure 2, middle school students in the current study were not sure about their responses so they did not seem to know that earthquakes are caused by release of energy stored in rocks or by the movement along faults.

B1: Earthquakes are caused by release of energy stored in rocks.

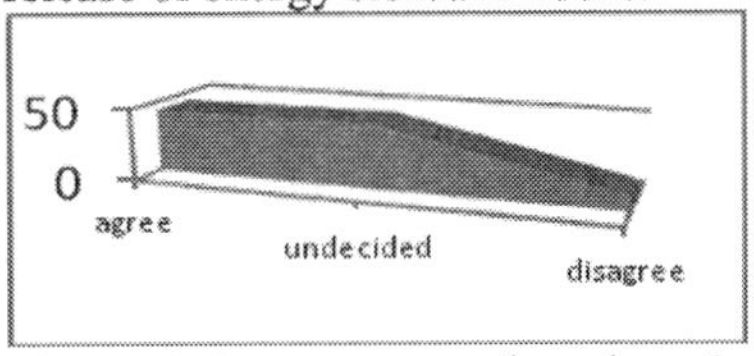

B2: Earthquakes are caused by the movement along faults.

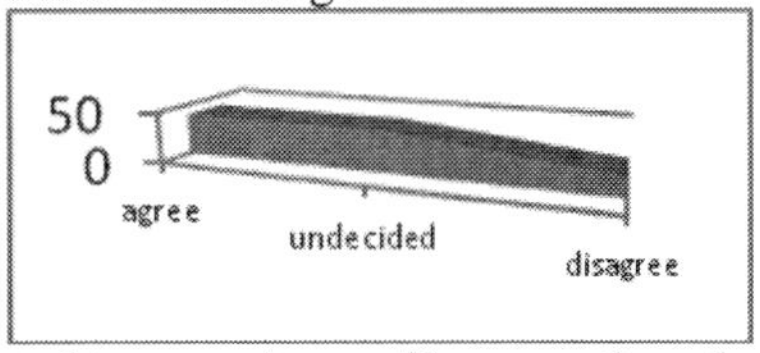

Figure 2. Percentage of students' responses related to questions of how earthquakes happen

B5: Earthquakes are caused testing.

B6: Earthquakes are caused by the Earth's core moving to the surface.

B14: Earthquakes are by nuclear caused by tides.

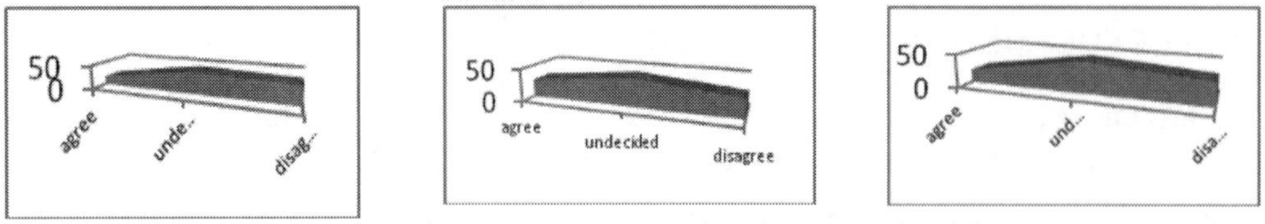

Figure 3. Percentage of students' responses related to unscientific statements of how earthquakes happen

Students in the current study seemed to have many misconceptions related to how earthquakes happen. In Figure 3, students seemed to be undecided that that testing, Earth's core moving to the surface, or tides can be reasons for earthquakes. Moreover, as seen in Figure 4, most of the students agreed with that deep noises vibrations or bad coming from under the ground can be reasons for earthquakes.

B13: Earthquakes are caused by the deep noises vibrations.

B15: Earthquakes are caused by bad coming from under the ground.

Figure 4. Percentage of students' misconceptions related to how earthquakes happen

Figure 5 shows percentage of students' responses of the effects of earthquakes. As seen in Figure 5, students seemed to have adequate knowledge about observable influences of earthquakes to daily life and social life. It is founded that students do not have clear understanding between earthquakes and volcanos. Many students agree with the items C3, C14, C15 about predictions of earthquakes as similar to common beliefs in society.

C2: Earthquakes can move faults.

C5: Earthquakes can make people have trouble walking

C6: Earthquakes can push move houses into the soil

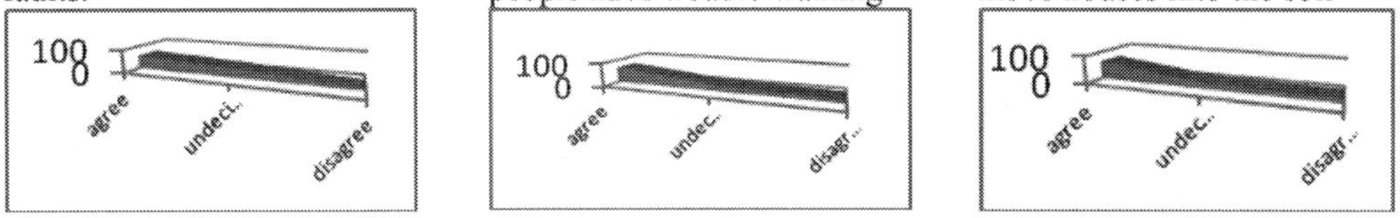

C7: Earthquakes can change the water level in wells.

C8: Earthquakes can shape the physical features of land.

C13: Earthquakes can cause volcanoes.

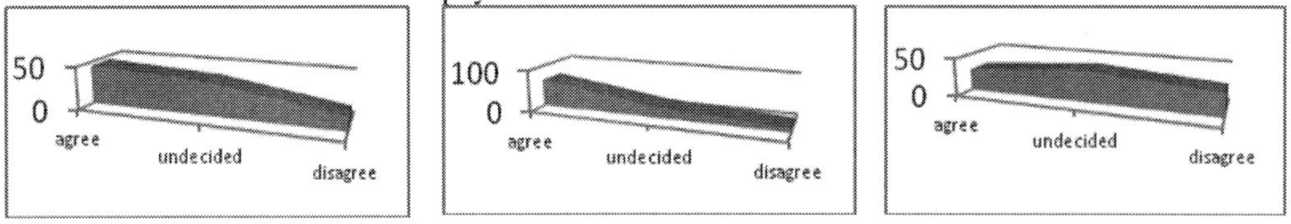

C3: Earthquakes can cause dog to bark just before it happens

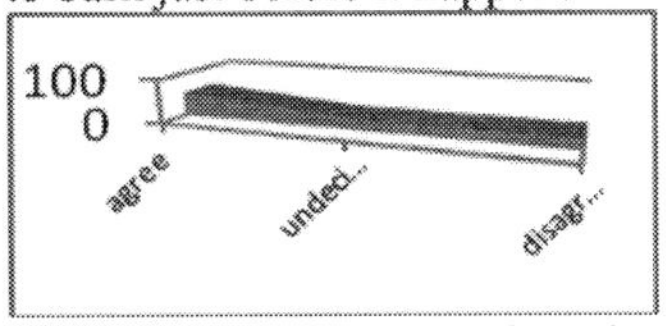

C14: Scientist can predict earthquakes.

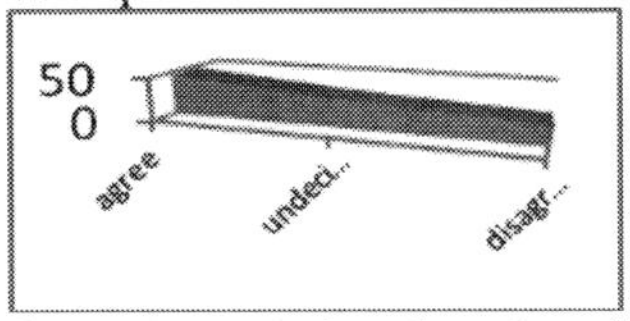

C15: Animals can predict earthquakes

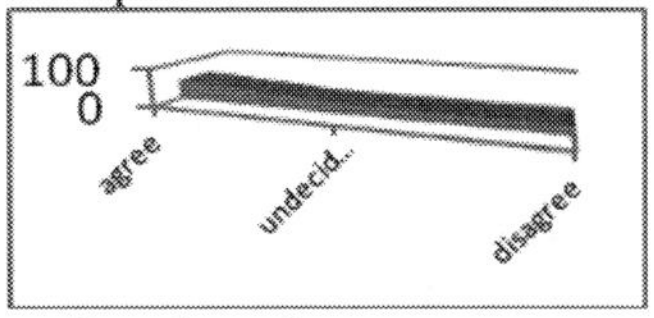

Figure 5. Percentage of students' responses related to the effects of earthquakes

Figure 6 indicates percentages of students' responses related to ways of protecting from earthquakes. Almost the half of the students disagreed with the items D2, D4, D10, D12 that include nonscientific ways of protection from earthquakes. However, students seemed to be not sure with respect to the items D6 and D7.

D2: Before earthquakes we should move heavy objects to high shelves because heavy objects can withstand quakes.

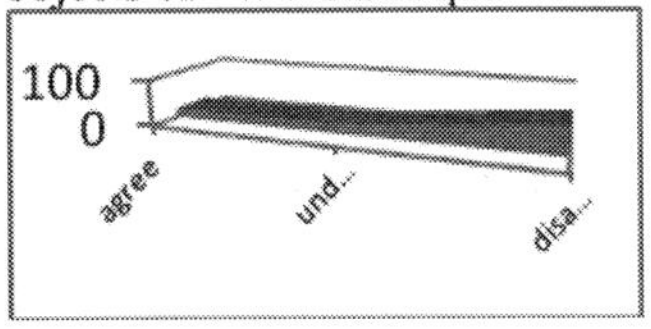

D4: Before earthquakes we should place beds by large windows so one can easily escape from the window.

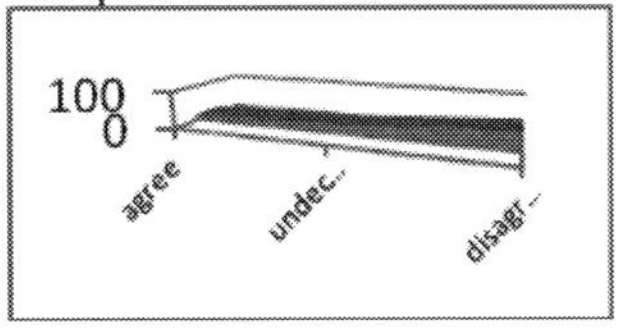

D9: During earthquakes we should get near a window.

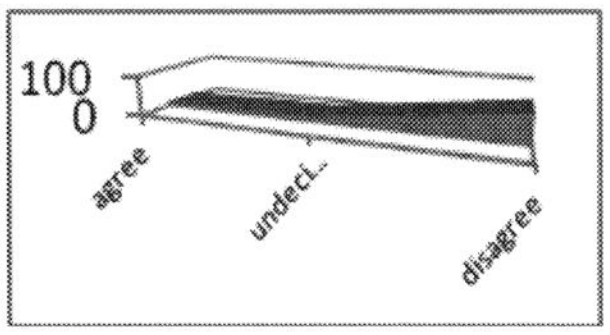

D10: During earthquakes we should stand under a tree.

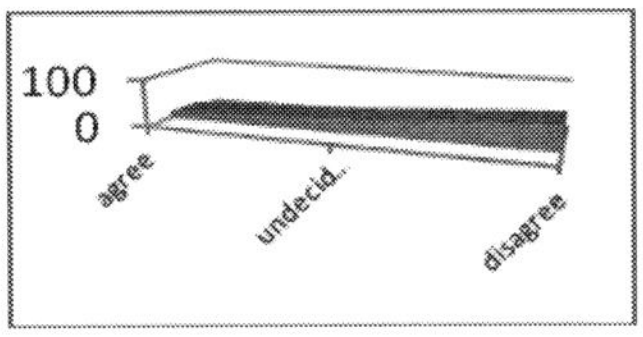

D12: During earthquakes if you find yourself indoors it is unusually better to rush outside.

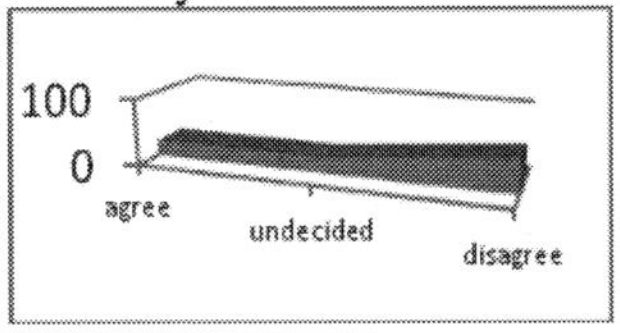

D6: Scientist can accurately predict earthquakes before it happens.

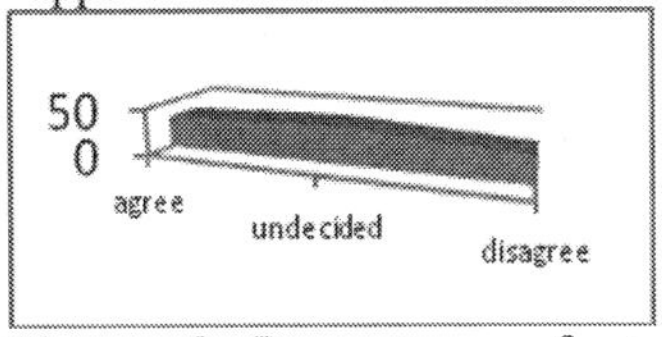

D7: During earthquakes we should hold on to something metal.

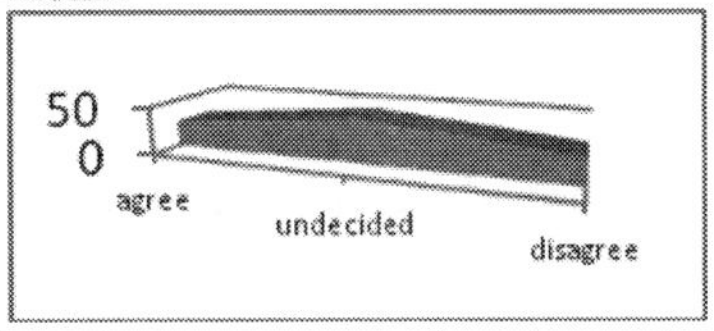

Figure 6. Percentage of students' responses related to the ways of protecting from earthquakes

In order to response research question 2, ANOVA test was done to investigate if there is any significant difference among students at different grade levels. Table 1 shows the result of statistical analysis with respect to what earthquakes are. As seen in Table 1, there is a statistical difference of students' conceptions of what earthquakes are in terms of grade level.

Table 1. Grade level comparison in terms of students' conception related to what earthquakes are

	SS	SD	Mean square	F	p	Significance
Between groups	61,13	3	20,64	4,45	,004	8-5,8-6,8-7
Within groups	4723,28	1019	4,63			
Total	4785,21	1022				

Table 2 shows the result of statistical analysis with respect to how earthquakes happen. As seen in Table 2, there is no statistical difference of students' conceptions of how earthquakes happen in terms of grade level.

Table 2. Grade level comparison in terms of students' conception related to how earthquakes happen

	SS	SD	Mean square	F	p	Significance
Between groups	59,41	3	19,80	3,76	,011	-
Within groups	5369,30	1020	5,26			
Total	5428,71	1023				

Table 3 indicates the result of statistical analysis with respect to effects of earthquakes. As seen in Table 3, there is a statistical difference of students' conceptions of effects of earthquakes in terms of grade level.

Table 3. Grade level comparison in terms of students' conception related to effects of earthquakes

	SS	SD	Mean square	F	p	Significance
Between groups	269,56	3	89,85	12,16	,000	8-5,8-6,8-7
Within groups	7535,31	1020	7,38			
Total	7804,88	1023				

Table 4 shows the result of statistical analysis with respect to ways of protection from earthquake damage. As seen in Table 4, there is a statistical difference between the fifth and the eighth grade students' conceptions of ways of protecting from earthquake damage.

Table 4. Grade level comparison in terms of students' conception related to ways of protection from earthquakes

	SS	SD	Mean square	F	p	Significance discrepancy
Between groups	38,38	3	12,79	2,82	,038	8-5
Within groups	4625,58	1020	4,53			
Total	4663,96	1023				

4 Discussion

This study investigated middle school students' conceptual understanding of earthquakes. Findings of the current study indicated that middle school students have difficulty to understand earthquake scientifically. Many students did not have scientific understanding of causes of earthquakes such as fault lines, seismic waves, and released energy stored in rocks. Some of the students believed that volcanism, tides, bad vibration and nuclear test can be causes of earthquakes. It is identified that students have belief about more occurrence of earthquakes in seas, dry regions and islands. Some of the students thought human actions like cutting trees, global warming, environmental pollution, over urbanization as causes of earthquakes. The findings of the research are similar with the results of previous studies [1, 10, 11, 12, 13, 14, 19, 20]. Findings of the current study indicated that some of the students believe that some animals can feel the earthquakes before it happens and scientist can predict earthquakes. Some of them stated that planting works, keeping environment clean, and less construction of buildings are necessary in order to prevent earthquakes. Students generally have lack of knowledge about causes of earthquakes and prediction about earthquakes. However, students at the upper grade level are more likely to have scientific understanding of earthquakes than those at the lower grades. The most difficult concept for students to understand were causes of earthquakes. This findings was consistent with the previous studies [6, 18, 19]. It is not surprising since science education curriculum does not cover sufficiently earthquakes topics.

5 Conclusion

The findings of the current study offers valuable implications for educators and future researchers. First of all, curriculum developers should include earthquake concepts especially the process about causes of them to the curriculum of primary and middle school since it is necessary to teach these concepts especially in Turkey. Secondly, teachers should have more scientific understanding of earthquakes and focus on more earthquake concepts in science classroom by a variety of instructional materials and methods. Finally, teacher education programs should organize seminars, conferences and other programs to increase knowledge and awareness of pre-service teachers and students.

Acknowledgment

This study is a partial of the first author's thesis. The project was supported by Istanbul University with a project no (will be added).

References

1. A. Oğuz, Unpublished PhD Dissertation Ohio State Uni. (2005)
2. O. Tan, M. C. Tapırdamaz, & A. Yörük, Turkish J. of Earth Sci. **17**, 405 (2008)
3. T. Taymaz, O. Tan, S. Yolsal, *The Proceedings of IWAM04*, (Mizunami Japan 2012)
4. A. Öcal Kastamonu Eğtim Dergisi. **15**, 1 (2007)
5. F. Aydın, Turkish Studies, **5**, 801 (2010)
6. E. Buluş-Kırıkkaya, O. Çakın, O., B. İmalı, & E. Bozkurt, Pro.Soc. Beh. Sci. **15**, 2305 (2011)
7. E. Buluş-Kırıkkaya, A. Oğuz-Ünver, & O. Çakın, Necatibey Eğt. Fak. Elekt.Fen ve Mat. Eğt. Der. **5**, 24 (2011)
8. C. Laçin-Şimşek, Jour.of Env. & Sci.Edu. **2**, 14 (2007).
9. A. Nalçacı, World Applied Sci. Jour. **12**, 1422 (2011).
10. M. Cin, H. Kara, A. Demir, *International Earthquake Symposium* (Kocaeli 2009)
11. M. Cin, Marmara Coğrafya Dergisi **22**, 70 (2010)
12. J. Dove, Res. Papers in Edu. **13**, 183 (1998)
13. S. Rakkapao, K. Arayathanitkul, P. Pananont, R. Chitaree, (2012)

14. K. E. K. Ross, T. Schuell *Northeastern Educational Research Association*, (Ellenville, NY 1990)
15. B. Aksoy, Jour. of World of Turks **5**, 247 (2013)
16. B. Aksoy, E. Sözen, Uşak Üni. Sos. Bil. Der. **7**, 279 (2014)
17. F. Aydın, ve M Coşkun, Int.Jour.of the Physical Sci. **5**, 1324 (2010)
18. H. Demirkaya, Türkiye Sos. Araş.Der. **3**, 38 (2007)
19. F. Savaşcı-Açıkalın, H. Uludüz, Asia-Pacific Forum on Sci.Learn. and Teach. **14**, 1 (2013)
20. Ü. Özdemir, M. Ertürk, İ Güner, M. K. Koca, Doğu Coğ.Der. **7**, 109 (2002)
21. A. D. Leather, Geology Teaching, **12** 102 (1987).
22. W. C. Philips, Science Teacher **58** 21 (1991)
23. S. Altay, Yüksek Lisans Tezi, Abant İzzet Baysal Üni.Sosyal Bil. Enst. (2008)

Assessment of problem solving proficiencies with self-efficacy perceptions of students in faculty of health sciences of cyprus international university

S.Yaprak Cetin[1,*], *Suat* Erel[2] and *Ozge* Ozalp[3]

[1] Akdeniz University, Department of Physiotherapy and Rehabilitation, Antalya, 70002, Turkey
[2] Pamukkale Univesity , School of Physical Therapy and Rehabilitation, Denizli, 20160, Turkey
[3] Cyprus International University, Health Sciences Faculty, Department of Physiotherapy and Rehabilitation, Nicosia, 99258, Turkish Republic of North Cyprus

Abstract. The aim of this study is to evaluate the self-efficacy perceptions and problem solving competencies of students of Health Sciences Faculty. The study included 150 students studying in 4th grade who completed the questionnaire completely. Self-efficacy-competence scale was used to evaluate students' self-efficacy perceptions, and Problem Solving Inventory was used to evaluate problem solving proficiencies. The mean age of the students included in the study was 22.26 ± 1.27 years and 59.3% [n = 89] were female students. It was determined that the self-efficacy perception scores of the students were 82.30 ± 14.37 and the problem solving ability scores were 103.65 ± 19.31. There was a significant relationship between self-efficacy perception and problem solving ability [r = -0,328, p: 0.01]. According to the results, it was determined that the students had a low level of self-efficacy perception and problem solving competencies.

Keywords: Student, Self-Efficacy ,Problem Solving, Health Sciences, Students

1 Introduction

Problem solving is "directing, respectively, the cognitive and effective behavioral activities such as giving behavioral reactions in order to adapt to complex internal and/or external wishes and desires" [1]. Problem solving competency involves many aspects including the self-belief of an individual in the cognitive process and problem solving.

The term self-efficacy was first introduced in 1977 by Bandura. Self-efficacy is described as a general capacity of an individual related to his/her belief of his/her competencies that can enable that individual to manage challenging situations that s/he has encountered or may encounter and a general capacity which involves cognitive, social,

*Corresponding author: fzt_s.yaprakulgen@hotmail.com

emotional and behavioral competencies and which has to be managed and organized for countless purposes [2]. A low perception of self-efficacy means the failure of an individual in believing his/her competencies and his/her perceiving challenges or tasks as problems. A high perception of self-efficacy, on the other hand, means considering the tasks with high levels of difficulty as opportunities that can be overcome, and thus managing to act more efficiently. Belief of self-efficacy has an influence on the way an individual thinks, feels, behaves and motivates himself/herself [2,3].

Regarding self-efficacy and learning strategies, Campbell and Hackett [1986], note that self-efficacy plays an important role in learning problem solving. The belief in self-efficacy can also influence the way individuals think as well as their emotional reactions. Individuals with low-self efficacy may tend to think that things are harder than they seem and may not be able to solve problems. Nevertheless, individuals with high self-efficacy approach more comfortably towards challenging tasks and problems and therefore can be more successful in solving the problems [4].

In literature, some studies have examined the perception of self-effectiveness/self-efficacy and problem solving proficiency separately and identified the factors determining these concepts. In literature, there is no study available that examines the self-efficacy/self-effectiveness perception and problem solving proficiency of students studying at faculty of health sciences.

The aim of this study is to evaluate the self-efficacy perceptions and problem solving proficiencies of students in the last semester of Health Sciences Faculty in Cyprus International University. It also examines whether there is a relationship between self-efficacy perceptions and problem solving proficiencies.

2 Method

2.1. Participants

The population of the research comprises of the students receiving education at Cyprus International University, Faculty of Health Sciences. The criteria of inclusion in the research necessitate being enrolled in one of the departments of Physiotherapy and Rehabilitation, Nutrition and Dietetics and Nursing departments within the faculty of health sciences, as well as volunteering to participate. The criterion of non-inclusion is he/she filling out the questionnaire incompletely.

2.2. Procedure

Problem Solving Inventory was used to evaluate problem solving proficiencies. The scale was developed by Heppner and Peterson in 1982 and adapted to Turkish by Sahin et.al in 1999 [5,6]. This Likert type scale consisting of 35 items and 3 sub-dimensions [confidence in problem solving ability, approach-avoidance, personal control] scored between 1-6; the lowest 32, the highest 192 can be taken. The high score indicates that the individual perceives himself / herself inadequately in problem solving skills and the low score indicates that he / she perceives himself / herself more adequately in problem solving skills [6].

Self-efficacy competence scale was used to evaluate students' self-efficacy perceptions. The scale was developed by Sherer et al. in 1982 and adapted to Turkish by Gozum and Aksayan in 1999 [7,8]. The scale consists of 23 items and 4 sub-dimensions [starting, maintaining, completing and interfering with behavior]. This Likert type scale scored between 1-5; the lowest score is 23, the highest score is 115. High score indicates high self-efficacy-competence perception, low score low self-efficacy-competence perception [8].

2.2.1 Statistical Analyses

Data collected by researchers was analyzed in SPSS 16.0 [Statistical Package for Social Science for Windows] package. In the evaluation mean, standard deviation and frequency distribution statistics were used. The Kolmogorov Smirnov Test was used to determine whether the data suit the normal distribution. Spearman correlation analysis was used for relationship between self-efficacy perception and problem solving ability because the data didn't suit the normal distribution. The Kruskal-Wallis test was used to determine whether there was a difference between self-efficacy and problem-solving ability among the sections. Mann Whitney U test was used in binary comparisons. Significance level was accepted as $p < 0.05$.

3 Results

The mean age of the students included in the study was 22.26 ± 1.27 years and 59.3% [n = 89] were female students [Table 1].

Table 1. Demographic variables of students

	X ±SD	min-max
Age [years]	22.26 ± 1.27	21-27
Weight (kg)	62.07±13.09	48-93
Height (cm)	168.53±11.14	158-182
Gender	**%**	**n**
Female	59.3	89
Male	40.7	61

It was found that the mean score of the self-efficiency/self-efficacy scale of students was 82.30±14.37 and the mean score of the problem solving inventory was 103.65 ± 19.31. There was a significant relationship in the negative direction between self-efficacy perception and problem solving ability [Table 2, $p<0.05$].

Table 2. Investigation of the relationship between problem solving proficiency and self-efficacy perception

	Problem Solving Inventory r[p*]
Problem Solving Inventory [score]	-
Self Efficacy Scale [score]	**-.328[0.01]**

*Spearman correlation analyses, $p<0.05$

It was also found that there is no difference among the departments regarding problem solving proficiency and self-efficacy perception [Table 3, $p<0.05$].

Table 3. Comparison of problem solving proficiency and self-efficacy perception of departments

	Physiotherapy and Rehabilitation X ±SD	Nutrition and dietetics X ±SD	Nursing X ±SD	$\chi 2$	p*	p**
PSI [score]	106.22±19.67	103.56±19.44	101.18±18.85	2.166	.339	.553[a]
						.148[b]
						.383[c]
SES [score]	84.80 ±15.13	81.42 ±14.57	80.70 ±13.30	2.710	.258	.676[a]
						.108[b]
						.255[c]

*Kruskal Wallis test, **Mann Whitney U test, X: mean, SD: standard deviation, PSI: problem solving inventory, SES: self efficacy scale, a: nutrition-physiotherapy, b: physiotherapy-nursing, c: nutrition-nursing

4 Discussion

The results of the study revealed that students have low level of problem solving proficiency and medium level of self-effectiveness/self-efficacy perception. Additionally, it was observed that there is a low level of correlation between problem solving proficiency and self-efficacy perception. In our study, students' self-efficacy perception increases; they perceived themselves more adequately about problem solving skills/proficiencies. It was found that there is no difference among the departments in terms of problem solving proficiencies and self-efficacy perception.

In literature, problem solving proficiencies and self-efficacy perceptions of students studying in the field of health sciences have been examined separately. Students that were involved in these studies are more generally students from nursing departments [9-12]. Our study is significant in the way that it determines altogether the problem solving proficiencies and self-efficacy perceptions of students from 3 different departments at the same faculty and also examines the relationship between them.

In a study conducted among nursing students, it is underlined that problem solving proficiencies are critical in all stages of health care system. It is highlighted that the art of caring entails problem solving proficiency, which sets the basis for knowledge, skills, expertise and effective medical practices [9] Moshirabadi et.al. [2015] notes that in order to improve the problem solving proficiency, educators need to help students overcome their emotional and cognitive challenges [10]. The studies conducted with Nursing Department students through making use of the Problem Solving Inventory have revealed that students have medium level of problem solving proficiencies [10-14]. Moreover, in some of the studies, it was observed that the problem solving proficiencies improved from the first grade to the fourth grade [10,15]. However, in our study, it was found that the problem solving proficiencies of students from all grades were at a low level. The fact that our results were found to be different than those in the literature can be related to such emotional factors as the upbringing, cultural background and educational background of the students. In the literature, it is underlined that problem solving proficiencies can be influenced by such characteristics [6,16].

The body of literature stresses that the beliefs of self-efficacy is practically important for health care workers and that it is also related to academic achievement [17]. Various methods have so far been used in the literature for the assessment of self-efficacy [18,19,20]. In a study that employed a different assessment method than our study, it was found that the self-efficacy of nursing students is at a high level [19]. In the study conducted by Orgun and Karaöz'ün with nursing students, the self-effectiveness/self-efficacy scale was used and it was observed that the self-efficacy of students was at a medium level [11]. In our study it was found that self-efficacy is at a medium level not only among nursing students but also among physiotherapy and rehabilitation, and nutrition and dietetics students.

In the literature, a study that evaluated the relation between problem solving proficiency and self-efficacy perception was not found. Bandura asserts that self-efficacy provides for effective problem solving. In a study, it is noted that the strategies for increasing self-efficacy could also help for the resolution of social problems [21]. In the study carried out with nursing students, it was also observed that there is a relation between academic self-efficacy perception and problem solving proficiency [22]. In a study conducted at the faculty of nursing, a positive, medium-level but statistically insignificant relation between post training problem-solving ability and self-efficacy has been found [23]. In our study, it was observed that the problem solving proficiencies and self-efficacy perceptions of the students that study at the physiotherapy and rehabilitation, nutrition and dietetics and nursing departments of the faculty of health sciences are related at a low level. As the students from all of the departments have low levels of problem solving proficiencies, we think that the relationship between problem solving proficiency and the perception of self-efficacy is at a low level.

The limitation of our study has been the fact that the study involved only the students from the 4th grade. Another limitation is that we were unable to include equal number of male and female students. Future studies may examine the problem solving proficiencies and self-efficacy perception of equal numbers of male and female students starting from the first grade and extending to upper grades.

Starting from the first year, we think that effective learning strategies during the undergraduate education can bring these characteristics to a better level than the last class. According to these results, the self-efficacy perception of the same group of students and problem solving proficiencies evaluation of Physiotherapy and rehabilitation, Nutrition and dietetics and Nursing education in last year is recommended.

References

1. P.P. Heppner, C.E. Baker, Applications of the Problem Solving Inventory. Meas Eval Couns Dev. ***29***, 4, 229-241 [1997]
2. A. Bandura, Self-efficacy: toward a unifying theory of behavioral change. *Psychol Rev.* **84**, 2, 191-215 [1977]
3. K. McLaughlin, M. Moutray, O. Muldoon, The role of personality ve self efficacy in the selection ve retention of successful nursing students: a longitudinal study. J Adv Nurs., **61**, 2, 211–221 [2007].
4. N. K. Campbell, G. Hackett, The effects of mathematics task performance on math self-efficacy and task interest. J Vocat Behav **28**, 2, 149-162 [1986]
5. P. P. Heppner, C. H. Petersen, The Development and Implications of a Personal Problem-Solving Inventory. J Couns Psychol. **29**, 1, 66-75 [1982]
6. N. Sahin, N. Sahin, P. Heppner. Psychometric properties of the Problem Solving Inventory in a group of Turkish University Students. Cog Theo Res, 17, 4 [1993]
7. M. Sherer, J.M. Maddux, The self-efficacy scale: Construction and Validation. Psychol Rep, **51**, 663-671 [1982]
8. S. Gozum, S. Aksayan. The reliability and validity of Turkish form of the self-efficacy scale. J Ataturk University School of Nursing, **2**,1 [1999]
9. J.J. Wang, K. Lo, Chi-Hui, K. Ya, Lie, Problem solving strategies integrated into nursing

process to promote clinical problem solving abilities of RN-BSN students. Nurse Educ Today, **24**, 589-595 [2004].

10. Z. Moshirabadi, N.Seyedfatemi, L. Borimnejad, H. Haghani, The Perceived Problem Solving Skill of Iranian Nursing Students. Client-Centered Nursing Care, **1**, 3 [2015]
11. F. Orgun, B. Karaoz, Epistemological beliefs and the Self-efficacy Scale in nursing students. Nurse Educ Today, **34**, 6, 37-40 [2014]
12. W.H. Jun , Anger expression, self-efficacy and interpersonal competency of Korean nursing students. Int Nurs Rev. 63, 4, 539-546 [2016]
13. N. Cinar, C. Sözeri, S. Sahin, R. Cevahir R, M. Say, Problem solving skills of the nursing and midwifery students and influential factors Rev Eletr Enf. **12**, 4, 601-606 [2010]
14. I. Altun, The perceived problem solving ability and values of student nurses and midwives, Nurse Educ Today, **23**, 575-584 [2003].
15. M. Uslu, C. Girgina, Effects of residential conditions on the problem solving skils of university students Procedia Soc Behav Sci, **2** , 3031–3035 [2010]
16. P.P. Heppner, C.E. Baker, Applications of the Problem Solving Inventory. Meas Eval Couns Dev. **29**, 4, 229-241 [1997]
17. J. Lane, A. Lane, Self-efficacy and academic performance. SBPJ. **29**, 687-694 [2001]
18. A.E. Durkin, R.S. Feinn, Traditional and Accelerated Baccalaureate Nursing Students' Self-Efficacy for Interprofessional Learning. Nurs Educ Perspect. **38**, 1, 23-28 [2017]
19. U. Karabacak, S. Serbest, Z. Kan Onturk, F. Eti Aslan , N. Olgun, Relationship between student nurses' self-efficacy and psychomotor skills competence. Int J Nurs Pract. **19**, 2, 124-130 [2013].
20. S.L. Casapulla, Self-efficacy of Osteopathic Medical Students in a Rural-Urban Underserved Pathway Program. J Am Osteopath Assoc. **117**, 9, 577-585 [2017]
21. A.D. Brown, M. L. Dorfman, C. R. Marmara, R.A. Bryant, The impact of perceived self-efficacy on mental time travel and social problem solving. Conscious Cogn, **21**, 1, 299-306 [2012]
22. F.F. Zhao, X.L. Lei, W. He, Y.H. Gu, D.W. Li, The study of perceived stress, coping strategy and self-efficacy of Chinese undergraduate nursing students in clinical practice Int J Nurs Pract. **21**, 401–409 [2015]
23. G. Angel, Problem solving training:effects on the problem solving skills and self efficacy of nursing students. Euro J Edu Res. **64**, 231-246 [2016]

Determining the learning preferences of the students of the faculty of health sciences in Cyprus International University

S.Yaprak Cetin[1,*] and *Suat* Erel[2]

[1]Akdeniz University, Department of Physiotherapy and Rehabilitation, Antalya, 70002, Turkey
[2]Pamukkale Univesity , School of Physical Therapy and Rehabilitation, Denizli, 20160, Turkey

Abstract. The purpose of the study is to examine the learning preferences of students at the Cyprus International University of Health Sciences and determine whether these preferences have changed according to department and sex. A total of 150 students participated in the study. While 61 of the students were female and 89 were male, the mean age was 22.06 ± 1.23 years. VARK [Visual, Aural, Read-write, Kinesthetic] Learning Preferences Inventory was used to determine students' learning preferences. As a result of the study participants mostly found "Kinesthetic" style (4.84 ± 2.13). However, there were no significant differences in terms of department and gender factors in any dimension ($p > 0.05$). Based on the results of this study, we think that determining the learning style that students are likely to lead to the selection of suitable techniques for the trainees.

Keywords: Learning preferences, students, health sciences faculty

1 Introduction

Students can learn in many ways [1]. Some students learn by seeing, some learn by hearing whereas some of them learn by drawing and creating mathematical models. Students from all age groups have ways of responding differently but coherently to the phenomenon of learning. These behaviors are called learning style or cognitive style [2]. In other words, the style of learning is a way of preserving new and difficult knowledge that begins with concentration, is processed and adopted. Methods of learning are also diverse. The amount of learning achieved by a student during class depends not only on that student's natural skills and preparation for the class but is also related to the student's style of learning and the educator's teaching method [3].

Educators are in pursuit of various strategies for their course sessions. As educators improve themselves in this direction, the quality of education increases [2].A student's determination and awareness of his/her own learning style, ensures better deliberation in the

* Corresponding author: fzt_s.yaprakulgen@hotmail.com

selection of materials, and in course design among the educators for improving the learning opportunities [1].

There is a variety of measuring tools in order to determine the learning style of a student. Developed by Fleming, the VARK [V: visual, A: aural, R: read-write, K: kineshtetic] model ofers a profile of students that enables the reception of knowledge and is based on sensual modalities. According to this model, students that prefer the visual style process knowledge through seeing. Students that prefer the aural style receive knowledge through hearing. For the read-write option, students prefer words to be written down. And the students that prefer the kinesthetic style acquire knowledge through experimentation and practice [2].

In literature, there are studies on learning preferences of students receiving education in a variety of fields [4, 5, 6, 7, 8]. Recent studies on students receiving education in the area of health are most generally carried out among faculties of medicine and faculties of nursing [7-10]. According to the results of these studies, it was observed that students studying in different departments have different learning styles [4-10). In these studies, it is also indicated that gender difference is a significant factor in terms of learning preference [11-13]. Additionally, in literature, there are also a few studies comparing the learning preferences among different departments [6, 14].

The aim of this study is to determine the learning preferences of the students receiving education at Physical Therapy and Rehabilitation, Nutrition and Dietetics and Nursing departments within the faculty of health sciences and to detect whether such preferences differ according to the varieties of grade and gender.

2 Methods

2.1. Participants

The population of the research comprises of the students receiving education at Cyprus International University, Faculty of Health Sciences. The criteria of inclusion in the research necessitate being enrolled in one of the departments of Physical Therapy and Rehabilitation, Nutrition and Dietetics and Nursing departments within the faculty of health sciences, as well as volunteering to participate. The criterion of non-inclusion is he filling out the questionnaire incompletely.

A total of 150 students in the Cyprus International University of Health Sciences Faculty in Physiotherapy and Rehabilitation [n:50], Nutrition and Dietetics [n:50], Nursing [n:50] department attending the 3rd and 4th semester in 2017-2018 academic year participated in the study. While 61 of the students were male and 89 were female, the mean age was 22.06 ± 1.23 years.

2.2. Procedure

VARK [Visual, Aural, Read-write, Kinesthetic] Learning Preferences Inventory was used to determine students' learning preferences. This test was developed by Fleming in 1987 and was later adapted to Turkish by Kalkan [15,16].

The scope of VARK inventory is defined as follows: the students that prefer learning in visual style make use of body language, mimics, diagrams, maps, graphics, pictures and tables in order to understand the contents of a course. The students that prefer aural tyle learning give importance to music and aural stimulants. Speaking, discussion, listening, narrating, tone fo voice and speaking speed are important for students that prefer this style. The students that prefer the read-write style garther information by reading or writing from published materials. The students that prefer the kinesthetic style learn through moving, touching and doing [17].

The VARK inventory consists of 16 questions in total. In the inventory, a different scenario is created for each question and the individual is asked about what action s/he would take in that scenario. The individual that prefers multiple ways can mark more than one option. The responses to the inventory questions are graded according to their being visual, aural, read-write and kinesthetic and total grades are obtained in these four dimensions. A higher grade in a dimension indicates that the related learning style is preferred on a higher degree [15]. A student responding to the questionnaire can prefer more than one learning style; and this reveals that an individual can be inclined to multi-dimensional learning style.

2.2.1 Statistical Analysis

The results of the study were analyzed with the SPSS 16.0 [Statistical Package for the Social Sciences] software. During this assessment, definitive statistics such as mean value, standard deviation and frequency distribution were used. Whether the data is coherent with the normal distribution was determined by use of the Kolmogorov Smirnov Test. The one-way analysis of variance "ANOVA" was used for comparing the department variables of the data whereas "Independent Samples T-Test" was used for the gender variable. Significance level was accepted as $p < 0.05$.

3 Results

Demographic data of the students are presented in Table 1.

Table 1. Demographics data of students

	X ±SD	**min-max**
Age (years)	22.26 ± 1.27	21-27
Weight (kg)	62.07±13.09	48-93
Height (cm)	168.53±11.14	158-182
Gender	**%**	**n**
Female	59.3	89
Male	40.7	61

It was found that the students mostly prefer the "Kinesthetic [K]" style [Table 2]. It was found that the students receiving education at Physical Therapy and Rehabilitation and Nursing mostly prefer the "Kinesthetic [K]" style; whereas the students at Nutrition and Dietetics prefer the "Aural [A]" style.

Table 2. Means of VARK's dimensions

VARK	X ±SD
Visual	3.38±2.08
Auditory	4.53±1.77
Read-write	4.01±1.76
Kinesthetic	4.84±2.13

X:mean, SD:Standart deviation

However, when the learning preferences were compared among the departments, a statistically meaningful difference could not be detected in any of the learning style dimensions [Table 3, $p<0.05$].

Table 3. Comparison between of departments of learning styles

VARK	Physitherapy X ±SD	Nutrition and dietetics X ±SD	Nursing X ±SD	F	p*
Visual	3.22±2.12	3.68±1.80	3.26±2.30	2.64	.07
Auditory	4.32±1.75	4.76±1.97	4.52±1.58	0.18	.82
Read-write	3.84±1.73	4.30±1.82	3.90±1.72	0.72	.48
Kinesthetic	5.02±2.12	4.52±2.19	4.98±2.08	0.09	.90

* ANOVA, $p<0.05$, X:mean, SD:Standart deviation

When the learning preferences were compared according to gender, a statistically meaningful difference could not be detected in any of the learning style dimensions [Table 4, $p<0.05$].

Table 4. Comparison of dimensions of VARK in terms of gender

VARK	X ±SD		F	p*
	Female	Male		
Visual	3.73±2.04	3.14±2.08	0.09	.08
Auditory	4.40±1.97	4.61±1.62	0.18	.49
Read-write	3.77±1.75	4.17±1.75	0.11	.16
Kinesthetic	4.70±1.79	4.93±2.34	2.47	.50

*Independent sample T test, $p<0.05$X:mean, SD:Standart deviation

4 Discussion and Conclusion

As a result of the study, it was observed that the students most generally prefer the "Kinesthetic [K]" style. It was found that the students receiving education at Physical Therapy and Rehabilitation and Nursing prefer the "Kinesthetic [K]" style; whereas the students at Nutrition and Dietetics prefer the "Aural [A]" style. However, the scale among the department did not reveal any meaningful difference. Similarly, in the comparison among departments and gender, a meaningful difference could not be detected in any dimension of the scale.

In literature, there are studies on learning preferences of students receiving education in a variety of fields (4-10). In a study in Iran carried out among medical students, it was found that the learning preference of students is Aural and Read-Write [9]. In another study, it was found that the students receiving education at the faculty of health sciences prefer the "Kinesthetic" style. The results obtained from this study have similarities with the study carried out by Baykan et. al [18]. We are in the opinion that this result depends on the fact that the courses at the faculty of health sciences are practical and require clinical experience [14,18].

In the literature, the results of the studies related to the comparison of learning preferences according to the gender are contradictory. In a study carried out with the students of Faculty of Medicine, in the Visual dimension, a meaningful result was found among female students [19]. In another study with the students at faculty of medicine, a gender difference could not be detected in any dimension of the VARK inventory. In a study carried out at a faculty of health sciences, a meaningful result was obtained among male students in the Kinesthetic style of the VARK inventory [18]. In a study with the dental school students, a difference according to gender could not be found [20]. In our study, a gender difference could not be found in any of the sub-dimensions of the VARK inventory. When the departments included in our study were compared with those in the study of Baykan et. al., a similarity was detected only with the Physical Therapy and Rehabilitation department. However, in this study, a different result among genders is not provided for the Physical Therapy and Rehabilitation department.

In literature, the results of the learning preferences of the students receiving education at different departments are diverse. In the studies, it was observed that the students at Physical Therapy and Rehabilitation department mostly prefer the Kinesthetic style [14]. According to the studies carried out with Nursing students in various universities, it was observed that the students prefer the kinesthetic style [21,22]. In another study, it was found that the physical therapy and nursing students also prefer kinesthetic style [23]. No study that determines the learning preferences of Nutrition and Dietetics students could be found in literature. In our study, in parallelism with the literature, it was found that physical therapy and rehabilitation and nursing students prefer the Kinesthetic style. In our opinion, the fact that the learning style of the nutrition and dietetics students is different is because the contents of the courses taught in this department are based mostly on theory.

The limitation in our study is the inequality of the number of male and female students. Another limitation is that in these departments, only the 3rd and 4th grade students were included in our study and that these students were taken as a single group and the differences among the grades was not taken into consideration.

According to the results of our study, the students receiving education at the faculty of health sciences most generally prefer the Kinesthetic style. Based on these results, it would be convenient for the educators at the faculty of health sciences to develop techniques according to this style while preparing the contents of their courses. Determination of the style that is mostly preferred by students could provide guidance for educators in selecting the right teaching technique. Thus, an increase in student achievements in their department courses can be provided.

References

1. R.M. Felder, L. K. Silverman. Learning and teaching styles in engineering education. Engr Education, **78**, 674-81 (1988)
2. N. D. Fleming, C. Mills. Not Another Inventory, Rather a Catalyst for reflection. To Improve the Academy, **11**, 137-55 (1992)

3. T. F. Hawk, A. J. Shah. Using learning style instruments to enhance student learning. Dec Sci J Innov Edu, **5**, 1-19 (2007)
4. S. Tuna. The Learning Styles of Art Education Students. Electro J Soc Sci, **25**, 252-261 (2008).
5. H. H. Bahar, R. Polat, M.R. Ozbas, Learning Styles of Art, Music and Physical Education Pre-Service Teachers. J Edu Fac, **18**, 409-424 (2016)
6. T. Brown, T. Cosgriff, G. French. Learning style preferences of occupational therapy, physiotherapy, and speech pathology students: a comparative study. J Allied Health, **6**,3 (2008)
7. P. Kharb, P. P. Samanta, M. Jındal, V. Singh. The learning styles and preferred teaching-learning strategies of first year medical students. J Clin Diagn Res. **7**, 6, 1089-1092 (2013).
8. I. M. Alkhasawneh, M.T. Mrayyan, C. Docherty, S. Alashram, H. Y. Yousef. Problem-based learning (PBL): assessing students' learning preferences using VARK. Nurse Educ Today, **28**, 5, 572-579 (2008).
9. H. Peyman , J. Sadeghifar, M. Alizadeh, M. Yaghoubi, M. Mohammad Hassan Nahal, N. Yamani, et al. Learning Styles of First Year Nursing and Midwifery Students in Ilam University of Medical Sciences. J Med Educ, **11**, 9, 1350-1358 (2012).
10. T.A. Meehan-Andrews. Teaching mode efficiency and learning preferences of first year nursing students. Nurse Educ Today, **29**, 1, 24-32 (2009).
11. R. Choudhary, P, Dullo, R.V. Tandon. Gender differences in learning style preferences of first year medical students. Pak J Physiol **7**,2 (2011).
12. E. A. Wehrwein, H. L. Lujan, S. E. DiCarlo. Gender differences in learning style preferences among undergraduate physiology students. Adv Physiol Educ. **31**, 2 ,153-157 (2007).
13. R. P. Urval, A. Kamath, S. Ullal, A. K. Shenoy, N. Shenoy, L. A. Udupa. Assessment of learning styles of undergraduate medical students using the VARK questionnaire and the influence of sex and academic performance. Adv Physiol Educ, **38**, 216–220 (2014).
14. S. A. Karaborklu, R. Mustafaoglu, G. Kus, A.R. Ozdincler. Determination of Learning Style Preferences in Students at the Faculty of Health Sciences. Clin Exp Health Sci, **7**, 146-151 (2017).
15. N. Fleming. VARK: A guide to learning styles Retrieved August 27, 2009, Available from: http://www. vark-learn. com/english/page. asp? p=research. (2001).
16. M. Kalkan. Learning preferences and problem-based discussion sessions: a study with Turkish university maritime students, SBPJ **36**, 1295-1302 (2008).
17. N. Fleming, C. Mills. Not another inventory, rather a catalyst for reflection, To improve the academy, **11**, 137 (1992).
18. Z. Baykan, M. Nacar. Learning styles of first year medical students attending Erciyes University in Kayscri,Turkey. Adv Physiol Educ. **31**,158–160 (2007).
19. R.S.Y. Wong, H.L. Siow, V. Kumarasamy, N.S.F. Suhaimi. Interdisciplinary and inter-institutional differences in learning preferences among Malaysian medical and health sciences students. J Adv Med E, **5**, 4, 164–171 (2017).
20. Z. Nasiri, S. Gharekhani, M. Ghasempour. Relationship between Learning Style and Academic Status of Babol Dental Students. Electron Physician. **8**, 5, 2340–2345 (2016).

21. L. McKenna, B. Copnell , A.E. Butler, R. Lau , Learning style preferences of Australian accelerated postgraduate pre-registration nursing students: A cross-sectional survey. Nurse Educ Pract, **28**, 280-284 (2018).
22. B.V. Stirling. Results of a study assessing teaching methods of faculty after measuring student learning style preference, Nurse Educ. Today. **55**, 107-111 (2017).
23. J.P. Good , D. Ramos , D.C. D'Amore. Learning style preferences and academic success of preclinical allied health students. J Allied Health. **42**, 4,81-90 (2013).

Research on the impact of recreational activities on the patients of schizophrenia

Yazgi Erdogan[1,*], *Faruk* Yamaner[1] and *Emrah* Karadere[2]

[1]Hitit University Sport Sciences Faculty, Corum, 19030, Turkey
[2]Hitit University Medical Faculty, Corum, 19030, Turkey

Abstract. This research was done for finding out the impacts of Recreational Activities on the Schizophrenic Patients. 30 patients diagnosed with schizophrenia registered in Hitit University Education and Research Hospital's Community Mental Health Centerwere included in the research. The patients were applied with educational games and folk dances as recreational activities three days a week for 12 weeks. In the research, Scale for the Assessment of the Negative Symptoms (SANS), Scale for the Assessment of the positive Symptoms (SAPS), Global Assessment of the Functioning (GAF) and Clinical Global Impression (CGI) scales were used as data collection tools at the beginning and the end of 12 weeks. In addition, body lipid percentages, body weights and body mass indexes (BMI) of the patients were calculated at the beginning and the end of the research by using TANITA device. According to the results of statistical analyses, the difference between start and end SANS (p=0,471), GAF (p=0,004), CGI (p=0,003) values and body lipid percentages (p=0,019) of the participants was statistically significant. However, the difference between start and end weight (p=0,406), BMI (p=0,471) and SAPS (p=0,081) rates was not statistically significant.

1 Introduction

Schizophrenia is a disease which starts at early ages, occur equally in both genders, can be seen in all societies and individuals in all socio-economic levels and continues with deformations, improvements and relapses in especially thought, deception and sensation areas (1, 2). According to a systematic review, life-long prevalence of schizophrenia in Turkey was determined as 8.9/1000 in general of the society (3).

In today's conditions, it gets harder day-by-day for a healthy individual to have a job, to continue his/her job and to become an economically free individual. This situation is harder for an individual diagnosed with schizophrenia than the healthy individuals (4).

Schizophrenia is a disease which effects a person's all cognitive functions (such as sensation, attention, memory), emotions, behaviors and judgment. It may create insufficiency in many areas such as relations between people, self-care and life abilities. The patients who lose their abilities, whose quality of life is impaired and who do not work are easy to be excluded from the society and to get blacklisted (5).

*Corresponding author: yzg.erdgnn@gmail.com

The signs of disease can be significantly removed with use of antipsychotic medicines and they are effective in all stages of antipsychotic treatment (start, fulminant and protective treatment (6).

However, rehabilitation programs which include art areas such as hand abilities, music, drawing, dance, folk dance are required in addition to the traditional treatment method evaluated as use of medicines (7).

It is thought that the physical activities impact the quality of life of the patients having mental diseases in two ways. The first one is that it increases physical health and the second is that it minimizes psychiatric and social discomfort (8).

The movements, pace, quickness, vitality, flexibility, force, stability in the folk dances are among important physical compatibility elements. The educational games also allow a person to relax physiologically and psychologically. It also eases compliance with the social life as well as it increases the impacts of treatment with game therapies. In this context, the purpose of this study is to review the impacts of 12-week educational games and folk dances to the treatment of the schizophrenia patients.

2 Method

2.1 Research Group

30 patients diagnosed with schizophrenia registered in Hitit University Education and Research Hospital's Community Mental Health Center were included in the research group.

2.2 Training Places and Durations

Trials were made under observation of the authorities for two weeks in order to provide adaptation, to see the lacks that may be present in the organization and to take feedbacks of the patients in terms of their motivations and the works were started after completing the lacks.

Educational games and folk dance works were done with the experimental group for totally twelve weeks as three times a week, for one hour on Monday, Wednesday and Friday in the sports hall of Hitit University's College of Medicine. The institution's psychiatrists and nurses took part in the works as observers.

Educational Games: Educational games were played between 10:00-11:00 on Monday and 10:00-10:30 on Friday for 12 weeks. The educational games included Twitch, Throw the Ball, Follow the Leader, Windmill Game, Run from the Rolling Ball, Taking and Giving up Hostage and Go Around and Get Position. It was given importance to make warm up for 10 minutes before the work and to make stretching moves for 10 minutes after the work.

Folk Dances: Folk dances were done between 10:00-11:00 on Wednesday and 10:30-11:00 on Friday for 12 weeks. In folk dance works, 'Ata Bari' of Artvin region, 'AgirGovend' of Bitlis region, 'Toycular' of Van region, 'Harmandali' of Izmir region and 'Kirikhan' of Gaziantep region were taught to the participants. While selecting the games, it was considered whether they are played as mixture of males and females, whether they have plain figures and whether they can be played by everyone without need of a unique player. It was given importance to make warm up for 10 minutes before the work and to make stretching moves for 10 minutes after the work.

2.3 Collection of Data

Body Composition Measurement: "Tanita Body Composition Analyze BC-418" bioelectric impedance analyzer was used for determination of body lipid percentages of the experiment group. The subjects were asked to stand on the platform with bare feet after entering the data to the analyzer's screen by reducing their lengths, ages, genders and weights of clothes for determining their body compositions. Body mass index (BMI), body lipid mass and body lipid percentage measurements were made.

Scale for the Assessment of the positive Symptoms (SAPS): It was developed by Andreasen in 1990 (9). In our country, availability and reliability works of this scale was made by Erkoç et al. in 1991. It consists of 34 items in total and 4 the sub scales as hallucinations, delusions, strange behaviors and formal thought disorders. Each item is assessed as *No symptom=0, *Suspicious=1, *Mild=2, *Middle=3, *Significant=4, *Strong=5 (10).

Scale for the Assessment of the Negative Symptoms (SANS): It was developed by Andreasen in 1990 (9). In our country, availability and reliability works of this scale was made by Erkoç et al. in 1991. It consists of totally 25 items and 5 sub scales as bluntness, alogia, decrease in energy and health, lack of enjoyment and social withdrawal and lack of attention. Each item is assessed as *No symptom=0, *Suspicious=1, *Mild=2, *Middle=3, *Significant=4, *Strong=5 (10).

Clinical Global Impression Scale (CGI): It was developed by Guy in 1976. It is a scale used by the observer for determining the strenght of mental disorders or the improvements in the observation. In the study, CGI-Strength form was used for assessment of the strength of disease. The observer scales the strength or improvement of the disease between *Not Sick=0 and *Very Sick=7 according to the general experience of the observer about the aforementioned disease (11).

Global Assessment of the Functioning (GAF): It was developed by Hall in 1995. It provides assessment of the general functioning related to the psychiatric symptoms. It is a scale assessed by the clinician based on the information identified with ranges of 10 points on the measurement scale with 100 points. It is a scale which helps observation of clinical processes of the individuals with a single scale in a general frame. High points in the scale show that the functioning is high (12).

2.4 Statistical Analysis

The data obtained in this study were analyzed with IBM SPSS Statistics Version 20 package program. While making research on the normal distribution base of the variants, Shapiro Wilk's was used due to the unit numbers. 0,05 was used as the significance level while interpreting the results and it was mentioned that the variants are not due to normal distribution when $p<0,05$ and variants are due to normal distribution when $p>0,05$.

While inspecting the difference between two related variants, Wilcoxon Test was used as they are not due to normal distribution.

0,05 was used as the significance level while interpreting the results and it was mentioned that there is a significant difference when $p<0,05$ and there is no significant difference when $p>0,05$.

3 Findings

Table 1. Frequency Distribution Table on Demographic Information

		n	%
Gender	Female	11	36.67
	Male	19	63.33
	Total	30	100
Marital Status	Single	18	60
	Married	10	33.33
	Divorced	2	6.67
	Total	30	100

36,67% of the participants are female and 63,33% are male. Regarding the marital status, 60% of them are single, 33,33% are married and 6,67% are divorced.

Table 2. Distribution Table on the Values

	n	Mean	Median	Min	Max	ss
Session Participation Rate	30	23.97	26	5	36	10.41
Age	30	41.23	40	24	64	10.22

The session participation rate is around 23.97. Age values are 41 in average.

Table 3. Results of Wilcoxon Test on the Difference between Times in terms of Weight Values

								Wilcoxon Test	
	n	Mean	Median	Min	Max	ss	Item Ave.	z	p
Weight 1	30	87.1	87	63	143	16.34	16.73	-0.688	0.492
Weight 2	30	85.03	84.5	61	145	17.42	11.46		

There is no statistically significant difference between times in terms of weight values (p>0,05). The value after weight is lower and it is not statistically significant.

Table 4. Results of Wilcoxon Test on the Difference between Times in terms of body mass index (BMI)

								Wilcoxon Test	
	n	Mean	Median	Min	Max	ss	Item Ave.	z	p
BMI 1	30	31.85	31.25	21.78	48.9	5.89	16.85	-0.721	0.471
BMI 2	30	31.04	30.08	23.04	49.59	6.2	11.36		

There is no statistically significant difference between times in terms of BMI values (p>0,05). The value after BMI is lower and it is not statistically significant.

Table 5. Results of Wilcoxon Test on the Difference between Times in terms of body lipid percentage

								Wilcoxon Test	
	n	Mean	Median	Min	Max	ss	Item Ave.	z	p
Body Lipid Percentage 1	18	35.97	37.55	21.7	50.6	8.7	9.69	-2.344	0,019*
Body Lipid Percentage 2	29	31.89	33	15.5	58.9	10.16	6.75		

There is no statistically significant difference between times in terms of body lipid percentage values (p>0,05). The value after body lipid percentage is significantly lower than the value before body lipid percentage.

Table 6. Results of Wilcoxon Test on the Difference between Times in terms of Points of Negative Symptom Scale

								Wilcoxon Test	
	n	Mean	Median	Min	Max	ss	Item Ave.	z	p
Negative Symptom Scale 1	30	42.3	41	9	81	17.77	13.26	-3.524	**0,001***
Negative Symptom Scale 2	30	41.17	40.5	10	80	18.05	6		

There is no statistically significant difference between times in terms of negative symptom scale points (p<0,05). The point after the negative symptom scale is significantly lower than the point before the negative symptom scale.

Table 7. Results of Wilcoxon Test on the Difference between Times in terms of Points of Positive Symptom Scale

								Wilcoxon Test	
	n	Mean	Median	Min	Max	ss	Item Ave.	z	p
Positive Symptom Scale 1	30	24.53	22	1	70	14.59	9.62	-1.743	0.081
Positive Symptom Scale 2	30	23.9	21	1	65	13.67	9.2		

There is no statistically significant difference between times in terms of positive symptom scale points (p>0,05). The value after the positive symptom scale is lower and it is not statistically significant.

Table 8. Results of Wilcoxon Test on the Difference between Times in terms of Points of General Assessment of Functioning

								Wilcoxon Test	
	n	Mean	Median	Min	Max	ss	Item Ave.	z	p
General Assessment of Functioning Scale 1	30	44.83	45	30	65	9.05	9.63	-2.912	0,004*
General Assessment of Functioning Scale 2	30	48.83	50	25	75	11.04	11.92		

There is no statistically significant difference between times in terms of General Assessment of Functioning Scale points (p<0,05). The point before the general assessment of functioning scale is significantly lower than the point after the general assessment of functioning scale.

Table 9. Results of Wilcoxon Test on the Difference between Times in terms of Points of Clinical Global Impression Scale

							Wilcoxon Test		
	n	Mean	Median	Min	Max	ss	Item Ave.	z	p
Clinical Global Impression Scale 1	30	4.77	5	4	6	0.77	8	-2.982	0,003*
Clinical Global Impression Scale 2	30	4.33	4	3	6	0.71	16		

There is no statistically significant difference between times in terms of clinical global impression scale points (p<0,05). The point after the clinical global impression scale is significantly lower than the point before the clinical global impression scale.

4 Conclusion, Discussion and Suggestions

As result of the research, it was found that there is reduction in the negative symptom levels of the schizophrenia patients and no reduction in the positive symptom levels (13) with the recreational activities. This finding is in compliance with the negative symptom scale in the other study findings that found reduction in psychiatric symptoms related to the increase of physical activities of schizophrenia patients, however, it is not in compliance with the positive symptom scale (14). In these researches, it is also mentioned that application of physical exercises is related to increase of quality of life (14, 15) and increase in functioning (15, 16). It is an expectable finding that we may have determined a significant increase in the points of general assessment of functioning as result of an approach that may increase quality of life and functioning. It can also be said that new socialization and entertainment possibilities offered by the recreational activities may have been effective in determination of these changes.

There was no significant change in body weights and BMIs of the schizophrenia patients after the recreational activities. It is claimed that the physical exercises have not been effective on weight loss induction (17). The fact that there has been no difference in the physical measurements although there have been increase in the psychiatric symptoms and quality of life as result of application of regular physical activities on the schizophrenia patients supports this claim (14). In another review, it was found that exercise approaches are not effective in BMI in schizophrenia (16). These literature findings support our study. It can also be said that the duration limited to 12 weeks and no diet program applied together with the physical exercises may have been effective in stability of measurements such as BMI and body weight in patients.

We can say that similar studies to be made on more schizophrenia patients with longer durations may present comprehensive findings in this field, thus they may contribute on treatments of schizophrenia patients by drawing attention on increase of approaches on applying more physical activities in the treatments.

This research and application study was limited to the patients diagnosed with schizophrenia in Hitit University Education and Research Hospital's Community Mental Health Center. In the research, educational games and folk dances were inspected as recreational activities. The suggestions developed as result of this research are given below.

- More added value can be provided on treatments of schizophrenia patients by increasing varieties of the educational games.
- Giving awards to the most successful ones among the schizophrenia patients during the educational games shall also be very important in learning and realizing the success criteria.
- More schizophrenia patients can be accessed by increasing the varieties of folk dances.They can have more energy and willingness in life.
- Positive feedbacks shall be taken if this kind of abilities are given also to the relatives of the schizophrenia patients. Because, self confidences of the patients shall increase as they start producing new things. And the families shall be the first ones to recognize these changes.
- They shall be able to actively live like the other individuals in the society.
- Comparisons can be made between those who newly begin the treatment and those who were treated before.

Generally, the schizophrenia patients have felt very well as they made sports and played games in this study. It was observed that the participants were generally very happy. It was observed that these people have socialized with the other patients. In addition, the patients who participated in this study mentioned that the mentors have been extremely helpful against them when they had difficulties in some games and sport activities. It is clear that activity treatment in schizophrenia patients shall have many benefits both nationally and internationally.

References

1. ArslantaşHülya, Adana Filiz, (2011), *Şizofreninin BakımVerenlereYükü. PsikiyatrideGüncelYaklaşımlar*, **3 (2)**, 251-277.
2. ÖzçelikBaşak,.(2002).,*SüregenpsikotikBozukluğu Olan HastalarınTedavi, BakımVeUyumSorunlarıBağlamındaBakırköyRuhVeSinirHastalıklarıEğitimVeAraştırmaHastanesi'ndekiUygulamalarVeYaşananGüçlükler. Düşünen Adam* 2002, **15(2)**: 85-89.
3. BinbayTolga, UlaşHalis, ElbiHayriye, AlptekinKöksal, (2011),*Türkiye'dePsikozEpidemiyolojisi: YaygınlıkTahminleriveBaşvuruOranlarıÜzerineSistemakBirGözdenGeçirme, TürkPsikiyatriDergisi*, **22**: 40-52.
4. Yıldız Mustafa. (2009).,*ŞizofreniRuhsalVeToplumsalTedaviGirişimleri. İçinde*: Ceylan E, Çetin M, Editörler. Şizofreni. **4Baskı**. İstanbul: İncekarakağıtMatbaası; 2009.1403-1413.
5. YanıkMedaim.(2007).,*TürkiyeRuhSağlığıSistemiÜzerineDeğerlendirmeVeÖneriler, RuhSağlığıEylemPlanıÖnerisi. PsikiyatrideDerlemeler, OlgularveVarsayımlar*;(özelsayı):16-20.
6. Remington GI, Adams ME (1994),.*Depotneuroleptics. Schizophrenia: ExploringtheSpectrum of Psychosis*, Editedby RJ Ancill, S Holliday, J Higenbotham, New York, Wiley.
7. KöroğluErtuğtul, GüleçCengiz.,(2007), *ŞizofreniIçinde. PsikiyatriTemelKitabı.* **2. Baskı**. Ankara: Hyb Basın Yayın;. 184-205.
8. Caroline, R.,Richardson M.D., Faulkner, G., McDevitt, J., SkrinarGary, S., Hutchinson, Dori S., Piette John D. (2005), *IntegratingPhysical Activity IntoMentalHealth Services forPersonsWithSerioucMentalIllness. Psychiatric Services.*;**Vol. 56No.3**, 30-50.
9. AndreasenNC., (1990),*Methods For Assessing Positive And Negative Symptoms. ProblPharmacopsychiatry*, 1990; **24**: 73-88

10. AydemirÖmer, KöroğluErtuğrul, (2006), *PsikiyatrideKullanılanKlinikÖlçekler*, **3**: 346-353.
11. Guy W. (1976),*ECDEUAssessment Manual for Psychopharmacology*, Revised US Dept Health, Education and Welfare publication (ADM), Rockville, National Institute of Mental Health, p.76-338.
12. Hall, R. C. (1995). *Global assessment of functioning: a modified scale.* Psychosomatics, **36(3)**, 267-275.
13. Açıl, Arzu Anıl, 2006, *ŞizofrenikHastalardaFizikselEgzersizinRuhsal Durum VeYaşamKalitesiÜzerineEtkisi*, CumhuriyetÜniversitesiSağlıkBilimleriEnstitüsüHemşirelikProgramı, YüksekLisansTezi, Sivas.
14. Sturludóttir K, Gestsdóttir S, Rafnsson RH, Jóhannsson E.(2015).,*The Effects Of Physical Activity İntervention On Symptoms İn Schizophrenia, Mental Well-Being And Body Composition In Young Adults*. Laeknabladid 2015;**101(11)**:519-24.
15. Dauwan M, Begemann MJ, Heringa SM, Sommer IE, (2016), *Exercise Improves Clinical Symptoms, Quality of Life, Global Functioning, and Depression in Schizophrenia: A Systematic Review and Meta-analysis. Schizophr Bull* 2016;42(3):588-99.
16. Firth J, Cotter J, Elliott R, French P, Yung AR.(2015),*A systematic review and meta-analysis of exercise interventions in schizophrenia patients*. Psychol Med. 2015;**45(7)**:1343-61.
17. Krogh J, Speyer H, Nørgaard HC, Moltke A, Nordentoft M.(2014),*Can Exercise Increase Fitness And Reduce Weight In Patients With Schizophrenia And Depression?* Front Psychiatry 2014;5:89.

A comparative study regarding secondary school students' satisfaction degree regarding the physical education class in Romanian and in Turkey

Teodora-Mihaela Iconomescu[1,*], *Veronica* Mindrescu[2], and *Ileana-Monica* Popovici[3]

[1]''Dunarea de Jos'' University, Domneasca Street, 47, Galati, 800008, Romania
[2]Transilvania University, Eroilor Street, 29, Brasov, 500036, Romania
[3]''Alexandru Ioan Cuza'' University, Carol I Street, 11, Iasi 700506, Romania

Abstract. In order for physical education classes in school to achieve their goals in the training and development of pupils, they must participate with pleasure, convinced that physical exercise helps them maintain an optimal state of health, a harmonious physical and personality development. For these reasons, it is important to know how students appreciate the physical education classes, how attractive they are to them, and what are their views on how to improve teaching techniques. The survey was conducted during school year 2015-2016, in November for the school from Turkey, on a number of 100 respondents and in March, for the schools from Romania, on a number of 94 respondents. The self-designed questionnaire represents the most widely used method in quantitative sociological research. The self-designed questionnaire contained a total of 10 questions that followed: In the first 4 questions, it was followed the pupils' opinion regarding the number of physical education classes in the school curriculum, the degree of satisfaction with the physical education classes in school, and the benefits that physical activity is believed to have. Questions 5-7 aimed at the rewards or sanctions received in the physical education class and the conflicts that may arise in the relationship between teacher and student. In both countries, physical education and sport require knowledge of all aspects associated with physical exercise, students' willingness to exercise and practise a sport, the desire to engage in physical exercises and their awareness of the influence that physical education has on their health.

Keywords: pupils, PE classes, attitudes

1 Introduction

Physical education has a predominant formative character, in a way that it prepares the subjects for life, and for the necessities of everyday life.

Physical education, being a part of the general education in schools of all degrees, has to fulfill the general needs of the youth: maintaining an optimal state of health, fostering harmonious physical development, improving the overall motor capacity, developing the

* Corresponding author: ticonomescu@ugal.ro, the present paper is the result of the equal contribution of all authors.

habit of practicing independent and systematic exercise, and the harmonious development of the subject's personality.

The discipline of "physical education" is provided in the curriculum for gymnasium education as a compulsory discipline in the schools in Romania and Turkey, the two countries in which the research was conducted.

The cultural and historical traditions are the most common reasons for choosing physical activities in schools. These are also reflected in the teaching of traditional dances and games, rooted in the culture of society. In gymnasium, the minimum recommended time for physical education is generally 6-8% of the total teaching time in most countries, while in Turkey the proportion is only 3-4% [9].

Improving the physical education lesson can attract the student to the enjoyment of movement so that he can continue to do physical activity, whether we are talking about outdoor games or various other sports, all being a good opportunity to socialize and to develop new and long-lasting friendships.

The educational value of practicing physical exercise depends decisively on how well students are attracted to the physical education class at school, and the degree of satisfaction of the lesson taught. The teacher will pursue didactic strategies designed to make physical education more effective, to educate students that physical education is a personal necessity for everyone, along with other daily necessities [4, 6].

The concept of Physical Education is a modern notion, being a new stage of gymnastics, as it was called in ancient times. Initially, Physical Education had some limited purposes, being regarded only as a mean of recreation after a more intense intellectual activity. Over time, Physical Education has diversified its content and gained deeper meanings.

Although for a long time Physical Education has been understood only as an action primarily aimed at fostering the right and harmonious growth of the youth body, endowing and developing the motor skills, abilities and habits, and preparing the youth for life, afterwards, after it expanded its scope and content of action, Physical Education became a permanent program that was extended to all categories of people.

As stated by Nicola [8], "the ideal of our education consider it to be an indispensable component that is contributing to the formation of human personality". Physical Education plays a decisive role by contributing to the harmonious development of personality and ensuring a functional balance between its components, particularly the physical and mental component.

In conclusion, Physical Education is not only aimed at achieving a limited and intrinsic purpose of physical development, but on the contrary it is a component of a system, and together with all the other components it acts on the integral development of personality, stimulating and strengthening its psychophysical qualities [1, 7]. Physical Education seeks to achieve a harmonious and psychophysical balance through the continuous development of biological and psychological elements.

Physical Education also reflects itself on the other aspects of education. By its specificity it contributes to the functional development of the nervous system, thus ensuring the favourable conditions for the successful development of the intellectual activity. The beauty of the movements and the rhythm of the deployment give many aesthetic valences.

2 Research methods

2.1 Procedure

The research was conducted in the school year 2015-2016, in November for the Turkish school and in March for the schools in Romania. The working method in the research undertaken was the data collection procedure using the self-designed questionnaire addressed to samples of pupils from the 7th and 8th grades from both research countries. As a tool for collecting the data used in the research, the researcher used the paper questionnaire handed directly to the subjects. For both countries, the self-designed questionnaire was given in the mother tongue and explained to the respondents how to complete and all the additional information they requested. The self-designed questionnaire represents the most widely used method in quantitative sociological research. The self-designed questionnaire contained a total of 10 questions that followed: In the first 4 questions, it was followed the pupils' opinion regarding the number of physical education classes in the school curriculum, the degree of satisfaction with the physical education classes in school, and the benefits that physical activity is believed to have. Questions 5-7 aimed at the rewards or sanctions received in the physical education class and the conflicts that may arise in the relationship between teacher and student. The last three questions addressed the student-teacher relationship and the conflicting nature that may arise.

2.2 The subjects

In Turkey, the research was conducted in Elazig on a sample of 100 subjects (55 boys and 45 girls), with the average age of 13.8 years. In Romania, the research was carried out in Galati on a sample of 94 subjects (50 boys and 44 girls), with an average age of 14.6. The age differences for similar classes are due to the fact that in Turkey children begin compulsory school at the age of 6.

3 Results and discussion

Throughout childhood and adolescence, physical education in school provides an excellent opportunity to learn and practice the skills needed to improve physical strength and health status throughout life. These daily activities can include running, swimming, cycling and climbing as well as more structured sports and games. Early acquisition of basic skills makes it crucial for young people to practice and better understand the value of these activities in their later education or as adults at work or in their leisure time.

In order for physical education classes in school to achieve their goals in the formation and development of pupils, they must participate with pleasure, convinced that physical activity helps them maintain an optimal state of health, harmonious physical development, and personality development.

From the considerations mentioned above, the self-drafted questionnaire presented in Table 1 was conducted in order to find out how students appreciate the physical education classes, how attractive they are to them, and what are their views on improving the teacher-student relationship.

Table 1. Content and comparative results between the two countries of the self-designed questionnaire

Nr.	Question	Answers	Romania	Turkey
1.	What do you think about physical education classes in the school curriculum?	There are too many	5.95%	6.00%
		There are too few	90.48%	93.00%
		There should not be any	3.57%	1.00%
2.	Are you satisfied with the way your physical education classes take place in your school?	Very satisfied	39.29%	34.00%
		Satisfied	41.67%	54.00%
		Dissatisfied	10.71%	9.00%
		Very dissatisfied	8.33%	3.00%

Table 1.*Continued*

3.	What is the main reason that you attend the physical education class?	To maintain my physical strength		20.24%	11.00%
		To improve my health		32.14%	36.00%
		To meet with my peers		2.38%	3.00%
		I like to socialize		1.19%	10.00%
		I can relax/get rid of the stress		14.29%	22.00%
		I improve my physical qualities		19.05%	4.00%
		I like the competition		7.14%	6.00%
		Other reason		3.57%	8.00%
4.	To what extent do you agree with the practice of physical activity?	To a very small extent		42.86%	48.00%
		To a small extent		38.10%	33.00%
		To a high extent		17.86%	17.00%
		To a very high extent		1.18%	2.00%
5.	Have you received rewards/sanctions during your physical education class? For what?	Rewards	yes	54.76%	43.00%
			no	45.24%,	57.00%
		Sanctions	yes	10.71%	25.00%
			no	89.29%	75.00%
6.	What was the reward/sanction?	Notes		91.46%	19.64%
		Diplomas		15.85%	14.29%
		Points		24.39%	16.07%
		Verbal appraisals		35.37%	62.86%
		Medal		4.88%	34.86%
		The decrease of the grade in behaviour		4.88%	0.00%
		Elimination		4.88%	12.50%
		Reprehension		7.32%	22.07%
7.	Did you tell your parents about the reward/sanction?	Rewards	yes	27,38%	38,00%
			no	72,62%	62,00%
		Sanctions	yes	57,14%	81,66%
			no	42,86%	18,34%
8.	What do you appreciate in a teacher?	Initiative		32.14%	16.00%
		Creativity		34.52%	29.00%
		Temperament		26.19%	21.00%
		The way he/she gets involved		60.71%	60.00%
		The teacher's communication skills		34.52%	39.00%
9.	Arrange in ascending order the causes of the student-teacher conflict.	Antipathy towards the object		11.90%	12,67%
		Antipathy towards the teacher		14.29%	7.00%
		Indiscipline		20.24%	30,09%
		Evaluation		23.81%	42,25%
		The communication method of the teacher		29.76%	7.00%
10.	How are student-teacher conflicts solved?	The student is punished(sanctioned)		17.86%	15.00%
		Through the communication between the teacher and the student		61.90%	65.00%
		By presenting the situation to the classroom teachers council		3.57%	6.00%
		By asking parents to come to the school		16.67%	14.00%

In the seventh grade, the school curriculum provides for 2 hours of physical education per week in Romania, and for similar classes in Turkey, only 1 hour of physical education per week. In the eighth grade, in both countries, it is only one hour per week. The number of physical education classes in the school curriculum is insufficient both in Romania and Turkey, this fact being confirmed by respondents' views on physical education classes that are very close and over 90% of the respondents consider that there are too few physical education classes, compared to those who consider them too many or would prefer not to have any at all. The answer confirms students' belief that physical education classes are beneficial to maintaining a good health and harmonious physical development.

Because students appreciate the physical education classes, I wanted to find out to what extent they are satisfied with the way in which physical education classes take place in the current format. The high number of students in Romania with a percentage of 41.67%, and in Turkey with a percentage of 54.00%, declared that they are satisfied and very satisfied about the way that physical education classes take place, confirming the answer to the previous question of increasing the number of physical education hours.

It was considered important for this research to know the extent to which participation in physical education is considered to be beneficial by pupils and, for that purpose, in question 3 of Table 1 we proposed a number of seven variants of answers and left a variant for one other reason than the seven proposed, to be mentioned by the respondent.

The main reason for the pupils in Romania and Turkey for attending the physical education class, according to the answers, is the improvement of the health status, response recorded in a percentage of 30%. That is why some authors consider that the systematic practice of physical exercises has a multilateral influence on the physical and harmonious development of the organism [5].

The answers of the questioned pupils in Turkey are different compared to those in Romania, the differences being illustrated in Fig. 1. A percentage of 36.00% of the pupils in Turkey compared to 32.14% in Romania are participating in the physical education class to improve their health and only a percentage of 4.00% of the students are doing it to maintain their physical appearance compared to 19.05% in Romania. In a higher percentage of 22.00% compared to 14.29% for those in Romania, they mentioned participation in physical education as a way to relieve stress and relax.

On the other hand, the students in Turkey consider the physical education class as a relaxing, stress-free and socializing occasion, with a percentage of 22% in Turkey, compared to 14.29% in Romania.

Respondents in Romania considered other reasons, which are: doing sports is something normal, and during the physical education classes they learn new exercises and moves. Respondents from Turkey referred to reasons other than those mentioned in the questionnaire, namely: they are attracted to the games during the hours; love sports activities; they are attracted by the proposed social and educational activities in physical education classes; have the opportunity to play football; participation in physical education classes is beneficial to their mental state; consider sport to be normal and necessary. It should be noted that no response, both for the Romanian and Turkish students, mentioned participation in physical education classes as an obligation in the curriculum, which proves the important role of physical education and sports in school.

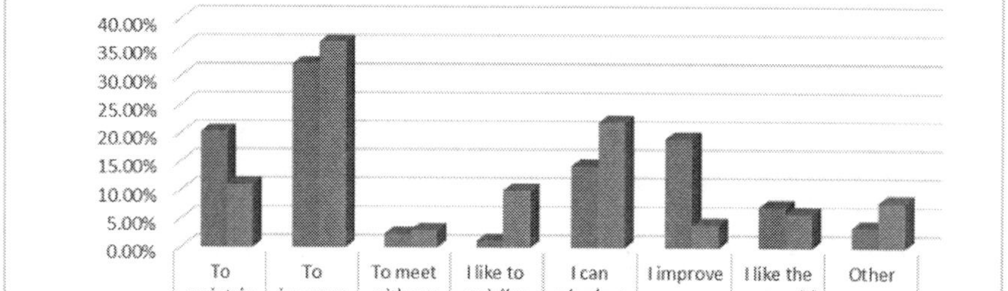

	To maintain my physical strength	To improve my health	To meet with my peers	I like to socialize	I can relax/get rid of the stress	I improve my physical qualities	I like the competiti on	Other reason
Romania	20.24%	32.14%	2.38%	1.19%	14.29%	19.05%	7.14%	3.57%
Turkey	11.00%	36%	3.00%	10.00%	22.00%	4.00%	6.00%	8.00%

Fig 1 Comparing answers to the question ``What is the main reason that you attend the physical education class?``

The conscious practice of various physical sports activities by the gymnasium students creates the premise that movement and physical exercise will become a concern for them when they become adults.

Physical activity is any form of body movement that involves energy consumption. So physical activity is not synonymous with physical exercise, although it involves it.

Physical activities should take into account leisure activities, physical exercise, sports activities, various forms of walking (walking, cycling, climbing stairs), physical activity during school hours and household chores. The results of numerous research have shown that a lack of physical activity and a sedentary lifestyle pose a threat to health. That is why the next question addressed to the respondents followed the attitude manifested by them regarding physical activity. A relatively high percentage of respondents in both Romania and Turkey stated that they practice physical activity to a very small extent (42.86% - Romania and 48% - Turkey), which shows that the only constant physical activity in their lives is the physical education class. This is also demonstrated by research in the past few years that has shown that there is a high percentage of children with a high degree of obesity due to lack of mainstream movement and unhealthy eating habits.

School regulations provide both rewards for students who achieve remarkable results in the physical education class and are distinguished by exemplary conduct and sanctions for students who violate regulations.

To find out to what extent the questioned pupils received rewards or sanctions in the physical education class, what the rewards or sanctions were, if they considered them to be deserved and if they were communicated to their parents, I asked them the following three questions, namely questions 5, 6 and 7.

The answers to the question about the rewards and sanctions received show that Romanian students received more rewards (54.76%) and fewer sanctions (10.71%) compared to Turkish students, where 43.00% received rewards and 25.00 % were sanctioned. The percentage differences between rewards and sanctions received by pupils at schools in both countries may be due both to students' behaviour during the physical education class and to school regulations that are not similar.

The reward/punishment system is a vicious system that, besides the positive influences it exerts on the student, it also contains negative aspects that may damage the student's status.

A reward is a form of praise in case of results that exceed the required level of demand, of results above the average of those usually obtained by regular students.

Research has shown that positive pedagogical methods (rewards, praises) have a stronger influence on pupils' outcomes and behaviour than negative pedagogical methods (sanctions, reprimands).

Students have a duty to learn for themselves and not for the fear of punishment or because they are attracted to the benefits of rewards because "We do not learn for school, we learn for life" [10].

In question 5, regarding the reward or sanction received, possible answers were suggested, but the free answer option was also provided if it was not a variant of the proposed ones. One response to the physical education sanction was the decrease in the behaviour grade. In this variation of an answer, it should be noted that in Turkey pupils do not receive grades for their behaviour in school, the deviations from the regulation being sanctioned by reprimand or removal from the hours.

The answers to the question as to what the reward or sanction was, were classified as: rewards - grades, diplomas, points, verbal appraisals, medals; sanctions - grades reduction, removal, reprimand.

Students in Romania mentioned notes as a reward in a percentage of 91.46% as opposed to students in Turkey where only 19.64% mentioned grades as a reward.

In a significant percentage, in both countries, the students mentioned 35.37% verbal appraisals in Romania and 62.86% in Turkey as rewards for physical education classes. This demonstrates a different degree of appreciation of how recipients receive the rewards and sanctions that are made in the classroom's moral conscience.

It is necessary to apply sanctions only after a careful and serious investigation, taking into account the reasons and the student's personality, so that the punishment can have a positive, educational effect.

By positively motivating the way students act and behave, the teacher with pedagogical tact will strengthen their confidence in their own forces to overcome inevitable difficulties.

To act and behave correctly from a pedagogical point of view is to resort to pedagogical methods of a positive and negative nature (to correctly use rewards and punishments in the broad sense of their acceptance).

In order to evaluate students' attitudes towards rewards or sanctions, we asked for clarification if the rewards or sanctions were brought to their parents' attention.

Most of the sanctions received were not communicated to the parents as opposed to rewards that were communicated to the parents. The percentage of those who did not communicate the sanctions received to parents was higher for Romanian students, namely 72.62%, compared to Turkey, 62.00%. Rewards were communicated to parents in a percentage of 57.14% by the Romanian pupils and 81.66% by the pupils in Turkey.

By comparing the answers, one can conclude that Turkish students communicated more to their parents both the sanctions and the rewards received, being aware of the actions that they foresee.

The relationship between teacher and student in the physical education class contributes greatly to motivating students to practice physical activity and sports.

Asked what they appreciate in a teacher at question 8, the majority of the answers given by the students were about the way the teacher gets involved, respectively 60.71% (Romania) and 60.00% (Turkey), after which they mentioned, approximately in the same order, the communication skills of the teacher (34.52%-Romania and 39,00%-Turkey), creativity (34.52%-Romania and 29.00%-Turkey), and temperament (26.19% in Romania and 21.00% in Turkey).

A significant proportion of pupils in Romania, respectively 32.14%, appreciates the teacher's initiative, unlike the pupils in Turkey where only 16.00% gave this answer.

The physical education lesson depends largely on the teacher's involvement, the way he communicates with the pupils, the interaction with each student's personality and the achievement of a homogeneous group. These are the basic qualities of the teacher in order to make the lesson more effective and attractive to students.

There may be conflicts between teachers and pupils, which are based on various causes. I mentioned five possible causes that respondents would arrange in ascending order. The pupils in Romania considered the teacher's communication skills as the main reason for the conflict (29.76%), followed by the evaluation (23.81%), the indiscipline (20.24%), the antipathy towards the teacher (14.29%), and, in the last place the antipathy towards the subject (11.90%). From their answers, it was concluded that in the physical education class the conflict arises because of a poor communication between the teacher and the student or because of the evaluation of the pupils on unknown criteria. They make the student have a negative attitude towards the physical education class and, even if he enjoys practicing physical activities, attending the lesson becomes a stress.

The pupils in Turkey mentioned the causes of the conflict as follows: the evaluation (42.25%), followed by indiscipline (30.09%), antipathy towards the object (12.67%), the teacher's communication skills (7.00%) and the antipathy towards the teacher (7%). From the respondents' answers, we can see that assessment is a cause of conflict between students and teachers and it is generally due to subjectivism.

Solving the conflict between the teacher and the student means to first acknowledge the cause that generated the conflict and, starting from the idea that conflicts can be generated by the lack of communication or the indiscipline of the student, I proposed variants of answers for these situations. Both students in Romania (69,05%) and those in Turkey (63,00%), placed on the first place the teacher-student communication, followed by the sanctioning of the student (17,86% in Romania and 15,00% in Turkey).

The next way to solve the conflict is considered by pupils in both countries to be the call of parents to school, 16.67% in Romania, and 11% in Turkey.

Solving the conflict between the teacher and the student in front of the teaching council is considered as a solution by only 61.90% of the respondents in Romania and 65.00% of the respondents in Turkey. The parties in the conflict have interdependent interests; conflicts are usually combinations of competitive and cooperative processes, and the course of the conflict will be determined by the nature of this combination. Conflict resolution can be achieved through interactive dialogue, bilateral feedback and mutual aid: the speaker must also listen and the listener must also communicate.

Ferriz et all [2] surveyed students' satisfaction in the Physical Education lesson (Spain) on a total of 405 boys and 453 girls aged between 15 to 21 and concluded that, in order to promote student satisfaction in PE, schools should promote educational environments that meet the students' needs for socialisation, competence, and autonomy by generating experiences in which students have fun and enjoy themselves.

Barney and Christenson [3] studied the attitudes of middle school students in physical education. The aim of this research was to determine the students' attitudes towards physical education. For this study, 227 midwestern middle school students from the United States were questioned, of which 28 students were interviewed regarding their attitudes towards physical education. It was found that middle school students tend to have positive attitudes towards physical education. Specifically, students considered physical education to be important for their general education and thought that the activities that they practice during the physical education classes are fun, considering physical education as being important in the day-to-day schooling of students.

The attitudes, motivations, and satisfaction of the gymnasium students vary from one country to another. This can be seen from the various research and their results. In order to achieve a high degree of satisfaction in the physical education class, the teacher has to orient his / her lesson objectives towards activities that please the pupils, stimulate them to participate in classes, and diversify the methods, exercises and sports materials. If a class of physical education is not appealing, the student attends the class but without the satisfaction of doing something useful and enjoyable.

4 Conclusion

After centralizing the data and analysing the answers, the opinions of the respondents, pupils in the 7th and 8th grades of the gymnasium cycle in Romania and Turkey, can be highlighted regarding the physical education classes in school.

It is worth noting that the use of the questionnaire with similar questions in the schools of the two countries with different cultural and religious traditions makes it difficult to compare the results.

The importance of the physical education class in the development and education of secondary school students is recognised in the curriculum of the two countries where the research was conducted.

In both countries, physical education and sports require knowledge of all aspects associated with physical exercise, students' willingness to exercise and play sports, the enjoyment of physical activity, and the knowledge of the physical education's influence on their health.

From the answers obtained through the questionnaire used in the research, one can draw the following conclusions:

-the pupils in both countries consider the number of physical education classes in the curriculum to be insufficient, respectively 90.48% in Romania and 54.00% in Turkey;

- the way that the physical education classes take place is to the liking of the majority of students in both countries, respectively 41.67% in Romania and 88.00% in Turkey;

The percentage of those dissatisfied with how physical education classes take place is a signal for teachers to make the classes more attractive by practicing sports games adapted to the age and skills of the students that they work with during the class.

- the main reason for the participation of students in physical education is the maintenance of their physical appearance and optimal health status, for 32.14% of the students surveyed in Romania and 36.00% of the students surveyed in Turkey.

Starting from the principle that regular exercise and more diversified physical exercise are necessary in maintaining physical appearance and optimal health, it can be considered that the number of those who have opted for this type of response is quite reduced.

- considering students' attitudes towards exercise and practicing physical activities, the answers received have shown that they are mostly interested in exercise and physical activity.

The teacher, as an expert in the teaching-learning act, can make decisions about everything that happens in the process of learning.

Being faced with developing human beings, the teacher must show great sensitivity, attachment, and respect towards them. A concrete expression is love for children. This implies first and foremost respect and confidence in the internal capabilities that every child possesses, and the sincere desire for these opportunities to develop along the way.

Particularly important is the attitude of the teacher in his / her relationship with students. His/her authoritative position, somewhat despotic, is not indicated. It creates affective blockages. Students are afraid to ask questions. The authority of a teacher is not based on constraint, on fear, but on his professional competence, on his objectivity and respectable posture. He must be close to the pupils, indulgent (within the permissible limits, human) and encourage imagination.

-conflicts between teacher and student for students of both countries have as their main 2 causes the evaluation and communication skills of the teacher, with the indication that they are seen in different percentages by the respondents. In Romania, the teacher's communication skills is in the first position with 34.52% whereas in Turkey, a percentage of 39% indicated the same cause. The evaluation is seen in close proportions as the cause of the teacher-student conflict, namely 29.76% in Romania and indiscipline with 30.09% in Turkey.

-for solving the conflict between teacher and student, the teacher-student communication is seen by the vast majority of respondents as a solution, namely 61.90% in Romania and 65.00% in Turkey.

A conflict is a social phenomenon that occurs when two or more interacting actors pursue incompatible goals or have incompatible intentions or values.

Conflicts between teachers and students may also be triggered by poor communication. Most conflicts can be attributed to the misunderstanding or erroneous perception of intentions, feelings, needs, and actions.

References

1. C. Alexandrache, Differentiated Education in The Service of Preventing / Reducing the School Conflict, Procedia - Social and Behavioral Sciences, 159 (2014), 433 – 436.
2. R Ferriz, A Sicilia, P Sáenz-Álvarez, Predicting satisfaction in physical education classes: A study based on self-determination theory, The Open Education Journal, 6 (2013), 1-7.
3. D Barney, R. Christenson, General attitudes of middle school students towards physical education. Asian Journal of Physical Education & Recreation, 18, (2), (2012)., 24-32.
4. G. Mocanu, L. Nanu, The experimental curricula planning strategy, aimed at the combined motor abilities development during the 8th grade physical education lessons, The Annals of "Dunărea de Jos" University of Galati 2011, Physical Education and Sport Management, XV 1 (2011), 37
5. I. Siclovan, Teoria educaţiei fizice şi sportului Editura Stadion, (1972).
6. L.G. Talaghir, M. Ion-Ene, A study of the implementation of the new curriculum for physical education in the romanian primary education, 9th International Conference on Education. New Learning Technologies, (2017), 486-495,
7. L.G. Talaghir, V. Mîndrescu, Study regarding the use of physical exercise in order to prevent school-age children from being overweight, SHS Web of Conference, 37 (2017).
8. I. Nicola, Tratat de pedagogie şcolară, ARAMIS PRINT, (2002), 317
9. European Commission / EACEA / Eurydice, (2013), 29
10. Seneca, Epistulae Morales ad Lucilium, A Loeb Classical Library Edition; 1 (1917)

Improving the Physical Education and Sport Faculty students' speed manifestation indices by means of the practical activities from the first year of study curriculum – bachelor's degree studies

Teodora-Mihaela Iconomescu[1,*], *George-Danut* Mocanu[1], and *Laurentiu-Gabriel* Talaghir[1]

[1]''Dunarea de Jos'' University, Faculty of Physical Education and Sports, Garii Stret, no 63-65, 800003, Romania

Abstract. Part of motor fitness, speed is an extremely important motor skill, which ensures the success and efficiency of the performed activities, being nevertheless dependent on the genetic component. Thus, this skill is difficult to train as compared to other motor skills. The experimental study included 31 girls and 59 boys, first year students at the Faculty of Physical Education and Sport from Galați, who were involved in the practical activities corresponding to the curriculum, comprising 7 subjects per semester and a number of 196 hours during 2015 – 2016 university year.
The difference between the averages obtained in the initial and final tests and the statistical processing of these results allowed us to determine both those speed manifestation forms for which progress is achievable and the situations in which the statistically significant progress is limited, regardless of the effort put in the activities and of the diversity of the stimuli used. The practical activities in which students were involved were varied and focused on different types of speed and its combination with other skills, the level of student involvement being high. The fact that the two groups obtained significant progress and similar correlation indices in most tests allowed us to draw some general conclusions. Nonetheless, for the studied groups, there were also some situations in which certain specific features had to be taken into account such as the sex or the level of motor skills, which influenced the final results. Students' progress in most tests highlight the optimization possibilities of the fitness level regarding speed and its combinations at a biological and chronological age for which the effort potential and the motor performance should be at an extremely high level.

Keywords: physical fitness, types of speed, sport branches, rapid motor structures

1 Introduction

Preparing specialists within the Faculty of Physical Education and Sport requires a rational combination of theoretical subjects – playing an extremely important part in understanding the domain-specific notions, in making the cause-effect connections regarding physical

* Corresponding author: ticonomescu@ugal.ro, the present paper is the result of the equal contribution of all authors.

effort, in planning and coordinating training plans for different sport branches in a scientific manner – with practical activities – whose goal is to consolidate or improve known skills, to get students familiar with the specific techniques of some sport branches, which haven't been practised previously but which are useful in shaping the motor skills of future domain-specialists. In addition to these practical activities, which focus mainly on the knowledge of sports technique and tactics or on the methodical method of practising them, the physical effort that characterizes these activities also influences the students' fitness level, ensuring, by means of their variety, certain effects on the coordinative and conditional motor skills - speed, strength and resistance. (1, 7)

Since the involvement in motor activities represents a normal aspect for the students from the Faculty of Physical Education and Sport (FPES), as compared to the students from other faculties – where the intellectual effort prevails and the physical effort is performed only occasionally – we may ask the question if, for the FPES students these practical activities, in which they must participate – according to the methodology in force – can contribute to some visible progress regarding their motor potential. If in the case of strength and resistance, the domain-specific literature confirms the chance of obvious qualitative leaps, in the case of speed, most specialists are more reserved because of the large number of factors which are difficult to perfect: analyser fineness and integrity, the rapidity of the nervous inflows transmitted via motor and sensitive ways, the type of innervation at motor level, the typology of muscle fibres, which is genetically determined, the alternation of excitatory and inhibitory processes in the brain, the energy sources such as phosphocreatine or the adenosine triphosphoric acid etc.

The progress rates are lower than in the case of other motor skills and are only possible by acting on those factors that are easier to improve: improving the quality of the execution technique through superior coordination, improving muscle contraction capacity/strength, improving flexibility and concentration (3, 4, 8).

Irrespective of the form of manifestation - simple reaction speed to visual, auditory or tactile, stimuli, complex reaction or decision speed, upper or lower limb execution speed, acceleration or deceleration speed, repetition speed, uniform or non-uniform speed, coordination speed, strength or resistance speed - these are not necessarily equally well developed in an individual, and there are cases in which even for performance athletes, the very good reaction speed is not accompanied by a higher repetition rate or cases in which the very good movement speed does not correspond to a very high execution speed (2, 3, 4).

The study aims to verify whether these ideas are valid, by studying the correlation coefficients between the various tests used, specific to various forms of speed manifestation.

Speed development methodology is extremely restrictive in terms of rules to be followed in order to install the desired progress and avoid possible injuries due to short but demanding efforts and these have been taken into account during all the practical activities in which the students have been involved : high-intensity exercises with few repetitions and long breaks to allow the body to rest and avoid fatigue, adapting distances to student possibilities, scheduling efforts in the first part of the class, often in combination with coordination –an exception from this rule may be considered the speed-resistance combination, the use of only those simple and well-known skills of the students, which do not pose risks in technical execution, efforts of 3-20 seconds, depending on the form of manifestation and the combination desired to be developed, diversified exercises to avoid monotony etc. (3, 5, 6).

2 Methods

The study was carried out during 2015 – 2016 university year and included only first year students majoring in Physical Education and Sport from Galați. The study focused on the students' constant involvement during the 7 practical activities included in the curriculum (athletics, gymnastics, football, volleyball, skating, swimming, and practice in mountain tourism). Each activity was allocated a number of 28 hours, the content having a diversified approach regarding the fitness level and a definite influence on the different forms of manifestations and combinations of speed as exemplified in fig. 1. The equipment belonging to the faculty, the Research centre within the faculty and the locations, where the practical activities took place, ensured optimal conditions for each activity. The practical activities were distributed in a balanced manner during the university year, 3 on each semester, and the internship in mountain tourism was carried out after the summer exams. Therefore, favourable conditions for a constant and systematic influence of speed were ensured by means of varied and attractive methods for students, fact which excludes the monotony or the boredom that may be generated by the constant use of the same methods.

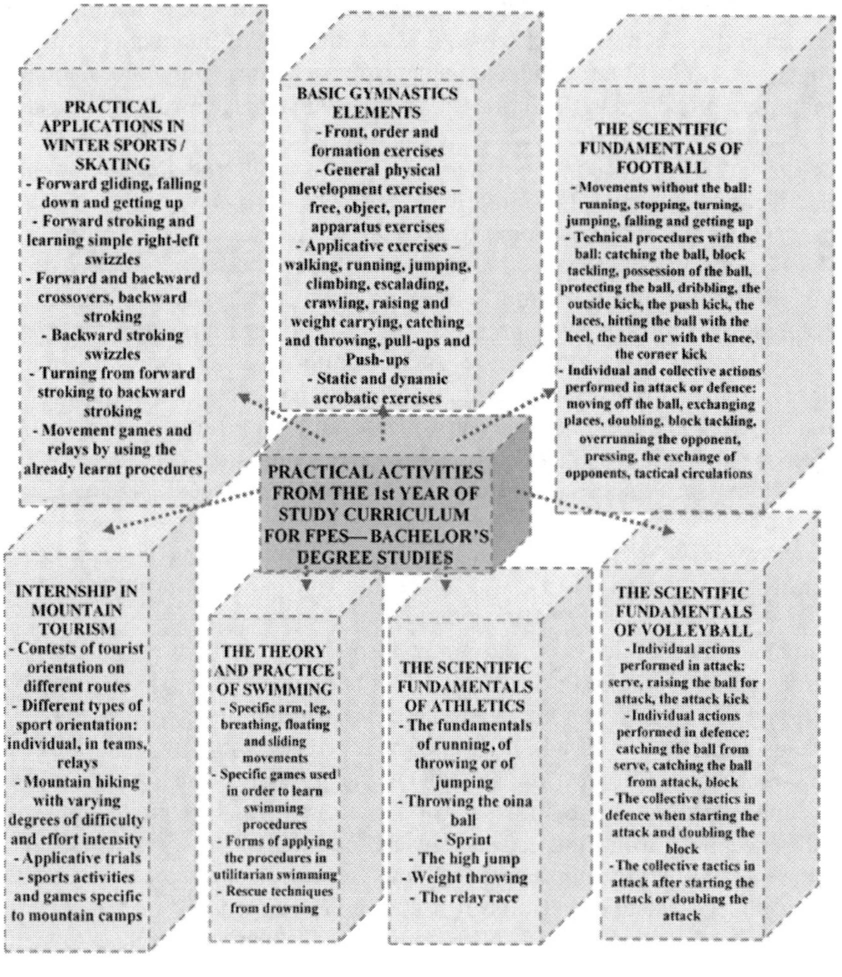

Fig 1. Practical activities from the 1st year of study curriculum for FPES – Bachelor's Degree studies

2.1 The subjects

The subjects of the research were represented by 59 boys and 31 girls, first-year students at the Faculty of Physical Education and Sport, majoring in Physical Education and Sport, who constantly participated in the previously mentioned 7 practical activities. The average age of the boys was of 21.9 and that of the girls of 21.6. The students who frequently missed classes during the university year were eliminated from the study in order not to influence the validity of the averages obtained by each group in the final tests and to be sure that the final results are primarily a consequence of the practical activities from the curriculum. Nevertheless, there is a stimulus variable, which couldn't be eliminated or controlled, represented by the performance sport physical activities or leisure activities, in which approximately a quarter of the tested students were constantly involved and which could influence the results of the final tests. The research activity was started only after obtaining the agreement of the management of the educational institution and after we described the objectives, the tests used and the working methodology to students.

2.2 The tests

The tapping Test determined the speed of the upper limbs while drawing some dots on paper, for 6 seconds. The falling baton test assessed the reaction time by catching a graded baton, which was left to fall. The Edgren Speed Test assessed the repetition speed of the lower limbs and involved the execution of lateral jumps for 10 seconds, on 3 parallel lines, situated at a distance of 1.2 metres. The 20-m agility test assessed the acceleration and change-of-direction ability by going along a route delimited by 3 lines, at a distance of 5m. one from the other. The Adams Speed Test assessed the repetition speed of the lower limbs, the orientation in space and the accuracy of movements through successive jumps on 4 numbers, separated by marks, which must not be stepped on. The 50-m movement speed test involved a race, which started from a standing position at an auditory signal. The visual-stimulus reaction time required an Internet connection and it involved touching the keyboard every time a square changed its colour. The speed test was used to assess acceleration, deceleration, agility, dynamic balance and orientation in space by dodging 8 cones, placed on both sides of a 14-metre line. The race was repeated twice. The acceleration capacity test involved an accelerated-speed sprint on a distance of 30 m. and then maintaining the speed achieved by running another 30-60 metres. The difference in point of time obtained between the 2 races expressed the acceleration capacity. The determination of the maximum running speed is given by the percentage between the 30 metre-sprint and the time obtained for the respective part. The 9-3-6-3-9 test assessed the speed of movement, the acceleration and deceleration capacity in running forwards or backwards, and the orientation in space on the volleyball court marks. The great marathon test assessed resistance running and agility while successively touching all the volleyball court marks and coming back to the first line, the race having a total of 90 metres.
The statistical calculation was performed with the help of the SPSS program.

3 Results and Discussion

The results of the average of the data, the values of t, the correlation coefficients and the significance limits obtained are included in tables 1 and 2.

In the tapping test – right, the group of girls obtained a difference of the average values corresponding to $t=-2.466$, result which corresponds to a limit $t=-2.466$, $p < .05$, significant only for the minimum possible limit.

The group of boys recorded a value of t=-.457, corresponding to a limit of p=.649, the result was > .05, which was insignificant form a statistical point of view.

In the tapping test – left, both groups recorded progress and insignificant limits: for the girl's t= -0.226, with a corresponding limit p=.823, p >.05, whereas for the boys' t=-0.460, with a limit p=.647, p >.05. We noticed that the fine and repeated movements, performed with the help of hands, are not frequently encountered in physical education and sport activities, fact which explains the lack of significant progress in these tests, in most situations the large segmental muscle groups being involved in the effort.

Testing the reaction time of the upper limbs by means of the trial The falling baton also recorded poor progress, which were insignificant from a statistical point of view for both sexes: the difference between the girls' averages records a t=0.183, value associated to a limit p=.856, result > .05, whereas the difference between the boys' averages corresponds to a t=0.570, value associated to a p=.571, result > .05. These results prove the difficulty in training the reaction time, the progress being thus limited by genetics and by the fact that the students from the FPES already reach at this age the superior values of motor reactions, which do not allow significant leaps in this direction.

In the Edgren test, both groups obtained a statistically significant difference: the girls recorded t=-7.439, associated to a limit of p=.000, p <.001, which is highly significant, whereas boys obtained a t=-3.020, associated to a limit p=.004, p <.01. The same situation was encountered in the agility test: the girls obtained a t=10.266, value which also corresponds to p=.000, p <.001, which is also highly significant from a statistic point of view. The improvement in the results is explained by the fact that these tests involve jumping, rapid changes of direction, accelerations, precise actions and orientation in space, the movements being already known, simple and frequently used in sports activity. A special situation was encountered in the two Adams tests - the correct jumps and incorrect jumps, where the girls obtained a superior average value of the correct number of jumps as compared to the boys, and an average of the incorrect jumps lower than the boys' average, the results being explained by the girls' better coordination and more accurate moves. The boys' mistakes were caused by imprecise movements and by not following the succession of numbers written on the ground.

Nevertheless, both sexes recorded significant progress: the girls scored in the correct Adams test a t = -8.778 and the boys a t = -4.461, the girls obtained in the wrong Adams test a t = 5.637 and the boys a t = 6.107, all of these values being associated with a limit p = .000, results <.001, which are significant from a statistical point of view. The same evolution is recorded by the differences in the averages for the 50-metre speed test: the group of girls obtained a t = 9.075 and the boys a t = 6.096, both values correspond to a limit p = .000, p <.001, which is statistically significant.

The reaction to visual stimuli test indicates a slight regression for girls, which statistically insignificant, the difference between the averages corresponds to a t = -0.283, a limit value p = .779, a result> .05, which is statistically insignificant. The boys recorded little progress, corresponding to a t = 2.315, a value corresponding to a limit p = .024, result <.05, which is significant only for the minimum limit. The fact that the test involved connecting to the Internet and making a quick movement whenever colours changed, which was unfamiliar to physical activities is an argument for the weaker results obtained in this situation. In the speed route test, both groups achieved a significant improvement in the results: the girls recorded a t = 7.461 and the boys t = 8.579, the results corresponding to a limit p = .000, p <.001, these qualitative leaps being explained by the fact that the agility movements, accelerations and decelerations specific to sporting game structures, are frequently performed by students.

Significant progress was achieved by both sexes for the 0-30m acceleration test: the girls recorded a t = 6.274 and the boys a t = 5.942, values associated with a limit p = .000, result <.001. The same situation is encountered for the 30-60m sprint test: the group of girls obtained a t = 7.050 and the boys a t = 6.207, both results corresponding to a limit p <.001, fact which demonstrates a strong and significant progress. However, the acceleration difference between the averages of the two tests is significant only for the group of boys with a t = 2.061, a value associated with a limit p = .044, a result <.05, which is significant only for the minimum limit accepted by statistics.

The girls record a t = -.0514, value associated with a p = .609, result> .05, which is statistically insignificant. A possible explanation for these differences is that boys have a better ability to maintain the maximum speed achieved over a range of 30-60 meters, while girls get tired more easily on the same distance, aspect which has generated more reduced values in the acceleration difference. However, the calculation of the maximum running speed revealed improvements for both groups, the girls obtaining a difference between the mean values corresponding to t = -8.109 and the boys to t = -6.553, results associated with a limit p <.001.

In the 9-3-6-3-9 test, significant progress was recorded for both genders: the girls obtained a t = 11.904 and the boys a t = 4.977, results corresponding to a limit p <.001. And for the great marathon test the same situation is reported, the group of girls obtained a t = 7.564, whereas the boys obtained a t = 9.763, both results being associated with a limit p <.001, which is strongly significant. Improvement in the results in these two tests is related to the fact that they involve the alternation of the acceleration and deceleration capacity, the adjustment of the frequency of the steps according to the length of the routes, the manifestation of the orientation in space and the agility abilities, the speed of the movement under resistance conditions etc., all of these elements being often addressed in the practical sports disciplines of the 1st year bachelor's degree studies curriculum.

Table 1. The significance of the difference in averages between the initial and final tests for the pair samples

GROUPS	PAIR SAMPLES – GROUPS FROM FPES							
	GILRS (N=31)				BOYS (N=59)			
TRIALS	T.I. $\bar{x} \pm m$	T.F. $\bar{x} \pm m$	t	P	T.I. $\bar{x} \pm m$	T.F. $\bar{x} \pm m$	t	P
TTR /points	50.0±1.514	50.6±1.434	-2.46	.020*	47.8±.82	48.0±.81	-.457	.649
TTL /points	44.4±1.201	44.4±1.192	-.22	.823	44.1±.66	44.2±.62	-.460	.647
FBT /cm	26.7±1.176	26.7±1.144	.18	.856	27.4±1.11	27.2±1.06	.570	.571
ET /points	14.0±.608	15.8±.465	-7.43	.000***	16.3±.26	16.6±.24	-3.020	.004**
AT /sec	5.9±.084	5.7±.080	10.26	.000***	5.3±.05	5.3±.05	4.155	.000***
ATC /no. of jumps	26.4±1.183	27.9±1.146	-8.77	.000***	23.7±.68	24.3±.62	-4.461	.000***
ATI/no. of jumps	3.0±.296	1.7±.158	5.67	.000***	5.2±.32	4.2±.26	6.107	.000***
50ST /sec	7.6±.078	7.5±.077	9.07	.000***	6.6±.06	6.6±.06	6.096	.000***
VSRT /sec	0.3±.011	0.3±.010	-.28	.779	0.36±.00	0.3±.00	2.315	.024*
SRT /sec	19.0±.420	18.7±.401	7.46	.000***	16.1±.15	16.1±.15	8.579	,000***
30AT /sec	5.0±.069	5.0±.070	6.27	.000***	4.5±.04	4.4±.04	5.942	.000***
ST /sec	4.5±.073	4.4±.071	7.05	.000***	3.9±.05	3.9±.05	6.207	.000***
ADT /sec	0.5±.049	0.5±.047	-.51	.609	0.5±.02	0.5±.03	2.061	.044*
MRS /m/sec	6.7±.107	6.7±.106	-8.10	.000***	7.7±.10	7.7±.10	-6.553	.000***
93639T /sec	8.8±.113	8.6±.110	11.90	.000***	8.1±.06	8.1±.06	4.977	.000***
GMT /sec	22.5±.246	22.1±.230	7.56	.000***	21.1±.15	21.0±.15	9.763	.000***

* P< 0.05, ** P< 0.01, *** P <0.001

In order to determine the association between the normal distribution tests, the Pearson correlation coefficient (r) was used; for all the other types of associations, the Spearman correlation coefficient (ρ) was used, the results being presented in Table 2. The correlation sign is determined by the type of the associated tests: for the typical ones, the increase in results implies an increase in performance (e.g. The Edgren test), for the atypical tests, an increase in results indicate a decrease in performance and vice versa (e.g. the 50-metre speed test).

Strong and significant associations are recorded between the tapping test right and the tapping test left, both assessing the repetition speed of the upper limbs, for girls ρ=.599 and for boys r=0.715, the results corresponding to a limit P <.01. Significant correlations are encountered only in the case of girls between the tapping test right and the agility test, with ρ=-.452 and P <.05, between the tapping test right and the 9-3-6-3-9 test, with ρ=-.358 and P < .05. Both sexes obtain significant correlations between the tapping test right and the Great marathon test, the girls with ρ=-.544 and P <.01, the boys with ρ=-.286 and P <.05.

The tapping test left records significant correlations with two tests, for both sexes: the Edgren test, in which the girls obtained a ρ=.394, with a limit P <.05, and the boys obtained a ρ=.433, with a P <.01, and the Great Marathon test, in which the girls obtained a ρ=-.378 and the boys obtained a ρ=-.286, both correlations having a P < .05.

The rest of the significant correlations of the tapping test left with other tests are different for the group of boys and girls, fact which proves that the sex particularities and the level of motor abilities influence the results of the tests. For the group of girls there are significant correlations between the tapping test left with the agility test (ρ=-.456 and P <.01) and with the Adams test – incorrect jumps (ρ=-.459 and P <.01), whereas for the group of boys there are significant correlations between the tapping test left and the Adams test – correct jumps (r=.405 and P <.01), with the 50-m. sprint test (ρ=-.280 and P <.05) and with the 9-3-6-3-9 test (ρ =-.350 and P <.01).

The falling baton test records few statistically significant correlations probably because the movement performed to catch the object is not frequently used in the usual sports activities, which often presuppose reactions towards objects, teammates or opponents in movement. This test has only one significant correlation with the Adams test – incorrect jumps (ρ =.454 and P < .05) for the group of girls and two significant correlations for the group of boys, one with the visual stimulus reaction test, which assesses the reaction time, but my means of another action n(ρ =.462 and P <.01), and the other one with the acceleration difference test, where the rapid reaction is associated with an increase in the difference between the two sprint routes (ρ=-.335 and P <.01).

The Edgren test records highly significant correlations for both sexes, with the following tests, which involve rapid movement, thus highlighting a correlation between the increase in the number of jumps and the decrease in the time obtained in the respective tests: The 50-metre sprint test (r =-.487 for girls and ρ=-.558 for boys, values corresponding to P <.01), the speed route test (r =-.735 for girls and ρ=-.456 for boys, values corresponding to P <.01), the 9-3-6-3-9 test (ρ =-.494 for girls and ρ=-.489 for boys, values corresponding to a P <.01).

For girls, a highly significant correlation is obtained with the agility test (r =-.847 and a P <.01), whereas for the boys, the correlation is weaker, but still statistically significant (ρ =-.275 and a P <.05).

Table 2. Pearson (r) and Spearman (ρ) Correlations – group of girls / N=31, group of boys / N=59

GIRLS / BOYS	TTR	TTL	FBT	ET	AT	ATC	ATI	50ST	VSRT	SRT	30AT	ST	ADT	MRS	93639T	GMT
TTR	1	ρ .599**	ρ .265	P. 470**	ρ -.452*	ρ .243	ρ .094	ρ .324	ρ .227	ρ .308	ρ .013	ρ .004	ρ .271	ρ .004	ρ .358*	ρ .544**
TTL	r .715**	1	ρ .038	ρ .394*	ρ -.456**	ρ .337	ρ -.459**	ρ .318	ρ .200	ρ .218	ρ .088	ρ .107	ρ-.043	ρ .107	ρ .313	ρ .378*
FBT	ρ .202	ρ -.183	1	ρ .074	ρ .101	ρ.006	ρ .454*	ρ .023	ρ .311	ρ .090	ρ .051	ρ .013	ρ .019	ρ -.013	ρ .055	ρ .223
ET	ρ .337**	ρ .433**	ρ .125	1	r -.847**	ρ .373*	r .036	r .487**	ρ .010	r .735**	ρ .369*	r .386*	r .091	r .428*	ρ .494**	ρ .145
AT	r .063	r .077	ρ .056	ρ-.275*	1	ρ .374*	r .080	r .544**	ρ .097	r .618**	ρ .484**	r .459**	r .156	r .492**	ρ .685**	ρ .244
ATC	r .261*	r .405**	ρ .178	ρ .428**	r .194	1	ρ -.098	ρ .413*	ρ .198	ρ -.510**	ρ .082	ρ .376*	ρ .072	ρ .376*	ρ .369*	ρ .566**
ATI	ρ .091	ρ .136	ρ .084	ρ-.246	ρ -.081	ρ -.536**	1	r .170	ρ -.056	r -.032	ρ .068	r -.045	r.,294	r .030	ρ .132	ρ .113
50ST	ρ .132	ρ .280*	ρ .240	ρ .558**	ρ .478**	ρ .258*	ρ .219	1	ρ .042	r .363*	ρ .593**	r .777**	r -.210	r .785**	ρ .623**	ρ .381*
VSRT	ρ .059	ρ .217	ρ .462**	ρ.287*	ρ -.054	ρ .387**	ρ .200	ρ .148	1	ρ .324	ρ .506**	ρ .349	ρ -.021	ρ .506**	ρ .164	ρ .277
SRT	ρ .055	ρ .102	ρ .212	ρ .456**	ρ .831**	ρ .114	ρ .049	ρ .403**	ρ .013	1	ρ .278	r .452*	r -.095	r .493**	ρ .514**	ρ .081
30AT	ρ .103	ρ .247	ρ .000	ρ .564**	ρ .387**	ρ -.259*	ρ .300*	ρ .832**	ρ .148	ρ .473**	1	ρ .617**	ρ .325	ρ .617**	ρ .461**	ρ .017
ST	r .035	r .136	ρ .176	ρ .477**	r .334**	r .338**	ρ .147	ρ .795**	ρ .333**	ρ .240	ρ .785**	1	r -.421*	r .992**	ρ .607**	ρ .298
ADT	r .166	r .201	ρ 335**	ρ .008	r ,109	r ,236	ρ .061	ρ .192	ρ .359**	ρ .227	ρ .028	r .493**	1	r..358*	ρ .152	ρ .047
MRS	r .020	r .115	ρ .177	ρ .477**	r -,293*	r .367**	ρ .146	ρ .795**	ρ .333**	ρ -.240	ρ .785**	r .990**	r .533**	1	ρ .607**	ρ .298
93639T	ρ .195	ρ .350**	ρ .086	ρ -.489**	ρ ,716**	ρ ,089	ρ .067	ρ .654**	ρ .034	ρ .728**	ρ .642**	ρ .94**	ρ .227	ρ .394**	1	ρ .311
GMT	ρ .286*	ρ .293*	ρ .174	ρ .607**	ρ .560**	ρ .215	ρ .025	ρ .751**	ρ .168	ρ .638**	ρ .727**	ρ .674**	ρ -.156	ρ .673**	ρ .753**	1

* The correlation is significant at the 0.05 level (2 tailed). ** The correlation is significant at the 0.01 level (2 tailed).

Tapping test Right – TTR; Tapping test Left – TTL; The falling baton test – FBT; The Edgren test-ET; The agility test – AT; Adams test correct – ATC; Adams test incorrect – ATI; The 50-metre speed test – 50ST; The visual stimulus reaction test – VSRT; The speed route test – SRT; The 0-30-metre acceleration test – 30AT; The 30-60 metre sprint test – ST; The acceleration difference test – ADT; The maximum running speed – MRS; The 9-3-6-3-9 test -93639T; The great marathon test – GMT.

The boys obtained significant correlations with the0-30-metre acceleration test (ρ =-.564 and a P <.01) and with the30-60-metre sprint (ρ =-.477 and a P <.01), whereas the girls obtained weaker correlations, but which are still statistically significant, for the above mentioned tests. (ρ =-.369 and ρ =-.386, respectively, both corresponding to a P <.05). Another major gender difference is recorded in the correlation with the Great marathon test, in which only the group of boys records a highly significant correlation, fact which highlights their ability to maintain a high frequency of motion movements under resistance conditions (ρ=-.607, with a P <.01).

The agility test has strong and statistically significant correlations for both groups with the following tests, all of which presuppose acceleration and speed of movement: the 50-metre speed test (r = .544 for girls and p = .478 for boys, values corresponding to a P <.01), The speed route test (r = .618 for girls and p = .831 for boys, values corresponding to a P <.01), the 0-30 metre acceleration test (p = .484 for girls and p = .387 for boys, P =.01), the 30-60-metre sprint test (r = .459 for girls and r = .334 for boys, values corresponding to a P <.01), the 9-3-6-3-9 test (p = .685 for girls and p = .716 for boys, values corresponding to a P <.01). The girls obtained a strong correlation with the speed of movement test (p = -.492, with a P <.01), while the boys recorded a significant correlation with the Great Marathon Test (p = .560 with a P <.01), a correlation that was not achieved by the girls, confirming the boys' ability to better exploit resistance.

The correct Adams test has strong but gender-differentiated correlations with the common tests for both groups, in which the significant correlations have lower limits, with P <.05. The girls recorded significant correlations with the speed route test (p = -.510) and the great marathon test (p = -.566), both results corresponding to a limit P <.01. The boys obtained significant correlations with the wrong Adams test, which highlights the association between increasing the number of correct jumps and lowering the incorrect ones (p = -.536), with the reaction to visual stimuli test (p = -.387), the 30-60-metresprint test (r = -.338) and the maximum running speed (r = .367), all these values corresponding to a limit P <.01.

The incorrect Adams test did not record any significant correlation with the tests that haven't been analysed yet, in the case of the group of girls, and for boys there is only one positive correlation with the rest of the tests, that is the 0-30-metre acceleration test, where ρ = .300, with a P <.05, which demonstrates an increase in the time obtained in accelerated running, along with the increase in the number of incorrect jumps, as a result of poor coordination.

The 50-meter sprint test showed strong correlations for both sexes with the following tests: the 0-30-metre acceleration test (p = .593 for girls and p = .832 for boys), the 30-60-metre sprint test (r = .777 for girls and p = .795 for boys), the maximum running speed test (r = -.785 for girls and p = -.795 for boys), the 9-3-6-3-9 test (p = .623 for girls and p = .654 for boys), all these correlations being associated with a limit P <.01. The boys obtained strong correlations with the speed route test (p = .403) and the great marathon test (p = .751) with significance limits P <.01, while the correlations of girls with these 2 tests are significant only for P <.05.

The reaction to visual stimuli test showed gender differences between the tests with which they make strong correlations. Of the tests that haven't been analysed, the only one where both groups achieved strong correlations is the maximum running speed (p = -.506 for girls and p = -.333 for boys with a limit P <.01). However, girls obtained a strong association with the 0-30-metre acceleration test, where reaction time is important in obtaining a superior result (p = .506 and a P <.01), but it is surprising that boys did not get a significant correlation in this case; however, they recorded a strong correlation with the 30-60-metre sprint, where the reaction time is not relevant, the test subjects already sprinting in this part of the route (p = .333 and a P <.01). Another significant correlation obtained by boys is the acceleration difference test (p = -.359 and a P <.01).

The speed route test correlates strongly for both groups with the 9-3-6-3-9 test (p = .514 for girls and p = .728 for boys, with a P <.01). For girls, a strong correlation was achieved with the maximum speed of movement test (r = -.493 and a P <.01), and for the boys with the 0-30-metre acceleration test (p = .473 and a P <.01) and with the great marathon test, respectively (p = .638 and a P <.01).

Another test with strong correlations for both genders is the 0-30-metre acceleration test, which reveals significant correlations with the 30-60-metre sprint test (p = .617 for girls and with p = .785 for boys at P <.01), with the maximum running speed test (p = -.617 for girls and with p = -.785 for boys at a P <.01), the 9-3-6-3-9 test (p = .461 for girls and p = .642 for boys with a P <.01). The boys obtained a strong correlation with the great marathon test (p =.727, with P <.01), whereas the girls recorded a small value in this correlation. The 30-60-metre sprint test has strong correlations with: the maximum running speed test (r = -.992 for girls and with p = -.990 for boys at P <.01), the 9-3-6-3 -9 test (p =.607 for girls and p = .394 for boys, with a P <.01). However, the boys' group also has strong correlations with the difference in acceleration test (r = -.493, with P <.01), and with the great marathon test, respectively (p = .674, with P <.01), where the girls' correlations are statistically insignificant.

Other strong correlations, explained by the similarity of movements and coordination processes, the existence of direction changes, the high intensity of effort and the energy mechanisms required are obtained between the 9-3-6-3-9 test and the maximum travel speed test (r = -.607 for girls and with p = -.394 for boys at a P <.01) or, for boys, between the great marathon test and the maximum running speed test (ρ = -.673, with P <.01) or the great marathon test and the 9-3-6-3-9 test (p = .753 with P <.01).

4 Conclusions

The above mentioned tests are completing a series of studies carried out with the FPES students in the previous years, which followed other elements of general fitness and motor fitness: muscle strength and coordination elements. The results obtained and their statistical processing partially confirm the possibilities for progress in speed motor skills, but show that the practical subjects and the number of hours allocated to them in the 1st year curriculum are sufficient in order to achieve statistically significant leaps for the groups studied. It should be noted here that these results contradict the opinion of many students who believe that there is an exaggerated number of theoretical subjects, which do not have a favourable contribution to their professional training.

Nevertheless, there is a certain reluctance in drawing some incontestable conclusions about improving students' performance, simply because approximately 25% of them are constantly involved in different sports or body fitness activities, and these physical activities certainly had an influence on the final results, without the possibility of being accurately quantified. However, the only stimuli to which all students studied were subjected throughout the academic year are the practical activities from the curriculum, so these requests are the main factors that have generated leaps in the motor performance achieved. The fact that there is significant progress in many of the tests used represents a favourable aspect, all the more so as the level of FPES students' training is higher than that of students from other faculties, and the improvement of the results is all the more difficult as the physical level of training is higher.

Significant differences between the performance of the two sexes are observed in the Tapping right and Tapping left tests, where the frequency of the upper limb executions is higher for the girls than for the boys even though the differences between the initial and the final tests indicated significant progress recorded by the girls only in the former test (the Tapping right test). The results obtained by the girls can be explained by superior manoeuvrability, by better coordination of arm movements in speed mode. Other tests, where progress is statistically insignificant or significant for the minimum limit ($P <.05$) are those evaluating the response rate in the upper limbs (The falling baton and the Reaction to visual stimuli test).

These results demonstrate the genetic conditioning of the reaction times and the difficulty of reducing them through training, especially since the skills required in the respective tests are not familiar to the students and are not used in practical activities, in which the reactions to auditory signals in athletics, or partner, object or opponent manipulation – in the case of sports games – are the most demanded.

For the rest of the tests that have common motor structures and which involve the use of the lower limbs such as jumps, accelerations, decelerations, rapid changes in direction, maintenance of the maximum tempo etc., we may notice the fact that both groups recorded statistically significant progress. One possible explanation is the fact that most sports branches - practised in the first year of study - require the practice of already known execution techniques, with strong influences on speed and its combinations with other motor skills. These types of skills are easily transferred by students and exploited in the speed assessment tests.

From the observations made during the initial and final tests, we could notice an active involvement of the students included in the study, but also a number of distinctive characteristics depending on the gender: in tests that were based on jumping, the boys are better, but are often hasty, pursuing a large number of executions and often not following the order of the markings, without paying much attention to coordination and the accuracy of the executions, whereas the girls have superior jumping control and fewer errors.

The correlative study of the tests highlighted the strong and significant associations between them, but it also emphasized the situations where they are very weak and statistically insignificant, for each gender being particular aspects to be mentioned regarding the obtained results. Firstly, there is a poor correlation between the Big Marathon Test and the rest of the tests for the group of girls, demonstrating that their adaptation to the resistance speed efforts is deficient, whereas in the case of boys there are, in most cases, recorded strong and significant correlations between the Great Marathon Test and the rest of the tests, which indicates a good exploitation of speed in longer efforts. An interesting aspect is related to the fact that the reaction rate assessment tests record, for both sexes, but more obviously in the case of the girls, the fewest statistically significant correlations with the rest of the tests, confirming that response times are a special form of speed manifestation, which are difficult to improve, and with less influence on the other forms of speed manifestation. A situation that is difficult to explain is that the two tests for response times (The falling baton and the reaction to visual stimuli test) are significantly correlated only in the case of boys, not girls.

Both groups frequently record strong and significant correlations between tests that involve speed of movement, acceleration and deceleration, agility, jumps, speed-coordination: the Edgren test, the agility test, the Adams test, the 50-metre sprint, the speed route test, the 0-30-metre sprint test, the 30-60-metre sprint test, the 9-3-6-3-9 test. The explanation is that all these involve the rapid action of the lower limbs in different contexts and usually on short distances, with or without a combination with coordination elements, and the results in these tests are thus favourably correlated.

The assessment of the speed level development must be done by taking into account the other motor skills that can condition and exploit it, such as the level of manifestation of the strength-speed combination, which is encountered in the domain-specific literature under the name of power, with multiple manifestations: starting power, acceleration and deceleration power, throwing power, separation power, landing power, reactive power. Studying the development level of this combination would allow a clearer overview on the motor possibilities of this age group.

References

1. C. Alexandrache, The development of self-reflective competences in actual Romanian educational system, Procedia - Social and Behavioral Sciences, 76, 54-60, (2013)
2. V. Albu, *The theory of physical education and sport*, Ex Ponto, (1999).
3. T.O Bompa, *The development of biomotor qualities*, Ex Ponto, (2001)
4. G. Rață, B.C. Rață., *Abilities in motor activity*, EduSoft, (2006).
5. Committee on Physical Activity and Physical Education in the School Environment; Food and Nutrition Board; Institute of Medicine; Kohl HW III, Cook HD, editors. Educating the Student Body: Taking Physical Activity and Physical Education to School. Washington (DC): National Academies Press (US); 2013, *Physical Activity, Fitness, and Physical Education: Effects on Academic Performance*. Available from: https://www.ncbi.nlm.nih.gov/books/NBK201501/
6. S. Pritam, S.B. Baljinder., S. Manjit, S. Sukhbir, A Comparative Analysis of Motor Fitness Components of Throwers: A Foundation for Success, *Res. J. Physical Education Sci.*, 2(10), 22-24, (2014)
7. Hashemi M., Study of Motor Fitness Among Students, *International Journal of Sports Sciences & Fitness*, 4 (1), 89-108, (2014)
8. R. Popović, A. Aleksić, D. Stojanović, M. Stefanović, S. Božić, M. Popović, Evaluation of the Physical Fitness Level in Physical Education Female Students Using "Eurofit-Test", International, *Journal of Sports Science and Physical Education*, 2, (1), 1-15, (2017)

A Comparison on illustration of story and narration of illustration

Selma Korkmaz[1,*]

[1]Near East University, Ataturk Faculty of Education, Department of Turkish Language Teaching, 99138 Nicosia, North Cyprus

Abstract. The purpose of Turkish classes is to equip students with the ability of comprehension and narration. Everyone knows that stories covered in Turkish courses are offered with visuals, meaning pictures, so that they could be more easily understood. Illustration of a read story and narration of a picture shown can help explore the extent to which the topic is comprehended and how it is narrated, meaning visual presentation and visual reading skills. The purpose of this study is to compare whether attention is paid to several elements such as event, time, place, persons, language and narration/visual language during the illustration of a story and narration of a picture shown, meaning whether a connection is established between the narrated story and drawn picture as well as between the shown picture and the narrated story. Study group consists of 35 pre-service teachers who are junior students at Turkish language teaching department of Atatürk Education Faculty at Near East University. Document analysis, which is a qualitative research method, was employed and several stories and pictures were used as data collection tools. Descriptive analysis, percentage and frequency were used in the analysis of data. Based on the obtained findings, we can claim that pre-service teachers are more skilled in narration of picture compared to illustration of stories, meaning that their visual reading skills are superior to their visual presentation skills.

1 Introduction

The purpose of Turkish courses is to equip students with the skill of understanding and narrating what they see, watch, listen and read. Visuals have a special place in the development of understanding and narrating skills. Everyone knows that stories covered in Turkish courses are offered with visuals, meaning pictures, so that they could be more easily understood. The purpose here is to facilitate the receipt of knowledge in the text, concretize the knowledge that is to be conveyed, display the knowledge in its entirety, ensure that the knowledge is easily recalled, facilitate the understandings of the knowledge, motivating the individual, attract attention and increase attractiveness. Ausburn claimed that visual thinking and learning improved narration skills, increased the interest and

* Corresponding author: selma.korkmaz@neu.edu.tr

motivation of students, contributed to the organization of opinions and self-expression, helped independent thinking and, most importantly, facilitated learning [1].

Pictures are among the first elements that come to mind when the word “visual” is mentioned. The major functions of pictures are emphasizing differences, establishing analogy relations, bringing attention to the forefront and ensuring that some elements are remembered. At this point, whether the preferred pictures are convenient for the topic and the purpose bears huge importance [2]. Başaran stated that concrete and abstract concepts could be described easily using pictures and the subject could be explained better and in a shorter period of time through visuals [3].

One can explore how a subject is understood and narrated through illustration of a read story and narration of a shown picture, which indicate visual presentation and reading skills. The purpose of this study is to compare whether attention is paid to several elements such as event, time, place, persons, language and narration/visual language during the illustration of a story and narration of a picture shown, meaning whether a connection is established between the narrated story and drawn picture as well as between the shown picture and the narrated story.

2 Method

2.1 Study Group

Our study group consists of 35 pre-service teachers who are junior students at Turkish language teaching department of Atatürk Education Faculty at Near East University. As the courses related to the four basic language skills are completed in the 3rd grade, it is believed that conducting this study with pre-service teachers studying at 3rd grade of Turkish language teaching department would be meaningful.

2.2 Collection of Data

During the collection of data, document analysis was employed which is a qualitative research method; as a result, several pictures and stories were used as data collection tools.

2.3 Analysis and Interpretation of Data

Descriptive analysis, percentage and frequency were used in the analysis of data. The opinions of two Turkish language experts and two drawing experts were consulted in the analysis of data.

3 Findings and Comments

3.1 Findings concerning the story line during the illustration of a read story and narration of a shown picture

Table 1. Frequency and percentage distribution of pre-service teachers concerning the story line during the illustration of a read story and narration of a shown picture

Group	f	%
Illustration of story	18	51,42
Narration of picture	32	91,42

An examination of table 1 shows that 51.42% of pre-service teachers conveyed the story line properly while illustrating the story whereas 91.42% conveyed the story line properly while narrating the picture.

In the story about two camping friends helping a person who was attacked by a bear, it is observed that most pre-service teachers drew people having fun in the camp.

In the picture, it is explained that children who go out to the street and park as the spring comes played ball and marbles, rode bicycles and people chatted at the park. However, it is observed that a few pre-service teachers misinterpreted the picture while telling the story line and mentioned the people who left the neighborhood and sad children.

3.2 Findings concerning the time during the illustration of a read story and narration of a shown picture

Table 2. Frequency and percentage distribution of pre-service teachers concerning the time during the illustration of a read story and narration of a shown picture

Group	f	%
Illustration of story	17	48,57
Narration of picture	29	82,85

An examination of table 2 shows that 48.57% of pre-service teachers conveyed the time properly while illustrating the story whereas 82.85% conveyed the time properly while narrating the picture.

Both the story and the picture mentions spring season but while narrating the story it is stated that there is still snow in the mountain although it is spring time. However, it is determined that a majority of pre-service teachers were mistaken about the time while illustrating the story whereas some were mistaken while narrating the picture; some even did not mention time at all. It is revealed that pre-service teachers mentioned time using such expressions as spring season, month of May while narrating the picture.

3.3 Findings concerning the place during the illustration of a read story and narration of a shown picture

Table 3. Frequency and percentage distribution of pre-service teachers concerning the place during the illustration of a read story and narration of a shown picture

Group	f	%
Illustration of story	32	91,42
Narration of picture	33	94,28

An examination of table 3 shows that 91.42% of pre-service teachers conveyed the place properly while illustrating the story whereas 94.28% conveyed the place properly while narrating the picture.

The story mentions a mountainous area. The picture is about a park, street or neighborhood in a village or town. It is explored that very few teacher candidates did not draw a mountainous region while illustrating the story and mention the place while narrating the picture.

3.4 Findings concerning the people during the illustration of a read story and narration of a shown picture

Table 4. Frequency and percentage distribution of pre-service teachers concerning the people during the illustration of a read story and narration of a shown picture

Group	f	%
Illustration of story	27	77,14
Narration of picture	34	97,14

In table 4, it is seen that 77.14% of pre-service teachers conveyed the people properly while illustrating the story whereas 97.14% conveyed the people properly while narrating the picture.

It is seen that there are three people in the story and several children and people in the picture. It is observed that while illustrating the story several pre-service teachers omitted some people whereas only one pre-service teacher did not mention people while narrating the picture.

3.5 Findings concerning the language and narration/visual language during the illustration of a read story and narration of a shown picture

Table 5. Frequency and percentage distribution of pre-service teachers concerning the language and narration/visual language during the illustration of a read story and narration of a shown picture

Group	f	%
Illustration of story	23	65,71
Narration of picture	33	94,28

An examination of table 5 shows that 65.71% of pre-service teachers used visual language properly while illustrating the story and described some materials used during camping and that 94.28% paid attention to using a plain and fluent language while illustrating the picture; they also made wide use of descriptions.

4 Discussion, Conclusion and Recommendations

Based on the obtained findings, it has been found out that pre-service teachers are more skilled in narration of picture compared to illustration of stories, meaning that their visual reading skills are superior to their visual presentation skills.

Despite the fact that spring time is mentioned both in the story and in the picture, as the venue of the event told in the picture is mountainous regions, it is told that there is still snow all around. However, an examination of the documents of pre-service teachers shows that they gave more accurate descriptions of the time in stories whereas many people misperceived the time in the pictures they drew.

It became clear that a majority of pre-service teachers conveyed the place accurately in the stories they told and the pictures they drew.

It has been found out that while pre-service teachers illustrated the story, they omitted some people but while they narrated the picture, they mentioned all the people in the picture.

It can be claimed that the language and narration used by pre-service teachers while narrating the picture is very good and they made better use of descriptions whereas while they illustrated stories their visual language was not that good as the omitted many descriptions which were included in the story.

In conclusion, we can claim that visual reading skills of pre-service teachers are much better than their visual presentation skills. It has been found out that pre-service teachers made sense of pictures accurately but many pre-service teachers failed to illustrate a story properly. This, in turn, makes clear that pre-service teachers have good comprehension of the elements in the picture but are unable to understand the elements in the story accurately or did not pay attention to these elements. Above all, pre-service teachers should know what the elements are that they must pay attention in both stories and pictures. Pre-service teachers can be taught how to use these elements and help them establish a meaning between the story and the picture. Köksal et al. stated that if the students are not taught how to use these elements, they cannot make effective sense between the story and the visual [4].

In addition, this result displays the fact that visual elements are more easily remembered but the elements in stories are forgotten more rapidly. It is believed that in order to make better sense of the story line and ensure permanence of the narration, stories should be handled along with visuals. It can be claimed that through visual presentations used during the transfer of knowledge the individual can perform visual reading and comprehend the information better; he/she can also ensure permanence of the information. Begoray displayed that visuals have essential contribution in the comprehension by students of the red or covered subject [5].

This study displays that written language skills of pre-service teachers is better than their visual language skills. Thus, it is possible to see the positive impact of pictures on comprehension and writing skills, which are among basic language skills in Turkish courses. Özbay also claimed that pictures have huge contribution in the development of comprehension and writing skills [6].

Based on this conclusion, it is believed that following the recommendations listed below would be beneficial:

- A course titled "visual reading and visual presentation" can be added to the Turkish language teaching program.
- Visual presentation skills of pre-service teachers can be improved through various activities.
- Panels and conferences can be organized for pre-service teachers and information can be given on visual presentation.
- It can be ensured that pre-service teachers have the awareness that visual presentation is as important as visual reading.

References

1. F. B. Ausburn, *A comparison of multiple and linear image presentations of a comparative visual location task with visual and haptic college students*, ERIC (1975).
2. H. Akyol, *Turkish teaching methods* Kök Publications, Ankara, (2006).
3. M. Başaran, *usage of teaching materials of 4th and 5th grade students at Turkish courses.* Unpublished MA Thesis, Gazi University. Gazi Graduate School of Education Sciences, Ankara, 21 (2003).
4. K. Köksal, T. Temur, H. Akçam, *A study on the visual reading skills of elementary first grade students,* National Classroom Teaching Congress, 14-16 April 2006, Gazi University, Ankara (2006).
5. D. Begoray, *Through a class darkly: Visual literacy in the classroom*, Canadian Journal of Education, **26**/2, 201-217 (2001).
6. M. Özbay, *Turkish special teaching methods I.* Öncü Books, Ankara, (2011).

Opinions of pre-school pre-service teachers concerning tales: The case of TRNC

Selma Korkmaz[1,*]

[1]Near East University, Ataturk Faculty of Education, Department of Turkish Language Teaching, 99138 Nicosia, North Cyprus

Abstract. Tales have an important place in the education lives of children. For this reason, attention should be paid to the qualifications of tales read to the children in pre-school period. Pre-school teachers have important roles to play in this regard. The purpose of this study is to obtain the opinions of pre-school pre-service teachers who will serve as preschool teachers in the future concerning tales and explore whether they have adequate knowledge and awareness. For this purpose, our study group consists of 60 pre-service teachers studying at 4th grade of Near East University Atatürk Education Faculty Preschool Teaching Department. Interview forms were used in the collection of data. Frequency, percentage and content analysis were used in the analysis of data. Based on the findings obtained, it is determined that pre-service teachers have a certain accumulation of knowledge concerning tales; however, it became evident that this knowledge is inadequate and that they are under the impact of foreign culture, and that they have little knowledge about Turkish tales although they are senior students. At the same time, pre-service teachers declare that when they become teachers they will teach some tales which they claim that have negative effects on children, which is an indication that they do not have conscious.

1 Introduction

Tales are defined as "a literary genre generally created by people, based on imagination, living in verbal tradition, and mostly citing the supernatural events that happen to people, animals, witches, goblins, giants, fairies etc." [1]. They are also defined as folk stories which mostly tell the narratives of extraordinary characters and adventures, and are based on imaginary subjects, which spread abroad from one person to another [2].

Tales have an important place in the culture, education and social life of a nation. Tales include several features concerning the ethical structure of a society, its traditions and customs, national elements, religious beliefs and national languages of a society and make considerable contribution in the members of a society in learning its cultural values. Tales also make contribution to the development of children in the field of education and have an important place in the acquisition of four basic language skills, namely reading, speaking writing and listening and teaching the richnesses of the native language. Individuals learn

* Corresponding author: selma.korkmaz@neu.edu.tr

how they should behave in social life based on human relations, friendship emotion, love for mother and father, keeping secrets, sense of sharing and amity in the tales.

Considering that tales are valuable in terms of preparing the child for life and giving him/her a favorable place in the society, preschool teachers have huge roles to play. Preschool teachers have to pay attention to the characteristics of the tales that children read. The purpose of this study is to obtain the opinions of preschool pre-service teachers who will work as preschool teachers in the future concerning tales and explore whether they have awareness about tales.

2 Method

2.1 Study Group

Our study group consists of 60 senior pre-service teachers studying at preschool teaching department of Atatürk Education Faculty of Near East University. The reason for preferring senior students at preschool teaching department is that they are believed to have wide knowledge accumulation on several topics concerning their profession and the necessary experience as they completed their internship program.

2.2 Collection of Data

Interview form was used in data collection. This interview form consists of the following 7 questions:

1. Which tales are you planning to read to your students when you become a teacher? Which criteria will you pay attention in choosing the tales that you will read?
2. In your opinion, which tales affect the children negatively? Why?
3. In your opinion, which elements affect the children negatively in tales?
4. Do you think that having elements contrary to our cultural values in the tales that you will read is inconvenient? Why?
5. In your opinion, what kind of an impact do the children have on the development of children?
6. Do you think that tales entail children to extreme imaginary worlds? Why?
7. What are your positive and negative opinions concerning the elements that belong to our culture in the tales?

2.3 Analysis and interpretation of data

Frequency, percentage and content analysis were used in the analysis of data. The data obtained from interview form were evaluated by creating various codes and themes and tabulation.

3 Findings and Comments

It is seen that pre-service teachers gave more than one answers to some questions in the interview form. For this reason all answers were included in the evaluation.

3.1 Findings concerning the tales that pre-service teachers are considering to read to their students when they become teachers and the criteria that they will consider in choosing these tales

Table 1. Frequency and percentage distribution of pre-service teachers concerning the tales that they consider reading to their students when they become teachers

Title of the tale	f	%
Snow-White and The Seven Dwarves	15	25,00
Little Red Riding Hood	10	16,66
Cinderella	9	15,00
Cicada and The Ant	7	11,66
Rapunzel	5	8,33
Pinocchio	4	6,66
Dede Korkut Tales	4	6,66
Sleeping Beauty	3	5,00
Frog and The Rabbit	1	1,66
Snow Queen	1	1,66
Little Mermaid	1	1,66
The Lion King	1	1,66
The Little Match Girl	1	1,66
Heidi	1	1,66
Liar Shepherd	1	1,66
Ali Baba and The Forty Thieves	1	1,66
Little Black Fish	1	1,66
Fairy Tale	1	1,66
La Fontaine Tales	1	1,66
Nasrettin Hodja Tales	1	1,66
Lion and The Mosquito	1	1,66
The Ugly Duckling	1	1,66
Alice in Wonderland	1	1,66
Crow and The Fox	1	1,66

According to table 1, 25% of pre-service teachers told that they would read Snow-White and The Seven Dwarves, 16.66% told that they would read the Little Red Riding Hood, 15% told that they would read Cinderella, 11.66% stated that they would read Cicada and The Ant, 8.33% told that they would read Rapunzel, 6.66% told that they would read Pinocchio, 6.66% told that they would read Dede Korkut, 5% told that they would read Sleeping Beauty and 26.66% told that they would read other tales to in the table to their students when they become teachers. Considering these tales, it is seen that teachers mostly consider foreign tales but do not even mention Turkish tales such as Keloğlan.

Table 2. Frequency and percentage distribution of pre-service teachers concerning the criteria that they will consider in choosing the tales that they are planning to read to their students when they become teachers

Theme	f	%
Being educative and didactic	29	48,33
Being suitable for the age group of the children	19	31,66
Strengthening the imagination	9	15,00
Including cultural elements	8	13,33
Relating to the daily life	7	11,66
Making considerable use of pictures	6	10,00
Being written with a clear and understandable language	6	10,00
Having and entertaining dimension	5	8,33
Making contribution to the development of the child	4	6,66
Tale cover being convenient to the content	1	1,66

The criteria that pre-service teachers would consider in choosing tales are given in Table 2. Accordingly, 48.33% of pre-service teachers stated that they chose the tales considering the criterion of being educative and didactic, 31.66% of pre-service teachers stated that they chose the tales considering the criterion of being suitable for the age group of children, 15% of pre-service teachers stated that they chose the tales considering the criterion of strengthening the imagination, 13.33% of pre-service teachers stated that they chose the tales considering the criterion of including cultural elements, 11.66% of pre-service teachers stated that they chose the tales considering the criterion of relating to daily life, 10% of pre-service teachers stated that they chose the tales considering the criterion of making considerable use of pictures, another 10% of pre-service teachers stated that they chose the tales considering the criterion of being written with a clear and understandable language, 8.33% of pre-service teachers stated that they chose the tales considering the criterion of having an entertaining dimension, 6.66% of pre-service teachers stated that they chose the tales considering the criterion of making contribution to the development of the child and 1.66% of pre-service teachers stated that they chose the tales considering the criterion of tale cover being convenient to the content. The most important reason of teaching tales from very early ages is to teach the child cultural elements, however, it has been found out that only 13.33% of pre-service teachers have such awareness.

3.2 Findings concerning which tales have negative impact on children and why these tales affect children negatively

Table 3. Frequency and percentage distribution of pre-service teachers concerning which tales affect children negatively

Title of the tale	f	%
Snow-White and The Seven Dwarves	9	15,00
Rapunzel	8	13,33
Cinderella	8	13,33
Little Red Riding Hood	7	11,66
Smurfs	5	8,33
Spider-Man	5	8,33
Batman	5	8,33
Pinocchio	5	8,33
Lucky Luke	4	6,66
Dede Korkut Tales	3	5,00
Ali Baba and The Forty Thieves	3	5,00
Hansel and Gretel	2	3,33
Heidi	1	1,66
Pollyanna	1	1,66
The Phoenix Tale	1	1,66
Beauty and The Beast	1	1,66
Cicada and The Ant	1	1,66
Puss in Boots	1	1,66
Arabian Nights Tales	1	1,66
Tin Soldier	1	1,66
The Ugly Duckling	1	1,66

A can be seen in table 3, 15% of pre-service teachers indicated Snow-White and The Seven Dwarves, 13.33% indicated Rapunzel, 13.33% indicated Cinderella, 11.66% indicated Little Red Riding Hood, 8.33% indicated Smurfs, 8.33% indicated Spider-Man, 8.33% indicated Batman, 8.33% indicated Pinocchio, 6.66% indicated Lucky Luke, 5% indicated Dede Korkut, 5% indicated Ali Baba and The Forty Thieves, 3.33% indicated Hansel and Gretel, and 15% indicated Heidi, Pollyanna, the Phoenix Tale, Beauty and The Beast, Cicada and The Ant, Puss in Boots, Arabian Nights, Tin Soldier and The Ugly

Duckling as the tales which affect children negatively. However, it is seen that pre-service teachers are under the effect of some cartoons and thought that such cartoons as Spider-Man, Batman and Lucky Luke are tales.

Table 4. Frequency and percentage distribution of pre-service teachers concerning the reasons of tales which affect children negatively

Theme	f	%
Including violence and horror elements	32	53,33
Being unrelated with reality	19	31,66
Being not convenient for cultural values	11	18,33

According to table 4, 53.33% of pre-service teachers think that tales which include violence and horror elements affect children negatively, 31.66% pre-service teachers think that tales which are unrelated to reality affect children negatively, and 18.33% of pre-service teachers think that tales which are not convenient for cultural values affect children negatively.

3.3 Findings on the elements in tales which affect children negatively

Table 5. Frequency and percentage distribution of pre-service teachers concerning the elements which affect children negatively in tales

Theme	f	%
Violence-war-fighting-guns	34	56,66
Dragons-monsters	20	33,33
Evil behaviors-evil	20	33,33
Witches	16	26,66
Magic-spell	16	26,66
Goblins	13	21,66
Fairies	11	18,33
Wolves	11	18,33
Strict rules	10	16,66
Theft	7	11,66
Giants	5	8,33
Negative wording	1	1,66

An examination of Table 5 shows that 56.66% of pre-service teachers think that such elements as violence, war, fighting and guns in tales affect children negatively, 33.33% think that such elements as dragons and monsters in tales affect children negatively, 33.33% think that such elements as evil behavior and evil in tales affect children negatively, 26.66% think that such elements as witches in tales affect children negatively, 26.66% think that such elements as magic or spell in tales affect children negatively, 21.66% think that such elements as goblins in tales affect children negatively, 18.33% think that such elements as fairies in tales affect children negatively, 18.33% think that such elements as wolves in tales affect children negatively, 16.66% think that such elements as strict rules in tales affect children negatively, 11.66% think that such elements as theft in tales affect children negatively, 8.33% think that such elements as giants in tales affect children negatively, and 1.66% think that such elements as negative wording in tales affect children negatively.

3.4 Findings as regards whether they find the elements in tales contrary to our cultural values inconvenient and why these elements are inconvenient

Table 6. Frequency and percentage distribution of pre-service teachers concerning whether they find the elements in tales contrary to our cultural values inconvenient and why these elements are inconvenient or not

Code	Theme	f	%
Inconvenient	As not everyone can learn their culture well and when children are learning their culture they suffer from confusions	36	60,00
	As the elements taught and experienced do not coincide	14	23,33
	As they are contrary to ethical rules	2	3,33
Not inconvenient	As they help children know different cultures	8	13,33

According to Table 6, 86.66% of pre-service teachers think that the elements which are contrary to our cultural values in tales are inconvenient, whereas 13.33% do not think that this is inconvenient. Sixty percent of pre-service teachers claim that they find inconvenience as not everyone can learn their culture properly and that children are suffering from confusions when they learn their culture, 23.33% think that they find inconvenience as the elements taught and experienced do not coincide, and 3.33% think that they find inconvenience as they are contrary to ethical rules whereas 8% think that they do not find inconvenience as they help children know different cultures.

3.5 Findings concerning the effect of tales on the development of children

Table 7. Frequency and percentage distribution of pre-service teachers concerning the effect of tales on the development of children

Theme	f	%
Improves imagination and creativity	39	65,00
Important in terms of cognitive and mental development	17	28,33
It has a didactic effect	10	16,66
Makes contribution to language development	10	16,66
Helps them give direction to their lives	3	5,00
Motivates reading	3	5,00
Ensures empathy development	3	5,00
Provides entertaining leisure time	2	3,33

All teachers stated that tales have positive effects on the development of children. As can be seen in table 7, 65% of pre-service teachers stated that tales were important as they improved imagination and creativity, 28.33% of pre-service teachers stated that tales were important as they ensured cognitive and mental development, 16.66% of pre-service teachers stated that tales were important as they had didactic effect, 16.66% of pre-service teachers stated that tales were important as they made contribution to language development, 5% of pre-service teachers stated that tales were important as they helped them give direction to their lives, 5% of pre-service teachers stated that tales were important as they motivated reading, 5% of pre-service teachers stated that tales were important as they ensured empathy development, and 3.33% of pre-service teachers stated that tales were important as they provided entertaining leisure time.

3.6 Findings concerning whether tales entail children to extreme imaginary worlds and its reasons

Table 8. Frequency and percentage distribution of pre-service teachers concerning whether tales entail children to extreme imaginary worlds and its reasons

Code	Theme	f	%
Yes, it entails to imaginary world	They try to be like tale characters and behave like them They believe in supernatural things	56	93,33
No, it does not entail to imaginary world	It motivates thinking It improves imagination	4	6,66

An examination of table 8 shows that 93.33% of pre-service teachers think that tales entail children to extreme imaginary worlds whereas 6.66% do not agree with this opinion. Pre-service teachers claim that tale tales entail children to imaginary worlds as they try to be like the tale characters and behave like them, and believe in supernatural things. However, according to pre-service teachers who do not agree with this opinion, tales motivate children for thinking and improve their imaginary worlds.

3.7 Findings concerning what we think positively and negatively about our cultural values in our tales

Table 9. Frequency and percentage distribution of pre-service teachers concerning what we think positively and negatively about the elements belonging to our cultural values in our tales

Code	Theme	f	%
Positive opinions	The child becomes aware of the cultural values	18	30,00
	The child knows different cultures	8	13,33
	The child learns cultural elements at an early age	7	11,66
	The child easily comprehends information concerning culture easily	6	10,00
Negative opinions	They do not reflect our culture totally	11	26,66
	They are contrary to our cultural elements	5	8,33
	They are not suitable for their age	5	8,33
	They include religious issues	5	8,33

Table 9 shows that 30% of pre-service teachers see positive aspects in tales as children become aware of their cultural values, 13.33% think that they know different cultures, 11.66% think that the child can learn cultural elements at an early age, and 10% believe that the child can easily comprehend the information given about culture. On the other hand, 26.66% of pre-service teachers see negative aspects in tales as they do not reflect our culture totally, 8.33% think that they are contrary to our cultural elements, 8.33% believe that they are not suitable for the age, and 8.33% think that they include religious issues.

4 Discussion, Conclusion and Recommendations

Although tales seem to be used in order to have fun and entertaining time, everyone knows that tales affect the development of children and that they have educative and didactic aspects. For this reason, it is needed that preschool pre-service teachers have a wide accumulation of knowledge as well as awareness concerning tales. It is observed that there is contradiction between the opinions of pre-service teachers concerning the tales that they will read to children when they become teachers and their opinions on the tales that have the worst negative effects on children. The fact that although pre-service teachers claim that some tales can affect children negatively they state that they will teach the same tales shows that they have certain knowledge accumulation but lack awareness. In addition, the fact that they think that some cartoons (Lucky Luke, Batman, Spider-Man etc.) are tales is an indicator of technology and that families cannot prevent this. It is evident that pre-service teachers are under the influence of foreign cultures and, although they are senior students, they have little information about Turkish tales. However, teachers who are supposed to raise next generation should be knowledgeable about tales which reflect our culture in the best manner and read and impose these tales to children. In this way we can choose tales belonging to our culture consciously and make considerable contribution to the development of children. Dilidüzgün believes that consciously choosing a tale to give to a child could eliminate possible inconveniencies [3].

It has been seen that pre-service teachers claimed that when choosing tales they would pay attention to such criteria as being educative and didactic, convenient for the age group of the children, improve imagination, include cultural elements, relate to daily life, make best use of pictures, are written in a clear and understandable language, are entertaining, make contribution to the development of the child and the tale cover is consistent with its content. However, none of the participants mentioned considering the interests and needs of the child. In their study, Kıldan and Bilgici concluded that children's books should be educative and didactic, improve imagination of children and especially address their interests and needs [4].

At the same time, it has been revealed that very few pre-service teachers are aware that cultural elements should be considered while choosing tales.

Pre-service teachers believe that tales which include elements of violence and horror, are unrelated to the reality and contrary to cultural values affect children in a negative direction.

They think that the elements which affect children negatively are violence-war-fighting-guns, dragons-monsters, evil behaviors-evil, witches, magic-spell, goblins, fairies, wolves, strict rules, theft, giants and negative wording.

Most of the pre-service teachers think that the elements in tales which are contrary to our cultural values is inconvenient whereas some believe that it is not inconvenient as it would be beneficial if children knew the characteristics of different cultures. Özünel mentioned the relation between tale and culture and stated that each tale reflected the unique viewpoint of the tale that it was told in and continued to include the features of other societies [5].

All pre-service teachers claimed that tales affected the development of children positively. They argued that tales improved imagination and creativity of children, were important in terms of their cognitive and mental development, had didactic impact, contributed to language development, helped them give direction to their lives, motivated reading, and ensured empathy development and having fun leisure time. According to Bilkan, tales improve the imagination of children and are important in terms of the development of native language [6]. Pilancı stated that the importance of tales in terms of language teaching, language usage and language awareness could not be disregarded [7]. Several researchers claimed that tales have important function in the education of native languages [8,9].

At the same time, it has been witnessed that several pre-service teachers agree that tales entail children to extremism in terms of imagination.

Pre-service teachers stated that tales are important in that children can become aware of their own cultural values, know different cultures, learn cultural elements in early ages, and easily comprehend the information given concerning culture; they also stated that they had negative opinions about tales which do not fully reflect our culture, are contrary to our cultural elements, are not suitable for the age of the child and include religious issues. Feyzioğlu claimed that tales were very important in the formation of a cultural identity [10].

As a result, it can be said that most pre-service teachers have a certain accumulation of knowledge about tales but lack the awareness of how to use them. Based on these findings, it is believed that pre-service teachers could benefit from the following recommendations:

- They have to become aware of the fact that tales are important in the education of pre-school children,
- They should know that the tales that they will read to the children will affect them either positively or negatively,
- They should consider the interests and needs of children while choosing tales,
- They should primarily prefer the tales which are convenient to our culture and then benefit from the tales in the world literature.

References

1. TDK, *Grand Turkish dictionary*, Turkish Language Institute Publications, Ankara, (2015).
2. *Meydan larousse*, C.8, Meydan Publications, İstanbul, (1972).
3. S. Dilidüzgün, *Contemporary children literature*, Yapı Kredi Publications, İstanbul, (1996).
4. A. O. Kıldan, B. G. Bilgici, *Determination of opinions of the parents of pre-school children concerning criteria for selecting children books*, National Education Journal, ***41***/192, 105-120 (2011).
5. E. Ö. Özünel, *Being a woman at tale place,* Geleneksel Publications, Ankara, (2006)
6. A. F. Bilkan, *Tale aesthetics*, Timaş Publications, İstanbul, (2009)
7. H. Pilancı, *Utilization of folk literature in modern education* (Anadolu University Publications, Ankara, (2008).
8. A. T. Görgü, *Contribution of tales to the cognitive and emotional development of children.* S. Sever (Ed.), II. National Children and Youth Literature Congress Proceedings Book, Ankara University Printing House, Ankara, 537–544 (2007).
9. Z. Gürel, F. Temizyürek, N. K. Şahbaz, *Children's literature*, Öncü Printing House, Ankara, (2007).
10. Y. Feyzioğlu, *Why are tales necessary for children?,* S. Sever (Ed.), II. National Children and Youth Literature Congress Proceedings Book, Ankara University Printing House, Ankara, 831–843 (2007).

A Comparison of fantacy–reality contradiction and melancholy themes in the works by Tevfik Fikret and Ahmet Tevfik, the first Turkish story-writer in Cyprus

Şevket Öznur[1,*]

[1]Near East University, Faculty of Arts and Sciences, Turkish Language and Literature, Nicosia-99138, North Cyprus

Abstract. The people representing Servet-i Fünun do not attend to social issues. They lock themselves in the house and are mostly interested in the nature and people they feel sorry about. The poets and writers of Servet-i Fünun literatures adapted Western literature and influenced many writers and poets of their time and later times by some changes in style, theme, and wording. The best sample of this interaction in literary periods can be observed in the comparative Works by the same community in different areas. In this study, a theme comparison will be done between the Work by Tevfik Fikret and the Turkish Cypriot writer and the theme interaction in Turkish Literature will be finalized. Tevfik Fikret is appointed as the Editor-in-chief of the Scientific and Science Journal. Then he converts the journal into Literature Journal and gathers young people around it. The Servet-i Fünun people use an arty language, peculiar to them, in expressing feelings and thoughts down to the last detail with ample images and characters. Most of the Servet-i Fünun writers and poets were raised in the same educational institutions, experienced the same political, social, and financial conditions, were engaged in the same issues, were almost at the same age generation from the middle-class, were educated in Western schools and with good knowledge of foreign languages. Naturally, these similarities created a common joy and culture among them. These writers and poets believed in strong family bonds and would take up the same motives when they were together to talk about literature issues. They influenced many writers and poets. Pessimism and tediousness, the basis of literature, became the main starting points for the whole literature. In his many poems, Tevfik Fikret treated compassion and reflected the grief of many poor and lonely people. In the 1970s Turkey adapted Western Literature type but this type of literature was introduced to Cyprus late, not before the 1890s. Even though, the Servet-i Fünun followers began to influence the literateurs and their Works in Cyprus. Soon after the British era in 1878 in Cyprus, tension between Moslem Turk and Christian Greek communities started to increase. In 1901, Ahmet Tevfik published the "Mir'at-ı Zaman" and in 1909 the "Kokonoz" newspapers. A fundamental change in the literature came about particularly when these newspapers

* Corresponding author: sevket.oznur@neu.edu.tr

were published in Cyprus. Tevfik Fikret brought up his views and his feelings about life in an allergoric and symbolic way. In both Works, the themes were full of pessimism and melancholy. While T. Fikret emphasized the fantasy-reality contradictions and the difference between thoughts and personalities of two lovers, the melancholy-pessimism theme was the priority in Ahmet Tevfik Efendi's work. In both works, the nature was explained with pessimism and melancholy and was symbolized as the place of love. The Servet-i Fünun followers were a family. Even more, it is emphasized that, in some Works the main characters are the writers and poets themselves. The Servet-i Fünun followers were effective in Abdülhamid II era, during which there was a pressure on the poets and writers. The pressure and censure took the writers and poets away from social issues and made them busy with an individual, pessimistic and sickly literature. This is why, melancholy and its analysis was amply mentioned in their Works. Turkish Story-writing started in 1897 in Cyprus. Ahmet Tevfik, who was in Istanbul then, was influenced by the Servet-i Fünun followers and took them as a model in his Works. They were strongly bound to the principles of arts. Although everything could be a topic for poems, but due to the political pressure of the day, they limited their Works to love, nature, family-life, and simple current issues. As the aim, the themes by the two writers will be compared and important parts of comparative studies in Turkish literature will be dealt with, to open a way to different comparisons.

1 Introduction

Arguments about traditional and contemporary literature went on for a long time and in the end the writers and poets who adapted contemporary literature began to discuss the issue among themselves. The problems created by these discussions were the groundwork for a new era. In 1895, Recaizade Mahmut Ekrem argues that "rhyme" is not visual, but audio and after long discussions of "fantacy-reality", he decides to establish a new magazine to advocate new ideas in literature. He appoints Tevfik Fikret as the author-in-chief of the Servet-i Fünun, a science magazine. Later, he names the magazine as "Literature Magazine" and calls the young genetation to suport it. In this new literature era, Halit Ziya Uşaklıgil, Tevfik Fikret, Cenab Şahabettin, Ahmet Şuayip, Mehmet Rauf, and Hüseyin Cahit Yalçın are the chief-representatives and Müftüoğlu Ahmet Fikret, Ali Ekrem, İsmail Safa, Faik Ali, Celal Sahir, Süleyman Nazif, Ahmet Reşit, Hüseyin Suat Safveti Ziya, Hüseyin Siyret, Safvet Nezihi, Ali Nusret [3], İsak Ferrera, an Ottoman Citizen, and Avram Naon are the representatives in the second or third places [6]. Nurettin Ferruh, a poet in Servet-i Fünun era, is always active in press, but kept in the background of the top poets or writers, brings up changes in style in poetry. He oficially registers his book called, "Şafak Sadaları" and his articles before the Servet-i Fünun era. The book "Şafak Sadaları", written before 1985, becomes an important source in terms of style in poetry for the Servet-i Fünun followers [8].

According to İsmail Parlatır, the themes of Servet-i Fünun are mostly fantasy-reality contradictions, running away, committing suicide, taking a shelter in the nature, and shedding tears. These themes have sub-motives. Tedium: Sadness, Pessimism: Melancholy, Broken-heart, broken stringed instrument-Rübab simile, Blind-love-Garam, Youth, Time concept and elapse of time, Art, Poetry, Natural Views, İmagination and disappointment Soul and Unhealthy soul, Love, Philosophy, Mercy, Brothers, Family and home, Wicked life, Flying- Wish to be a bird, Unrevealed feeling of freedom, Death- grave, Homeland and portraits [4].

The Servet-i Fünun magazine, first published in (1886) is closed in 1901. However the influence of this new literature lasts until 1914, the beginning of World War 1. Tevfik Fikret, the author-in-chief of the Servet-i Fünun magazine and the poet with the best examples of poems dies in 1915. He influences many writers and poets. The basics of his literature, pessimism and melancholy become the foundation of a literature. T.Fikret writes several poems in which he deals with sadness and worries about poor and homeless people. Before he starts for the magazine, he writes poems in old style. In 1893-1895, he discovers his own style and becomes more confident of himself. French poetry and Western writers help him find his own style. He can not travel particularly to remote places and this strengthens fantacy-reality contradictions in his poems. He writes the book "Rübab-ı Şikeste" between 1986-1900. The theme "fantacy and reality contradictions " in the poem "Süha and Pervin", in his book, is the topic. He also includes the nature, love, and pessimism in his motives [3].

1.1 The first works of contemporary Turkish literature in Cyprus

Turkey adapted Western type of literature in the 1870s, but its reflection in Cyprus was not before the 1890s. Even though, from 1890 onwards, the Servet-i Fünun followers were able to influence the litereteurs and their works. After 1878, clashes between the Moslem Turk and Christian Greek communities gradually became more severe. In 1883, Aşık Kenzi produced one of the most beautiful examples of folk-poems called "Cyprus Epic". In 1901, Ahmed Tevfik published "Mir'at-ı Zaman" and in 1909 "Kokonoz" newspapers. Fundamental changes happened in literature particularly when publishing newspapers started in Cyprus. Kaytazzade Mehmet Nazım wrote the first examples of poems in Western style. Ahmet Tevfik is the following important name followed by Urkiye Mine Balman, Engin Gönül, Pembe Marmara, Osman Türkay, Özker Yaşın, Nazif Süleyman Ebeoğlu, Semih Sami Umar, and Necla Salih Suphi in the British Colonial period. Kaytazzade Mehmet Nazım, one of the youngsters raised by Namık Kemal, produced his first work called "Yadigar-ı Muhabbet" in 1896. The first novel "İntibah" was writing in Cyprus by Namık Kemal during his detention on the island. Following this, Hikmet Afif Mapolar had a great influence on the Cyprus Turkish literature by publishing his novels and stories, some of which are; "Kahraman Kaplan" (1936), "Son Damla" (1937), "Diken Çiçeği" (1938), "Son Çıldırış" (1939), and "Kendime Dönüyorum" (1943). The first theatres were "Hicran-ı Ebedi" written in 1895 and "Safa" or "Netice-i İptila" by Kaytazzade Mehmet Nazım . Namık Kemal "Vatan yahut Silistre" play was on the stage 20 years after his death, as the first local play on stage in Cyprus. Following min Nihat Bey's Müsameret-name", one of the first most important stories was " Bir Manzara-i Dil-Güşa" by Ahmet Tevfik Efendi in 1897, which is also assumed as the beginning of Turkish story writing in Cyprus. Ahmet Tevfik, in Istanbul on those days, is influenced by the Servet-i Fünun followers and takes them as the model in his writings. The first story book is "Gülünçlü İbret-amiz Hikayeler", written by Ahmed Nuri Müdürzade, in 1908. This is followed by the long story "Son Çıldırış" by Hikmet Afif Mapolar, in 1939 [7].

2 A comparative study of Süha and Pervin and Bir Manzara-i Dil Güşa

2.1 Thematic study 1: Ahmed Tevfik Efendi's story "Bir Manzara-i Dil Güşa"

We overviewed A.Tevfik Efendi's themes and motives in his story "Bir manzara-i Dil-Güşa" and noticed he mostly emphasized Pessimism and melancholy and conveyed this to his reader through the nature. He presented the motive of nature intermingled with pessimism . Below are some examples from the story;

It was a lively time in Spring. The shining moon glistened the world with its dazzling light going through the branches of every tree making new leaves look like embroidered with silver wire [2].

This is the introduction part of the text. The scene of the nature is used describe the spring motive with the darkness.

She was in her late fourteens, but the change on her shining face reflected the signs of a strong ongoing anxiety in her heart.

Angel is the girl in the story, still in her late fourteens, which displays the beauty and the motives of young age.

The dinner- bell rings to invite the households to dinner. The girl, once more, looks at herself admiringly in the mirror for the final touches and walks out of her room. There were no guests at the dinner- table. Although the girl was attractive, nobody noticed her since they were busy eating.

After the meal everybody took a seat in the sitting-room, but the girl would stand up every five minutes and walk up and down in the room as if she was very restless.

In these sections, the evening-meal and the households sitting positions are explained. The girl's nervousness and tediousness is reflected together with the family motif.

Just as everything in the world rapidly comes to an end, the unbearable nervousness of the girl ended after two hours.

The headiness, the girl experienced as the main character in the story, caused by a wave of excitement mixed with joy and elapse of time is expressed with time motif.

Every two minutes she would look at the clock angrily and would curse the time for being late.

Angel's feeling pessimistic and angry about the slow elapse of time is reflected in time motif. She is experiencing a feeling of seesaw between e happiness and pessimism because of elapse of time.

This time they were frustrated and all their sweet dreams turned into a painful, unendurable heart- beat and an ongoing trembling.

As she is secretly trying to run away from home, Anjel has the feeling that she will not be able to fulfill her ambitions and this makes her unhappy. This situation is described together with disappointment motif.

The grief, ill-luck the poor experienced from the very minute after leaving the room, should have been more than enough that the janitor stretches his hand from the window, opens it and pulls the poor inside.

The main character, Anjel, is pessimistic about all the bad experiences she has. Even a very trifle event eradicates all the good things in hurt mind and starts to feel pessimistic. The melancholy motif is exhibited throughout the story.

He would leave a trace along the way so as not lose his directions. For example, he would put little stones, very close to each other, along the direction he followed. He would not miss the stones in the moonlight.

Along the way she was going to meet her lover in the forest, Anjel would leave little stones on the way so as not to be lost on the way back. This section talks about the beauty of the moon and the open country in the description of the nature.

I can't call this bad luck, because I found myself in this dilemma. I asked for it. I am in such a hopeless situation that I may dishonour myself.

Anjel meets a shepherd in the forest on her way to meet her lover and she starts to feel very pessimistic with the fear of being caught. This melancholic situation is always keeps Anjel's mind busy throughout the story, and this causes her the worst uneasiness.

Shadows of trees in the moonlight are fearful scenes and the crooked shadows from branches are frightening because they look like the shadows of watchers following them.

The feeling of desperation and confusion experienced here due to meeting secretly and the fear of being caught, is reflected to the nature and the trees look like someone preventing them from meeting.

Yes! A forest! A dreadful place. Among these tall cypress tress, listening the the silence, one feels himself lying in a grave.

The silence of the nature is likened to a grave and this displays the most probable melancholic situation. Likening silence to a grave, reminds us the motif of death.

While everybody is falling asleep in the moonlight, stretched in their comfortable beds, feeling their lovers' hair, I am wondering in the forest just like wild monsters.

Marki describes the forest, where he meets his lover secretly, as a place full of monsters. He feels totally disappointed because of his thoughts. The place, which is full of beauty, is a bad place because of silence and his pessimistic thought.

The young man: Anjel, my love! Yes! My second sould! You were waiting for me in the forest, weren't you?

Anjel: Not only in the forest, but I would never be afraid of waiting for you even in hell.

In Anjel's and Marki's conversation, the motif of love is clearly expressed. This mutual love is, from time to time, is reflected with pleasing words.

During this sweet conversation, their fear is still continuing as the birds fly among tree branches and the sudden image of shadow of the trees that looks like someone watching them.

The fear of being caught, due to Anjel's ongoing negative and pessimistic thoughts, her animating and likening the nature is everywhere in the story. This fear causes anxiety, but not peace when they meet.

Marki, accepting your proposal is not possible. You know that very well. I'll go back to my room, Marki. I'm sorry,but It is not decent to meet in your room right now

Anjel's objection to the meeting place disappoints Marki and they keep crying until the next meeting. In this part also, there is pessimism and tears.

2.2 Thematic study II: The poem "Süha and Pervin" by Tevfik Fikret

The poem begins after Süha and Pervin meet in a forest. The nature and the shelter for the two lovers are described in a decent language.

Süha prefers to be in a different place where nobody can reach easily, rather than the one he is in with Pervin. He does not feel comfortable at his present place. This feeling can be noticed on his face (Imagination).

Pervin is worried about Suha's fancy to be at an imaginary place and this worries her. She questions him on his unhappiness with his life (Reality).

Süha imagines himself at an unknown place where he can be happy. The life he wishes for is at a place where he will not be disturbed in his conversations with the sky and God. The running away motif is presented in the theme of an imaginary place.

Good news! The clouds are dispersing. Wow! We did not have the sunshine for days.

Pervin is a realistic character. She likes the sun and light. Süha, on the other hand, reflects his pessimism to the nature and describes it. Even more, Pervin still treats Süha as a child.

Treating Süha as a child and voicing it disappoints Süha. This disappointment is hidden in his looks.

Pervin can not put up with Süha's childishness and insists on living real love. Under those prevailing circumstances she wants to live her love freely, but Süha's imaginary character disappoints her.

Reality does not fit Süha's character. For him, regarding love and sex equal means deceiving oneself. Süha and Pervin have different perceptves regarding love (Realistic-Imaginative).

No matter what Pervin says, Süha is still in an imaginary world. He argues that sadness is a part of his life. The tediousness motif has the priority.

Süha believes that negative thoughts do not give one any harm. He is happy to be in this group. (There is sentimentality, getting pleasure from sadness. Masochism). Trying to prove something becomes an obstacle in understanding life. Thus, we can not notice the beauties of life.

Süha pictures the place he imagines pessimistically as he describes the nature. He describes this place tediously. He enjoys tediousness.

Just like Tevfik Fikret, Süha enjoys being imaginative and he relates this characteristic to his nature.

Süha wants to die. He hopes that he can be with his love next to his grave even after death. This displays the death motif.

2.3 Stylistic study I: Ahmed Tevfik Efendi

Ahmed Tevfik Efendi has several poems written in satirical and humorous styles. He includes local expressions and idioms in his poems and writings. His poems usually have an addressing style. From time to time, he includes imitative styles in his writings [1]. In his story, "Bir Manzara-i Dil-Güşa" A.Tevfik Efendi uses Arabic and Persian words, but they are easy to understand. These foreign words are scattered around in certain parts of the story and they can be worked out easily. The main characters in the story have Western names.

2.4 Stylistic study II: Tevfik Fikret

As a poet using synonyms, Tevfik Fikret uses Turkish, Arabic, and Persian words corresponding to the same feelings, the same beings, and the same thoughts in his work. He tries art of speech in poetry language to convey an expression and concept in a more effective, intensive, and aesthetic way . He frequently includes in his work natural symbols and considers the nature as a shelter. According to Mehmet Kaplan. Tevfik Fikret is a paradoxical poet. The words, reality-lie, darkness- light prove this issue. The writer is very strict about dictation marks in his poems. At first look, his style seems incomprehensible because of the foreign words he uses [4]. In general he deals with the fear of reality, the rest of the world, timidness, and imagination even if it is deceptive. This can be observed in the poem "Süha and Pervin". In Tevfik Fikret's style there is an image of "trembling", which has an important feature.

3 Conclusion

In his poem "Süha and Pervin", Tevfik Fikret displays his view of life and perceptions in an allegoric and symbolic style. There are ample themes full of sadness and pessimism. In

Tevfik Fikret's work there is reality-fantacy contradiction, and the difference between the two lovers' thoughts and characters. On the other hand, melancholy-pessimism theme stand out. In both works the nature is described with the feeling of pessimism and sadness and as the symbol of love [5]. When the place for the topic and the dialogue between the two lovers are considered, a striking similarity between the two Works can easily be noticed. In this regard, Ahmed Tevfik Fikret Efendi might have been influenced by Tevfik Fikret's Work. One of the two differences between them is that in Tevfik Fikret's Work Süha is the pessimistic character, whereas in Ahmed Tevfik Fikret's Work Anjel is the pessimistic character. The second difference is that in Tevfik Fikret's Work, Süha is deserted because of his being pessimistic, but in Ahmed Tevfik Efendi's Work both lovers leave each other in pessimism and sadness to meet again.

As we study their style, we can observe that Ahmed Fikret Efendi's Work is more comprehensible compared to Tevfik Fikret's Work and this is because A.Tevfik Efendi used foreign words and the language is clearer. Tevfik Fikret, on the other hand, had a more arty style. That is, Ahmed Tevfik Efendi included more public language.

References

1. Emin Onuş, *Ahmed Tevfik Efendi'nin Teselya Savaşı İle İlgili Yazıları ve Şiirleri,* Doğu Akdeniz Üniversitesi Yüksek Lisans Tezi, *10*, (2012).
2. Harid Fedai, *Kıbrıs Türk Kültürü Makaleler* 1, SAMTAY Mağusa Tarihini Araştırma ve Yazın Vakfı Yayımı, 104-115, (2004).
3. İnci Enginün, *Yeni Türk Edebiyatı Tanzimat'tan Cumhuriyet'e (1839-1923),* DergâhYayınları, 533-534,535-538, (2014).
4. İsmail Parlatır,*Tevfik Fikret,*Akçağ Yayınları,100-120, (2014).
5. Macit Balık, *Sühâ Ve Pervîn"De Narsist Kimliğin Görünümleri*, Akademik Sosyal Araştırmalar Dergisi,Yıl: *3*(11),Tevfik Fikret Özel Sayısı. 160-175, (Nisan 2015).
6. Oğuz Karakartal, *Tevfik Fikret'in İzinde İki Şair Avram Naon ve İsak Ferera,* Eren Yayıncılık,50-51,(2006).
7. Şevket Öznur, Kıbrıs Türk Edebiyatı, 50-51, (2014).
8. Sevim Şermet, *Serbest Şiirin Tarihine Girişte Unutulan Bir İsim: Nurettin Ferruh ve Şiir Sanatı*,(Turkish Studies International Periodical For the Languages, Literature and History of Turkish or Turkic Volume *5*/2 Spring,160-175, (2010).

Investigation of World assumption, personal attributes and gender roles of adolescents

Meral Sert Ağır[1,*]

[1]Marmara University, Atatürk Faculty of Education, Department of Educational Sciences, Psychological Counseling and Guidance Department, Göztepe Istanbul, Turkey

Abstract. This research aims to examine adolescents' world assumptions, personal attributes and gender roles. The research has attempted to examine the thoughts of adolescents about the world and the ways in which they define themselves as a man or a woman by considering the fact that their lives are affected not only by "traumatic" events but also by several family and environmental dynamics affecting their quality of life. Data was obtained from randomly selected 407 high school students from Kadıköy district in Istanbul province, by applying "World Assumptions Scale (WAS)", "Extended Personal Attributes Questionnaire (EPAQ)", "Gender Roles Attitude Scale (GRAS)", and "Data Collection Form". Our results showed that there was a significant difference in the scales and sub-dimensions used in the research with respect to gender, grade, family characteristics as well as life standards, balance of standards, adequacy of/change in family income, living with the family without problems, level of satisfaction with the environment, and the desire to change the living environment. In addition to a positive relationship between world assumptions and personal attributes, various correlations in different directions were also found between the sub-dimensions of the scales. Our research has shown that adolescents' life dynamics can make a difference in their perception of the world and their assumptions about perceiving themselves as moral and valuable individuals, as well as their personal attributes and perceptions about gender roles.

Keywords: World assumptions, personal attributes, gender roles, quality of life, adolescence, gender identity and sex role behaviors

1 Introduction

Each person's reality contains comments about what is happening and what will happen in the shadow of perceptions and schemas that are linked to their experiences and the traces left behind by these experiences [1]. A schema is the knowledge of the human about the world. Schemas are acquired through the mental processes of human beings [2,3]. Human beings perceive the world, define what they perceive, and their definitions bring explanations about the meaning of life. Each of these explanations contains comments that

* Corresponding author: meralagir@marmara.edu.tr – meralagir@yahoo.com

carry traces of previous experiences. Therefore, although the building blocks of people are the same, thoughts, feelings and behaviors regarding life are different. This difference is a sign of the understanding and expectation of each person in terms of life [4]. In a sense, human beings manage their lives through definitions and explanations about the world in which they live in and motivate themselves to live. Thus, they adopt a particular attitude by means of thoughts and beliefs that they formed in the face of the changing dynamics of life [5,6].

According to the cognitive theory, human beings fundamentally have positive assumptions about themselves and the world, but their interactions can lead to a change of positive beliefs [7]. In recent years, theoreticians have conceptualized beliefs and thoughts about stressful events that change behavior styles of individuals as "casual attributions", "coping potential" and "meaning". Attribution is positive or negative characteristic explanations formed against encountered events, and coping skills are emotion-oriented and problem-based behavioral strategies. The assumptions are the ideas and beliefs developed based on schemas [8].

According to the Theory of Basic Assumptions, which explains human thoughts and behaviors with cognitive understanding, three basic assumptions define behavior: "benevolence of the world", "meaningfulness of the world" and "perceived benevolence of the world". These assumptions are supported by eight hypotheses [9] (see Table 1).

Table 1. World Assumptions and related hypotheses

Assumptions	Benevolence of the world	Meaningfulness of the world	Worthiness of self
Hypotheses	Benevolence of the world Benevolence of human beings	Justice Control Randomness	Self-worth Self-control Luck

According to the theory, three basic assumptions involving eight hypotheses are based on the schemas that the world we live in is a safer place and not a hurtful place. As they are formed with interactions, these schemas may produce an effort to cope with the challenges related to empowerment and development but may also have the opposite effect. According to the relevant literature, the formation of negative assumptions of humans with "traumatic events", experiences that deeply influence the natural course of life as opposed to anticipation or expectation. In other words, while the innate and positive assumption that the world is a safe and invulnerable (place will be replaced by negative assumptions about "benevolence of the world, meaningfulness of the world, and worthiness of self" after traumatic experiences, it differentiates the style of behaviors as well [10,11,12,13].

As can be seen, the assumptions (beliefs) that arise as a result of past learning can make a difference in terms of meeting life functions.

Human life is the process of learning, change and development including opportunities and challenges. Humans should strive and struggle to gain the competences at each step of the development process and to fulfill the functions of future life. In addition, each step in the progressional process has a critical importance in order to survive in terms of acquiring certain features [14]. Among these, adolescence is a transitional period with critical importance that enables human beings who are dependent from birth due to developmental dynamics to mature into independent individuals. Adolescence is the questioning period where one decides "who s/he will be", i.e. the period where the style of performing life functions/duties is decided upon. In a sense, humans decide what their thoughts about themselves and the world should be during adolescence and how they will meet the functions of following periods of life [15,16]. The style of fulfilling "gender identity" and "sex roles" that carry a psychological, sociological and cultural meaning within the context of social roles and definitions highlight adolescents' definition of "identity" about themselves. Thus, they distinguish themselves beyond the notions of "men" and "women" of biological origin, by using "masculinity" and "femininity", which correspond to the way of carrying out functions in life [17,18].

The way of coping with the environmental difficulties of the period as well as the developmental difficulties form within the context of adolescent's thoughts on him/herself and life [19]. In the context of cognitive theory, the adolescent's interactions may affect the attributions about the world, the way of meaningfulness, and his/her capacity to cope with problems. In other words, the behavior generated by the assumptions that the world is a safe place where the people are helpful and get what they deserve, can make a difference with their behavior, and they are valuable in this word and protect themselves from evil with correct behaviors will not be the same with the behavior produced by the opposite assumptions [20]. Therefore, adolescents' definition of "identity" about what kind of an adult one will be, and the "masculinity" and "femininity" role behaviors described by the concept of "gender identity" can change [21].

In the light of these theoretical dynamics, "traumatic events" that are effective on world assumptions were analyzed in this research in the context of quality of life [22,23,24,25], based on the literature on the importance of having a life that fits "life standards" for adolescents. The research was conducted in the context of socio-economic factors to explain adolescent's world assumptions and role definitions of gender identity. In this respect, the research aimed to examine adolescents' world assumptions and personal attributions (in terms of gender identity) and sex role behaviors in relation to quality of life standards.

2 Method

2.1 Research Method

This research examined adolescents' world assumptions, personal attributions and sex roles. The relational screening model was used in the research.

2.2 Study Group

Study group consisted of 407 randomly selected students (169 male, 238 female) studying at 9th, 10th, 11th grades in Kadıköy district of İstanbul province in 2015-2016 academic year.

2.3 Data Collection Tools

Institutional approval was obtained from İstanbul Governorship Provincial Directorate of Education Number: 59090411-20-E.4529708, Dated:21.04.2016. Data were collected by "World Assumptions Scale" standardized by Yılmaz [26], "Extended Personal Attributes Questionnaire" standardized by Demirtaş-Mardan [27], "Gender Roles Attitude Scale" developed by Zeyneloğlu [28] and "Personal Information Form" prepared by the researcher.

2.4 Data Analysis

The data were analyzed in SPSS computer program using t test, one-way analysis of variance and relationship techniques. Gender were investigated by t Test, whereas differences with respect to some variables were investigated by one way analysis of variance.

3 Results

Results of this research are listed below.
3.1. According to the gender characteristic, a significant difference is found in the random dimension, one of the sub-dimensions of the World Assumptions Scale (WAS), and in the negative and positive masculinity sub-dimensions of Extended Personal Attributes Questionnaire (EPAQ) in favor of men, and in the "equalitarian gender role, female gender role, marriage gender role, traditional gender role, male gender role", in the sub-dimensions of the Gender Roles Attitude Scale (GRAS), in favor of women.

Table 2. T test results of scales and sub-dimensions according to gender variable

Scales/Subdimensions	t	p	$\bar{x}$ MALE	$\bar{x}$ FEMALE
Randomness	3.400	0.001	20.48	18.94
Negative masculinity	2.854	0.005	16.62	15.45
Positive femininity	-2.970	0.003	27.90	29.47
Masculinity-femininity	-4.814	0.000	24.96	27.42
Positive masculinity	3.547	0.000	29.75	27.57
Negative femininity (verbal)	-4.190	0.000	10.17	11.63
Gender Roles Attitude Scale	-8.416	0.000	132.82	153.08
Equalitarian gender role	-5.203	0.000	31.31	34.77
Female gender role	-5.474	0.000	24.95	28.62
Marriage gender role	-6.857	0.000	30.86	35.05
Traditional gender role	-9.122	0.000	23.92	29.97
Masculine gender role	-5.613	0.000	21.76	24.66

3.2. According to the grade, in the random sub-dimension of WAS a difference is found between 9th and 10th grade students in favor of 9th grade students; between 10th and 11th grade students in favor of 11th grade students; in the marriage gender role sub-dimension of GRAS, a difference is found between 9th and 10th grade students in favor of 10th students.

Table 3. One-way Analysis of Variance (ANOVA) Results of Scales and Sub-Dimensions According to Grade Variable

Grade	F	p
Randomness	5.103	0.006
Marriage gender role	4.919	0.008

3.3. According to the mother's education level, in the luck sub-dimension of WAS, a significant difference is found between those whose mothers are graduated from high school and whose mothers are illiterate in favor of high school graduates. There is a significant difference found between those whose mothers are graduated from the university and those whose mothers are illiterate in favor of students whose mothers are university graduates. In the female gender role sub-dimension of the GRAS, a significant difference is found between those whose mothers are graduated from the university and those whose mothers are graduated from elementary school in favor of students whose mothers are university graduates. In the traditional gender role sub-dimension, a significant difference is found between those whose mothers are graduated from high school and those whose mothers are graduated from elementary school in favor of high school graduates. According to the level of father's education, no significant difference is found in the related scales and their sub-dimensions.

Table 4. One-way analysis of variance (Anova) results of scales and sub-dimensions according to mother educational status variable

Mother Educational Status	F	p
Luck	4.380	0.002
Gender Roles Attitude Scale	3.641	0.006
Traditional gender role	3.115	0.015

3.4. According to the mother's employment level, in the total scores of GRAS, a significant difference is found between those whose mothers work full time and those whose mothers are housewife in favor of those working full time; in terms of female gender role, a significant difference is found between those whose mothers work full time and those whose mothers are housewife in favor of those working full time, and between those whose mothers are retired and those whose mothers are housewife in favor of those retired.

Table 5. One-way analysis of variance (Anova) results of scales and sub-dimensions according to mother's employment level variable

Mother's Employment Level	F	p
Gender Roles Attitude Scale	3.808	0.010
Female gender role	8.686	0.000

3.5 According to father's working level, in the justice sub-dimension of WAS, a significant difference is found among those whose fathers are retired, those whose fathers work full time and those whose fathers work half-time in favor of those retired; in the negative masculine sub-dimension of the EPAQ, a significant difference is found between those whose fathers work half-time and those whose fathers work full-time in favor of those working half-time.

Table 6. One-way analysis of variance (Anova) results of scales and sub-dimensions according to father's employment level variable

Father's Employment Level	F	p
Justice	3.437	0.017
Negative masculinity	3.128	0.026

3.6. In the WAS and its sub-dimensions justice, luck, self-worth, according to the situation of a crisis related to the income of the family (dismissal of the family member, income drop) experienced in the last 5 years, a significant difference is found in favor of those who haven't had a crisis. In the negative masculine sub-dimension of the EPAQ, female gender role and traditional gender role sub-dimensions of GRAS, there is a significant difference in favor of those who have had a crisis.

Table 7. T test results of scales and sub-dimensions according to crises in the family variable

The situation of a crisis related to the income of the family experienced in the last 5 years	**t**	**p**	**$\bar{x}$ (Yes)**	**$\bar{x}$ (No)**
World Assumptions Scale	-2.807	0.005	106.96	113.35
Justice	-2.540	0.011	17.98	20.18
Luck	-2.204	0.028	14.67	16.16
Self-worth	-2.743	0.006	15.43	16.95
Negative masculinity	2.248	0.025	16.85	15.71
Gender Roles Attitude Scale	2.025	0.044	149.86	143.37
Female gender role	3.100	0.002	29.20	26.57
Traditional gender role	1.996	0.047	28.89	27.10

3.7 In the relevant WAS and its sub-dimension of justice, according to whether there has been an increase in family income over the last 5 years, there is a significant difference found in favor of those that had an increase. In the negative femininity (relational) sub-dimension of the EPAQ and the female gender role and traditional gender role sub-dimensions of GRAS, a significant difference is found in favor of those that does not have an increase.

Table 8. T test results of scales and sub-dimensions according to increase in family income over the last 5 years variable

Increase in family income over the last 5 years	**t**	**p**	**$\bar{x}$ (Yes)**	**$\bar{x}$ (No)**
World Assumptions Scale	2.397	0.017	114.37	110.00
Justice	2.175	0.030	20.53	19.02
Negative femininity (relational)	-2.052	0.041	9.24	9.86
Gender Roles Attitude Scale	-2.341	0.020	26.26	27.85
Traditional gender role	-2.154	0.032	26.65	28.19

3.8. In the WAS, according to the situation of thinking that you are living without economic difficulties with your family, a significant difference is found between those who have given the answer always and sometimes in favor of those who say always. In favor of those who say frequently between those who have given the answer frequently and sometimes; and in the justice, luck and control sub-dimensions, there is a significant difference found in favor of those who say always between those who have given the answer always and sometimes; in the self-worth sub-dimension a significant difference is found in favor of those who say always among those who have given the answer always and sometimes and never; in the positive masculine sub-dimension of the EPAQ, a significant difference is found in favor of those who say always among those who have given the answer always and never; in favor of those who say frequently between those who have given the answer frequently and never; in the negative femininity (relational) sub-dimension, there is a significant difference found in favor of those who say always among those who have given the answer always and sometimes.

Table 9. One-way analysis of variance (Anova) results of scales and sub-dimensions according to the situation of thinking that living without economic difficulties with your family variable

The situation of thinking that you are living without economic difficulties with your family	F	p
World Assumptions Scale	9.098	0.000
Justice	4.083	0.003
Luck	4.072	0.003
Self-worth	8.891	0.000
Control	4.501	0.001
Positive masculinity	3.307	0.011
Negative femininity (relational)	3.397	0.009

3.9. In the WAS according to the situation of whether being satisfied with the district /living area, there is a significant difference found between those who have given the answer always and never in favor of those who say always; between those who have given the answer frequently and never in favor of those who say frequently; and between those who have given the answer sometimes and never in favor of those who say sometimes; in the sub-dimensions justice, benevolence, self-worth, control, there is a significant difference found between those who have given the answer always and never in favor of those who say always. In the positive femininity sub-dimensions of EPAQ, there is a significant difference found between those who have given the answer always and never in favor of those who say always; regarding the GRAS total score, a significant difference is found in favor of those who say never among those who have given the answer never and always; in the dimensions of female gender role and marriage gender role, there is a significant difference found in favor of those who say never among those who have given the answer never, always and frequently; in the sub-dimensions traditional gender role and male gender role, there is a significant difference found in favor of those who say sometimes among those who have given the answer sometimes and always.

Table 10. One-way analysis of variance (Anova) results of scales and sub-dimensions according to the situation of whether being satisfied with the district /living area variable

The Situation of Whether Being Satisfied With the District /Living	F	p
World Assumptions Scale	9.051	0.000
Justice	8.782	0.000
Benevolence	2.720	0.029
Self-worth	7.581	0.000
Control	2.799	0.026
Positive femininity	2.985	0.019
Gender Roles Attitude Scale	3.322	0.011
Female gender role	3.515	0.008
Marriage gender role	3.374	0.010
Traditional gender role	3.018	0.018
Masculine gender role	2.409	0.049

3.10. In the WAS and justice sub-dimension, according to the situation of desiring to change the environment they are in, there is a significant difference found between those who have given the answer never and always in favor of those who say never; in the dimension of luck, between those who say never and frequently in favor of those who say never; in the dimension self-worth, between those who say sometimes and always in favor of those who say sometimes and between those who say rarely and always in favor of those who say rarely; in the traditional gender role sub-dimension of GRAS, there is a significant difference found between those who say never and sometimes in favor of those who say never.

Table 11. One-way analysis of variance (Anova) results of scales and sub-dimensions according to the situation of desiring to change the environment they are in variable

The situation of desiring to change the environment they are in	F	p
World Assumptions Scale	5.770	0.000
Justice	5.791	0.000
Luck	3.693	0.006
Self worth	6.366	0.000
Traditional gender role	2.401	0.049

3.11. In the WAS and its sub-dimensions justice, benevolence, self-worth, according to the situation of thinking a positive change will occur in their lives within 5 years, there is a significant difference found in favor those who say yes and in the negative masculine sub-dimension of EPAQ, in favor of those who say no; in the equalitarian gender role sub-dimension of GRAS, there is a significant difference found in favor those who say yes.

Table 12. T test results of scales and sub-dimensions according to the situation of thinking a positive change will occur in their lives within 5 years variable

The situation of thinking a positive change will occur in their lives within 5 years	t	p	$\bar{x}$ (Yes)	$\bar{x}$ (No)
World Assumptions Scale	3.901	0.000	113.44	103.00
Justice	2.023	0.044	20.01	17.92
Benevolence	3.432	0.001	31.46	27.72
Self-worth	3.399	0.001	16.94	14.72
Negative masculinity	-2.865	0.004	15.71	17.43
Equalitarian gender role	2.144	0.033	33.62	31.47

3.12. In the EPAQ sub-dimension positive femininity, in the GRAS and its sub-dimensions equalitarian gender role, marriage gender role and male gender role; according to the situation of thinking a positive change will occur in their lives within 5 years with the education received, there is a significant difference found in favor of those who say yes.

Table 13. T test results of scales and sub-dimensions according to the situation of thinking a positive change will occur in their lives within 5 years with the education received variable

The situation of thinking a positive change will occur in their lives within 5 years with the education received	t	p	$\bar{x}$ (Yes)	$\bar{x}$ (No)
Positive femininity	2,414	0,016	29,07	27,20
Gender Roles Attitude Scale	2,566	0,011	145,95	136,30
Equalitarian gender role	3,056	0,002	33,74	30,72
Marriage gender role	2,082	0,038	33,57	31,63
Masculine gender role	2,107	0,039	23,71	21,85

3.13. In the positive femininity, one of the EPAQ sub-dimensions, and female gender role and traditional gender role sub-dimensions of GRAS; according to the situation that additional training should be taken to change/improve life, there is a significant difference found in favor of those who say yes.

Table14. T test results of scales and sub-dimensions according to the situation that additional training should be taken to change/improve life variable

The situation that additional training should be taken to change/improve life	t	p	$\bar{x}$ (Yes)	$\bar{x}$ (No)
Positive femininity	2.207	0.028	29.15	27.83
Gender Roles Attitude Scale	2.195	0.029	146.30	139.84
Female gender role	2.750	0.006	27.64	25.50
Traditional gender role	2.016	0.044	27.88	26.22

3.14. As a result of correlation analyses, positive correlation (r = 0.116) was observed between WAS and EPAQ, moreover, it is observed that there are positive and negative relationships among the sub-dimensions of the features of the research topic.

Table 15. Correlation table between the scales

		World Assumptions Scale	Extended personal attributes	Gender Roles Attitude Scale
World Assumptions Scale	Pearson Correlation	1	.116*	-.057
	Sig. (2-tailed)		.020	.252
	N	407	407	407
Extended personal attributes	Pearson Correlation	.116*	1	-,015
	Sig. (2-tailed)	,020		.762
	N	407	407	407
Gender Roles Attitude Scale	Pearson Correlation	-.057	-.015	1
	Sig. (2-tailed)	.252	.762	
	N	407	407	407

4 Discussion

4.1. In the random sub-dimension of the world assumptions questionnaire (WAS), according to gender feature difference is found in favor of boys (Male $\bar{x}$=20.48; Female $\bar{x}$=18.94). Depending on the proposition of "justice, controllability and random" of the meaningfulness of world assumption of the relevant scale, it involves thoughts about how much people can get or deserve according to various criteria (according to the individual's schema). As a requirement of the just world, it emphasizes that everybody can get what they deserve as well as the link between behavior and outcomes [29]. Coincidence in this dimension explains that the events have a natural course and that making effort is meaningless, vain behavior. In this dimension, the difference in favor of boys suggests that boys believe that the effort to change their lives is meaningless. In the negative masculinity sub-dimension of the Extended Personal Attributes Questionnaire (EPAQ) (Male $\bar{x}$=16.62; Female $\bar{x}$=15.45) and in the positive masculinity (Male $\bar{x}$=29.75 ; Female $\bar{x}$=27.57) sub-dimension, there is a significant difference found in favor of boys; in the masculinity-femininity (Male $\bar{x}$=24.96); Female $\bar{x}$=27.42), positive femininity (Male $\bar{x}$=27.90; Female $\bar{x}$=29.47), negative femininity (verbal) (Male $\bar{x}$=10.17; Female $\bar{x}$=11.63) sub-dimensions, there is a significant difference found in favor of girls. The negative masculinity dimension corresponds to the negative role behaviors such as arrogance, selfishness, dictatorship, hostility whereas the positive masculinity dimension corresponds to the positive role behaviors such as ambition, independence, being active, competitiveness, easy decision making, self-confidence, pressure resistance. In terms of these characteristics, boys getting higher scores than girls show positive gender identity behaviors on the one hand and their inclination to the negative identity behaviors on the other hand. Considering that the average of random dimension is higher in boys' assumptions about the world, it is thought that their assumptions about life is negative and that their negative masculine behavior tendencies as gender identity behaviors are consistent with this knowledge. That the average of girls in masculinity femininity is higher than boys in the sub-dimensions of the EPAQ, is consistent with the finding obtained from the standardization study of the scale. This dimension includes both positive and negative features of the masculine and femininity traits; for example, dominant, liking to serve others, materialist, easily feeling panic in the moment of a crisis, aggressive; and the positive femininity qualities of girls corresponding to qualities such as emotional, being able to dedicate oneself to others, polite, helpful, understanding, sincere. In addition to the fact that the positive femininity point averages of girls are high, the difference among the average scores of negative female (verbal) characteristics (grouchy, constantly whining, grumbler, elaborative, choosy) is consistent with the literature as in boys [31]. In the studies on gender identity, as a human being, neither "female" nor "male" has pure positive or negative characteristics.

Gender Roles Attitude Scale (GRAS) total point averages (Male $\bar{x}$=132.82; Female $\bar{x}$=153,08) and there has been a difference in favor of females in the sub-dimension of "equalitarian gender role (Male $\bar{x}$=31.31; Female $\bar{x}$=34,77), female gender role (Male $\bar{x}$=24.95; Female $\bar{x}$=28.62), marriage gender role (Male $\bar{x}$=30.86; Female $\bar{x}$=35.05), traditional gender role (Male $\bar{x}$=23,92; Female $\bar{x}$=29,97), male gender role (Male $\bar{x}$=23.92; Female $\bar{x}$=29.97)". It is supported by the data regarding socio-cultural dynamics that girls participating in the research differ from the relevant sub-dimensions of the relevant boys in gender roles [32].

4.2. In the sub-dimension of "random" sub-dimension of the WAS, according to the grades, there is a difference found in the score averages of 9th grades ($\bar{x}$=19.89) from 10th grades ($\bar{x}$=18.39), 11th grades ($\bar{x}$=20.15). This finding suggests that students differ in the way they make sense of the world depending on the class level. In the GRAS sub-dimension "marriage gender role", there is a difference found in favor of 10th grade between the scores of 10th grade ($\bar{x}$=34.95) and 9th grade $\bar{x}$=32.60). It is observed that there is a difference in the way of 10th grade students' perception regarding male and female roles within the marriage institution defined by the society.

4.3. According to the mother's education level, there is a significant difference found in the WAS total scores in favor of high school graduates between those whose mothers are graduated from high school ($\bar{x}$=112.90) and whose mothers are illiterate ($\bar{x}$=98.11); there is a significant difference found in favor of university graduates between those whose mothers are graduated from university ($\bar{x}$=115.03) and those whose mothers are illiterate ($\bar{x}$=98.11). The difference in this dimension shows that the educational level of the mother can make a difference in their positive thoughts and beliefs in their assumptions about the world. In the "luck" sub-dimension of WAS, according to the education level of the mother, there is a significant difference found in favor of university graduates between those whose mothers are graduated from university ($\bar{x}$=16.98) and those whose mothers are graduated from secondary school ($\bar{x}$=14.20). The difference in this dimension can work according to the improbability principle in the context of random proposition of the assumption of meaningfulness of the world, however the individual has the belief that he can protect himself from bad luck. Therefore, according to the sub-proposal of the self-worth assumption of the mother's education level, it is possible to say that the belief that they can protect themselves from bad luck can make a difference and this result is consistent with the previous finding about the level of education of the mother. In the "female gender role" sub-dimension of GRAS, there is a significant difference found between those whose mothers are graduated from university ($\bar{x}$=28.49) and those whose mothers are graduated from elementary school ($\bar{x}$=25.25) in favor of university graduates. In the "traditional gender role" sub-dimension of GRAS, there is a significant difference found between those whose mothers are graduated from high school ($\bar{x}$=28.76) and those whose mothers are graduated from elementary school ($\bar{x}$=25.79) in favor of high school graduates. Both findings of the relevant scale show that the level of education of their mother can make a difference on student's perceptions of female gender role and traditional gender role [32].

4.4. According to mother's working status, in the total GRAS scores, there is a significant difference found between those whose mothers work full-time ($\bar{x}$=150.21) and those whose mothers are housewife ($\bar{x}$=142.19) in favor of those working full-time. According to mother's working status, the female gender role sub-dimension of GRAS, there is a significant difference between those whose mothers work full-time ($\bar{x}$=29.56) and those whose mothers are housewife ($\bar{x}$=26.03) in favor of those whose mothers work full time and there is a significant difference between those whose mothers are retired ($\bar{x}$=31.20) and those whose mothers are housewife ($\bar{x}$=26.03) in favor of those whose mothers are retired. It shows that the mother is working or has worked can change the perception regarding the communal gender roles. This finding is in line with findings on the level of maternal education and is supported by the literature on studies related to gender equality [34,35,36].

4.5. According to the father's working level, in the justice sub-dimension of WAS, there is a significant difference found between those who have retired fathers ($\bar{x}$=22.40), those who have fathers working full-time ($\bar{x}$=19.56) and those who have fathers working half-time, ($\bar{x}$=17.18). The difference in justice dimension is based on the belief that the world has a fair order that provides results that are appropriate for everyone's behavior regarding the assumptions about the world. The difference of the scores of those whose fathers have retired shows that these students have significant thoughts about world being a fair place, in other words everyone can get results in the direction of their effort [37]. Considering that retirement period is a dynamic related to the performance that the individual has shown in his or her working life, it is thought that finding gives information about the difference of the assumptions on world of the students whose fathers are still working, the effect of socioeconomic dynamics on young people. In the negative masculine sub-dimension of EPAQ, there is a significant difference found between those whose fathers work half-time ($\bar{x}$=30.18) and those whose fathers work full-time ($\bar{x}$=28.29). It is seen that negative male role behaviors such as selfishness, hostility and dictatorship are role models in the definition of male gender role in those whose fathers work half-time. It is thought that this situation is related to the psychological dynamics that father working half-time can create on the relationship with himself and his immediate environment as "an individual". This finding is in favor with those whose fathers are retired and consistent with the finding related to the justice sub-dimension of the WAS. The difference that is created by the working status of the father both in the WAS and EPAQ sub-dimensions can be supported by the findings of interdisciplinary studies [38,39].

4.6. According to whether a crisis had been faced related to the income of the family (dismissal of a family member, loss of income) in the last five years, there is a significant difference in WAS total scores and justice, luck and self-worth sub-dimensions of WAS in favor of those who did not experience a crisis [40]. This finding shows those who did not face an economic crisis have positive beliefs concerning "benevolence of the world, meaningfulness of the world". There is a significant difference between the negative masculine sub-dimension of EPAQ, the female gender role and traditional gender role sub-dimensions of GRAS and GRAS in favor of those who did not experience a crisis. This finding shows facing a crisis is one of the factors that affect negative masculine behavior. Similarly, it can be said that the effects of experiencing a crisis on female gender role and traditional gender role differ. Accordingly, experiencing an economic crisis can change the student's perception of the world that it will be safe and invulnerable, as well as in the gender identity perception and role specifications.

4.7. According to an increase in the income of the family in the last five years, there is a significant difference found in WAS (Y$\bar{x}$=114.37; N$\bar{x}$=110.00) and in the justice sub-dimension of WAS (Y$\bar{x}$=20.53; N$\bar{x}$=19.02) in favor of those who have an increase (who responded yes). This difference shows, it can be effective in developing positive thoughts in respect of the world being safe and them not being vulnerable. There is a significant difference found in negative femininity (relational) sub-dimension of EPAQ (Y$\bar{x}$=9.24; N$\bar{x}$=9.86), female gender role sub-dimension of GRAS (Y$\bar{x}$=26.26; N$\bar{x}$=27.85) and the traditional gender role sub-dimension (Y$\bar{x}$=26.65; N$\bar{x}$=28.19) in favor of those who did not have an increase (who responded no). The result acquired with the aspect of WAS and justice sub-dimension in favor of those who have an increase in income within the last five years, and the results related to whether having a crisis in the family income or not in within the last five years support each other. The differentiation of the condition of not having an increase in income with regards to negative femininity (relational) sub-dimension of EPAQ, female gender role sub-dimension of GRAS and the traditional gender role emphasizes the importance of social roles and expectations attributed to women concerning economic changes. In addition, interdisciplinary studies on the subject, research on gender equality and domestic violence support this result as well.

4.8. According to living with one's family without having financial difficulties, there is a significant difference found between those who have given the answer always and sometimes in favor of those who say always in WAS and its sub-dimensions justice, luck, control and self-worth.

(WAS $\bar{x}$=116.92 / $\bar{x}$=102.26; Justice $\bar{x}$=20.94 / $\bar{x}$=17.02; Luck $\bar{x}$=16.89 / $\bar{x}$=13.94; Control $\bar{x}$=11.81 / $\bar{x}$=10.09; Self-worth $\bar{x}$=17.63/ $\bar{x}$=14.37/ Never $\bar{x}$=13.53). In addition. there is a significant difference found between those who have given the answer frequently ($\bar{x}$=16.82). sometimes ($\bar{x}$=14.37) and never ($\bar{x}$=13,53) in favor of those who say frequently in self-worth sub-dimension. According to living with one's family without having financial difficulties, the difference in WAS and its sub-dimensions justice, luck, control and self-worth in favor of those who say always, shows that the perception regarding not having any financial difficulties can make a difference in the world assumptions.

According to living with one's family without having financial difficulties, there is a significant difference found between those who have given the answer always ($\bar{x}$=29.12) and never ($\bar{x}$=24.79) in favor of those who say always, and between those who have given the answer frequently ($\bar{x}$=28.86) and never ($\bar{x}$=24.79) in favor of those who say never in positive masculine sub-dimension of EPAQ. The finding draws attention to the perception regarding the function of the male gender related to family welfare, considering the positive masculine sub-dimension of EPAQ in favor of those who say always; and frequently in the positive masculine sub-dimension. Positive masculine features contain ambition, independence, being active, competitiveness, easy decision making, not giving up, self-confidence, pressure resistance and superior self-perception. Therefore, it is possible to say that, in terms of sustaining the prosperity of the family, the students care about the mentioned features.

According to living with one's family without having financial difficulties, there is a significant difference found between those who have given the answer sometimes ($\bar{x}$=10.43) and always ($\bar{x}$=9.14) in favor of those who say sometimes in negative femininity sub-dimension of EPAQ. It is thought that the result obtained in favor of those who say sometimes in the EPAQ negative femininity (relational) sub-dimension can be evaluated with the features of respective sub-dimension and having these features in terms of the society. According to the respective sub-dimension, the woman is an unscrupulous, flaccid, self-deprecating, self-derogatory, gullible, easily-tricked individual. Since an individual with these features is not expected to be able to use family's resources effectively, this person will also be considered responsible. While afore said result draws attention to the perception of "women" roles and duties when the family's financial prosperity can be sustained, it is necessary to consider that the young ones grow with the values of the society they are in. Moreover, studies related to family and women as well as socio-psychological research support the result [41, 42].

4.9. There is a significant difference found between those who have given the answer always ($\bar{x}$=116.93) and never ($\bar{x}$=99.60) in favor of those who say always; between those who have given the answer frequently ($\bar{x}$=112.41) and never ($\bar{x}$=99.60) in favor of those who say frequently, and between those who have given the answer sometimes ($\bar{x}$=111.00) and never ($\bar{x}$=99.60) in favor of those who say sometimes among WAS total scores according to the satisfaction condition of neighborhood / living environment.

There is a significant difference found between those who have given the answer always ($\bar{x}$=21.53) and never ($\bar{x}$=15.14) in favor of those who say always; between those who have given the answer frequently ($\bar{x}$=19.86) and never ($\bar{x}$=15.14) in favor of those who say frequently and between sometimes ($\bar{x}$=19.83) and never ($\bar{x}$=15.14) in favor of those who say sometimes among justice scores, sub-dimension of WAS according to the satisfaction condition of neighborhood / living environment.

There is a significant difference found between those who have given the answer always ($\bar{x}$=32.20) and never ($\bar{x}$=28.42) in favor of those who say always in benevolence of people scores, sub-dimension of WAS according to the satisfaction condition of neighborhood / living environment.

There is a significant difference found between those who have given the answer always ($\bar{x}$=17.58) and never ($\bar{x}$=13.80) in favor of those who say always and between those who have given the answer frequently ($\bar{x}$=17.08) and never ($\bar{x}$=13.80) in favor of those who say frequently among self-worth scores, sub-dimension of WAS according to the satisfaction condition of neighborhood / living environment.

There is a significant difference found between those who have given the answer always ($\bar{x}$=11.77) and never ($\bar{x}$=10.44) in favor of those who say always in control scores, a sub-dimension of WAS according to the satisfaction condition of neighborhood / living environment.

The variation comprising in favor of the students stating, they are always pleased according to the satisfaction characteristics of neighborhood / living environment shows that being satisfied with the social-cultural-economic environment that is being lived in can make difference in the meaningfulness of the world, benevolence of the world and the self-worth among WAS scale total scores in terms of the satisfaction condition of neighborhood / living environment and sub-dimensions of justice, benevolence of people, self-worth and control. In this context, the features of the socio-economic-cultural environment that is being lived in support the faith in the benevolence of people, charity and being courteous while the assumption of justice supports the belief that everyone will acquire the consequences of their behavior in a just world order, In addition, concerning the self-worth, the result related to the students who state that they are always satisfied with the environment they live in, shows that they see themselves as moral, well-behaved and valuable, and that their self-perceptions are positive. A similar result for the control sub-dimension indicates that students' beliefs about behaviors that can control the outcomes with appropriate acts can be affected by the level of satisfaction with the environment in which they live.

There is a significant difference between those who have given the answer always ($\bar{x}$=29.52) and never ($\bar{x}$=27.24) in favor of those who say always among positive femininity scores, sub-dimension of EPAQ according to the satisfaction condition of neighborhood

/living environment. The results acquired show that the environment can create evaluation regarding the socio-economic conditions and variation of perception concerning the role of women.

There is a significant difference found between those who have given the answer never ($\bar{x}$=154.14) and always ($\bar{x}$=140.99) in favor of those who say never among GRAS total scores according to the satisfaction condition of neighborhood / living environment.

There is a significant difference between those who have given the answer never ($\bar{x}$=30.22), always ($\bar{x}$=26.34) and frequently ($\bar{x}$=26.33) in favor of those who say never among female gender role scores, sub-dimension of GRAS according to the satisfaction condition of neighborhood / living environment.

There is a significant difference between those who have given the answer never ($\bar{x}$=35.58), always ($\bar{x}$=32.50) frequently ($\bar{x}$=32.56) in favor of those who say never among marriage gender role scores, sub-dimension of GRAS according to the satisfaction condition of neighborhood / living environment.

There is a significant difference between those who have given the answer sometimes ($\bar{x}$=29.26) and always ($\bar{x}$=26.41) in favor of those who say sometimes among traditional gender role scores, sub-dimension of GRAS according to the satisfaction condition of neighborhood / living environment.

There is a significant difference between those who have given the answer sometimes ($\bar{x}$=24.20) and always ($\bar{x}$=22.65) in favor sometimes and never ($\bar{x}$=24.98) and always ($\bar{x}$=22.65) in favor of those who say never among male gender role scores, sub-dimension of GRAS according to the satisfaction condition of neighborhood / living environment.

GRAS scale and its sub-dimensions of female gender role, marriage gender role, traditional gender role and masculine gender role and their results, variation emerging in terms of low level of satisfaction or no satisfaction condition regarding the living environment shows that the students evaluate the characteristics of the socio-economic cultural environment which they live in from the point of functions related to role and roles.

4.10. There is a significant difference between those who have given the answer never ($\bar{x}$=117.79) and always ($\bar{x}$=107.11) in favor of those who say never among WAS total scores according to the situation of desiring to change the environment they are in.

There is a significant difference between those who have given the answer never ($\bar{x}$=21.89) and always ($\bar{x}$=17.69) in favor of those who say never among justice scores, sub-dimension of WAS according to the situation of desiring to change the environment they are in.

There is a significant difference between those who have given the answer never ($\bar{x}$=17.04) and frequently ($\bar{x}$=14.51) in favor never, and between those who have given the answer rarely ($\bar{x}$=17.40) and frequently (14.51) in favor of those who say rarely among luck scores, sub-dimension of WAS according to the situation of desiring to change the environment they are in.

There is a significant difference between those who have given the answer sometimes ($\bar{x}$=17.81) and always ($\bar{x}$=15.32) in favor of those who say sometimes, and between those who have given the answer rarely ($\bar{x}$=18.12) and always ($\bar{x}$=15.32) in favor of those who say rarely among self-worth scores, sub-dimension of WAS in terms of the condition demanding to change the living environment if possible. Among the total WAS scores according to the situation of desiring to change the environment they are in. According to the situation of desiring to change the environment they are in, WAS total scores, and its sub-dimensions of justice and luck, the result that is obtained supports the variation in favor of the students who stated that they never want to change the environment they live in. Students who think that they do not want to change the environment they live in have positive perceptions about the world being safe and will not allow them to get in a vulnerable situation. The justice dimension states the assumption of the students living in a fair world in relation to the distribution of the consequences of their behaviors and the luck dimension states the assumption of them having the luck to protect themselves from evil. Accordingly, it can be said that the students who do not consider changing the environment they live in, have the assumption that appropriate behaviors can ensure this circumstance and that they are the ones who can be protected from evil generated by the coincidences. The result of self-worth sub-dimension of the WAS with regards to those who consider changing the environment they live in and those who rarely think, between those who have given the answer rarely and always, the difference according to those who have given the answer rarely, the individuals who think to change the environment they live in have low self-perception and self-esteem.

There is a significant difference found between those who have given the answer never ($\bar{x}$=25.33) and sometimes ($\bar{x}$=28.73) in favor of those who say never among traditional gender role scores, sub-dimension of GRAS. The result obtained from the GRAS perspective suggests that the traditional gender role behaviors of those who have given the answer never differ in the sense of traditional gender role. Therefore, it is possible to say that the traditional gender role definitions of those who do not want to change the environment they live in differ from the egalitarian gender role definitions of the other group.

4.11. According to thinking whether or not a positive change will occur in their lives over the next five years, there is significant difference in the total WAS scores (Y$\bar{x}$=113.44 / N$\bar{x}$=103.00), sub-dimensions of WAS justice score (Y$\bar{x}$=20.01 / N$\bar{x}$=17.92), benevolence of the world score (Y$\bar{x}$=31.46/ N$\bar{x}$=27.72), self-worth score (Y$\bar{x}$=16,94 / N$\bar{x}$=14,72), in the equalitarian gender role sub-dimension of GRAS (Y$\bar{x}$=33.62 / N$\bar{x}$=31.47), in favor of those who think there will be a positive change, and in the negative masculine sub-dimension of EPAQ (Y$\bar{x}$=15.71 / N$\bar{x}$=17.43) there is significant difference found in favor of those who do not think that there will be a positive change. The difference in favor of the students who think there will be a positive change in their lives; in WAS total score and its sub-dimensions justice, benevolence, self-worth; reveal that there are positive thoughts about the benevolence of the world, the significance of the world, and the assumptions of self-worth. In other words, the world is a safe place with features that can meet the expectations of the students and will not allow them to get in a vulnerable situation. At the same time, the world has a just order where it gives everyone his or her right, everyone gets what they deserve; therefore, they will be rewarded for their effort within the five-years. It is because the finding of self-worth assumptions shows that they perceive themselves as good, ethical, and valuable, and that their self-esteem is high. The world is a safe place which has an order that gives value to good, ethical and valuable people. The finding obtained in the equality gender sub-dimension of GRAS in favor of the students who think that there will be a positive change in their lives, in the negative masculine sub-dimension of the EPAQ in favor of the students who think that there will be no change in their lives are consistent with the WAS and its sub-dimensions. GRAS equality gender sub-dimension bases the role descriptions of both sexual identities related to each other on equality, cooperation, respect and similar principles through democratic life values, independent of socio-cultural expectations [43]. Therefore, we can say that the individuals who think that there will be a positive change in their life within the next five years believe that they will realize this idea based on the definition of the equalitarian gender role. The significant difference in the negative masculine sub-dimension of EPAQ, in favor of the students who believe that there will be no change in the future makes us think that the negative role behaviors such as arrogance, selfishness, hostility, suspicion, dictatorship are related to the feeling of despair about the future [44]. When considered in terms of difference in WAS and its sub-dimensions in favor of the students who think that their future can change positively, it is thought that negative thinking about the future may also be associated with the negative

WAS. The finding suggests that the personal attributes regarding gender identity behaviors of the students, who do not believe that there will be a positive change in their future, are not positive. Moreover, this result can be supported by the findings of psycho-social researches on anger, violence and aggression as well as researches on hope and hopelessness in the context of positive psychology and cognitive psychology [45,46,47,48].

4.12. According to the situation of thinking a positive change will occur in their lives within 5 years with the education received in the positive femininity sub-dimension of EPAQ (Y$\bar{x}$=29.07 / N$\bar{x}$=27.20), GRAS total scores (Y$\bar{x}$=145.95 / N$\bar{x}$=136.30), the equalitarian gender role sub-dimension of GRAS (Y$\bar{x}$=33.74 / N$\bar{x}$=30,72), marriage gender role (Y$\bar{x}$=33.57 / N$\bar{x}$=31.63), male gender role (Y$\bar{x}$=23.71 /N$\bar{x}$=21.85); there is significant difference found in favor of those who think there will be difference in their lives with the education. We can say that the difference in the femininity dimension of EPAQ and its sub-dimensions equalitarian gender role, marriage gender role and male gender role in favor of the individuals who think that there will be a positive change in the way of life through education, shows that the students give importance to their positive role behaviors as individuals who are open to development as women and men [49,50].

4.13. According to the situation that additional trainings must be taken to change/improve life in the positive femininity sub-dimension of EPAQ (Y$\bar{x}$=29.15 / N$\bar{x}$=27.83), total GRAS scores (Y$\bar{x}$=146.30 / N$\bar{x}$=139.84), female gender role (Y$\bar{x}$=27.64 /N$\bar{x}$=25.50), traditional gender role (Y$\bar{x}$=27.88 /N$\bar{x}$=26.22) sub-dimensions of GRAS, there is significant difference in favor of those who think trainings must be received. Regarding the EPAQ and GRAS, the significant difference about students who think they need to receive additional trainings makes us think that they give importance to empowerment of women. Moreover, the difference in positive femininity sub-dimension of EPAQ and the difference in the traditional gender role of GRAS of those who think it is necessary to receive training make us think that it is necessary for students to perceive change as a form of behavior required by positive femininity.

4.14. As a result of the correlation analyses, a positive correlation (r=0.116) is observed between the assumptions related to world and personal attributes. Furthermore, the sub-dimensions of the characteristics that constitute the research theme are also related to each other in positive and negative aspects. According to the correlation analysis, in line with the correlation analysis between WAS and EPAQ, as the WAS score increases, difference in the EPAQ scores can be observed.

5 Conclusion and recommendations

According to the World Health Organization, the quality of life is the perception of the people's own life in a sociological system by their goals, expectations, standards and interests. The relevant literature however defines the quality of life based on the objective criteria related to the right to live, such as education, health, income, profession, physical environment etc. Both perspectives include people's experiences of life and information on how they may be affected by them. In this context, the study aimed to examine world assumptions, personal implications and social gender role behaviors in relation to perceptions of adolescents' own quality of life, taking objective criteria into account.

In the study, adolescents' perceptions of their quality of life were evaluated with the questions related to the "past, the period in which the research was conducted and the future". The education level and working status were also considered.

The results of the study show difference in terms of world assumptions, personal attributes and social role behaviors between the male and female students. It is observed that the mother's education level, and the working status of the father and mother cause a difference in world assumptions, personal attributes and social role behaviors of the students.

Education and working status of parents provide information about the standards regarding the quality and quantity of the environment in which the child lives. Thus, the acquired information is thought to be important in terms of the studies towards adolescents.
Students' perceptions of the economic and social situations that may affect their lives were obtained with answers to the questions related to the last five years (including the process in which the research was conducted) and within the next five-year period. With these questions students' world assumptions, interpersonal implications and social gender roles in the context of past, present and the future were examined. With the questions in this context, difference was found between those who experienced a positive event (increase in life standard/income) and who experienced a negative event (economic crisis, dismissal of a family member); between those who think they live suitable to their expectancy of life with their family and who think the opposite; between those who do not think to change the current environment and are happy with their physical and social environment and who are not; and between those who think there might be a positive change in their lives within the next five years and who not; with respect to world assumptions, personal relations and social gender roles. The world assumptions of the students who answer to relevant questions positively (who has not experienced a crisis, are happy with their social environment, believe in positive changes in the future) are found positive with regards to the world assumptions, meaningfulness of the world, benevolence of world and self-worth. It is found that the students' relative results were distributed among dimensions of "Total scores of world assumptions and justice, control, self-worth, luck and benevolence of people"; and the results of the students who answered negatively were distributed more in the random dimension. The results of the positive responding students regarding their interpersonal attributes are related to their differences in positive masculine and positive femininity dimensions. Among the results of students who responded negatively, the difference in negative masculine, negative femininity (verbal) and negative femininity (relational) dimensions is remarkable. While the results of the traditional gender role highlight the female role expectations in the society; the students responding positively with regards to social gender roles, show difference in female gender role, male gender role and egalitarian gender role dimensions. Moreover, according to the correlation analysis carried out in the study, a low but positive correlation was found between the world assumptions scale scores and personal attributes.
As a conclusion, it has been found that the adolescents' perception of their quality of life in the context of "past, present and future" may differentiate their thoughts on world, life, themselves, and in this regard the definitions of gender identity and role behaviors in social relationship. In this sense, it is possible to say that the socio-economic experiences which adolescents experience with their families do not only remain for that period, but also create a change in definitions towards the future world and therefore their interpersonal attributes and the perceptions of gender roles may change. In addition; considering that the research features are related to many factors; it is important to repeat the related studies in a multi-dimensional way regarding the "adolescents".

References

1. Damian, R. I., & Robins, R. W. (2012). Investigations into the human self: A naturalist perspective. *Social Cognition*, ***30***(4), 431-448.
2. Axelrod, R. (1973). Schema theory: An information processing model of perception and cognition. *American Political Science Review*, ***67***(4), 1248-1266.
3. Thompson, S. C., & Janigian, A. S. (1988). Life schemes: A framework for understanding the search for meaning. *Journal of Social and Clinical Psychology*, *7*(2-3), 260-280.

4. Bratman, G. N., Hamilton, J. P., & Daily, G. C. (2012). The impacts of nature experience on human cognitive function and mental health. *Annals of the New York Academy of Sciences*, ***1249***(1), 118-136.
5. Janoff-Bulman, R. (1989). The benefits of illusions, the threat of disillusionment, and the limitations of inaccuracy. *Journal of Social and Clinical Psychology*, ***8***(2), 158-175.
6. Mikulincer, M., Shaver, P. R., & Pereg, D. (2003). Attachment theory and affect regulation: The dynamics, development, and cognitive consequences of attachment-related strategies. *Motivation and Emotion*, ***27***(2), 77-102.
7. Jeavons, S., & Greenwood, K. M. (2007). World assumptions, coping and attributions. *Personality and Individual Differences*, ***42***(7), 1427-1437.
8. Janoff-Bulman, R., & Schwartzberg, S. S. (1991). Toward a general model of personal change. *Handbook of social and clinical psychology: The health Perspective*, 488-508.
9. Janoff-Bulman, R. (2010). *Shattered assumptions*. USA: The Free Press.
10. Lilly, M. M., Valdez, C. E., & Graham-Bermann, S. A. (2011). The mediating effect of world assumptions on the relationship between trauma exposure and depression. *Journal of Interpersonal Violence*, ***26***(12), 2499-2516.
11. Maschi, T., Macmillan, T., Morgen, K., Gibson, S., & Stimmel, M. (2010). Trauma, world assumptions, and coping resources among youthful offenders: Social work, mental health, and criminal justice implications. *Child and Adolescent Social Work Journal*, ***27***(6), 377-393.
12. Dekel, R., Solomon, Z., Elklit, A., & Ginzburg, K. (2004). World assumptions and combat-related posttraumatic stress disorder. *The Journal of Social Psychology*, ***144***(4), 407-420.
13. Steinberg, L., & Morris, A. S. (2001). Adolescent development. *Annual Review of Psychology*, ***52***(1), 83-110.
14. Susman, E. And Alan Rogal . (2004). *Puberty and Psychological Development. Richard M. Lerner and Laurence Steinberg* (ed.)((15-45). Handbook of Adolescent Psychologhy (second Edition) New Jersey: John Wiley&Sons, Inc.
15. Marcia, J. E. (1966). Development and validation of ego-identity status. *Journal of Personality andSsocial Psychology*, ***3***(5), 551.
16. Rose, A. J., & Rudolph, K. D. (2006). A review of sex differences in peer relationship processes: potential trade-offs for the emotional and behavioral development of girls and boys. *Psychological Bulletin*, ***132***(1), 98.
17. Bem, S. L. (1981). Gender schema theory: A cognitive account of sex typing. *Psychological Review*, ***88***(4), 354.
18. Arnett, J. J. (2007). Suffering, selfish, slackers? Myths and reality about emerging adults. *Journal of Youth and Adolescence*, ***36***(1), 23-29.
19. Lilly, M. M., Howell, K. H., & Graham-Bermann, S. (2015). World assumptions, religiosity, and PTSD in survivors of intimate partner violence. *Violence Against Women*, ***21***(1), 87-104.
20. Elklit, A., Shevlin, M., Solomon, Z., & Dekel, R. (2007). Factor structure and concurrent validity of the world assumptions scale. *Journal of Traumatic Stress: Official Publication of The International Society for Traumatic Stress Studies*, ***20***(3), 291-301.
21. Butler, T., Giordano, S., & Neren, S. (1985). Gender and sex-role attributes as predictors of utilization of natural support systems during personal stress events. *Sex Roles*, ***13***(9-10), 515-524.

22. WHOQOL GROUP. (1995). The World Health Organization quality of life assessment (WHOQOL): position paper from the World Health Organization. *Social science & medicine*, ***41***(10), 1403-1409.
23. Hofstede, G. (1984). The cultural relativity of the quality of life concept. *Academy of Management Review*, ***9***(3), 389-398.
24. Wallander, J. L., Schmitt, M., & Koot, H. M. (2001). Quality of life measurement in children and adolescents: issues, instruments, and applications. *Journal of Clinical Psychology*, ***57***(4), 571-585.
25. Topolski, T. D., Patrick, D. L., Edwards, T. C., Huebner, C. E., Connell, F. A., & Mount, K. K. (2001). Quality of life and health-risk behaviors among adolescents. *Journal of Adolescent Health*, ***29***(6), 426-435.
26. Yilmaz, B. (2008). Dunyaya Iliskin varsayimlar Olcegi gecerlik ve guvenirlik calismasi: On calisma [Reliability and validity study of World Assumptions Scale: Pilot study]. *Turk Psikoloji Yazilari*, ***11***(21), 41-51.
27. Demirtaş-Madran, H. A. (2016). Genişletilmiş Kişisel Yüklemeler Ölçeğinin Türkçe formunun geçerlilik ve güvenilirlik çalışması. *Anatolian Journal of Psychiatry/Anadolu Psikiyatri Dergisi*, ***17***.
28. Zeyneloğlu, S., & Terzioğlu, F. (2011). Toplumsal cinsiyet rolleri tutum ölçeğinin geliştirilmesi ve psikometrik özellikleri. *Hacettepe Üniversitesi Eğitim Fakültesi Dergisi*, ***40***, 409-420.
29. Gebauer, M. (2017). *The role of world assumptions in the development of PTSD: Cultural differences between western and non-western respondents* (Bachelor's thesis, University of Twente).
30. Helmreich, R. L., Spence, J. T., & Wilhelm, J. A. (1981). A psychometric analysis of the Personal Attributes Questionnaire. *Sex Roles*, *7*(11), 1097-1108.
31. Demirtaş-Madran, H. A. (2016). Genişletilmiş Kişisel Yüklemeler Ölçeğinin Türkçe formunun geçerlilik ve güvenilirlik çalışması. *Anatolian Journal of Psychiatry/Anadolu Psikiyatri Dergisi*, ***17***(Supplement 1), 60-68.
32. Esen, E., Siyez, D., Soylu, Y., & Demirgürz, G. (2017). Üniversite öğrencilerinde toplumsal cinsiyet algısının toplumsal cinsiyet rolü ve cinsiyet değişkenlerine göre incelenmesi//Examination of gender perception of university students according to sex and sex roles. *e-International Journal of Educational Research*, ***8***(1).
33. Collins, W. A. and Brett Laurse. (2004). Parent-adolescent relationships and ınfluences. Richard M. Lerner and Laurence Steinberg (ed.) (331-361). *Handbook of Adolescent Psychologhy* (second Edition) New Jersey: John Wiley&Sons, Inc
34. Yüksel, Ö. (2013). *Kadınlarda evlilik uyumu ve psikolojik belirtiler arasındaki ilişki: Stresle baş etme biçimleri ve toplumsal cinsiyet rolü tutumlarının aracı rolleri.* (Yayımlanmamış doktora tezi/yüksek lisans tezi). Hacettepe Üniversitesi. Ankara.
35. Kurt, Ş. (2006). İşsizliğin psiko-sosyal sonuçları ve Türkiye üzerine muhtemel etkileri. *Sosyal Siyaset Konferansları Dergisi*, (51), 357-379.
36. Çelik, A. S., Pasinlioğlu, T., Gonca, T. A. N., & Koyuncu, H. (2013). Üniversite öğrencilerinin cinsiyet eşitliği tutumlarinin belirlenmesi. *Florence Nightingale Hemşirelik Dergisi*, ***21***(3), 181-186.
37. Yilmaz, B. (2008). Dünyaya iliskin varsayımlar ölçeği geçerlik ve güvenirlik çalışması: Ön çalışma: [Reliability and validity study of World Assumptions Scale: Pilot study]. *Türk Psikoloji Yazıları*, ***11***(21), 41-51.
38. Sümer, N., Solak, N., & Harma, M. (2013). *İşsiz yaşam: İşsizliğin ve iş güvencesizliğinin birey ve aile üzerindeki etkileri.* Koç Üniversitesi Yayınları.
39. Özmen, S. K. (2004). Aile içinde öfke ve saldırganlığın yansımaları. *Ankara Üniversitesi Eğitim Bilimleri Fakültesi Dergisi*, ***37***(2), 27-39.

40. Kurt, Ş. (2006). İşsizliğin psiko-sosyal sonuçları ve Türkiye üzerine muhtemel etkileri. *Sosyal Siyaset Konferansları Dergisi*, (51), 357-379.
41. Can, Y. (2014). Türk ailesinde aile içi şiddetin kültürel dinamikleri. *Electronic Turkish Studies*, *9*(8). 13-19.
42. Karakaya, Handan. Algısı, Toplumsal cinsiyet algısı, din ve kadın. *Journal of Analytic Divinity*, **(*2*)**2, 36-62.
43. Gebauer, M. (2017). *The role of world assumptions in the development of PTSD: Cultural differences between western and non-western respondents* (Bachelor's thesis, University of Twente).
44. Eisler, R. M., Skidmore, J. R., & Ward, C. H. (1988). Masculine gender-role stress: Predictor of anger, anxiety, and health-risk behaviors. *Journal of Personality Assessment*, ***52***(1), 133-141.
45. Eryılmaz, A. (2011). Ergen öznel iyi oluşu ile olumlu gelecek beklentisi arasındaki ilişkinin incelenmesi. *Dusunen Adam: Journal of Psychiatry & Neurological Sciences*, ***24***(3). 209-215.
46. Tümkaya, S., Aybek, B., & Çelik, M. (2010). Yoksul ailelerden gelen ergenlerde psiko-sosyal bir olgu olarak umutsuzluk ve boyun eğici davranışların incelenmesi. *Uluslararası İnsan Bilimleri Dergisi*, *7*(1), 970-984.
47. Uluçay, T., Özpolat, A. R., İşgör, İ. Y., & Taşkesen, O. (2014). Lise öğrencilerinin gelecek beklentileri üzerine bir araştırma. *Education Sciences*, ***9***(2), 234-247.
48. Brems, C., & Johnson, M. E. (1989). Problem-solving appraisal and coping style: The influence of sex-role orientation and gender. *The Journal of Psychology*, ***123***(2), 187-194.
49. Özaydınlık, K. (2014). Toplumsal cinsiyet temelinde Türkiye'de kadın ve eğitim. *Sosyal Politika Çalışmaları Dergisi*, (33). 93-112.
50. Prentice, D. A., & Carranza, E. (2002). What women and men should be, shouldn't be, are allowed to be, and don't have to be: The contents of prescriptive gender stereotypes. *Psychology of women quarterly*, ***26***(4), 269-281.

Investigation of emotions management skills, perceived social competence, friendship quality, social exclusion and need to belong in adolescents

Meral Sert Agır[1,*]

[1]Marmara University, Atatürk Faculty of Education, Department of Educational Sciences, Psychological Counseling and Guidance Department, Göztepe, Istanbul, Turkey

Abstract. The research was conducted to investigate the dynamics between emotional management skills, perceived social competence, friendship quality, social exclusion, and need to belong in adolescents. Previous studies emphasize the importance of competencies in adolescents related to emotional management skills in social and academic life as well as in the family. In this context, emotional management skills gain an importance as a feature that can help adolescents become a member of a group and meet the need to belong by positively changing the perception of the social competence of the individual, increasing social harmony, and developing meaningful and supportive friendships. Research data was obtained by applying "Emotions Management Skills Scale", "Perceived Social Competence Scale", "Friendship Quality Scale", "Social Exclusion Scale", "Need to Belong Scale" and "Personal Information Form" on 431 students (195 male, 236 female) in 9th, 10th, and 11th Grades in Kadıköy district, Istanbul province. Significant differences were found in friendship quality, perceived social competence, and emotions management with respect to gender. In addition, differences were found in investigated characteristics with respect to age, grade, academic achievement, family dynamics and, a negative relationship was found between social exclusion and emotions management skills, perceived social competence, and friendship quality.

Keywords: Adolescence Period; Emotions Management Skills; Perceived Social Competence; Social Exclusion; Friendship Quality; Need to Belong

1 Introduction

Each period of human development involves many different competences, struggles and opportunities [1]. Among these, adolescence is a critical period in which the neurobiological processes underlying higher cognitive functions and social and emotional behavior matures and change and development take place as individuals overcome many

* Corresponding author: meralagir@marmara.edu.tr – meralagir@yahoo.com

difficulties in all areas of development [2,3]. Adolescence is the transition period to adulthood, where the individual forms his or her identity through relationships. Definitions of what kind of a person an individual will become are shaped during adolescence [4]. The relationship of adolescents with their family and peers differentiate and prepare them for adulthood as individuals [4]. In this period, the interaction of the individual with his or her family, peers and school environment refer not only to the period of adolescence but also to a process of maturation affecting the whole life [5]. Maturing on the path to become an individual requires independence from childhood to adulthood and being able to assume the responsibilities of being an adult [6]. The adolescence period characterizes the difficulties of the transformation process from the parent-dependent identity structure of childhood to autonomous individuals, and the competences needed to overcome these difficulties and become a healthy adult [7,8]. One of the most important emphases of the period is the dynamics of emotional-social development in the context of personality development. The literature on adolescents characterizes this period with rapidly changing emotional states over a short time period [9]. For adolescents, the changing emotional states can be regarded as a sign of development and change to gain emotional competences required throughout life, including the neurophysiological, mental, social, and complex processes of emotion [10,11]. In other words, physical changes accompanying emotions give clues about being an "adult" depending on thought and behavior styles, maturation of inherent cognitive and emotional competences, and the process of socialization [12]. Thus, in adolescence, the change and development of emotional behaviors and gaining emotional competence is influential on not only emotions but also development of competences in all developmental areas. Although studies on academic preparations since childhood overshadow emotional and social development, the research shows that emotional-social competences are correlated with school achievement and family-peer interaction quality. Findings indicate that children with emotional and social competences have better school achievement and adaptation and less risk than children having significant emotional and social difficulties [13,14,15,16]. The American School Counselors Association also emphasizes the need for a holistic approach of the social-emotional development, academic success and career preparation studies of young people in the information age we live in [17]. In addition, when the content of career preparation/readiness efforts, which have gained more importance in recent years –critical thinking/problem solving, verbal and written communication, leadership, teamwork and collaboration, professional ethics competencies, global-intercultural communication– is taken into account, it is seen that emotion management in terms of social and emotional competences and communication and interaction with other people are effective also in life after adolescence [18,19,20,21]. Thus, the ability of adolescents to be aware of, express, control their emotions and adapt to their own and others' emotions will support the emotional maturation process as an individual and the maturation process in other developmental areas [22]. In this context, emotions management skills can provide a positive change in the perception of the individual's social competence, friendships and membership of a group, especially in their relationships with their peers [23]. These dynamics are even more important when one considers that a person is a social being and creates its identity through others. The skills and competences of social interactions for adolescents who turn towards their peers more than their parents during the process of gaining independence and creating an identity take the function of a mirror to get to know themselves [24,25]. Adolescents form a definition of "social competence" related to their own social skills and performance in relation to their own and others' opinions. Social competence (competence), addressed by some specialists in conjunction with the concept of social skill, is the judgment and verdicts about the assessment of the individual's performance in tasks within the context of social interactions depending on certain criteria given by the individual himself or others –parents, teachers, peer groups, etc. [26,27]. Perhaps the most important agent of the judgments and verdicts for adolescents is their peer groups, i.e. friends. Thus, the ability of adolescents to initiate and maintain emotional and social relationships enable them to experience the thought and feeling of "being valuable and liked" as well as belonging – "being accepted" [28,29]. In this context, a young person who is able to perceive him/herself as socially competent experiences the proofs by the status of being accepted by his/her peers, and otherwise becomes excluded or neglected [30,31]. Being a socially accepted non-excluded person enables being perceived as socially competent, which includes characteristics such as emotions management skills, friendship in the context of effective communication skills, trustworthiness, etc. These interacting dynamics can support the healthier development and maturation of an adolescent's identity [33,34].

As can be seen, the level of awareness of the adolescent regarding emotional processes and his/her way of using these is one of the dynamics that influence the perception of social competence and being accepted by peers. In other words, the competency of emotions management skills, together with the need to belong to a group, can affect whether adolescents are excluded by their peers, and their status of being competent/capable individuals. The experiences related to these dynamics leave effects during adolescence, which has a critical importance for identity development, that carry their traces all the way to adulthood.

In this context, this research was conducted to examine adolescents' emotions management skills, perceived social competence, friendship quality, social exclusion, and need to belong.

2.1 Research Method

This research was based on the descriptive relational screening model.

2.2 Study Group

The study group was selected randomly and consisted of 431 students (195 male, 236 female) from 9th, 10th, 11th Grades studying in public high schools in Kadıköy district, Istanbul during 2015-2016 academic year.

2.3 Data Collection Tools

For this research, institutional approval was obtained from Istanbul Governorship, Ministry of National Education Issue: 59090411-20-E.4519169 and Date: 21.04.2016. Research data was obtained by using the "Emotions Management Skills Scale" developed by Rezzan Çeçen (internal consistency coefficient of the scale was 0.83 whereas the cronbach alpha value obtained within this research) [35], "Perceived Social Competence Scale" adapted into Turkish by Sarıçam et al. [36], "Friendship Quality Scale" [37], "Social Exclusion Scale" [38], "Need to Belong Scale" [39] adapted into Turkish by Akın et al., and "Personal Information Form" developed by the researcher.

2.4 Data Analysis

The data were analyzed in SPSS computer program using t test, one-way analysis of variance and relationship techniques. Differences in social exclusion, need to belong, emotions management skills, perceived social competence and friendship quality with respect to gender were investigated by t test, whereas differences with respect to age, grade, student achievement in the current academic year in which the research was carried out and the previous academic year (based on student statement), family characteristics (nuclear, extended, fragmented), number of siblings, parent educational status, parent working status were investigated by one way analysis of variance.

In addition, relationship analysis was performed to determine whether there is a relationship between these characteristics of adolescents.

3 Results

Results of this research are listed below.

3.1. There was a significant difference in favor of girls in terms of gender with respect to friendship quality and perceived social competence accordingly. A significant difference in favor of girls was found in the verbal expression sub-dimension of emotions management skills, whereas a significant difference in favor of boys was found in control of negative body response and anger management sub-dimensions.

Table 1. T test results of scales and sub-dimensions according to gender variable

Scale/Subcale	t	p	$\bar{x}$ Male	$\bar{x}$ Female
Friendship quality	-2.23	0.026	86.98	91.29
Closeness	-3.27	0.001	25.87	28.03
Acceptance	-1.97	0.050	17.95	18.81
Help	-3.42	0.001	8.38	9.29
Social competence	-3.83	0.000	23.85	25.61
Expression of emotions as a verbal	-2.58	0.010	22.73	24.24
Control of negative body response	5.099	0.000	13.48	11.83
Management of anger	2.773	0.006	8.92	8.39

3.2. Significant differences were found in terms of social exclusion, friendship quality, security, proximity, acceptance, and assistance scores with respect to the age variable.

Table 2. One-way analysis of variance (Anova) results of scales and sub-dimensions according to age variable

Age	F	p
Social exclusion	3.159	0.043
Friendship Quality	8.410	0.000
Safety	3.823	0.023
Closeness	5.878	0.003
Acceptance	9.403	0.000
Help	10.000	0.000

3.3. No significant difference was found in the scales applied and the sub-dimension scores with respect to the grade level of students.

3.4. A significant difference was found in terms of friendship quality, security, assistance, belonging and achievement scores with respect to student achievement in the current academic period.

Table 3. One-way analysis of variance (Anova) results of scales and sub-dimensions according to student achievement variable

Student Achievement	F	p
Friendship Quality	3.048	0.017
Security	3.118	0.015
Help	3.781	0.005
Belonging need	2.699	0.030
Coping	2.743	0.028

3.5. A significant difference was found in terms of social competent scores with respect to academic achievement status in the previous academic period.

Table 4. One-way analysis of variance (Anova) results of scales and sub-dimensions according to previous academic period student achievement variable

Previous Academic Period Student Achievement	F	p
Social competence	2.443	0.046

3.6. A significant difference was found in the belonging, emotions management skills, and coping scores within emotions management skills with respect to the number of siblings.

Table 5. One-way analysis of variance (Anova) results of scales and sub-dimensions according to number of siblings variable

Number of Siblings	F	p
Belonging need	3.263	0.012
Emotion management skills	4.073	0.003
Coping	2.931	0.021

3.7. A difference was found in terms of emotions management skills with respect to parents being together.

Table 6. One-way analysis of variance (Anova) results of scales and sub-dimensions according to parents living together variable

Parents Living Together	F	p
Emotion management skills	3.176	0.043

3.8. A significant difference was found in terms of acceptance, emotions management skills, and verbal expression scores with respect to mother educational status.

Table 7. One-way analysis of variance (Anova) results of scales and sub-dimensions according to mother educational status variable

Mother Educational Status	F	p
Acceptance	2.771	0.027
Emotion management skills	2.929	0.021
Expression of emotions as a verbal	2.961	0.020

3.9. Significant difference was found in terms of acceptance, emotions management skills, and verbal expression scores with respect to father educational status.

Table 8. One-way analysis of variance (anova) results of scales and sub-dimensions according to father educational status variable

Father Educational Status	F	p
Emotion management skills	2.754	0.028
Expression of emotions as a verbal	2.456	0.045

https://doi.org/10.1051/shsconf/20184801034

3.10. According to the results of relationship analysis conducted to determine the relationships between scales, a negative relationship was found between social exclusion and emotions management skills, perceived social competence and friendship quality.

A positive relationship was found between friendship quality and belonging, social competence, and emotions management skills.

A positive relationship was found between belonging and social competence, whereas a negative relationship was found between belonging and emotions management skills.

Table 9. Correlation table between the scales

		Social exclusion	**Friendshi p quality**	**Belonging need**	**Social competences**	**Emotion managemen t skills**
Social exclusion	Pearson Corr.	1	-.418**	-.031	-.437**	-.397**
	p		.000	.522	.000	.000
	N	431	431	431	431	431
Friendship quality	Pearson Corr.	-.418**	1	.217**	.419**	.213**
	p	.000		.000	.000	.000
	N	431	431	431	431	431
Belonging need	Pearson Corr.	-.031	.217**	1	.148**	-.223**
	p	.522	.000		.002	.000
	N	431	431	431	431	431
Social competences	Pearson Corr.	-.437**	.419**	.148**	1	.279**
	p	.000	.000	.002		.000
	N	431	431	431	431	431
Emotion management skills	Pearson Corr.	-.397**	.213**	-.223**	.279**	1
	p	.000	.000	.000	.000	
	N	431	431	431	431	431

4 Discussion

According to the gender feature, the average scores of social competences scale perceived as "proximity, help and acceptance" dimensions of friendship quality scale and subscale were found to differ from males in favor of females. It shows that female students find the quality of friendship more positive than male students and find themselves more competent in social relations. This result is consistent with the finding that the mean scores of the "verbal self-expression" dimension from the subscales of emotion management scale differ in favor of female students. In addition, the result that the mean scores of "expression of emotions as they are" and "control of negative body response and anger management" scales differed in favor of male students from emotion management subscales also supported the finding that female students differed in their average level of friendship and perceived social competence. Considering that emotional control and friendship quality are accepted as factors influencing social competence, it is seen that the scores of females are supported by the literature [40,41,42]. Similarly, the results regarding other life periods as well as the literature on adolescents have supported emotional management skills and the ability of the individual to find himself or herself socially satisfactory in terms of establishing positive friendships [43]. The mean scores of "control negative body response" and "anger management" dimensions of emotions management skill subscale differ in favor of male students, indicating that male students have more positive qualities than girls in terms of these characteristics. This result makes us think that male students may also differ positively in terms of friendship and perceived social competence levels. However, no differences were found in favor of females with respect to qualifications. It is believed that it may be related to the differences in the level of expressing emotions as verbal in male and female students.

Significant differences were found in terms of social exclusion and friendship quality scores with respect to the age of the students. The total scores of friendships quality also differed between the mean scores of security, proximity, acceptance and help subscales. The average scores of the friendship quality scale and the mean scores of the three sub-dimensions in question differ from the adolescents aged 16 and 17 in favor of the adolescents aged 15. In other words, it is possible to state that quality of friendship relations perceived more positively by adolescents aged 15 than adolescents aged 16 and 17, and their security, proximity and acceptance feelings are more intense in friendships. This result can be supported by the literature that 15-year-old adolescents can maintain their definition of "friendship" in secondary school age and their relationship while their self-definition can vary depending on the psychosocial development patterns when they are at the age of 16 and 17. The stated result can be supported by the finding that the mean scores of the social exclusion scale are at the highest level in the age of 16.

According to the grades of the students, no significant difference was found in terms of the related scale scores. While there was no difference according to the grades, the difference according to the age has suggested that the age factor may be more important in the regulation of the peer relations in terms of related characteristics [44].

In terms of student achievement during the study period, significant differences were found in terms of friendship quality and belonging scores. It was found that the averages of friendship quality scores were higher than those who defined 'very good', 'not bad', 'bad' and 'very bad' in favor of those who defined academic success as good (based on student statement). The fact that students who defined academic achievement as 'very good' had lower average scores of friendship quality ($\bar{x}$=80.31) than those of other academic achievement categories, suggesting that these students devote less time to social connections due to academic achievement expectations. The average score of the students who see their academic achievement as 'not bad' in terms of the average score of need to belong is higher ($\bar{x}$=32.48) than the students in the other academic achievement categories. The lowest score average ($\bar{x}$=28.42) belongs to the students who regard their academic success as 'bad'. This suggests that the need of belonging is more in the students who see themselves in the average. The fact that students evaluating themselves as 'bad' for academic achievement have lower average score of need to belong than students evaluating themselves 'very bad' may be related to the defensive mechanisms that adolescents may have developed about the problems they experience. The fact that the students with perceived academic achievement as 'very bad' ($\bar{x}$=30.40) and those who perceive as 'very good' ($\bar{x}$=30.66) are close to each other can be explained that they are located at both ends of the class average according to the normal distribution curve in both groups [45,46,47,48].

A significant difference was found in terms of social competence scores with respect to academic achievement in the previous semester. Accordingly, the students whose academic achievement is very low ($\bar{x}$=20.67), have a lower social competence score average than the other academic achievement average scores. Students that perceive themselves average ($\bar{x}$=25.48) and above average ($\bar{x}$=25.20) have higher average scores. This situation may be regarded as a social psychological phenomenon, although it appears to be in conflict with the result that average students' need to belong in the previous finding are high. In the light of sociology and social psychology, the middle class in the theory of social stratification can perceive itself more competently than the lower class while experiencing the need to be accepted by the upper class.

According to the sibling numbers, there was a difference in terms of total score of emotion management skills and sub dimension of coping with. In terms of emotion management skills regarding sibling number, it has been found that children without siblings ($\bar{x}$=96.44) have higher score of emotion management than children with 2-3 and 4 siblings. Children with 4 siblings ($\bar{x}$=85.41) have lower scores on emotion management skills than others. The average scores of coping skills of single children was found ($\bar{x}$=13.79) higher than other groups (the average score of children with 2 or more siblings respectively; ($\bar{x}$=12.74; $\bar{x}$=12.95; $\bar{x}$=11.48; $\bar{x}$=12.75). It is considered that this result is consistent with preference of having one child or two children increases with the education level according to population growth data of Turkey [49,50]. In terms of the literature related to the adolescents, evaluations related to the emotional and social development of the children with siblings are considered together with various factors [51,52,53]. Although it is thought that having a sibling may be more positive than being a single child, this feature requires many familial factors to be dealt with together.

A difference was found in emotion management skills according to the marital state of parents. 384 of the participants in the research reported that their parents live together, 36 have divorced, and 11 reported that their parents live separately. Although the family togetherness is expected to make a difference among young people in terms of dynamics of the study, it is considered that this characteristic should be taken into account with other dynamics related to the family [54,55].

According to the characteristics of maternal education level, there were differences in acceptance sub dimension of friendship quality scale and average total score of emotional management and its sub dimension and sub dimension of expressing verbally. A significant difference was found in terms of friendship quality scores according to maternal education level. Average score of friendship quality of children's mothers who are illiterate ($\bar{x}$=78,29) or primary school graduate ($\bar{x}$=83.77) and the total score of emotional management skills of secondary school, high school and university graduates is also considered. Total average score of emotional management skill is lower in those whose mothers are illiterate ($\bar{x}$=86.57) than mothers graduated from high school ($\bar{x}$=94.52) or university ($\bar{x}$=93.93). The psychology literature and a large number of researches emphasize the importance of the individual's qualifications regarding "mother's" characteristics and "motherhood roles and functions" as individuals at every stage of her life. Therefore, the obtained result is consistent with the relevant literature data in terms of maternal education level and friendship quality scale and emotion management skills, and once again emphasizes the importance of this subject [56].

It has also been found that father's education level differs in terms of emotion management skills and expressing verbally in its sub dimensions. It was found that, in terms of average total score of emotion management skills, children having illiterate father ($\bar{x}$=87.67) differs from primary school graduates ($\bar{x}$=90.47), secondary school graduates ($\bar{x}$=89.26), high school graduates ($\bar{x}$=92.47) and university graduates ($\bar{x}$=94.59). In the average total score of sub dimensions of expressing the scale verbally in children's father that are illiterate ($\bar{x}$=24.67) are higher than other groups (respectively $\bar{x}$=22.16; $\bar{x}$=22.51; $\bar{x}$=23.76; $\bar{x}$=24.56) The fact that the ones whose father is illiterate and the ones whose father is university graduate are close in terms of total average score of sub dimensions of expressing themselves verbally makes us think that illiterate individuals need more verbal expression to sustain their daily lives. In addition, whether the patterns of expressing verbally are same among educated individuals are evaluated in terms of emotions management skills total score and it has been revealed that it is significant for fathers to be educated as well as mothers.

According to the results of the relationship analysis, a negative relationship was found between social exclusion and emotion management skills, perceived social competence and friendship quality. A positive relationship was found between emotion management skills and perceived social competence and friendship quality whereas a negative relationship was found between emotions management skills and social exclusion. The increase in social exclusion informs young people in terms of emotion management skills and perceived social competence that they need support, and their friendship qualities do not have supportive qualifications. In other words, when competence related to emotion management skills increase in young people, communication with their peers, positive perception level of their competences and their friendships quality become supportive and enhancing while social exclusion and neglection by peers decrease. The result obtained supports the relevant literature in terms of research subject [57,58,59,60].

5 Conclusion and Recommendations

The results of the study have shown that in the process of acquiring a healthy identity; regulation of emotion management skills and peer relationships, and the importance of self-competence perception as well as studies related to the subject should be approached multi-dimensionally. In this context, it is believed that emotion management skills should be regulated in order to support all its dimensions and social exclusion should be evaluated together with "peer victimization", and incentives of extracurricular activities should be increased to improve friendships. In addition, structuring educational institutions' functions to be comprehensive rather than acquiring "academic qualification" in order to include all individuals, children and the youth can contribute to the healthy development of young individuals. It is suggested that all social institutions and organizations for young people should be in cooperation and coordination for the works supporting young individuals and their families in order to raise awareness for the importance of taking preventive and remedial roles.

References

1. Bandura, A. Adolescence Development from an Agentic Perspective. Tim Urdan and Frank Pajares (Eds.) Self Efficacy Beliefs of Adolescence (1-47). USA: Information Age Publishing. (2005).
2. Yurgelun, Todd D. Emotional and cognitive changes during adolescence. *Current Opinion in Neurobiology*, **17**(2), 251-257. (2007).
3. McLaughlin, K. A, Megan C. Garrard and Leah H. Somerville. What develops during emotional development? A component process approach to identifying sources of psychopathology risk in adolescence. *Dialogues in Clinical Neuroscience,* **17**(4), 403. (2015).
4. Malatesta, C. Z. The role of emotions in the development and organization of personality. In *Nebraska symposium on motivation* (Vol. **36**, pp. 1-56). (1990, January).
5. Zimmer- Gembeck, M. J. and W. Andrew Collins. Autonomy Development during Adolescence. Gerald R. Adams and Micheal D. Berzonsky (Eds.) *Blackwell handbook of adolescence* (175-200). UK: Blackwell Publishing. (2006).
6. Zimmerman, B., J. & Timothy J Cleary. Adolescent's development of personal agency, The role of self- efficacy beliefs and self regulatory skill. Tim Urdan and Frank Pajares (Eds.) *Self efficacy beliefs of adolescence* (45-69). USA: Information Age Publishing. (2005).

7. Schunk, Dale H. & Judith L. Meece. Self-efficacy development in adolesence. Tim Urdan and Frank Pajares (Eds.) *Self-Efficacy beliefs of adolescence* (71-96). USA: Information Age Publishing. (2005).
8. Dusek, J. B. & Julie Guay McIntyre. Self-concept and self-esteem development. Gerald R. Adams and Micheal D. Berzonsky (Eds.) *Blackwell handbook of adolescence* (290-300). UK: Blackwell Publishing. (2006).
9. Crone EA, Dahl RE. Understanding adolescence as a period of social-affective engagement and goal flexibility. *Nature Reviews. Neuroscience.***13**:636–650. (2012).
10. McLaughlin, K. A, Megan C. Garrard and Leah H. Somerville. What develops during emotional development? A component process approach to identifying sources of psychopathology risk in adolescence. *Dialogues in Clinical Neuroscience,* **17**(4), 403-410. (2015).
11. Konrad, K., Firk, C., & Uhlhaas, P. J. Brain development during adolescence: neuroscientific insights into this developmental period. *Deutsches Ärzteblatt International*, ***110*** (25), 425. (2013).
12. Susman,E. And Alan Rogal . Puberty and Psychological Development. Richard M. Lerner and Laurence Steinberg (Eds.) *Handbook of adolescent psychology* (second Edition) (15-45). New Jersey: John Wiley&Sons, Inc. (2004).
13. Raver, C. C. Young Children's Emotional Development and School Readiness. ERIC Digest. (2003).
14. Nurmi, J-E. Socialization and self-development channeling, selection, adjustment and reflection. Richard M. Lerner and Laurence Steinberg (Eds.) *Handbook of adolescent psychologhy* (second Edition) (85-124). New Jersey: John Wiley&Sons, Inc. (2004).
15. Collins, W. A. &Brett Laurse. Parent-adolescent relationships and influences. Richard M. Lerner and Laurence Steinberg (Eds.) *Handbook of adolescent psychologhy* (331-361), (second Edition). New Jersey: John Wiley&Sons, Inc. (2004).
16. Brown, B. *Adolescents' relationships with peers.* Richard M. Lerner and Laurence Steinberg (Eds.) *Handbook of adolescent psychologhy* (363-394), (second Edition). New Jersey: John Wiley&Sons, Inc. (2004).
17. American School Counselor Association. ASCA national model: A framework for school counseling programs. American School Counselor Association. (2012).
18. Dymnicki, A., Sambolt, M., & Kidron, Y. *Improving college and career readiness by incorporating social and emotional learning*. College and Career Readiness and Success Center. (2013).
19. Kavanagh, M. H., & Drennan, L. What skills and attributes does an accounting graduate need? Evidence from student perceptions and employer expectations. *Accounting & Finance*, **48** (2), 279-300. (2008).
20. Robles, M. M. Executive perceptions of the top 10 soft skills needed in today's workplace. *Business Communication Quarterly*, **75**(4), 453-465. (2012).
21. English, D., Manton, E. J., SAMI, A. R., & Dubey, A. A comparison of the views of college of business graduate and undergraduate students on qualities needed in the workplace. *College Student Journal*, **46** (2), 427-435. (2012).
22. Thompson, R. A. Emotional regulation and emotional development. *Educational Psychology Review*, **3**(4), 269-307. (1991).
23. Brown, B. B. and Christia Klute Friendships, cliques and crowds. Gerald R. Adams and Micheal D. Berzonsky (Eds.) *Blackwell handbook of adolescence* (330-349). UK: Blackwell Publishing. (2006).

24. Rose, A. J., & Rudolph, K. D. A review of sex differences in peer relationship processes: potential trade-offs for the emotional and behavioral development of girls and boys. *Psychological Bulletin*, ***132*** (1), 98. (2006).
25. Galambos, N. L., & Costigan, C. L. Emotional and personality development in adolescence. *Handbook of Psychology*, 351-372. (2003).
26. Connolly, J. Social self-efficacy in adolescence: Relations with self-concept, social adjustment, and mental health. *Canadian Journal Of Behavioural Science/Revue Canadienne Des Sciences Du Comportement*, ***21***(3), 258. (1989).
27. Bandura, A., Barbaranelli, C., Caprara, G. V., & Pastorelli, C. Self-efficacy beliefs as shapers of children's aspirations and career trajectories. *Child Development*, ***72***(1), 187-206. (2001).
28. Bacchini, D., & Magliulo, F. Self-image and perceived self-efficacy during adolescence. *Journal of Youth And Adolescence*, ***32***(5), 337-349.(2003).
29. Anderson, S. L., & Betz, N. E. Sources of social self-efficacy expectations: Their measurement and relation to career development. *Journal of Vocational Behaviour*, ***58***(1), 98-117. (2001).
30. Baumeister, R. F., DeWall, C. N., Ciarocco, N. J., & Twenge, J. M. Social exclusion impairs self-regulation. *Journal Of Personality And Social Psychology*, ***88***(4), 589. (2005).
31. Leary, M. R. Responses to social exclusion: Social anxiety, jealousy, loneliness, depression, and low self-esteem. *Journal of Social and Clinical Psychology*, ***9***(2), 221-229. (1990).
32. Anderman, L. H.). Academic and social perceptions as predictors of change in middle school students' sense of school belonging. *The Journal of Experimental Education*, ***72***(1), 5-22. (2003
33. Wilkinson, R. G., & Marmot, M. (Eds.). *Social determinants of health: the solid facts*. World Health Organization. (2003).
34. Derfler-Rozin, R., Pillutla, M., & Thau, S. Social reconnection revisited: The effects of social exclusion risk on reciprocity, trust, and general risk-taking. *Organizational Behavior and Human Decision Processes*, ***112***(2), 140-150. (2010).
35. Çeçen, A. R. Duyguları yönetme becerileri ölçeğinin geliştirilmesi: Geçerlik ve güvenirlik çalışmaları. *Türk Psikolojik Danışma ve Rehberlik Dergisi*, ***3***(26), 101-113. (2006).
36. Sarıçam, H., Akın, A., Akın, Ü., & Çardak, M. Algılanan Sosyal Yetkinlik Ölçeğinin Türkçeye uyarlanması: Geçerlik ve güvenirlik çalışması. *The Journal of Academic Social Science Studies, **6**(3), 591-600.* (2013).
37. Akın, A., Karduz Adam, F. F., & Akın, Ü. Arkadaşlık kalitesi ölçeği Türkçe formunun geçerlik ve güvenirliği. *Journal of Research in Education and Teaching*, **3**(4), 378-383. (2014).
38. Akın, A., Doğan, R., Gönülalan, G. D., Atik, R., Çebiş, T., Akın, U. Ergenler için sosyal dışlanma ölçeği Türkçe formunun geçerlik ve güvenirliği. *Paper presented at the 1st Eurasian Educational Research Congress*, April, 24-26, İstanbul, Türkiye. (2014).
39. Akın, A. Ait Olma ihtiyacı ölçeği. Ahmet Akın. (Eds.) *Psikolojide kullanılan güncel ölçme araçları* . İstanbul: Nobel. (2015).

40. Silvers, J. A., McRae, K., Gabrieli, J. D., Gross, J. J., Remy, K. A., Ochsner, K. N. Age-related differences in emotional reactivity, regulation, and rejection sensitivity in adolescence. *Emotion*, ***12***(6), 1235. (2012).
41. Carlo, G., Crockett, L. J., Wolff, J. M., & Beal, S. J. The role of emotional reactivity, self-regulation, and puberty in adolescents' prosocial behaviors. *Social Development*, ***21***(4), 667-685. (2012).
42. Myin-Germeys, I., Van Os, J., Schwartz, J. E., Stone, A. A., & Delespaul, P. A. Emotional reactivity to daily life stress in psychosis. *Archives of General Psychiatry*, ***58***(12), 1137-1144. (2001).
43. Li, Y., Doyle Lynch, A., Kalvin, C., Liu, J., & Lerner, R. M. Peer relationships as a context for the development of school engagement during early adolescence. *International Journal of Behavioural Development*, ***35***(4), 329-342. (2011).
44. Birditt, K. S., Fingerman, K. L., & Almeida, D. M. Age differences in exposure and reactions to interpersonal tensions: a daily diary study. *Psychology and Aging*, ***20***(2), 330. (2005).
45. Pajares, F.. Self-efficacy beliefs in academic settings. *Review of Educational Research*, ***66***(4), 543-578. (1996)
46. Pajares, F., &Schunk, D. The development of academic self-efficacy. *Development of Achievement Motivation. United States*, *7*. (2001).
47. Bong, M., & Skaalvik, E. M. Academic self-concept and self-efficacy: How different are they really?. *Educational Psychology Review*, ***15***(1), 1-40. (2003).
48. Pintrich, P. R., & Zusho, A. The development of academic self-regulation: The role of cognitive and motivational factors. In A. Wigfield & J. S. Eccles (Eds.), *A Vol. in the educational psychology series. Development of achievement motivation* (pp. 249-284). San Diego, CA, US: Academic Press. (2002). http://dx.doi.org/10.1016/B978-012750053-9/50012-7
49. ÇobanN, A. İ., & Özbesler, C. Türkiye'de aileye yönelik sosyal politika ve hizmetler. *Sosyal Politika Çalışmaları Dergisi*, ***18***(18), 31-41. (2009).
50. Akça, H., & Ela, M. Türkiye'de eğitim, doğurganlık ve işsizlik ilişkisinin analizi. *Maliye Dergisi*, ***163***, 223-242. (2012).
51. Katz, L. F., Kramer, L., & Gottman, J. M. Conflict and emotions in marital, sibling, and peer relationships. *Conflict in Child and Adolescent Development*, 122-149. (1992).
52. Brody, G. H. Sibling relationship quality: Its causes and consequences. *Annual Review of Psychology*, ***49***(1), 1-24. (1998).
53. Brody, G. H. Siblings' direct and indirect contributions to child development. *Current Directions in Psychological Science*, ***13***(3), 124-126. (2004).
54. Morris, A. S., Silk, J. S., Steinberg, L., Myers, S. S., & Robinson, L. R. The role of the family context in the development of emotion regulation. *Social Development*, ***16***(2), 361-388. (2007).
55. Buehler, C., & Welsh, D. P. A process model of adolescents' triangulation into parents' marital conflict: The role of emotional reactivity. *Journal of Family Psychology*, ***23***(2), 167. (2009).
56. Fox, N. A., & Calkins, S. D. The development of self-control of emotion: Intrinsic and extrinsic influences. *Motivation and Emotion*, ***27***(1), 7-26. (2003).
57. Connolly, J. Social self-efficacy in adolescence: Relations with self-concept, social adjustment, and mental health. *Canadian Journal of Behavioural Science/Revue Canadienne des Sciences du Comportement*, ***21***(3), 258. (1989).

58. Twenge, J. M., Baumeister, R. F., DeWall, C. N., Ciarocco, N. J., & Bartels, J. M. Social exclusion decreases prosocial behavior. *Journal of Personality and Social Psychology*, ***92***(1), 56. (2007).
59. Carthy, T., Horesh, N., Apter, A., & Gross, J. J. Patterns of emotional reactivity and regulation in children with anxiety disorders. *Journal of Psychopathology and Behavioral Assessment*, ***32***(1), 23-36. (2010).
60. Urdan, T., & Schoenfelder, E. Classroom effects on student motivation: Goal structures, social relationships, and competence beliefs. *Journal of School Psychology*, ***44***(5), 331-349. (2006).

An evaluation of language philosophy of Yunus Emre and Mevlana

Esra Karabacak[1,*], and *Aslı* Piro[2]

[1]Near East University, Faculty of Arts and Sciences, Turkish Language and Literature, Nicosia-99138, North Cyprus
[2]Near East University, Faculty of Arts and Sciences, Turkish Language and Literature, Nicosia-99138, North Cyprus

Abstract. Philosophers express, share with other people and convey them their opinions through language. We can define language as a system of symbols which is used for expressing any mental activity and its transfer from one mind to another. Language plays an essential role in the spreading and sharing of philosophy. Language is an essential tool of communication for conveying opinions. As Mevlana stated, "no matter how much you know, what you say is not more than what others understand." Mevlana's poems, his poetry and the meanings he added to statements and words are very important for literature and its history. What is the place of literary works in language philosophy in Turkish literature? This is worth examining. Words have gained new meanings and their meanings extended to abstractions as a result of certain developments in the poetry tradition in the East. Likewise, the philosophical dimension of language can be solved based on the works of poets and authors who are considered as close to each other. Yunus Emre emphasized the supremacy of meaning and valuelessness of material things which integrated carrying the load of Islamic Sufism. Scientists who study Yunus Emre claim that he widely read and internalized the poems of poets who came before him. In addition to the general style characteristics of the poet, he also has some peculiar features. Choosing examples from the poems of Mevlana and Yunus Emre, evaluations will be made in terms of language and philosophy which will explore similar characteristics.

1 Introduction

Human mind has the ability of creating concepts through abstractions. Human beings want to create some propositions from these concepts and express what they want to tell. Language is a system of symbols which is used for expressing any mental activity and its transfer from one mind to another. Abstract thinking power provided by language is the most important factor in conceptualization of the reality of people outside themselves and establishment of relations with the community. It is through language that we can perceive

* Corresponding author: esra.karabacak@neu.edu.tr

reality. We are able to produce knowledge about values through language. Language has an essential role in the spreading and sharing of philosophy. Language is an essential means of communication. The interaction between minds is only possible through language. Language is the means of conveying opinions. In Mevlana's words, "no matter how much you know, what you say is not more than what others understand" [1].

The literary aspect of Mevlana and his poet personality is essential in terms of meanings that he added to words. That words gain new meanings and the expression extends from concrete to abstract is the result of certain developments in the poetry tradition in the East. The differentiation in style in Persian poetry in Seljukian period and theme preferences is explained as *Seljukian Style*. In this period poet personality also went through differentiation. Mevlana was an exception to classical court poet personality and affected the direction of poetry. Mevlana and his son Sultan Veled claimed that meaning had supremacy and material things were valueless. The path of creating new and different meanings with old words was approved and reinforced by Mevlana who considerably benefited from literary tradition. Mevlana's poetry bears general style characteristics of Persian poetry as well as some unique features.

Language philosophy is a part belonging to human beings, a branch of philosophy which deals with unique problems just like history philosophy. Language philosophy does not examine the mutual relations between elements which form a language; it examines the relations between them and the world. Language can serve as a means of communication only through this type of relationships. Language philosophy tries to explain how language works, how it can be useful and how it is used for communication. How and according to which rules is the function of indicating these beings performed? Several approaches on Mevlana are very meaningful; but the topic of language must also be examined. Yet, his philosophical opinions, socio-cultural viewpoints and didactic-educating dimensions are also remarkable in addition to his literary personality [2].

As a result, according to Mevlana the peace among opposites on earth tells that it is the most important and inevitable reality for the creatures so that they can live their lives. Certainly the side effects that controversies will create must not be forgotten. He believed that contrasts make the universe dynamic in a harmonious order and ensure the movement among themselves and progress. Besides, by explaining this reality, he even watches negative events with tolerance and tries to explain the contrasts among them as the reflection of peace. Mevlana explains the following reality: "in the universe of the one and godhead, there is no problem of contrast any more. There is equality and sameness. Every object, event etc. that we think as contrasting are actions that will take us to greatness. Accepting this action is peace itself!" [3].

I am silence, thought, language and voice
I am the sound of ney.

With these words, Mevlana asks the question of *how is the language processed and woven? What is the opinion-based impact on language?* This can be solved by examining his general philosophy and then its reflection on language.

2 Examination

Wisdom in Mevlana's thought, which is reflected on language, is expressed in concrete terms instead of abstract terms. He follows the topic of wisdom in the society. In this context, he does not reprimand the contrasts and classifications among people and thinks that mutual cooperation and convergence among people is a peace factor based on "the principle of integration". With this opinion, it is possible to accept the "peace in contrast" of Mevlana as an intellectual way of thinking.

As is known, there are three pre-eminent personalities in Mevlana. This means that there is vertical personality instead of horizontal personality. In other words, his personality in the field of science and wisdom has three stages; it gains meaning with Crudity, Maturity and Burning. He defines life as a process and explains that it gains meaning not with horizontal movement but with vertical movement towards greatness. In the crude (raw) period everything must be tolerated, as all events are caused by lack of knowledge and education; however, in maturity period everything finds its place and then gains meaning from Beka-Billah (Reaching the endless life in the existence of God) to fenafillah (Perishing in the existence of God). Contrast is caused by crudity, whereas consensus and peace is caused by maturity. As a result, burning with the love of God is gaining meaning in Him. Mevlana explains the maturity of human beings in this regard and states that peace can be ensured only in this direction. He inherited the regular meaning search concerning peace from his father, Burhaneddin Muhakkik-i Termezî, and Şems-i Tebrizî [4].

The subject or theme in the focus of language philosophy is meaning and its nature. The topic of meaning is an essential point where all researches in language philosophy intersect. The question in language philosophy is not like *what does this word mean?* The question is more like *what does it mean when something tells another thing?* This question can also be asked as *what does it mean when a part in a language system tells something outside that language system?* The elements belonging to language are words, meaning names, noun phrases, adjectives, conjunctions, adverbs, prepositions etc., simple-complicated sentences, written texts or cliché expressions. Concepts which indicate all kinds of beings including abstract, concrete, material or spiritual are extremely essential while examining a literary type.

It is clear that Mevlana is knowledgeable about Greek philosophy. He mentions Plato, Calinus and sophists in Mesnevi. His closeness to philosophy is also reflected on his usage of language. He also includes the opinions of Gazali and Avicenna in his works who examined Greek philosophy. Therefore, with the impact of this philosophy he moves words in word groups around a main center while using language. He thinks that every word is the cornerstone of poetry. Every word has a different meaning. However, in poetry and especially in lyric and pastoral poetry moving words just like the notes in music is the effect of a part of philosophy.

I am both me and you not only in me but also in you,
I am both mine and yours, and you are mine,
So weird have I become that
I do not know if you are me, or I am you.

Mevlana criticized the thinkers who accept mind as basis. He cites the friendship of a Bedouin and a philosopher on the road: the Bedouin loaded two full bags on his camel. One bag had wheat and the other had sand. The philosopher warned the Bedouin that he should pour sand and divide the wheat into two bags in equal amounts so that the load would be lighter. The Bedouin adored this opinion and became the zealot of the philosopher. In the end, the Bedouin understood that the philosopher is a penniless and troublesome person and moved away from him. He said words meaning *your intelligence and wisdom is useless* and broke with the philosopher. Mevlana mostly defines thinkers deprived of faith by the word "philosopher". He ended his story as following: *the wisdom based on nature and consisting of imagination is a wisdom deprived of the inspiration of the light of God.* Using the words philosopher, Bedouin, imagination and wisdom here actually shows that he chose complementary elements in terms of meaning. Certainly the words used in a narrative constitute the internal part of the expression; this means that it is the main element. Mevlana is one of the authors and poems who use narrative expression best. Especially in his poems the effect of narrative can be witnessed [5].

Next thing you know they deceive me with gold,
Next thing you know they deceive me with fame and honor.
However I did not want gold or anything from him,
And it has been a long time since I ignored fame and honor.

I am an iron,
Running from magnet.
I am a straw,
Which sidestepped to magnets.

Language philosophy examines and compares expression patterns, determines the strengths and weaknesses in the form of a theory and tries to implement a more ideal meaning theory. It is important to determine the manner with which the author employs language for customized uses. What we obtain by looking at the vocabulary is not the meaning of word, but the definition of a word by a series of other words.

I am an iron, running from magnet.
I am a straw, which sidestepped to magnets.
I am such a particle that I revolted against entire worlds.
I revolted against the air and soil, fire and water.

Water, fire, air and soil, which were frequently used in ancient philosophy, are among impressive elements in Mevlana. In the verses given above, *iron, magnet, particle, straw, fire, water, air and soil* are used in a philosophical order related to the word *revolt.* In the end, it is finalized with an expression which is opposite to but supportive of "revolt". And the movement was based on freedom of opinion.

Since ancient times, thinkers have been asking themselves how beings came to existence. Some Greek thinkers claimed that the first element of existence was water, air, fire or soil. In Islam, the emphasis is on that the existence came into being with the will of God. Those who adopted midway in Islam believe that beings are created with the words *kün feyekün,* meaning "comes into existence when He says 'be'". However, there are different comments in Islam related to existence. Mevlana tried to express the unity of beings. In essence, the unity in existence philosophy was deducted from the hadiths of Muhammed the Prophet on the topic.

While Mevlana explains responsibility, which is one of the most important elements in human life, the processing of language is essential: a man entered into a vineyard, shook the apricot tree and began to eat the fruits. The owner of the vineyard saw him and said: "Are you not afraid of God?" The man answered: "Why should I be? The tree is God's tree, I am God's subject, and God's subject is eating God's property." The owner of the vineyard tied him to a tree and began to beat the hell out of him with a stick. The man could not stand the pain of the stick and asked the owner: "Are you not afraid of God?" The owner answered: "Why should I be? You are God's subject, this is God's stick, I am beating God's subject". Thus Mevlana explained that the man was responsible for the act of stealing.

The wisdom in Mevlana's thought is explained not in abstract but in concrete terms. He follows the topic of wisdom in the society. In this context, he does not reprimand the contrasts and classifications among people and thinks that mutual cooperation and convergence among people is a peace factor based on "the principle of integration". With this opinion, it is possible to accept the "peace in contrast" of Mevlana as an intellectual way of thinking [6].

Mevlana gave a superior value to human beings and saw them as beings that deserve the love of God. He sought everything in humans. He thought that as a human being becomes more refined in terms of spirituality, he comprehends that everything is just a dream, and that only God exists as being. According to Mevlana, He is the one who constitutes chemistry. What is chemistry after all? One has to vanish vis-à-vis his existence. What is existence in his presence? It is just a meaningless thing. The failure to know that this existence can come into being only with the existence of God is the evidence of blindness. Such expressions of belief display the connection of opinion-based language philosophy with human philosophy in the clearest and most beautiful manner.

Mevlana's explanation of death is also very critical in terms of language. Death is inevitable for human life. It is putting a full-stop to the life in this world. Mevlana is not afraid of death and he almost tries to endear death to people. According to his philosophy, human beings are in this universe because God wished so. Human beings are part of the existence. He thinks that a lover does not fear from reaching his beloved one. This is what death is like. It is being elevated to the level of God. Here opposite words express an entirety. However, exactly the opposite was expected. Complementary expressions give the wording more strength.

He always states that reality and things cannot be comprehended with the mind. By doing this, he moves words and criticizes the disarrangement of the mind. A deep system can be noticed in his works. He claims that a disorganized mind is illuminated with light. A deep system can be noticed in his works. The words are ordered according to this system. Even interacted concepts are presented in a more understandable method and style. Mevlana believes that it is material and form which interests mind. Similar to Islamic philosophers, Mevlana accepts some Aristotelean opinions and supports them with words. He intertwines concepts which are among the most important elements of language philosophy [7].

Do you think that I can recruit a rose if I saw a thorn? If you do not saw one, no sapling gives you a rose. Streams are just like wheat and the world is like a windmill; if you take adobe to the windmill all you obtain is soil.

Here the word *rose* connects sentences with different meanings. The usage of repetitions is one of the most important elements of language features. The analogy between world and windmill is important as an example of emulating art in prose.

A human being is an eye; beyond him there is nothing more than skin and meat. The value of human is equal to what his eyes see. Here "eye" accommodates several meanings; what matters is just what a person sees. What they see are put into words within a system of thought during when the relation between language and philosophy emerges and completes each other.

"Heart, word and love will blend in poetry; and illuminate hearts without love". With these expressions, he emphasized that internal structure and external features can be expressed with poetry. Emotions are fed in poetry and cast into words.

My friend, I am you and you are me.
Come here, come closer…
It is that you are me and I am you,
Then what is that you and me for?

Here language moves through personal pronouns. Expressions are based on pronouns.

The meaning is reinforced with repetition group and duplexing with pronouns. Certainly while assigning this task to meaning, the relation between language and opinion is completed. As can be seen, his poems are easily understandable for all cultures and the entire humanity. The words he uses belong to the common language which can be generally understood by everyone.

Did not I tell you not to go there?
Did not I tell you that only I could know you?
Did not I tell you I am the fountain of life in this country of absence?
Even if you become angry and desert me,

Even if you go to a distance of one hundred thousand years, did I not tell you that I am what you will come back and reach?

A general opinion is conveyed with the question expressions above. Conditional sentences completed these expressions. The repetition of "did I not tell you" turns negativity into positivity. Although it is a small element, it conveys an important way of thinking into language [8].

One of the most beautiful and meaningful verses;
Be like the sun in compassion and mercy,
Be like the night in covering the mistakes of others,
Be like a river in goodness and generosity,
Be like a dead in anger and quick temper,
Be like soil in humility and modesty,
Be like a sea in tolerance,
Either seem as you are or be as you seem…

are the fundamental philosophy of life. And these opinions are reflected to the words only in a certain unity of emotions. By using analogies and different words with the same meaning, emphasis has been put on how human beings would be in life. Mevlana almost became the language of all creatures.

As for Yunus Emre…

When Yunus is mentioned, Anatolia comes to mind. His poems are unadorned, far from vanity and highly sincere. Anatolian people found themselves in the poems of Yunus. According to Yunus Emre, a person must first know the language of his society, and speak that language. Yunus Emre was a man of the people and he used folk language. His expressions in his poems are very clear and plain.

The language of Yunus Emre is Old Oghuz Turkish. The century when Yunus lived iswas a transition period for the history of Turkish language. On one side there were the traces of old Turkish; on the other side there were the traces of newly shaped Old Anatolian Turkish; both of them can be found in the poems of Yunus. In other words, almost all of the poets in this period have similar characteristics. Yunus Emre used several words which have the traces of Old Turkish [9].

My life, you are deceiving me
Oh, my life, what shall I do with you?
You made me unable to move
Oh, my life, what shall I do with you?
All I had was you
You were soul in my soul
You were sultan to me

Oh, my life, what shall I do with you?
Even someone who knows a lot needs suggestion
He who wants to reach the destination should appear in sorrow
This road is evil distant the world is a trap for it
Those who fall in this trap should repel their guides

It is not easy to find any poems similar to his plain but beautiful poems which were written without concern for art. The hardly pronounceable opinions and excitements of Islamic Sufism can be seen instantly in his poems. Yunus Emre approved and reinforced the way of creating new and different meanings with old words and literary tradition was utilized considerably. As he was very close to philosophy, Yunus Emre used language as a philosophical element and brought a soft comment to his writings in every topic and even added an interpretation full of love to Islam religion and contributed to the spreading of love for human beings, solidarity and sincere love for religion. Language philosophy examines and compares patterns of expressions, determines their strong and weak points in the form of a theory and, as a result, tries to apply a more ideal theory of meaning [10].

Poems of Yunus Emre express the feelings, enthusiasm, longings and dreams of human beings in a unique language. It makes language more vivid, beautiful and effective and adds it a personality. Poet chose the words in daily language with care. He added them brand new meanings. He added new values and meanings to the used language. He included analogies and metaphors. He turned concrete beings into abstract beings and vice versa. As a result, he added a depth of meaning to feelings and opinions. Art was utilized in order to avoid monotony in the poems:

Your love took me from myself
I need you and only you
I burn yesterday and today
I need you and only you

I am not happy with wealth
I am not sad with poverty
Diverting myself with your love
I need you and only you

The poet expressed his feelings, opinions and dreams with sentences. Daily speaking language and poetry language are different from each other. Poet chose the words in daily language with care and added them brand new meanings. He madeuse of dreams, images and impression while explaining them. He also utilized some analogies and metaphors in addition to the form, rhyme, measure, harmony, emphasis and toning of the poem while using words. He turned concrete beings into abstract beings and vice versa. As a result, he added a depth of meaning to feelings and opinions. Some figures of speech are used in order to increase the power of word in poems. Figures of speech add depth to the meaning and elegance to feelings in poetry.

If the poem is not only a sum of the words that constitute it but is well beyond this compilation with some divine characteristic, the viewpoint of the poet towards life and his stance can be explained better:

Falls upon mountain and makes it ash,
Falls upon hearts and makes a road,
Turns sultans into slaves,
Love is an erudite object.
Whom did the arrow touch?
There is no resent and anxiety.
Ferhad and his sighs are high,
Love is an object of absence.

3 Conclusion

Yunus Emre and Mevlana are among the writers who make best use of language. They explained the topic of unity especially in the enthusiasm of love for God and brought vividness to Islamic Sufism. While using language, human philosophy was emphasized. Language gave life a meaning, and it was given a prominent place while evaluating the place of human in universe. While creating a symbol in poetry, comparisons, exaggerations, and metaphors are used. Human mind has the ability of creating concepts by abstraction.

People create propositions from these concepts and try to express their intentions. From this perspective, especially poetry language is easily shared with other people and transferred to them. Yunus Emre added new meanings to words in addition to their lexical meaning and took them out of the sentence structure within the general rules of language and created different compositions of words. The power of abstract thinking provided by Yunus Emre's poems have become the most important factor in the conceptualization of reality by people and their ability to establish relations with their environment.

Mevlana is one of the writers who make best use of the relation between language and opinion. He especially explained the topic of unity in the enthusiasm of love for God and brought vividness to Islamic Sufism. While using language, human philosophy was emphasized. Language gave life a meaning, and it was given a prominent place while evaluating the place of human in universe. He acted as the pioneer of narrative expression. However, we understand from the foregoing that language, religion, philosophy, sociology, history and literature are all intertwined, or rather, complete each other. Mevlana's words have a wide prominence in several world languages in folk poems and mystic philosophy.

Mevlana's Dewan and Mesnevi are translated in several languages. His works are affected by both Eastern and Western thought. He is a major Turkish thinker. Although more than seven centuries passed, his philosophy is still being read and adopted by people. It is beyond doubt that Mevlana has an important place in Islamic philosophy. In addition, he played an essential role in literature in his use of language and expression techniques. Mevlana gave huge importance to the freedom of conscious. He brought a soft interpretation to the Islam religion. In ethical terms, he recommended behaviors which would end with happiness. He gave importance to good intentions and the power of will. In all these expressions, he brought language to the fore. These philosophical opinions have become the most beautiful examples of language philosophy.

The examination which began with the following words:

> I am silence, thought, language and voice.
> I am the sound of ney.

emphasises that the operation of language in Mevlana is intertwined with word patterns, and opinion-based impact in language. It is possible that Mevlana is a good beginning and an important example in terms of language philosophy. It will be suitable to complete with an important saying of Mevlana. Do not look for our grave on the ground after we die. Our grave is in the hearts of the wise… And when we enter the hearts, we enter language.

References

1. D. Aksan, *Semantics and Turkish semantics,* (Ankara University Faculty of Language and History-Geography Publications, Ankara, 1978)
2. Z. Özcan, *Language Philosophy I-II,* (Sentez Publications, Ankara, 2014)
3. Gölpınarlı, *Mevlana Celâleddin,* (İnkılap Publications, Ankara 1999)
4. G. Golkarian, Mevlana and His Philosophy. *Sohan Journal*, **6/3** (2014)
5. M. Tatcı, *Yunus Emre Dewan-text with Criticism-II,* (Ministry of Culture Publications, Ankara, 1990)
6. G. Golkarian, Peace and Consensus Understanding in Mevlana's Views, *Doğu Esintileri (Eastern Breeze)*, **4**, (2017)
7. S. Eyüboğlu, *Yunus Emre* (Cem Publications, İstanbul, 1971)
8. Kabaklı, *Mevlana*, (Toker Publications, İstanbul, 1972)
9. E. J. W. Gibb, *History of Ottoman Poetry*. Translated by Ali Çavuşoğlu, (Akçağ Publications, Ankara, 1999)
10. A. Kemal, *Yunus Emre*, (Parıltı Publications, İstanbul, 2004).

A linguistic evaluation of the preface of "Mikyasu'l-Lisan Kıstasu'l-Beyan" by Abdurrahman Fevzi Efendi

Esra Karabacak[1,*]

[1]Near East University, Faculty of Arts and Sciences, Turkish Language and Literature, Nicosia-99138, North Cyprus

Abstract. *Mikyasü'l lisan Kıstasül-beyan*, which is the only known work of Abdurrahman Fevzi, is accepted by researchers as the first Turkish grammar book of Tanzimat based on the date when its writing began (1846) and its author is given the title of the first Turkish grammarian; however, considering its completion (1861) and publication dates (1881), the first printed grammar is *Medhal-i Kavîd* (1851) which was co-authored by Keçecizade Mehmed Fuad and Ahmed Cevdet Pasha that played a critical role as a school textbook for half a century. Unprepared and uneducated in Turkish grammar writing, first period Tanzimat intellectuals lacked a national system which could set an example of the work that they needed in education and teaching and had passed through madrasah training; thus, grammar method developed for Classical Arabic which they knew best was the first example of their works. This pattern was applied in *Müyessiretü'l Ulûm* (1530) which was the first Turkish grammar book in Anatolian land, but in terms of its structure and origins, this effort handled Turkish from the perspective of a different language, as a result of which it did not yield any results. In the 300 years that passed thereafter, a new step was not taken in this area. Thus, the fact that Bergamalı Kadri's work has only a few copies is an indicator that it failed to create an impact in the world of scholarship. The compiled Turkish grammars of 19th century show similarities with the method of the first grammar written in Anatolian land previously. Those who came to the world of scholarship from madrasah with Arabic "iştikak" (etymology) knowledge performed conceptualizations based on this infrastructure. The operation system brought knowledge of patterns to the forefront. Right thereafter the results of the first contacts with the West would show itself in the field of Turkish grammar science but this time the operation of language would drift to a wrong course and French grammar method would

* Corresponding author: esra.karabacak@neu.edu.tr

gain dominance. In this context, necessary examinations will be made in line with the collected data and the results will be discussed within the literature in the light of the obtained findings.

1 Introduction

The examination and study of language in terms of grammar is based on the methods developed by certain rules. Grammar is derived from the word *gramma* which means "writing" in Greek, and is defined as the examination of a language consisting of systematic group of words which show certain regularities in terms of pattern, pronunciation, sentence structure, meaning and history of words. When we examine this system for Turkish language, we can see that it was not given importance until Tanzimat and that Arabic grammar was given precedence. In the first Ottoman madrasahs, Arabic teaching was importance as a continuation of the past. Naturally due to the relation of Turkish with Arabic and Persian, Turkish teaching was not handled comprehensively. In Anatolian Chiefdoms, more importance was given to Turkish and several works were authored.

Turkish grammar science was created by Kaşgarlı Mahmud. The most important grammar of Kaşgarlı Mahmud titled *Kitâbu Cevâhirü'n-Nahv fî Lugati't-Türk* is lost; however, in his *Kitâbu Divâni Lugâti't-Türk* [1] which was written with the purpose of teaching Turkish to Arabs gives rules about Karahanli Turkish. The book titled *Müyessiretü'l-Ulûm* which was presented in 1530 to Ibrahim Pasha (1493-1536), the Sadrazam of Suleiman the Magnificent (1494-1536) by Bergamalı Kadri, is the first Turkish grammar book [2]. After a period of stillness in terms of grammar, Tanzimat intellectuals believed that Turkish should be taught in the new schools and took action believing that there is a huge gap in Turkish teaching. However, due to the lack of a founded resource and their madrasah background, they tried to see an example for Turkish in the classical language, Arabic, which they knew best. In the meantime several grammar books were written. The first grammar books were *Medhal-i Kavâid* by Ahmet Cevdet Pasha and *Kavâid-i Osmâniye* which was co-authored by Ahmet Cevdet Pasha and Keçecizade Mehmed Fuat, who later became a member of the General Council on Education [3, 4]. *Mikyâsü'l-Lisân Kıstâsu'l- Beyân* by Kütahyalı Abdurrahman Fevzi Efendi was completed in 1847 before Ahmed Cevdet Pasha's work and accepted by Ministry of Education; however, it was printed in 1882 after the death of its author [5]. The first study on this book was conducted by Ali Ulvi Elöve [6]. Later, after the adoption of the new Turkish alphabet in 1928, a new era was opened in Turkish grammar works. The first grammar trial with new Turkish alphabet was *Brief Turkish Grammar* which was prepared by Turkish Language Committee. Grammar writing activities began in Republican era with this book and several books have been written until today.

2 Examination

Abdurrahman Fevzi Efendi was an important grammarian educated in Kütahya who served Turkish language. He was born in Kütahya in 1802. His full name was Seyyid Abdurrahman Halvetî er-Rufai el-Kütahî. His father was Sadıkzade Mustafa Efendi, who was a scholar of Kütahya. He received his first education in his hometown from his father in the form of religious education (1828); in 1829 he went to Istanbul to receive madrasah education. He received lectures from Mudarris Imam Zade Esat Efendi. He completed his graduate education and received his diploma in 1833. He became a mudarris (madrasah teacher). In 1834 he was assigned as mudarris at *Dâru'l-Hadis Valide Sultan* in Istanbul.

One year later (1835) he was assigned to the Military School as Arabic teacher. He gave Turkish, Arabic and history classes here for twenty consecutive years. He was promoted to the rank of Sofia Charter (1858). He retired in 1863 and died one year later (1864) in Istanbul. He was buried in *Yâvedud Cemetery* in Eyüp Defterdar Street in Istanbul. Abdurrahman Fevzi Efendi was pictured as a man of good ethics and intellect who knew the nuances of the science and a mature man. Bursalı Mehmet Tahir reports in his book *Ottoman Authors* that Abdurrahman Fevzi Efendi was known as *Kitabsız (bookless)* at the Military School and was the son of Mustafa Pasha, who was an Ottoman mathematician [7].

Abdurrahman Fevzi Efendi was raised in an era when importance was given to the learning and teaching of Turkish; adapting the fashion of the time, he wrote his book titled *Mikyasu'l-Lisan Kıstasu'l-Beyan* which explained the rules of Turkish language and offered a huge service to the Turkish language. He began writing his book in 1847 and completed the work in 1851. Later he extended the book with some corrections. The book was examined by a commission and seen as valuable in terms of grammar; as a result, it was decided to print the book which was after the death of its author. It was printed on behalf of Darüşşafaka in 1882 and the Turkish lessons were offered based on this book. It was accepted as the first Turkish grammar book of Tanzimat and its author was given the title of the first Turkish grammarian of Tanzimat; however, considering its completion (1861) and publication dates (1881), the first printed grammar book is *Medhal-i Kavîd* (1851) which was co-authored by Keçecizade Mehmed Fuad and Ahmed Cevdet Pasha which was sued as school textbook for half a century.

Unprepared and uneducated in Turkish grammar writing, first period Tanzimat intellectuals lacked a national system which could set an example of the work that they needed in education and teaching and had passed through madrasah training; thus, grammar method developed for Classical Arabic which they knew best was the first example of their works. This pattern was applied in *Müyessiretü'l Ulûm* (1530) which was the first Turkish grammar book in Anatolian land, but in terms of its structure and origins, this effort handled Turkish from the perspective of a different language, as a result of which it did not yield any results. A new study was not performed in the period which passed thereafter. Turkish grammar books written in 19th century have similarities with the method of the first grammar book written in the Anatolian land previously.

The method followed by Abdurrahman Fevzi had differences from his contemporaries in two points: first of all, he identified the terms on which he would found the grammar. In the introduction to his book, the terms were given with their equivalents under the title *Istılâhât-i Mevzû'a ve Unvânât-i Muhteri'a.* Adding the new terms that he scattered to the entire book, there is an abundance of such terms. The book is also essential in terms of grammar terms which are produced from Arabic origins but identified according to the structure of Turkish language. All derivational affixes and inflexional suffixes were given with different terms and a new term was provided for each meaning value. In the book, a term production system is noticed which aims at identifying the distinguishing points for meanings. Ali Ulvi Elöve, an expert at Turkish Language Institute, prepared the first sixty two terms with the equivalents that he produced and presented at the Fourth Turkish Language Council (1940) [8]. In the book, the idea that a new alphabet should be developed by comparing the sound values of Turkish and Arabic alphabet was defended. Abdurrahman Fevzi Efendi was the forerunner of the Latin alphabet which was based on the principle of "a letter for every sound, a sound for every letter" and he offered his new proposals with the purpose of ensuring that language could be read and understood easily and education and teaching could gain speed. His most important opinion was that under the title *grammar,* spelling, morphology (knowledge of structure), syntax and etymology should be united and that usage of vowels was inevitable. He emphasized that in order to show the vowel system of Turkish, letters which are similar to the signs called vowel in the West should be used and that the thin and bold ordered forms of each letter should be developed. He believed that lack of a spelling book made learning word phrases more difficult and led to loss of time.

The richness of pure Turkish words that he used in morphology did not attract attention until Republican era. Turkish Language Institute launched a project in 1933 for identifying the Turkish vocabulary which included the examination of *Mikyasü'l-Lisan ve Kıstasü'l-Beyan* by İshak Refet. Later, this book laid the foundations of Ali Ulvi Elöve's translation of *Grammaire de la Langue Turque (dialecte Osmanli)* by Jean Deny [9].

In the introduction of *Külliyât-ı Kavâid-i Osmâniye* by Manastırlı Rıfat Efendi [10] and in *The History of Education* by Osman Ergin thereafter [11], it is stated that *Mikyasü'l-Lisan ve Kıstasü'l-Beyan* actually consisted of two volumes and that only the first volume was published by Mustafa Safvet, son of Fevzi. Ergin stated that he thought that the second volume of the book was in Hamidiye Library [12].

The book is accepted as the second grammar book of Turkish language after *Müyessiretü'l-Ulûm* of Bergamalı Kadri (1530). The first grammar study in Anatolian field with Ottoman Turkish is *Müyessiretü'l-Ulûm* of Bergamalı Kadri which was written in 1530. Years after the writing of this book, grammar studies began to be conducted in 19th century. *Mikyasu'l-Lisan Kıstasu'l-Beyan* by Abdurrahman Fevzi Efendi is one of the books written in this period. This book is the first grammar book written after *Müyessiretü'l-Ulûm* as of its printing date and writing date. The book was printed in Mahmut Beg Printing House in Istanbul upon permission of Education Council in 1299 (1882). We used this edition when examining the book. This edition is registered with 29442 shelf number at Beyazıt State Library Ottoman Works Section.

The text section of *Mikyasu'l-Lisan Kıstasu'l-Beyan* consists of 177 pages and 17 chapters. In the beginning of the book the contents section, a section where terms are explained, and another section which gives information on the author and its printing place can be found, which consists of 22 pages. In the end of the book there is a true-false table of 8 pages. The 22 pages in the beginning, the text and the true-false table are numbered separately. Thus, the book consists of 207 pages in total. Each page in the text section consists of 35 lines. The book consists of a preface, five purpose sections and a conclusion. After the basic information part, the book is separated into topics and the topics are separated into sections.

The book begins with basmala, and continues with a section which praises God and the Prophet. The section titled *Ammâ ba'd* can be accepted as a preface where the importance given to the language by Abdurrahman Fevzi Efendi is explained by himself.

The author explained the reasons for which he wrote the book and emphasized the importance of language education. He explained how language education was given attention in Europe and underlined that we should pay attention to this topic as well.

The preface of the book consists of the opinions of Abdurrahman Fevzi Efendi on Turkish language. In this paper, the opinions of Abdurrahman Fevzi Efendi on Turkish language will be examined based on the preface of this book which can be seen as an important step in Turkish grammar scholarship [13].

According to Abdurrahman Fevzi Efendi, linguistics is a supreme art which compiles many benefits; however, scholars who are superior to their equivalents in producing good works did not write in this area and direct their opinions in this direction. Writing such a book was his chance. When he was teaching Arabic sciences to high school students, he noticed that fifteen or sixteen years old teenagers who came to Islamic countries from European schools had completed the grammar of several foreign languages after learning the grammar of their native language, and had studied drawing, essay-writing, geography and several other sciences; as a result, they learned and memorized Arabic and Persian faster than their contemporaries. Considering all the foregoing, he dreamed of writing an essential Turkish grammar book. He decided to write a book which would examine the types, genres and qualifications of Turkish letters and vowel points, especially the types, genres and qualifications of pure Turkish words written using these letters, their changing patterns, and the types of phrases and sentences and compile the rules which show the right way of writing these words; the book would also be full of examples which explain the foregoing. Accordingly, he examined the input and output of this language and investigated all related issues and searched a way to display the treasury of Turkish language. However, as the case in every age, some people who wanted to restrain him emerged in this age, too. But these efforts almost supported him more. In addition, Sultan Abdülaziz Han (1830-1876) who was the son of Sultan Gazi Mahmud Han (1784-1839) believed and decided that a qualified person like him could overcome this task. As a result, he began to work even harder and completed the book in 1847. The author believed that the fact that singular 2nd person imperative, which is one of the changing word types, could be transformed into several different patterns and that there were rules without exception concerning all simple and united forms each of which had related resources, meaning that Turkish was a grand language. However, Arabic language had no equivalent or equal in every aspect, Arabic was superior to all other languages. It had rules and did not have any exceptions. Turkish was about to vanish due to the association of Arabic and Persian. For this reason, Turkish had to be freed from Arabic forms and examined according to its own features as far as possible. In this case, Turkish could surpass Arabic. Arabic alphabet was not suitable for Turkish language. Especially the vowel points could not correspond to all vowel sounds in Turkish. Some changes were required absolutely. Writing an organized book by preserving the changes of a language which came to the point of absolute destruction and recording each to the place it deserves proved to be a challenge. It should be known that there was a single branch of science which explained the various patterns of words in a language and several issues of that language, which was called "linguistics". In that way the grammar of each language was an art consisting of several ordered issues which showed the ways of speaking and writing that language accurately. Issues related to language in Arabic were divided into four sections by scholars, namely "morphology, etymology, syntax and lettering". In some Arabic words the issues that show the way of easing the pronunciation of some difficult words were compiled under the title of "morphology". New words were derived from some words in different patterns which was termed "etymology". The need for identifying the place of some words in the sentence and the type of sentence was explained by the word "syntax". An effort was paid to determine the shape of letters and vowel points and prevent misspellings, which was called "lettering".

According to Abdurrahman Fevzi Efendi, most of the books and booklets written in sciences of religion and sharia and other fields were displayed in western and other languages whereas Qur'an and hadiths were written in Arabic language. For this reason, the meaning of these books should be learned and their expression should be translated into Turkish as the first step so that these languages could be learned better in a short period of time. And these languages could be learned and completed in that manner only by reading and completing Arabic language sciences known as syntax, morphology, etymology and lettering and the grammars of other languages which also consist of these four parts. For this effect, the following three tasks should be undertaken as necessary:

First of all, a book should be written so that the rules concerning letters and vowel points used in Turkish letters could be understood perfectly and pronounced and written in an accurate manner. Unless we had such a book, the rules concerning the changes of other languages cannot be measured and weighed with the rules of our language and thus the ways of writing Turkish words accurately could be known; as a result, it could not be possible to learn the changing rules of foreign languages in a short period of time and to translate the expressions of books in foreign languages in our language. This shows that Abdurrahman Fevzi Efendi paid attention to language education and that in those years we had to know the grammar of our language very well in order to make a good translation and that language was an essential factor so that nations could know each other better.

Secondly, Arabic alphabet was defective in terms of expressing the vowels and consonants of Turkish, and by keeping some shapes and eliminating others which were used for this purpose or by distinguishing them with some signs and correcting them altogether is needed. As the shapes of letters and vowel points was the foundation of spelling and writing, unless they were corrected, a book which compiled all of the issues related to the transformation of Turkish words and their shaping in writing could give proper guidance in pronouncing and writing Turkish words accurately; however, they could not adopt the desired shapes and patterns as the used shapes were incomplete. For this reason, the necessity of using foreign languages emerged which could not be understood by new beginners in the books translated from other languages. Another problem could be that there would be no time left to learn and complete the sciences and arts by taking several pains in learning Turkish spelling which had always been the case. At this point, the necessity of having an alphabet convenient to the spelling system of Turkish in those times was emphasized.

Thirdly, as the most important Arabic books had to be taught and learned which were hadith and interpretation books, they had to be printed with vowel points such as med, kasr, teşdid, vakf and vasl. In order to make sense of hadiths and other books, they had to be read and memorised accurately, and their accurate reading depended on the usage of such signs. Traditionally when these signs were not used, the words could be understood only by finding their meanings first because signs and words could not be read accurately and we had to check glossaries for corrections which led to loss of time. Even texts had to be applied for some signs in these books. Regardless of the time of their writing, in order to understand Qur'an and hadiths, it must be remembered that some phrases should be known and glossaries should be consulted. The same is valid for today, too.

The second of these three tasks is easier but more important than the other two as it will explore the types, genres and qualifications of words. The traditional word patterns would require slight changes which required the agreement and approval of scholars just like in the second and third tasks; thus, this was renounced. It is beyond everything that all kinds of Turkish words are accurately read and written in a short period of time and thus those able to write do not spend their entire life for learning how to spell and find the time to complete religious sciences and arts in their youth; it is also essential that they can complete Arabic language and the sciences in other languages which ensure that we obtain and learn these sciences. Thus, they would not lose time for learning Arabic and deal with Qur'an sciences and sharia laws, and save time for learning Turkish spelling rules. According to this book, conflicts can arise between nations with different languages even if they are under one rule as they do not know the languages of each other. However, if each nation learns the language of other nations, agreement can continue between them even if they are different nations; the language used by the state should be known and used by all tribes and clans which is more important than everything.

3 Conclusion

The author claims that first and foremost a language should be adopted with its grammar. Arabic and Persian should be minimized for Turkish so that this language can be freed from these two languages. These two languages can also be learned whenever necessary. This is very important especially in the period when this book was written. Not only in religious affairs but in all matters knowledge could be obtained with these languages. This was a requirement in order to be a cultivated person. In addition, one of the western languages had to be learned properly. If we transfer this opinion to the present time, especially in topics related to our cultural history, Arabic and Persian as well as a western language has to be known very well in order to study in such fields as history of natural sciences, astronomy, mathematics, history of medicine, Turkish language and literature and history, as there are several hand-written and printed books on these topics in Arabic and Persian. Especially in natural sciences field there are several works translated from ancient Greek to Arabic. One has to have access to these books in order to have in-depth knowledge and conduct study in these areas.

The opinions of Abdurrahman Fevzi Efendi concerning language are clearly expressed in the introduction to his book titled "Mikyâsu'l-Lisan Kıstâsu'l-Beyân". Bergamalı Kadri and Ahmet Cevdet Pasha were among the pioneers who played important role with Kütahyalı Abdurrahman Fevzi Efendi in the emergence of Turkish grammar. A general look at their works shows that they agree with the opinions indicated in the introduction to "Mikyâsu'l-Lisan Kıstâsu'l-Beyân". Those who tried to write on Turkish grammar after Abdurrahman Fevzi Efendi attempted to adopt the same opinions and apply them in accordance with their term. This can be observed only by examining the books that they authored. It is possible that some people did not see or pay attention to this book but still wrote their books in line with similar opinions. We can claim that Kütahyalı Abdurrahman Fevzi Efendi was the first person to convey his opinions on language at first hand in the history of Turkish grammar science. His work titled "Mikyâsu'l-Lisan Kıstâsu'l-Beyân" occupies an essential place in the history of Turkish grammar science especially with its introduction.

4. Text: Translation of Text [5]

Bismillâhirrahmanirrahîm

Erbâb-ı vukûf ve eshâb-ı ma'ârife tezkîr ve ihtârdan müstagnî olduğu üzere dinin kıyam ve devamına ve dünyanın kıvâm ve nizamına bâdî ve sebeb-i adî olan ulûm-ı diniyye ve şer'iyyeye da'ir ve ma'arif-i dünyeviyye ve sınâ'iyyeye müteda'ir olan kütüb-i musannafa ve resâ'il-i mü'ennifenin çoğu elsine-i Arabiyye ve sa'ireden bulunduğundan ve ale'l-husus bâ'is-i salâh ve dâ'i-i fellâhımız bulunan Kur'an-ı mübîn ve ehâdîs-i fahru'l-mürselîn Arabiyyu'n-nazm ve'l-ibare olduğundan gerek Kur'an-ı azîmu'ş-şânın ve ehâdîs-i kudsiyye ve nebeviyyenin nazm-ı şerîf ve me'âl-i münîflerine bi-kadri't-tâka kesb-i vukuf etmez için gerek kütüb-i mesfûrenin me'âllerini tahsil bile elfâza ve ibaretini lisân-ı Türkiyye nakl ve tahvil eylemez için ol emrde ol elsineyi az vaktte gereği gibi tahsil etmez umûr-ı lâzımadan idiği derkârdır ve bizce ise elsine-i markûmayı vech-i mezkûr üzere tahsil ve tekmil hususu ol elsineyi ya'ni (nahv) (sarf) (iştikâk) (hat) isimleriyle mersûm olan ulûm-ı Arabiyyeyi ve fünûn-ı erba'a-i mezkûreden ibaret olan elsine-i ecnebiyye gramerlerini kırâ'at ve tekmilden başka bir suretle uyamıyacağı vâreste-i kayd ve iş'ârdır. Halbuki bizim fünûn-ı markûmayı az vaktde gereği gibi tahsil ederek (3) makâsid-i diniyye ve metâlib-i dünyeviyyeye da'ir kütüb ve resâ'ilin hem me'âl hem mü'eddâlarını kesb-i vukûf etmez ve hem de ibarelerini lisanımızda peyderpey nakl ve tahvil eylemez. Âti'l-beyân umûr-ı selâsenin muktezâsını icraya menût ve mütevakkıfdır.

Birincisi, kelimât-ı Türkiyyenin ve ol kelimâta mevzu ve dâl olan suver-i hurûf ve nukûş-ı harekâtın hey'ât-ı tagayyür ve tahavvülünü ve keyfiyyât-ı teşekkül ve tebeddülünü i'lâm ve inhâ ve doğru söylenip yazmalarının tarikini ifhâm ve inbâ eder bir mecelle ve risalenin bulunmasına mütevaffıkdır. Zira elde öyle bir kitabımız olmadıkça elsine-i sa'irenin keyfiyyât-ı tagayyürüne da'ir nizamâtı lisanımızın nizamıyla mukayese ve muvazene olunamayacağından başka kelimât-ı Türkiyyenin bi-lâ karîne okunacak surette yazılmalarının tariki dahi bilinemeyeceğinden ne elsine-i ecnebiyyenin kavânîn-i tagyîresini beyan eden fünûn-ı mâra'z-zikrâ az vaktte gereği gibi tahsil ve tekmil hususu olabilir ve ne de lisan-ı âherde bulunan kütüb-i diniyye ve dünyeviyyenin ibarelerini lisanımıza nakl ve tebdil emri uyabilir.

İkincisi, fi'l-asl hurûf-ı Arabiyyeden yirmi iki nev ve hurûf-ı Farisiyye ve Türkiyyeden iki nev ve ancak hurûf-ı Türkiyyeden bir nev harfe mevzu olup hurûf ve harekât-ı Türkiyyede müştereken ve müterâdifen müsta'mel olan âti'l-beyan yirmi beş türlü suver-i hurûfa nukûş-ı harekâtın maksad-ı evvel âti'z-zikrin birinci babından anlaşılacağı vecihle hurûf ve harekât-ı Türkiyyeyi ifadede kusurları olduğundan ol suver ve nukûş-ı müsta'meleyi ya mahv ve isbat ile bâb-ı mezkûrda mebsût olan turuk-ı selâsenin birine ircâ ederek tashih veyahut suver ve nukûş-ı müsta'meleyi ba'zı alâmât ile takyîd ederek fi'l-cümle ıslah etmeğe mütevaffıkdır. Zira eşkâl-i hurûf ve nukûş-ı harekât suver-i kitabet ve imlânın huyûlu ve maddesi menzilesinde olmalarıyla vech-i mezkûr üzere tashih veya ıslah olunmadıkça kelimât-ı Türkiyyenin keyfiyyât-ı tagayyür ve tahavvülünden ve eşkâl ve nukûş-ı muharrirenin hey'ât-ı teşekkül ve tebeddülünden bahseden mesâ'ilin kâffesini mütekeffil ve müştemil olmak üzere tertip ve tanzim olunmuş olan işbu kitap ve mecelle her ne kadar kelimât-ı Türkiyyeyi doğru söylemenin tarikini bildirdiği gibi doğru yazmanın tarikini dahi bildirirse de eşkâl ve nukûş-ı müsta'mele artık ve eksik olduğu cihetle suver ve kavâlib-i matlûbadan her birine isâga ve ifrâ olunamayacağından hem mübtedîler için lisanımıza nakl ve tahvil olunacak kütübde kütüb-i Türkiyye-i mevcudede olduğu meselli anlamayacakları lugat-ı ecnebiyyeyi isti'male mecburiyet lâzım gelecektir ve hem de kitâbet-i Türkiyyeyi tahsil yolunda olageldiği üzere pek çok zahmet çekilerek tekmil fünûn ve ulûma vakit kalmayacaktır.

Üçüncüsü, kütüb-i Arabiyyeden evvel-be-evvel okunması veya mütalâ'a olunması ehem ve akdam olanların husûsen kütüb-i ehâdîs ve tefâsîrin mushaf-ı şerif meselli hareke ve sükûn ve medde kasr ve temsil olunmalarına mütevaffıkdır. Zira hem ehâdîs-i nebeviyyenin ve hem kütüb-i sa'irenin me'âl ve mü'eddâları istihrâc ve istinbât olunma ibarelerinin doğru okunup zabt olunmasına marbût ve ol ibarelerin doğru okunması dahi alâmât-ı markûma ile mukayyet olmalarına manût olup halbuki ibârât-ı mezkûre yazılageldiği üzere alâmât-ı markûma ile mukayyet olmadığı surette ol ibâratın doğru okunup zabt olunması bi'l-aks me'âllerini istihrâc ve istinbâta tevakkuf edeceğinden ve bu ise devr-i batılı müstelzim olmakla ibârât-ı markûma herhalde doğru okunamayacağından bi'z-zarure tashih-i ibare ve kelimât için metûn-ı lugata müraca'atla izâ'a-i evkât etmez lâzım gelecektir. Ve egerçi mesâ'il ve mübâhisine hariçten vukûf ve ittilâsıyla ba'zı ibareleri doğru okunmuş olsa bile ol vukûf ve ittilâ'ın ibârât arasında bulunan esâmî ve elkâb meselli kelimâtı doğru okumamız hakkında bir fa'idesi olmayacağından bu cihetle yine metûn-ı lugata müraca'attan kurtulunmayacaktır.

İmdi lâzımu'l-icra olan umûr-ı selâse-i mesrûdeden ikinci emr ya'ni hurûf (4) ve harekât-ı Türkiyyede müsta'mel olan yirmi beş türlü nukûş ve eşkâli ya âti'l-beyân turuk-ı selâsenin birine ircâ ile tashih yahut birkaç alâmet ihdâs ve vaz ile nukûş ve eşkâl-i müsta'meleyi ıslah ederek kelimât-ı Türkiyyeyi söylendiği gibi yazılma ve yazılanı bi-lâ karîne okunma kabiline ifrâ birle kitâbet-i Türkiyyeyi hat-ı Arabî-i mukayyet meselli silk-i nizama rabt ve hadd-i matlûba iblâ etme hususu egerçi hurûf ve harekât-ı Türkiyyenin ecnâs ve envâ ve havâsı bi'l-külliyye zahire ihraç olunmuş olduğu cihetle umûr-ı selâse-i mesrûdenin cümlesinden ehven ve eshel ve bununla bile fevâ'id ve menâfi'i eşmel ve ekmel bulunmuş ise de bi-lâ nizam yazıla gelen eşkâl-i kelimât-ı me'lûfeyi bir mikdar tagyîr ve tebdil etme lâzım geleceğinden husus-ı markûmı icra ikinci ve üçüncü emirler meselli ulemâ-ı milletin icmâ ve ittihâfına ve vükelâ-yı devletin kabul ve tasdikine mukârin irade-i gayr-ı te'âde-i mulûkânenin şeref-i sudûrına mevkûl-ı mevâdden bulunmuş olduğundan bundan sarf-ı nazar olunmuş ve birinci emir ise ya'ni kelimât-ı Türkiyyenin keyfiyyât-ı tagayyür ve tahavvülünden ve devâlî bulunan suver-i hurûf ve nukûş-ı harekâtın hey'ât-ı tebeddül ve teşekkülünden bahs eden mesâ'ilin kâfesini şâmil-i kütüb ve resâ'il tertip ve tanzim olunma hususu ise iş'âr mâra'z-zikrden müstebân olduğu üzere hem kelimât-ı Türkiyyenin her nev ve kısmını az vaktte doğru okuyup yazmamız ve bu cihetle erbâb-ı kalem tahsil-i kitabette ifnâ-i i'mar etmeyerek ulûm-ı diniyye ve funûn-ı hükmiyye ve sınâ'iyyeyi eyyâm-ı şebâbette tekmile vakit bulmaları için ve hem ulûm-ı diniyye ve fünûn-ı hükmiyye ve sınâ'iyyeyi ahz ve tahsilimize vesile olan fünûn-ı elsine-i Arabiyye ve sa'ireyi az vakitte tekmil etmez ve bu cihetle talebe-i ulûm-ı fünûn-ı Arabiyyeyi tahsilde izâga-i evkât etmeyerek maksad-ı aslı olan ulûm-ı Kur'aniyye ve ehâdis-i nebeviyye ve şer'iyye ile istagâle ve hem de kitabet-i Türkiyyeyi tahsile ihtilâs-ı vakt eylemeleri için akdem-i umûrdan bulunduğu gibi hükümet-i vâhide dâhilinde bulunan akvâm-ı muhtelifetü'l-elsine birbirlerinin lisanlarına arif olmadıkları surette her ne kadar müttahidetü'l-millet olsalar bile beynlerinde bu cihetle vahşet ve menâfiretin kıyamı ve her biri diğerlerinin lisanlarına vakıf oldukları surette muhtelifetü'l-millet bulunsalar bile aralarında bu yüzden ülfet ve mevâlâtın devamı umûr-ı tabî'iyyeden olduğuna nazaran devletimizin kullandığı lisânı zîr-i hükümetinde dâhil ve âsûde-i hâl olan gerek müslim gerek sa'ir bunca kabâ'il ve aşâ'irin bilip kullanmaları için dahi akdam-ı umûrdan bulunmuştur. Bu surette her ne kadar müttahidetü'l-millet olsalar bile beynlerinde bu cihetle vahşet ve menâfiretin kıyamı ve her biri diğerlerinin lisanlarına vakıf oldukları surette muhtelifetü'l-millet bulunsalar bile aralarında bu yüzden ülfet ve mevâlâtın devamı umûr-ı tabî'iyyeden olduğuna nazaran devletimizin kullandığı lisânı zîr-i hükümetinde dâhil ve âsûde-i hâl olan gerek müslim gerek sa'ir bunca kabâ'il ve aşâ'irin bilip kullanmaları için dahi akdam-ı umûrdan bulunmuştur.

Bu surette ilm-i lisan böyle menâfi'-i adîdeyi müştemil bir fen-i celîlu'ş-şan iken ibrâz-ı mü'essir-i cemîlede fâ'iku'l-emsâl zevât-ı zevi'l-kemâlden hiç birinin kemmiyyet-i hâmme-i himmeti bu muzmâr fevâ'id-i medâr cihetine sevk ve icâle ve cuybâr-ı medrâr fikr ve ru'yeti ol vâdî semtine icra ve isâle olunması meğerse ke'l-misli's-sa'ir elsine-i ekâbirde mütedâ'ir işbu (kem terku'l-evvel li'l-âhirîn) kelâmında meram şa'ir istifham alâ vechi'l-inkâr olması ihtimaline da'ir makaleden sırr-ı Ebu's-Su'ûdî kabâle-i ahbâra imâle hikmetine mebnî ve irâ'a tettakî gaybdan bu emrin fıtk ve rıtkı mevâlîden talib-i feyz-i ilâhî müznib muhattî sâhi seyyid Abdu'r-rahman el-Halvetî er-Rufâ'î el-Kutâhînin ahde-i ubûdiyyetlerine tefvîz ve ihale buyrulması olmuş ki mekteb-i ma'ârif-i i'dâdiyye şâkirdânına ulûm-ı Arabiyye vesa'ireyi ta'limi hengâmında (5) Avrupa mektepleri şâkirdânından dahil-i havza islâm olmuş on beş on altı yaşında efendiler eyyâm-ı sibâvetlerinde mâder-zâd lisanlarının gramerlerini okumuş oldukları cihetiyle birkaç elsine-i ecnebiyye gramerlerinii tekmil ve resm ve inşâ ve coğrafya ve vâfir ulûm-ı riyâziyyeyi okumuş ve tahsil etmiş olduklarını ve bu zâde fünûn-ı Arabiyye ve Farisiyyeyi dahi hoca efendilerin takrîrât ve ta'bîrât-ı Türkiyyelerini henüz iyice fehm ve idrak edemedikleri hâlde hem-sâlleri ve zekâda emsal ve hemhâlleri bulunan şürekâlarından daha ziyade öğrenip bilmediklerini kerrâren ve merrâren müşahade etmekle evvel-be-evvel merci-i erbâb-ı ilm ve ma'rifet ve ma'haz-ı eshâb-ı rakam ve kitabet olmak emeliyle hurûf ve harekât-ı Türkiyyenin ecnâs ve envâ ve havâs ve evsâfından vâvu'l-hurûf ve harekâta vaz ve ta'yin olunması lâzım gelen nukûş ve alâmâtın hâlât-ı intikâş ve irtisâmından ve hurûf-ı mezkûreden mürekkep olup dâru's-saltanati's-seniyye ve memâlik-i sa'ire-i Osmaniyyede müsta'mel olan kelimât-ı Türkiyyu'l-aslın ecnâs ve envâ ve evsâfından ve keyfiyyât-ı tagayyür ve tahavvülünden ve mürekkebâtın envâ ve aksâmından ve keyfiyyât-ı Türkiyyeden ve kelimât-ı markûmeye delâlet eden nukûş-ı mürekkebe ve eşkâl-i mü'ellifenin hey'ât-ı tebeddül ve teşekkülünden bahsederek kelimât-ı mezkûreyi doğru söyleyip yazmanın tarîkini bildirir. Kavâ'id ve zavâbitin kâfesini hâvî ve hâfil ve ol kavâ'id ve zavâbiti şerh ve izah eder. Emsile ve şevâhidin âmmesini kâfi ve kâfil bir kitab-ı saht-nisâb tanzim ve tertip etme hülyasına dûçâr olmuş olmakla bî-ihtiyâr lisan-ı garib garîbi'l-beniyyâtın medâhil ve mehâricine em'ân ve enzâr ve ma'âkil ve ma'âricine i'mâl-i hendese efkâr ederek kâfe-i ahvâl ve mesâ'ilini ve her birinin mevâzi-i zikr ve mihâlini hâtır-ı fâtir ve zihn-i kâsırında icmâlen zabt ve ihzâr etmiş idi. Egerçi ikmâl-i esbâb-ı rufâh hâl-i enbâ cins ve himemleti için dil-i viranesinde nihân ve muzmar olan gencine-i lisan-ı Türkiyyu'l-beyanı ibrâz ve izhâra bir yol arardı. Lâkin her asırda bulunduğu vecihle tarrârân ve gaddârân kırd-ı nihâd ve hisâd-ı ümmü'l-fesâd Ebû Cehl Nejadların fevâ'id ve menâfi'ini inkâr etmeleri hatırasıyla da'vasından nukûl ve izhârdan yine izmâra udûl eder idi. Çünkü her şeyin verâ-ı ıstâr-ı gaybdan ref-i nikâb-ı adem ve âlem-i şahâdete izhâr-ı dîdâr vücûd ve vaz-ı kadem etmesi bir vakte merhûn bir sebebe makrûn olduğundan naçar husul-ı meramının zuhuru hengâmına dîde-dûz intizâr olarak beyn-i akdâm ve ahcâm etmekte iken e'âzim-i vükelâ-yı nâdiri'l-emsâlden bir sahib-i fazl ve kemal ile vuku bulan mebâhisât-ı ilmiyye hilâlinda ilm-i lisanın fevâ'id ve menâfi'ine da'ir tarafeynden tûl ve derâz-ı makalât cereyan etmekle hakkında hüsn-i zanların mahz-ı ibrâz-ı ma'nasında şöyle buyurdular ki el-hâletu hâzihi kavâ'id-i Türkiyyeyi câmi bir kitab-ı nâfi'in te'lif ve tertip olunması saltanat-ı seniyyenin pek aşırı emel ve matlûbu olmakla evliyâ-ı umûr-ı kemal-i huyûr ve surûr ile çaresini aramakta bulunmuştur. Bu surette devlet ve milletimize bir hizmet-i mahsusa olmak üzere ber vech-i matlûb bir kitap tertip etmiş olsa Gazâlî yevmu'l-kıyam ibkâ-i nîk-nâm ile be-kâm ve mazhar-ı iddi'a-i hayriyye has u âm olmakla beyne'l-en'âm makza'l-meram olurdunuz gibi hikmet-âmîz ve gayret-engîz kelimât ile tahrîz ve igrâ buyurmaları akdamca cây-gîr zamiri olan halât ve hülyayı mâ ra'z-zikrâ tehyîc ve beş on gün murûrunda ulûm-ı Arabiyyede kesb-i maharet ve tahsil-i ülfet etmiş hoca efendilerden bi'l-intihâb üç beş zevât ma'ârif-i semâtın tavsî da'ire-i ma'lûmât ederek kitab-ı matlûbı tanzim ve tertîbe kesb-i miknet ve kudret eylemeleri için cânib-i devletten pârsa isbâl ve isrâ buyrulmaları dahi tehyîc-i mezkûru tervîc etmekle (mütevekkilen ale'l-meliki'l-allâm) sâlifu'l-beyân kitabı kendi matlûbu üzere tanzîm ve terkîme altmış üçte vaz-ı kalem-i ikdâm ve tahrik berâ'a-i ihtimâm (ve elhamdulillahi'l-mufazzali'l-men'âm) altmış sekizde peyveste hayr-ı intizam ve ihtimam eylemişti. Ancak ba'zı ibârât ve ifâdâtını ıslah ve izah ile kâlib-i mergûb ve makbûle isâga ve ifrâ[a] etmek ve ba'zı fevâ'id ve zevâ'id ferâ'id-i izâfe ve ilâvesiyle mümkün mertebe had-i kemâle îsâl ve iblâ etmekte iken (sübhâne'l-mukaddem ve'l-mu'ahhar bi-yedihi melekût küllü şey'in ve hüve alâ külli şey'in kadîr) enfusu ve afâkı ketâ'ib ve nevâ'ib ve sihâm-ı mesâ'ibin hücum ve nüşûbu ile şikeste-bâl ve şûrîde-hayal olmakla bir mikdarını ma'a'l-futûr tastîr ve tahrîr ve bir mikdarını dahi (li'l-eyyâm en yentefise) (6) ve tîresi iktibâz-ı asrın inbisât-ı yusra tebeddülü eyyâmına te'cil ve te'hir etmişti. (Lehu'l-minne) Pâdişâh-ı Cem Haşm ve Şehinşâh-ı merza'l-şiyem Sultan Abdülaziz Han İbnu's-Sultâni'l-Gâzi Mahmûd Han (lâ zâlet şumûs-ı şevkete şârikatu müda'd-duhûr ve'l-eyyâm ve mâ barihat akmâr re'fetuhu bârikatun alâ mefâriki'l-enâm) efendimiz hazretleri bi't-te'yidi'r-rabbânî ve'l-avni's-samadânî serîr-i hilâfet-masîr Osmânî ve Evreng mu'allâ-yı cihân-bânî üzere culûs-ı hümâyûn Şevket Makrûn buyurdular. Rûz-ı fîrûz ma'delet-burûzdan beri seciyye-i zekiyye-i mülûkâne ve şehinşeh-i marziyye-i padişahâneleri muktezâsı memâlik-i mahrûsa-i şahanelerinde mekîn ve zill-i zelil bî-adîl mülûkânelerinde asayişkarîn olan sunûf-ı tab'a-i saltanatlarının tezâyüd-i asayiş-i bâl ve refâh halleri esbâb-ı kâmilesini istihsâl-i emr ehemmine sarf-ı makdûr ve esbâb-ı mezkûreyi istihsâl ise (a'ti'l-kavs bârîhâ) zabıtası her umûru ehl ve erbâbına sipariş ve tefvîzinden başka bir suretle uyamayacağı kalb-i keramet meheb gîtî sitânelerine lâyıh ve ind-i âlem-pesend mülûkânelerinde vazıh olmaktan nâşî teveccühat-ı sa'adet gayât tâcdârânelerin mevhibe-i sübhaniye ve atiye-i rabbânîh olan akl ve irfân ile ihmal-i zat ve istihsâl-i ulûm ve ma'arif ile tekmil sıfât etmiş eshâb-ı kemalâta ma'tûf ve maksûr buyurma menvî zamir-i şahaneleri idiği evzâ-ı padişahânelerinden ma'lûm-ı ekâbir ve asâgir olmakla (lâ cerem) bâzâr-ı kemal ve ma'arif-i zaman-ı Yemen iktirân-ı hâkânîlerinde revâcîni bulma alâmât ve emârâtı be-dîdâr olmuş ve bu cihetle dâ'iyân-ı devlet-i âliye ve tab'a-i saltanat-ı seniyye evlat ve ahfâdı sâye-i mulûkânelerinde tevârî (gıyâbetü'l-ceb) cehl ve nâdânîden vâreste ve zîbâyiş-i ulûm ve ma'arif ile ârâste olmak için esbâb ve vesâ'il-i tahsilâta teşebbüse ibtidâr etmede olmalarıyla asr-ı meyâmin hasr-ı mülûkâneleri (savânu'l-hükm ve'l-ma'arif) ünvanına sezâvâr nuhbe-i a'sâr-ı rüzgâr olacağı âşikâr olmuştur. Yenâ alâ zâlike yâdigâr-ı ahd-ı hilâfet penâhı ve ömr-i sânî abd-ı bâ'is fakir-i Kütahî olmak ümit ve eminesiyle bâ akdâm ve ihtimam-ı aceleti'l-vakt ikmâl ve itmâm "Mikyâsu'l-Lisan Kıstâsu'l-Beyan" namıyla be-nâm eylemiştir. Bu da mahfî olmaya ki lisan-ı Arabın kavâ'id-i tagyîriye ve zevâbıt-ı tahviliyyesini zabt ve her birini mahall-i lâyıkına vaz ile taht-ı nizama rabt ederek bir kitap vaz ve ibdâ itmek ulûm-ı sa'irenin mesâ'ilini tanzim ve tertip etmeden es'ab olduğu (evvelen delil-i lemî) ilm-i lisân-ı Arab merâtib-i ulûm-ı kesbiyyenin en nihayetinde vakı ilm-i ictihâdın a'zam-ı erkânı olmasından müstebân (sâniyen delil-i ânî) lisan-ı mezkûrun ahvâl-i tagyîriyye-i mütenevvi'asını mübeyyen mufassal ve mücmel-i kutub-ı mü'ellife ve resâ'il-i mürettibenin kesretinden ve izah-ı ahvâl-i tagyîriyye beyan-ı ma'ânî-i külliyye ve cüz'iyye hususlarında e'imme lugatından sâdir olan kelimât-ı muhtelife ve ahvâl-i muztaribenin vefretinden zahir ve nümâyân olur. Egerçi elsine-i aklâm ve elsine-i a'lâm-ı mütesâviyetu'l-akdâm ve elsine-i a'lâm-ı mütesâviyetu'l-akdâm olmadığı meselli elsine-i tavâ'if ve ümem dahi mütesâviyetu'l-akdâm olmadığından lisan-ı Araba her cihetle müsâvî ve mu'âdil-i lisan bulunmayacağı derkâr ise de lisân-ı Türkî dahi kendisinde vâki kelimât-ı mütegayyire envâ'ından ez cümle emr-i hâzır-ı vâhid kalilu'l-elfâz kesiru'l-ma'ânî yüz bin sîgaya kadr-ı tebdil ve tahvil olunduğundan ve hey'ât-ı külliye-i efrâdiyye ve terkîbiyyesine da'ir kâfe-i kavâ'id ve zavâbiti ise şuzûddan beri ve istisnadan ârî ve her birinin uyûn ve enhârı mütesâvi'l-mecârî bulunduğundan isbat-ı sânî babında kâtı'a ve ba's-ı rusul vuku'unda âyet-i sâtı'a garîbu'l-bünyân bir lisân-ı acîbu'ş-şân olduğu vâreste-i kayd ve eş'ârdır. Bu surette lisân-ı Türkî bi'l-külliye zayi olma derecesine gelmiş iken ahvâl-i tagyîriyesini bi-cemî envâ'ihâ ve aksâmihâ zabt ve her birini mahall-i lâyıkına kayıt ile taht-ı nizama rabt ederek bir kitab-ı lisân-ı Arabın ahvâl-i tagyîriyesini zabt ve rabtın su'ûbetinden dûn ve noksan olmadığı ifade-i sabıkadan be-dîdâr ve bu cümleyi kutub-ı sarf ve nahivden her biriyle muvazeneden zahir ve aşikar olmakla mütalâ'aya rağbet buyuran ehl-i kemâl-i hasebu'l-beşeriyye sudûru derkâr olan hafvât ve aserât ve galatât ve saktâtını ma'ânînin kemal-i dikkatinden dolayı ifâdât-ı lâzımanın şiddet-i su'ûbetine hamle lutfen ve keremen tashihe himmet buyuralar. (Ceza'llahu anhu mak'ad saddaka men zekerehu bi-lisani sıdkin ve bi'llahi't-tevfik ni'ami'l-mevlâ ve ni'ami'r-refik.)

(7) **Meşrû-ı ulûm-ı lisandan nahv sarf iştikâk-ı hattın fenn-i vâhid olması beyanındadır.**

Ma'lûm ola ki kelimât-ı Arabiyye ve sa'irenin tagayyürat-ı muhtelifelerinden ve ol kelimâta delâlet eden suver-i hurûf ve nukûş-ı harekâtın teşekkülât-ı mütenevvi'alarından bahs eden mesâ'il-i mütekessireyi lisan ve imlâyı hıfz ve vikâye-i emrinde birleştikleri cihete nazaran ilm-i vâhid addetme sureti ca'iz olduğu gibi ol mesâ'ilin mevzu'at ve fevâ'idi âti'l-beyân dört nev mevzu ve fa'ideye raci ve muvazzi olduğu cihete nazaran dört nev ilm ad ve i'tibar etme sureti dahi ca'iz olur. Pes elsine-i ecnebiyyede vâkı kelimâtın ve ol kelimâta delâlet eden suver ve nukûşun tagayyürât-ı mütenevvi'a ve teşekkülât-ı muhtelifelerini ifade eden mesâ'il-i mütekessireyi cem ve te'lif hakkında suret-i evveli münasib olma'ın elsine-i mezkûre eshâbı ol kelâmın tagayyüratını suver ve nukûşunun teşekkülâtını ifade ve i'lâm eden mesâ'il-i mütekessireyi bir mahalde kayıt ve (gramer) namıyla ilm-i vâhid addetmişler. Bu surette her lisanın (grameri) ol lisanda bulunan kelimâtı ve ol kelimâtın nukûş ve eşkâlini ta'bir ve tahvil ve tersîm ve teşkil etmenin tarikini beyan zımnında doğru söyleyip yazmanın tarikini îzân eden mesâ'il-i kesîre-i mü'ellifeden ibaret bir fen olmuş olur ve lisân-ı Arabda vâkı kelimâtın ve ol kelimâta dâl olan suver-i hurûf ve nukûş-ı harekâtın tagayyürat-ı mütenevvi'a ve teşekkülât-ı muhtelifelerini beyan eden mesâ'il-i mütekessireyi cem ve te'lif hakkında suret-i sâniye münasip olma'ın e'imme-i lugat-ı Arabiyye dahi ol kelimâtı ve devâlî olan suver ve nukûşu tagayyür ve teşkil etmenin tarihini ifade eden mesâ'il-i mütekessireyi dört kısma taksim ve ol kısımları (sarf) (iştikâk) (nahv) (hat) isimleriyle birbirlerinden temeyyüz ve başka başka tertip ve tanzim etmişler. Şöyle ki ba'zı kelimât-ı Arabiyyenin lisanca sakil olan harflerini iskân ve kalb ve hazf ve idgâm ve teshîl ile hey'âtını tagayyür ve tebdil etmenin tarihini beyan zımnında telaffuzâtını tahfîf ve ta'dil etmenin yolunu gösteren mesâ'il-i mütekessireyi ayrıca cem ve te'lif edip (sarf) ismiyle tesmiye ve tavsif etmişler ve ba'zı kelimâtın evâ'il ve evâsit ve ahirinde hurûf ve harekât ziyade ve tenkîs ederek suretlerini tagyîr ve suver-i mütenevvi'a ve emsile-i muhtelifeye tahvil etmenin tarihini beyan zımnında ma'nasına münasip olan ma'na-yı mütenevvi'a-i matlûbayı ahzar-ı vech üzere tahsil etmenin yolunu ifade eden mesâ'ili başkaca tertip ve tensîk edip (iştikâk) namıyla fünûn-ı sa'ireden temeyyüz ve tefrik etmişler ve ba'zı kelimâtın dahi terkibde vuku'u cihetinden dolayı ancak ahirinde ya harf veya hareke veya tenkîs ederek suretlerini tagyîr ve tebdil etmenin yolunu irâ'e zımnında ma'ânilerine alâ vechi't-tevârüd ârız olan (fâ'iliyyet) ve (mef'ûliyyet) ve (izâfet) meselli ma'ânî hafiyyeleri tahsil ve ifade etmenin tariki i'lâm eden mesâ'ili cem ve tertip edip nahiv ismini tensip etmişler ve eşkâl-i hurûf ve nukûş-ı harekâtı tersîm ve teşkil ve suver-i matlûbaya tebdil ve tahvil etmek tarihini beyan zımnında imlâyı hatâdan s,n ve vikâye etmenin yolunu ifade eden mesâ'ili dahi başkaca zabt edip (hat) namını i'tâ etmişler. İmdi kelimât-ı Türkiyyenin tagayyürât-ı muhtelifelerini ve devâlî olan suver-i hurûf ve nukûş-ı harekâtın teşekkülât-ı mütenevvi'alarını beyan eden mesâ'il-i mütekessireyi dahi kelimât-ı Arabiyyenin ve devâlî olan suver-i hurûf ve nukûş-ı harekâtın tagayyürat ve teşekkülâtını ifade eden mesâ'il-i mütekessire meselli dört kısma taksim ve her kısmı bir râsimle başka başka tertip ve tanzim sureti uyabilirse de mesâ'il-i mezkûrenin ekseri mütedâhile olduğundan elsine-i ecnebiyyede vâkı kelimâtın ve devâlî olan nukûş ve eşkâlin keyfiyyât-ı tagayyür ve teşekkülünü ifade eden mesâ'il meselli bir mecellede zabt ve kayıt ve bir nam ile ilm-i vâhid addetme sureti daha münasip olduğundan mesâ'il-i mütekessire-i merkûmenin kâfesi mukteżâ-yı lisan-ı Türkî üzere tanzim ve tevsîk ve ifadeye enseb ve elyak ve ahz ve telâkkiye akrab ve vâfık surette tertip ve tensîk olunarak bir mukaddime, beş maksat, bir hâtimeye tevzi ve tefrik olunmuştur.

References

1. B. Atalay, *Divanü Lugati't-Türk Traslation, I-III; Divânü Lugati't-Türk Index "Index", IV*, Turkish Language Institute, Ankara, (1985-1986).
2. B. Atalay, *Bergamalı Kadri, Müyessiretü'l-Ulûm (Facsimile, -Transcripted Text and Index),* Turkish Language Institute, İstanbul, (1946).
3. Ahmet Cevdet Pasha, *Medhal-i Kavâid*, İstanbul, (1851).
4. Ahmet Cevdet Pasha and Fuat Pasha, *Kavâid-i Osmâniye*, İstanbul, (1858).
5. Kütahyalı Abdurrahman Fevzi Efendi, *Mikyâsü'l-Lisân Kıstâsu'l-Beyân*, İstanbul, (1847).
6. A.U. Elöve, *Kütahyalı Abdurrahman Hoca Mikyasüllisan ve Kıstasülbeyan*, Turkish Language Institute Publications, İstanbul, (1942).
7. Bursalı Mehmet Tahir, *Ottoman Authors* , v. I, İstanbul, (1914).
8. Kütahyalı Abdurrahman Hoca. Translated by Ali Ulvi Elüve. *Mıkyasüllisan ve Kıstasülbeyan*, İstanbul, (1942).
9. A.U. Elöve, *Mikyasü'l-Lisan Kıstasü'l-Beyan.*, İstanbul, (1962).
10. Manastırlı Rıfat. *Külliyât-ı Kavâid-i Osmaniye*. İstanbul, (1303).
11. O. Ergin, *History of Turkish Education*. İstanbul, (1977).
12. M. Koç, *Abdurrahman Fevzi, Encyclopedia of Ottomans with their Lives and Works I*, 27-29, İstanbul, (2008).

English language teaching for students of management of travel and tourism

Jaroslav Kacetl[1,*]

[1]University of Hradec Kralove, Rokitanskeho 62, Hradec Kralove 500 03, Czech Republic

Abstract. English has become the lingua franca in a lot of areas, including tourism industry. The aim of this contribution was to explain the way English is taught to students of Management of Travel and Tourism at the Faculty of Informatics and Management, University of Hradec Kralove, Czech Republic. The basic teaching approaches were described, and justified. Methods of collecting as well as creating teaching materials were exemplified. The resulting syllabi should be implemented in the coming years. Prior to this implementation, the whole curriculum of Management of Travel and Tourism has to be revised as the new accreditation is due in 2019. The new approach takes into account the fact that people working in tourism need to master especially speaking and listening as they are expected to communicate with foreigners.

1 Introduction

The Department of Applied Linguistics, Faculty of Informatics and Management (FIM), University of Hradec Kralove, provides English language lessons for all FIM students, including those who study Management of Travel and Tourism. Management of Travel and Tourism is the most language-oriented field of study at FIM. Its students can focus either on English or German. As Semradova and Hubackova [1] summarised, language teaching to full-time students of Management of Travel and Tourism may extends to 8-10 lessons a week. Two lessons of practical language usage skills a week are compulsory, the student can also attend optional subjects focusing on realia, translating, and literature and cultural studies of the countries where English or German are spoken. Nonetheless, this contribution focuses entirely on English language teaching.

With an impending date of accreditation renewal, it is necessary to revise and possibly improve the curriculum and syllabi of all subjects taught to the students of Management of Travel and Tourism, particularly the compulsory ones, i.e. in case of English language lessons Practical English Language 1 - 4. The whole procedure is quite complicated as new syllabi as well as e-learning courses should be created. For language teachers this includes finding as well as creating relevant study materials and textbooks and all this in close cooperation with teachers from the Department of Recreology and Tourism, who are responsible for courses focusing on geography and tourism.

* Corresponding author: jaroslav.kacetl@uhk.cz

This contribution aims at providing information about the way the compulsory subject called Practical English Language 1 – 4 should be taught in the coming years. With respect to the overall orientation of FIM as well as current worldwide trends, information and communication technologies (ICT) are going to play an important part in teaching. As Kacetl and Frydrychova-Klimova [2] emphasized, ICT are an inseparable part of current university education. In other words, although ICT have already been used at FIM for some time, the new syllabi count on using the Internet and ICT even more frequently.

Language teachers have been using ICT for some time. In case of Practical English Language 1 – 4, the most frequently used source is video from the Internet. This practice is recommended by authors like Bull and Bell [3], Muniandy and Veloo [4], all of whom suggest various websites including, among others, Discovery Education, MSN Soapbox, Next Vista for Learning, OneWorld TV, or YouTube, which is praised by Mullen and Wedwick [5] as an unfathomable well of resources. Other authors do research on and write about using video clips in education. Among others, Canning-Wilson [6] maintain that students like language classes using video in class and lists other advantages of this practice. They claim that it provides visual stimuli and contextual clues, generates prediction, helps learners to predict information and infer ideas, allows the learner to see authentic body rhythm and speech rhythm in second language discourse. McKinnon [7] divides in-class activities involving video into pre-viewing, while-viewing and post-viewing tasks. Çakir [8] provides a list of techniques for using video in class, including active viewing, freeze framing and prediction, silent viewing, sound on and vision off activity, repetition and role-play, reproduction activity, dubbing activity, and follow-up activity.

The way English is taught at FIM can be labelled as Teaching English as a Foreign Language (TEFL), which is according to Griffith [9] the practice of linguistically educating those for whom English is not their native language. English is increasingly becoming the dominant medium in every domain of communication, including the tourism sector, within both local and global contexts, resulting in high demand for English speakers [10-11].

Mastering various English language skills is essential for people working in the tourism sector as it is the means for communicating with tourists and understanding cultural differences, and for increasing employees' job opportunities in this international industry [12]. English for tourism is viewed as an area of business English [13], and integrates business English and English for academic purposes by bridging workplace communication and classroom use [14]. It can be said that English for tourism deals with teaching the language needed for communication and interaction between people of different cultures in airports, tourism and travel firms, markets and hospitality (e.g. [15]). It seems that the knowledge of English should be one of the major criteria in hiring people in the tourism sector. As Ghany and Latif [16] claim, English is used as a lingua franca to communicate with international tourists in many countries. It is not surprising, therefore, that English is taught as a core subject at tourism and hospitality higher education, which applies to FIM, too.

As e.g. Prachanant [17] maintains, needs analysis plays a vital role in developing English for specific purposes curriculum. The results of Prachanant's study include the following problem areas: inability to understand foreigners' accents, inappropriate words and expressions, inadequate vocabulary, and lack of grammar knowledge. The author claims that tourism employees use English as a means to communicate, negotiate, and execute transactions with tourists. The findings showed that the majority of the tourism employees rated all four skills as highly needed. Most of them perceived speaking as the most important skill, followed by listening, reading and writing, respectively. Whereas speaking and listening are vital for face to face communication and reading is used because a lot of information sources are in English, writing is viewed as the least important skill by tourism employees (compare [17]).

2 Methods

At FIM, the language teachers agree that the students of Management of Travel and Tourism need to possess not only the four skills (speaking, listening, reading, writing) but should also be aware of the currently used specialized vocabulary applicable to their field of study and they should have a good knowledge of English grammar as both these skills are vital to their ability to communicate in the target language.

Still, the author focuses in particular on listening and speaking as tourism employees tend to consider these two skills to be the most important ones (e.g. [17]). It goes hand in hand with what Semradova and Hubackova [1], both of whom teach German at FIM, suggest, namely that in teaching the teacher must aspire to change the instructive concept of education, which leads to instant knowledge, into the communicative concept. They add that language teaching, which is clearly aimed at developing communicative competences, provides suitable conditions to make this turn.

In order to practise listening skills with the students of Management of Travel and Tourism, videos from the Internet have been used for almost ten years. As it was necessary to create worksheets for students to use before, while and after watching the video clips, a literature review of articles about using video recordings in class was employed. Another literature review looked into basic information on language teaching for travel and tourism students and employees. Then, the way of making worksheets used for practising listening and speaking was described.

The latter activity had one unexpected results. Transcripts of video recordings used in class provide material for studying the language of tourism. Collected transcripts can be used as a corpus for a subsequent frequency analysis resulting in making a list of currently used specialized vocabulary in the field of travel and tourism. Based on all the above-mentioned preliminary activities, new syllabi for teaching Practical English Language 1 – 4 have been made.

2 Results

2.1 Video

Video recordings from the Internet have been used in class at FIM since 2010. Video clips used in class are around four minutes long. This is because students would not pay attention to longer ones. Moreover, the video clips selected for teaching purposes are not monotonous. There are usually several different people speaking in them about a few topics, which makes the clips easier to follow. The language used in these clips is both standard and non-standard English. In fact, students can hear different "Englishes". As Crystal [18] claims, English has become a pluricentric language, which means that its norms and functions vary globally and students ought to be aware of this phenomenon. Moreover, the video clips help students improve their command of currently used English vocabulary for tourism. Therefore, all video clips selected for teaching purposes focus on travel and tourism. The most frequently used website is Deutsche Welle (DW), which contains hundreds of video clips in different languages. DW makes various series of clips, for instance Euromaxx City, presenting European cities as tourist destinations, but also shorter ones containing a limited number of parts, like Great Gardens, Holiday Challenge,

Market Tales, or Regional Success Stories, which provide interesting information about culture, history, politics, institutions and more.

As it has been mentioned above, there are different ways how to use video in class and it should always be well-prepared. The most suitable format for Management of Travel and Tourism students is a one-page worksheet (see Fig. 1) containing the video clip title, the website, a short text introducing the topic, key vocabulary, and exercises. Teachers use a two-page version with key. As of June 2018, there are more than one hundred worksheets to their corresponding English language video clips for the students of Management of Travel and Tourism. Another outcome are two textbooks English Listening Exercises [19] and English Listening Exercises II [20] with 40 and 50 worksheets, respectively. Seventy of these worksheets are meant for the students of Management of Travel and Tourism.

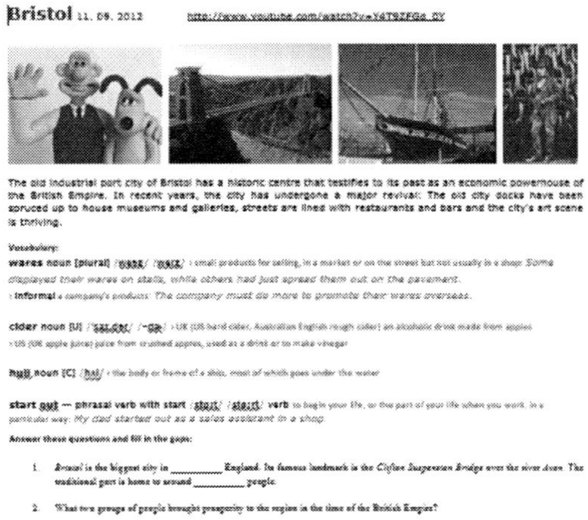
Bristol 11. 09. 2012

The old industrial port city of Bristol has a historic centre that testifies to its past as an economic powerhouse of the British Empire. In recent years, the city has undergone a major revival: The old city docks have been spruced up to house museums and galleries, streets are lined with restaurants and bars and the city's art scene is thriving.

Vocabulary:

wares noun [plural] small products for selling, in a market or on the street but not usually in a shop: *Some displayed their wares on stalls, while others had just spread them out on the pavement.*

informal a company's products: *The company must do more to promote their wares overseas.*

cider noun [U] UK (US hard cider, Australian English rough cider) an alcoholic drink made from apples

US (UK apple juice) juice from crushed apples, used as a drink or to make vinegar

hull noun [C] the body or frame of a ship, most of which goes under the water

start out — phrasal verb with start verb to begin your life, or the part of your life when you work, in a particular way: *My dad started out as a sales assistant in a shop.*

Answer these questions and fill in the gaps:

1. *Bristol* is the biggest city in ________ England. Its famous landmark is the *Clifton Suspension Bridge* over the river *Avon*. The traditional port is home to around ________ people.
2. What two groups of people brought prosperity to the region in the time of the British Empire?

Fig. 1. The layout of listening worksheets – an example.

2.2 Vocabulary and dictionaries

The approach to teaching vocabulary is threefold. First, vocabulary from the course book CAE Result and selected keywords included in the above mentioned worksheets to video clips are taught in classes and then tested. Second, transcripts of tourism-related video clips were analysed by means of the corpus approach and the results have been taken into consideration in selecting vocabulary taught in classes and/or meant for self-study and testing, too. Last but not least, close cooperation between the Department of Applied Linguistics and the Department of Recreology and Tourism resulted in determining the most important areas of vocabulary the students of Management of Travel and Tourism should be able to use.

Whereas the first group of vocabulary does not need any further explanation, the latter two do. The electronic version of video clip transcripts proved to be a good source of material to be analysed by means of the British National Corpus, more specifically through a word frequency analysis done by the Sketch Engine. As Kacetl and Klimova [21] inform, as of April 2015, the studied file contained 24,177 tokens. For instance, seven broad categories of frequently used nouns were identified: places (and place names), time, architecture, people, culture, food and drink, numbers. Consequently, the corresponding vocabulary is taught. First, geographical names, their spelling, pronunciation and the usage of the definite article are taught. Similarly, teachers also focus on the correct usage of time expressions, words related to architectural styles and their most significant features, or vocabulary categorised by arts (painting, sculpting, or music). Gastronomy is another broad area of lexical interest in the field of tourism. Last but not least, correct saying numbers is important, too (compare [21]).

So far, there have been created several short dictionaries (or lists of selected vocabulary), which are divided as follows: trees and bushes, flowers and plants, animals, fish, architecture, or culture. For teaching and learning purposes, all these dictionaries are bilingual. Nonetheless, picture dictionaries are sometimes used, too. The extent of compulsory vocabulary depends on the actual level of students who attend the class in question and common knowledge of the population of the Czech Republic.

2.3 Speaking

Once again, with respect to the content of various textbook for English in travel and tourism and in cooperation with the Department of Recreology and Tourism, twelve topic areas were identified as significant in relation to teaching English for the students of Management of Travel and Tourism. These topics were divided into four groups of three as there are four semesters for teaching them. The selected topics are as follows: Social Media in Tourism, Reasons for Travel, Trends in Tourism; Means of Transport – land, Means of Transport - air and water, Accommodation Facilities; Cultural Heritage (attractions and events), Natural Heritage, Gastronomy; Jobs in Tourism, Marketing in Tourism, Geographical Terms.

Means of Transport - land

1. What means of transport are depicted in the pictures below?
2. Which of these means of transport do you like most and why?
3. Which of the scenes is the closest to your ideal way of travelling?

Fig. 2. The layout of speaking worksheets – an example.

These topics for speaking are practised in a way similar to the collaborative task of either First Certificate in English (FCE) or Certificate in Advanced English (CAE) speaking examination. There are worksheets (see Fig. 2) with several questions and visual materials. Students work in pair and are should interact only with each other for several minutes, usually three to five.

2.4 Grammar

As for grammar, Practical English Language 1and Practical English Language 2, which are taught in the first year, focus on revising and consolidation of intermediate grammar. On the other hand, grammar taught in Practical English Language 3 and Practical English Language 4, which are studied by second-year students of Management of Travel and Tourism, is much more demanding.

The list of English grammar areas in Practical English Language 3 include: review of tenses, participle clauses, relative clauses, conditionals, wishes, gerunds or infinitives (verb patterns), modal auxiliary verbs, passive voice, distancing the facts (seem/appear), inversions (emphasis), avoiding repetition. The areas causing problems to students are particularly inversions and distancing the fact.

Practical English Language 4 contains the following English grammar areas: prepositions, real and unreal tense usage, collocations and similes (adverb collocations, intensifying adverbs), linking devices, discourse markers, conjunctions, articles (geographical expressions), adjectives – order, phrasal verbs, British English versus American English. Among these areas, there are more problematic issues like order of adjectives, articles, linking devices and discourse markers.

2.5 Syllabi

The new syllabi for Practical English Language 1 – 4 are primarily based on the course book CAE Result [21]. The whole textbook consist of 12 units. Consequently, three units are taught during each semester. The course book material is supplemented with additional materials created by teachers (see Fig. 1 and Fig. 2).

Each unit is taught in three ninety-minute long classes. Speaking exercises focused on selected topics are done in once in three classes. Listening exercises based on selected videos are done in every single class as well as grammar, the latter only in case of Practical English Language 3 – 4 courses. Practical English Language 1 – 2 courses contain intermediate grammar, which does not need such a thorough practice. Of course, there is a lack of time to do the grammar in detail. Students are therefore advised to self-study additional grammar exercises based on explanations, instructions and examples given in class.

3 Conclusion

Video clips (listening) as well as speaking exercises are done in more or less all classes, advanced grammar is taught in Practical English Language 3 – 4 courses. Dictionaries with specialised vocabulary are based on listening exercises and materials recommended by the Department of Recreology and Tourism. Some vocabulary is meant for self-study. All courses should be supported by corresponding e-learning courses, which will be created in the coming months.

The most significant outcomes achieved, based on the need to focus language classes on topics for state examinations from Management of Travel and Tourism, include the fact that there were identified ways of adjusting suitable and up-to-date material from the Internet, and the most frequently used vocabulary. Furthermore, as the students of Management of Travel and Tourism may undergo practical training in a geopark or national park, they ought to be aware of basic vocabulary linked to topics like geology, botany, or zoology, too. All in all, the most important skills to be worked on are listening, speaking and vocabulary. As it can be expected, all of these with special attention to the field of travel and tourism. Last but not least, advanced grammar should be taught, too. The reason being that it is desirable for most tourism employees to master the English language at the best possible level.

This article is supported by the Internal Grant Project of the Faculty of Informatics and Management, University of Hradec Kralove ID: 1903.

References

1. I. Semradova, S. Hubackova. Characteristics of Language Teaching for Travel and Tourism Management Students at the Faculty of Informatics and Management. *Procedia - Social and Behavioral Sciences*. **93**, 665-669 (2013) [online] Available at: <https://www.sciencedirect.com/science/article/pii/S1877042813033612> [Accessed 25 June 2018].
2. J. Kacetl, B. Frydrychova-Klimova. English Vocabulary in Video Clips on Travel and Tourism. *Procedia Social and Behavioral Sciences*, **182**, 364-368 (2015)
3. L. Bell, G. Bull. Digital video and teaching. Contemporary Issues in Technology and Teacher Education, **10(1)** (2010) [online] Available at: <http://www.citejournal.org/vol10/iss1/editorial/article1.cfm> [Accessed 5 April 2014].
4. B. Muniandy, S. Veloo. Managing and Utilizing Online Video Clips for Teaching English Language: Views of TESOL Pre Service Teachers. 2nd International Conference on Education and Management Technology, IPEDR, **13**, 173-178 (2011) [online] Available at: <http://www.ipedr.net/vol13/34-T00063.pdf> [Accessed 7 January 2012].
5. R. Mullen, L. Wedwick. Avoiding the Digital Abyss: Getting Started in the Classroom with YouTube, Digital Stories and Blogs, **82(2)**, 66-69 (2008) [online] Available at: <http://www.academia.edu/930232/Avoiding_the_digital_abyss_Getting_started_in_the_classroom_with_YouTube_digital_stories_and_blogs> [Accessed 5 April 2014].
6. C. Canning-Wilson. Practical Aspects of Using Video in the Foreign Language Classroom, The Internet TESL Journal, **VI**, No. 11 (2000) [online] Available at: <http://iteslj.org/Articles/Canning-Video.html> [Accessed 5 April 2014].
7. M. McKinnon. Teaching technologies: teaching English using video, (2011?) [online] Available at: <http://www.onestopenglish.com/support/methodology/teaching-technologies/teaching-technologies-teaching-english-using-video/146527.article> [Accessed 6 April 2014].
8. İ. Çakir. The Use of Video as an Audio-Visual Material in Foreign Language Teaching Classroom, The Turkish Online Journal of Educational Technology – TOJET October 2006 ISSN: 1303-6521 **5**, Issue 4 Article 9 (2006) [online] Available at: <http://www.tojet.net/articles/v5i4/549.pdf> [Accessed 5 April 2014].
9. S. Griffith. *Teaching English abroad: Talk your way around the world* (13th ed.). Oxford: Vacation Work (2014)
10. A. Khamkhien. Teaching English Speaking and English Speaking Tests in the Thai Context: A Reflection from Thai Perspective. English Language Teaching Journal, **3(1)**, 184-200 (2010) [online] Available at: <http://www.ccsenet.org/journal/index.php/elt/article/view/5253> [Accessed 25 June 2018].
11. P. Punthumasen. International Program for Teacher Education: An Approach to Tackling Problems of English Education in Thailand. (2007) [online] Available at:

<http://backoffice.onec.go.th/uploaded/Category/EngBook/ProblemEngEd13dec07-03-03-2011.pdf> [Accessed 25 June 2018].

12. D. Leslie, H. Russell. The importance of foreign language skills in the tourism sector: A comparative study of student perceptions in the UK and continental Europe. Tourism Management **27** 1397–1407 (2006). [online] Available at: <http://isiarticles.com/bundles/Article/pre/pdf/21038.pdf> [Accessed 25 June 2018].
13. B. Cho. Usefulness and Enjoyment of Simulation Activities for Tourism Major Students, Modern English Education, **6(1)**, 3-17 (2005) [online] Available at: <http://210.101.116.28/W_files/kiss61/1f100038_pv.pdf> [Accessed 25 June 2018].
14. A. C. Fuentes. The use of corpora and IT in evaluating oral task competence for tourism English, CALICO Journal, **22(1)**, 5-24 (2004)
15. K. Afzali, M. Fakharzadeh. A needs analysis survey: The case of tourism letter writing in Iran, ESP World, **8**, Issue 1 (22), (2009) [online] Available at: <http://www.esp-world.info. http://www.esp-world.info/Articles_22/PDF/A%20needs%20analysis%20survey.pdf> [Accessed 25 June 2018].
16. S. Y. A. Ghany, M. M. A. Latif. English language preparation of tourism and hospitality undergraduates in Egypt: Does it meet their future workplace requirements? Journal of Hospitality, Leisure, Sport & Tourism Education **11**, 93–100 (2012) [online] Available at: <http://daneshyari.com/article/preview/1011330.pdf> [Accessed 25 June 2018].
17. N. Prachanant. Needs Analysis on English Language Use in Tourism Industry. *Procedia - Social and Behavioral Sciences 66*, 117–125 (2012) [online] Available at: <https://ac.els-cdn.com/S187704281205238X/1-s2.0-S187704281205238X-main.pdf?_tid=73aa1fd9-66e0-40aa-b185-1aac6f96e09c&acdnat=1529923226_9b9e263cd0316f863e711bbe5b52a0fb> [Accessed 25 June 2018].
18. D. Crystal, *The Stories of English*. Overlook Press (2004)
19. J. Kacetl. *English Listening Exercises*. Hradec Králové: Gaudeamus (2011)
20. J. Kacetl. *English Listening Exercises II*. Hradec Králové: Gaudeamus (2014)
21. J. Kacetl, B. Klimova. English Vocabulary for Tourism – A Corpus-Based Approach. In: Christiansen H., Stojanovic I., Papadopoulos G. (eds) *Modeling and Using Context*. CONTEXT 2015. Lecture Notes in Computer Science, **9405**. Springer, Cham (2015)
22. K. Gude, M. Stephens. CAE Result. Oxford (2008)

Turkish adaptation of the comprehensive inventory of mindfulness experiences-adolescents: A reliability and validity study

Beyza Kırca[1,*] and *Halil* Ekşi[2]

[1]Faculty of Education, Department of Educational Sciences, Istanbul Sabahattin Zaim University, Istanbul Halkalı Campus 34303, Turkey
[2]Faculty of Education, Department of Educational Sciences, Marmara University, İstanbul Göztepe Campus 34722, Turkey

Abstract. In this study, it was aimed to adapt the Comprehensive Inventory of Mindfulness Experiences-Adolescents into Turkish, and to analyze the measure's validity and reliability. The sample of the study consisted of 415 high school students. Confirmatory factor analysis confirmed the original eight-factor structure. Cronbach alpha coefficient for the overall scale is 0.70 and the coefficients differ from 0.48 to 0.69 for the sub-scales. Corrected item-total correlations are found to be between 0.20 and 0.55. The convergent and divergent validity was examined and statistically significant relations were found. The study showed that the Turkish adaptation of The Comprehensive Inventory of Mindfulness Experiences-Adolescents is a reliable and valid scale for measuring mindfulness in adolescents.

1 Introduction

In recent years, interest in Eastern psychology has increased in the West, and it has been a time of increased work of investigating the effectiveness of the use of Buddhism-originated practices in clinical settings [1]. The discipline, which is described as the heart of Buddhism-based psychology and which constitutes its essence, is mindfulness [2]. The widespread use of mindfulness-based practices brought about various studies about the effectiveness of these practices and these understandings and practices, which are rooted in the East, have been transferred to the West with a trans-epistemological approach [1].

1.1 What is Mindfulness?

Mindfulness is one of the basic elements of Buddhism, which has a history of 2500 years [3]. With the use of Buddha, the word mindfulness got the meaning of memorizing certain facts, remembering and being aware of them. Of these facts, the most important ones are that all physical and mental phenomena are temporary and awareness must be applied

* Corresponding author: beyza.kirca@izu.edu.tr

repeatedly, to every life experience, from a moral point of view [4]. According to one of the pioneers of mindfulness-based therapeutic practices, Jon Kabat-Zinn [5], mindfulness is the state of awareness that arises as a result of paying attention to the moment deliberately and without judgement. According to another definition, mindfulness is a self-regulation of attention which enables the attention to focus on the moment of experience and to recognize the cognitive activities of oneself. This is the first component of mindfulness. The second component is to approach one's experiences, in the moment, with curiosity, open heartedness and acceptance [6].

Grossman [7], emphasizes that mindfulness makes it possible to move away from the daily affairs of everyday life and in that sense, it is a transformative pathway. While aiming to direct attention to the present time and to pursue it, mindfulness is not only about staying in the moment; at the same time, it regulates "how" to stay in the moment [8]. Jon Kabat-Zinn [9], summarizes the qualities which support and reinforces mindfulness as acceptance, non-judgemental stance, to let it go, patience, nonstriving, trust, a beginner's mind, gratitude and generosity. Wolf and Serpa [8], added curiosity, kindness and humor to these qualities.

1.2 Mindfulness in Adolescence

The elements of executive function, which is defined as the purposeful control of thoughts, actions and feelings; and which includes cognitive flexibility, inhibitory control and working memory [10], appear in infancy, show significant changes in the pre-school period and reach the point of competence in adolescence and young adulthood [11]. Along with the metacognitive abilities that develop during adolescence, when neural plasticity still occurs at high levels, the self-regulation processes of the person become more conscious and controlled, but again, arousal and anxiety can undermine these processes. At this point, it is stated that mindfulness may be a very appropriate intervention in self-regulation for adolescents with a balancing task by strengthening executive function and reducing the influence of emotions on the one hand [12].

Scientific research is important for ensuring that practices are not harmful and for the correct understanding of the mechanisms that enable change. Until recently, the interest was on whether those practices were effective or not. As studies increased the confidence in the efficacy of those psychological treatments, interest has shifted to investigating the processes [13].

A number of scales about mindfulness have been developed, some of which have been adapted to Turkish language. Due to the fact that mindfulness is a relatively new subject in the scientific world and it has a complex structure, criticisms have been made to the existing scales in the sense that multidimensional linear and additive models cannot encompass the synergistic and reciprocal structure of mindfulness [14] and that the investigation of the interaction of different dimensions will be useful for a better understanding of the mechanisms of change [15]. Considering these issues, it was stated that the measurement of mindfulness should be improved [16].

While there are many studies on mindfulness in adults, mindfulness in adolescents is a newly emerging field and there are a limited number of measurement tools [17]. Several mindfulness scales are available in Turkish but there isn't any mindfulness scale developed for adolescents. The importance of this study is that it is the first Turkish mindfulness inventory which was developed for adolescents and it enables examining separately the sub-factors mentioned as necessary to understand the mechanisms of change.

In this study, it was aimed to adapt the Comprehensive Inventory of Mindfulness Experiences-Adolescents, developed by Johnson, Burke, Brinkman and Wade [17] into Turkish and to analyze its validity and reliability.

2 Method

In this study the quantitative descriptive survey method was adopted accordingly with the aim of examining the statistical sufficiency of a measurement tool.

2.1 Participants

The sample of the study was selected according to the multistage sampling method from the high school students of Suleymanpaşa District of Tekirdağ Province during the 2016-2017 academic year. Firstly, all the schools in the Süleymanpaşa District were accepted as a cluster and then students from each school (Social Sciences High School, Science High School, Anatolian High School) were selected by simple random sampling technique according to their own ratios. For the criterion-dependent validity as well as for other analyzes, 94 students from a school (Anatolian Religous Studies High School) from the district of Güngören in Istanbul were included in the sample. The sample was constituted of 415 high school students (291 girls, 124 boys) from preparation class, 9th grade, 10th grade, 11th grade and 12th grade of four different schools types.

2.2 Measures

2.2.1 The Comprehensive Inventory of Mindfulness Experiences – Adolescents (Chime-A) (Turkish version)

It was originally developed by Johnson, Burke, Brinkman and Wade [17]. It is a modified version of the 37-item Comprehensive Inventory of Mindfulness Experiences developed by Bergomi, Tschacher and Kupper [18] for adults. The adolescent version consists of 25 items and 8 factors. The inventory is a 5-point Likert-type scale and high scores indicate a high level of mindfulness experience. There are 8 reverse items at the end of the scale. The eight factors are Awareness of Internal Experiences, Awareness of External Experiences, Acting with Awareness, Accepting and Non-judgemental Orientation, Decentering and Non-reactivity, Openness to Experience, Relativity of Thoughts and Insightful Understanding.

2.2.2 The EPOCH Measure of Adolescent Well-Being

The EPOCH Measure of Adolescent Well-Being was developed by Kern, Benson, Steinberg and Steinberg [19] and it was adapted to Turkish by Demirci and Ekşi [20]. The scale consists of 20 items and 5 sub-factors and also provides a total score of well-being. The sub-factors are Engagement, Perseverance, Optimism, Connectedness and Happiness. The internal consistency coefficient of the scale was reported to be .95 while the internal consistency coefficients of the subscales were reported to range from .72 to .88. Significant relationships have also been reported as a result of criterion-related validity analysis.

2.2.3 The Mindful Attention Awareness Scale

The scale was developed by Brown and Ryan [21] and it was adapted to Turkish by Özyeşil, Arslan, Kesici and Deniz [22]. It consists of 15 items. It is a 6-point Likert-type scale and has a one-factor structure. The internal consistency coefficient of the scale was reported to be .80 and item factor loadings were reported to range from .48 to .81. Test-retest correlation was .86. Significant relationships have also been reported as a result of criterion-related validity analysis.

2.3 Procedure

After obtaining the necessary permissions, for providing linguistic equivalence, four advanced level English speakers, two of whom were bilinguals, translated the inventory and then three academicians different from the translators, one in the field of English Language Teaching and the other two in the field of Counseling and Psychological Counseling, put the inventory into the final form. After the data were collected, missing data analysis was performed and it was observed that there was no participant with more than 5% of data loss. Data were completed with expectation maximization method in order to perform factor analysis. As a result of singular and multivariate normality evaluations, there were no outliers in terms of singular normality, whereas in the case of multivariate normality, 3 individuals were determined to be outliers and these 3 persons were left out of the analysis.

The suitability of the data for factor analysis was tested by Kaiser-Meyer-Olkin (KMO) coefficient and Bartlett test; and found to be suitable. Confirmatory factor analysis was performed and the results were analyzed according to the model fit indices. Criteria-related validity analysis was conducted within the scope of validity analysis. The Mindful Attention Awareness Scale [22] for convergent validity and The EPOCH Measure of Adolescent Well-Being [20] for the divergent validity were included for the analyses. Finally, Cronbach alpha coefficients, corrected item-total score correlations, and item mean scores of the lower 27% and upper 27% of the total scores of the factors were examined.

3 Results

3.1 Validity Analysis

3.1.1 Construct Validity

The suitability of the data for factor analysis was tested by Kaiser-Meyer-Olkin (KMO) coefficient and Bartlett test. The KMO coefficient is expected to be greater than .60 in terms of suitability for factoring. The Bartlett sphericity test examines whether there is a relationship between variables by looking at partial correlations and it is an evidence of normality [23]. The KMO coefficient was greater than .60 (KMO = .77) and the chi-square value was found to be statistically significant (Chi-Square $\chi 2$ =2368,55; p=0,00). This indicated that the sample size was sufficient and the normality of distribution assumption was satisfied.

3.1.2 Confirmatory Factor Analysis

Confirmatory factor analysis was applied to the data from 412 students using the IBM SPSS AMOS 23 program to analyze the construct validity of the Comprehensive Inventory of Mindfulness Experiences-Adolescents. The results of the analysis showed that the 8-factor structure is a good fit as it is in the original study ($\chi 2$= 568.143., sd= 247, $\chi 2$/sd= 2,3, RMSEA= ,056, GFI= .90, AGFI= .87, CFI= .85, SRMR= .074) according to the model fit indices.

3.1.3 Criterion-related Validity

The Mindful Attention Awareness Scale [22] was included to examine convergent validation and The EPOCH Measure of Adolescent Well-Being [20] was included to examine divergent validation with the CHIME-A Turkish version. The relationships were analyzed with Pearson correlation coefficient method and the results are shown in the Table 1 and 2.

Table 1. Convergent validity analysis with the MAAS

Subscale		MAAS
Awareness of Internal Experiences	r	-,113
	p	,277
Awareness of External Experiences	r	-,006
	p	,952
Acting with Awareness	r	,532*
	p	,000
Accepting and Non-judgemental Orientation	r	,311*
	p	,002
Decentering and Non-reactivity	r	,284*
	p	,006
Openness to Experience	r	,298*
	p	,004

*significant correlations with p<.01

As shown in the Table 1, positively significant correlations were found between the factors Acting with Awareness, Accepting and Non-judgemental Orientation, Decentering and Non-reactivity, Openness to Experience and The Mindful Attention Awareness Scale ($p<.01$). In other words the The Mindful Attention Awareness Scale shows good convergent validity with the Acting with Awareness ($r=.53$), Accepting and Non-judgemental Orientation ($r=.31$), Decentering and Non-reactivity ($r=.28$), Openness to Experience subscales ($r=.29$).

As shown in the Table 2, positively significant correlations were found between Awareness of Internal Experiences, Awareness of External Experiences, Accepting and Non-judgemental orientation, Decentering and Non-reactivity, Insightful Understanding subscales and The EPOCH Measure of Adolescent Well-Being total score and all of its subscales ($p<0.01$). Positively significant correlations were found between Acting with Awareness factor and all of the subscales of the EPOCH Measure of Adolescent Well-Being except the total score and the Engagement subscale ($p<0.01$). A negatively significant correlation was found between Openness to Experience and the Engagement subscale of the EPOCH Measure of Adolescent Well-Being ($p<0.01$). Finally, positively significant correlations were found between the Relativity of Thoughts factor and the Engagement, Optimism subscales of the EPOCH Measure of Adolescent Well-Being and its total score ($p<0.01$). These results indicate that the EPOCH Measure of Adolescent Well-Being shows good divergent validity with the Comprehensive Inventory of Mindfulness Experiences – Adolescents Turkish version.

Table 2. Divergent validity analysis with the EPOCH Measure of Adolescent Well-Being

Subscale		Engagement	Perseverence	Optimism	Connectedness	Happiness	EPOCH
Awareness of Internal Experiences	r	,174*	,151*	,139*	,171*	,137*	,210*
	p	,000	,002	,005	,000	,005	,000
Awareness of External Experiences	r	,233*	,256*	,227*	206*	,217*	,310*
	p	,000	,000	,000	,000	,000	,000
Acting with Awareness	r	-,011	,291*	,234*	,161*	,214*	,242*
	p	,825	,000	,000	,000	,000	,000
Accepting and Non-judgemental Orientation	r	,144*	,312*	,399*	,147*	,347*	,372*
	p	,003	,000	,000	,003	,000	,000
Decentering and Non-reactivity	r	,237*	,326*	,396*	,197*	,308*	,401*
	p	,000	,000	,000	,000	,000	,000
Openness to Experience	r	-,150*	,011	-,039	,007	-,017	-,052
	p	,002	,817	,432	,880	,725	,292
Relativity of Thoughts	r	,116*	-,004	,125	,077	,041	,099
	p	,018	,932	,011	,117	,411	,045
Insightful Understanding	r	,220*	,154*	,148*	,130*	,200*	,233*
	p	,000	,002	,003	,008	,000	,000

* Significant correlations with p<.01

3.2 Reliability Analysis

3.2.1 Internal Consistency Analysis

As a result of the internal consistency analyses, the Cronbach alpha value was found to be α=.70 for the overall inventory. The effect of any item that has a declining effect on the Cronbach alpha value was determined not to be greater than 0.003. The internal consistency reliability coefficient of .70 is regarded as sufficient for newly developed tests [23]. The internal consistency coefficients of the subscales were found to be α =.57 for Awareness of Internal Experiences, α =.67 for Awareness of External Experiences, α =.66 for Acting with Awareness, α =.48 for Accepting and Non-judgemental orientation, α =.60 for Decentering and Non-reactivity, α =.64 for Openness to Experience, α =.54 for Relativity of Thoughts and α =.69 for Insightful Understanding.

3.2.2 Corrected Item-Total Score Correlations

The corrected item-total score correlations, describe the relationship between the points taken from the items and the total score. Positive and high correlations of item-total scores are accepted as indicators of measuring similar behavior and high internal consistency of the test. .30 and above are indicative of good discrimination, values between .20 and .30 are indicative that the item may be protected if compulsory, and values below .20 are recommended not to be taken into the test [23]. The corrected item-total score correlations of the factors of the Comprehensive Inventory of Mindfulness Experiences – Adolescents-Turkish version were ranged between 0.55 (item 22) 0.20 (item 24). The values between

0.20-0.30 were protected because there were few items in the inventory and 3-4 items in each of the factors.

In the scope of the item analysis, the differences between the item mean scores of the lower 27% and upper 27% of the total scores of the factors were examined by independent samples t-tests and statistically significant results were found ($p<0.01$).

4 Discussion

In this study, it was aimed to adapt the Comprehensive Inventory of Mindfulness Experiences-Adolescents, developed by Johnson, Burke, Brinkman and Wade [17] into Turkish and to analyze the measure's validity and reliability. Confirmatory factor analysis was performed and the results were analyzed according to the model fit indices. Confirmatory factor analysis confirmed the original eight-factor structure. Therefore, the Comprehensive Inventory of Mindfulness Experiences-Adolescents (Turkish version) consists of 25 items and 8 factors. The inventory is a 5-point Likert-type scale and high scores indicate a high level of mindfulness experience. There are 8 reverse items at the end of the scale. The eight factors are Awareness of Internal Experiences, Awareness of External Experiences, Acting with Awareness, Accepting and Non-judgemental orientation, Decentering and Non-reactivity, Openness to Experience, Relativity of Thoughts and Insightful Understanding.

The internal consistency coefficient of the scale is α =.80 and the internal consistency coefficients of the sub-factors are between α =.48 and α =.69. Corrected item-total correlations are found to be between 0.20 and 0.55. The convergent and divergent validity were examined and statistically significant relations were found. The study showed that the Turkish adaptation of The Comprehensive Inventory of Mindfulness Experiences-Adolescents is a reliable and valid scale for measuring mindfulness in adolescents.

References

1. F. Didonna, *Introduction: Where new and old paths to dealing with suffering meet. In Clinical handbook of mindfulness* (Springer, New York, 2009)
2. N. Thera, *Satipatthana: The heart of Buddhist meditation: A handbook of mental training based on the Buddha's way of mindfulness* (Rider, 1962)
3. R. D. Siegel, C. K. Germer, A. Olendzki, *Mindfulness: What is it? Where did it come from?. In Clinical handbook of mindfulness* (Springer, New York, 2009)
4. B. Bodhi, CB, **12** (01), 19-39, (2011)
5. J. Kabat-Zinn, CP: Science and practice, **10**(2), 144-156, (2003)
6. S. R. Bishop, M. Lau, S. Shapiro, L. Carlson, N. D. Anderson, J. Carmody, G. Devins, CP: Science and practice, **11**(3), 230-241, (2004)
7. P. Grossman, Mindfulness, **1.2**, 87-97, (2010)
8. C. Wolf, J. G. *Serpa, A Clinician's Guide to Teaching Mindfulness: The Comprehensive Session-by-Session Program for Mental Health Professionals and Health Care Provider,* (New Harbinger Publications, 2015)
9. J. Kabat-Zinn, *Full catastrophe living: The program of the stress reduction clinic at the University of Massachusetts Medical Center,* (Delta, New York, 1990)
10. A. Miyake, N. P. Friedman, M. J. Emerson, A. H.Witzki, A. Howerter, T. Wagar, Cog. Psy., **41**, 49–100, (2000)
11. S. M. Carlson, Dev. Neuropsy., **28**, 595–616, (2005)

12. P. D. Zelazo, K. E. Lyons, Child Dev. Pers., **6,** 154–160, (2012)
13. R. A. Baer, Cont. Buddhism, **12**(01), 241-261, (2011)
14. M. Christopher, B. Gilbert, Faculty Scholarship (SPP), **2**, (2007)
15. T. A. Eisenlohr-Moul, E. C. Walsh, R. J. Charnigo Jr, D. R. Lynam, R. A. Baer, Assessment, **19**(3), 276-286, (2012)
16. P. Grossman, N. T. Van Dam, Cont. Buddhism, **12**(01), 219-239, (2011)
17. C. Johnson, C. Burke, S. Brinkman, T. Wade, Psy. Assessment, **29**(3), 264, (2007)
18. C. Bergomi, W. Tschacher, Z. Kupper, Diagnostica, (2014)
19. M. L. Kern, L. Benson, E. A. Steinberg, L. Steinberg, Psy. assessment, 28(5), 586, (2016)
20. İ. Demirci, F. Ekşi, Gençlik Araştırmaları Dergisi, 3(3), 9-30, (2015)
21. K. W. Brown,R. M. Ryan, J. of personality and social psy., **84**(4), 822, (2003)
22. Z. Özyeşil, C. Arslan, Ş. Kesici, M. E. Deniz, Eğitim ve Bilim, **36**(160), 224-235, (2011)
23. Ş. Büyüköztürk, *Veri analizi el kitabi*, (Pegem Akademi, Ankara, (2012)

Exploration of Climate Change in Architectural Design Studio

Eray Bozkurt[1,*]

[1]Izmir Yasar University, Department of Architecture, Selcuk Yasar Campus, 35310 Bornova-Izmir, Turkey

Abstract. Many researches reveal that climate change is a significant public issue. With the rising awareness of climate change impacts by both national and international bodies, building climate resilience has become a major goal for many institutions. This influence began to find path in architectural design education. Architectural design education is mostly given in the design studios. Each semester, the studio instructors prepare design briefs that need to be completed in a required period of time with given constraints. This is an opportunity for the design studios to adapt new theories and approaches like climate change into the design study. This article describes the experiences of the studio team after the design work proposed for climate. The study explains the transition from research to design stage. The studio tutors collected data after close observations on 42 students from Yasar University, School of Architecture third year studio.

1 Introduction

Conventional building systems of the Modern era have aimed to resist the outdoor environment, instead of being responsive to local climate conditions. Vernacular and traditional architecture styles before the Modern era used the local climate opportunities like the orientation towards the sun, the ratio of the building surface and the cultural traditions, etc., to sustain thermal comfort inside the spaces. The conventional building systems have ignored the relationship between human and nature. These systems have triggered today's energy-hungry construction methods.

Climate change is a recent topic that needs to be addressed much more in architectural design education to prepare students for the unforeseen challenges. It will become necessary that more schools will address this issue in their future curriculum and that more tutors acquire sufficient basic climate design knowledge to be able to guide such studios.

Climate resilience efforts cover social, economic, technological, and political strategies that are being implemented at all scales of society. From local community action to global treaties, addressing climate resilience is becoming a priority in urban environments. The key focus of climate resilience efforts is to address the vulnerability of human existence

* Corresponding author: eray.bozkurt@yasar.edu.tr

that communities currently have, concerning the environmental consequences of climate change. The possible relations between climate resilience and the built environment need to be explored for further adjustments.

2 Climate change and architectural design education

Current debates about climate change circle around the necessary speed of action to tackle with the problem. Some experts defend the fact that the idea of climate change is a hoax because of the lack of evidence. However, the catastrophic events acquiring around the world reveal that the transformation of climate has already began especially locations near the sea. The melting down the ice caps, have been changing the sea levels, which is a strong proof for the upcoming disasters of the future. As seen in Figure 1, Izmir bay area effected from excessive rain and storm, caused serious damages to the facilities near the sea.

Many disciplines still is not prepared enough for the climate change conditions; lack of knowledge and awareness about the topic. Many people have been ignoring the possible disasters, even the professionals in the built environment. The forefront role of the climate change has not developed mutual strategies to tackle the problem. Especially, architectural schools need to educate future architects to correct this situation.

Fig. 1. After heavy rain and storm, Izmir Kordon was underwater in February 2018.

Different disciplines are not yet ready for the transformations that climate change will create on the Earth Systems. Many communities are not paying enough attention to the problems about the changes that may occur in the near future.

Design studios are interdisciplinary zones to imply new theories and approaches. Altomente et al. mentioned the barriers for design education and discussed the insufficient training of experts and architects. Lack of knowledge transfer between professional domains reduce the quality of the architectural design education. Altomente et al. states that conventional teaching and learning approaches may not be appropriate for addressing education for sustainability. It will become necessary that more schools will address this issue in their future curricula and that more tutors acquire sufficient basic climate knowledge to be able to guide such studios [1].

1.1 The description of the studio

A studio is a workspace where students explore a set of skills with or without the presence of an instructor. Studios engage students with architectural knowledge using various projects.

Third year architectural design studio prepares students to organize their own architectural design building proposals. This is almost valid for all architectural schools around the world. The current case study took place in Yasar University, school of architecture. It's a young university that tries to evolve to sustainable education. For this purpose, the department wanted to change the conventional system. The studio coordinator suggested an atelier system, but the resources were not enough to run the system. Unit system suggested instead. Four units created to study the climate change topic in four different approaches. First unit titled 'Sustainable Heritage' asked to design an accommodation in a historical context. They concentrated more on preserving the historical buildings with adaptive reuse strategy. Second unit concentrated on the low carbon strategies. Students developed projects related with the topic. Third unit decided to build an expo center on a large-scale site. Forth group worked on energy efficiency subject. The case study will focus on second unit and 42 students' experiences.

1.2 The advantages of design brief

The brief describes the requirements of the design studio, is an opportunity to communicate with the students to describe the challenges and the limits of the proposed project. The theme of the project can be explained in the brief to guide the students for one semester period, let them focus on particular subjects, tools and methods. Second unit designed areas in Urla, related to their researches and site investigations. The design brief guided them through the beginning till end of the project. All the requirements and constraints described in the brief document. The requirements were given in the project brief before the course period starts. The aim of the brief is not to give all the clues, researches, notes and discussions done on the particular theme. The design tutors persuade students research and collect data for them to discover their own innovative ideas. The design tutors instructed not to give any design suggestions. However, their role is to evaluate whether their project worth doing for 14 weeks of studio period.

1.3 Adaptation of climate change

Another problem of the adaptation of the climate change is the level of knowledge of the students and tutors. The tutors hold strong backgrounds on building design, structure studies, energy efficiency and sustainable topics. These make them eligible for the current positions. Students before they attend the studio, they practiced how to present architectural idea and learned how to use visual presentations. Another advantage of the students is they studied 'Environmental Control Systems and Energy Efficiency' theory course before they enter the third-year level. They took also, 'Sustainable Buildings and the Cities' course parallel to their studio. Some theoretical backgrounds were discussed during the course hours and even some exercises introduced related with the sustainable topics. They used the outcomes of their designs in 'Computational Design' course, submitted all the technical issues about their projects.

3 Methodology

The purpose of third year studio is to provide students with experience designing in a sustainable approach. This study collects students' opinions about their learning experiences in the proposed unit system. It addresses the design studio learning experiences of third year architectural students in Unit 2. The basic structure of the unit persuaded students to form a group of three. In total, 14 groups conducted a site analysis in Urla / Izmir. To boost their creativity, the groups were free to find their own site and develop their own program considering climate change design brief and low carbon issue.

First four weeks, students conducted an intensive research on climate change and low carbon emissions. Before they visit the site in Urla, they excavated all historical and technical information about the surrounding. They checked whether there is any initiative about climate change ideas. There were three institutions; one is an underwater archaeological team from Ankara University, second is shipping technologies group from Dokuz Eylül University, and third group is aqua cultural engineering from Ege University. All the activities of these institutions provided necessary conditions for innovative design solutions.

After the completion of the research period, students prepared two design options for a chosen area. Most of the ideas emerged with the influences of the research and site investigations. Most of the fourteen group designed a research centre, under different themes.

Students got support from the desk critics given by their tutors. They can access the studio space 7 days and 24 hours. Lectures planned about the climate change, delivering expert opinions about the research field.

4 Results

Students' capability with the design process developed technical solutions by employing the fundamental processes associated with sustainable and innovative solutions. All units discussed the adaptation of climate change as a concept idea, learning experiences, and their design findings. Although students had personal views on the sustainable design and other subjects, they limited themselves to couple of influential ideas. Among all 42 students, they considered the ideas mostly related with sea level rising, renewable energy sources, food production and floating structures.

The findings show that the students described their learning experiences as innovative, improved their knowledge and design abilities. They claimed that they observed new viewpoints in their conceptual thinking.

5 Conclusions

Climate change is a significant issue, especially in the built environment. The concept idea of protecting the planet is out there since 1970s oil crisis. Since then, many efforts were given on energy and environment issues. Architecture Schools had contributed many attempts to transform the conventional building systems into more sustainable and environmentally friendly design solutions. However, the expected rapid development never happened due to lack of interest towards climate change.

The study proved that it is possible to adapt the climate change theme in a design studio. The consequences are the level of knowledge and expertise, finding the right tools for further investigations, and supporting long lasting design solutions.

References

1. Altomonte, S., Rutherford, P. & Wilson, R. Mapping the way forward: Education for sustainability in architecture and urban design. *Corp. Soc. Responsib. Environ. Manag.* **21,** 143–154 (2014).
2. Tascı, B. G. "Sustainability" Education by Sustainable School Design. *Procedia - Soc. Behav. Sci.* **186,** 868–873 (2015).
3. Stieldorf, K. Building physics, design, and the collaborative build: Sustainability and resilience in architectural education. *Archit. Des.* **88,** 102–109 (2018).
4. van den Branden, K. Sustainable education: Basic principles and strategic recommendations. *Sch. Eff. Sch. Improv.* **23,** 285–304 (2012).
5. Lenzholzer, S. & Brown, R. D. Climate-responsive landscape architecture design education. *J. Clean. Prod.* **61,** 89–99 (2013).
6. Stubbs, E. A., Zimmerman, A. R., Warner, L. A. & Myers, B. E. Reflecting on a multidisciplinary collaboration to design a general education climate change course. *J. Environ. Stud. Sci.* **8,** 32–38 (2018).
7. Jacobson, M. J. *et al.* Designs for learning about climate change as a complex system. *Learn. Instr.* **52,** 1–14 (2017).
8. Anthony, K. H. Journal of Architectural Education Designing for Diversity: Implications for Architectural Education in the Twenty-first Century Designing for Diversity: Implications for Architectural Education in the Twenty-rst Century. *J. Archit. Educ.* 257–267 (2016). doi:10.1162/104648802753657969
9. Birks, F. & Prater, K. Adapting to global change: Ageing, urbanisation and resilience. *Archit. Des.* **84,** 28–35 (2014).
10. Carmody, J. The role of architectural research centers in addressing climate change. *Enquiry* **6,** 33–39 (2009).
11. Loftness, V., Lam, K. P. & Hartkopf, V. Education and environmental performance-based design: A Carnegie Mellon perspective. *Building Research and Information* **33,** 196–203 (2005).
12. Stupar, A., Mihajlov, V. & Simic, I. Towards the conceptual changes in architectural education: Adjusting to climate change. *Sustain.* **9,** (2017).
13. Stevenson, F., Roberts, A. & Altomonte, S. Designs on the planet: A workshop series on architectural education and the challenges of climate change. in *PLEA 2009 - Architecture Energy and the Occupant's Perspective: Proceedings of the 26th International Conference on Passive and Low Energy Architecture* (2009).
14. McMahon, M. J., Dascalu, S. M., Harris, F. C., Strachan, S. & Biondi, F. Architecting climate change data infrastructure for Nevada. in *Lecture Notes in Business Information Processing* **83 LNBIP,** 354–365 (2011).
15. Zari, M. P. Biomimetic design for climate change adaptation and mitigation. *Archit. Sci. Rev.* **53,** 172–183 (2010).
16. Pedersen Zari, M. Bioinspired architectural design to adapt to climate change. *World Sustainable Building Conference SB08* (2008).

Adaptation of the proposed unit system for third year architectural design studio

Eray Bozkurt[1,*]

[1]Assist.Prof.Dr., Izmir Yasar University, Department of Architecture, Selcuk Yasar Campus, Bornova, Izmir -35310 Turkey

Abstract. Architectural design studios aim to teach students the fundamental design thinking. Well-structured studio may help the students to explore the global responses and develop projects focused on the current conditions of the society. This study focuses on the adaptation of the proposed unit system for third year architectural design studio. The adaptation process of the proposed unit system analyzed with the description of the previous system. This study discusses the positive outcomes of the new proposed unit teaching method at School of Architecture, Yasar University.

1 Introduction

Architectural studio is the main core of education for design based architectural schools. These architectural design studios are continuously exploring many learning environments. They have studio coordinators that provide organized working environment. It is hard to define the correct path to follow, however studio coordinators' attempts can provide new opportunities that will tackle the current needs of the constantly changing challenges in architectural design education.

Architectural design education has remained the same for many centuries [1], however there is a growing dissatisfaction appears to be the main concern of researchers and academicians around the world. In the study environment of architectural studio, design tutors play an important role to educate the registered university students. The minimum requirement expected from design tutors is their previous practice experiences. However, the academic requirements are more tough compared to their practice careers. The expected level of academic career involves being expert on a particular architectural subject, and good pedagogical mentality to teach architecture students. The quality of the tutors can increase the flexibility potential of the studio's main frame. If any modification occurs in the studio teaching system, they have many years of experiences to adapt themselves to new conditions. Students' reactions are more important at this stage. They can suffer from the unexpected changes in the studio environment.

* Corresponding author: eray.bozkurt@yasar.edu.tr

The current study was structured in Yaşar University's school of architecture in Izmir. The observation evaluated the students who attended third year studio in Spring 2018. They were the first group of students who experienced the proposed unit system teaching.

Conventional studio system given before Spring 2018 semester, focused on one particular type of design project. The brief was about the design of an education facilities in a given location. This approach was questioned in many occasions as placing studio away from the current debates in architectural education and society. The expectations of society is rapidly changing in many directions. The proposed unit system teaching has emerged to resolve the problems about how to adapt the studio environment to rapid changes in building industry and society. The proposed unit system provides variety of interesting subjects to choose from and give more freedom for the students to explore their abilities in a desired working environment.

2 Adapting the architectural education to current debates

It's not wrong to claim that sustainable, energy conscious and environmentally responsive design approaches have been contributing to reduce the carbon emissions. The sustainable design approaches have been in action since 1970s oil crisis, contributed in many occasions to lower the carbon emissions. It's needless to say that sustainable, environment and energy topics will be valid for the next generations. Any architectural school should develop curriculum that considers sustainable strategies, climate change, energy efficiency, waste management, resource deflation etc.

Generally architectural education consists of two parts. The first part is the studio-based design education where students explore their design projects and implement practical solutions with their theoretical background. The second part is the theoretical part, which improves the students' knowledge about the architectural discipline. The flexibility of the architectural studio environments can help to adjust to study the current debates in international society.

3 Architectural studio education

Architectural schools are organizations that are frequently quite stable in the short term, but inevitably evolving over the longer term in response to changes in conditions. Many architectural schools have launched programs aiming to imply changes in the theoretical lessons and design studios. There are various debates for changing non-renewable with more renewable and efficient teaching methods. The conventional teaching and learning approaches may not be appropriate for addressing the current undergraduate education.

The discussions on the curriculum changes is always valid in Turkey because of country's dynamic nature. Any new developments can find response from communities; however it can fade away very quickly to open a newer development. Architectural education is also in constant change due to the expectations of communities. Students before they enter the university, don't have right and sufficient skills to complete the undergraduate curriculum. Universities' architecture schools facing this problem, spend most of their tutors' time and resources to train students to tackle undergraduate curriculum. Another part of the problem is, students who will attend third year design studio, entered the university with the Turkish national exam. They needed to collect enough scores to be successful candidates. They had sufficient skills in science and math subjects, however the exam system does not provide valuable information about their art and entrepreneur skills. After entering the university, these skills were triggered by the first-year design tutors. When students reached to their third-year level, they were all ready to work on full program architectural design projects. This effects the universities main targets, leaving less time for research activities till their graduations.

The proposed unit system aims to trigger research capacity of the students and help them to experience more innovative design solutions. This way, more time will be given to the research related study environment. That improves the education quality of architectural schools.

3.1 Conventional studio description

Conventional architectural studio is influenced from Bauhaus traditions and pick adaptations on the way. Architectural schools may change the original structure depending on the geographical location and their communities' expectations. Before Spring 2018, architecture school at Yasar University structured its third year conventional architectural studio with the strategy on a design program dedicated to one particular building type; education facility. The brief asked students to design a school project for a given location. The minimum requirements were the spatial sizes and their functions provided to the students. Students distributed among the design tutors randomly and were reviewed by at most two tutors till the end. During the design period, students may focus more on representation and improvements of their proposed education facility rather than showing efforts on the new design and construction developments. This approach weakened the strength of their projects innovative nature. During the assessment period, the external examiners gave comments to students' projects without grading them. The group tutors gave their own decisions with or without considering the contributions of external examiners. The projects' performances were under the control of the groups' design tutors. This leads the speculation about the tutors' attitude. At some stages of the projects, it's claimed by some students that the design tutors' personal interests helped students to develop their ideas.

3.2 Proposed unit system

The aim of the study is to analyse the adaptation of the unit system strategy in third year architectural studio in Izmir Yasar University. The university's physical environment is not sufficient to support atelier system, existing spaces are shared by different departments. The atelier system needs studio spaces for each design topic that can be used by only by architecture students, twenty-four hours in a day and seven days a week. The third-year coordinator checked the physical conditions and decided not to proceed on the atelier system. Instead of the atelier system, the students were divided into four parts, represented as unit. These four units explored the current trends in the architecture field. The course coordinator organized the fourteen weeks of the studio period, depending on the submission requirements. Each unit had two instructors with similar academic subjects. They controlled their units' learning environment and helped students to explore various design thinking. The course coordinator organized the assessment process and the correlations between the units according the given targets. The site visit was conducted at the beginning of the semester. Before the site visit, the students researched the area. Later, they combined their knowledge with on-site investigations. The students formed a group of three, in the end there were 56 groups in total. The design programs for each group were emerged from their researches on their interests and site investigation reports. In the semester plan, the students experimented ideas on the design concept, structure, environmental control systems, materials, and presentation techniques. Each unit was assessed by its two-unit instructors. During the major assessment periods like open juries, other unit instructor and an external examiner joined to the unit team. The course coordinator assigned external examiner from the professional practice who had various expertise on the construction and design of influential buildings. This approach helped students to interact with the professional people in the architecture field. Four jury members at the end, formed an assessment panel with equal amount of grading percentage. As a result, students made less complaints about their tutors being not fair to them.

3.3 Discussion

Design teaching is given in the architectural design studios planned in a one semester or yearly. The whole education weeks in a semester period, planned to organise the students to trigger different approaches of design solutions. The conventional method brought limitations and constraints on the design program possibilities. The conventional method expected students to concentrate over the guidelines given by the instructors more strictly. The new teaching approach has triggered the creativity of design thinking process. The students explored the different perspectives of the design approaches and dedicated more on their researches.

The students' creative thinking process were observed to measure the opportunities of the new method. In all cases, the development of the design thinking process is key to any similar studies.

4 Conclusion

Architecture field is an extremely complex professional that it's hard to predict where architects' role will be useful on different types and scaled projects. One day it's possible for an architect to design a concert hall or next year, will put all the efforts on climate research center project. The quality of the university education at that level comes to discussion. If one to describe a successful architecture school, definitely is a place that provides the necessary skills and research abilities for its graduates. Architecture school that influences future architects to work in harmony with other professionals, can make their graduates more competent in international society. Architectural design studio environment is a valuable asset for school of architectures to increase the quality of their curriculums. However, they need more interdisciplinary connections and researches to handle the sustainability in building industry. However, the real problem is to adapt a suitable teaching method to challenge current trends.

It's crystal clear that architectural studios must adapt sustainable topics into their learning environment. Many experts claimed that sustainability is the only model for the next generation.

References

1. Bashier, F. Reflections on architectural design education: The return of rationalism in the studio. Front. Archit. Res. **3**, 424–430 (2014).
2. Haase, J. Changing Trends in Architectural Design Education. in The International Conference of the Center for the Study of architecture in the Arab Region 520–534 (2006).
3. Lueth, P. L. O. The architectural design studio as a learning environment: A qualitative exploration of architecture design student learning experiences in design studios from first- through fourth-year. 238 (2008). doi:10.1017/CBO9781107415324.004.
4. Riley, S. et al. Designing the future - are our university staff up to it? 9th International

Conference on Engineering & Product Design Education: Shaping the Future? 361–366 (2007).

5. Aydemir, Z. Connotations in Architectural Design Education. in Contemporary Discussions and Design Methodologies in Architecture ARCHDESIGN '14 / Architectural Design Conference Proceedings 91–100 (2014).
6. Gerards, S., Bleeckere, S. De & (Hasselt University, Hasselt, B. Narrative Thinking in Architectural Education. in ARCC/EAAE 2014 | Beyond Architecture: New Intersections & Connections Methods: Agents of Change in Changing Paradigms. Scientifi c, Technological, Strategic, Intuitive, and Pragmatic. 305–311 (2005).
7. Cheng, R. Designers designing design education. J. Archit. Educ. **68**, 12–14 (2014).
8. Kahvecioğlu, N. P. Architectural design studio organization and creativity. A|Z ITU J. Fac. Archit. **4**, 6–26 (2007).
9. Savage, K. & O'Brien, M. Architectural education-studio based learning. DS 38 Proc. E DPE 2006, 8th Int. Conf. Eng. Prod. Des. Educ. 87–94 (2006).
10. Ascher, B. E. The bauhaus: Case study experiments in education. Archit. Des. **85**, 30–33 (2015).
11. Ibrahim, N. L. N. & Utaberta, N. Learning in Architecture Design Studio. Procedia - Soc. Behav. Sci. **60**, 30–35 (2012).
12. Seelig, M. & Seelig, J. Architectural education: On flies, bees, and the architectural studio. Archit. Rec. **173**, 51–55 (1985).
13. Mathew, L. Future Directions in Architectural Design Education-Parametric Modeling. QRS Repos. 13 (2011). doi:10.5339/qnrs.2011.13

How the seventh grade students visualize atomic structure and models

Rüveyda Yavuz [1,*], and *Funda* Savaşcı-Açıkalın[2]

[1]Graduate Student, Istanbul University-Cerrahpaşa Graduate School Istanbul Turkey
[2]Associate Professor, Istanbul University-Cerrahpaşa Hasan Ali Yucel Faculty of Education, Istanbul Turkey

Abstract. The purpose of this study is to examine how the seventh-grade students visualize the atomic structure and models in their minds. The problem of the study is "How do the seventh grade students visualize the atomic structure and models?" This study is conducted with 25 seventh-grade students in a state school, Bursa. Qualitative research methodology was adopted in the study. As data collection tools, worksheets were collected via four different activities by the researcher. Data collection process took two weeks (eight lessons). Worksheets consist of different questions about atom and structure and also atom models. For the validity and objective evaluation of the worksheets, an analysis schema was prepared for four different activities by a subject instructor and two science teachers with two or four years teaching experiences. Analysis schema and worksheets were re-evaluated by the science teacher with three years of teaching experiences. Consequently, students' visualization of the atom structures do not match with the scientific models. And also, students confuse the basic concepts about atomic structure.

1 Introduction

Science requires more thinking and comprehension activity because it contains abstract concepts to understand difficulty [1]. The particulate nature of matter is one of the abstract concepts that need to be learned precisely in chemistry at the elementary level and forms the basis of chemistry education [2]. It is difficult for middle school students to teach atom and structure which is abstract and difficult to learn [3]. Since atoms and atoms models are abstract concepts, it is important to identify how students visualize these concepts in their minds and compare them with the scientific models [4]. Moreover, since they are fundamental concepts, learning them are required for understanding other concepts in science [5]. It is easily seen that students also try to create concepts related to this subject through their own experiences and prior knowledge in their minds [6]. Much information about atomic and structure is on the submicroscopic level, so it is not accessible for direct observation [7].

* Corresponding author: fsavasci@istanbul.edu.tr

1.1 Multiple Representations

Students should associate three levels of representation, macroscopic, submicroscopic and symbolic, with each other properly in order to develop a scientific understanding of this subject [8]. Macroscopic levels refer to the visible aspects of the material; submicroscopic levels provide information about the atomic, molecular, and kinetic aspects of matter, and also symbolic levels include the use of symbols such as formulas [7]. Students use macroscopic features to explain submicroscopic levels, so they cannot differentiate between macroscopic and submicroscopic ones each other [9]. Thus, students have difficulty to visualize atomic structure and models due to the relationship between multiple representations [10]. Furthermore, they have many misconceptions about these abstract concepts such as atom models, protons, neutrons, electrons, ions and models have been identified in the literature [11-17]. Some of misconceptions are listed in Table 1 and Table 2.

Table 1. Misconceptions about atomic structure

Misconceptions	References
Electrons and protons have the same weight.	Valanides, 2000
Electrons are heavier and smaller than proton.	Olsen,2002
Copper atoms are different from each other.	Olsen,2002
Negative charges in atoms are less than positive charges.	Gilbert et all,2004
Electron and neutron in the nucleus, the proton is in orbit.	Gilbert et all,2004
The atom can be seen under a microscope.	Coll&Taylor,2007
Atom particles do not move.	Coll&Taylor,2007
The atom cannot be broken apart, because the nuclei cannot be broken.	Papageorgiou et al.,2016
Atom is the smallest structure of matter.	Papageorgiou et al.,2016
If the material is compressed, the shape of the atom changes.	Kapıcı&Akçay,2016
Atom is alive because the electrons move.	Mishra,2017
Atom is small enough to be visible.	Mishra,2017
Electron and proton in the orbit, neutron in the nucleus.	Fitriza & Gazali,2018

According to other studies in the literature [9-10], [18-28].on the teaching of atom and structure, limited number of studies are about not only atom and structure but also atom models. And also, they do not include all learning outcomes. For these reasons, it is found to have no effect on the students' learning at the expected level. Thus, this study is important that it includes both the atomic structure and models with considering both the basic knowledge and learning outcomes, as well as multiple representations. Overall, the aim of this study is to examine how the seventh-grade students visualize the atomic structure and models in their minds. And the research question is 'How do the seventh grade students visualize the atomic structure and models?'

Table 2. Misconceptions about atom models

Misconceptions	References
Atom is square.	Bajah & Teibo,2000
Atom is moving wave.	Bajah & Teibo,2000
Atom is straight.	Park & Light,2009
Atom looks like clouds.	Park & Light, 2009
According to the Bohr Atom model, the electrons in the H atom move freely in the nucleus and resemble the Grape Cake model.	Kahraman & Demir, 2011
According to the Modern Atom model, electrons in the H atom are drawn as moving particles in the orbits around the nucleus and mixed with the Bohr Atom model.	Kahraman & Demir, 2011
According to the Bohr Atom model, protons are at the center, and according to Modern Atom model, protons are distributed in equal amounts everywhere.	Kahraman & Demir, 2011
Atomic structure resembles the solar system. Accordingly, the sun is similar to the atomic nucleus, the planets are similar to electrons, and they act in certain orbits like electrons.	Kapıcı & Akçay, 2016
The atom is similar to a globe with a core in it. Like the Earth, it is round and central. The Moon, which is the world's satellites, resembles electrons. In this model, the number of electrons is low and the atomic nucleus and electron are under the same shell.	Kapıcı & Akçay, 2016
The atomic structure resembles a spinner, with the nucleus in the middle and round, with all of the electrons revolving around this nucleus in a single orbital granular shape.	Papageorgiou et all,2016
Atom looks like the Earth.	Mishra, 2017
Atom is square.	Fitriza & Gazali, 2018

2 Methodology

Qualitative research methodology was adopted in the study [29]. This study is conducted with the 25 seventh-grade students as 10 girls and 15 boys in state school, Bursa. As data collection tools, worksheets were collected via four different activities organized by the researcher. Worksheets consist different questions about atom and structure and also atom models. Data collection process took two weeks (eight lessons).

2.1 Analysis

For the validity and objective evaluation of the worksheets, an analysis schema was prepared for four different activities by a subject instructor and two science teachers with two or four years teaching experiences. Analysis schema and worksheets were reevaluated by the science teacher with three years of teaching experiences.

3 Findings

Table 3. Findings about students' models of particles in atom

		Scientific		Partial		None	
		f	%	f	%	f	%
Initial	Shape	16	**64**	6	24	3	12
	Representation	19	**76**	3	12	3	12
	Space	13	**42**	6	24	6	24
	Explanation	2	8	1	4	22	**88**
	Shape	4	16	17	**68**	4	16
Heated	Representation	5	20	15	**60**	5	20
	Space	2	8	1	4	22	88
	Explanation	1	4	1	4	23	92
	Shape	6	24	15	**60**	4	16
Bent	Representation	8	32	13	**42**	4	16
and	Space	5	20	1	4	19	**76**
Twisted	Explanation	5	20	3	12	17	**68**

As seen in Table 3, students have difficulty in explaining the shape and size of the change in their particles by heating or bending the material. For example, the percent of students who scientifically explain the particles of copper plate before heating is 64% while the percentage of students who scientifically explain the shape of the particles is 16% when the copper plate is heated and the percentage of the students who scientifically explain the shape of the particles scientifically when the plate is bent is 24%. And also, percentage of students who scientifically explain the particle size of the copper plate before heating is 76% while the percentage of the student who scientifically explains the size of the particles is 20% when the copper plate is heated and 32% of the students explain the shape of the particles when the plate is bent scientifically. On the other hand, students also often have difficulty explaining the space between particles initial and after the material is heated and bent. Moreover, 42% of students explain the gap between pre-heated particles of copper plate and the 8% of students explain the gap between particles when the copper plate is heated and 20% of students explain the gap between particles when the plate is bent scientifically.

Table 4. Findings about students' design of atom models

	Scientific		Partial		None	
	f	%	f	%	f	%
Shape	14	**64**	2	8	9	36
Use of Imagination	14	**64**	11	44	0	0
Explanation	3	12	3	12	19	**76**

Table 4 shows that, when asked to design atom models, 64% of students design scientific models in terms of shapes, while 36% design non-scientific models. In terms of use of creativity, 64% of the students used their creativity while designing the model, partially using 44%. And also, 76% of the students did not adequately explain these atom models.

Table 5. Findings about students' drawings of atomic structure

	Scientific		Partial		None	
	f	%	f	%	f	%
Shape	7	28	8	32	10	**40**
Name of particle	7	28	2	8	16	**64**
Color	3	12	0	0	22	**88**
Mobility	0	0	0	0	0	0
Explanation	0	0	0	0	0	0

Table 5 revealed that the student who explains shape and particle name scientifically is 28% while the ratio of students who do not base on scientific explanation is 40% in shape and 64% in name of particle. While 88% of the students are not scientific in their atomic and structure models, only 12% can be considered scientific. It has been determined that students are not sufficient in general explanations of mobility and so, models about atomic structure seem to be not scientific.

Table 6. Findings about students' atom models

	Scientific		Partial		None	
	f	%	f	%	f	%
Name of Atom Model	23	**92**	2	8	0	0
Name of Scientist	22	**88**	3	12	0	0
Model Drawing and Explanation	9	36	15	**60**	1	4
Consistent with Textbook	16	**64**	8	32	1	4

As seen in Table 6, the atomic models that 92% of the students made are scientific, not the non-scientific model. Moreover, 88% of the students state the name of the scientist scientifically. Although 60% of the students draw the model correctly, they do not base on any scientific explanation. In addition, it is realized that 64% of the students draw the same models as the models in the textbook.

4 Discussions

Based on these findings, students have some misconceptions about atomic structure because the phenomenon of atom is carried out in the submicroscopic level, it is difficult for students to comprehend and to create a mental model [30].Similarly, students cannot explain the atom models properly and they have some misconceptions about the model. Since they use macroscopic features to explain submicroscopic events, so they can not differentiate between macroscopic and submicroscopic ones each other [9].When the explanations about atomic structure of students are investigated, it is stated that students try to explain the concepts related to this subject through their own experiences and prior knowledge in their minds [31]. Also, in the study of Baybars & Küçüközer [11] listed that a lot of misconceptions about the topic of atom such as atom models, proton, neutron, and electron.

5 Conclusion

It is found that students have difficulty in explaining the space between particles in the case that before and after the material was unheated and bent and twisted. Moreover, it is defined that due to the heating or bending of the material, they have some misconceptions in terms of size and shape such as the adhesion of the atoms to each other and the decrease in the number of atoms. On the other hand, even though most of the students (64%) design scientific atomic models as shapes, but a large majority (76%) are not adequately enough to explain these models or explain some misconceptions such as the charge of proton is – and the ones of neutron is +. It is discovered that after the atomic models are introduced to the students, the vast majority (92%) made atom models scientifically and also although the majority of the drawn models (64%) are the same as the visuals in the textbook; they have no scientific knowledge such as what it is or how it is developed. At the end of the research, the following suggestions can be made:

1. Since there is no difference in conceptual learning of students and it is difficult to change this with a short term, long-term studies should be designed to make difference in conceptual learning of students.
2. Students should make the atom models thanks to student-centered activities.
3. Students should design the atomic structure and models by animating or simulating to learn through experience.

References

1. A. Ayas, B. Coştu, *Yeni Bin Yılın Basında Fen Bilimleri Eğitimi Sempozyumu* (İstanbul, 2001)
2. Z. Yaseen, S. Akaygün, Mehmet Akif Ersoy Üni. Eğt. Fak. Der. **40**, 469 (2016)
3. G. Demircioğlu, M. A. Aydın, H. Demircioğlu, Bayburt Üni. Eğt. Fak. Der. **6**, 70 (2012)
4. G. Tsaparlis, G. Papaphotis, Int. Jour. of Sci. Edu. **31**, 895 (2009)
5. M. Duran, B. Ballıel, S. Bilgili, *2nd International Conference on New Trends in Education and Their Implications*. (Ankara, 2011)
6. D. L. Gabel, Jour. of Che. Edu., **70**, 193 (1993).
7. D. L. Gabel, *International Handbook of Science Education* (London,1998)
8. J. Gobert, L. O'Dwyer, P. Hortwiz, B. Buckley, S. T. Levy, U. Wilensky, Int. Jour. of Sci. Edu. **33**, 653 (2011)
9. D. Yeğnidemir, *Yüksek lisans tezi. Gazi Üniversitesi*. (Ankara, 2000)
10. S. T. Bajah, B. O. Teibo, *Senior Secondary Chemistry Book* (Longman, 2000)
11. M. G. Baybars, H. Küçüközer, Eği. ve Öğr. Araş. Der., **3**, 405 (2014)
12. Z. Fitriza, F. Gazali, F. (2018). Jour. of Phys. Con. Seri, **1013**, 87 (2018).
13. R. E. Mayer, R. Moreno, (2002). Edu. Psyc. Rev., **1**, 87 (2002)
14. B. Mishra, Int. Jour. of Adv. Res., **5**, 1957 (2017)
15. S. Özgür, A. Bostan, E-Jour. of New Wor. Sci. Aca, **3**, 214 (2007)
16. G. Papageorgiou, A. Markos, N. Zarkadis, Sci. Edu. Int., **27**, 464 (2016)
17. N. Valanides, Che. Edu.: Res. and Pra., **1**, 249 (2000)
18. A. K. Griffiths,K. R. Preston, Jour. of Res. in Sci. Teac., **29**, 611 (1992)
19. A. G. Harrison, D. F. Treagust, Sci. Edu., **80**, 509 (1996)
20. C. Tsai, Int. Jour. of Sci. Edu., **22**, 285 (2000)
21. C. Nakiboğlu, Gazi Üni. Eğt. Fak. Der., **21**, 131 (2001)
22. R. V. Olsen, Int. Jour. of Sci. Edu., **24**, 565 (2002)
23. H. Tezcan, H., Ç. Salmaz, Gazi Üni. Eğt. Fak. Der., **25**, 41 (2005)
24. N. Kavak, Gazi Üni. Eğt. Fak. Der., **27**, 327 (2007)
25. R. K. Coll, N. Taylor, Res. in Sci. and Tech. Edu., **19**, 171 (2001)
26. H. Tezcan, T. Çelik, Türk Eğt. Bil. Der., **7**, 49 (2009)
27. E. J. Park, G. Light, Int. Jour. of Sci. Edu., **31**, 233 (2009)
28. S. Kahraman, Y. Demir, Erzincan Üni. Eğt. Fak. Der., **13**, 173 (2011)
29. J. W. Creswell, *Eğiten Kitap* (Ankara, 2013)
30. F. Kaya, F. (2010). *Yayımlanmamış Yüksek Lisans Tezi Pamukkale Üniversitesi* (Denizli,2010)
31. H.Ö. Kapıcı, H. Akçay, Euro. Jour. of Edu. Stu., **2**, 43 (2016)

Simulation-based first aid training of students of health sciences

Brigita Marc[1,*], *Eva* Dolenc[2], and *Damjan* Slabe[1]

[1]University of Ljubljana, Faculty of Health Sciences, Zdravstvena pot 5, 1000 Ljubljana, Slovenia
[2] University of Ljubljana, Faculty of Health Sciences, Zdravstvena pot 5, 1000 Ljubljana, Slovenia

Abstract. To achieve desired goals in the first aid training, we can use different learning methods. We can choose simulation, which represents one of the active forms of learning. Within the simulations, we can select simulated scenarios to bring more reality into the learning process. With our research we wanted to evaluate the effectiveness of scenario-based first aid training. We included 65 students of Faculty of Health Sciences, University of Ljubljana. The experimental group was unlike the control group exposed to scenario-based learning during one-week first aid training. We collected the data with a questionnaire and evaluation paper, which enabled us to assess the students during the practical test. Our research has shown that pre-training with simulated scenarios improves provided first aid in case of a simulated accident. Keywords: scenarios; teaching; active learning; first aid

1 Introduction

The purpose of first-aid training is to increase the learners' knowledge, skills, confidence and willingness to apply first aid competencies [1]. In order to achieve the aims and objectives of training, different approaches and learning methods can be used. The traditional teaching methods are not always the most appropriate and effective [2], because they rarely include active forms of learning and thus do not fully involve participants in the learning process. Most adults find it easy to accept information in interactive environments [3] and when they are actively involved in the learning process [4]. The advantages of active forms of teaching and learning in comparison with more passive ones are primarily in achieving better results in terms of acquired knowledge and skills, increased motivation for learning and better critical thinking [5,6,7]. Simulations are one of the options that may offer an additional benefit to traditional training [8].

Simulations are one of the active forms of learning [9] that combine problem-based and experiential learning. It is an innovative approach to learning and teaching [10], supported by the principles of adult education [3], as it meets the adult learners' needs [11]. Simulations are based on situations and events from real life and enable learning in a safe, controlled environment [12]. The purpose of simulation-based learning is to achieve specific learning objectives [13]. Simulations offer a valuable learning experience [14] and

* Corresponding author: slabed@zf.uni-lj.si

enable learners to acquire relevant knowledge and skills, encourage critical thinking [15], improve skills and, consequently, self-confidence [16,17]. They also help in reducing the gap between theory and practice [18,19]. Simulations enable a better awareness of the complexity of emergencies and help to facilitate the retrieval of essential information when necessary [20]. They allow a systematic approach, adapting the learning process to the individual and his or her knowledge [15] and repeated implementation until the required level of knowledge or acquired skills and procedures have been reached [8,9]. Implementation of simulations in the educational program may represent a challenge, but its advantages outweigh the disadvantages [19]. The use of simulations in teaching basic resuscitation procedures is supported by the European Resuscitation Council guidelines for resuscitation 2015 [21], as they contribute to better knowledge and skills in comparison with training without simulations. Research also suggests that nursing students want more simulations for learning skills [19]. They are also mentioned in the International guidelines for first aid and resuscitation as an effective method of teaching [22].

Scenarios can form the basis of training through simulations [23,24]. Scenarios are structured descriptions of events or problems from the real world. They allow learners to deepen into a specific real-life problem and to find solutions to this problem. They must use their already acquired knowledge, cognitive and social skills, and solve the problem or task [25]. It is a method that allows learning in an authentic context [26], and tries to put learners in a more active role [27]. Scenarios can create a very rich learning environment [28].

The purpose of simulation-based training is to learn specific concepts or procedures [29]. Scenario-based simulation training supports the development of knowledge and skills [30], enables the adoption of certain procedures and strategies for problem solving [31], in-depth understanding [27] and the development of competences [28]. At the same time, learners become more confident in providing first aid [30]. When faced with real injuries, it will be easier for them, their approach will be less emotional and adopted measures more professional and more effective [32]. Through scenarios, we can also expose or present possible risks that could occur in certain situations [28].

Designing and preparing scenarios are not simple tasks [26]. It is necessary to define how the process will proceed, describe the activity of the participants in the training, determine the roles they will take and the tools they will need [26,31]. It is important to provide the most realistic environment for students to get accustomed to such situations [12]. A key consideration in any simulation activity is a debriefing that should follow immediately after the end of the scenario [33,34]. It is advisable to start with open questions [14]. Participation in the scenario may be a stressful and emotional experience [11], and the debriefing at the end of the scenario can help reduce pressure and at the same time incorporate the experience into the knowledge [34]. During the debriefing, participants of the training have the opportunity to present their experience with simulation activity, their thoughts, their views and the reasons for their decisions and actions, give an assessment of the work, highlight what has been done well and what needs to be improved and how [14,33,35]. It is important to include also those participants who have participated in the scenario only as observers, as this is a key element in the scenario-based training [14].

The literature supports the use of scenarios as a learning and teaching strategy, but there are very few theoretical basis for this field. These would be very useful and necessary to enable this method of training to be integrated into training as effectively as possible [36].

2 Purpose

The purpose is to evaluate the effectiveness of scenario-based first aid training. The aim is to determine whether the use of scenarios improves the provided first aid, how the participants of training assess the usefulness of scenarios, and whether they would like to practice more with this method.

3 Method

We used the experimental method. In the academic year 2016-2017, we conducted the research in the classroom for first aid training at the Faculty of Health Sciences, University of Ljubljana. We included 65 students of the Faculty of Health Sciences. Unlike the control group, the experimental group was exposed to scenario-based learning during first aid training. The experimental group included 27 students, in the control group there were 38 students. We collected the data with a questionnaire and evaluation paper, which enabled us to assess students during the practical test. Evaluation paper included nine categories – checking for safety, use of protective gloves, assessing consciousness, opening the airway of the victim, checking for breathing, putting the victim in the recovery position, calling 112, examination of the injured person and dressing the wound. The assessment was based on the criteria for assessing the practical test, which we previously prepared and defined. We used evaluation papers at the end of the one-week training course. Before the practical test, which was evaluated with the aforementioned evaluation papers, we asked all student from the group to leave the classroom. Meanwhile we prepared everything that was needed for the practical test, and then students entered the classroom one by one. The same scenario was prepared for all students, and we provided the same description of the imaginary situation to all students before they entered the classroom. Students were asked to provide first aid to a person who was lying on the ground in the lobby of the faculty. It was an unconscious person who has received an electric shock and was still breathing. Students were observed as they were providing fist aid, and evaluated with the use of evaluation papers. Participation in the practical test was voluntary and anonymous.

We measured the satisfaction of students with first aid training and their opinion about scenario-based training with a questionnaire. We gave the questionnaires to students after the practical test. The questionnaire was anonymous and contained 4 closed questions.

At the end we calculated the average values. We processed the data obtained through questionnaires and evaluation papers with Microsoft Office Excel 2013. We presented the data graphically and descriptively.

4 Results

4.1 The data obtained through evaluation paper.

Figure 1 shows the average number of points achieved for each measure in the experimental (first-aid training included scenarios) and control (in the first-aid training scenarios were not included) group. The lowest average score was 0.5 and the highest 9.8.

The apparent differences in the average number of points achieved between the experimental group and the control group are in putting the victim in the recovery position and in examination. For putting the victim in the recovery position, students from the experimental group received 8.9 points on average, and students from the control group 4.5 points. The difference is also noticeable in examination of the victim, where the average value for the experimental group is 4.3 and for the control 1.4 points. From the graph in Figure 1 it is also evident at which measures students gathered a smaller number of points – in using protective gloves, where the students from the experimental group reached an average of 2.2 points and the members of control group an average of 0.5 points. Less points were also collected in checking for safety – students from the experimental group collected 2.6 points on average and students from the control group 1.1 points.

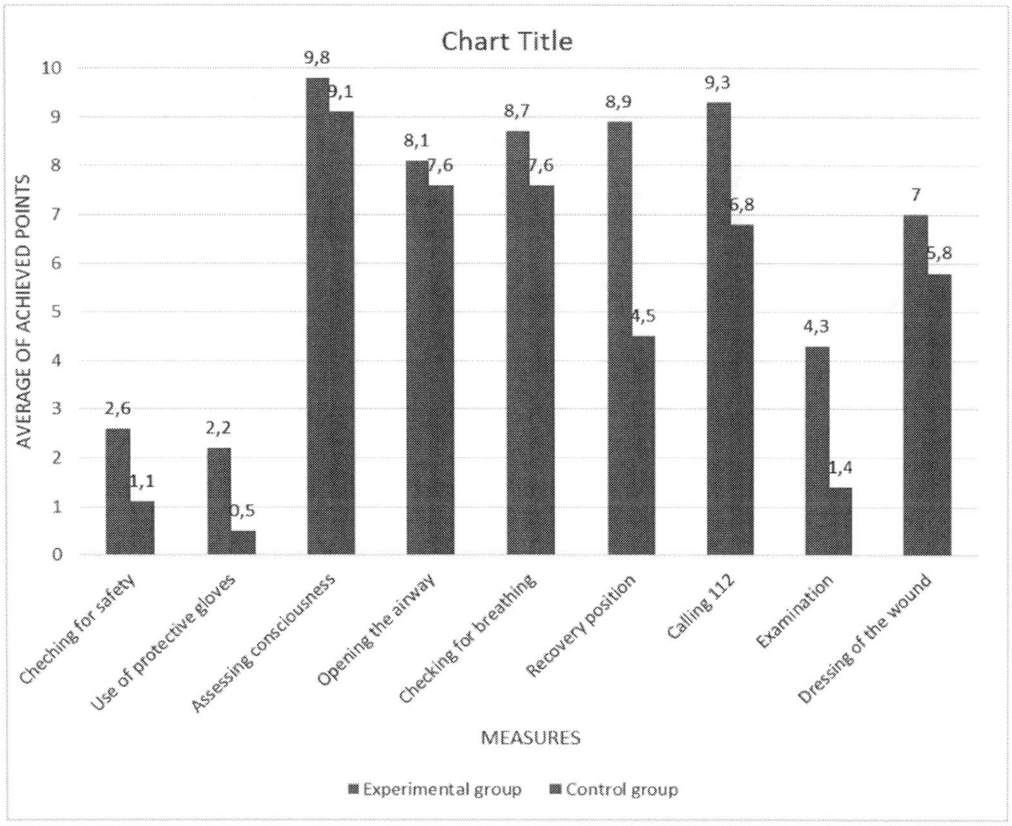

Fig. 1. The average number of points achieved in the experimental and control group.

4.2 The data obtained through questionnaire

Students could rate the themes, tools and methods with minimum rating 1 and maximum 5.

As can be seen from Figure 2, students have evaluated cardiopulmonary resuscitation and scenarios with the most points. The cardiopulmonary resuscitation was evaluated by the students of experimental group with an average score of 4.9 and by the students of control group with an average score of 4.8. The scenarios were evaluated with an average score of 4.8 by both groups.

To the second question (»What do you think about scenario-based training in terms of usefulness? «) students from both groups answered that they think that it is useful for their knowledge.

All students from the experimental groups and all students from the control group would like to take even more practice using scenarios.

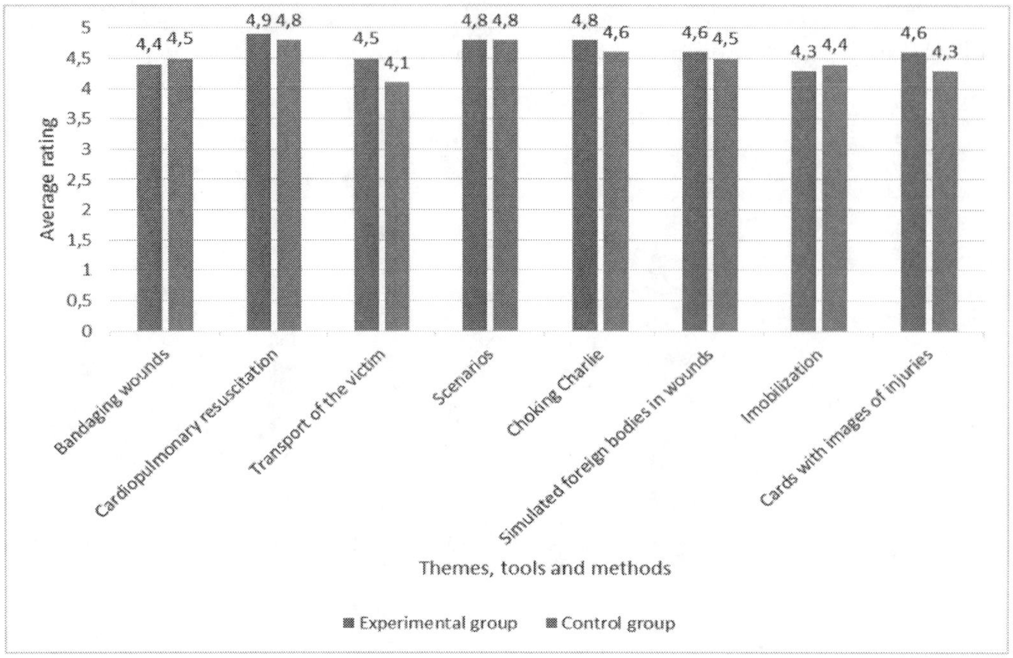

Fig. 2. Average assessment of themes, tools and methods.

Students could only assess the mentioned methods and forms of work with a minimum rating of 1 and a maximum of 5.

As can be seen from Figure 3, students rated the scenarios with the most points. These were assessed with an average rating of 3.9 by students from the experimental group and 4.6 by students in the control group.

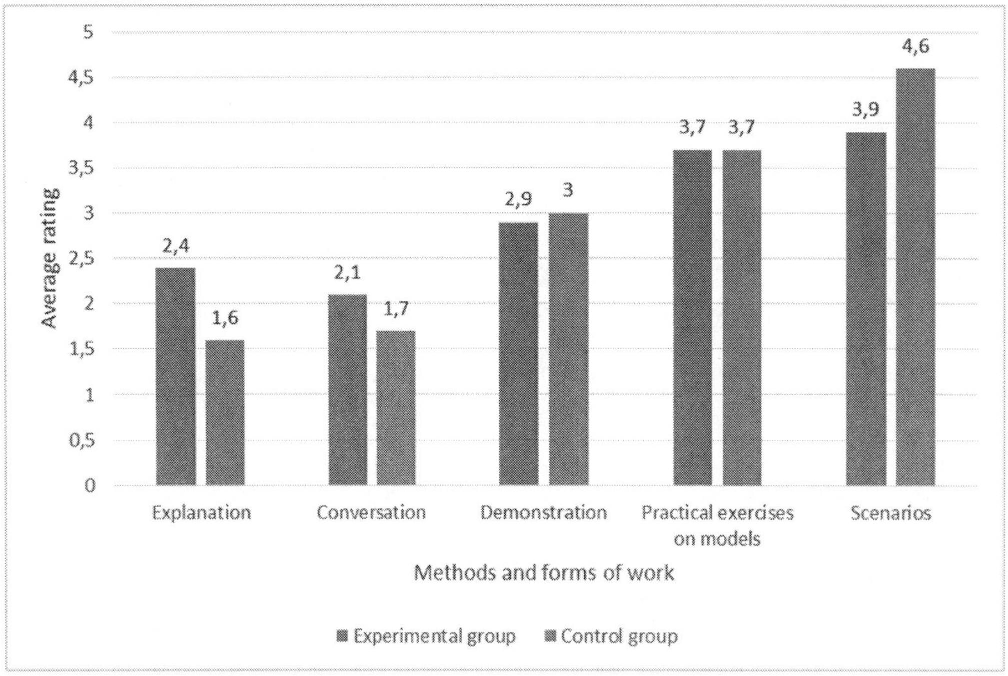

Fig. 3. Average rating of methods and forms of work.

5 Discussion and conclusion

When first aid is provided, the safety of first aid providers must be always considered. It may happen that the rescuer gets injured or ill, and then he or she cannot help. Before they come to the victim they must be convinced that they are not at risk or they must eliminate the risk [37]. As can be seen from Figure 1, students from both the experimental and the control group got a few points on average. Only a few students have checked whether it is safe to come near the victim and then properly eliminated the danger (electric cable) – 7 students from the experimental group and 4 students from the control group. Some students just said that they would check for safety before helping the victim, but they did not do it or they did not notice the electric cable and remove it. Some of the students noticed the electric cable later when they were already providing first aid. Some of them noticed the cable but did not properly remove it with a non-conductive object. The obtained data is a little bit worrying. We would like to have a greater proportion of students who would properly check for safety, as in a real situation serious injuries could have occurred. The analyses of work of Civil Protection and Red Cross first aid teams also show insufficient safetycare so it would be sensible to prepare more casualty simulations, focusing on safety precautions [38,39].

Only a few students have thought about using protective gloves (six students from the experimental group and two students from the control group). Protective gloves prevent direct contact of the rescuer with the injured person (with blood and body fluids) [40], and are very important when providing first aid – because of the rescuer's protection and the protection of injured person. The main reason for forgetting to put on protective gloves as stated by students was that they forgot about them in panic, but they would definitely use them in the real situation.

When assessing consciousness, students performed much better. Most of them gently shaked the victim, asked if they are OK, and they also called for help as it is recommended in the latest resuscitation guidelines [21].

When opening the airway and checking for breathing some of the students had some problems because they did not tilt the head back enough or were not checking the breathing for enough time. The most common cause for airway obstruction in the unconscious person are the loose throat muscles that are restricting the flow of air. The head-tilt/ chin-lift maneuver can enable the victim to breathe, therefore it is crucial that is performed correctly [40].

When putting the victim into the recovery position, the students from the experimental group got more points on average, while the students from the control group had some problems with this measure. Some of them first applied a bandage or called 112, and then placed the victim in the appropriate position, which does not correspond to the correct sequence of measures, as the injured person can stop breathing while the rescuer is calling an ambulance. Some of the students turned the victim in the opposite direction (away from themselves) or were handling the victim roughly. Some of the students placed the injured person in an adequate and very stable position, but at the end they did not tilt the victim's head back to open their airway.

The examination of the injured person was generally performed more negligently and the wound was mostly noticed by coincidence. Some of the students rinsed the wound, some cooled it and then used the Aluplast Swab, most of them applied a sterile gauze swab and attached it with a bandage, as recommended by Ahčan [41]. Some students did not notice the wound.

First aid, provided by students during the practical test was satisfactory, with the exception of checking for safety and using protective gloves. In first aid training a great emphasis is given to security and protection, however, according to the results of our research, these two key aspects of providing first aid should be given an even greater emphasis or should be emphasised in some other way. For example, different scenarios could be used to highlight various hazards (fire, gas, traffic, chemicals, slippery surfaces, danger of explosions…).

As can be seen from Figure 1, students from the experimental group (in which scenarios were used during the training) showed a slightly higher level of knowledge at the practical test in comparison with the students from the control group although the difference was small. The apparent difference is evident in putting the victim in the recovery position and also in examination of the victim (even though the students from both groups performed it quite superficially). We can conclude that pre-training with simulated scenarios is the reason for a better performance in measures of first aid of the students from the experimental group, but there are also some other variables that could affect the results. For example, one of them is the structure of groups. In the sample we included students from different study programmes, and at the same time different knowledge and experience with first aid, which we did not check, but it would likely make a reasonable difference in results. In addition the sample was small and therefore the results can not be generalized.

As can be seen from Figure 2, students from the experimental and control groups prefer the cardiopulmonary resuscitation and scenarios from all listed themes, tools and methods, then Choking Charlie Mannequin for training of the Heimlich abdominal thrust maneuver, and cards with images of realistic injuries. Based on the results obtained, we can conclude that students mostly like more interactive methods, as they can be more actively involved. Within scenarios and while teaching cardiopulmonary resuscitation a story or a description of events is given to students, in order to make it easier and to enable them to better experience the situation. Based on the description of the situation, students are presented with a problem which they must solve. This allows them to be actively involved in the learning process. The importance and effectiveness of this is highlighted by many researches, as it helps them to achieve better results in terms of knowledge and skills [5,7].

Based on the results of the second and third question, students think that scenario-based training is a useful method for learning and they would like this method to be used more often. Bellack [42] emphasizes that it is very important to take into account the opinions and wishes of students about the methods of teaching which they want to be used, and select the ones that are the most appropriate for them. Therefore, the data obtained is very important as it indicates that it would be reasonable to include more simulated scenarios in first aid training.

From Figure 3 it can be seen that the students from the experimental and control group prefer scenarios, then follow practical exercises on models, demonstration and, finally, conversation and explanation. At this question students had to classify the methods and forms of work (and not to evaluate them as at the first question), which is why the difference is more noticeable. The results show that, in comparison with traditional teaching methods (such as, for example, explanation), students are more interested in active methods of work, including simulated scenarios.

Based on these findings, it can be summarized that scenario-based training appears to be an effective method for students, and that they would like this method to be used more often. In addition, the results showed that students from the experimental group who were exposed to scenario-based learning during first aid training showed a higher level of knowledge in comparison with students from the control group. In spite of small sample included in the research, based on the results obtained, it can be concluded that this method can have a very important contribution to the acquired knowledge and skills. Therefore it would be reasonable to use it repeatedly in first aid training. At the same time, it would be necessary to undertake more research on this topic, as there is no theoretical basis and there are no studies that would contribute to a greater and effective use of this teaching method.

References

1. International Federation of Red Cross and Red Crescent Societies. International first aid and resuscitation guidelines 2016. Geneva. Accessed via: http://www.ifrc.org/Global/Publications/Health/First-Aid-2016-Guidelines_EN.pdf (2016)
2. J. Lippmann, P. Livingston, M. Craike, Health Educ J, **70**, 2 (2011)
3. B. A. LaVelle, J. J. McLaughlin, Simulation-based education improves patient safety in ambulatory care. In: K. Henriksen, J. B. Battles, M. A. Keyes, M. L. Grady, Advances in patient safety: new direction and alternative approaches. Rockville: Agency for Healthcare Research Quality, 225–244 (2008)
4. R. Clemow, Nurse Educ Today, **27**, 1 (2007)
5. K. Jakee, Int J Teach Learn High Educ, **23**, 1 (2011)
6. G. Norton, M. Taylor, T. Stewart et al., Australas J Educ Technol, **28**, 7 (2012)
7. R. S. Rosa, G. J. C. Sanches, I. C. R. Gomes, M. L. M. Silva, A. C. Santos Duarte, R. N. S. Boery, J Nurs, **11**, 2 (2017)
8. F. Lateef, J Emerg Trauma Shock, **3**, 4 (2010)
9. B. Žvanut, S. Jurgec, I. Karnjuš, Obzor Zdr N **47**, 1 (2013)
10. K. Edgecombe, P. Seaton, K. Monahan, S. Meyer, S. LePage, G. Erlam, Clinical simulation in nursing: a literature review and guidelines for practice. Wellington: Ako Aotearoa.
Accessed via: https://akoaotearoa.ac.nz/download/ng/file/group-6261/clinical-simulation-in-nursing-a-literature-review-and-guidelines-for-practice.pdf (2013)
11. E. A. Hunt, M. Fiedor- Hamilton, W. J. Eppich, Pediatr Clin N Am, **55**, 4 (2008)
12. C. Arthur, T. Levett-Jones, A. Kable, Nurse Educ Today, **33**, 11 (2013)
13. T. Valler- Jones, R. Meechan, H. Jones, Br J Nurs, **20**, 10 (2011)
14. K. T. Waxman, J Nurs Educ, **49**, 1 (2010)
15. I. Karnjuš, P. Pucer, Obzor Zdr N, **46**, 1 (2012)
16. A. H. Al-Elq, J Family Community Med, **17**, 1 (2010)
17. G. D. Perkins, Resuscitation, **73**, 2 (2007)
18. D. Tschannen, M. Aebersold, E. McLaughlin, J. Bowen, J. Fairchld, J Nurs Educ Pract, **2**, 3 (2012)
19. J. McCallum, Nurse Educ Today, **27**, 8 (2007)
20. J. Mikkelsen, M. Hegg Reime, A. K. Harris, Nurse Educ Today, **28**, 664–671 (2008)
21. P. Gradišek, M. Grošelj Grenc, A. Strdin Košir et al., Smernice za oživljanje 2015 Evropskega reanimacijskega sveta. 1. izd. Ljubljana: Slovensko združenje za urgentno medicino.
Accessed via: http://www.szum.si/media/uploads/files/ERC_2015_slo-1.pdf (2015)
22. U. Kovačič, D. Slabe, eds., Mednarodne smernice za prvo pomoč in oživljanje 2011. Ljubljana: Rdeči križ Slovenije, 112–113 (2013)
23. J. A. Cannon-Bowers, Curr Opin Anaesthesiol, **21**, 6 (2008)
24. K. A. Yaeger, J. M. R. Arafeh, J Perinat Neonat Nurs, **22**, 2 (2008)
25. S. Erol, A. Jäger, P. Hold, K. Ott, W. Sihn, Procedia CIRP, **54**, 13–18 (2016)
26. S. S. Yetik, H. I. Akyuz, H. Keser, Turk Online J Distance Educ, **13**, 2 (2012)
27. R. Sorin, E. Errington, L. Ireland, A. Nickson, M. Caltabiano, Journal of the NUS Teaching academy, **2**, 4 (2012)
28. T. Zakšek, Obzor Zdr N, **42**, 3 (2008)
29. R. Clark, T+D, **63**, 1 (2009)
30. P. Moule, A. Wilford, R. Sales, L. Lockyer, Nurse Educ Today, **28**, 7 (2008)
31. E. P. Errington, Int J Interdiscip Soc Sci, **3**, 3 (2008)
32. M. Steinbuch, Ujma, **26**, 238–242 (2012)

33. D. Van Niekerk, C. Coetzee, D. Botha et al., J Homel Secur Emerg Manag, **12**, 1 (2014)
34. M. A. Cantrell, Clin Simul Nurs, **4**, 2 (2008)
35. K. T. Dreifuerst, Nurs Educ Perspect, **30**, 2 (2009)
36. J. B. Moats, T. J. Chermack, L. M. Dooley, Adv Dev Hum Resour, **10**, 3 (2008)
37. D. Vlahovič, Pristop k poškodovancu ali nenadno obolelemu. In: *Prva pomoč: priročnik za bolničarje*. Ljubljana: Rdeči križ Slovenije (2008)
38. D. Slabe, L. Kosec, D. Horvat, R. Šutanovac, Ujma, **23**, 196–204 (2009)
39. D. Slabe, L. Kosec, D. Horvat, J. Melanšek, Ujma, **26**, 222–229 (2012)
40. D. Slabe, I. Šterbenc, Obzor Zdr N, **45**, 1 (2009)
41. U. G. Ahčan, Celostna obravnava opeklinskih poškodb. In: *Prva pomoč: priročnik za bolničarje*. Ljubljana: Rdeči križ Slovenije (2008)
42. J. P. Bellack, J Nurs Educ, **47**, 10 (2008)

Polish education system under 2017 reform: Assumptions, aims and controversies

Justyna Wojniak[1,*], and *Marta* Majorek[2]

[1] Pedagogical University of Krakow, Podchorążych 2, 30-084 Kraków, Poland
[2] Andrzej Frycz Modrzewski Krakow University, Herlinga – Grudzińskiego 1, Kraków 30-705, Poland

Abstract. The paper analyzes some current changes in the Polish education system. The comprehensive reform of the system was undertaken in 2016, and the new system was introduced in the school year 2016/2017, changing the structure of the education cycle as well as the teaching content and the handbooks. The aim of the Ministry of National Education was to create a "good school" for students, teachers and parents. The reform, however, triggered a national discussion on its aims and assumptions, as it is accompanied by a number of controversies and strong differences of opinions in the Polish society.

Keywords: Education system, education reform, Poland

1 Introduction

Current discussion around the reform of Polish education system has proven a visible split of the opinions concerning the idea of such a profound change of the school life, not only among the politicians, but in the general public opinion as well. First of all, controversies have aroused around the aim of the reform itself. Before the reform, the Polish education system had been assumed as an effective one according to a number of surveys and research. Moreover, the pace of introducing such fundamental changes was also quite short, which demanded a lot of organizational and financial efforts taken particularly by the local authorities which are responsible for effective performance of educational institutions in Poland. Even though the first school year under the new educational provisions has already finished, the controversies still exist and the discussion on the reform is quite lively, and it is not only within the groups of parents or teachers who are at the center of the transformation. The public opinion in Poland demonstrates a visible split in the points of view on this matter, which is strongly connected with their political attitudes towards the government.

2 On the verge of the reform - reasons of the change

According to the official information published on the Ministry of National Education website: "The developed reform of education meets the expectations of the majority of

* Corresponding author's e-mail: justyna.wojniak@up.krakow.pl

Poles who want a modern school, and at the same time one that is strongly rooted in our tradition. The changes are well-thought and have been planned for numerous years. It is important to us that every student, regardless of their origin and the material status of their parents, has a good school and good education. The reform of education is not just a change in the school system. It is also a proposal of new solutions in the development of vocational education strongly linked to the labor market and changes in the organization and functioning of schools and educational institutions" [1].

2.1 Key features of the new education system

The reform of education in question was introduced at the beginning of 2017. Its main objective is to prepare the students who complete the entire education cycle to meet the needs of individual development and those of a modern labor market, which requires some solid grounds in a form of general education.

The key elements of the reform are as follows:

- Change in the structure of the education system consisting in the introduction of a long 8-grade school (primary and four-year high school and five-year technical high school).
- The obligation for a one-year pre-school preparation for 6-year-olds, when the child learns some basic skills - its teaching, like learning at school, is covered by an educational subvention from the state budget.
- Providing free textbooks.
- Strengthening the general and vocational education in secondary schools by extending the learning cycle by one year.
- Introduction of a 3-year branch education (1 qualification in a given profession) with the possibility of acquiring further qualifications and preparation for the matriculation exam in a 2-year second-degree industry school.
- Propagation of a dual education implemented in cooperation with entrepreneurs.
- Increasing the participation of employers in co-financing the vocational education by establishing the Fund for Development of Vocational Education [2].

The changes entered into force in the 2017/2018 school year. Students completing the 6th grade of primary school in the 2016/2017 school year became students of the 7th grade of a primary school. Structural changes are introduced pursuant to the Act of 14 December 2016 on "Law on School Education" and the Act on "Legislation introducing the Act - Law on School Education" of the same date.

The target structure of education will include:

- 8-year primary school;
- 4-year general high school;
- 5-year technical college;
- 3-year industry school of the first degree;
- 2-year industry school of the second degree;
- 3-year special training school for work;
- Post-secondary school.

The industry-oriented primary school replaced the basic vocational school on 1 September 2017. The second-cycle industry school for graduates of the industry-first school will be introduced as of the school year 2020/2021. Compulsory education is 10 years in Poland and includes the last year of the pre-school education, a 6-year primary school and a 3-year junior high school. As regards the education system's reform adopted in 2017, compulsory education is 9 years now and covers the last year of pre-school education and an 8-year primary school. The schooling obligation and the obligation to learn were separated in the Polish education system. The schooling obligation (i.e. the obligation to attend primary and lower secondary school, in a new structure covering the 8-year primary school) is imposed on children and juveniles aged 7-16 (in the new structure they are 7-15 years old). The compulsory education applies to young people aged 16-18 (15-18 years old in a new structure) and the duty can be fulfilled in a school or out-of-school form (implementation of professional training at the employer's) [3].

2.2 Structure of the national compulsory education system

2.2.1 Early education and care

Facilities for children aged 0-3:

- Nurseries,
- Children's clubs.

There is no obligation to attend nurseries. They are not a part of the education system but are governed by The Ministry of Family, Labor and Social Policy.

Facilities for children aged 3-6:

- Kindergartens,
- Pre-school departments in primary schools,
- Pre-school education teams,
- Pre-school points.

Pre-school education has been optional for children aged 3-5 and obligatory for 6-year-olds since September 2016. Every 4- and 5-year-old is entitled to a place in kindergarten. From September 2017, this right have also applied to 3-year-old children. From the 2016/17 school year, parents of 6-year-olds have the right to choose - they can send a 6-year-old to the 1st grade of primary school or allow to continue its education in a pre-school education center. 7-year-old children begin compulsory education from the 1st class of primary school.

Basic education

Prior to the reform, education had been carried out in 6-year compulsory primary schools for pupils aged 6/7-13.

Education included two stages:

- Classes 1-3 (early school education),
- Grades 4-6, where the teaching is divided into subjects.

At the end of the primary school there was an external test conducted, bearing solely an informative function.

After the reform

The reform consists of introducing a single-structure comprising of ISCED 1 and ISCED 2 levels (primary and lower secondary education). It is an 8-year primary school for pupils aged 6/7 to 15 years. Learning in an 8-year primary school includes two stages:

- Classes 1-3 (early school education),
- Grades 4-8, where teaching is divided into subjects [4].

2.2.2 Lower secondary education

Before the reform, the education had been carried out in obligatory 3-year gymnasiums (youth aged 13-16). At the end of the gymnasium, an external exam was conducted, the results of which decided on admission to upper secondary schools.

After the reform

From 2017, gymnasiums have been gradually eliminated from the system. Students completing their studies in the 6th grade of an elementary school become students of the 7th grade of the new 8-year primary school. From the school year 2018/19, the obligatory external examination will take place in the 8th grade of primary school.

2.2.3 Secondary education

The vast majority of junior high school graduates continue their education in upper secondary general or vocational schools, although it is not compulsory (students are only subject to the schooling obligation, however it ceases to apply after the student turns 18).

This stage includes learning in the following types of schools:

- 3-year general secondary schools,
- 4-year technical upper secondary school,
- 3-year basic vocational schools.

Secondary school is attended by young people aged 16-19 (16-20 years old in the case of technical secondary schools).

After the reform

The reform of lower secondary schools will begin in the 2019/2020 and end in the 2023/2024 school year.

New types of secondary (secondary) schools:

- 4-year general high school,
- 5-year technical upper secondary school,
- 3-year industry school (1st degree) (it has been operating since September 2017),
- 2-year industry school (second cycle),

Students of the 1st level trade school (before the reform of the main vocational school) and the technical school may take confirmation exams during or after their graduation qualifications in a given profession and obtain a diploma confirming their professional qualifications. High school and technical high school students can take an external matriculation examination after finishing the school. It allows to obtain a matriculation certificate, which is a prerequisite for admission to higher education schools. Students from the second-level industry school will also have this option [5].

2.2.4 Post-secondary education

This stage of education is covered by the secondary education in the Polish education system. Post-secondary schools are intended for people with general secondary education and offer a diploma confirming professional qualifications provided that the student passes the exam. The course of post-secondary education is from 1 to 2.5 years. The post-secondary school students sit the same vocational examinations as students of basic vocational and technical schools. Post-secondary schools are not subject to any structural changes due to the reform [6].

3 Discussion

The Constitution of The Republic of Poland, adopted by the National Assembly on 2 April 2 1997 provides for regulations related to the education. It guarantees the right to learn, but at the same time it imposed the schooling obligation until the age of 18. The Constitution confirms that education in public schools is free of any charges. Parents have the freedom to choose other than public schools for their children and are entitled to establish such facilities. At the same time, the Constitution stipulates that all citizens are guaranteed with universal and equal access to education [7]. For this purpose, public authorities are obliged to create and support systems of individual financial aid for pupils and students.

According to the assumptions made by the educational transformation, it is indispensable to achieve the following goals:

- Raising the level of public education through propagation of the secondary and higher education;
- Equalizing educational opportunities;
- Encouraging the improvement of the educational quality, understood as an integral process of upbringing and education [8].

Therefore, the reform of education was carried out among others to meet the postulate of equalizing educational opportunities. It was recognized that the pre-reform school was not conducive to achieving equality in this area, and education was not of egalitarian character [9]. The system of education functioning before 1999, in the opinion of the reformers, was elitist or even exclusive. The low participation of young people who obtained secondary and higher education was indicated in order to confirm that argument. It was noted that secondary school and higher education were primarily available for students coming from families of a high social status [10].

The changes introduced by the latest reform may have a negative impact on the equalization of opportunities. First of all, we are talking about shortening the schooling obligation by one year, and also about withdrawing from the idea of an earlier education obligation for the youngest children. Five-year-old children covered by the educational obligation, who reach the nets and kindergartens, benefit the most. The earliest possible inclusion of a child into the education system is extremely important. Unfortunately, these chances have been taken away from them. Under the influence of social protests, 5-year-old children were excluded from the school duty. Unfortunately, the rejection of equalizing educational opportunities in the pre-school age can be never made up. Meanwhile, research confirms that each additional year in the kindergarten improves results in mathematics. It is then that shaping of competences takes place at a later age [11].

Children from the age of seven have been required to attend school from the 2016/2017 school year. A 6-year-old child have the right to start education in the first grade of primary school if he / she has benefited from pre-school education in the school year preceding the school year in which he or she is to start the school. If a 6-year-old did not attend a kindergarten, the parents are still able to enroll their child in the first grade. In this case, however, it will be necessary to consult the psychological and pedagogical specialist about the possibility of beginning the primary school education [12].

It follows that parents who want to send a 6-year-old child to the primary school will encounter a number of problems, which in turn will lead to a shift in the school-leaving age. The European Union also encourages parents to send their children to kindergarten and school as early as possible. In 2011, the European Commission created the document entitled "Early Childhood Education and Care: we will guarantee all children in the EU a good start in the future." The authors emphasize that "early education and childcare is the foundation for successful lifelong learning, social integration and personal development, and at a later stage - a factor that increases employability"[13].

There is a tendency in the European Union to lower the age at which the compulsory education begins. Several countries have decided to do so, and the last pre-school class became the first class of primary school. It could be stated that Poland took the same path. Five other EU member states reduced the age of starting compulsory education, apart from Poland. In Romania, not seven-year-old but six-year-old children go to school, however, in Slovenia the last grade of kindergarten was transferred to schools. In Greece, Cyprus and

Latvia, primary education has not changed, but the compulsory pre-school education now starts one year, a year and four months and two years earlier respectively [14]. In the light of the change which was carried out in 2016, the possibility of early education of children was basically withdrawn. The regulations indicate that children will have the guaranteed pre-school education from the age of 3, which is not feasible in the current circumstances. The problem is the availability of the pre-school education. Poland suffers from a deficit in the number of kindergartens and the state does not guarantee that 3-year-old children will be able to begin their education. This will have some measurable impact on the careers of active mothers who will be excluded from the labor market for the period of childcare, as they will not have a possibility to send their children to kindergartens. What is more, it is well-known that a long break in the professional activity evidently practically results in eliminating an employee (in this case a mother) from the labor market.

Junior high schools and in general the whole Polish education system is not perfect - no one has created such a system in the world so far. However, the collected data suggest that the introduction of junior high school in 1999 was an idea that brought more good than harm. Although some people may find it surprising, gymnasium is the strongest element of Polish education. This is the result of all available research - both Polish and international. Before the introduction of junior high schools, we had over 80% of students who did not cope with reading comprehension in vocational schools. They were simply functional illiterates. After the reform, we gradually improved these results until we reached the top in the OECD. Now we have, for example, more good students in mathematics than Finland, famous for its education system [15]. PISA (international survey of skills of 15-year-olds) and PIAAC (International Adult Competence Research) show that young Poles are really well-educated [16]. Polish students between 16 and 19 years of age have several points more than the average for the OECD countries in reading comprehension, and they reach this average in mathematics. The younger colleagues examined in the PISA study achieved even better results. The output is also quite good for 16-24-year-old students. Only the elders - those who did not graduate from gymnasiums, only 8-year primary school - lower these results [17]. Currently, we are dealing with the notorious undermining of the results of the above-mentioned research - mainly the PISA surveys - by the governing party politicians. It is the largest measurement of students' skills in the world in three basic areas: reading and interpretation, mathematics and reasoning in natural sciences, developed by an international consortium of the best OECD experts [18]. Of course, it can be argued that it does not include knowledge of religion, history and Polish literature, but these are not the key skills to succeed in international competition.

One of the most repeated arguments of the reformers is that the middle school is the breeding ground of the worst youth pathology. A deep analysis performed by the Institute for Educational Research, based on several both domestic and international studies, gave quite different results. According to estimates, bullying affects about 10 percent of Polish students [19]. As verified in the HBSC study in the 2009/2010 school year, the victims of bullying (those bullied at least two-three times a month in the last few months) accounted for around 14% among 11-year-old, 11% among 13-year-old and 7% among 15-year-old students. The scale of bullying in Polish schools is average when compared to almost 40 countries or regions [20]. In addition, it is not true that it is getting worse. Research conducted in 1997, 2003 and 2007 indicates the stability or even a slight reduction in the scale of aggression and violence in schools. And what is most important, it is not so intense in junior high schools at all. The study entitled "School without Violence" conducted in 2011 shows, for example, that physical aggression was encountered by 49% of students in primary schools, 36% in junior high schools and 18% in high school [21].

Concerning the industry schools, the communist authorities abolished lower secondary schools in 1948, justifying the reform with the need to quickly prepare professional personnel for the economy, and above all, with the industry which reported the demand for skilled workers - thus, two big economic plans were implemented in Poland at that time: 3 years at first (1947-1949) and 6 years afterwards (1950-1955) [22]. An element of the education reform introduced by the communists was the simultaneous expansion of vocational education - basic vocational schools with a duration of education from 2 to 3.5 years and a very narrow curriculum for teaching humanities and general subjects were introduced. There was also a technique with a 5-year learning cycle, where the emphasis was placed on vocational and specialist education, and vocational high schools oriented on preparing graduates directly for work [23]. Even if we sometimes miss a locksmith who would replace a door lock or a shoemaker who would repair our favorite shoes, skilled manual workers are less needed in the modern economy than they were in the era of rapid industrialization. And in a moment, along with the progressing automation, not only in industry but also in services, the demand for them will be even lower. This whole model from the past does not match the challenges of today's world thus, the workers are not any as busy twisting the devices on the belt, as they were a hundred years ago in Ford plants.

Introduction of junior high schools was guided by the idea of equal opportunities. The Minister of Education, Mirosław Handke, employed this level of education in 1999, wishing, among other things, to help children from poorer families, from neglected rural areas, with a lower socio-economic status. And research confirms that it has succeeded to a certain extend [24]. Michał Sitek states that from his own analyzes (carried out on the basis of PISA data) it appears that between 2000-2012 the differences in educational output were levelled, which was mainly due to the improvement in results achieved by the weakest students [25]. Differences between students with low and high socio-economic statuses have decreased, and so has the influence of social origin on the selection of upper secondary school. Equally, Hungarian researchers L. F. Drucker and D. Horn appreciated the equalization of opportunities by Polish junior high schools. Their report shows that equalizing opportunities by Polish junior high schools has a long-lasting effect. The lower secondary school reform in Poland improved the chances of graduates to find a job and influenced the increase in their remuneration. These effects occurred especially in the group of students achieving the lowest educational results [26]. An interesting problem arises here, why Polish lower secondary schools have helped the weakest students and low socio-economic status. Many researchers associate this with the extension of one year of general education. A weakness of education systems which quickly select students is their large stratification. Children from poorer families, national minorities, children of less educated parents go to vocational schools - this is the case, for example, in Germany, and this problem was noticed by the Hungarians who transformed their post-communist educational system adopting the German model, and the y are now thinking about changing it again.

It is no coincidence that the above-mentioned PISA tests examine the students' skills related to reading comprehension, logical thinking, math and knowledge in the field of natural sciences. These are the skills that today are crucial for development of a modern and innovative economy, as the politicians like to say. Only by having these skills, can we successfully compete in the world. Will we continue to intensively develop and promote them in the new educational system, without lower secondary schools? There are some serious doubts. Elimination of the obligatory test of nature at the end of the primary school will cause, for example, a significant part of children to lose motivation to learn nature. There will also be very little IT teaching hours in the new high school program. On the other hand, there will be more teaching hours of history in all types of schools.

What is more, some serious doubts may arise from the form of preparing the reform, in particular the new core curriculum for the reformed school. Not only the negation of the previous reform, the lack of reliable arguments supporting the change of the system, but also the lack of reference to authorities in the field of education can be questionable from the perspective of the quality of changes. The Ombudsman joined the appeal proceedings in the case. He assessed that the Voivodeship Administrative Court correctly recognized that the experts who worked on the core curriculum for mathematics in the primary and general secondary schools are individuals holding public functions and contractors of the Ministry. This means that information about them is subject to disclosure under the Act on Access to Public Information. On 22 November 2017, the VAC in Warsaw (file reference number II Sa / Wa 1094/17) quashed the two refusal decisions appealed by the Minister of National Education regarding the disclosure of public information. It was a question of the composition of a team of experts preparing a new core curriculum - related to the reform of education introduced on 1 September 2017; names of team members and information about their academic degrees and institutions which they are employed in. The resort referred to the protection of experts' privacy. In the opinion of the Ministry of National Education, they were not persons holding any public functions within the meaning of the Act on Access to Public Information. The Minister indicated that there is a contract concluded with those individuals. They also had no impact on the extent to which the materials they developed would be used in legislative work. In addition, the Ministry did not receive their statements about the resignation of their right to privacy protection. The Provincial Administrative Court ruled that the minister had committed a violation of law. This violation considered improper application of the restriction in access to public information - and thus violation of the rule of law. The court ruled that since these persons had influenced the shape of the adopted core curriculum to some extent, and thus the content of decisions of a general social nature, it is justified to treat them as holding public functions. The court stated that their data cannot be excluded due to privacy. The fact of concluding the civil law contracts with with those individuals additionally spoke for the necessity of disclosing their names and surnames. According to the court, in order to implement the constitutional principle of transparency of public administration activities and transparency of spending public funds, it is necessary to provide citizens with full knowledge of who - by concluding contracts with state authorities - becomes a beneficiary of public funds. It also makes it possible to assess whether the task was entrusted to persons with appropriate knowledge, and the contract itself was not in fact a camouflaged mean of unauthorized flow of public funds to private individuals. In its opinion, the conflict between the right to access public information should prevail over the right to the protection of personal data. As part of the market economy, there is no obligation to enter into contracts with public entities - the court highlighted. The Minister of Education filed an appeal to the Supreme Administrative Court. She allegedly violated the rules of the VAC, including by giving prevalence to the right to access public information. She also argued that the criterion of "a person holding public functions" is to have decision-making powers in the scope of the content of a normative act.

In the Ombudsman's opinion, who fully agrees with the verdict of the VAC, the complaints are unjustified. The court correctly claimed that persons working on the development of the core curriculum are individuals who hold public functions and contractors of the Ministry of National Education. The Ombudsman stressed that the VAC's findings are based on the wide-ranging understanding of the term "a person holding a public function" adopted in the case-law. It does not matter on what basis the person holds the public function. Undoubtedly, in the case of experts preparing the core curriculum, we are dealing with the decision-making dimension of their competence - as the Ombudsman, Adam Bodnar, wrote [27]. The Ombudsman claimed that these individuals were assigned to develop a new core curriculum, so they had some real (not only hypothetical) impact on the legal situation of other people. It is also impossible to accept the standpoint of the Ministry of Education that their work was of an advisory and consultative nature, since the body itself admitted that the experts prepared specific parts of the assumptions to the core. The principle of disclosure of personal data of the entities - parties to contracts concluded with public bodies and using public assets - is underlined in the currently uniform ruling system of the Supreme Administrative Court. Every contractor of a public authority which benefits from public funds is a person holding public functions. To the extent that the information refers to this relationship, they are subject to public disclosure [28].

Another issue worth pointing out is the huge cost of the changes implemented in the education system. Despite the assurances from the current authorities, it turns out that the majority of expenditures will be borne by local governments. Local governments submit applications to the Ministry of Education for reimbursement of costs incurred for education reform. For example, the authorities of Poznań stated that they had to contribute PLN 16 million from the local budget for this purpose. The local government in Łódź, in turn, speaks of over PLN 52 million. Anna Zalewska, the Minister of National Education, when asked about this issue, assured that the Ministry regularly allocates money to local governments. As "Rzeczpospolita" reported, the Ministry of National Education has received 1131 applications from local governments so far, demanding reimbursement of costs incurred prior to the education reform [29]. Local authorities complain that they had to use their own budgets to cover the costs of retrofitting classrooms or severance payable to the exempted teachers. Local government: the cost of reforming education is enormous. For example, the authorities of Poznań reported that they spent PLN 16 million, the local government of city of Gdańsk spoke about PLN 8 million, and the authorities of Łódź gave the amount of PLN 52.6 million [30].

A significant change concerns the teaching of children with different types of disabilities. So far, the integration of disabled children has been as close as possible, through the creation of integration classes and the implementation of various assumptions aimed at including this group of children in the general education system. In response, this is what the reformed system has to offer: shorter education of children with more severe disabilities, individual teaching of children with Asperger, only at home, a longer path to obtain a decision on special education. This is just a part of the consequences of the reform of education for parents of children with disabilities. Educational subsidies for students with autism, Asperger's syndrome and conjugate disabilities are 9.5 times higher than for a healthy student. Parents suspect that the government intends to lower subventions in search of savings and exclude the pupils with Asperger's syndrome from the group receiving the ruling on special education, which is significantly more expensive than education of a healthy student. As a result of the changes, children with various types of disabilities, especially those intellectual, would be eliminated from the inclusive educational processes carried out in groups. This may cause isolation and lack of social development, but it can also lead to reduction in the degree of tolerance from healthy students who will be deprived of contact with children with disabilities.

4 Conclusion

As the Polish school system has been working within the frames of new regulations for one school year, it is difficult to already assess its effectiveness or its strengths and weaknesses. The fact is that the way of introducing the reform, the dynamic pace of this process and a number of new regulations have triggered the discussion and certain controversies, particularly due to the insufficient consultations with the teachers' community, the groups of parents and the non-governmental organizations which are active in the field of education.

One of the main doubts over the change of the system structure was the notion of the extent, to which the previous system proved its lack of effectiveness or quality. The international surveys assessing the level of performance of Polish youth showed that there were no significant discrepancies between them and their peers from other countries. Moreover, the organizational matters, particularly those related to adaptation of the existing educational institutions to the demands of the reform - what is the responsibility of local governments - required an apparent financial effort, and the state support turned out to be insufficient. Hence, the local authorities decided to present their complaints on this matter to the Voivodeship Administrative Court.

The reform has also its impact on the teachers' situation. One of the most important assumptions concerning their career is the duration of their professional path. The new regulation makes this path longer than it was before the reform, as the period for gaining the second rank was extended by one year, and the elongation of the period of break between getting one rank and beginning the internship to the next level of professional promotion. It has also its impact on the teachers' salaries level. Another negative aspect of the change within the structure of the school system is a decreasing number of teachers. Plenty of them have lost their jobs and a significant number of those professionally active were forced to work in a part-time system. There is a noticeable number of teachers who have to combine employment in more than one educational institution in order to reach a satisfying level of income. For obvious reasons, this situation causes rising disappointment among the teachers, and the two main Polish teachers unions present their discontent with these provisions.

As it was emphasized above, it would be too early to make an attempt of an assessment the reform at the moment. However, it is worth bringing forward the main assumptions of this serious change together with the doubts and concerns that still exist in the Polish society after the first school year under the new regulations.

References

1. Ministry of National Education, *O reformie.* Available at: http://reformaedukacji.men.gov.pl. (2018)
2. Eurydice, *Krótka informacja o polskim systemie edukacji 2017/2018.* Available at: http://eurydice.org.pl/wp-content/uploads/2017/10/System-edukacji-w-Polsce_2017_2018_PL.pdf. (2017)
3. *Dobra Szkoła. Reforma systemu edukacji. Struktura szkól.* Available at: https://reformaedukacji.men.gov.pl (2017)
4. Eurydice, op. cit.
5. Ibid.
6. Ibid.
7. *Constitution of The Republic of Poland.* Article 70. Available at: http://www.sejm.gov.pl/prawo/konst/angielski/kon1.htm (1997).
8. Ministerstwo Edukacji Narodowej, *Reforma systemu edukacji. Projekt*, Warszawa (1998).
9. P. Długosz, *Elitaryzm versus egalitaryzm systemu oświatowego. Analiza aspiracji edukacyjnych gimnazjalistów polski południowej.* In M. Niezgoda (ed.), *Społeczne skutkizmiany oświatowej w Polsce*, Kraków: WUJ , pp. 129-132 (2011)
10. N. Stępień, *Wyrównywanie szans edukacyjnych w warunkach polskiej szkoły po 1989 roku. O potrzebie polityki wyrównywania szans edukacyjnych*, Studia Politicae Universitatis Silesiensis, T. 14, p. 128 (2015)
11. D. Zielińska, *Jedynie wspólny front nauczycieli i rodziców może powstrzymać reformę edukacji.* Available at: mediumpubliczne.pl. (2016)
12. Serwis Samorządowy PAP, *Zmiany w szkole. MEN przypomina skutki nowelizacji systemu oświaty.* Available at: http://samorzad.pap.pl/depesze/wiadomosci_centralne/160007 (2016)

13. Komunikat Komisji Europejskiej, *Wczesna edukacja i opieka nad dzieckiem: zagwarantujmy wszystkim dzieciom w UE dobry start w przyszłość.* Brussels. Available at: https://eur-lex.europa.eu/legal-content/pl/txt/?uri=celex%3a52011dc0066 (2011)
14. M. Herbst, P. Strawinski, *Early effects of an early start: Evidence from lowering the school starting age in Poland.* Educational Research Institute. Available at: https://www.researchgate.net/publication/283355035_Early_effects_of_an_early_start_Evidence_from_lowering_the_school_starting_age_in_Poland (2015)
15. OECD, *Education Policy Outlook: Poland.* Available at: http://www.oecd.org/education/pol-country-profile.pdf (2015)
16. PISA, *PISA - key findings for Poland.* Available at: http://www.oecd.org/poland/pisa-2015-poland.htm (2015)
17. K. McCann, *Teenagers in the UK lag behind their peers in countries like Singapore, Japan and Poland in maths, science and reading, a major international report has found*, The Telegraph. Available at: https://www.telegraph.co.uk/education/2016/12/06/uk-teenagers-lag-behind-peers-maths-science-reading-global-report/) (2016)
18. J. Suchecka, *Polscy uczniowie znów wysoko w teście PISA. Ministerstwo Edukacji bagatelizuje ich sukces*, Gazeta Wyborcza. Available at: http://wyborcza.pl/7,75398,21082119,polscy-uczniowie-znow-wysoko-w-tescie-pisa-ministerstwo-edukacji.html?disableRedirects=true (2016)
19. J. Przewłocka, *Bezpieczeństwo uczniów i klimat społeczny w polskich szkołach. Raport z badania*, Warszawa (2015)
20. Instytut Badań Edukacyjnych, *Przemoc w polskiej szkole.* Available at: http://www.ibe.edu.pl/pl/publikacje/analizy-ibe/38-aktualnosci/525-przemoc-w-polskiej-szkole (2015)
21. A. Komendant-Brodowska, *Przemoc w szkole. Raport z badań*, Warszawa: Instytut Socjologii Uniwersytetu Warszawskiego (2011)
22. Muzeum Historii Polski. *Plan Trzyletni.* Available at: http://muzhp.pl/pl/e/1698/plan-trzyletni) (2013).
23. Pyter M, *Legal Principles of Functioning of Education in People's Republic of Poland*, Studia Iuridica Lublinensia, **XXIV**, 4. (2015)
24. M. Zahorska, *Successes and failures of the education reform*, Przegląd Socjologiczny, **58**, 3, pp. 119-142 (2009)
25. M. Sitek, *Changes in educational inequalities in Poland. A polemic against the article of Zbigniew Sawiński. Gimnazja wobec nierówności społecznych*, Edukacja, **2,** 137, pp. 113–130 (2016)
26. L. F. Drucker, D. Horn, *Decreased tracking, increased earning: Evidence from the comprehensive Polish educational reform of 1999*, Budapest Working Papers On The Labour Market. BWP nr 2 (2016)
27. Edukacja i Wychowanie, *Reforma edukacji: RPO żąda ujawnienia autorów podstawy programowej z matematyki*, Rzeczpospolita, Available at: http://www.rp.pl/Edukacja-i-wychowanie/304059964-Reforma-edukacji-RPO-zada-ujawnienia-autorow-podstawy-programowej-z-matematyki.html (2018)
28. RPO, *Rzecznik Praw Obywatelskich za ujawnieniem autorów nowej podstawy programowej z matematyki.* Available at: https://www.rpo.gov.pl/pl/content/rpo-za-ujawnieniem-autorow-nowej-podstawy-programowej-z-matematyki (2018)
29. *Miliony za zmiany w szkołach.* Rzeczpospolita. Available at: http://www.rp.pl/Polityka/302229871-Miliony-za-zmiany-w-szkolach.html. (2018)

30. *Zwrot kosztów reformy edukacji*. Available at: www.tvn24.pl/wiadomosci-z-kraju,3/zwrot-kosztow-reformy-edukacji-i-remontow-szkol-tego-chca-samorzady,817456.html (2018)

Media labs–creative cooperation and mutual learning: Case studies across Europe

Marta du Vall[1,*], and *Marta* Majorek[2]

[1]Andrzej Frycz Modrzewski Krakow University, Herlinga – Grudzińskiego 1, Kraków 30 - 705, Poland
[2]Andrzej Frycz Modrzewski Krakow University, Herlinga – Grudzińskiego 1, Kraków 30 - 705, Poland

Abstract. The idea of a media lab is not strictly defined. Media labs, in general, are experimental projects combining creative, research and education activities. As some researchers have concluded, "Media lab is not a name, only a tag that you can describe a specific type of place and - as with tags - use freely, according to and contributing to its conceptual meaning." The study will present the most contemporary, important theoretical issues regarding media labs which, by creating a platform for exchanging experience and knowledge between people representing different professional groups, such as programmers, culture animators and academic researchers, enable work on projects seeking convergence of knowledge, multimedia and technology. The authors will also focus on case studies to indicate the wide range of possibilities for applying this model of creative cooperation.

Key words. digital tools, media lab, education, cooperation, knowledge, technology

1 What is a media lab?

At the beginning, it is worth noting that there is no precise definition of a media appealing because its impreciseness, which is not reckless, makes it open and ready to respond dynamically to change. Furthermore, there is no single media lab model. The simplest definition, which we can find on the internet reads that "A media lab is a form of institution that enables joint work and learning by people with different skills over projects that use new media and technologies." [1] It is assumed that by intensifying the exchange of experience and knowledge between people representing various professional groups (artists, designers, programmers, cultural animators, academic researchers), it is possible to work on projects which strive to converge multimedia and technology.

Some researchers claim that the idea of a media lab is so appealing because its impreciseness, which is not reckless, makes it open and ready to be able to respond

* Corresponding author's e-mail: mduvall@afm.edu.pl

dynamically to change. Media lab is not a name, only a tag that can be used to describe a specific type of place and it can be used freely. [2]

The concept of a media lab is associated with the idea of "Makers" which is propagated by Dale Dougherty. In his TED Talk [3], Dougherty claims that all people are makers. We all have the ability to make and create things. Makers are enthusiasts, who today harvest the technology from places around us and create and explore new areas. Makers are sources of innovation. Dougherty, in his article in "Make", wrote: "More than mere consumers of technology, we are makers, adapting technology to our needs and integrating it into our lives". [4] Dougherty claims, and he is not alone, that the idea of makers should be propagated in education. It is hard to disagree. School should develop creativity – giving young minds the possibility to plan an action and its implementation, even if it fails. A teacher should stand aside, but also be an active observer and respond to each call by advising students or talking to them about the causes of failures. [5]

A media lab, as an idea, can be treated as an experimental educational laboratory. It is worth referring to Grzegorz Stunża's (Polish researcher and media educator) analysis here [6]:

- A media lab is primarily education about and using new media.
- Workshop activities of media labs should be treated as critical and dialogic education. They focus on awakening critical awareness.
- Another thing is freedom of projects implemented by media labs, which manifests in the possibility of benefiting from the experiences of other participants interested in similar activities.
- Activities integrating people who are interested in cooperation and in the idea of a media lab, as well as the media lab's community with the local community, have the dimension of educational exchange.
- Idea of a media lab stands in opposition to the "traditional" pedagogy of the school, where hierarchical communication is still dominant, focused on gathering knowledge. Variability of position in the course of education - transitivity of the role of a teacher and a student is an extremely important and creative experience, not yet explored by numerous institutions.

Returning to the main thread of the deliberations, media labs sometimes pose sources of real technological innovation; they also generate new forms of art and creativity. [7] A media lab is a type of institution that combines innovative trends developed in the field of culture and science with technology and the idea of creative workshops. As we can read on the website of the oldest media lab: "In a world where radical advances in technology are taken for granted, media lab researchers design technologies for people to create a better future". [8] In general, we can describe a media lab as an experimental project combining creative, research and education activities. It helps to bring ideas (even those seemingly crazy at first) into reality.

It is recognized that the first media lab in the world was established as the Department of Architecture and Urbanism School which is a part of the Massachusetts Institute of Technology. The MIT Media Lab was founded by professor Nicholas Negroponte and former rector of the university Jerome Wiesner in 1985. As we can read on the CBS NEWS website "for more than 30 years, MIT has been recruiting people with crazy ideas to work in their media lab, where life-changing inventions are created". [9] noteworthy are The following fragments from the mentioned article published on the CBS News website perfectly reflecting the ideas of a media lab are noteworthy:

"The Media Lab is this glorious mixture, this renaissance, where we break down these formal disciplines and we mix it all up and we see what pops out".

"Ideas are the currency of MIT's Media Lab. The lab is a six-story tower of Babel where 230 graduate students speak dialects of art, engineering, biology, physics and coding, all translated into innovation".

"We really select for people who have a passion. We don't have to tell them to work hard. We have to tell them to work less hard and to get sleep, occasionally."

"The uncommon growth of the Media Lab flows from its refusal to be bound to goals, contracts, or next quarter's profits. It is simply a ship of exploration going wherever a crazy idea may lead."

On the MIT Media Lab website, under *A Unique Perspective* tab we can find the following information: "The MIT Media Lab is a unique resource to help companies address these issues via its facilities and faculty, which support more than 25 research groups and initiatives and more than 450 projects, ranging from smart prostheses for amputees, to creative computation for kids, to designing cities of the future. Broad research foci include synthetic neurobiology, digital currencies, extended intelligence, wellbeing, affective computing, innovative interfaces, and sociable robots". [10] In turn, the *The MIT Media Lab at a Glance* tab reads as follows: „The MIT Media Lab transcends known boundaries and disciplines by actively promoting a unique, antidisciplinary culture that emboldens unconventional mixing and matching of seemingly disparate research areas". [11]

It is not difficult to see that the idea of a media lab makes it possible to create new quality, new technologies, convergence of media and technology through joint work on projects. All these give the opportunity to create modern teaching methods and techniques. The media lab is deeply rooted in the idea of media education, which assumes not only the ability to critical reception of media messages, but also to participate in the creation of content. Media labs can be treated as a new approach to new media and new technologies that are increasingly absorbing most of us. It is also necessary to mention that, unfortunately, numerous education systems fail to keep up with the new media and technological novelties. Hence, the idea of a media lab, as a kind of fun and experimenting, seems to be particularly interesting. Media lab is for all those who the idea of cooperation is close for. It gives opportunities to try one's own skills in practice in an interdisciplinary team, acquiring new competences and implementing some exceptional projects. Everyone can participate in media lab's activities, regardless of their education or age. The media lab is characterized by its anti-disciplinary nature. Antidisciplinarity requires that media lab participants have different competences and skills. It is assumed that each participant has specific knowledge and skills and is expected to actively use them in the educational process. Combining various points of view and competences serves to open the hermetic worlds of individual disciplines. [12] The idea of a media lab changes the perspective from *Do It Yourself* (DIY) to *Do It Together*. The media lab combines social activism, education and technology. It creates some space for experiment and cooperation, sharing knowledge and searching for solutions.

While closing the subject of the general definition of a media lab, it is worth noting that the activity described in the article can also be defined by other terms, such as: Fablab, Futurelab, Thinklab, Idealab, Hackerspace. We could also describe it as simply as workshops or laboratories. We can refer all the indicated terms to the new spaces of cooperation and creativity. Kevin Flanagan recalled: „Whether you were born into the networks or simply interested in digital creation, nowadays there are places and communities where you can learn, create and share knowledge. These laboratories (labs) are mediation spaces dedicated to practice, expression and creation as much as critical commitment on the role of technology in art and society. Individual users, artists, engineers, researchers and designers go there to research and produce in the free culture spirit". [13]

2 Case studies - media labs in Europe

One of the most popular media lab in Europe is *MediaLab Prado.* It is „a citizens' laboratory that serves as a place of encounter for the production of open cultural projects. Anybody can make proposals or sign up for proposals made by someone else and carry them out on a collaborative basis. Activities are structured around work groups, open calls for the production of projects, collaborative research and learning communities that address a very wide range of topics". [14] The main goals which have been set are: building, promoting and sustaining learning and hands-on communities which see people from highly different worlds (in terms of education and experience, interests, background or social status) work together on development of specific projects; improving and evaluating collaborative work methodologies and modus operandi at various levels of action: institutional in general, within the organization itself and in users' development of projects. The MediaLab Prado consists of six thematic laboratories: Creative Prototyping Lab, Collective Intelligence Laboratory for Democratic Participation, Citizen Innovation Lab, Open Data Lab, Citizen Science Lab, Audio/Video Experimentation Lab. It is worth indicating selected programmes implemented in MediaLab Prado. From the authors' point of view, *Collective Intelligence for Democracy* programme seems to be very interesting. „During a period of fifteen days, ten multidisciplinary teams participate in the workshop of Collective Intelligence for Democracy, creating prototypes to activate collective intelligence, improving democracy and citizen commitment". [15] Another interesting programme is *Inclusiva-net.* It „is a platform dedicated to the research, documentation, and circulation of network culture theory. Its main study and documentation areas are the processes of social and cultural inclusion of telecommunication networks and their effects in the development of new artistic practices and critical knowledge production". [16]

The Digital World Research Centre [17] is a research network at the University of Surrey. It brings engineering, communication, social science, business, design and arts together to work on media innovation projects which have some particular impact on the society and culture. The Center conducts interdisciplinary research into new media platforms, content and experiences, and strives to commercialize and apply the research findings in the society. The main focus in on understanding new forms of digital media production and consumption, and on developing ways of supporting them with novel media genres, formats, devices and services. Currently, the Center is carrying out, among others, the following projects: *Media parcels: facilitated media sharing to promote feelings of social connectedness in older adults.* As we can read on project website „This project is a collaborative research activity and network between the University of Surrey, University of Sao Paulo (USP) and Federal University of Sao Carlos UFSCAR). It tries to fill a gap in the research and development of mobile device applications for older users, including tools for assisted living, monitoring, e-health care and wellbeing". [18]

In the Netherlands, the *Hackastory* is worth mentioning, which main purpose is to teach coders and journalists how to collaborate. *Hackastory* refers to the previously mentioned idea suggested by Dougherty. We can read what follows on the media lab website: „We are doers. We get things done for you". [19] The founder of *Hackastory* emphasizes that the main activity is organization of the Hackathons journalism where multidisciplinary teams of designers, coders and journalists work together. The *Hacakstory* team has created a very interesting thing - namely a handpicked list of tools and resources to help build digital story. [20] It provides some information and links to useful applications helpful in creating various kinds of materials: multimedia, infographic, mapping, video, photo, audio, mojo, data, verification, social media, VR, animation, design. There are also such tabs as: library, inspiration and brainstorm.

NxtMedia, a Norwegian technology cluster [21], conducts activities aimed at stimulating journalism innovation through encouraging partnerships, research and product development across international media, technology and academic boundaries. Rolf Dyrnes Svendsen, an editor and a chairman at *NxtMedia* claims that this media lab is driven by two priorities: networking and enabling. Members of the network are focused on common goals or interest areas, and supported in finding opportunities and resources to implement the projects. Svendsen explains that the process "identifies possibilities according to partner's and member's interests and accelerates projects from idea to execution". [22]

In turn, in one of the Polish media lab – *Medialab Katowice* - participants of interdisciplinary projects carried out at the point where art, design and technology meet, use digital media to study the city and create new narratives for the city of Katowice. The project includes workshops, interventions in the public space, exhibitions, lectures and discussions. The medialab's activities take place in several thematic blocks: Shared Cities, Data Science, BudgetsLab, ByteLab and Kosciuszko's project. [23] A particularly interesting project implemented by the *Medialab Katowice* was *Urban Data Stories* – „an interdisciplinary meeting of designers, developers, planners, activists, journalists and all others interested in the acquisition, processing and analysis of data to create meaningful stories about the city". [24] The *Medialab Katowice* follows the cultural activity in the city by collecting, studying and visualizing data on participants of cultural events and social media users. [25]

Designers, engineers and psychologists work together in the media lab located in Lausanne, France. The *EPFL+ECAL Lab* aims to explore the potential of emerging technologies through design research. As we can read on the lab's website [26]: it fosters innovation at the crossroads between technology, design and architecture. The *EPFL-ECAL Lab* bases its „activities along three axes: giving new meaning to technologies, fueling innovation by widening the scope of designers' work and forming new links between research and applications for society". [27] The worth mentioning projects are among others e.g. *Solidarity Network* – its aim is to give digital technologies a social purpose for older people; *Massive is Light* – it offers digital solutions to manage big data for everyday use; *La Porte des Savoirs* - it focuses on experience of immersion and information flow; *Give me more* - its purpose is to change the relationship between the physical and digital worlds.

A media lab located in Greece carries out an interesting and important activity. The *InVID* project embarked on a mission to create a platform to detect, authenticate and check the reliability and accuracy of newsworthy video files and video content spread via social media. [28] In response to the growing attention for the fake news problem, InVID released a free browser plug-in to help journalists verify images and videos and to debunk fake video news - the InVID Verification Plugin. [29] The plugin code has been provided in open source under a MIT license. Making the tool as widely available as possible allows to get feedback from users, so products can be improved. [30] In turn, the InVID Verification Application is a web-based integrated toolset for the verification of videos and their context. [31] The InVID Multimodal Analytics Dashboard is a visual search and information exploration platform to identify and track evolving stories across multiple social media platforms – including participating actors (persons, organizations) and the relations among them. [32] Some examples of the use of tools created by the InVID team can be found on the project website.

3 Conclusion

As it has been shown above, media labs can cover a wide spectrum of activities. They can also successfully generate a wide range of pedagogical activities - from artistic education, through education in the use of technology, construction of new technological solutions, music education, historical education and any other, through a combination of the theory of action developed in the dialogue, implementation based on various, often open source media tools. [33]

The media labs indicate the direction which changes in the education system should go in. The modern education systems should give the choice (freedom), be personalized (adapted to each student individually), transparent and reliable (and therefore respond to the need for criticism and give a sense of integrity with the student's experience); they should also allow for cooperation in a group and be fun, and also take advantage of speed and innovation (in terms of methods and tasks). [34]

The change of thinking is made due to the social need and maladjustment of the education system to the dynamics of cultural and communication changes under the pressure of new technologies. The most important factor influencing the attractiveness of the media lab idea is its bottom-up character, flexibility and openness to various environments, especially from outside of the academy or the field of education. The media labs are often educational and cultural institutions which are rooted in the need to jointly develop some interests of certain individuals, with the desire to create a place for meetings for people working together on the web on specific projects. [35] Undoubtedly, the possibilities of practical use of digital tools by all (not only young) people in educational, cultural, social and technological projects are an investment in the future. The media labs, despite being on the margin of the academy and the education system, can be tools for change. They indicate new patterns of action, new ways of thinking and new forms of cooperation.

References

1. Wikipedia. Available at: https://pl.wikipedia.org/wiki/Media_Lab (2018)
2. M. Filiciak, A. Tarkowski, *Medialab.a sprawa polska.* in: M. Filiciak, A. Tarkowski, A. Jałosińska, *Medialab. Instrukcja Obsługi.* Chrzelice, p. 11-12 (2011).
3. D. Dougherty, *TED Talk.* Available at: https://www.ted.com/talks/dale_dougherty_we_are_makers (2011)
4. D. Dougherty, *The makers of Make*, Make **vol. 1**, p. 7 (2005)
5. G. Tulley, *TED Talk.* Available at: https://www.ted.com/talks/gever_tulley_s_tinkering_school_in_action (2009)
6. G. Stunża, *Edukator Medialny.* Available at: http://edukatormedialny.pl/2011/01/06/medialab-laboratorium-edukacji-medialnej/ (2011)
7. M. Filiciak, A. Tarkowski, *Medialab.a sprawa polska.* in: M. Filiciak, A. Tarkowski, A. Jałosińska, *Medialab. Instrukcja Obsługi.* Chrzelice, p. 13, (2011).
8. MIT Media Lab. (2018). Available at: https://www.media.mit.edu/about/mission-history/ (2018)
9. S. Pelley, *CBS News.* Available at: https://www.cbsnews.com/news/mit-media-lab-making-ideas-into-reality-future-factory/ (2018)
10. MIT Media Lab. Available at: https://dam-prod.media.mit.edu/x/2018/05/24/Unique%20Perspective%20May%202018_tNbz4ms.pdf (2018)

11. MIT Media Lab. Available at: https://dam-prod.media.mit.edu/x/2018/05/07/at-a-glance.pdf (2018)
12. A. Słodownik, *Dwutygodnik.com. Strona kultury*. Available at: http://www.dwutygodnik.com/artykul/4912-medialaby-czyli-jak-mozna.html (2013)
13. K. Flanagan, *P2P Foundation*. Available at: https://blog.p2pfoundation.net/media-labs-in-europe-mapping-places-and-networks/2014/10/12 (2014)
14. MediaLab Prado. Available at: https://www.medialab-prado.es/en/medialab/more-info/about (2018)
15. MediaLab Prado. Available at: https://www.medialab-prado.es/en/programs/collective-intelligence-democracy (2018)
16. MediaLab Prado. Available at: https://www.medialab-prado.es/en/programs/inclusiva-net (2018)
17. Digital World Research Center. Available at: https://www.surrey.ac.uk/digital-world-research-centre (2018)
18. Digital World Research Center. https://www.surrey.ac.uk/digital-world-research-centre/funded-projects/uk-brazil-sprint-network-assistive-media-health-and (2018)
19. Hackastory. Available at: https://hackastory.com/about-hackastory/ (2018)
20. Hackastory. Available at: https://tools.hackastory.com/ (2018)
21. NxtMedia. Available at: https://nxtmedia.no (2018)
22. Media Innovation News. Available at: https://media-innovation.news/media-lab/nxtmedia-a-collaborative-network-for-innovation/ (2018)
23. Medialab Katowice. Available at: https://medialabkatowice.eu/o-medialabie/ (2018)
24. Urban Data Stories. Available at:http://urbandatastories.eu/ (2018)
25. Blog. Medialab Katowice. Available at: https://blog.medialabkatowice.eu/en/ (2018)
26. EPFL-ECAL Lab. Available at: http://www.epfl-ecal-lab.ch/ (2018)
27. ibid
28. InVID Project. Available at: http://www.invid-project.eu/description/ (2018)
29. InVID Verification Plugin. Available at: http://www.invid-project.eu/invid-verification-application/ (2018)
30. Media Innovation News. Available at: https://media-innovation.news/media-lab/invid-video-verification-project-involving-developers-academics-journalists/ (2018)
31. InVID Verification Application. Available at: http://www.invid-project.eu/invid-verification-application/ (2018)
32. InVID Multimodal Analytics Dashboard. Available at: http://www.invid-project.eu/invid-multimodal-analytics-dashboard/ (2018)
33. G. Stunża, *Edukator Medialny*. Available at: http://edukatormedialny.pl/2011/01/06/medialab-laboratorium-edukacji-medialnej/ (2011)
34. A. Maj, *Medialaby, fablaby i banki wiedzy jako nowe modele instytucji edukacyjnych.* Państwo i Społeczeństwo, **vol.3**, p. 94. (2017).
35. ibid.

Empowering civil society through educating about responsible research and innovation

Marta Majorek [1,*] and *Marta* du Vall[2]

[1] Andrzej Frycz Modrzewski Krakow University, Herlinga – Grudzińskiego 1, Kraków 30-705, Poland
[2] Andrzej Frycz Modrzewski Krakow University, Herlinga – Grudzińskiego 1, Kraków 30-705, Poland

Abstract. Number of factors may be indicated that can negatively affect the willingness of third sector actors and citizens to get involved with research and innovation policy. It is worth referring to these factors as barriers to societal engagement. Six key barriers can be identified: lack of knowledge and skills, lack of relevance, lack of impact, lack of trust and critical views of others, lack of time and finances, and lack of legitimacy. The main purpose of this article is to present some policies and practice options that can help to overcome these barriers. The main focus will be on solving the lack of knowledge and skills of social actors. In this context, the fact that citizens and third sector actors may perceive an engagement process as not relevant to their own interests, concerns, and goals may be indicated as the main cause for their non-involvement. Citizens and third sector actors may refrain from engagement when they fear they lack the necessary knowledge and skills to engage in research or in research and innovation policy. They may also be reluctant to participate when they do not have the basic understanding of science and scientific working methods. The article will propose an overview of policies and activities that can effectively overcome the indicated barriers to engagement.

Keywords. Civil society, education, RRI, societal engagement

1 Introduction

The Responsible Research and Innovation tool was created to build effective cooperation between science and society in order to acquire new talents for research and innovation and to combine scientific excellence with social awareness and responsibility. Contribution to solving European social problems identified in Horizon 2020, building capacity and developing innovative methods for inclusion of science into the society are some of its main goals. Therefore, learning will become more attractive (especially for young people), the interest of the society in innovation will increase and further research and innovation activities will be possible.

* Corresponding author's e-mail: mmajorek@afm.edu.pl

As a part of the program, all social actors (scientists, citizens, policy makers, businesses, third sector organizations, etc.) have the opportunity to cooperate throughout the research and innovation process in order to adapt both the process and its results to values, needs and expectations of the European society to a greater extent. The RRI aims to ensure cooperation between social actors throughout the entire research and innovation process. In general terms, the RRI stands for anticipating and evaluating potential social effects and expectations in relation to research and innovation [1].

In practice, responsible research and innovation consists of the design and implementation of research and innovation policy which will broadly involve society in its research and innovation activities, increase access to scientific research results, ensure gender equality, both in the research process and the scope of research being carried out, consider the ethical dimension, promote formal and informal education in science education. The basic idea lying under the RRI is that given the significant impact that ICT innovation has on our world, the whole society should be involved in the process. This means that research and innovation projects come from a closed world of experts in "hard science", opening up to social sciences and humanities, as well as citizens and civil society organizations which can offer various perspectives and creativity as well as foster some more socially relevant outcomes. Another important dimension of the RRI is the development of open access, promotion of science education, care for gender equality and ethical standards [2]. In this context, it is worth considering the role of the Responsible Research and Innovation in promoting attitudes of social involvement, and in particular the role of education in development of attitudes which are open to cooperation and joint action in the field of science and innovation. In the first place, the issues related to the problem of no social involvement and its effects that can currently be noticed in contemporary societies will be discussed in a comprehensive way. Afterwards, the solutions offered by the tools which are created as part of the project of responsible research and innovation with particular emphasis on the sphere of knowledge and education will be indicated. Particular emphasis in this respect will be placed on the social actors, who bear the burden of involvement in social innovation processes, and whose participation in projects aimed at creating and implementing modern solutions in the social area is often insufficient.

2 From civil society to global civil society

The very idea of civil society as such is an issue considered by the philosophy of politics almost from the very beginning of reflection on the idea of state and citizenship. It consists a number of issues which, among others, allow to categorize the relations between the state, the authorities and citizens. Its function is to establish relations within the society or to present a way of an individual's life in order to become a citizen. So far, the research has focused mainly on the idea of civil society as a local mechanism of action in the area of relations between the state and its citizens [3]. It is worth pointing to one, indispensable element based on which a civil society is formed. It is the acceptance and absolute respect for certain norms and values with clearly liberal roots. These norms include, above all, tolerance, mutual respect and trust, pluralism, as well as a sense of identification and solidarity with the community, responsibility for its fate, and readiness to actively work for its well-being and in its defense [4].

Along with the dynamic development of the new information and communication technologies, the perception of a civil society has also deeply changed. There was a need to create a new theoretical framework, for the sake of changing conditions. It seems, therefore, that the most adequate statement is the attempted definition of a civil society at the global level as a network of interrelated and mutually dependent social organizations, what is related to their activities carried out beyond the closest local surroundings, intended for (as grand as it sounds) improvement of the overall situation of the organizations trying to implement and respect human rights, improve working conditions, and take care of the environmental protection etc. The global civil society is a creation that transcends national borders and states, at the same time being rooted in them and this rooting does not renounce. It is a collection of individuals, organizations, sometimes companies, which, while operating under local laws and conditions, deal with issues of broadly understood globalization in economic, cultural and social dimensions. However, the interrelations and interdependencies among these individuals or organizations which are created at a level exceeding geographical, ideological, and cultural boundaries are the key here [5]. Due to social, cultural and economic changes caused by the expansion of new technologies, the very construction of the civil society has changed, which nowadays tend to detach from its global connotations. Therefore, the European Union programs and tools created for the purpose of connecting citizens with the area of science and innovation and strengthening their involvement in the process of developing and implementing modern solutions, must take into account the transnational aspect and work to strengthen the supra-social ties and structures. It is necessary to consider the importance of multicultural approaches while creating such tools. Development of universal tools and processes is not an easy task and it requires reflection on the shape of contemporary, diversified social recipients.

3 Meaning and significance of social engagement

Nowadays, we observe a significant growth of interest in publicly engaged and participatory research. Discussions devoted to engagement, the democratization of knowledge generation and societal participation in decision making are, of course, not a new subject of interest. As Nick Mahony and Hilde C. Stephansen highlighted, this growing body of literature on public engagement with socio-cultural research is currently missing an analysis that encompasses developments in public engagement and participation beyond academia based on contemporary practice. As is well-documented, recent years have been characterized by a 'participatory turn' in a number of domains, including higher education, science and technology, environment, urban regeneration, arts and policy making [6].

The main question arises - what the societal engagement means? The simplest answer is that this is the ability to work constructively within and between social groups to create more resilient and sustainable communities. The indicated definition appears to be highly simplified, but it contains numerous meanings. Social involvement may be manifested in many activities, but nowadays, we deal with its decreasing extent. The inability to see the world from the vantage point of others is a key factor behind both the local and civil conflict. It can also lead to less violent but equally harmful problems of alienation, marginalization and exclusion. We develop our identity by comparing ourselves to like and unlike groups, but this can lead to jumping at assumptions and stereotyping as people struggle to make sense of who they are. Understanding how identity categories are created and how labels can be attached to determine people as insiders or outsiders is important in developing more resilient and sustainable communities. Although learners may have covered the notion of citizenship at school, rarely does the citizenship education include any personal reflection or experiential learning and it may not implement any democratic classroom practices. Learners talk about differences and equalities in a multicultural world, but with the limited direct experience of the range of people that make up any community, they may not have the emotional literacy or the skills to deal with it. Building equal relationships and finding some common grounds with those individuals, when this is not immediately obvious, requires a certain level of some personal confidence which the learners can only develop for themselves [7].

Merrifield, in the research carried out on 'learning citizenship', concluded that 'civic education framed in terms of knowledge and perhaps values but without an experiential component has little impact on behavior' [8]. The popular theory of Putnam's social capital is widely adopted to aid in the analysis of social engagement. His extensive study of American society at the end of the 20th century identified a growing sense of fear and isolation and the demise of trust, support and belonging. He sees the development of social networks as important to the well-being of individuals and groups and differentiates between the notion of bonding and bridging the social capital. Bonding involves reciprocal relationships between known groups that grow out of doing things for people you know will do things for you in return. But by focusing on similarities and facilitating inclusion, this can reinforce divisions between identity groups. Bridging the social capital, on the other hand, involves reciprocal relationships between unlike groups, doing things for people you do not necessarily know, and a more generalized reciprocity. It stems from the belief that borader contribution to a trustful and giving society will eventually benefit us all [9]. The social capital is a concept often defined through the prism of social relations and benefits gained by a local community, within which it is developed.

The main element creating the social capital is trust, which is the basis for development to strengthen local networks. Social cooperation is another key term for the development of social capital., Development of the social capital is important for non-governmental organizations and it coincides with their mission and goals. It allows to use the existing networks of relationships for cooperation, making contacts, implementing plans in a new group, as it makes it easier to establish contacts. This improves the resources and strengthens the efficiency of functioning. In addition, greater public confidence is also reflected in the level of intersectoral cooperation with public administration and business, where the culture of cooperation and prejudice towards NGOs pose a problem [10].

4 Involving social actors in creation of science and innovation policy

Engaging societal actors in the research and innovation (R&I) activities is beneficial for the researchers as well as the public in general. Societal engagement can be pursued for both democratic (citizens having a say on research agendas) and instrumental reasons (more appropriate research results by including societal knowledge, ideas and capacities; higher awareness of science and technology with citizens) [11]. There are specific groups of actors, which should be involved in science and innovation policy: CSOs (such as patient organizations or environmental NGOs) and citizens, especially those with regard to democratic motives [12]. The Engage2020 program identified 6 forms, or dimensions, of policy and activity support, which are relevant to encouraging public engagement in science and research and provided its recommendations based on the following categories: Rules and regulations. This is the most formal effort to integrate public engagement in the R&I policy making and practice; Funding and other incentives which constitute a very effective lever to direct research activities; Promotion which is next to the strong "formal" incentives. Some "soft" promotion activities are proposed as they have the potential to raise interest in engagement in innovation processes on a broad and continuing basis. However, from the point of view of this subject of analysis, the most crucial aspects are among others teaching and training. It is especially demanding to conduct an engagement process and to get relevant results out of it. Even if a participative process was conducted in the best methodical manner, it is not certain whether the results of the process would be used and kept by the political institutions which initiated the participation process. In order to introduce the processes into the Research & Innovation actions undertaken by the European Commission, of national or regional R&I structures, and to have the involved administrative bodies employed the results, it is especially important to directly address and educate various groups of people which are a part of the public engagement process. Various specialists can be involved in this process, from EC administrators and advisors to national policy-makers and government experts, scientists, and other public actors. Successful integration of engagement requires not only theoretical and methodical knowledge about diverse forms and methods of participation. It also demands certain "participative" competences, e.g. discursive, analytical, or moderation skills, which should be trained. In our understanding, the RRI requires research to be anticipatory, inclusive, and reflexive. It should be also responsive, and here is a vital role of citizens, stakeholders and users to be played in embodying the RRI vision. Today, tens of thousands of Europeans are involved in participatory processes every year, and institutions see the benefits. Most participants and creators of RRI tools believe that the future of the European science and technology field depends on proper implementation of this concept. Strong engagement from European citizens, stakeholders and users is a crucial part of this emerging landscape. Regardless of what role any individual plays in the research and innovation in the future, they will definitely need to consider how the social actors can work to address the societal challenges [13].

5 More knowledge - more innovation and engagement

Undoubtedly, we have a lot to do within the area of innovation. In the Global Innovation Index 2015 rank, which determined the level of innovativeness of individual countries, Poland holds the 46th place in the world, out of 141 classified countries [14]. Why such a weak result? Well, the reasons should be seen in the still unfavorable market situation and in the lack of comprehensive support for innovative investments. An investor will provide funds to implement a specific idea if the chances of success are sensibly calculated. If the risk does not bring any profits because the environment is not conducive to its taking, and the reimbursement of costs incurred takes too long or is uncertain, no one will fund even the most promising investment. This is one side of the coin. The second one is actually education. However, we should go a little further here: the university level complements the educational path, which starts much earlier and is unfortunately not a success in our case [15]. We do not teach children and youth how to cooperate, we do not show that it is worth risking. Instead, we instill a lot of doubt in them, the fear of public ridicule, and patterns of thinking and acting. This happens long before the stage of choosing between a humanist and a strict discipline. Yet another issue is a completely false division, placing the humanists overloaded with the impractical knowledge on one side of the reconstructive barricades, while the innovative researchers and engineers remain on the other. This should not be and is not present in any of the countries in the top places of the Global Innovation Index [16]. Everyone should create innovations, not just scientists and engineers. Hence, involvement of other sectors is so significant, not directly related to the sphere of research and innovation

When it comes to research and research and innovation policy, citizens and third sector actors may fear they lack the necessary knowledge and skills to engage. This inevitably leads to a situation of fear of involvement. Due to the lack of knowledge about science and scientific topics citizens can refrain from participation when they have no basic understanding of science and scientific working methods. They may also be reluctant to participate when they lack knowledge about a given scientific topic. The topic may have not been of interest to them so far or it may be that there is hardly any knowledge available because the respective research or innovation field is still at a very early stage. In these cases, citizens may not feel confident to discuss certain issues with other citizens and/or to exchange their views with experts. Plenty of third sector actors are not experienced or equipped for engaging with research and research and innovation policy. Low levels of topic-related knowledge and lack of competent individuals or personnel to actively and effectively take part in an engagement process can deter them from becoming involved [17]. Citizens in particular may think they lack the communicative skills to participate in dialogues and discussions. When engagement includes the use of technical devices such as web-based tools, microphones for making one's own contributions, or video/audio recording, and when citizens are not familiar with such devices, this can have an additional discouraging effect. It is especially likely in the case of less privileged individuals. Societal engagement and political participation generally tend to be dominated by people of higher socio-economic status, such as the middle classes. Depending on how it is designed, societal engagement in research and in research and innovation policy bears the risk of perpetuating the peripheral role of the less privileged. When self-recruitment is adopted for selection of participants, and when the citizens are invited to deal with highly abstract and unpopular topics, when the engagement is only about exchange of arguments (and not for instance, about exchange of personal experiences and views), these are the marginalized groups such as migrants, the socially vulnerable, and the less educated who are most likely to be deterred from getting involved.

A huge problem that can be identified is that third sector actors may not get involved in research projects because they have little or no understanding of the research system in their country and at the EU level. They may not be aware of research funding opportunities for third sector actors or they may have no knowledge of how to (jointly) set up a project proposal and what is required from beneficiaries of publicly funded research in terms of research and administrative tasks and responsibilities [18].

One possibility to deal with the indicated problems is to try to embed engagement more widely into the education system. Teaching on civic engagement and engagement in research and in research and innovation policy can be included in classes on science, citizenship or similar subjects in secondary schools. Building capacities and developing innovative ways of connecting science to society is a priority under Horizon 2020 [19]. Knowledge of science is integral to preparing our population to be actively engaged and responsible citizens, creative and innovative, able to work collaboratively, and fully aware of and conversant with the complex challenges that the society needs to face. It helps us to explain and understand our world, to guide technological development and innovation, and to forecast and plan for the future [20]. It can promote citizens‘ awareness, interest, and willingness to be engaged in scientific debates from an early age and increase their confidence that they can be valuable partners in science and governance of science. Educational organizations can furthermore integrate elements of engagement into school life. They can make use for instance, of debating clubs, school parliaments or class councils in which the pupils debate, discuss and decide on topics of their choice. In addition, societal debates on research and innovation can be simulated in science classes. Use of such formats can help develop competences early on in community-building, dialogue, discussion, and participation. The Erasmus+ programme of the EU could showcase examples of societal engagement in research and innovation in order to attract applications in this field. Erasmus+ is the new EU programme for education, training, youth, and sport which includes (amongst others) the Lifelong Learning Programme (LLP) and the Youth in Action Programme [21]. Another helpful element can be promotion of science education. This promotion can be attempted to achieve by including principles of scientific thinking more widely in the school education curricula. When citizens have a basic understanding of the principles based on which the science works, it may appear less daunting. This may encourage greater contact with scientists. Science journalism can help explain scientific facts and findings and stimulate interest in research and innovation and thereby contribute to ensuring that societal needs and concerns feed more effectively into the research and innovation systems. One way to strengthen science journalism is to make it an integral part of the education of journalists at universities. Another way is to establish structures for dialogue between policy, science, and journalists [22].

Providing support through National Contact Points: The existing network of National Contact Points (NCPs) is the main structure to provide guidance, practical information, and assistance on all aspects of participation in the EU research programmes. The NCPs are established at a national level and give personalized Relevance Impact Trust Knowledge & Skills Time & Resources Legitimacy [23]. They could contribute to capacity-building for third sector actors by serving also as contact points for societal engagement in research. They would build up competence for offering their basic services also in relation to participatory and collaborative research, for instance, in terms of assistance in partner search or guidance on choosing relevant topics and types of action. The support of initiatives and projects involving researchers and societal actors could be explicitly included in their mandate. Opening up advisory boards to third sector organizations: Capacity-building for third sector actors can also occur through learning by doing. This can take place, for instance, through participation in committees that advise on funding programmes and policy [24].

6 Conclusion

Innovation is a change that leads to new quality, a new relationship, a new way of acting or a new solution. And speaking even more succinctly and settling the matter in the market realities: change, as a result of which a new service or new product is created. I will use an example: we introduce some unexpected elements to an existing set of blocks. It leads to development of a different set of blocks which better meets the current needs of users, opens up some new opportunities for builders and at the same time affects the other sets of blocks. However, this is not the case, for example, a new variant of the building, made up of known elements. It is a different way of thinking, followed by innovative actions or previously non-existing relationships [24]. Citizens and third sector actors may be more willing to get involved when they learn that special care has been taken to present balanced information, for instance through expert contributions that include diverse perspectives. Possibilities for self-learning such as interactive websites or a list of relevant web-links can meet the demands of those who wish to obtain more in-depth information and may mitigate the concerns of those who fear restricted and biased information. The more abstract and technical the issues to be dealt with in the engagement process, the more important it is to offer information in different ways.

References

1. Krajowy Punkt Kontaktowy, *Nauka z udziałem społeczeństwa i dla społeczeństwa*. Available at: https://www.kpk.gov.pl/?page_id=10560 (2016)
2. CORDIS, *Nadszedł czas na odpowiedzialne badania naukowe i innowacje (RRI) w ICT*. Available at: https://cordis.europa.eu/news/rcn/123625_pl.html (2015)
3. J. Wrede, *Czym jest Globalne społeczeństwo obywatelskie*. In: J. Miklaszewska, J. Szczepański , *Filozofia polityczna po roku 1989 Teoria – historia – praktyka*. Kraków: WUJ (2012)
4. M. Majorek, *Pomiędzy społeczeństwem obywatelskim a obywatelskim nieposłuszeństwem. Kontestacja społeczna jako forma współczesnej postawy obywatelskie*. In B. Krauz-Mozer, P. Borowiec, *Samotność idei. Społeczeństwo obywatelskie we współczesnym świecie*. Krakow, p.36 (2007)

5. J. Wrede, *Czym jest Globalne społeczeństwo obywatelskie*. In: J. Miklaszewska, J. Szczepański , *Filozofia polityczna po roku 1989 Teoria – historia – praktyka*. Kraków: WUJ (2012)
6. N. Mahony, H.C. Stephansen, *Engaging with the public in public engagement with research*. Res. for All. **1** (1), pp. 35–51 (2017)
7. J. Millican, *Social Engagement*. Available at: http://arts.brighton.ac.uk/__data/assets/pdf_file/0019/6274/Social-Engagement-2.pdf. (2018)
8. J. Merrifield, *Learning citizenship*. IDS working paper 158. Sussex: IDS. (2002)
9. R. Putnam, *Bowling alone. The collapse and revival of American community*. New York: Simon and Schuster. (2000)
10. M. Teodorczyk, *Współpraca organizacji pozarządowych z otoczeniem*. Available at: http://meakultura.pl/edukatornia/wspolpraca-organizacji-pozarzadowych-z-otoczeniem-1909. (2017)
11. *Policies and Activities Supporting Societal Engagement in Research and Innovation*. Available at: http://engage2020.eu/media/Engage2020-Policy-Brief-Issue-1_final.pdf. . (2014)
12. I. Newman, *Public engagement: a dynamo of democracy*. In E. Andersson, S. Bussu, H. Davis , *Engage 2020. Science, Society and Engagement. An e-anthology*. London, p. 27. Available at: http://engage2020.eu/media/Engage2020_withVideo.pdf. (2015)
13. S. Bussu, H. Mulder, S. Pfersdorf, R. Kuhn, G. Mbungu, L. Nierling, *Public Engagement in R&I*. London: The Involve Foundation, p. 40. (2015)
14. S. Dutta, B. Lanvin, S. Wunsch-Vincent (eds.), *The Global Innovation Index 2015. Effective Innovation, Policies for Development*. Cornell University. (2015)
15. M. Bukowski, A. Szpor, A. Śniegocki, *Potencjał i bariery polskiej innowacyjności*. Warszawa: IBS. (2012)
16. S. Dutta, B. Lanvin, S. Wunsch-Vincent (eds.), *The Global Innovation Index 2015. Effective Innovation, Policies for Development*. Cornell University. (2015)
17. P. Adamiak, *Zaangażowanie społeczne Polek i Polaków. Wolontariat, filantropia, 1% i wizerunek organizacji pozarządowych*. Stowarzyszenie Klon/Jawor, Warszawa. (2014)
18. M. Dreyer, H. Kosow, F. Dratsdrummer, *Engaging Society For Responsible Research And Innovation Lowering Barriers – Innovating Policies And Practices*. PROSO Project. (2018)
19. Komisja Europejska - Dyrekcja Generalna ds. Badań i Innowacji, *Horizon 2020 w skrócie. Program ramowy UE w zakresie badań naukowych i innowacji. Luksemburg*. (2014)
20. *Science education policies in the European Commission: towards responsible citizenship*. Science with and for Society. Policy Brief. **2**. Available at: www.sisnetwork.eu. (2016).
21. CORDIS, *Responsible Research and Innovation in Higher Education Curricula*. Available at: https://cordis.europa.eu/programme/rcn/665135_en.html. (2014)
22. M. Dreyer, H. Kosow, F. Dratsdrummer, *Engaging Society For Responsible Research And Innovation Lowering Barriers – Innovating Policies And Practices*. PROSO Project. (2018)
23. Ibid.
24. Ibid.
25. K. Charewicz-Jakubowska, *Skąd się biorą innowacje?* Blog SWPS. Available at: https://www.swps.pl/nauka-i-badania/blog-naukowy/5897-skad-sie-biora-innowacje. (2016)

Threshold Approaches to Architectural Design Studio

Ebru Alakavuk[1,*]

[1]Yasar University, Üniversite Street No:37-39 Ağaçlıyol Bornova, İzmir, Turkey

Abstract. Threshold is a popular design theory in architecture that can be defined in many ways. One definition is "a barrier space that is located for separating the volumes". This is "dictionary definition" of the threshold, but in fact this term can has various meanings according to the different perspectives. The threshold can be physical, psychological, emotional, social, economic, etc. definitions. There are many ways of expressing threshold in to architectural design considering the terms mentioned above. In this paper different ways of expressing "threshold" term in to the architectural design is discussed. For this purpose third year architecture design studio is taken as a case study. The student projects by the ways of defining and expressing the threshold term in to design is taken in consideration. The aim of this paper to put forward the integration of various meanings of threshold in to the architectural design by the case studies that are obtained from the architectural design studio.

Keywords: Architectural Design, Threshold, Architectural Education

1 Introduction

Threshold is; "the floor of an entrance to a building or room" according to the Cambridge Dictionary. In Longman Dictionary the definitions for threshold are; "the level at which something starts to happen or have an effect" and "at the beginning of a new and important event or development. This is the physical definition of threshold that in this definition threshold is taken account just like a separation or connection element located between different spaces. But as it is known threshold does not have only this meaning. It also has physical, psychological, emotional, social, economical, etc. meanings. The problem is how to apply different meanings of threshold on architectural design and also putting forward the importance of designing with threshold.

Walter Benjamin notes: The threshold must be carefully distinguished from the boundary. A Schwelle "threshold" is a zone. Transformation, passage, wave action are in the word Schwellen swell, and etymology ought not to overlook these senses. On the other hand, it is necessary to keep in mind the immediate tectonic and ceremonial context which has brought the word to its current meaning [3]. Till Boettger notes that thresholds are spatial conditions that create openings in boundaries allowing for movement and transition in space [4].

* Corresponding author: ebru.alakavuk@yasar.edu.tr

The transactions between the two distinct spatial environments include movement of people through thresholds such as doors, verandahs, colonnades, porches, triumphal arches, terraces, marquees, stairways, patios, loggias, and stoops. Besides the passage of people across a physical boundary, mediation across environmental, acoustic, and visual boundaries includes flow of air, light, sound, and odor through thresholds such as doors, windows, louvers, and screens. While allowing transition, mediation, and passage through boundaries, thresholds are associated with specific symbolic meanings, rituals, and socio-cultural behavioral codes [5].

A threshold concept is fundamentally transformative: it may be considered 'akin to a portal, opening up a new and previously inaccessible way of thinking about something . . . it represents a transformed way of understanding, or interpreting, or viewing . . . without which the learner cannot progress' [6].

Threshold: what is it? Catherine Dee in her book 'Form and Fabric in Architecture' regards it as a spatial component which provides for integrated, subtle and complex transitions. The threshold is the space that links spaces, mediums or objects [7].

2 Threshold approaches to architectural design studio

As mentioned above threshold is not only the entrance of the buildings. It has different meanings more than that. Expressing the meaning of threshold in to architectural design is not an easy thing.

In this paper meanings, influence and effects of threshold on design is discussed in the third year architecture design studio course. Methods that are used in this study are literature review, evaluation of design with threshold and observing the architectural design process. Firstly, students are asked to question the meaning of the threshold. And then they applied the threshold on their projects. The students are asked to create a threshold in their design. The meaning and ways for applying threshold in their design are up to students. Every student takes the term in different perspective. Some take physical while others take psychological threshold. The objective of this paper is putting forward the effect of understanding of threshold on design process. For this purpose students design their projects with threshold and reflect this term on their design with the meaning they want. Some of them thought threshold as a separator that divides spaces in to zones while some thought threshold as an intersection, gathering point. By naming and designing road, walkways as threshold the students designed a physical threshold. They divide the architectural design in zones like public, semi public and private areas with the physical threshold as roads. With these roads the boundaries of the zones are defined in a natural way. There is no need to put any other architectural element for emphasizing the boundaries. On the other hand some students thought threshold as a connection element for different functions. They combine old places or areas with new ones by the help of threshold. Or they combine underwater places with upper ones by using thresholds.

Taking account threshold in design process, affects the main design idea and maybe sometimes concept. Evaluation the importance of threshold in architectural design is the significance of this paper. Because understanding the aim of threshold in designs can let us understand the architectural design correctly and easily. Every perspective towards and also including threshold can have different point of view.

In one of the student project threshold creates the connectivity between nature and the built environment. Threshold guided the design of the project and revealed structures with two separate functions. Threshold provides fresh air and access in between spaces. And this Project named as sense of time scale, (Fig 1).

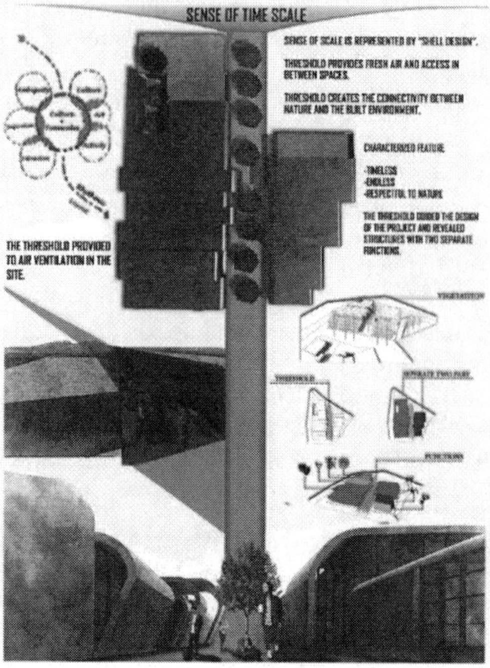

Fig1. Student project in which threshold taken in consideration as a physical separator.

In another student project; there is a blue zone. This blue zone seperates the functions into two main axis such as social and medical axis, divide building to private and public parts. Blue zone is a doorway for patient to heal with social areas, accomadation, meditation,yoga parts and natural walkway. With the blue zone project is divided into zones according to public, semi public and private, (fig 2).

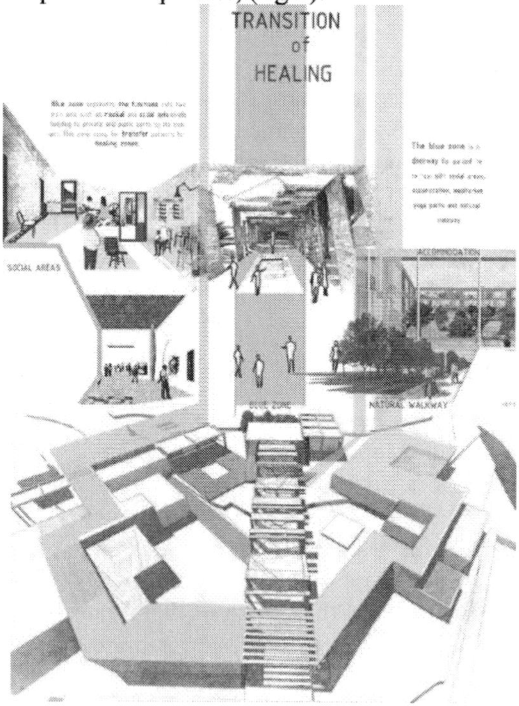

Fig 2. Student project in which threshold taken in consideration as a privacy seperator.

 https://doi.org/10.1051/shsconf/20184801046

The results of this study are interesting. As threshold has many meanings, almost every project take threshold in different perspectives. In the architectural design studio, many different thresholds come apart. In this study some projects of student that have different perspectives are explained. Ways of applying threshold is discussed in this paper. By this acknowledgement can be done for the ones who prefer to use threshold in their architectural design.

References

1. https://dictionary.cambridge.org/tr/
2. https://www.ldoceonline.com/
3. Walter Benjamin and Rolf Tiedemann, *The Arcades Project* (Cambridge, Mass: Belknap Press), 494, (1999).
4. Till Boettger, *Threshold Spaces: Transitions in Architecture Analysis and Design Tools* (Basel, Switzerland: Birkhäuser), 15–51, (2014).
5. Quentin Stevens, *"Betwixt and Between: Building Thresholds, Liminality and Public Space," in Loose Space: Possibility and Diversity in Urban Life*, ed. Karen A. Franck and Quentin Stevens (London; New York: Routledge), 73–92, (2007).
6. Land, R., Meyer, J.H.F. and Baillie, C., *Editors' Preface: Threshold Concepts and Transformational Learning,in: Threshold Concepts and Transformational Learning*, Land, R., Meyer, J.H.F. and Baillie, C., (eds), Sense Publishers, Rotterdam, pp. ix-xlii, (2010).
7. Catherine Dee in her book '*Form and Fabric in Architecture*', Spon Press, London and New York, (2001).

Structure and Material Usages Concerning Sustainability in Architectural Design Studio

Ebru Alakavuk[1*]

[1]Yasar University, Üniversite Street No:37-39 Ağaçlıyol Bornova, İzmir, Turkey

Abstract. Sustainability is a term that there is no exact definition that is accepted for everyone. But the main acceptance is that goods and services that use resources that can be replaced. As it is clear that climate change is one of the big problems of the world nowadays, sustainability becomes an important subject of the world. Day by day people become more conscious about sustainability and try to live environmentally friendly. In such a condition sustainability in architectural design becomes more important. In this paper applying sustainability concepts on architectural design is discussed. In the third year architectural design studio students are supposed to design a sustainable project that is respectable to the environment and also using renewable energy sources. The aim of this paper is to put forward integration of sustainability with respect to material usage in architectural design. The projects of third year studio students are taken as a case study and integration of sustainable structures and materials to architectural design is discussed.

1 Introduction

Climate change is one of the global problems that world faces in nowadays. As the climate changes, sea level has risen, typhoons may cause more damage, average rainfall has increased, hot temperatures can be dangeruos for human health and also changing weather conditions can effect the ranges of plants and animals. For reducing the impacts of climate change people has to take precautions. One of the precaution that can be done is being sustainable. As buildings consume most of the energy, sustainability of the buildings is important. Architects must think about energy consumption and sustainability for living in healthy environment.

There is much talk of 'sustainable development' and little comprehension of its meaning. It is very evident that those involved in the so-called 'green' movement are characterized by their passion, [1]. Estimates of likely future adaptations are an essential ingredient in impact and vulnerability assessments. The extent to which ecosystems, food supplies, and sustainable development are vulnerable or "in danger" depends both on exposure to changes in climate and on the ability of the impacted system to adapt. In addition, adaptation is an important policy response option, along with mitigation. There is a need for the development and assessment of planned adaptation initiatives to help manage the risks of climate change [2].

Adaptation also is considered an important response option or s t r a t e g y, along with mitigation [3, 4, 5, 6]. Even with reductions in greenhouse gas (GHG) emissions, global temperatures are expected to increase, other changes in climate—including extremes—are likely, and sea level will continue to rise [7, 8, 9]. Hence, development of planned adaptation strategies to deal with these risks is regarded as a necessary complement to mitigation actions [10, 11, 12, 13]. Article 4.1 of the UNFCCC commits parties to formulating, cooperating on, and implementing "measures to facilitate adequate adaptation to climate change." The Kyoto Protocol (Article 10) also commits parties to promote and facilitate adaptation and deploy adaptation technologies to address climate change.

One of the ways of adaptation to the climate change is being sustainable. As most of the energy consumption is done by the buildings, being sustainable and using sustainable principles in buildings is getting important day by day.

2 Structure and material usages concerning sustainability in architectural design studio

Mostly every architecture faculty has theoretical courses including sustainability. But ıntegrating sustainability principles in to architectural design is difficult. In this paper adaptation of the sustainability principles to architectural design and how to make the building sustainable by using different materials and structures is discussed. To emphasize and to achieve a consciousness of the sustainability, third year architecture design studio focused on it. Third year architecture design studio and it's outcomes is taken as a case study of this paper.

It was a challenge for students to design with sustainable principles. As sustainability has many ways to apply, students tried to adapt different principles of it into their design. They firstly tried to find new methods, systems, structures and materials for their designs. After that they searched deeply the applicability of the systems. Some of the projects have used different materials and methods for cleaning the surrounding air, collecting rain water, producing energy from sun and waves, using natural ventilation, using biomass and using wind energy. Whereas one of the project used fibre forced polyester for a temporary sustainable project. In this design besides sustainability it can take precautions for climate change. As it is known one of the results of the climate change is the rising the level of sea. This project and the interior spaces of it will not have any damage even if it goes under water. Another project work on the materials for producing energy with algae. This project designed algae producing units as façade elements in building scale and also as separation elements in landscape. The ones that are used on façade are also has the function of shading and providing privacy. As the algae in tubes get larger in volume, the colour of the water in the tubes located on facade get darker achieving the function of sun shading (fig1, fig2). Students learned how to design sustainable project by hands on doing method.

Fig 1. Experiment with algea tubes

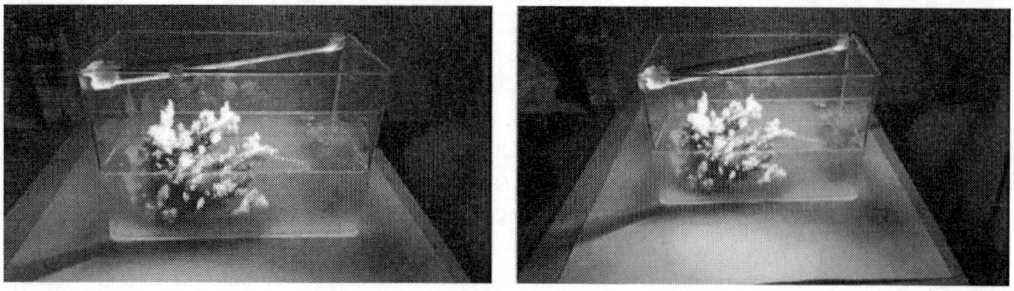

Fig 2. Experiment with algea aquarium

In design process concerning sustainability is important for living in a healthy world. Using renewable sources and energy efficiently can make big changes in our lives quality. Evaluation the importance of sustainability in architectural design is the significance of this paper. Because sustainability in designs can let the architectural design be environmentally friendly. By being sustainable, effects of the serious problems of the world which is climate change and be decreased. In this paper several methods are used. These are; literature review, evaluation of design with sustainability and observing the architectural design process.

The results of this study point out the integration of sustainability principles to architectural design. With this awareness of sustainability on design the energy consumption of buildings can be decreased. Different materials and structures concerning sustainability are put forward by this paper. And with case studies taken from the third year architectural design studio, the application methods of these systems to architectural design is introduced.

References

1. Smith, Peter F., *Architecture in a Climate of Change, A guide to sustainable design* Architectural Press, in Great Britain, p2, (2001).
2. B. Smit, O. Pilifosova *Adaptation to Climate Change in the Context of Sustainable Development and Equity*, p879
3. Fankhauser, S., *The potential costs of climate change adaptation*. In: Adapting to Climate Change: An International Perspective [Smith, J., N. Bhatti, G. Menzhulin, R. Benioff, M.I. Budyko, M. Campos, B. Jallow, and F. Rijsberman (eds.)]. Springer-Verlag, New York, NY, USA, pp. 80–96, (1996).
4. Smith, J.B. and S.S. Lenhart, Climate change adaptation policy options. Climate Research, **6**(2), 193–201, (1996)
5. Pielke, R.A., Rethinking the role of adaptation in climate policy. Global Environmental Change, **8**(2), 159–170, (1998).
6. Kane, S.M. and J.F. Shogren, Linking adaptation and mitigation in c l imate change policy. Climatic Change, **45**(1), 75–102, (2000).
7. Raper, S.C.B., T.M.L. Wigley, and R.A. Warrick, *Global sea level rise: past and future*. In: Sea Level Rise and Coastal Subsidence: Causes, Consequences and Strategies [Milliman, J.D. and B.U. Haq (eds.)]. J. Kluwer Academic Publishers, Dordrecht, The Netherlands, pp. 11–45, (1996).
8. White, R. and D. Etkin, Climate change, extreme events and the Canadian insurance industry. Natural Hazards, **16**, 135–163, (1997).

9. Wigley, T.M.L., *The Science of Climate Change: Global and U.S. Perspectives*. Pew Center for Climate Change, Washington, DC, USA, 48 pp, (1999).
10. Burton, I., *The growth of adaptation capacity: practice and policy*. In: Adapting to Climate Change: An International Perspective [Smith, J., N. Bhatti, G. Menzhulin, R. Benioff, M.I. Budyko, M. Campos, B. Jallow, and F. Rijsberman (eds.)]. Springer-Verlag, New York, NY, USA, pp. 55–67, (1996).
11. Parry, M., N. Arnell, M. Hulme, R. Nicholls, and M. Livermore, Adapting to the inevitable. Nature, **395**, 741–742, (1998).
12. Smit, B., D. McNabb, and J. Smithers, Agricultural adaptation to climate change. Climatic Change, **33**, 7–29, (1996).
13. Parry, M., N. Arnell, M. Hulme, R. Nicholls, and M. Livermore, Adapting to the inevitable. Nature, **395**, 741–742, (1998).
14. Smit, B., I. Burton, R.J.T. Klein, and R. Street, The science of adaptation: a framework for assessment. Mitigation and Adaptation Strategies for Global Change, **4**, 199–213, (1999).

Investigate the effect of bicycle education provided for children with autism on recognising bicycle and cycling skill

Bircan Kavlak[a*] , *Zekiye* Başaran[b] , *Serap* Çolak[c], *Mecit* Kılınç[e] and *Osman* Arslan[d]

[abcd]Kocaeli University Sport Sciences Faculty 41380 Umuttepe Kocaeli / Türkiye
[e]Mavi Otizm Sports Club Association President Tekirdağ / Türkiye

Abstract. The purpose of this study is to investigate the effect of bicycle training on children with autism on their ability to recognize and ride cycling. The sample of the study consisted of 33 children aged 5-17 years. The prepared program was applied for 3 days per week and 2 sessions for each child separately. "Cycling riding skill observation form for autistic individuals" which prepared by Kavlak was used as a data collection tool. The data obtained from the form was analyzed with the SPSS 22 packet program. Descriptive statistics and from dependent variables Wilcoxon Test was applied to non-normal distribution data ($p<0.05$). At the end of study; a statistically significant difference (p =. 000) was found between the pre-test / post-test scores of the cycling skill observation form. This difference was also found in all the items on the form. Bicycle Skill Training has been a positive influence on children with autism. And all the children who participated in the exercise learned to use bicycles. Such special trainings will help their development and maintain a happier life.

Keywords: Autism, Child, Cycling.

1 Introduction and purpose

Autism term was defined as "to absent itself from participating in social world" by Bleuler. Autism is a lifetime discrepancy which generally shows indications in first three years of life. [1] It is a complicated neurological disorder with multiple causes which indicates stereotype behaviors and language, communication and social interaction skills incapability [2,3,4,5,6].

Many individuals with autism have different features and they aren't always at the same similarity level. Autism intensities may be classified according to perception capabilities of individuals. Therefore, autism is not defined as illness but as a disorder [7].

Cause of autism is not known yet; however it is dwelled on that functional disorders, imbalances of releasing chemical substances in body, genetic susceptibility, environmental factors and socio-psychological reasons may be the causes [8,9].

* Corresponding author: bircankav@gmail.com

Doing physical activities regularly provides physiological, psychological and sociological benefits to people. These benefits are quite important for individuals with autism. Sports activities help children with autism to strengthen their muscles, hand-eye coordination, balance development and especially to establish social relationships which is their biggest problem. It helps to reduce adjustment disturbing behaviors. Therefore it eases to have a place in communal living for them [10].

Bicycle which became a part of daily life is a way to entertain as much as being a means of transport. Riding requires ability but everybody can learn how to ride. However a special education method is required for disadvantageous groups such as individuals with autism. Therefore to examine the effect of bicycle education provided for children with autism on recognizing bicycle and cycling skill in this study is the purpose of our research.

2 Material method

2.1 Research group

18 males and 2 females from France Agir Vivre L'autisme with 11,2 (±2.7) age average and 13 male with autism from İzmit Autism Sports Club Association with 12.2 (±2.8) age average participated in research voluntarily by permission of their parents.

2.2 Research method

Researches were made on different dates for each individual for three days and 2 sessions (40 ±7 min.) in a week. Individualized educations designed by special education specialists based on students' perception capacities were applied one-to-one. Applied behavior analysis method focused on how to learn and how to change behaviors based on learning principles is used at researches [11]. To be a model, method to absent clue with physical help and verbal helps were applied. Researchers were attentive to apply education cascades in same order in both countries. Educational games were added into sessions and it was taken care of children to learn entertainingly.

2.3 Data collection tool

"Cycling skill of individuals with autism observation test" developed by Kaylak; one of researchers was used. Movements of children during the tests were videotaped. Then 3 trainers graded videotapes by first shoots and latest shoots according to prepared form and averaged. This from consisting on ten questions is triple likert-type and four questions evaluate level of recognizing bicycle and six questions evaluate cycling skill.

2.4 Data analysis

Data obtained from surveys were analyzed in SPSS 22 packaged software. Definitive statistics, frequency (F) and percent (%) data belonging to personal information were obtained. Also nonparametric Wilcoxon Test was applied in order to test dependent variables ($p<0.05$). Cronbach's Alpha was determined as 918.

Table.1 Definitive Statistics belonging to Participants

	N	Minimum	Maximum	Mean	Std. Deviation
AGE	33	5	17	11,64	2,859
SIZE (CM)	33	115,0	175,0	148,3333	15,46501
KILOGRAM (KG)	33	22	83	47,79	16,221

Age range is 5-17 in sample group. Age average is 11,64 (±2,859)

Table 2. Gender

	Turkish		French	
Sex	**N**	**%**	**N**	**%**
Women	-		2	10
Men	13	100	18	90
Total	13	100	20	100

There are 2 females and 31 males in application group.

Table 3. Distribution of age by countries

Age		f	%
Turkish Children	8	2	11,8
	9	4	23,5
	11	1	5,9
	12	5	29,4
	13	1	5,9
	15	2	11,8
	16	1	5,9
	17	1	5,9
	Total	13	100,0
French Children	5	1	6,3
	6	1	6,3
	9	1	6,3
	10	1	6,3
	11	3	18,8
	12	2	12,5
	13	3	18,8
	14	2	12,5
	15	1	6,3
	16	1	6,3
	Total	20	100,0

It was determined that Turkish children are mainly at the ages of 8,9 and 12 and French children are in 11-14 age range by means of distribution of ages by countries.

Table 4. Cycling Learning Sessions of Children

Seans	F	%
3	1	3,0
5	2	6,1
6	1	3,0
8	2	6,1
10	3	9,1
12	4	12,1
15	3	9,1
17	1	3,0
18	2	6,1
20	1	3,0
22	1	3,0
25	3	9,1
26	1	3,0
30	3	9,1
31	1	3,0
35	1	3,0
36	1	3,0
39	1	3,0
40	1	3,0
Total	**33**	**100**

Considering cycling learning sessions of children, we see it is in 3-40 sessions range. Considering percent; we can say that more children became skillful at cycling between 10-15 sessions.

Table 5. Comparison of Cycling Skills Preliminary Test/Last Data

	N	Mean	Std. Deviation	Minimum	Maximum	Z	P
First TEST	33	12,91	4,397	10	22	-5,021	**,000**
Last TEST	33	26,21	4,256	18	30		

When comparing total points of preliminary test and posttest of cycling skills; a statistically meaningful difference was found.

Table 6. Pre test-Post test Data of Articles in Bicycle Observation Form (Survey)

	Saddle know	Pedal know	Handle Bar know	Brake know	Sit on a bicycle	Right pedaling on the bicycle	Reading bicycle on balance	Turning bicycle with balance	Acceralation by the bicycle	Brake on bicycle
Z	-4,137	-4,137	-4,137	-4,137	-4,625	-5,200	-5,745	-5,745	-4,730	-4,363
P	**,000**	**,000**	**,000**	**,000**	**,000**	**,000**	**,000**	**,000**	**,000**	**,000**

Considering questions of survey by articles, statistically meaningful difference was determined at all parameters.

3 Discussion and conclusion

It is emphasized in studies that activities including sports improved communication skills and physical capacities of children with autism and made current situation better. Bicycle as a sport and daily vehicle might be effective on children for recreation, communicating with friends, to improve physical capacity, to make contribution to consciousness and to grow self-confidence.

Recognizing bicycle and cycling skills of children with autism who need special support to maintain daily life and for social harmony were wanted to grow. There are 33 children in total including 20 French and 13 Turkish children with 5-17 age range. Studies carried out separately for each one lasted for 40 sessions and required skills were obtained between 5-40 sessions.

Considering cycling pre test/post test averages of our study; cycling skill which is $12{,}91 \pm 4{,}397$ at pre test increased to $26{,}21 \pm 4{,}256$ at posttest. Statistically meaningful difference was found at $p<0.05$ level(,000).

Ardahan and Mert [12] researched the relation between students' physical conditions and duration of cycling learning and stated that children who like to move learn to cycle faster.

MacDonald and friends [13] applied individualized education method to children at at cycling upskilling study carried out with 30 individual with down syndrome and 41 individuals with autism. It was observed that 73.3% of children with down syndrome and 85.4% of children with autism could cycle for a distance longer than 100 meters at the end of 5 days of study.

Although duration of learning differs, every person in sample group participated in our research could obtain skill to cycle for more than 10 minutes.

Considering pre test and post test results of study carried out for children to recognize "saddle, pedal, handlebar and brake" which are parts of bicycle, statistically meaningful differences were determined (,000). We believe that children with autism learn concrete conceptions easier as they have trouble learning abstract conceptions. Using sports activity in teaching concepts will contribute education.

Doğru and friends [14] To ride a bicycle with balanced tires is taught 3 children with autism in 3-6 age range by direct education method. However, we think that riding bicycle with balanced tires causes to delay riding bicycles with two tires and leads individuals with autism having habit to put their weight on one side.

Statistically meaningful differences were determined as a result of pre test and post test comparison of behaviors including ability to sit on bicycle (saddle), to cycle correctly, to balance on bicycle, to make turns on bicycle, ability to brake, to make departure on bicycle on our study made concerning ability to ride bicycle with two tires(,000).

Yanardağ and friends [15], Elaltunkara and Cengiz [16], Gök and Başaran [10] stated that 16-weeks exercise education they provided for children with autism affected their basic motor skills and subjects on daily life positively, improved them and increased their life quality Alp and Çamlıyer [17] observed decrease in problematical behaviors of children who do physical activity. It was seen that individual with autism who does physical activity grows better comparing with individual with autism who does not do physical activity. [18, 19, 20].

As a conclusion: Education to recognize bicycle and to cycle affected children with autism positively and all children in our sample group learnt how to ride bicycle with two tires. This result was found meaningful in pre test and post test point results statistically. Skills and disciplines brought by correct approaches to groups needing this type special education in order to maintain their daily life will help them to grow and to maintain a happier life.

3.1 Recommendations

- Only education to recognize bicycle and to cycle was given in this study. Education programs for requested behavior change or skill acquisition may be prepared and given depending on child's capacity.
- As this study is based on one-to-one teaching method, it was carried out with limited number of students. Its background may be prepared by the state in order to apply this on all children with autism.
- As this kind of education requires a special leadership and fund of knowledge, sufficient number of leaders should be raised. It should be followed step by step as it is in coaching.

References

1. E. T. İftar, *Otizm Spektrum Bozukluğu Olan Çocuklar ve Eğitimleri* , 3.baskı Vize Yayıncılık, Ankara (2014)
2. O. I. Lovaas, *Ben Kitabı* (Çevirmen: Sorias, O, Gürkan, A., Tekinsav Sütçü, S., Çengelci, B., Yılmaz Irmak T.) Sistem yayınevi, İstanbul 1.Baskı ISBN No: 9753224036 (2005)
3. L. Wing, *Otizm El Rehber* (Çevirmen: Kurt S.) Yayınevi Sistem İstanbul 3. Baskı ISBN No: 9786054463657 (2010)
4. A. Özen, *Özel Gereksinimli Bireyler Ve Bakım Hizmetleri* Anadolu Üniversitesi Yayınları p.15-43 Eskişehir (2012)
5. A. Baniel, *Sınırları Aşan Çocuklar* (Çevirmen: Dalar, Y.), Doğan Yayınevi, İstanbul, ISSN 9786050930955 (2015)
6. B. Korkmaz *Ah şu Otizm* Aba yayınevi, İstanbul, ISBN: 978-605-66593-7-9 (2017)

7. N. Motavalli, *Oizm Spektrum Bozuklukları,* Erişim Tarihi: 19.03.2018 http://www.inca2014.com/sunular/turkce/Nahit%20Motavalli%20Mukaddes.pdf (2014)
8. W. Chung, *Otizm Hakkında Bildiklerimiz ve Henüz Bilmediklerimiz* Erişim Tarihi : 15 Mayıs 2018 https://www.youtube.com/watch?v=JzRsYJ0bzE8 (2014)
9. S. Benson, *What is autism spectrum disorder,* Erişim Tarihi: 19 Mart 2018, https://www.psychiatry.org/patients-families/autism/what-is-autism-spectrum-disorder (2016)
10. E. Gök, Z. Başaran, Spor Eğitimin 6-17 Yaş Otistik Çocuklarda Duyusal ve Davranış Problemlerine Etkisi, Uluslararası Herkes İçin Spor ve Wellness Kongresi, 05-08 Nisan 2018, Antalya, Alanya (2018)
11. D. Erbaş, Y.Ş. Özkan, *Uygulamalı Davranış Analizi* Yayınevi, Pagem, İstanbul, ISBN: 6052411414 (2017)
12. F. Ardahan, M. Mert, *Bisiklet Kullanan Bireylerin Profillerinin Belirlenmesi ve Bireyleri Bisiklet Kullanmaya Motive Eden Faktörlerin Çeşitli Demografik Değişkenlere Göre Değerlendirilmesi: Türkiye Örneği,* Türkiye Klinikleri Journal of Sports Sciences, **6(2)**: 53-67 (2014)
13. M. Macdonald, P. Esposito, J. Hauck, I. Jeong, J. Hornyak, A. Argento, D.A Ulrich, *Bicycle Training For Youth With Down Syndrome And Autism Spectrum Disorders* Focus On Autism And Other Developmental Disabilities :**27(1)** p: 12-21 (2012)
14. S.S.Y. Doğru, Ö.B.Y Önal, H. Bek, *Teaching How Tor İde A Blanche Wheeled Bicycle To Autistic Children Using The Direct Instruction Method,* Selçuk Üniversitesi Sosyal Bilimler Enstitüsü Dergisi **(18)** p:245-256 ISSN No: 1302-1796 (2007)
15. M. Yanardağ, N. Ergun, Y. İlker, *Otistik Çocuklarda Adapte Edilmiş Egzersiz Eğitiminin Fiziksel Uygunluk Düzeyine Etkisi* Fizyoterapi Rehabilitasyon **20(1)** p:25-31 (2009)
16. C. Elaltunkara, R. Cengiz, *16 Haftalık Spor Eğitiminin Otizmli Çocuklarda Temel Motor Becerileri Üzerine Etkisi,* Bartın Üniversitesi Beden Eğitimi ve Spor Öğretmenliği Anabilim Dalı, Yayınlanmamış Yüksek Lisans Tezi, Bartın (2017)
17. H. Alp, H. Çamlıyer, *Otistik Çocuklarda Görülen Davranış Problemlerinin Düzeltilmesiyle Hareket Eğitimi Ve Fiziksel Aktivitelerin İlişkisi,* Eğitim ve Öğretim Araştırmaları Dergisi, **5(2/26)**: 252-264, ISSN: 2146-9199 (2016)
18. S. Namlı, *Spor Yapan ve Yapmayan Otistik Engelli Bireylerin Davranış Ve Motor Performanslarının Karşılaştırılması* (Yayınlanmamış Yüksek Lisans Tezi). Sakarya Üniversitesi, Eğitim Bilimleri Enstitüsü, Sakarya (2012)
19. B. Görgün, M.A. Melekoğlu, *Otizm Spektrum Bozukluğu (Osb) Olan Bireylerin Fiziksel Aktivitelerine İlişkin Yapılan Çalışmaların Gözden Geçirilmesi,* Ankara Üniversitesi Eğitim Bilimleri Fakültesi Özel Eğitim Dergisi, **17(3)**, p: 347-376 (2016)
20. B. Kavlak, B. Bayazıt, *Otizmli Bireylere Uygulanan Bireyselleştirilmiş Egzersiz Eğitiminin Motor Gelişimine Etkisi,* Uluslararası Rekreasyon ve Spor Yönetimi Kongresi, 10-13 Mayıs 2018, Bodrum-Türkiye (2018)

An Examination of the Relationship between High School Students' Self-efficacy Perceptions Concerning Electromagnetism and Their Academic Success

Sevim Bezen[1*], *Işıl* Aykutlu[1], and *Celal* Bayrak[1]

[1] Hacettepe University, Faculty of Education, Ankara, Turkey

Abstract. In the study, "Magnetism and Electromagnetic Induction" topic, which is part of the unit titled Electricity and Magnetism within the 11th grade Physics program that came into effect in 2013. In this study that aims to examine the relationship between high school students' self-efficacy perceptions concerning electromagnetism and their academic success, study group consists of students who are enrolled at the 11th grade of Anatolian high schools in Ankara. Selection criterion was that students have completed covering "Magnetism and Electromagnetic Induction" topic. Within the scope of the study, answers to following questions were sought: "What is the self-efficacy level of 11th-grade students concerning electromagnetism?", "What is the academic success levels of 11th grade students concerning electromagnetism?" and "Is there a meaningful relationship between students' perception of self-efficacy concerning electromagnetism and their academic success?". At the end of the study, it was revealed that students experience problems with electromagnetism, and thus they do not have a high perception of self-efficacy.

1 Introduction

Learning is a complex and multidimensional process. In this process, cognitive and sensory proficiencies affect learning. Among sensory factors are proficiencies, beliefs, thoughts, and motivations [1]. Self-efficacy, which is one of the motivational sources, shapes people's thoughts [2] self-efficacy is among the basic factors that affect the realization of learning objectives and student success during all learning steps. With self-efficacy perception students' beliefs concerning what they could do under various circumstances are revealed [1]. It can be said that students with high self-efficacy perception are more determined, willing, and insistent on succeeding [3]. It can be said that there is a difference between a student who says I can and who says I cannot in their tendency to learn. In this respect, there is a positive relation between self-efficacy and academic achievement [4]. In general, it is expected that students with high self-efficacy perception have a high academic success [2], because it is known that with the high level of self-efficacy perception students

* Corresponding author: sevimbezen@hacettepe.edu.tr

will have a higher motivation and they will focus on the topic more, and they will be more willing to try to learn. At the same time, it is thought that students should reach a consistent result between their self-efficacy and academic success in order to manage their own learning processes [5, 6]. In literature, there are studies on whether high school students' self-efficacy and academic success can be predicted. At the end of these studies, it was seen that self-efficacy is a significant variable that predicts student success especially in the fields of mathematics and positive sciences [7, 8, 9]. In this study, electromagnetism is taken as the subject matter in the examination of the relationship between self-efficacy perception and success. It this thought that students experience difficulties in learning electromagnetism as a topic, and it is thought that the reason for this is that students have a low self-efficacy perception on this topic [10]. Indeed, electromagnetism as a topic includes such abstract concepts that cannot be explained by direct observation, and these concepts are used in various places and fields such as compasses, electricity, loudspeakers, usb's, and many other fields [11]. Students get the chance to employ their skills of three-dimensional thinking and visualization for the first time during this particular topic [12]. At the same time, electromagnetism affects not only the lives of humans but also the lives of other beings. At this point, the importance of teaching the basic concepts of this topic is obvious [13]. To this end, in this study, "Magnetism and Electromagnetic Induction" which is included in the 11th grade Physics curriculum. In the study, the aim was to examine the relationship between academic success and 11th graders' self-efficacy perceptions concerning electromagnetism, and answers to following questions were sought:

What is the self-efficacy perception of 11th graders concerning electromagnetism?

What is the academic success of 11th graders concerning electromagnetism?

Is there a meaningful relationship between 11th graders' self-efficacy perceptions concerning electromagnetism and academic success?

2 Methodology

2.1 Pattern

This study was patterned in accordance with the relational survey model because the aim was to describe the relationship between self-efficacy perception levels of students concerning electromagnetism, which is part of the physics course, and their academic success levels. In this model, the aim is to describe the situation as it is without any external influence or interference to the circumstances of students [14]. In the study, quantitative data gathering and analysis methods were used.

2.2 Sampling

Study universe consists of 11th grade science and math students during the 2017-2018 academic year Spring semester in Ankara. Sampling was formed with the participation of a total of 200 students from 3 high schools. In the study, criterion for inclusion was that "Magnetism and Electromagnetic Induction" topic should be completed in class. At the end of the data gathering process, data obtained from 200 students were taken into account.

2.3 Data gathering tools

Data of the study were gathered with the help of "Self-Efficacy Form Concerning Electromagnetism" and "Electromagnetism Conceptual Success Test." In this respect, the study was limited within the frame of students' perception of their self-efficacy and their academic success. The self-efficacy form, which was developed by the researchers, was designed by examining the outcomes that exist within the field of this particular topic, and giving behavior expressions that could signify the acquisition of these outcomes (I can write down …., I can understand …., etc.). Items in the form were graded as "Always, Often, Undecided, Rarely, and Never." Moreover, at the beginning of the form there was an explanation part where the aim of the study was explained; and the positive and negative items were put randomly in the form so as not to cause any manipulation. Then, this self-efficacy form was examined by three experts who hold PhDs in this field. Based on the views and suggestions of the experts, the form was re-arranged, and it took its final form. The final form consists of 15 items. Cronbach alpha coefficient was calculated to be 0.84 after the reliability test of the measurements obtained from the form. In this respect, it can be said that the measurements have a good reliability level. Another data gathering tool to be used in the study was the "Electromagnetism Conceptual Success Test," designed by [15]. Electromagnetism Conceptual Success Test was designed based on the outcomes that are given in the curriculum, and it consists of 12 multiple-choice questions. The first four questions in the form are graded five points, and the other questions are 10 points. Reliability coefficient of the "Electromagnetism Conceptual Success Test" was found to be 0.768.

2.4 Process and data analysis

Because the study was conducted according to relational survey model, the self-efficacy concerning electromagnetism form and conceptual success test were handed to the students all together. Data obtained from the study were first of all arranged and the forms of those who completed both forms completely were taken into consideration. Then, students' answers were examined by the researchers separately and they were scored. In the success test, students' scores were calculated based on their answers and their final success scores were calculated. The lowest score students can get from the success test is 0, and the highest they can get is 100. In the form with which their self-efficacy perception is determined, positive and negative items were scored in reverse in that the lowest self-efficacy perception was given and coded as 1, and the highest five. Then, total score each student receives from the self-efficacy form was calculated. According to this, high scores students get in this form indicate high self-efficacy perception, and low scores indicate low self-efficacy perception. Lowest possible score students may get from the self-efficacy form is 15, and the highest possible score is 75. Interval coefficient of this form according to this was calculated to be 12: Never (1): 15-27, Sometimes (2): 27-39; Undecided (3): 39-51; Frequently (4) 51-63; Always (5): 63-75. Data were analyzed through SPSS in accordance with quantitative data analysis techniques. In this respect, students' self-efficacy levels and success levels were analyzed by using descriptive statistical analysis techniques (arithmetic average, standard deviation), and the relationship between self-efficacy scores and success scores was analyzed with the help of Pearson correlation coefficient technique.

3 Findings

In the study, findings of the study, which were obtained after the data analysis collected through "Self-Efficacy Form Concerning Electromagnetism" and "Electromagnetism Conceptual Success Test," were gathered under three headings according to the research questions. Under the first and second headings were presented the findings obtained from the success test and the self-efficacy form as a result of descriptive statistics; and under the third heading were given the correlation analysis results that examine the relationship between students' self-efficacy perceptions and their success scores.

3.1 Findings concerning self-efficacy perception levels

In this section, an answer to the following research question was sought: "What is the level of self-efficacy perception of 11th graders concerning electromagnetism?" First of all, students' scores concerning self-efficacy form were analyzed through descriptive statistics analysis in order for the research question to be answered, and results of the analysis can be seen in Table 1.

Table 1. Minimum, Maximum, Arithmetic Average, Standard Deviation Values of Students' Self-Efficacy Scores.

	n	Minimum	Maximum	Arithmetic Aver.	Standard Deviation
Scores of Self-Efficacy Form	200	22.00	79.00	53.03	10.24346

According to Table1, the lowest score students got from the self-efficacy form is 22, and the highest is 79. Arithmetic average of their scores is 53.03. arithmetic average of students' self-efficacy perception in the sampling falls in "Frequently (3): 51-63" category. According to this, it can be said that students' self-efficacy perception level is intermediate.

3.2 Findings concerning success levels

The second research question was "What is the academic success of 11th graders concerning electromagnetism?" Descriptive statistics analysis results concerning student success, which was measured by the success test designed for electromagnetism, are given in Table 2.

Table 2. Minimum, Maximum, Arithmetic Average, Standard Deviation Values of Students' Success Test Scores.

	n	Minimum	Maximum	Arithmetic Aver.	Standard Deviation
Success Test Scores	200	00.00	80.00	36.13	19.234

When Table 2 is examined, it can be the lowest score students got from the test is 0, and the highest is 80. Arithmetic average of their scores is 36,13. Since students can get 0 the lowest and 100 the highest from the test, it can be said that students' general success levels are low.

3.3 Findings related to the relationship between self-efficacy and success

The third research question was "Is there a meaningful relationship between 11th graders' self-efficacy perception concerning electromagnetism and their success levels?" Whether the there is a meaningful relationship between the two, it was tested by calculating the Pearson moments multiplication coefficient. Analysis results are given in Table 3.

Table 3. Correlation Results between Students' Self-Efficacy Perception and Their Success Level Concerning Electromagnetism.

		Self-Efficacy Perception
Success	r	,279**
	p	,000
	n	200

**p<.01

According to Table 3, there is a positive, low level yet meaningful relationship between students' self-efficacy perception concerning electromagnetism and their success levels ($r=0,279$; $p<.01$). This relationship can be read as follows: the more self-efficacy students have the more successful they will be; likewise the less self-efficacy they have, the less successful they will be.

4 Conclusion and discussion

In this study, 11th graders' self-efficacy perception concerning electromagnetism and their success levels as well as the relationship between the two was examined. Findings of the study show that students' success levels in electromagnetism are generally low and their self-efficacy levels are intermediate. It was determined that the relationship between the two is low but meaningful in a positive way. According to this, it can be said that students' self-efficacy perception and success increase or decrease in parallel to their each other. As far as electromagnetism is concerned, it is known that it is part of daily life and that learning it is effective in daily life [11]. However, finding of the result shows that students have a low success level on this topic. This makes one think that objectives have not been properly achieved in physics classes concerning electromagnetism. It can be argued that problems faced in this topic, which plays an important role in the acquisition of basic knowledge and skills of the field, can have a negative effect in students' future learning experiences. It is thought that this may stem from teachers, student, and the learning process. When literature is examined, there were such expressions that indicate the need for preferring active learning methods to eliminate such problems [16]. It is contended that by using active learning methods success and attitude of students towards the topic would increase. Moreover, literature shows that studies on electromagnetism are generally on conceptual comprehension [17, 18]. It can be said that the reason for this is the fact that electromagnetism includes abstract concepts and that it is difficult to learn electromagnetism conceptually. In addition to this, no study has been found that examine the relationship between high school students' self-efficacy perceptions and their academic success levels. However, it is seen that the result of this study, which contends that there is a meaningful relationship between self-efficacy perception and academic success, is supported by other studies conducted with high school students [7, 8, 19]. For example, [20] and [21] researched whether students' self-efficacy beliefs is a predictor of their success in mathematics classes. At the end of the study, it was revealed that self-efficacy beliefs have an effect on academic success. Likewise, [9] and [22] researched the effect of self-efficacy belief on success in science classes, and they reached the same conclusion. In this respect, it is thought that students' self-efficacy perceptions should be strengthened, and that students should be able to determine their own objectives concerning these. Students should be supported in selecting an appropriate strategy, in progressing with the way they have planned things, and in being able to evaluate the conclusion they have reached. At the same time, it can be suggested that new studies may focus on putting forth a model for determining which factors other than self-efficacy perceptions affect students' success in what levels and in which ways. Since self-efficacy is a factor that affects the whole learning process, it is expected that this relationship between self-efficacy and success will be reflected in the attitude towards electromagnetism or the physics classes. In this respect, examining the relationship between self-efficacy, success, and attitude all together would be good, and it is believed that such studies will fill a gap in the field.

References

1. A. Bandura, *Self-efficacy: The exercise of control* (W. H. Freedman and Company, 1997).
2. D. H. Schunk, Educational Psychologist, **26** (1991).
3. H. Margolis, P. P. Mccabe, Intervention in School and Clinic, **41,** 4 (2006).
4. S. Kurbanoğlu, Information World, **5,** 2 (2004).
5. F. Pajares, M. D. Miller, Journal of Educational Psychology, **86,** 2 (1994).
6. F. Pajares, Contemporary Educational Psychology, **21** (1996).
7. J. Gold, *The relationship between self-efficacy and achievement in at-risk high school students* (Walden University College of Education, 2010).
8. Ş. Keleşoğlu, *A study on the predictive power of the variables of learning styles, academic self- efficacy, the scores of level determination exams and student characteristics in predicting the academic success of 1st grade of high school* (Ankara University, Ankara, 2011).
9. M. Pektaş, *Some of factors affecting science achievement in sampling of Turkey that trends in International Mathematics and Science Study (TIMSS)* (Hacettepe University, Ankara, 2010).
10. N. Yiğit, A. R. Akdeniz, Ş. Kurt, *Fizik öğretiminde çalışma yapraklarının geliştirilmesi [Development of working leaves in physics teaching]* (Maltepe University, İstanbul, 2001).
11. Ş. Aycan, A. Yumuşak, National Education, **159** (2003).
12. E. Bagno, B. S. Eylon, American Journal of Physics, **65**, 8 (1997).
13. R. Chabay, B. Sherwood, American Journal of Physics, **74**, 4 (2006).
14. N. Karasar, *Scientific research method* (Nobel Company, Ankara, 2005).
15. Ü. Turgut, R. Salar, A. Çolak, Bayburt Eğitim Fakültesi Dergisi, **11**, 1 (2016).
16. F. Akşit, *The effect of active learning on academic success in geography teaching* (Gazi University, Ankara, 2007).
17. G. M. Paulus, D. F. Treagust, Journal of Science and Mathematics Education in South East Asia, **14**, 2 (1991).
18. A. Hapkiewicz, MSTA Newsletter, **28** (1992).
19. J. Saunders, L. Davis, T. Williams, J. H. Williams, Journal of Youth and Adolescence, **33**, 1 (2004).
20. F. Barış, *The investigate of TIMSS-R and TIMSS-2007 examinations for the purposes of factors that affected the student's achievement* (Hacettepe University, Ankara, 2009).
21. S. Akarsu, *A cross-national study on self-efficacy, motivation and pisa 2003 mathematics literacy: Turkey and Finland* (Abant Izzet Baysal University, Bolu, 2009).
22. A. Mutlu, *Self-efficacy, learning strategies, task value and gender: Predictors of 11th grade biology achievement* (Middle East Technical University, Ankara, 2012).

George Z. F. Bereday (Zygmunt Fijałkowski) and his comparative method in educational research

Justyna Wojniak

Pedagogical University of Krakow, Podchorążych 2, 30-084 Kraków, Poland

Abstract. The paper concerns George Bereday's (Zygmunt Fijałkowski - 1920-1983) scientific activities and his contribution to the development of comparative education as a scientific discipline. Bereday was a researcher of Polish origin and a professor of Columbia University. His works concern methodological aspects of comparative research in education, and his key study is entitled Comparative Method in Education. The main assumption of this method is to analyze educational facts in a broad social and political context. Bereday also examined the education system and policy in the Soviet Union, as well as in the United States and Japan. An important issue of his interest was mass education, including that on a university level, from the point of view of American and European experiences.

Keywords: comparative education, comparative method, political geography

1 Introduction - Bereday's life and scientific career

George Bereday (Zygmunt Fijałkowski - 1920-1983) was a researcher of Polish origin and a professor of Columbia University. Despite his unquestionable contribution to the development of comparative education as a scientific discipline, both Bereday himself and his achievements remain insufficiently recognized in science of education worldwide. Also in Poland, his native country, his works were not analyzed too deeply due to the lack of their translations. The basic information available is limited to short references, thus the topic remains unknown even on the Polish ground.

The information on Bereday's personal life is scarce. The data available in the archives of Columbia University is rather brief and limited to a few facts [1]. In his Curriculum Vitae of 1978, Bereday provided some information on his birth date and place, which is July 15th 1920, Warsaw (Poland), and he described his personal situation: married to Mary Hale Gillam of Minneapolis, father of three children: Mariko (Japanese-American), Cornelia Krystyna and Thaddeus Matthew Sigmund. The Curriculum Vitae also includes the information on Bereday's military service: during the World War II he served in the Polish Cavalry and the British Parachute Regiment. He was awarded the War Order of Virtuti Militari, Poland's highest military decoration, for his contribution as a parachute

[1] Corresponding author: justyna.wojniak@up.krakow.pl

battalion commander in the Arnhem Airborne Operation in Holland [2] (*Comparative Education*, 1984, p. 5).

After the World War II, he decided to stay abroad, first in the UK, and then he moved to the US. There is a need for a more detailed insight to Bereday's life in order to reconstruct the circumstances of his decision on the immigration, as well as his earlier life - family background in the context of pre-war situation in Poland. It is an important part of the research, especially from the perspective of his individual access to education, which was quite limited in Poland of that time, and Bereday's choice of his university faculties, as well as in terms of his further standpoint on the matter of public education, its inclusion and availability not only for the elite [3].

As for Bereday's educational background, his comprehensive education and studies in a number of disciplines such as economics, sociology, history, political science and law are worth emphasizing. Bereday held bachelor's and master's degrees from few higher education institutions: London University (economics and sociology, 1940-1944, B.Sc.), Oxford University (history, political science, 1947-1950, B.A., 1953 M.A.), Harvard University (sociology, comparative education, 1950-1953, M.A.), and Columbia University (Law, 1976, J.D.) (Bereday, 1978). He was developing his academic career from 1955 at Teachers College of Columbia University. Furthermore, he cooperated with Moscow University (1961), Tokyo University (1962), or University of Hawaii (1969-1970), and many others as Warsaw, Edinburgh, Heidelberg, Barcelona, Paris, Stockholm, Singapore, Kuala Lumpur, playing a role of an exchange or visiting professor. Besides his scientific and didactic activities, Bereday was also involved in political and diplomatic work in the field of culture education. He was a member of cultural missions to USSR (1958), representing the US Department of Education, and to Finland (1966), representing the US Department of State. In 1969, he was appointed by the US Department of State as a member of delegation to the US-Japan Cultural Conference, and in 1970 he was nominated a chief of the US Department of State Short Term American Grantee Mission to Western Europe. His expertise in the field of education was of great value also for some international organizations - between 1970-1971, Bereday served as a consultant for the Organization for Economic Cooperation and Development in Paris, and in 1971, also in Paris, he held a function of a principal consultant and an editor of the United Nations Feasibility Study for UNESCO.

Bereday was a founding editor of the "Comparative Education Review" and a joint editor of the "Year Book of Worlds Education" for numerous years. His books and articles were published in eight languages, as he was proficient in Polish (native), English, French, German, Russian, Italian, Spanish and Japanese. In his research, Bereday specialized in studies of the Soviet Union education policy, as well as American, Japanese and Western Europe education systems and their social and political context [4].

2 The purpose of comparative research in education

Although Bereday's key topic of interest was comparison of education practices and experiences of various nations, he should not be viewed as a "founding father" of the comparative education phenomenon. One must take into consideration that the origins of such investigations date back to the first half of 19th century, and the first researcher who explored this field was Marc Antoine Jullien de Paris, whose work entitled *Esquisse et vues préliminaires d'un ouvrage sur l'éducation comparée, et séries de questions sur l'éducation* of 1817, has been viewed as the "field's originating source" [5].

Development of comparative studies and a comparative method in education research might be divided into three phases, as Bereday described it [6]. The first phase was called a period of "borrowing" related to Marc Antoine Jullien de Paris, and it included collecting and cataloguing descriptive educational data. The best practices of one country were gathered in order to transplant them to others. The aim was to follow the systems which were considered effective, and to develop or improve those which were recognized as underdeveloped or imperfect. Bereday mentioned Domingo Sarmiento in Argentina or Horace Mann in America, who studied foreign education systems and expressed their strong belief that their countries should borrow the best practices from other states, namely the West European nations. It was also a typical practice of French and British empires in Africa, India etc., and a part of their general policy during the colonial period, when the mother country attempted to extend and to retain its control over a particular territory, exercising its own political and social practices.

The second period - of "prediction" - was founded by Michael Sadler and a series of his *Special Reports on Educational Subjects* of 1897-1902 and reports of 1903-1906, developed for local British education authorities for the purpose of reorganization their educational regulations after the Education Act 1902. In this case, the preparatory process before the transplantation was emphasized. The borrowing was not automated, as Sadler advised taking into account the principles which a particular nation is attached to and which determine effectiveness of an education system in a given country. Mistakes and achievements of other countries may only pose an example, and their experiences were never completely identical. What is important is the fact that Sadler's successors - Friedrich Schneider, Nicolas Hans or Pedro Roselló - paid their attention to the foundations of education - the social causes behind the pedagogical scene [7].

The third phase was described as a period of "analysis" and linked to Isaac Kandel and his *Comparative Education*. In his view, "The factors and forces outside the school matter even more than what goes on inside it" [8]. In other words, school reflects social and political ideals of a particular nation, and the main value of the comparative approach should be analysis of the causes which produced whole "educational machinery". Starting with the analysis of differences between national systems of education and their origins and then studying the solutions introduced might bring a more comprehensive view on education than just the interpretation of this process as a set of schoolroom procedures. This approach led to development of "internationalism", arising from appreciative understanding of other as well as one's own nation. For that reason, comparative education studies were conducted as deep, emotionless analytical works aimed at lowering the barriers of ethnocentrism and contributing to better understanding between the nations [9].

Based on the contribution made by the mentioned authors, Bereday claimed that the knowledge on other nations delivered by the comparison is a matter of not only curiosity but also necessity. First, it may be used to make conclusions from achievements and mistakes of other nations, to generate some practical clues for a particular society, which may turn out helpful in the development of their own education system. What is more, foreign education studies help a nation to become more aware of its roots and heritage, and to evaluate the educational issues from a global rather than ethnocentric point of view, at the same time being aware of diversified perspectives. Dealing with two or more cultures leads to better understanding of others and of ourselves.

3 Bereday's comparative method in education

For this author, the social and political circumstances of education system were the key point of interest, which he expressed in one of his best-known works entitled *Comparative Method in Education* (1964). In his opinion they, were the most important determinants of the school life and its development in a particular country, as they are "deeply enmeshed in a matrix of social circumstances". Therefore, "they cannot be compared without a careful accounting for a total situation" [10].

The central point which the research method should be focused on was development of a correct way of making comparisons, which brought comparative education close to other disciplines, within which the political systems could be compared or intercultural studies conducted. According to Bereday, the discussed field of knowledge was deeply rooted in the science of politics or geography. It was also based on methods adopted in philosophy, psychology, literature or statistics. Its proper task was, as Bereday stated it, to combine the subject of interest in the humanities and social sciences with the geographical perspective of education. For this reason, comparative education cannot be treated simply as a history of education or educational thought, but rather as a "current history of education", thus referring to phenomena which occur dynamically while observed and participated in [11].

As far as this domain was located within the social sciences, it could be a part of anthropology, sociology or economics of education, but it could not be identified with any particular discipline. It should be treated as a combination of certain or all elements. Therefore, comparative education was a "political geography of schools" and its role was to search knowledge about various variants of educational practice in various societies, leaning on research methods used by other above-mentioned disciplines.

As for the "technical" side of research, Bereday saw two stages here. The first included a descriptive study of a specific region (area studies), a kind of "educational geography" within which specific data and information were collected. While the second had its clear explanatory dimension and was also referred to as a social analysis - this is when the scholar applied methods and tools employed in other fields of social sciences in order to interpret the previously obtained data. Mutual confrontation of these data was the starting point for comparisons in the international dimension.

Bereday stressed that the area studies demanded not only knowledge of the foreign language or living abroad, but also extreme watchfulness in the observation process. First of all, the researcher had to be aware and at the same time disciplined enough to control any cultural stereotypes and personal prejudices that he might manifest in everyday life. It is worth noting that a demand of scientific objectivity is somehow interfered with in the very decision on the topic of research, as it is governed by a personal interest and an individual attitude displayed by the scholar who considers a particular problem as worth of his or her analysis.

Referring to his temporal stay in the examined territory, Bereday - following Edmund King - suggested that this solution may interfere with the condition of objectivity, as it could induce a sense of alienation, excessive distance, and thus lack of understanding of cultural or social nuances. The opposite situation is also possible, namely the far-reaching degree of integration with the analyzed environment, the sense of identification with the region (country) or establishing social or friendly ties with the local community [12].

Bereday suggested the use of documents and materials available without visiting a specific place as an alternative or a supplementing source of information. Establishing some contact with entities from a given region or country, institutions as well as individuals, for example foreign teachers seemed to be the most natural way. Bereday added the need for the researcher's constant participation in the examined country's culture. This can be achieved through various media: listening to the radio, reading the press, as well as accessing some photographic materials and cinematography which are channels enabling mediated, but also systematic contact with political, social and cultural conditions of a given country or region. They are indispensable elements providing a cultural context for any implemented educational projects, reforms or priorities that are formulated in the field of education and training.

For obvious reasons, this type of research activity, both covering temporary presence in the studied area, and focusing on indirect access to important information and data from the research point of view, would be impossible without at least elementary knowledge of the language. Translator's assistance could turn out significant here, however, this was the researcher's linguistic competence what was of crucial importance. Language skills sharpened the perception of certain phenomena, seemingly irrelevant, which might be consequently important to explain certain phenomena. In addition, as Bereday pointed it out, only the knowledge of the language gives the researcher a chance to "fuse" with the culture he or she examined.

Bereday also referred in detail to the interpretation of data obtained in the process of observation. For this purpose, the knowledge in several areas that could be considered as auxiliary in relation to education, such as history, sociology or economics was essential. What is more, all fields of social sciences and humanities should be treated as a kind of intellectual background, broadening horizons and research perspectives in the area of education. In this context, Bereday again formulated the thesis that adopting the political science (political geography) as a superior discipline would provide the researchers with more courage in discovering the links between educational processes and diverse social and cultural issues. Hence, reaching for knowledge in the field of literature, demography or religion studies could ensure some significant explanatory tools.

Gathering relevant data on education in a given area or areas (regions or countries), regardless of whether the description will be expanded by an attempt to explain the regularities to the broadest extent or not, allow to generate the definitions of comparative research in education. At this stage, it is necessary to switch to real comparative studies. The comparison, however, cannot be based on the articulation of statements about the observed facts. In order to be able to talk about the comparison of the studied phenomena, it is necessary to juxtapose them. It demanded enumeration of education practices in selected countries to trace an issue which was interesting for the researcher. The next step was to review the data under the leading phenomenon and to sum them up in the hypothesis stating the essence of the comparison to be undertaken. As Bereday put it: "Even the most superficial comparison opens the eyes of the student to the truly broadening vistas. This extra dimension to the total thinking processes is the most substantial contribution that comparative studies in general have to offer" [13].

4 Soviet school

Besides the methodological aspects of comparative education studies, Bereday - as an author and editor - examined some selected education systems, placing them in a wide socio-political context, according to his view on the discipline. One of the countries and systems of his interest was the Soviet Union.

In *Modernization and Diversity in Soviet Education with Special Reference to Nationality Groups* this country was described as a Third New Nation, following The United States and Japan in its development as a modern political and economic power [14].

Bereday started with general characteristic of the Soviet school development, determined by pre-revolutionary history and Tsarist educational policy, particularly ineffective in increasing literacy level of the society. In the early years of Soviet regime, the main goal was to "train all the people to build the socialist and industrial state that would devote itself in time to the increased well-being of the population as a whole" [15]. Among the key determinants of the rise of Soviet power, Bereday indicated education and modernization, having pointed out the correlation between them and the Soviet political and economic development. Although it was hardly possible to track the result of such an interaction precisely, some aspects of this process could be documented. Successes in the field of military-technological achievements, such as rocket technology or launching of satellites attracted the world's attention causing the technical education in the USSR to become a topic of discussion abroad [16].

Despite the Soviet government's attempts to expand the educational opportunities for everyone, there were certain difficulties that occurred. This situation was partially determined by the Soviet social specificity and diversity which was forced by the federal system. As a consequence, heterogeneity of nations, languages, religions followed by different aspirations, needs and demands of particular groups, shaped the Soviet educational reforms and practice. Taking into account the presence of such various nations and cultures as Ukrainians, Balts as well as people of Asian and Caucasian origin, some difficulties in performing consistent educational policy could be easily observed.

The main goal of the educational efforts undertaken by the Soviet authorities was its contribution to modernization of the country, which included development of vocational education and so-called polytechnization of education [17]. It also demanded assimilation under the leadership of the politically dominant Russian ethnic group. This assimilation was forced by the Russian language of instruction and Russian textbooks at primary and secondary level of education. It was perceived as a vital condition of professional and academic education of an individual. Although the demand of free and open access to education was one of the core elements of a communist party's program, this access was significantly limited: "The official formula of Soviet administration is democratic centralization", which ensured the strict uniformity of school organization and policy, typical for the communist system [18]. For that reason, Bereday called the Soviet system as the one aimed at diversity within unity - contrary to the American system of education [19].

5 American-Japanese program

The education in the United States and Japan was a topic of Bereday's *American Education through Japanese Eyes* written together with Shigeo Masui from the National Institute for Educational Research in Tokyo. In this publication, Bereday's fascination with Japanese culture and civilization can be easily noticed. He focused his attention on the postwar modernization of the country and the society especially in terms of transformations observed in the young generation lifestyle. The school had a key role to play in those processes [20].

The program was held between 1964-1968. It is worth noting that the initiative was undertaken by Japanese businessmen, as they perceived it as a part of social responsibility of business. The idea was supported politically by Robert Kennedy, who visited Japan and whose involvement in the project resulted in financial support from the Ford Foundation. The Program was supervised by Columbia University, represented by G. Bereday, and Kyushiu University. The main idea of the project was to invite Japanese teachers to the United States. The number of participants during the whole period of four years was 150, and each of them was supposed to spend two months in the US. They lived with selected American families and they visited schools. No particular aim was specified - the only condition was to record the teachers' observations and to disseminate this content in Japan. As a result, there were hundreds of papers, reports and essays published in Japan, triggering high interest among the educational authorities, other teachers and the public opinion in general [21].

The purpose of this idea was not only to acquaint the guests with American school life, but first of all to overcome the stereotypical views or even mutual hostility existing in both societies due to the historical and political reasons. It was a fruitful experience for both sides: on the one hand Japanese teachers had an opportunity to confront themselves with a decentralized model of school administration which was they were completely unfamiliar with. The Americans on the other hand gained an opportunity to "face the others", not only on the professional ground at schools visited by those Japanese teachers, but also on private terms, as the hosts of guests from Japan. "Many participants expressed that the Project not only added new knowledge and information on American things, but also changed their views and images of America completely" [22].

One of the most evident differences in American and Japanese school administration was decentralization vs. centralization of the system. Japanese teachers were aware of this American specificity, as they had participated in seminars and lectures on American education before their visit to the US. However, when confronted with it, they were shocked and bewildered, but also able to notice some positive output of this solution. Moreover, they were fascinated by the degree of American teachers' participation in the decision-making process concerning the school life. They were impressed by the plurality of relationships among various groups involved in the process of education, but they were also concerned about the lack of "formal ritualistic rigidities", what was caused by Japanese customs and tradition [23].

The teaching content also posed an interesting area of differences between both countries. For example, this was the case with the field of moral education, one of the core elements within Japanese school curriculum, apart from physical and intellectual education, in fact one of three major areas of the development of the youth. In the American school this issue occurred to a quite limited extent, as it was diffused in various subjects, left to the parents or omitted for the purpose of educating individuals who act independently and are not attached to a single specific way of behavior. From that point of view, according to the Bereday's way of perceiving the role of comparative studies not only in the field education, a significant element is to provide knowledge which allows the students to see a "true face of foreign people and to show their own faces reflected in foreigners' eyes" [24].

Apart from Japanese criticism towards selected American educational practices, the program helped to overcome the national bias of both nationalities. What appeared one of the most interesting results of the Japanese visit to the US was the noticeable homogenization of views concerning not only the school life - there were some observations about American education which became postulates for Japanese education. This process had its manifestation also in the attitude towards current political issues of that time, namely Vietnam war, atomic stockpiles or the Okinawa case. The Japanese teachers discovered that plenty of Americans shared their points of view which had a calming effect and opened the way for intellectual homogenization. It was a determining step towards "international community of teachers", as Bereday and Masui concluded [25].

6 Academic education

Another topic of Bereday's interest was the issue of mass education, including university level, in relation to the education of professionals. In his book entitled *Universities for All,* he asked a provocative question of whether a department for engineers should exist side by side with a department for plumbers, "both instructed in their skill with the addition of a healthy dose of Plato". Anticipating the controversy which might arise, Bereday claimed that in the world where 60% of population was still illiterate, even one-year universal schooling was an extremely ambitious goal, taking into account that even the access to the compulsory education was limited in the industrialized countries of that time [26].

The ideal, as Bereday described it, would have been if all human beings were admitted to graduation without exclusion. Nevertheless, it was hard to imagine that accessibility of higher education on a mass level would ever come true. Although Universities were described as a bastion of cultural stability, their role raised (and still does today) some controversies. There was a sort of clash between academic activities, namely research and teaching, as it was extremely difficult to combine those two areas. Another field of academic activity and responsibility is the public service, particularly in terms of shaping the public opinion. Modernization of social life and industrialization of economy were the main reasons why the university was not able to perform these complex roles effectively. A university was rather expected to meet the aims of a modern industrialized society, which involved educating professionals of various fields. As a consequence, scholars became the teaching staff rather than the contemplative academicians. Therefore, a major thrust of that time was in "the direction of the university as a school" [27].

An answer for the public demand on access to universities could have been be a sort of a union between intellectual elitism and mass opportunity, a popular model emerging in European educational institutions, which Bereday called as hybridized. The weakness of this concept was a division between university and non-university institutions which caused some tensions between "first-rate and second-rate minds" which might lead to destruction of the academy" [28].

In this context, Bereday underlined the fact that higher education should not only concentrate on young adults, but it should also include education "from cradle to grave - lifelong education". Many governments, partially inspired by egalitarian ideas and social equality, became more aware of people's expectations and ambitions, as well as the role of the educated population in the national growth. Hence, such solutions as establishing higher education institutions in rural areas, developing a network of student dormitories, providing work-study programs and organizing some financial assistance for the students, shaped the frames for democratization of higher education. Although the situation of women and minorities was improved, there still was a significant gap between particular groups, depending on their socio-economic status as well as customs and traditions existing in a given nation or region [29].

For that reason, Bereday's aim, from the comparative education point of view, was to create a theory for the mass higher education. The arguments Bereday adopted for his concept, grasped the idea of to use the human potential. He claimed that open admission did not mean a lower quality, and the high standards would have not been damaged if they were more flexible and less pedantic. This situation might lead to effective use of the people's ambitions. Another argument for mass higher education was an educational upgrade of all professions, as according to Bereday, there was no such a thing as overproduction of people with high qualifications. Besides, mass education did not mean egalitarian but rather an open school: "The curriculum must give most to those who have the least in order to increase the academic comprehension of the mass rather than simply reinforce existing disparities" [30].

The conclusive argument supporting such a solution, in spite of potential controversies or even resistance of conservative academic institutions, was the fact that: "The many new opportunities for higher studies help to create resourceful, well-motivated and critical population. Higher education is correctly thought to be a precondition of good democracy" [31].

7 Juvenile law

Bereday focused his research also on the activities in the field of juvenile law systems, in the comparative view, taking into account the competent institutions and applicable provisions existing in the US, the USSR, China, Sweden, Japan and France. What is significant is that after 20 years as a university professor, he decided to enroll as a first-year student at Columbia Law School for that purpose [32].

Juvenile law was defined as all legal matters concerning minors, to avoid isolating legal issues of this field from one another [33]. It is important to mention that the range of the topics was highly extensive, from defending the rights to property of unborn as a descendant, through suing for malparenting, right to bilingual education, to trials before the court. According to this variety of issues, the juvenile law might be divided into five sections: 1) law of life, 2) law of infants, 3) civic law, 4) school law, 5) juvenile justice (court law) [34].

The first section addressed the issues concerning prenatal life, related to abortion. Bereday referred to the 19th century views and the catholic standpoint assuming it is a manslaughter and underlining the rights of adults, namely of mothers who cannot not be described as instruments of ensuring human race's future and their right to the privacy of their bodies which prevailed. The juvenile law was therefore reflected in the rule that life of an adult was still superior to the life of a being about to be born. Further issues discussed in this section were: contraceptives, sterilization [35]. In another manuscript, Bereday introduced a classification, where those three elements were included in the "Prevention" category. There was also the "Protection" category added, including artificial insemination (previously under the "Prevention" category), surrogate mothers and prenatal torts [36].

The second section, law of infants, concerned the rights of infants that started with the time of their birth. They regulated the parents' position in their children' lives as well as the state's position and the instruments its institutions might use in case of any mistreatment of the children. This area comprised of such problems as the best interest of the child in terms of custody, contacting natural parents, children's financial support, or the so-called childsnatching. Another topic was illegitimacy of children and their unequal treatment as a consequence of such a distinction. Bereday referred to the problem of adoption, foster families, the domicile arrangements in case of the parents' divorce.

Civic law put forward the question in what extent the minors should have been treated as adults. It concerned various rights and duties in connection with parental guidance responsible for the general control of their children. For example: issuing driving license to juveniles, employment of minors, medical consent, inheritance and administration of their own property, voting rights.

School law addressed the issues of the state-church relationship and the secular vs. religious training, students' freedom to express their opinion, search and seizure, suspension and expulsion. Other topics are censorship of school newspapers, sexual education, bilingual education of immigrant children, equal educational opportunities for disabled children.

Juvenile justice was the most noticeable area of juvenile law, commonly recognized by the public opinion, and those terms were often used interchangeably. The former, however, applies to children in front of the court, as victims and as offenders. Bereday mentioned neglected and abused children in the first group. Several groups depending on the sort of crime they committed may be distinguished among the offenders. Regardless of whether they are tried in front of a family, a juvenile or an adult court, they had the right to be heard, and in the case of the adult court, the right to a counsel, the trial by jury and to plea bargaining, as well as they were placed in separate parts of penitentiaries if incarcerated [37].

Among the reasons for examination of this topic, Bereday mentioned that it is a history and civilization demand, as the equal protection of various groups was developed within the course of years, including social classes, race and ethnic minorities. The remained category to protect would be therefore only the one distinguished by the age, and the recognition of the importance of law affecting minors is getting public attention [38]. From this point of view, it was rather an innovative attitude, more typical for the present decades, when awareness of the children's rights promotion and protection has become widely discussed worldwide.

As some of Bereday's and his colleagues works above-mentioned have never been published, it can be assumed that they were prepared for the didactics purposes, as the materials for the lectures or seminars addressed to students. Gottesman Library at Teachers College of Columbia University has also a draft of article entitled *An Introduction to*

Juvenile Law and Its Bibliography in its archive. The research was supported by a grant from the Richard Lounsberry Foundation, a draft includes names of the assistants who cooperated with Bereday in its preparation, but there is no date when it was written. The article includes references to books and papers published in 1981 and earlier, therefore on it may be assumed that Bereday was not able to publish it before his death in 1983. It may be the reason why there are only few Bereday's publications concerning the topic are available.

8 Conclusion - Bereday's impact today

Although Bereday's activity fell on the second half of 20th century, his influence on contemporary shape of science of education is indisputable. Taking into account his contribution to research on methodology, some authors [39] ascribe him with the four steps of comparison model (description – interpretation – juxtaposition – comparison: "First description, the systematic collection of pedagogical information in one country, then interpretation, the analysis in terms of social sciences, then juxtaposition, a simultaneous review of several systems to determine the framework in which to compare them, and finally comparison, first of select problems and then of the total relevance of education in several countries – these four steps point the way to the future for comparative education" [40].

However, other authors attribute this invention to Franz Hilker, explaining that he could be possibly forgotten, as his works were published in German and he was not able to become popular in English-speaking community of researchers [41]. Bereday was familiar with Hilker's book entitled *Vergleichende Pädagogik* of 1964, as he in his letter to Hilker clearly referred to this matter, informing Hilker that the book was going to be reviewed for "Comparative Education Review" by William Brickman. Bereday was a bit critical towards the concept - he was appreciative but he thought that "it deals with mechanics rather than the content of analysis" [42]. Therefore, it is quite obvious that both authors knew each other's works, discussed them and treated them as an inspiration for their further research activity. Taking into account the concept of four steps of the comparison model, it is worth underlining that while discussing the two main 'purposes of comparison' – interpretive or causal-analytic - Bereday's approach could be described as the interpretive one [43]. Despite of the limitations brought by the four steps model, it has led to new and different methodologies today [44].

Moreover, Bereday and Hilker were leading figures in the beginnings of academic associations in comparative education. Bereday's name should be mentioned in a context of the origins of the US-based Comparative Education Society (CES) founded in 1956, which was renamed as the Comparative and International Education Society (CIES) in 1969. The idea for an international conference in London in May 1961 led to the founding of the Comparative Education Society in Europe (CESE). In 1957, Bereday became the first editor of the "Comparative Education Review", the society journal of the US-based CES (later CIES), the academic journal that still exists today.

William Brickman, the president of the Comparative Education Society, in his editorial note in the first issue explained the aims of this publication: "It aspires to be a clearing house of basic data and resources for the effective teaching of comparative education at the colleges and universities" [45]. In the eulogy after Bereday's death, Phillip Altbach highlighted his "commitment to reflect a broader parameter of the field rather than to shape a journal in the image of one scholarly approach or ideology" [46].

In 1980, the first award committee was formed to review articles published in the "Comparative Education Review". The mandate was to review all the articles published in the preceding year in terms of their significance for shaping the field, analytic merit, policy implications, concern for theoretical constructs and implications for future research. In 1989, the CIES Awards Committee formally named the award as: The George Bereday Annual Best CER Article Award. The award was first granted in 1981 and has been granted every year since then [47]. In 2017, the award was presented to Francine Menashy for the article entitled *The Limits of Multistakeholder Governance: The Case of the Global Partnership for Education and Private Schooling*".

Taking into account all scientific and academic activities that George Z. F. Bereday performed, a wide range of his interests, including not only methodological issues in educational research, but their application in his works concerning various topics he examined can be noticed. William Brickman described him as an extraordinarily talented and gifted personality: "Professor Bereday represented a rare blend of the classical and the modern, of Eastern and Western European education and scholarship, and of the Occidental and Oriental cultures," and that he "exhibited endless evidence of humanism toward other cultures and humanitarianism toward persons of all ethnic, racial, and national backgrounds" [48].

References

1. G. Z. F. Bereday, *Vita*, Gottesman Libraries, Teachers College, Columbia University NY (1978, May)
2. *Professor George Bereday,* Comparative Education, **20**, 1, p. 5 (1984)
3. D. Coldrin, *Interview with dr Bereday, Your School Report Today,* Columbus OH (1973, August)
4. *G. Z. F. Bereday Dead; Educator, Author and Editor*, The New York Times (1983, October 26).
5. E. H. Epstein, *Is Marc-Antoine Jullien de Paris the 'father' of comparative education?*, Compare: A Journal of Comparative and International Education, **47**, 3, doi: 10.1080/03057925.2016.1254542, p. 317 (2017).
6. G. Z. F. Bereday, *Comparative Method in Education*, New York NY: Holt, Rinehart and Winston Inc., pp. 7-10 (1964)
7. Ibid., p. 8.
8. I. L. Kandel *Comparative Education,* Cambridge MA: The Riverside Press, Introduction, xix (1933)
9. Ibid., Introduction xxv
10. G. Z. F. Bereday, op. cit., Preface, ix (1964)
11. Ibid., Preface, x
12. E. King, *Students, Teachers, and Researchers in Comparative Education*, Comparative Education Review, **3**, 1, p. 34 (1959)
13. G. Z. F. Bereday, op. cit., p. 23 (1964).
14. G. Z. F. Bereday, J. Pennar, I. Bakalo, *Modernization and Diversity in Soviet Education*, New York NY: Praeger Publishers, Preface, v (1971)
15. Ibid., p. 31.
16. R. Karça, *A General View of Soviet Education.* In G. Z. F. Bereday, J. Pennar (eds.), *The Politics of Soviet Union,* New York NY: Frederick A. Praeger, p. 3 (1959)
17. G. Z. F. Bereday, *American and Soviet Scientific Potential*, Social Problems, **4,** 3, p. 213 (1957)

18. G. Z. F. Bereday, *Changes in Soviet Educational Administration, School and Society*, 86 (2124), p. 38 (1958, January 18)
19. G. Z. F. Bereday, J. Pennar, I. Bakalo, op. cit., p. 341 (1971)
20. G. Z. F. Bereday, S. Masui, *American Education through Japanese Eyes*, Honolulu: The University Press of Hawaii, Preface, vii (1973)
21. T. Kobayashi, *On the Japanese-American Teachers Project: A Report to the Director*, Gottesman Libraries, Teachers College, Columbia University NY, pp. 1-12 (1964, November)
22. Ibid., p. 10.
23. G. Z. F. Bereday, S. Masui, op. cit., pp. 3-23 (1973)
24. G. Z. F Bereday, op. cit., p. 6 (1964)
25. G. Z. F. Bereday, S. Masui , op. cit., p. 227 (1973).
26. G. Z. F. Bereday, *Universities for All*, San Francisco CA: Jossey-Bass Publishers, pp. 1-2.(1973)
27. Ibid., p. 14
28. Ibid., p. 16
29. 29.G. Z. F. Bereday, *Democratization of Higher Education,* Educational Information and Documentation. Bulletin of International Bureau of Education, **53,** 210, Paris-Geneva: UNESCO, pp. 14-16 (1979),
30. G. Z. F. Bereday, op. cit., pp. 139-145 (1973)
31. G. Z. F. Bereday, op. cit., p. 16 (1979)
32. G. Z. F. Bereday, *First Semester at Law School*, Intellect. Law&Justice, pp. 460-463 (1975, April)
33. G. Z. F. Bereday, *The General Parameters of Juvenile Law,* Hawaii Bar Journal, **17**, 2, pp. 87-103(1982)
34. G. Z. F. Bereday, B. L, Morton, R. Galbraith, *Comparative Juvenile Law. Outline of Research* (manuscript), Gottesman Libraries, Teachers College, Columbia University NY, p. 3
35. Ibid., p. 13
36. G. Z. F. Bereday., *American Juvenile Law. Cases and Materials* (manuscript), Gottesman Libraries, Teachers College, Columbia University NY
37. G. Z. F. Bereday, *Juvenile Deliquents, the Deprived and the Acculturation Process*. In *Vergleichende Erziehungswissenchaft*, U. Baumann, V. Lenhart, A. Zimmermann (eds.), Wiesbaden: Akademische Verlagsgesellschaft, p. 255 (1981)
38. G. Z. F. Bereday, *The Basic Premises of Juvenile Law and an Introductory Reading* (manuscript), Gottesman Libraries, Teachers College, Columbia University NY
39. M. Manzon, *Comparing Places*. In *Comparative Education Research. Approaches and Methods*, M. Bray, B. Adamson, M. Mason (eds.), Hong Kong-Dordrecht: Springer, p. 99.(2007)
40. G. Z. F. Bereday, op. cit, pp. 27-28 (1964)
41. Ch. Adick, *Bereday and Hilker: Origins of the 'Four Steps of Comparison' Model*, Comparative Education, **54,** 1, doi: 10.1080/03050068.2017.1396088, p. 36 (2018)
42. G. Z. F. Bereday, *Letter to Franz Hilker*, Gottesman Libraries, Teachers College, Columbia University NY (1962, October 31)
43. M. Manzon , op. cit, p. 99

44. Ch. Adick, op. cit, p. 44
45. W. Brickman , A New Journal in Comparative Education, Comparative Education Review, **1,** 1, p. 1
46. J. Cossa, Shaping the Intellectual Landscape. In *Crafting a Global Field. Six Decades of the Comparative and International Education Society*, E. H. Epstein (ed.), Hong Kong: Springer, p. 132 (2016)
47. Comparative and International Education Society *George Bereday Award*, https://www.cies.us/general/custom.asp?page=BeredayAward (2018), Accessed: 27.06.2018.
48. Comparative Education Review, George Z. F. Bereday Award for 2015, **60,** 2, pp. 420-421. (2016, May)

Determinants of General Chemistry Success of Engineering Students in PLTL and Traditional Classroom: State Anxiety and Test Anxiety

Ece N. Eren-Sisman[1*], *Ceyhan* Cigdemoglu[2] and *Ömer* Geban[1]

[1]Department of Mathematics and Science Education, Middle East Technical University, 06800, Ankara, Turkey
[2]Department of Educational Sciences, Atılım University, 06830, Ankara, Turkey

Abstract. The purpose is to find out whether state and test anxiety can predict general chemistry grade in peer-led team learning group (PLTL) and non-PLTL groups and to explore their predictability of the grade after controlling the influence of trait anxiety. The sample consisted of a total 128 freshman engineering students attending general chemistry in a private university. STAI and RTT instruments and exams were used to generate data which were analyzed by using standard and hierarchical multiple regression. The findings revealed that in both groups the combination of predictors is significantly related to general chemistry grade, having the strongest unique contribution of test anxiety; however, it was only statistically significant for PLTL group. After controlling the effect of trait anxiety, test anxiety still makes a unique significant contribution for PLTL group. Accordingly, test anxiety can be used to predict the general chemistry grade of PLTL students.

1 Introduction

1.1 Anxiety experiences

Anxiety as an element of the affective domain of learning is a significant factor since they can influence students' understanding of science [1]. Anxiety is also classified as trait anxiety and state anxiety by Spielberger et al. [2], who define the state anxiety as an interpretation of a particularly stressful situation at a particular time while trait anxiety was defined as a permanent personality characteristic or a general feeling of anxiety. Some studies confirmed that state and trait anxiety can be a significant predictor of academic achievement, in others, there are findings contrary to this view. Besides, test anxiety refers to the experience of the high level of anxiety elicited by testing in academic settings [3]. They also stressed that it is an important issue that can associate with the academic performance of college students.

* Corresponding author: neren@metu.edu.tr

1.2 Peer-led team learning

Peer-led team learning (PLTL) model was first introduced in general chemistry classes as at The City College of New York (CCNY) for a systemic initiative in chemistry in the early 1990s and was disseminated by many institutions nationwide across all STEM disciplines in the US [4].

In PLTL model, lectures are first introduced by the course instructors and then these lectures are supplemented with weekly PLTL workshops in which a successful undergraduate student (peer leader) guides a group of 6–8 students for one or two hours per week to solve problems developed by the course instructor [4]. Peer leaders also meet with the instructor to discuss the topics and solve the problems correlated with the course content by providing conceptual understanding and critical thinking. Unlike a teacher in the traditional sense of lecturing or a teaching assistant in demonstrating how to solve the problem, "peer leader" is a facilitator or guide who earned at least a B in the same course in the previous years.

All conditions regarding six critical components of the model, namely involvement of faculty members, integration of the workshops to the lecture, good leader selection and training, appropriate materials, appropriate organizational arrangements and administrative supports should be met for implementation and dissemination of the model since it was advised to be implemented properly so as to achieve highly remarkable results [4].

1.3 Purpose and research questions

This study aimed at finding out whether state and test anxiety can predict general chemistry grade of engineering students in PLTL and non-PLTL groups and which anxiety is the best predictor of the success. Additionally, we aimed at exploring whether they are still able to predict the general chemistry grade in the case of controlling the possible effect of trait anxiety.

As a result, the research questions were established as follows:

1. How well do the two measures of anxiety (state and test anxiety scores) predict general chemistry grade of PLTL and non-PLTL groups? How much variance in general chemistry grade can be explained by scores on two measures for PLTL and non-PLTL groups?
2. Which is the best predictor of general chemistry grade for PLTL and non-PLTL groups: state anxiety, or test anxiety?
3. If we control the possible effect of trait anxiety, is this set of variables still able to predict a significant amount of the variance in general chemistry grade?

2 Methods

This paper employed the predictive study type of the correlational research. If there is a relationship with sufficient magnitude between two variables, one variable can be used to predict the other variable [5]. Therefore, in the current study state anxiety and test anxiety were used to make the prediction (predictor variables) about the general chemistry grade (criterion variable) of students in PLTL and non-PLTL groups.

2.1 Context and sample of the study

The sample consisted of two groups of students who were total 128 freshman engineering students in Atılım University in Turkey. Two intact sections of General Chemistry course taught by the same instructor were selected. 68 students in one section attended PLTL while

60 students in other section of the course participated in the traditional instruction group. In the PLTL group, in two-thirds of the class time instructor explained the concepts as in the traditional classroom and in the remaining time, students solve a set of structured problems under the guidance of a peer leader who has completed the course successfully and trained in accordance with the framework of PLTL. Throughout the semester students attended six workshops twice a week and in addition to the workshops, team leaders participated in eight training sessions. In the traditional group, the same instructor described the topics and solve problems simultaneously in whole lecture time. At the beginning of the semester, all students informed about the study and signed the voluntary participation form.

2.2 Data collection tools

2.2.1 State-trait anxiety inventory (STAI)

It was used to measure two distinct anxiety concepts: state and trait anxiety. The inventory consists of 2 subscales: state anxiety scale and trait anxiety scale. It has a total of 40 items: Items 1 - 20 measure situational or state anxiety (STAI-S) and items 21 - 40 measure trait anxiety (STAI-T). After reversing scores for positively-worded items, a total score of a student get from each scale was minimum 20 and maximum 80. The high score shows a high level of anxiety.

2.2.2 Reaction to test (RTT)

It was used to measure the presence of test anxiety. It consisted of 20-item. Total score of a student get from this inventory was minimum 20 and maximum 80. High scores show a high level of test anxiety.

2.2.3. General chemistry (GC) grade

It was calculated from the raw score in points required from two midterms, one final exam and a laboratory work. All exams were scored out of 100 so maximum score that a student can obtain from these exams was 100 and the minimum score was 0. Their contribution rates were 25% for each midterm, 35 % for the final exam and 15% for laboratory work of the total grade

2.3 Data analysis

STAI and RTT instruments were used to generate data about trait and state anxiety and test anxiety respectively while students' general chemistry grade was calculated from the exams and a laboratory work. These data were analyzed by using standard multiple regression to address first and second research questions and were analyzed by hierarchical multiple regression to address third research question via IBM SPSS (Statistical Package for the Social Sciences) Statistics 24.0 program for Windows. Before conducting a regression analysis, all assumptions were satisfied.

3 Results and discussion

3.1 Correlational results

According to Table 1 below, for PLTL group students there was a statistically significant association between test anxiety and general chemistry (GC) grade while for non-PLTL group students there was a statistically significant association between trait anxiety, state anxiety, test anxiety and general chemistry (GC) grade. Thus, they could be used as predictor variables. Additionally, all anxiety-related variables showed high correlation with each other. Since trait anxiety as a permanent personality characteristic is difficult to change easily by using teaching methods or strategy, it was used as a covariate in the study.

Table 1. Correlations among all variables

	PLTL group				NON-PLTL group			
Variable	**GC grade**	**Trait anxiety**	**State anxiety**	**Test anxiety**	**GC grade**	**Trait anxiety**	**State anxiety**	**Test anxiety**
GC grade	–	-.159	-.168	-.315**	–	-.270*	-.314*	-.355**
Trait anxiety	-.159	–	.769**	.609**	-.270*	–	-762**	.706**
State anxiety	-.168	.769**	–	.492**	-.314*	-762**	–	.572**
Test anxiety	-.315**	.609**	.492**	–	- .355**	.706**	.572**	–

* Correlations significant at the 0.05 level, p<.05 ** Correlations significant at the 0.01 level, p<.01

3.2 Addressing the first research question: The prediction of GC grade from the combination of two variables

In order to answer the questions of "How well do the two measures of anxiety (state and test anxiety scores) predict general chemistry grade of PLTL and non-PLTL groups?" and "How much variance in general chemistry grade can be explained by scores on two measures for PLTL and non-PLTL groups?" the Table 2 and 3 were analyzed. The coefficients of multiple regression which were .315 for PLTL and .380 for a non-PLTL group indicates a medium level correlation between the combination of predictor variables (state and test anxiety) and a criterion variable (general chemistry grade). The R square value (coefficient of determination) in Table 2 tell us how much of the variance in total grade is explained by the model (which includes the state and test anxiety). In the study, this value was .099 for PLTL group students and .144 for non-PLTL group students which referred that our model explained 9.9 % and 14.4 % of the variance in general chemistry grade for PLTL and non-PLTL group respectively. Consequently, they were better predictors for the non-PLTL group.

Table 2. The coefficients of both multiple regression and determination

PLTL group				NON-PLTL group		
Model	**R**	**R Square**	**Adjusted R Square**	**R**	**R Square**	**Adjusted R Square**
1	.315	.099	.072	.380	.144	.114

Model 1. Predictors: (Constant), state and test anxiety

To assess the statistical significance of the result, it was necessary to look in Table 3 below. The combination of the predictor (state and test anxiety) was significantly related to general chemistry grade, $F(2, 65) = 3.59$, $p = .033$ for PLTL, $F(2, 57) = 4.81$, $p = .012$ for the non-PLTL group. Therefore, state and test anxiety can be used to predict the GC grade of engineering students in both groups.

Table 3. ANOVA results

Model		PLTL group					NON-PLTL group				
		SS	**df**	**MS**	**F**	**Sig.**	**SS**	**df**	**MS**	**F**	**Sig.**
1	Regression	1160.54	2	580.27	3.59	.033	1879.05	2	939.52	4.81	.012
	Residual	10505.89	65	161.63			11133.84	57	195.33		
	Total	11666.43	67				13012.88	59			

Note: Model 1. Predictors: (Constant), state and test anxiety.
SS: Sum of Squares, MS: Mean Square

Additionally, the regression equations were written with the B value in Table 4. Equation 1 could be used to predict the total grade of PLTL students while equation 2 could be used to predict the total grade of non-PLTL students

$$Y\text{ (total grade)} = 80{,}93\,X - 0{,}017\text{ (state anxiety)} - 0{,}333\text{ (test anxiety)} \quad (1)$$

$$Y\text{ (total grade)} = 86{,}28\,X - 0{,}212\text{ (state anxiety)} - 0{,}324\text{ (test anxiety)} \quad (2)$$

3.3 Addressing the second research question: Determination of the best predictor

For the comparison of the contribution of each anxiety variable, beta values in Table 4 were used. The largest beta coefficient belonged to test anxiety whose beta values were -.307 for PLTL and -.260 for non-PLTL groups. This meant that this variable made the strongest unique contribution to explaining the general chemistry grade when the variance explained by all other variables in the model was controlled for. Besides, the beta value for state anxiety was lower compared to test anxiety, indicating that it made less of a unique contribution.

Table 4. Coefficients for each of the predictors

Group	Model	B	Beta	Sig	Correlations			
					Zero-order	**Partial**	**Part**	**Part square**
PLTL	(Constant)	80.93		.000				
	State anxiety	-.017	-.017	.902	-.168	-.015	-.015	.000225
	Test anxiety	-.333	-.307	.027	-.315	-.271	-.267	.0713
Non-PLTL	(Constant)	86.28	-.260	.000				
	State anxiety	-.212	-.165	.273	-.314	-.145	-.136	.0184
	Test anxiety	-.324	-.260	.087	-.355	-.225	-.214	.0467

When the sig value was examined, for PLTL group test anxiety made a statistically significant unique contribution to the prediction of total score (p=0.027); however, state anxiety did not make any unique contribution. In addition, for the non-PLTL group, although the combination of state and test anxiety has a statistical significance to predict their GC grade. Statistically, insignificance in the results may be due to the overlap between independent variables in the model since the shared variance was excluded from the results. According to Pallant [6], this is very dependent on which variables are included in the equation and how much overlap there is among them.

The part correlation coefficient in Table 4 referred to the semi-partial correlations coefficients. The square of this value was the indication of the contribution of that variable to the total R square. Test anxiety had a unique contribution of 7.13 percent to the explanation of variance in GC grade of PLTL students. 4.67 % of total variance in general chemistry grade of non-PLTL students is uniquely explained by test anxiety while 1.84 % of total variance in general chemistry grade of non-PLTL students is uniquely explained by state anxiety.

Accordingly, since test anxiety had a significant unique contribution, it could be used to predict the GC grade of PLTL students. It was also possible to predict that PLTL students having a high level of test anxiety tend to get low GC grade.

3.4 Addressing the third research question: Control for the possible effect of trait anxiety

Table 5. Model summary for predicting general chemistry grade after controlling trait anxiety

Group	Model	R	R Square	R Square Change	Change Statistics			
					F Change	df1	df2	Sig. F Change
PLTL	1	.159	.025	.025	1.710	1	66	.195
	2	.323	.104	.079	2.829	2	64	.066
Non-PLTL	1	.270	.073	.073	4.575	1	58	.037
	2	.387	.149	.076	2.513	2	56	.090

Note: Model 1. Predictors: (Constant), trait anxiety
Model 2. Predictors: (Constant), trait, state, and test anxiety

After trait anxiety was entered, model 1 (takes unique contr. plus shared variance) explained 2.5% of the variance and after both state anxiety and test anxiety were entered the overall model 2 explained 10.4 % of the variance. Moreover, after the effect of trait anxiety was removed, state and test anxiety explained an additional 7.9 % of the variance in general chemistry grade of PLTL group, R square change=.079, F change (2,64) =2,829, p>0.05. Similarly, state and test anxiety explained an additional 7.6 % of the variance in general chemistry grade of the non-PLTL group after the effect of trait anxiety was removed, R square change=.076, F change (2,56) =2,513, p>0.05. However, those were not a significant contribution, as indicated by the Sig. F change in Table 5. This can be due to the presence of a high correlation between them.

Table 6. ANOVA results of two models for both PLTL and non-PLTL group

		PLTL group					NON-PLTL group				
Model		SS	df	MS	F	Sig.	SS	df	MS	F	Sig.
1	Regression	294.68	1	294.68	1.71	.195	951.32	1	951.33	4.58	.037
	Residual	11371.75	66	172.30			12061.57	58	207.96		
	Total	11666.43	67				13012.88	59			
2	Regression	1218.46	3	406.15	2.49	.068	1944.55	3	648.18	3.28	.027
	Residual	10447.97	64	163.25			11068.34	56	197.65		
	Total	11666.43	67				13012.88	59			

Note: Model 1. Predictors: (Constant), trait anxiety
Model 2. Predictors: (Constant), trait, state, and test anxiety
SS: Sum of Squares, MS: Mean Square

The ANOVA table indicated that the model as a whole was not statistically significant for PLTL group (F (3, 64) =2,49, p=0.068) while it was statistically significant for the non-PLTL group (F (3, 56) =3,28, p=0.027).

Table 7. Coefficients of predictors for model 1 and 2

Model	Predictors	PLTL group			NON-PLTL group		
		B	Beta	Sig.	B	Beta	Sig.
1	(Constant)	73.34		.000	78.54		.000
	Trait anxiety	-.176	-.159	.195	-.362	-.270	.037
2	(Constant)	80.25		.000	85.43		.000
	Trait anxiety	.134	.121	.554	.171	.127	.567
	State anxiety	-.095	-.092	.622	-.300	-.233	.227
	Test anxiety	-.373	-.344	.025	-.387	-.311	.080

Note: Model 1. Predictors: (Constant), trait anxiety
Model 2. Predictors: (Constant), trait, state, and test anxiety

To find out how well each of the variables contributes to the final equation, we need to look in model 2 row in Table 7. Scanning the sig. column, there was only one variable that made a unique statistically significant contribution in the final model with a higher beta value (beta=-.344, p=0.025) that represented the unique contribution of test anxiety when the overlapping effects of all other variables were statistically removed.

4 Conclusion

Consequently, test anxiety can be used to predict the general chemistry grade of PLTL students. Due to significant negative correlation (r= -.315), low test-anxious students in PLTL are likely to succeed in or get higher grades in general chemistry. Implementing innovative and effective teaching methods such as PLTL may not be sufficient to increase student understanding and enhance their performance if they have especially high anxiety. At the beginning of the semester, the instructor can use a diagnostic test to measure the test anxiety of the students as well as suggest some strategies that high test anxious students may use.

References

1. J. Osborne, S. Simon, S. Collins, Attitudes towards science: A review of the literature and its implications, *Int. J. Sci. Educ.*, **25**, 1049–1079 (2003).
2. C. D. Spielberger, R. L. Gorsuch, R. Lushene, P. R. Vagg, G. A. Jacobs, *Manual for the state-trait anxiety inventory (Form Y),* Palo Alto, CA: Consulting Psychologists Press (1983).
3. D. D. Szafranski, T. L. Barrera, P. J. Norton, Test anxiety inventory: 30 years later. *Anxiety, Stress, & Coping*, **25**, 667-677 (2012).
4. L. Gafney, P. Varma-Nelson, *Innovations in science education and technology: Vol. 16. Peer-led team learning: Evaluation, dissemination, and institutionalization of a college level initiative.* Weston, MA: Springer (2008).
5. J. R. Fraenkel, N. E. Wallen, H. H. Hyun, *How to design and evaluate research in education (8th ed.).* New York: McGraw-Hill (2012).
6. J. Pallant, *SPSS survival manual: A step by step guide to data analysis using the SPSS program, 4th Edition,* Allen & Unwin, Berkshire (2011)

Creative Thinking in Interior Architecture Education: Basic Design Courses

Gülsüm Damla Aşkın[1]*

[1]Mimar Sinan Fine Arts University, Department of Interior Architecture, Istanbul 34427, Turkey

Abstract. Basic Design courses aim to enable the students to produce creative designs with original and aesthetic perspectives in Interior Architecture Education in Turkey. In this study, it was aimed to develop the skill to use creative thinking of the students studying Interior Architecture and to bring the childish creativity back in the Basic Design course. Firstly, the Interior Architecture students were made to prepare an individual preliminary design work within the workshop carried out for this purpose. One week after the individual work, a workshop was held together with the kindergarten students. The aim of the workshops held in the scope of Basic Design course is to make the students generate ideas more quickly, be aware of the new design methods, and to gain the skill of working with individuals from various age groups in harmony. A survey was carried out with the participation of 16 academicians in the field of Interior Architecture and the designs obtained in the beginning and end of the study were evaluated by comparing them in terms of the use of creative thinking. To conclude, it can be said that the interior architecture students used creative thinking more effectively together with kindergarten students.

Keywords: Interior architecture, education, basic design, creative thinking

1 Introduction

The first stage of the design education constitutes Basic Design courses in İnterior Architecture education in Turkey. Basic Design courses aim to enable the students to produce creative designs with original and aesthetic perspectives that meet the requirements of the current social, cultural, and technological developments. In this respect, the Basic Design course plays an important role in the development of the creativity.

The freshmen of the Interior Architecture begin design education after getting training to improve their behaviour in the secondary and high school. The students are involved in the mental learning and teaching process together with the primary school period. The mental processes play an active role in each stage of the basic design course. The fact that the students had an education based on rote-learning from a kindergarten to the university makes it difficult for them to perceive the mental design process [1]. At the age of thirteen, the creativity reaches its peak and it lies fallow by the time unless it is recalled [2]. The

* Corresponding author: damlaaskin@sehir.edu.tr

creativity is formed by what the individual learns throughout his/her life. However, it is known that the period when the creativity develops the most is the kindergarten period. The self-expression methods of the children who go to kindergarten before compulsory education are more original and creative than adults [3]. The goal of design education, which is given in the first year of the Interior Architecture education, is to recall the creativity that has begun to vanish over time and to develop the skill to use creative thinking of the students.

Within the Basic Design courses in Interior Architecture, the disciplines such as music, literature, graphic design, cinema, plays, performance arts, visual and digital arts are used to improve creative thinking. In this study, it is aimed to recall the creative thinking skill gained in the past by working together with the kindergarten students. Accordingly, it is aimed to transform the free drawings of the children going to kindergarten into the design and to enable the Interior Architecture students to use creative thinking effectively.

The purpose of this research is to provide interior design students with new methods to improve their ability to interpret other disciplines that require creativity, to use childish creative thinking effectively, and to work in harmony with the various age groups. Therefore, the qualitative data analysis was carried out by examining the current Basic Design education and its methods at first. Within the scope of the research, a workshop was held with the freshmen of Interior Architecture who took Basic Design course at Işık University in the fall semester in 2017-2018. The interior architecture students and the theme of the work were considered as constants, and the working method was considered as a variable. In the study, upper year students taking project course were excluded. At the first stage of the study, the students were asked to design a one-story playhouse in the activity area in Ayazağa Işık Kindergarten in. According to the kindergarten manager, playhouse was a significant necessity for school. The 6-year-old children, who study at Işık Kindergarten, were also asked to draw the picture of the playhouse to be constructed in the activity area.

One week after the preliminary work, each Interior Architecture student was asked to repeat the same design process together with a kindergarten student. In the same working environment, the interior architecture students are expected to be inspired by the children's imagination and their drawings. The purpose of the workshop is not to deliver a finished project but to shape the functions and form of the playhouse with the ideas of kindergarten students. After the collaborative work, the Interior Architecture students transformed their design ideas into physical forms as models. In the last stage of the study, the students' works designed with both perspectives were evaluated by 16 Interior Architecture academicians using a survey.

2 Importance of basic design courses in interior architecture education

Interior Architecture is a field of occupation that uses scientific and technical data for meeting the requests of the user as well as satisfying functional needs [4]. Interior architecture departments established under architecture, fine arts and design faculties, provide education with influences from different disciplines based on the characteristics of its faculty.

Interior architecture students are expected to interpret all disciplines and develop designs within the integrity of the space [5]. Within this context, it is only possible with basic design courses that students can provide solutions for problems, state their ideas and put them into practice.

In the 21st century, when the knowledge is constantly updated, interior design students must also react to this change, produce new ways of thinking and designs. The Basic

Design course taken in the first year of interior architecture program lays the professional foundations, affect future project courses [6]. Within this respect, Basic Design courses gain more importance in the interior architecture education.

Purpose of Basic Design courses has been freeing students of conditioning and giving creativity, imagination, personal expression opportunities prominence ever since the school of Bauhaus [7]. Basic Design education is a process that activates intellectual stages of students such as perception, impression, observation, researching, association, invention, knowledge and assessment and transforms such stages into originals forms. The design process consists of knowledge, analysis of knowledge, research, thinking, discussion, sketches leading to creative results, presentation boards, search for the proper material for the study and the final outcome [8].

As the goal of design education is to guide creative individuals with aesthetical perceptions, Interior Architecture education must also be improved so that it supports creativity [9]. Especially in the information and communication age, needs and personal choices become more and more various, and the role of creativity in interior architecture design gets more and more significant. Gropius stated that the purpose of education is teaching a way, method for approaching problems rather than providing a certain information-skill. Considering that the design education is a process of creating, experiencing and researching, methods that support such process and bring creativity forward become more important [10]. A design education is provided in consideration of basic designing principals such as color, ratio, difference, integrity, rhythm, balance, and contrast in order to contribute to visual and intuitive developments of students. Creativity is improved through working, experiencing, observing, the researching and perceiving. Principals adopted in Basic Design courses improve the perceptions and experiences of students and contribute to their creativity.

3 Basic design courses and creativity

According to Torance, creativity is researching spaces, disturbing or missing elements and making assumptions, testing them; comparing the results and attaining an outcome [11]. Within this respect, creativity refers to a process that includes innovation and improves with environmental effect.

Thinking, creating new things, assessing objects and situations from different points of view with the help of education is defined as creativity, and it involves curiosity, imagination, invention, and originality [12]. In other words, thinking leading to new ideas is centered around creativity.

Creativity requires developing original designs through benefiting from experiences and new information. Creativity is encountered in first years of life and demonstrated in a child's play for the first time. Children find a chance to express themselves through painting, listening to musing in different activities in kindergartens. Furthermore, as a result of the "Torrance Test of Creative Thinking'' [13], it has been determined that creative thinking scores of children receiving preschool education are significantly higher than children not receiving preschool education [14]. Kindergarten period affects the whole life of children when their creativity improves the most. With the primary school period, students get involved with the education system towards behavior correction. And at the age of 13, creativity reaches its peak and lies fallow unless recalled [15]. Purpose of the Basic Design course provided in the first year of Interior Architecture education is to ensure that students produce more original projects by recalling the fading creativity.

4 Workshop processes

Creative design process improves perception, understanding, interpreting and expressing skills of students. Applied education programs, in which students actively participate in courses, are more commonly preferred in Basic Design courses [16]. Within this respect, a workshop has been held between the Işık University Interior Architecture Department students and Işık Ayazağa Kindergarten 6-age group students in the 2017-2018 Fall semester within the University. The workshop has been held with the approval and opinions of the principal of Işık Ayazağa Kindergarten.

4.1 Project area

Maximum 20 m² part of the activity hall, of which is approximately 35-40 m², can be used for creating a playhouse. Determining the location of the house within the hall has been left to the students, there has not been a limitation.

4.2 Objective

It has been aimed with the workshop that the creativity of interior architecture students had before the education system towards behavior correction is recalled through designing along with kindergarten students within the same room. The purpose of the workshop has been ensuring that students get knowledge on basic design principals and methods, develop ideas from a two-dimensional, abstract image, and get used to teamwork for exchanging ideas. It has been expected that, following the idea generation stage, skills towards creating a form and conceiving a structure are improved. As a result of the study, it will be ensured that previously existing creativity skills of interior architecture students are recalled while creative thinking skills of kindergarten students are improved.

4.3 Sample

The study has been conducted between Interior Architecture junior year students having received the Basic Design course in Işık University and the 6-age group students in Işık Kindergarten. In the study, students not having received the Basic Design course or higher year students taking project courses have been left outside the scope of the study.

4.4 Methodology

The workshop includes a 3-week process, consisting of personal market production, joint workshop study, and final market study. What is expected in the workshop is not delivery of a completed project, but shaping the functions and form of the playhouse with the ideas of kindergarten students.

4.4.1 First step

First year students of Interior Architecture department have been asked to make models of the playhouse to be located in the activity area in Işık Ayazağa Kindergarten.

Fig. 1. Basic Design Studies of Interior Architecture Students

4.4.2 Second step

6-age group students in Işık Kindergartens have been asked to draw the pictures of the playhouse to be located in the activity area in their school. Kindergarten students take a weekly course in which they make models from discarded materials. Therefore, material and color choices have been left to students' preferences.

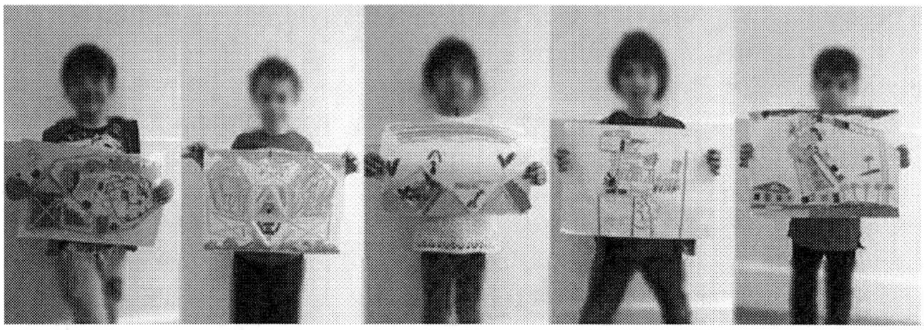

Fig. 2. Design Studies of Kindergarten Students

4.4.3 Third step

Interior Architecture students have been paired off with the kindergarten students, thus ensuring that they repeat the same design process together. In this process, ideas of the kindergarten students have been received, and they expressed the playhouse they imagined on their drawings. Afterwards, Interior Architecture students have designed a model with the help of drawings by kindergarten students. During the process, students have had the opportunity to have one-to-one discussions and help each other.

Fig. 3. Students Working Together

Fig. 4. Design Studies of Interior Architecture Students Together with Kindergarten Students

4.5 Results

A survey was carried out with the participation of 16 academicians in the field of Interior Architecture and the designs obtained in the beginning and end of the study were evaluated by comparing them in terms of the originality, use of creative thinking, childish creativity, working in harmony and contribution to basic design courses.

Table 1. Results of Survey

Survey Questions		Originality	Use of Creative Thinking	Childish Creativity	Working in Harmony	Contribution to Basic Design
Number of Academics (16)	available	13	14	14	16	16
	not	3	2	2	0	0
Percentage of Success		81,25%	87,50%	87,50%	100%	100%

The result of the survey study revealed that 81.25% of the academicians making the evaluations stated their opinion that the design works obtained at the end of the workshop were more original than the preliminary works and that the students could use creative thinking more effectively. 87.5% of the academics think that the Interior Design students could bring out their childish creativity through their designs. The time was recorded during the workshop and it was observed that all of the students decided on their design ideas easier and applied it more quickly by taking advantage of the pictures of the kindergarten students. The Interior Architecture students and the Kindergarten students worked in harmony in the same environment and the students realized that there may have been new design methods.

5 Conclusion

Changing environmental conditions, technology and a variety of problems indicate the need for more original and creative solutions. As I mentioned above, students with different pasts, coming from different conditions, try to provide creative solutions for today's problems during and after the Interior Architecture education. In Basic Design courses provided in the first year of Interior Architecture education, students acquire the skill to formalize their ideas. Within this sense, it is concluded that Basic Design courses establish a transition stage between secondary education and university.

Within the scope of the study, a case workshop has been conducted in order to ensure that interior architecture students can satisfy needs such as creativity in design, transforming the available knowledge to what is new, providing alternative solutions, questioning and discussing. A playhouse has been designed for the activity area in Ayazağa Işık Kindergarten with two different points of view within the workshop. Contributions have been made to the improvement of creativity skills of both Interior Architecture students and kindergarten students in order to establish an interactive working environment.

As a result of the conducted workshop, Interior Architecture students have had an idea of basic design principles, developed design ideas from two-dimensional drawings, and been involved in teamwork. They have harmoniously created a new form after the idea generation stage. Furthermore, it has been ensured that the creative thinking skills of kindergarten students are improved while the previously existing creative ideas of interior architecture students are recalled.

A survey was carried out with the participation of 16 academicians in the field of Interior Architecture and the designs obtained in the beginning and end of the study were evaluated by comparing them in terms of the use of creative thinking. In this process, attention has been drawn to the necessity of co-working with different age groups and using different disciplines during the study within the scope of Basic Design courses in Interior Architecture education. As a result, it can be said that the Interior Design students can use creative thinking more effectively during the joint workshop, the produced models contribute directly to the Basic Design course and allow the development of new design methods.

References

1. T. Zorlu, B. Akgül, vs., A Different View of First Year Design Studios in Interior Architecture Education; space from picture; Kandinsky, *İÇMEK / 2nd National Congress of Interior Architecture Education, Istanbul, Turkey* (2012)
2. E. Aslan, E. Aktan, I. Kamaraj, The Effect of Kindergarten Education on Creativity and Creative Problem-Solving Ability, *M.U. Atatürk Education Faculty Journal of Educational Sciences,* **9**, 37-48 (1997, 2001)
3. M. Yaşar, N. Aral, The Impact of Pre-School Education on Creative Thinking Skills, *Educationscience*, **3 (2)**, 201-209 (2010)
4. Ç. B. Gökhan, A. Atasoy, A Model Proposal for Interior Architecture Education Program Design and Development, *ITU Journal,* **4/2,** 25-36 (2005)
5. L. Arıdağ, A. E. Aslan, Design Studies-1 Effect of Creative Drama Activities on the Development of Creative Thinking Skills of Architectural Students, *Megaron*, **7(1)**: 49-66 (2012)
6. H. T. Örmecioğlu, A. Uçar, First Design Studio Experience in Education of Interior Architecture: an Example of Akdeniz University, *Procedia - Social and Behavioral Sciences*, **51**, 1107 – 1111 (2012)
7. L. Arıdağ, A. E. Aslan, Design Studies-1 Effect of Creative Drama Activities on the Development of Creative Thinking Skills of Architectural Students, *Megaron*, **7(1)**: 49-66 (2012)
8. İ. San, Arts Education Theories, *Utopia Publishing,* (2010)

9. A. Akyıldız, Hatırnaz, Design Suggestion for Developing Creativity in Design Education: Design Cycle, Proficiency in Art Thesis, Mimar Sinan Fine Arts University, Institute of Science, (2010)
10. U. T. Karslı, S. Özker, The contributions of workshops on formal interior architecture education. *Procedia-Social and Behavioral Sciences*, **152**, 47-52 (2014)
11. E. P. Torrance; E. B. Orlow, Test of Creative Thinking, norms and technical Manual, *bensenville Scholastic testing service Inc,* (1974)
12. A. Besgen, Teaching/Learning Strategies Through Art: Painting and Basic Design Education, *Procedia-Social and Behavioral Sciences*, **182**, 420-427 (2015)
13. A. E. Aslan, Puccio, G., Developing and Testing A Turkish Version of Torrance Tests of Creative Thinking: A Study of Adults. *Journal of Creative Behavior, Massachusetts,* **40 (3),** 163-178 (2006)
14. D. Onur, T. Zorlu, Training Methods and Creativity Relevant to Design Studios, *www. tojdac. org*., (2017)
15. M. Yaşar, N. Aral, The Impact of Pre-School Education on Creative Thinking Skills, *Educationscience*, **3 (2)**, 201-209 (2010)
16. H. Kılıçaslan, B. E. Ziyrek, A Research About Creativity in Design Education, *Procedia - Social and Behavioral Sciences*, **46**, 1461-1464, (2012)

Two new scales in the field of couples and marriage counseling: The inclusion of other in the self scale and Turkish self-change in romantic relationships scale

Duygu Dincer[1*], *Halil* Eksi[2], and *Arthur* Aron[3]

[1]Ibn Haldun University, Department of Counseling Psychology, 34494 Istanbul, Turkey
[2]Marmara University, Department of Counseling Psychology, 34722 Istanbul, Turkey
[3]Stony Brook University, Department of Psychology, 11794 New York, USA

Abstract. This study had two aims. One aim was to adapt the Inclusion of Other in the Self (IOS) Scale into the Turkish cultural context. The second aim was to develop the Turkish Self-Change in Romantic Relationships Scale (TSCRRS) based on the existing Relational Self-Change Scale. The research process for this study consisted of four stages. In the first stage, forward-backward translation of the IOS Scale was performed to determine bilingual equivalence. In the second stage, an item-pool was created to measure self-change in romantic relationships. In the third stage, data were collected to determine the reliability and validity of the TSCRRS (N = 426). In the fourth stage, new data were collected to determine the validity and reliability of the IOS Scale and the TSCRRS (N = 348). All of the participants were in a romantic relationship. The findings revealed that both the TSCRRS and the IOS Scale have good reliability and validity.

Keywords: romantic relationships, self-change, the inclusion of other in the self, scale adaptation, scale development, culture

1 Introduction

People in a romantic relationship can experience positive and negative changes related to their self-concepts. In 2014, three social psychology researchers, Brent Mattingly, Gary Lewandowski, and Kevin McIntyre proposed a new psychological model called the Two-dimensional Model of Relational Self-change to conceptualize these self-changes, and they developed a scale based on their model [1]. According to this model, self-changes in a romantic relationship can occur based on two dimensions: direction and valence [1, 2]. The concept of direction refers to a quantitative self-change and the concept of valence refers to a qualitative self-change. Thus, the direction of the self-concept is related to increases or decreases in the content of an individual's self-concept, but the direction of the self-concept is associated with the subjective aspects of the changes in that person's self-concept [1, 2]. Based on this conceptualization, there are four types of self-concept changes: self-expansion, self-pruning, self-contraction, and self-adulteration [1]. These self-concept changes can be formularized as follows:

* Corresponding author: drduygudincer@gmail.com

- Self-expansion = Positive content of self-concept ↑
- Self-contraction = Positive content of self-concept ↓
- Self-adulteration = Negative content of self-concept ↑
- Self-pruning = Negative content of self-concept ↓

Although this model introduced and conceptualized the terms of self-pruning, self-contraction, and self-adulteration for the first time, the concept of self-expansion has been known for many years. Almost three decades ago, two social psychology researchers, Arthur Aron and Elaine Aron, developed the Self-expansion Theory that assumes people have a motive to expand their selves, and one of the best ways of accomplishing that is to establish and maintain close relationships, especially romantic relationships [3, 4]. According to this theory, people seek out and create an optimal close relationship [3], and they tend to include in the self the other's social, intellectual, and financial resources, worldview, and identities [5]; thus, they become a collective unit and begin to see and experience the world from their partner's viewpoint [6].

Although many researchers from all over the world have examined the ideas stated above, there seems to have been little interest in the Turkish close relationships literature on self-changes and the inclusion of other in the self. Thus, the present study aimed to draw attention to these relational dynamics and provide psychological tools to measure these relational constructs. For this reason, we tested the validity and reliability of the Inclusion of Other in the Self (IOS) Scale [7] and we developed a new scale to assess self-change in romantic relationships based on the Two-dimensional Model of Relational Self-change.

2 Method

2.1 Sample and procedures

In the first stage of this study, forward-backward translation of the IOS Scale [7] was performed to determine bilingual equivalence. Then, 31 students (all currently in a dating relationship) from the English Teaching Department, who were assumed to be fluent in both English and Turkish, participated in a bilingual equivalence study. Twenty-five of the participants (80.6%) were female, and six (19.4%) were male. The participants ranged in age from 18 to 39; the mean was 22.6 years (DF = 3.68). The length of their relationships ranged from 5 months to 120 months; the mean relationship length was 28.9 months (DF = 2.47),

In the second stage, based on the existing Relational Self-Change Scale (RSCS) [1], the Two-dimensional Model of the Relational Self-change [1], and a focus group conducted with Turkish college students were used to create an item-pool to measure self-change processes in romantic relationships. Then, these items were examined by four specialists in the field of close relationships. Based on that feedback, the authors created the final item-pool [8, 9]

In the third stage, data were collected to determine the reliability and validity of the Turkish Self-Change in Romantic Relationships Scale (TSCRRS) (N = 426, all currently in a romantic relationship). Of the 426 participants in this stage of the study, 210 (49.3%) were female and 216 (50.7%) were male. Moreover, 70.1% (N = 285) of the participants were dating, 14.6% (N = 62) were engaged, and 18.3% (N = 78) were married. The participants' ages ranged from 18 to 40; the mean age was 23.88 years (DF = 4.63). The length of the participants' relationships ranged from 1 month to 192 months; the mean relationship length was 31.7 months (DF = 31.22). In this sample, exploratory factor analysis (EFA) was applied to discover the factor structure of the scale and to examine its internal reliability.

In the fourth stage, new data were collected to determine the construct validity (via confirmatory factor analysis [CFA]) and the parallel test reliability of the TSCRRS, and to assess the criterion validity of the IOS Scale and the TSCRRS (N = 348, all currently in a romantic relationship). Of the 348 participants in this stage of the study, 141 (40.5%) were female and 207 (59.5%) were male; moreover, 70.0% (N = 240) of the participants were dating, 13.5% (N = 47) were engaged, and 17.5% (N = 61) were married. The participants ranged in age from 18 to 40; the mean age was 23.71 years (*DF* = 4.60). The length of the relationships ranged from 1 month to 144 months; the mean relationship length was 30.3 months (*DF* = 29.98). The existing RSCS [1] was used as a parallel test of the TSCRRS (Actually, the TSCRRS was developed as the parallel test of the RSCS in the first author's dissertation [8]). Furthermore, the Relationship Assessment Scale (RAS) [10] were used to determine the criterion validity of the TSCRRS. At the same time, the RAS and the RSCS were used to determine criterion validity of the IOS Scale.

2.2 Materials

In this study, the participants completed the IOS Scale, the Turkish version of the RSCS, the RAS, and the TSCRRS. They also completed a brief demographic information sheet which consisted of some questions about their gender, age, current relationship status, type of relationship, and the duration of the relationship.

2.2.1 The Inclusion of Other into the Self (IOS) Scale:

The one-item pictorial IOS Scale was developed to assess the self-other overlap in romantic relationships [7]. The scale consists of seven paired circles. In each pair, one circle represents the self, and one circle represents the other (partner). The degree of intersection indicates the degree of closeness and intimacy, and the extent to which the other is included in the self. In the original study, the scale demonstrated good reliability (α = .95; and test-retest reliability was .85) and validity (As expected, the IOS Scale was positively related to the Sternberg Intimacy Scale and the Subjective Closeness Index) [7].

2.2.2 The Relational Self-Change Scale (RSCS):

The RSCS was developed to assess changes in self-concepts [1]. It consists of four subscales: self-expansion, self-contraction, self-pruning, and self-adulteration. Each subscale contains three items. Sample items include: "I have learned many great new things" (self-expansion), "My positive attributes have decreased" (self-contraction), "My bad habits have diminished" (self-pruning), and "I have more negative qualities" (self-adulteration). The RSCS is rated on a 7-point scale (1 = not very much and 7 = very much). In the original research, each subscale demonstrated good reliability. In the first study at Time 1 (the first time the RSCS was administered), the following reliability results were obtained: self-expansion (α = .81), self-contraction (α = .72), self-pruning (α = .78), and self-adulteration (α = .72). At Time 2 (the second time the RSCS was administered) the reliability results were: self-expansion (α = .85), self-contraction (α = .84), self-pruning (α = .78), and self-adulteration (α = .72). In the second study, the reliability results were: self-expansion (α = .84), self-contraction (α = .92), self-pruning (α = .92), and self-adulteration (α = .78). Consistent with these findings, in another study conducted by the same authors, each subscale again demonstrated good reliability. At Time 1, the following reliability results were found: self-expansion (α = .81), self-contraction (α = .72), self-pruning (α = .78), and self-adulteration (α = .72). At Time 2, the reliability results were: self-expansion (α = .85), self-contraction (α = .84), pruning (α = .88), and adulteration (α = .79). The scale was adapted to the Turkish cultural context by the authors of the current paper [8, 9]. The findings revealed that the goodness of fit index values were good [x^2/DF = 2.34, x^2 = 112.18, DF = 48, CFI = .98, NFI= .96, GFI = .96, RMSEA = .06 (N = 426)]. Moreover, Cronbach's alpha coefficients of .84, .84, .89, and .76 were obtained for the self-expansion, self-contraction, self-pruning, and self-adulteration subscales. It was shown that the inclusion of other in the self and relationship satisfaction were positively correlated to self-expansion (.33, $p < .01$; .42, $p < .01$) and self-pruning (.27, $p < .01$; .25, $p < .01$), and they were negatively correlated to self-contraction (-.19, $p < .01$; -.45, $p < .01$) [1, 2].

2.2.3 The Relationship Assessment Scale (RAS):

The 7-item and single structure RAS was developed to assess global relationship satisfaction [10]. It is rated on a 5-point scale (1 = low satisfaction and 7 = high satisfaction). Sample items include: "How good is your relationship compared to most?" and "To what extent has your relationship met your original expectations?". In the original study, the scale demonstrated good reliability (α = .86) and validity; in fact, the explained variance was high (46%) [10]. The RAS was adapted to the Turkish cultural context [11], and it was found that the scale had good validity and reliability (α = .86; the explained variance was 52% in the total sample).

1.2.4 The Turkish Self-Change in Romantic Relationships Scale (TSCRRS):

The authors of the current paper developed the 16-item TSCRRS based on the existing Relational Self-Change Scale (RSCS) [1], the Two-dimensional Model of the Relational Self-change [1], and a focus group conducted with Turkish college students to assess the perceived self-change processes in couple relationships. The TSCRRS consists of four subscales: self-expansion (5 items), self-contraction (5 items), self-pruning (3 items), and self-adulteration (3 items). The TSCRRS is rated on a 7-point scale (1 = not very much and 7 = very much). Moreover, it contains several culture-specific items based on a focus group.

3 Results

3.1 The validity of the TSCRRS

3.1.1 EFA

The Kaiser-Meyer-Olkin (KMO) score for the TSCRRS was 0.89, and Bartlett's Test of Sphericity (χ^2 = 4113.31, DF = 231, $p < .00$) was found to be significant. Based on the KMO and Bartlett's Test of Sphericity scores, factor analysis was conducted. EFA was performed to evaluate the TSCRRS. The EFA results support the use of a 16-item four-factor solution as the best fitting model for the data, and the explained variance was high (62.34% in the third stage sample).

3.1.2 CFA

Next, CFA was performed for a new dataset (N = 348), and it revealed that the goodness of fit index values were $x^2/DF = 1.97$, $x^2 = 192.74$, DF = 97, CFI = .93, NFI = .90, GFI = .93, RMSEA = .05 (in the fourth stage sample).

3.2 The reliability of the TSCRRS

3.2.1 Internal reliability

Cronbach's alpha coefficients of .80, .85, .76, .63 (in the third stage sample) and .80, .85, .74, .61 (in the fourth stage sample) were obtained for the self-expansion, self-contraction, self-pruning, and self-adulteration subscales.

3.2.2 Parallel tests reliability

Pearson's correlations among the subscales of the TSCRRS and the RSCS were statistically significant ($p < .01$) (Table 1).

Table 1. Correlations among the subscales of the TSCRRS and the RSCS

Variables	1	2	3	4	5	6	7	8
1. RSCS self-expansion	1	-.26**	.45**	.10	.70**	-.06	.33**	.13*
2. RSCS self-contraction		1	-.12*	.42**	-.14**	.53**	-.05	.27**
3. RSCS self-pruning			1	.20**	.48**	.11*	.52**	.32**
4. RSCS self-adulteration				1	.28**	.78**	.12*	.30**
5. TSCRRS self-expansion					1	-.02	.38**	.14**
6. TSCRRS self-contraction						1	.01	.42**
7. TSCRRS self-pruning							1	.12*
8. TSCRRS self-adulteration								1
x	5.08	2.07	4.31	3.07	4.51	3.02	3.98	3.57
DF	1.28	1.31	1.55	1.20	1.24	1.43	1.55	1.47
Cronbach's alpha	.82	.84	.89	.77	.80	.85	.74	.61

***p < .01, *p < .05*

3.2.3 Item-total correlations

To examine the correlations, each item score and overall assessment score of the item-total correlations were calculated. The corrected item-total correlations ranged between .28 and .48 (in the fourth stage sample).

3.3 The validity and reliability of the IOS Scale

We only assessed the test-retest reliability and criterion-related validity of the IOS Scale because this scale only contains one item.

3.3.1 Test-retest reliability

To examine the test–retest reliability of the IOS Scale, 31 students were re-administered the IOS Scale two weeks after they were first administered it. The results showed that the test-retest reliability of the scale was .57.

3.3.2 The criterion-related validity

To check the correlations between the inclusion of other in the self and the external variables (relationship satisfaction and self-change), the RAS and the RSCS were used. The results revealed that the criterion-related validity of the IOS Scale was satisfactory (Table 2).

Table 2. The criterion-related validity of the IOS Scale

Variables	1	2	3	4	5	6
1. RSCS self-expansion	1	-.26**	.45**	.10	.42**	.33**
2. RSCS self-contraction		1	-.12*	.42**	-.45**	-.19*
3. RSCS self-pruning			1	.20**	.25**	.27**
4. RSCS self-adulteration				1	-.11	.06
5. Relationship satisfaction					1	.46**
6. Inclusion of other in the self						1
X	5.08	2,07	4,31	3,07	5.65	5.60
DF	1.28	1.31	1.55	1.20	1.13	1.55
Cronbach's alpha	.82	.84	.89	.77	.89	-

**$p < .01$, *$p < .05$

4 Conclusion

This study had two aims. One aim was to adapt the IOS Scale into the Turkish cultural context. The second aim was to develop the TSCRRS based on the Two-dimensional Relational Self-change Model. To adapt the IOS Scale, linguistic equivalence was tested at the beginning of the study, and the result showed that the Turkish version of the scale had good linguistic equivalence. After testing for linguistic equivalence, the validity and reliability analyses (only test-retest reliability and criterion-related validity) of the IOS Scale were run. The analyses revealed that the IOS Scale had good validity and reliability. As we expected, there were significant correlations between the IOS Scale and the subscales of the RSCS. At the same time, we created an item-pool to develop the TSCRRS and to measure self-change processes in romantic relationships based on the existing RSCS, the Two-dimensional Model of the Relational Self-change, and a focus group conducted with Turkish college students. After these items were examined by four specialists in the field of close relationships, the authors created the final item-pool. Then, EFA, CFA, parallel-test validity, and criterion-related reliability were performed. The findings demonstrated that the TSCRRS had good validity and reliability. Moreover, as we expected, there were significant correlations between the subscales of TSCRRS and the original RSCS. In conclusion, it is clear that the results regarding the psychometric properties of the TSCRRS and the IOS Scale guarantee that they can be used confidently in couples and marriage counseling research and practices.

Although this study represents a remarkable effort to enrich the close relationships literature, it has several limitations. First, the study sample only consisted of undergraduate students in Turkey. In other words, the present study validated the TSCRRS only in the Turkish cultural context. Although it contains several culture-specific items based on a focus group, in future studies, researchers could validate the TSCRRS in different cultures (i.e., collectivistic and individualistic cultures) in countries around the world and so, they examine the cross-cultural differences on self-change processes. Second, the educational level of the participants was relatively high because the data were collected from an educated sample (university students). In the future, studies could examine these self-change processes in romantic relationships in low educated samples.

Acknowledgements

The authors would like to thank the Scientific and Technological Research Council of Turkey (TUBITAK) 2214/A International Doctoral Research Fellowship Program for supporting this study (and Dr. Duygu Dincer's dissertation) financially.

References

1. B. A. Mattingly, G. W. Lewandowski, & K. McIntyre "You make me a better/worse person: A two-dimensional model of relationship self-change." Pers Relationship, **21**, 176-190 (2014)
2. K. McIntyre, B.A. Mattingly, & G. W. Lewandowski When "we" changes "me": The two-dimensional model of relational self-change and relationship outcomes. J Soc Pers Relat, **32**(2), 857-878 (2015)
3. A. Aron, & A. Aron. *Love and expansion of self: Understanding attraction and satisfaction* (Hemisphere publishing Corporation, New York, 1986)
4. A. Aron, & E. Aron Self-expansion motivation and including other in the self. In S. Duck (Ed.), *Handbook of personal relationships* (2nd ed., pp. 251–270). (Wiley, Chichester, UK, 1997)
5. D. Mashek, B. Le, K. Israel, & A. Aron Wanting less closeness in romantic relationships. Basic Appl SocPsych, **33**, 333-345 (2011)
6. A. P. Aron, D. J. Mashek, & E. A. Aron Closeness a including other in the self. In D.J. Mashek & A. Aron (Eds.) *Handbook of closeness and intimacy* (pp. 27-43). (Lawrence Erlbaum Associates, Inc., Publishers, New Jersey, 2008)
7. A. Aron, E. N. Aron, & D. Smollan Inclusion of other in the self scale and the structure of interpersonal closeness. J Pers Soc Psychol, **63**, 596-612 (1992)
8. D. Dincer *Factors predicting relationship satisfaction and life satisfaction in romantic relationships: The two-dimensional model of relational self-change* (Unpublished dissertation) (Marmara University, Istanbul, Turkey, 2017)
9. D. Dincer, H. Eksi, & A. Aron Psychometric properties of the Turkish version of the Relational Self-Change Scale. Paper presented at 2nd Eurasian Congress on Positive Psychology, Istanbul, Turkey (2017).
10. S. S. Hendrick A generic measure of relationship satisfaction. J Marriage Fam, **50**, 93–98 (1988)
11. F. Curun *The effects of sexism and sex role orientation on romantic relationship satisfaction* (Unpublished thesis). (Middle East Technical University, Ankara, Turkey, 2001)

A Qualitative Evaluation on Fiqh Education from İmam Hatip High Schools to Theology Faculties

Samira Hasanova*

Near East University, Faculty of Teology, Nicosia-99280, North Cyprus

Abstract: Fiqh (Islamic law) has a central place in religious education. This paper attempts to attract attention to the central position of fiqh, which is defined as knowing one's rights and duties; for this purpose the historical background of fiqh education from Ottoman madrasahs to the present is briefly covered, and its relation with basic Islamic sciences and Arabic, which is known as instrumental sciences, is displayed in the context of quality of education. In the paper the negative and positive aspects of the reflection of acquisitions on faculty education of İmam Hatip high school graduates in the case that they enter theology faculty are examined. Fiqh is related to such disciplines as construction, hadith and kalam based on religion; but it is also connected with such disciplines as philosophy, sociology and psychology which are not based on religion. The paper emphasizes the importance of including new fields such as Islamic law sociology and Islamic law philosophy in theology curricula and discussion is made on the necessity to open a space in the curriculum for these fields. The purpose here is to examine the problems in fiqh education in the process from İmam Hatip high schools to university and evaluate them from the perspective of students, lecturers and the curriculum.

1 Introduction

1.1 Purpose

The purpose of my study is to question the quality of fiqh education, which is also known as Islamic law. The reason is my concerns about the adequacy of the acquisitions of individuals who graduate from İmam Hatip High Schools and prefer Theology Faculties. I aim to analyze and explore the reasons of the problems I encounter as someone who gives fiqh education at Theology Faculty.

1.2 Method

The paper follows literature review and on-site monitoring/case analysis method.

* Corresponding author: samira.hasanova@neu.edu.tr

2 Fiqh and its place in Islamic sciences

In the geography that we live, we sometimes witness rising tensions, conflicts and disagreements. It is a reality that these disagreements and conflicts are based on religion. However, we cannot claim that religion is the reason of these conflicts. Misunderstandings in the interpretation of religion lead to wars and conflicts. If we talk about the special case of Islam religion, we can say that it consists of three main elements: Belief/kalam, deeds/fiqh and ethic/sufism. It should be noted that understanding and teaching these three elements as a whole is an important step in terms of preventing possible conflicts. Different schools have occurred in our tradition concerning the understanding of the three elements of religion. These schools were formed in a systematic and consistent manner as a result of an intellectual mental activity; at the same time they are responses to the different interpretations in their ages. Maturidi and Eşari schools which were formed in the field of belief are expressions of a stance towards other salafi, exotic and dissenter schools. The same also goes for fiqh sects. There are several reasons for the fact that some sects are accepted and some have become materials of history in our tradition. However, we can say that the search for social peace is effective in the mentioned preference. Religious-based conflicts in our region are connected to the past in terms of origin and mentality and they are not new interpretations. Therefore, we have to understand the experience that our tradition produces against the understandings which lead to conflict and wars and transfer it to generations. Religious education and its quality bear huge importance in terms of protecting our generations from this kind of conflicts.

Knowing the Islamic laws in any manners or ways with self-diligence. Base on curriculum of Islamic school, Fiqh is the field of Islamic study which is designed to prepare students to recognize, appreciate and practice the Islamic law, which later became the basis of life view through the activities of counseling, instruction, training and experience practice. Based on the explanation above, the authors concluded that the jurisprudence is a science in the Islamic Shari"ah which specifically discuss the issue of Islamic rules which is relating to the person, either permitted or forbidden and compulsory or permissible and human relationships with each other, based on postulates of the verses of Al Qur"an and Sunnah of the Prophet[1].

Fiqh, on the other hand, is a discipline which regulates, directs and manages the behaviors of Muslims. Almost all of the religious knowledge obtained from main sources with mental effort is fiqh; it is also called the knowledge of rights and liabilities of a person. Fiqh is the name of the science which consists of knowledge and judgments on the descendants of religion and practical life and until today catechism, law and its methodology, economics, politics, administrative sciences and institutions related to these sciences have been seen and examined in fiqh branch among Islamic sciences. Fiqh is the changing aspect of the changing face of Muslim world; to tell the truth, it is the changeable aspect. This is to say that fiqh consists of prayers, transactions and punishments. Prayers is the unchanging aspect of fiqh as its boundaries are determined in Qur'an and Sunnah and it cannot change. Transactions is the part which regulates interpersonal relations. This is the part which changes with time, place and circumstances. In other words, this is the part which adapts to the changing worlds and innovations. Fiqh procedures sciences, which is not in Qur'an and Sunnah or, even if it is in Qur'an and Sunnah but is required to give new judgments in the face of new conditions, is also known as fiqh methodology and is now a part of fiqh. Fiqh procedures also serves as the sociology and philosophy of fiqh. Therefore, in order to know a fiqh science branch, one has to know the elements which constitute the content of fiqh very well. As our main sources are in Arabic, one has to have good command of Arabic language naturally in order to be able to read Fiqh.

In general it can be said that the study of Islamic knowledge cannot be separated from the Arabic language. The great body of work on Islamic knowledge that are used as main references or considered to be important work are almost all written in the Arabic language and text. Therefore, the mastery of the Arabic language is a prerequisite for those who wish to study Islam from its original sources. Among the problems faced by lecturers involved in this research is the university students' weak grasp of the Arabic language. Most of the reference books used by lecturers are almost entirely in Arabic. It would be fair to say that there are no precise, concise and in depth literature on usul al-fiqh available in other languages besides Arabic. Therefore the students' dependency on Arabic literature on the subject is paramount. The study also shows that all the lecturers involved in the teaching of usul al-fiqh rely on literatures in Arabic and use them as their main textbooks. Thus this study concludes that the students' weakness in Arabic is the main challenge faced in the study of usul al-fiqh. To overcome this problem, serious long term actions must be taken by the Islamic faculties in the public universities to rectify this situation. Other than the above, this study further reveals that majority of the lecturers/tutors have not fully used Arabic as the medium as they have to explain and elaborate in Malay so that the students could properly understand the contents [2].

The level of Arabic command among students needs to be paid great attention. Due to the present level of Arabic command amongst students, lecturers focuses much of their attention either to explain the meaning of words and sentences or to translate the whole texts of relevant books. This is certainly a waste of valuable time that could be put to better use to deal with the subject matter in more depth.

We will try to examine the extent to which this content of fiqh is visible today.

3 Ottoman period madrasah education

As is known, religion continued its existence in the society in different forms since the creation of humankind and preserved its place as the basic factor in the formation of civilizations. Relatedly, importance has been given to religious education by all societies. Our purpose is not to emphasize the importance of religious education or display its history. Our purpose is to emphasize its importance in the geography we live. Religious education has been offered in madrasahs from Karahanlis and Seljukians in Anatolian soil, which dates back to 11th and 12th centuries.

In terms of foundation history, the structure of madrasah system was based on a legal foundation which was defined, interpreted and protected by fiqh science experts. In terms of organization, priority was given to fiqh and its auxiliary fields in the education offered at madrasahs [3]. Even before Nizamiye madrasahs, some madrasahs were founded to offer a fiqh-only education [4]. When we look at Anatolian Seljukian madrasahs, it can be seen that there was more specialization. Madrasahs were classified as daru'l-hadis, fiqh madrasah and medicine madrasah according to the topics covered. The Madrasah with Thin Minaret in Konya (1258) was a daru'l-hadis, Sırçalı Madrasah in Konya (1242) was a fiqh madrasah, and the eastern side of Double Madrasah in Kayseri was a medicine madrasah [5]. In this case, we can see that education in madrasahs was not single-sided based on religious education. E. İhsanoğlu explains the following concerning the first Ottoman madrasahs:

"Before Mehmed the Conqueror (Fatih), education in Ottoman madrasahs continued based on the tradition of Nizamiye Madrasahs with the basic purpose of covering religious sciences and popularization of fiqh education. However, the fact that some Seljukian madrasahs were founded next to hospitals and that there were observer wells next to some madrasahs gives some clues about the fact that astronomy and medicine were also studied in these madrasahs. Philosophical, mathematical and natural sciences which were not classified among religious sciences in Seljukian and pre-Fatih Ottoman period were studied in the houses of non-madrasah scientists or hospitals according to the traditions which continued since the past."

The abovementioned tradition continued without any degeneracy and by strengthening the education system in natural sciences. Indeed, the madrasah structure that Ottomans inherited from Seljukians showed considerable development in terms of curriculum and architecture. Fatih madrasahs constituted the infrastructure of the later Ottoman madrasahs.

In Ottoman madrasahs sciences called "Ulum-u 'aliye" (علوم عالية) such as kalam, logic, rhetoric, dictionary, syntax, mathematics, astronomy, philosophy, history and geography and sciences called "Ulum-u 'aliye" (علوم عالية) such as Qur'an sciences, hadith and fiqh were studied. After the reign of Suleiman the Magnificent, there were Umımi (General) madrasahs where Islamic sciences and the sciences which entered Islamic world later were studied and mudarrises, muftis and kadis were raised as well as *Expertise Madrasahs* which aimed at teaching one of the Islamic sciences or sciences that entered Islamic world later which were called Ulum-i Dahiliye (internal sciences) [6].

The mudarrises/scholars who lectured at these madrasahs were perceived as fatwa authorities of their region. They were seen as the first actors in such topics as funerals, marriages, divorces, condolences, inheritance, interpersonal disagreements, peace, shopping etc. From this perspective, madrasah scholars enjoyed a position which directed and executed social events. This is still the case. The fiqh knowledge which is covered theoretically at madrasahs is put into practice in such social topics as divorce, marriage, commerce and other disagreements. Therefore, the fiqh education provided is not restricted to the madrasah; it flows into life via mudarris and students.

In this case, student profile becomes important. Teaching period at madrasahs were mostly dependent on the diligence of students and their ability to pass required classes and exams; it was not organized based on the years and grades in today's sense. Students who studied the offered courses and passed the required exams with success were given a graduation certificate called "deed" which allowed the student to enter a high-degree madrasah. A student who was graduated from a high-degree madrasah with success was given a diploma which allowed for lecturing at any madrasah or working as kadı [7]. Thus, although there was not a grade system in today's fashion, we can talk about the existence of exams which measured success and determined whether the student passed to a higher grade. It can be explained that this system was similar to the present system of passing from elementary school to secondary school, to university and then to master and PhD programs in order to complete the education at the highest level.

The education style which was formed before Ottomans continued at general measures in Ottoman period, too. Education and teaching activities continued at Ottoman madrasahs according to the level of students. It is known that in education book-passing was the principle, courses were recited with frequent repetitions and mutual negotiations and in the mosques or prayer rooms close to the classroom, the knowledge acquired was put into practice [8].

This order continued after the dissolution of Ottoman Empire including the courses delivered and textbooks covered; although they were not organized by a single institution, the same curriculum was followed in all madrasahs.

As a result, we can say that fiqh education and teaching constituted the foundation of this curriculum and covered an important place. In the examined madrasahs, fiqh books were the most widely used sources after the basic sources studied in order to ensure that Arabic, which is known as instrumental sciences, could be better understood.

4 Fiqh education at present imam hatip high schools

Religious education in Turkey is offered on a formal and non-formal basis. Religious education is provided with religious culture and ethical knowledge courses which are compulsory until the end of high school education. In addition, students can obtain more knowledge about religion through prophetic biography, Qur'an-ı Qerim etc. courses which are provided on an elective basis at these grades. Similarly, there are İmam Hatip schools with their secondary and high school sections which focus on religious education. These schools offer field/vocational "must" courses such as Arabic, Qur'an, prophetic biography, fiqh and kalam in addition to the curricula of other schools which apply normal curriculum. In their high school period of eight years (four years secondary + four years) the students of İmam Hatip schools also receive scientific courses such as mathematics and chemistry as well as social courses such as history and geography and artistic courses like drawing and music which are covered in other schools. Here we can see that İmam Hatip high schools are not much different from Ottoman madrasah system structurally. Both religious and non-religious sciences are covered in General Madrasahs in the same curriculum. However, considering the curriculum and its objectives, we can say that it is heading towards a slope compared to madrasah system. Yet, both schools produce specialized persons. These are individuals who can be assigned as Religious Culture teachers even on a contractual basis. Even if they cannot receive a task, they prefer Theology faculties.

Fiqh, which forms the backbone of basic Islamic sciences and is the most important course for expertise, is covered as fiqh and basic Islamic knowledge (catechism) at İmam Hatip high schools and an elective course with the title "readings in fiqh" is offered. The question is: is it adequate? When does this question emerge? Naturally, when the inadequacy of İmam Hatip high school graduates is observed in field courses.

Yes, it is a reality that the curriculum makes students inadequate. However, is this the only reason? As education is a whole consisting of curriculum, teacher and student, any problem in any one of them affects the other negatively. Students have difficulties due to the infrastructure problems in fiqh courses. In the system where Arabic language is not lectured adequately, they suffer from disconnection with Islamic sciences and they become unfamiliar with the terms and concepts in the course content, which suffocates students and drives them to despair.

In our country the age of religious education is unfortunately high; therefore, students who come from İmam Hatip schools see themselves as experts in religious matters. The religious groups which want to gain them also make some contributions as they take pains to keep in their monopoly the religious education of the person they influence. Due to this attitude, students question in their minds the religious group of the teachers before they begin the lecturing and feel sympathy or antipathy for the teacher according to the result.

In this case, it will not be true to argue that the only factor which creates the failure of the course to reach its objective is the curriculum.

5 Fiqh education at universities

Students graduated from Theology faculties work as İmam Hatip, preacher and mufti at different levels of Directorate of Religious Affairs, and teacher at public and private schools under the Ministry of National Education; but can they make the best of their duties?

Can the theology faculties which aim at equipping students with the knowledge and ability of reading and evaluating Islamic sciences from its resources, obtaining adequate knowledge in relevant social and religious sciences and relating them with their fields, expressing the things they learn in writing systematically, producing solutions to the problems they encounter concerning their field and sharing them with the society, and practicing vocational applications, obtain the efficiency that they target?

First of all, it should be noted that one of the most important factors is that students who come to theology faculties from İmam Hatip high schools come to theology faculties with the problems that we mentioned. Later, let us review the area that fiqh course covers in the curriculum of theology faculties.

In the course curriculum of theology faculties, Fiqh is offered in such courses as Islamic prayer principles, introduction to Islamic law, Islamic law procedure I and II, and Islamic law I and II. When this course which is given as 18 credits in total is divided into grades, it is seen that it is inadequate in terms of conveying of fiqh, and is covered very superficially. As a matter of fact, successful students who want to have a master's degree in the field of fiqh can become successful in master's program without infrastructure preparation.

One of the missing points in fiqh education in theology faculties is that the relation of fiqh with non-religious sciences is not mentioned in the curriculum at all. Thus, the social and worldly dimension of fiqh obliges it to relate to non-religious disciplines. That is to say that fiqh procedures which is a methodology of fiqh in that it enjoys logical consistency, examines the origins of legal principles, imposes general principles related to high ideas, Islamic terminology and commands, and teaches the general concepts of law, is also fiqh philosophy. Usul al-fiqh (Principles of Islamic Jurisprudence) is undoubtedly a core and important discipline in shariah studies. The term usul al-fiqh is actually derived from two words; usul (singular of asl) and fiqh. Each of the words has its own meanings; either literal or technical. However the term usul al-fiqh could be defined as follows: "the principles by the use of which the mujtahid arrives at the legal rules through specific evidences". Therefore, this discipline directly concerns the mujtahidin, scholars who have the qualification and ability to exercise and deduce Islamic rulings from recognized sources of laws especially al-Qur'an and al-Sunnah. By having knowledge of primary sources of Islamic law, an establishment of Islamic rulings can be done by utilizing other recognized derivative sources. As far as Shariah studies in the higher institutes and universities are concerned, the introduction of usul al-fiqh in its curriculum is crucial. It is undoubtedly that mastery of this discipline is necessary, for it is a very basic principle in deducing Islamic rulings in Islam

Its social dimension keeps its relation with sociology and psychology alive. This means that in topics for which judgement is sought without research, meaning daily matters, judgement cannot be made and fatwa cannot be given. Fiqh produces solution to the problems of the society on an Islamic ground and the contribution of the case law to solution depends on the knowledge of the interpreter of Islamic law about his time and society. Such that as indicated by İbn Abidin the mufti who will give fatwa has to know the traditions of the time and the status of the society. Therefore, it is essential in terms of fiqh education that new areas such as Islamic law philosophy and Islamic law sociology are included in theology curricula.

6 Conclusion

Students who are graduated from İmam Hatip high schools are inadequate in their fields of expertise and they carry this inadequacy to the society.

İmam Hatip graduates who prefer theology faculties have overconfidence like "I know everything"; as a result, they are graduated from faculty with unsuccessful degrees. The successful students reach this level only with their own effort.

The credit of must courses in theology faculty curriculum is not adequate in order to complete fiqh education. The courses teaching the relation of fiqh with non-religious sciences is not given any place in the curriculum. This makes the education of an individual who is respectful to traditions, have a vision and is creative impossible and creates a mentality which is disconnected with the world they live in.

I tried to display that it is compulsory that the teaching of fiqh, which is one of the three pillars of basic Islamic sciences, begins in small ages, that the course curricula at İmam Hatip high schools should be reviewed and people who will become theologists should be educated, curricula which would consider and support the existing deficiencies and fiqh education should be given more space in the curricula in theology faculties and number of its credits should be increased.

İt is imperative to move beyond an exclusively doctrinal, literal and inflexible approach to the teaching and learning experiences in Islamic law.

References

1. A. Sabri, Gusmaneli, The Using of Media in Learning Fiqh to the Islamic Education Department of Education and Teacher Faculty of IAIN Imam Bonjol Padang. J. Al-Ta'lim **22 (2),** 180 (2015)
2. N.N.A. Rahman, A.K. Ali, R. Ramli, M.S. Ismail, The Teaching And Learning Of Usul Al Fiqh In Public Universities In Malaysia: Reality And Challenges, Shariah J. **16**, 535 (2008)
3. E. İhsanoğlu, *Osmanlı Medeniyeti Tarihi*, **1,** 232 (1999)
4. Z. Kazıcı, *Ana Hatlarıyla İslam Eğitim Tarihi*, 48 (1995)
5. İ. Kayaoğlu (1994). *İslam Kurumları Tarihi,* **2**, 54 (1994)
6. Z. Kazıcı, *İslâm Medeniyeti ve Müesseseleri Tarihi,* 372 (2003)
7. Y. Sarıkaya, *Medreseler ve Modernleşme*, 36 (1997)
8. C. Baltacı, *XV. ve XVI. Asırlar Osmanlı Medreseleri,* 45 (1976)

Knowledge Status of X-Ray Department Managers of Istanbul Private Hospitals about Hospital Accreditation

Nuran Akyurt[1, *]

[1]Marmara University, Vocational School of Health Services, D-100 Güney Yanyolu Üzeri, Cevizli Mahallesi, 34865 Kartal – Istanbul, Turkey

Abstract. JCI accreditation standards are an undertaking that provides continuity of improvement and development work that is guided by the development of patient care quality at the most appropriate level, the provision of a reliable patient care environment, and the reduction of the risks of patient and service providers. The purpose of our work is to determine the extent to which x-ray department managers from the Istanbul city's private hospitals who are preparing for accreditation or have successfully completed the accreditation can apply the JCI accreditation standards, their knowledge level and their attitude about it. The study's universe constitutes a total of 111 people serving as managers in the radiology departments of private hospitals operating in the province of Istanbul. A survey form was applied in the study. As a result, the education of the managers of the radiology services should be under the management of the persons with the expertise and experience.

1 Accreditation in health organizations

In the world countries, recent developments and changes in health sector have caused significant changes in the physical and functional structure of developed country hospitals. Medical technology, developed for the diagnosis and treatment of disease as well as for the protection of patients from disease has led to a decrease in hospitalization times for patients admitted to bedside services and an increase in bed turnover rates. This change affects the structure of the hospital, its design and functions, and provides a quality health care service in a very short time.

The health sector is an important sector around the world where, for a long time, standards and models have been launched based on the continual notion of improvement. Increased healthcare spending, gained importance of patient safety and continuous development idea at service providers and service receivers have led to healthcare organizations establishing quality management systems, applying international standards and constantly improving mechanisms.

[*] Corresponding author: nakyurt@hotmail.com

In order to satisfy patients' need for medical care at a satisfactory level, efforts to provide quality services that have started in private hospitals and in a short time also applied in public hospitals are at the level of documenting the quality of health care services by an impartial external body.

The need to document the quality of health care services by an impartial external organization has emerged in the United States (USA) for the first time. The accreditation document for the health organizations operating in the USA started to be given by the "Joint Commission Accreditation For Health Organization" (JCAHO). This development in the field of health in the USA, has been a study that attracts the attention of world countries since 1990. Hospital accreditation in the international arena is made by Joint Commission International (JCI), a subdivision of JCAHO. Joint Commission International (JCI) works to improve patient safety and quality of health care in the international community by offering education, publications, advisory services, and international accreditation and certification. In more than 100 countries, JCI partners with hospitals, clinics, and academic medical centers; health systems and agencies; government ministries; academia; and international advocates to promote rigorous standards of care and to provide solutions for achieving peak performance.

Within health services, hospitals have always had a special place, as most of the resources in the entire service chain are consumed in hospitals. Approximately 40% of the expenditures in the Ministry of Health budget in our country are always allocated to hospital services. In this case, hospitals are obliged to place principles such as efficiency, activity and equity in health care. In particular, resources for in-hospital patients and advanced laboratory tests have two major impacts on hospital costs. For this reason, developed countries make great efforts to minimize hospital stay, to improve the success and to increase the number of the outpatient clinics and to avoid unnecessary laboratory use, [1].

Patients who do not need close supervision by the doctor or nursing care are closely followed in the hostels, which are built adjacent to the hospital. The purpose of these applications is to improve the quality of service provided to the patient and to reduce health expenditures, [2]. Providing quality goods or services is cheaper than what is known. Considering the sum of all income earned in the countries, the high spending on health care for many governments makes it difficult to control hospital costs and to implement health system reforms, [3]. Considering the situation in our country, the following should be taken into account: the rapid increase in the number of private hospitals over the last five years, the growing importance of health for the citizens and their families and the expectation of qualified health services.

Parallel to the developments in the world, important steps on accreditation are also being taken in our country. The Turkish Accreditation Authority (TURKAK) was established with the Law No. 4457 published on November 4, 1999 in order to accredit the conformity assessment activities in our country, [4]. In order to establish the "National Health Accreditation System", the Ministry of Health initiated a series of studies under the health transformation project. In these studies conducted under the leadership of the Ministry of Health, great importance is attached to the participation of all stakeholders in the health sector and the international experience in this area, [5]. As the Ministry of Health, negotiations are underway with the Joint Commission International (JCI) regarding the establishment of the National Health Accreditation System (Institutional Evaluation Hospital Accreditation System). The business alliance, which started with Joint Commission International (JCI), took concrete steps in structuring the National Accreditation System, assessed the situation in different working groups, and signed a protocol with JCI officials in 2004, [6]. Ministry of Health and JCI business association protocol includes the structuring of the national health accreditation system, the development of standards, quality and monitoring systems, the training of auditors and the creation of databases.

2 International accreditation standards in hospitals

JCI accreditation audit process is seen as an assessing of general policies and values of the hospital, organization structure, service activities, services provided, environmental management, communication network, information use, operational policies, employee skills and training, and quality management.

There is experiences that a two-year preparatory process is needed (preparing for the standards and transitional stages) for hospitals in order to get accredited from JCI, [7]. Hospitals have to form "councils and committees" within their own organization to implement and oversee 440 standards that the JCI organization has collected under 11 main headings.

The hospital needs to establish its mission, vision, policies and strategies before entering the JCI accreditation audit. After the mission and vision of the institution is determined, there are opinions that the institution should set a number of goals and targets that will guide the strategies for the future and help them to be measured and assessed, [8]. After the missions, vision and strategies that the hospital management has established, it is necessary to establish "quality improvement council" in order to determine "quality indicators follow-up procedures" for JCI accreditation standards and measurable elements and to follow them.

Figure 2.2: Structure of the Quality Improvement Council

Source: Mücella Tokatlıoğlu, "Uluslararası Akreditasyon Standartları", IQ Uluslararası Kalite Danışmanlık Organizasyon AŞ Dokümanları, p. 250.

There are views on the necessity of using guidelines in clinical practice in order to collect, analyze and continuously improve the data of clinical and administrative procedures designed to provide quality patient care within the scope of the hospital's mission, vision and quality management improvement goals, [9, 10].

Follow-up procedures should be established in order to evaluate the services provided by the hospitals. These follow-up procedures show the result of a time-out or outcome performance of all efforts and processes undertaken to realize the mission, vision and policies of the hospital. Planned by the quality management council, prepared in line with the quality management and improvement program, units in the scope of specific strategic follow-up and reporting plan of the departments within the flow of the quality indicator follow-up procedure have to determine the processes they consider to follow, the quality indicators and their targets. The quality council and the leaders determine which processes should be monitored and improved on a priority basis, the priority and the frequency of data collection. These priorities should include critical, high-risk and problem-prone areas. Today, there is a great increase in the medical information, with the technology development in measuring and imaging methods, medical tests, analysis and monitoring devices, also in data and information gathered from individuals and patients. In an environment where the level of knowledge of individuals is high, patient protection methods are in the foreground, the context of fast and effective treatment is of high expectations and institutions are increasingly specialized, it is now one of the priority requirements to receive care services in different phases as integrated and continuous services. The condition of the patient, radiological requirements and interventions depend on the ability of the hospital which has fully implemented the informational strategies.

Hospital management, requesting JCI accreditation is required to establish the quality management program for the radiology department so that the accreditation standards can be used and applied. With the participation of the radiology department manager (leader), "strategy and reporting follow-up process" for the department should first be prepared. Radiology manager should show all services in the department during the strategy and reporting follow-up process. In the strategy follow-up process, the radiology department should detail its aim, vision, mission, goals, measurements needed to achieve these goals, and specific performance criteria for the segmentation.

3 Methods

The purpose of our work is to determine the extent to which x-ray department managers from the Istanbul city's private hospitals who are preparing for accreditation or have successfully completed the accreditation can apply the JCI accreditation standards, their knowledge level and their attitude about it.

3.1 Universe and sampling

The study's universe constitutes a total of 111 people serving as managers in the radiology departments of private hospitals operating in the province of Istanbul. Scientific data related to the hospitals were prepared taking into account the "Statistical Yearbook of Hospitalized Treatment Institutions" published by the Ministry of Health.

3.2 Data collection tools

Research is a descriptive work. Survey form was created and applied in the survey. The accreditation standards developed by the JCI accreditation organization for radiology departments were taken as basis in the creation of the statements in the questionnaire, [11]. For the statements in the questionnaire, the 13 standards and measurable components prepared for these standards which were defined by JCI accreditation organization (patient evaluating) for evaluating radiology services were used, [12].

The accreditation standards for the radiology departments of the JCI organization are as shown below. These standards are, [13];

HD.6 Radiology services are available to meet the needs of patients and they must comply with all regional / national standards, laws and regulations.

HD.6.1 Diagnostic imaging services must be provided by the institution or linked to external resources that are ready for use at any time.

HD.6.2 The radiation protection program should be available, followed and documented.

D.6.3 The implementation and interpretation of the tests should be carried out by appropriately trained, competent and experienced specialists.

HD.6.4 Radiology results should be given within a period defined by the institution.

HD.6.5 All radiology equipment should be regularly checked, maintained, calibrated and kept in a register of these activities.

HD.6.6 X-ray films and other materials should be available on a regular basis.

HD.6.7 The management of diagnostic radiology services should be the responsibility of the expert (s).

HD.6.8 Quality control procedures should be established, followed and documented.

HD.6.9 The institution should regularly check the quality control results of the products coming to the radiology service from outside.

HD.6.10 The institution should have the necessary infrastructure to be able to apply to specialists in highly specialized diagnostic areas.

HD.7 Patient-care medical, nursing and other persons and services must be in a business alliance to analyze and integrate patient assessment.

HD.7.1 The most urgent and important maintenance needs must be identified.

In the first part of the questionnaire, there are questions about determining the demographic information of the managers in the radiology departments.

In the second part of the questionnaire, there are questions about the departments of radiology managers.

In the third part of the questionnaire, we tried to determine the JCI standards developed for the evaluation of the services provided in the radiology departments of the hospitals, which would mainly require accreditation supervision, and the participation rates in the areas that managers should comply with when fulfilling them.

3.3 Analysis of data

The obtained data were analyzed by using SPSS data analysis program. As statistical analysis technique, [14, 15, 16, 17, 18]; Frequency distribution, Independent Sampling t-Test, One-Way ANOVA and Tukey Multiple Comparison Method (Post-Hoc) were used.

4 Results

When we examined the results, 29.7% of the 111 radiology managers participated in the survey were women, 70.3% were men; 44.3% of them are working as managers for 0-5 years; 44,1% are radiologists, 43,2% are vocational school of health graduates and 12,7% are vocational high school graduates.

When we examined the results of the questions concerning the departments, it was found that 57.1% (n = 28) of them had a quality certificate, 24.5% (n = 12) of this certificate had ISO 9001 quality certificate and 14.3% (n = 7) documented that they are documentary. Do you have a vision and mission in your department and they have answered with 61.2% (n = 30) yes of them.

When we examine the answers to the accreditation criteria of the radiology departments of hospitals seeking to be accredited, I agree with 45.9% (n = 51) of the expression "radiology services are available to meet the needs of HD 6 patients and they must comply with all regional / national standards, laws and regulations" , 43.2% (n = 48) completely agree with each other. Since the unit is on institutions Turkey Atomic Energy Agency (TAEK) is operated under license from operating certificate issued by the phrase to agree 28.2% (n = 31) I totally agree 71.8% (n = 79) percent gave the answer, "HD.6.6 X-ray films and other materials for use as a regular 53.6% (n = 59) agree completely, 31.9% (n = 35) agree completely. For the failure of the radiology services, X-ray films have been participated at high level since the purchase of X-ray films has to be well followed up from the storage to the storage, as well as to the presentation of the extraction rooms.

Also we aim to determine the consistency of the statements made by us with respect to the accreditation standards, to evaluate the homogeneity by subjecting it to reliability analysis and different statistical tests. The Cronbach Alpha value was calculated to determine the reliability of the data obtained by the questionnaire. We can say that our questionnaire is reliable since alpha values are very close to 1.00, which is considered as full reliability.

5 Discussion

"Accreditation"; is a formal process by which a health facility conforms to pre-established and published standards, which are evaluated and approved by the JCI accreditation organization. The decision on accreditation of a specific health institution is made after an on-site audit by accreditation auditors.

There is a difference of opinion between educational status and age groups in the extent to which JCI accreditation standards are fulfilled by those who have assumed the role of manager in the radiology units of private hospitals. The difference of opinion among the managers regarding these standards lies between the young group managers (the newly completed group of specialization / university education) and the age group who have been for many years serving in the radiology units and are in the pension stage. In these two age groups, radiology specialist managers over 45 years old have had a more positive view of their implementation in the parts of accreditation standards. The same situation has also been observed among the radiology specialists who have successfully completed speciality medicine and the radiology department graduates of the vocational school of health. While the radiology specialist gives a more positive opinion in the fulfillment and implementation of some JCI standards, the vocational college graduate thinks differently. This is also seen between managers of the vocational school of health services graduates and managers of the vocational high school graduates in the fulfillment and implementation of some JCI standards. In order to overcome the disparity between the education and age groups that we are trying to summarize above, the meaning of the JCI standards and how it should be applied/implemented in the radiology departments has to explained with trainings given by the experts of this subject. We think that this training about the standards can be regarded as a positive contribution to the elimination of differences of view and application.

6 Conclusion

Hospital accreditation is a vocational assessment and scorecard work carried out by professionals. In short, it certifies that the hospital radiology services that have received the accreditation document are also provided at a desirable level, that is, it is committed that the employees' opinions are valued, the safety and security of the patients and employees are provided, the team work is emphasized and the professional education and progress of the employees are supported.

The accreditation standards developed by the JCI organization for the radiology department include the staff, the patients and their relatives, and the safe operation of the functioning devices in the department. The standards established by the JCI organization for the radiology departments are based on national, international laws and regulations. Therefore, in order to perform ideal radiology services in private hospitals radiology managers who have fulfilled the requirements of the JCI accreditation standards have also fulfilled the ideal radiology service. In short, we believe that ideal radiology services can be provided with ideal radiology units that protect patients and employees, respect patient rights, inform patients, have calibrated all the devices actively used, and take into account other issues that we have already mentioned. As a result of our work, the requirements for hospital management and radiology managers who wants to be accredited by the JCI organization are listed as a suggestion.

6.1 Suggestions

- Radiology managers should be able to create organizational charts for their departments including the competency and responsibilities of the employees.
- Radiology managers need to create a device management program for all devices in their units. This program should contain all information about the devices. It is necessary to use specialist experts in selecting and purchasing radiology devices. In the accreditation process, formal entry of radiology devices becomes important.
- Hospital senior management must regularly document records of radiology devices. For this purpose, medical physicians should be employed in the units.
- The hospital senior management is required to set up units to carry out periodic maintenance and repair and calibration plans of all medical and radiological devices. Calibration procedures for all devices in the hospital must be followed by biomedical engineering. The biomedical departments of the hospital should create a staff planning to coordinate with these, the established plans for the medical devices.
- Calibrations of mammography, computerized tomography, magnetic resonance imaging (MRI), nuclear medicine, etc. devices from the radiology departments should be performed using phantoms approved by international organizations. It is necessary to make quality measurements for the acquired image and to keep records for radiology management.
- Instructions should be made by the administrators regarding the storage and service of the kit, film and other materials used in the radiology units and the materials should be shipped in accordance with this instruction (instructions for storing radiology materials).

- In situations such as fluoroscopic procedures used in radiology units, catheter guidance in angiography units, the x-ray machine should be used as short as possible. Radiology managers should refer to x-ray attenuation methods in such cases.
- Radiology managers should be able to provide personal protection for employees by ensuring that personnel working in the units are provided with eyes protection, thyroid protective accessories, lead, glass plate, lead screen, lead gloves, gonod protectors and lead aprons.
- Lead aprons, lead curtains, lead gloves, gonod protectors and thyroid protectors used for the purpose of protecting the radiology workers and their patients should be checked at least once a year for cracks, holes or tears under fluoroscopy and these procedures should be recorded.
- Before starting the radiological examination, it is necessary to develop and implement a method for obtaining the written confirmation form of the patient, which provides the accuracy of the patient's identity information and the information of the requesting patient and the patients who have special circumstances, especially in the units where the interventional procedures are performed.
- Before starting the radiological examination, especially in the units where the interventional procedures are performed, it is necessary to develop and implement a method which provides the accuracy of the patient's identity information with the identity information on the request sheet and which obtain the written consent form from patients with special circumstances.
- Patient preparation instructions should be drawn up for all examinations to be made in radiology units and personnel should be trained about these instructions.
- Radiology managers need to establish a follow-up process to identify processes that are problematic or potentially problematic in order to improve the radiological services provided in their departments.
- Radiology managers need to apply the shift system to increase the usage capacities of the medical devices used in the units and to keep them active 24 hours a day. Accordingly, rotation plans for the personnel in the shift system must be established. Radiology services should be provided for emergency services except working hours.
- Radiology administrators should create an operational program that allows them to monitor the performance of their departments on a regular basis, to review test results and to track material flow on a regular basis, and periodically document records associated with this program.
- Radiology managers should identify specialists who will be needed in specific diagnostic areas, such as radiation physics, nuclear medicine radiation oncology, where appropriate, and determine a method to be able to contact them any time.
- There should be an active radiation safety program at the level required by the risks / hazards encountered / may encountered throughout the hospital. The program should specify safety practices and preventive measures for the radiology team, other teams and patients. The program should be coordinated with the institution's safety management program.
- Reliable quality control systems need to be established to provide excellent radiology services in radiology units.
- Radiology managers should be able to ensure that all devices operate at acceptable levels and are safe for the user (radiology personnel).
- In order to make a decision for recruiting, the radiology managers should organize orientation training and rotation for new personnel where they should make different

number of shots in different radiology units. The managers should support all its employees in recruitment, training, development and continuing education programs.

- Radiology managers should organize continuing education programs in relation to the services they provide to their staff and patients. They should create a budget for annual scientific activities for the staff of the department and direct their staff to this activities.
- Radiology managers should be able to create a team-based, mutually respectful environment for all of their employees.
- Radiology managers should be able to take measures to reduce bureaucracy in the department. Radiology managers should be able to conduct internal and external researches on patient expectations.
- Radiology managers should be able to create mechanisms for facilitating new ideas about the department (suggestion boxes, awarding of best ideas, etc.).
- Radiology administrators should be able to create procedures and instructions for all radiological examinations performed in their units and ensure that all employees are properly trained in this area.
- In interventional radiological procedures, radiology managers should be able to include the patient, patient family and persons who decides in behalf of the patient in the decision process.
- Radiology managers need to establish a method to ensure that information (patient datas) of patients arriving at the units to be examined is kept properly.
- Radiology managers should lead the creation of a safety committee based on the size of the hospital they are working in, and should take part in the execution of the program.
- Valuable data should be provided to monitor all aspects of the program, to develop the program, and to reduce the probability of risks within the organization.

References

1. Haydar Sur, "Hastanelerde Kaynak İsrafı: Nasıl Önüne Geçmeli?" (Çevrimiçi) http://www.merih.net/m1/0mangmt.html, (30 Kasım 2006).
2. Murat Yerebakan, Özel Hastaneler Araştırması Mevcut Durum Sorunlar ve Çözüm Önerileri, İstanbul Ticaret Odası Yayın No: 2000–26, , s.46 (İstanbul 2000).
3. R. L. Williams, "JCAHO Accreditation. Is It Necessary?", Nurs Manage, Nov, 28(11), pp. 60-63 (1997).
4. http://www.turkak.org.tr/literat/mkl1.html, (Çevrimiçi), (16 Agustos 2004).
5. George Purvis, "Kurumsal Değerlendirme Hastane Akreditasyon Sistemi" raporu, Kalite ve Akreditasyon Çalıştayı (Antalya), JCI International Summer Practicum on Quality Improvement and Accredidation, 12–16 Temmuz 2004; Sağlık Hizmetlerinde Akreditasyon, 23 Eylül 2004, JCI ile işbirliği anlaşması (İstanbul) ; Sağlık Hizmetlerinde Kalite ve Akreditasyon, Bursa (18 Aralık 2004).
6. Recep Akdağ, "Sağlık Sektöründe Akraditasyon" (Çevrimiçi) http://www.akreditasyon2004.org/pdf/Bakan.pdf, (22 Ekim 2004).
7. İrem Ergun Öcal, "JCI Standartları ve Uluslararası Kalite", SB Diyalog, s. 30 (Eylül 2005).
8. Hayri Ülgen, S. Kadri Mirze, İşletmelerde Stratejik Yönetim, Literatür Yayınları No:113, s. 69 (2004, Ocak).

9. A. A. Boxwala, S. W. Tu, M. Peleg, Q. Zeng, O. Ogunyemi, R. A. Greenes, et. al., "Toward a representation format for sharable clinical guidelines", J Biomed Inform, 34 (3), p. 157 (2001 Jun).
10. S. T. M. Shaneyfelt, M. F. Mayo-Smith, J. Rothwangl, "Are Guidelines Following Guidelines? The Methodological Quality of Clinical Practice Guidelines in The Peer Reviewed Medical Literature", Journal of the American Medical Association (JAMA), 281, p. 1902, (1999).
11. Uluslararası Birleşik Komisyon, Hastaneler için Akreditasyon Standartları, s. 56-61.
12. A. e., s. 41–63.
13. Joint Commission International (JCI) Accreditation Standards for Hospitals, Effective, 2. Edition, pp. 45–46 (January 2003).
14. Ayhan Ural, İbrahim Kılıç, Bilimsel Araştırma Süreci ve SPSS İle Veri Analizi, Detay Yayıncılık, Ankara, s. 151, 185, 172, 192 (Ocak 2005).
15. Yahşi Yazıcıoğlu, Samiye Erdoğan, SPSS Uygulamalı Bilimsel Araştırma Yöntemleri, Detay Yayıncılık, Ankara, s. 203, 239, (Ocak 2005).
16. Remzi Altunışık, Recai Coşkun, Serkan Bayraktaroğlu, Engin Yıldırım, Sosyal Bilimlerde Araştırma Yöntemleri, SPSS Uygulamalı, Sakarya Kitabevi, Sakarya, s.318–328, 114 (Ekim 2005).
17. Aziz Akgül, Osman Çevik, İstatiksel Analiz Teknikleri SPSS'te İşletme Yönetimi Uygulamaları, Emek Ofset Ltd. Şti., Ankara, s. 3, 170, 185, 434 (2005)
18. Nural Bekiroğlu, Açıklamalı Bioistatistik Terimleri Sözlüğü, Nobel Tıp Kitapevleri, İstanbul, s. 44 (1998).

Determination of the Communication Skills of University Students by Sociodemographic Features

Nuran Akyurt[1, *]

[1]Marmara University, Vocational School of Health Services, D-100 Güney Yanyolu Üzeri, Cevizli Mahallesi, 34865 Kartal – Istanbul, Turkey

Abstract. As a social being, human life continues in communities with other people. Human being is the only entity that communicates with highly complex learned behaviors that include best use of gestures and mimics, advanced reflex and instinct language as well as language. In our study, we wanted to determine the communication skills of university students with their socio-demographic characteristics. Two separate forms were used in the study. The evaluation of the obtained data was done by SPSS (Version 16.0) Statistical Package Program. The target population of the study is composed of students studying at Marmara University. In the direction of the data obtained within the scope of the research it was observed that the communication skills of the students studying in the departments providing health education are higher. University students are encouraged to develop listening skills and create an environment in which they can express themselves better.

1 Communication concept and definition

As a social being, human lives in communities with other people. Thus it is possible for him to satisfy his social needs and overcome the troubles caused by personal inadequacies. Through the unity and solidarity with other people, it is easier and faster for him to fulfill his needs, to promote individual development and to overcome environmental factors, [1]. Communication is as old as human history; Mankind finds himself in a network of relationships with himself and his surroundings from the first moment that he exists, [2]. The word communication is used as a counterpart in our language of the word "Communication" derived from the root of "communis", which means "common" in Latin. The word "communication" means partnership, socialization, coexistence because of its origins. The existing rules, values and beliefs of the community in which the individual lives are transmitted through communication.

There are different definitions of communication concept in the literature. For the first time in the 5th and 4th centuries BC, Aristotle defined communication as "skill and art of an orator to influence and to convince audiences in any way with his speech, [2]. Eren defined communication as a process of passing information, ideas and feelings from one person to another, [3]. According to Paksoy, a communication takes place when the sender

* Corresponding author: nakyurt@hotmail.com

sends something to which a meaning is attached and the receiver interprets this as well, [4]. According to Koçel, communication is expressed as the transmission of information, data and understanding from one person to another, [5]. According to another definition, communication is a system which has temporal, objective and social dimensions, which enables the parties to act together to establish attitudes and behaviors and social structures, [6]. According to another definition, communication is "to send information from one place to another via the means of symbols", [7]. Burgoon, Buller and Woodall discuss the relationship and differences between the concepts of information, behavior and communication in order to enable a better understanding of the concept of communication in a personal sense, [8], [9].

In the common expressions given in the literature, communication includes various systems, written, verbal and nonverbal forms of messages in the transfer of information, data, perception, understanding and intuition. Therefore, although communication seems simple, it is a process that carries many problems in its own right.

1.1 Elements of the communication process

Transferring information, datas, ideas, thoughts, perceptions, understanding, approach, intuition, desire, wish and feelings from one to another to have mutual interaction is named as communication process [1]. In the communication process, the transmitter (sender, source) creates a message and transfers it to the receiver (destination). The recipient interprets this message and responds satisfactorily to the sender (feedback). Many models have been developed to explain the communication process. One of these oldest and most widely known model in the literature is Shannon and Weaver's communication model (Figure 1). This model includes all functions such as coding, sending, receiving and feedback during the transmission of certain news or information from a transmitter to a receiver.

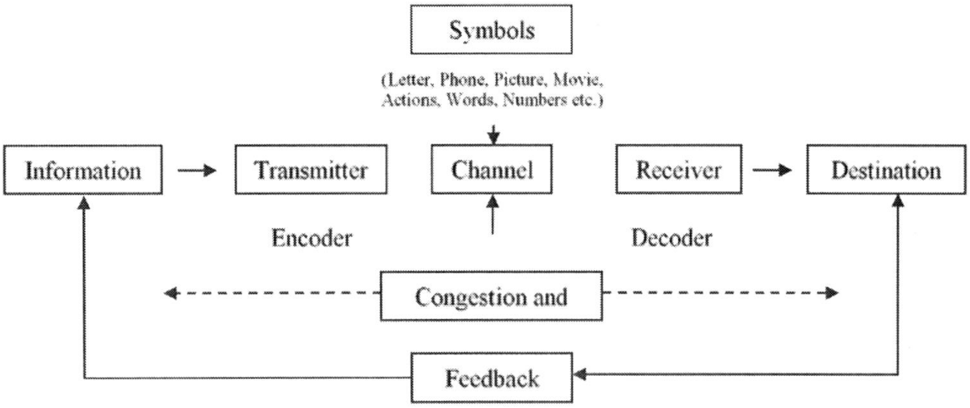

Figure 1. Communication Process
Source: C. E. Shannon, "A Mathematical Theory of Communication" Reprinted with corrections from The Bell System Technical Journal, Vol. 27, pp. 379–423, 623–656, July, October, 1948

Shannon-Weaver's communication model has been made in the sense of communication and continues to be valid today. According to this highly objective and technical model, the main elements of the communication process can be listed as transmitter, receiver, message, communication channel, congestion, hitch and feedback, [6]. In the given model, the source unit, which is called the sender or transmitter, is the person or group sending gathered and created informations, emotions, thoughts and ideas to the receiver. The sender passes the generated message through a communication channel to the receiver. The message in the communication process is transmitted from the sender to the recipient by certain means. If the recipient does not give the message a meaning close to the sender's meaning, it means that it has not been reached for the purpose of communication. Therefore, the message needs to reach the recipient which means the receiver must be a good listener.

Obstructions and obstacles are the negative elements that arise during the communication process, which degrade communication, impair the authenticity and reliability of the communication. Feedback is the sender's response to the recipient's message, taking a significant place in the communication process and indicating that the communication process is complete, [1].

1.2 Effective communication process

There are similar expressions in the literature for an effective communication process. According to Koçel, [5], in order for communication to be complete, the symbols that indicate the message must be identified by the receiver. Bozdoğan, states that there are three basic conditions: naturalness, acceptance/respect and empathy, [10]. According to this; The naturalness is that the individual is open and honest. Acceptance/respect is that people respect each other's existence and accept this person with his or her own qualities. Empathy is that individuals can put themselves in their place, that is, they can evaluate events from the point of view. Empathy is a difficult skill to win.

According to Hodgetts, an effective communication process in working life occurs in four stages; Empathy, attention, understanding, acceptance and existing response, [11]. Attention is to make the receiver listen to the message that is attempted to be transmitted, to force the receiver to listen. If the transmitter cannot attract the attention of the receiver, communication will not be possible and continuation will not be possible. Understanding is that the recipient understands the content of the message and perceives the message. Acceptance can be explained as the recipient's obedience to the message. The response is the phase in which communication takes place and requires the implementation of the message. Effective listening and effective response is summarized by Korkut as the ability of a healthy communication, [12]. These skills classified as follows; Asking questions, summarizing, repetition, reacting with keywords, identifying and reflecting the behavior, words and feelings of the other person, testing whether they understand or not, and giving effective feedback, [13]. Korkut states that one of the most effective communication skills is effective listening and that the majority of communication problems are due to poor listening, [14].

In order to have better human relationships and to get better in contact besides the good use of body the individual need to be reach emotional maturity. Emotional maturity is that the individual understands his own feelings and arranges the way he can raise his or her level of life, empathizing for the feelings of others. Instead of emotional maturity concept, self-awareness and delayed gratification (delayed gratification) concepts is used. This feature is called "emotional reason", indicating that the individual's success in life will depend on the degree to which he possesses these skills. This concept was later described as "emotional intelligence" and is defined as the individual being aware of their own feelings, [21].

The effective communication process, in which the principal elements are given above, is not fully operational in practice. Communication barriers arise from the fact that lack of communication is effective in this process.

1.3 Communication skills required by different professional groups

Communication has its own place and importance in working life. Individuals, working in industrial enterprises while they found in positive or negative behaviors against the environment benefit from a wide range of communication tools. Whatever the purpose is, businesses, which are part of the social structure, maintain their lives within the framework of internal and external relations. The communication mechanism that is inherent in social life and which is the essence of the organizational structure is a phenomenon aiming to establish relations between individuals, groups and organizations, [22].

Organizations are units created by people who have come together for "production", have different opinions and knowledge, dependent to each other to reach different but common purposes. The most important element of organizations are people who are in continuous interaction with each other. Organizational communication systems that connect these people to one another are systems for providing reconciliation for production. From a broader perspective, organizations today are not only having efforts for production, intra-organizational collaboration and providing feedback. Beside these they have to communicate with "outside world", to transfer information's got from environment to information-processing centers in the organization in order to create a strategy for ambiguous, competitive and dynamic environment.

Just as in every field of social life, communication skills in business life have a great importance. Communication skills are among the interpersonal skills required for almost every type of business, in other words, the overall business dimensions required for success in an enterprise. Therefore, the skills of individuals in communication are an important advantage in a large majority of occupations. Communication skills are important for virtually every profession and every position. Because of the importance of communication skills in business life, employers also attach importance to communication skills when hiring. Thus, communication skills are often referred as the skills required to perform a job well. It has been revealed that the most wanted skills in job advertisements is success in human relations, in other words communication skills. Organizations continue their existence through the interactions of the business potential that they have in their possession.

The better the personal relations of the employees of the organization, the better it is to develop the organization, and if it is bad, the organization is in danger. Any kind of behavior that the person exhibits with the knowledge, skills and abilities that he possesses affects his working life. In order for the individual to achieve success and satisfaction in his working life; knowledge, skills and abilities, personality characteristics and interests that are possessed are relevant to the chosen occupation is important. Orientation to a profession appropriate to the characteristics of the individual, it is an important and a big step in professional life. From this point of action, individual must know himself and what qualifications are required of the profession he chooses. Every profession requires different knowledge, skills and abilities. One of the basic skills that is important for almost all professions is "communication skills".

2 Method

2.1 Purpose and design of research

In this study, aimed to determine whether there are differences in communication skills between students who receive vocational education in different fields at Marmara University and whether communication skills of these students differ or not in terms of socio demographic variables. In addition, the influence of the advanced communication skills on professional success in different professions is examined. Within the scope of the research, a sample of students in the fields of health, technical, educational sciences was used to represent different professional orientations. In the creation of the sample, the "Change over Years in the Distribution of Students among Academic Units" statistics published by Marmara University was used. During the application of the questionnaire to the university students studying in vocational branches, the necessary permissions were taken from the top management. During the application of the forms, explanations were made about the purpose of the study each class separately and verbal approval received. Participation in the study was voluntary, and the name and personal information of the student were not included in the questionnaire.

2.2 Sampling

The target population of the study is composed of 1116 students who are studying in the fields of health, technical and educational sciences. The universe of the research is limited with students studying in the fields of health, technology and education.

2.3 Data collection tools

Two separate forms were used as data collection tools in the study. The first form was developed by the researchers through a literature review and included 34 questions of information such as age, gender, parental education status, income status, participation in cultural and artistic activities, and follow-up of written and verbal communication tools and materials in order to determine the socio- demographic characteristics of the students.

The second form used in the study is "Communication Skills Inventory" developed by Ersanlı and Balcı, [17]. "Communication Skills Inventory" used by the researchers to measure the communication skills of the vocational students was first developed and used by Balcı. The required validity and reliability studies are 70 items in this first version of the inventory. The inventory was then applied again to a sample of 500 university students and the number of items was reduced to 45 as a result of factor analysis. The inventory, finalized by Ersan and Balcı, consists of Likert type 45 questions. Inventory measures mental, emotional and behavioral communication skills. There are 15 items measuring each dimension. The following items appear in each dimension:

Mental: 1, 3, 6, 12, 15, 17, 18, 20, 24, 28, 30, 33, 37, 43, 45

Emotional: 5, 9, 11, 26, 27, 29, 31, 34, 35, 36, 38, 39, 40, 42, 44

Behavioral: 2, 4, 7, 8, 10, 13, 14, 16, 19, 21, 22, 23, 25, 32, 41

Materials; "Always", "Usually", "Sometimes", "Rarely", "Never". Higher scores in size and overall (total) communication skills correspond to higher communication skills.

As a means of collecting data, a questionnaire form prepared by the researchers was distributed to the students who want to fill in "Communication Skills Inventory" voluntarily.

2.4 Analysis of data

The evaluation of the obtained data was done with SPSS Statistical Package Program (16.0 version). As a statistical analysis technique, (Ural and Kılıç, 2005; Yazıcıoğlu and Erdoğan, 2005; Altunışık et al., 2005; Akgül and Çevik, 2005; Bekiroğlu, 1998) frequency distributions, "Independent Sampling T-Test", "Single Factor Analysis of Variance" (One-Way ANOVA) and Tukey Multiple Comparison Test (Post-Hoc) were used, [18], [19], [20], [21], [22].

2.5 Hypotheses

Based on the various literatures given in the general theoretical framework, the following hypotheses have been formulated.

Hypothesis 1. There is a difference between educations field of the students and communication skills (mental, emotional, behavioral) inventory average scores.

Hypothesis 2. There is a difference between gender and communication skills (mental, emotional, behavioral) inventory average scores.

Hypothesis 3. There is a difference between socioeconomic status and communication skills (mental, emotional, behavioral) inventory average scores.

3 Findings and discussion

According to the results obtained in the research, when the genders of the vocational educated youth are examined, it is found that more than half of them are female students (63.6%); in terms of education fields; 31,3% in health fields (Vocational High School), 37,3% in technical fields, 31,4% in education and technical fields (Bachelor) (31,4%). The vast majority of the ongoing vocational education students (55.2%) stated that they did not study in the section they had imagined. The result is similar to the result that Yiğit and his colleagues reached in 2007 as they have been researching on the same subject at university students, [23]. In this study, 55.2% of the students indicated that they are not studying at the university and area that they have dreamed of. The majority of the students (60.4%) are living in the city. Başer, reached on the research with Hacettepe University nursing students that most of the students (48,2%) were of urban origin, [24].

Most of the university students who participated in the survey lived with their families (62.5%) while the other part (16.5%) reside with their friends. In the research of Yiğit and his colleagues in 2007, 37.6% of the students are living with their families, 31.2% in student dormitories, and 31.2% living together with other students. It can be seen that the percentage distribution is very close together. The difference between these two surveys can be interpreted as the fact that the majority of the students in our study consisted of vocational high school students and according to the transition system without examination the students were preferentially directed to Marmara University which is located in their Vocational and Technical Education Region and their families also reside in this region.

When the educational status of the parents of the students is examined (**Table 1a**); A majority of the parents, mother (47%) and father (32.8%), were primary school graduates. In other studies on youth receiving vocational education, similar results were obtained regarding the educational status of parents, [25].

If we look to the reading habit of the students (Table 1b) it is seen that most of the vocational education students do not have the habit of reading books (27.5%), and it is observed that the majority of the same students are not participating to courses (82.3%) and to sport activities (62.4%). In this case, university administrations should open courses and sports activities in which students can actively participate and they have to orient the students to these activities.

From the data of research, we have seen the following: the vast majority of students have vocational high school graduate (73.3%), more than half of the students are studying in the first year at the university (58.3%), 60,6% of the students are living their life in the city center, from 39.2% the family members consist of 4 persons, from 27.2% of 5 persons and from 14% of 6 persons. As a family income, participants reported the following: between 1000 TL and less (37.1%), between 1000 - 1500 TL (35.6%), between 1500 - 2000 TL (12.4%); Their own expenditures were as follows: between 200 and less (28,2%), between 200 and 300 TL (% 31.2), between 300 and 400 TL (17.3%), between 400 TL and above (22.5%).

Table 1a. Socio-Demographic Characteristics of Students

		n	Percentage
Gender	Male	710	63,62%
	Female	406	36,38%
	Total	**1116**	100,00%
Faculty or College of Education	Faculty of Education	191	17,11%
	Faculty of Technical Education	160	14,34%
	Vocational School of Health Services	349	31,27%
	Vocational School of Technical Sciences	416	37,28%
	Total	**1116**	**100,00%**
Is the chosen subject of study the subject you imagine?	Yes	499	44,71%
	No	615	55,11%
	No Answer	2	0,18%
	Total	**1116**	**100,00%**
Whom do you live with?	with the family	698	62,54%
	with relatives	67	6,00%
	by itself	26	2,33%
	with a friend	184	16,49%
	State Dorm	57	5,11%
	Private Dorm	70	6,27%
	Housing	14	1,25%
	Total	**1116**	**100,00%**
Mother's education	Illiterate	66	5,91%
	Can Read and Write	51	4,57%
	Primary School Graduate	524	46,95%
	Secondary School graduate	206	18,46%
	High school graduate	201	18,01%
	Graduated from a University	56	5,02%
	I do not know	7	0,63%
	No Answer	5	0,45%
	Total	**1116**	**100,00%**
Father's Education	Illiterate	6	0,54%
	Can Read and Write	22	1,97%
	Primary School Graduate	366	32,80%
	Secondary School graduate	243	21,77%
	High school graduate	309	27,69%
	Graduated from a University	147	13,17%
	I do not know	12	1,08%
	No Answer	11	0,99%
	Total	**1116**	**100,00%**

Table 1b. Socio-Demographic Characteristics of Students

		n	Percentage
Socio-Economic Level	Lower income group	166	14,87%
	Middle income group	871	78,05%
	Upper income group	68	6,09%
	No Answer	11	0,99%
	Total	**1116**	100,00%
Do you receive a scholarship?	Yes	298	26,70%
	No	808	72,40%
	No Answer	10	0,90%
	Total	**1116**	100,00%
Book Reading Habit	Yes	801	71,77%
	No	307	27,51%
	No Answer	8	0,72%
	Total	**1116**	100,00%
Newspaper / Magazine Reading Habit	Yes	969	86,83%
	No	136	12,19%
	No Answer	11	0,99%
	Total	**1116**	100,00%
Participation in Cultural Activities	Yes	606	54,30%
	No	503	45,07%
	No Answer	7	0,63%
	Total	**1116**	100,00%
Participation in Courses	Yes	179	16,04%
	No	919	82,35%
	No Answer	18	1,61%
	Total	**1116**	100,00%
Participation in Sportive Activities	Yes	386	34,59%
	No	716	64,16%
	No Answer	14	1,25%
	Total	**1116**	100,00%

As seen in Table 2, there was a significant difference between the field of education of vocational education students at Marmara University and the communication skills (mental, emotional, behavioral) inventory average scores ($p < 0.05$). The H0 hypothesis has been rejected. Toy achieved similar results in his work on engineering and law faculty students in 2007. It seems to be similar to the results obtained in this study, [26].

It was seen that university students had a meaningful difference between their field of study and their communication skills and that this difference was caused by the questions that measured communication skills in behavioral, mental and emotional dimensions and the general sum of these questions ($p < 0.05$).

As shown in Table 3, a multiple comparison Tukey statistic test was done to show the difference between the students' total scores of Communication Skills Inventory and the area they studied. The differences; Behavioral, mental, emotional, and general totals were found to have originated from the technical and health sciences by occupation. In the research; The fact that the communication skills average scores of the students in the health field are higher than in the other fields requires strong communication skills to be established with patients, health personnel and patient relatives in order to carry out health services effectively. From this point of view, behavioral sciences and communication skills lessons in schools offering health education can be considered as effective in the curriculum.

Tablo 2. Meslek Alanlarına Göre İletişim Becerileri Farklılığı Testi (ANOVA)

Communication Skills Inventory / Question No.	Sum of Squares	Degree of Freedom	Mean Square	F	P
Behavioral Question: 2, 4, 7, 8, 10, 13, 14, 16, 19, 21, 22, 23, 25, 32, 41	1209.997	3	403.332	12.595	**.000**
	35608.737	1112	32.022		
	36818.734	1115			
Mental Question: 1, 3, 6, 12, 15, 17, 18, 20, 24, 28, 30, 33, 37, 43, 45	1542.641	3	514.214	11.798	**.000**
	48467.134	1112	43.586		
	50009.774	1115			
Emotional Question: 5, 9, 11, 26, 27, 29, 31, 34, 35, 36, 38, 39, 40, 42, 44	506.085	3	168.695	5.127	**.002**
	36589.937	1112	32.905		
	37096.022	1115			
Total	8987.791	3	2995.93	14.045	**.000**
	237206.819	1112	213.315		
	246194.609	1115			

Table 3. Determination of Source of Difference according to Learning Appearance Areas (Multiple Comparison Analysis Post Hoc Tests) Tukey Test

Communication Skills Inventory / Question No.	Area of Study	Area of Study	Mean Difference	Standard Error	P Değeri
BehavioralQuestion: 2, 4, 7, 8, 10, 13, 14, 16, 19, 21, 22, 23, 25, 32, 41	**Educational Sciences**	Faculty of Technical Education	.59617	.60646	.759
		Vocational School of Health Services	**2.02309(*)**	.50932	**.000**
		Vocational School of Technical Sciences	-.42402	.49460	.827
	Technical Sciences	Faculty of Education	-.59617	.60646	.759
		Vocational School of Health Services	**1.42692(*)**	.54027	**.042**
		Vocational School of Technical Sciences	-102.019	.52642	.213
	Health Sciences (Associate degree)	Faculty of Education	**-2.02309(*)**	.50932	**.000**
		Faculty of Technical Education	**-1.42692(*)**	.54027	**.042**
		Vocational School of Technical Sciences	**-2.44711(*)**	.41077	**.000**
	Technical Sciences (Associate degree)	Faculty of Education	.42402	.49460	.827
		Faculty of Technical Education	102.019	.52642	.213

		Vocational School of Health Services	**2.44711(*)**	.41077	**.000**

Table 3. *Continued*

MentalQuestion: 1, 3, 6, 12, 15, 17, 18, 20, 24, 28, 30, 33, 37, 43, 45	**Educational Sciences**	Faculty of Technical Education	.47925	.70754	.906
		Vocational School of Health Services	**2.65916(*)**	.59421	**.000**
		Vocational School of Technical Sciences	.07877	.57704	.999
	Technical Sciences	Faculty of Education	-.47925	.70754	.906
		Vocational School of Health Services	**2.17991(*)**	.63031	**.003**
		Vocational School of Technical Sciences	-.40048	.61415	.915
	Health Sciences (Associate degree)	Faculty of Education	**-2.65916(*)**	.59421	**.000**
		Faculty of Technical Education	**-2.17991(*)**	.63031	**.003**
		Vocational School of Technical Sciences	**-2.58039(*)**	.47923	**.000**
	Technical Sciences (Associate degree)	Faculty of Education	-.07877	.57704	.999
		Faculty of Technical Education	.40048	.61415	.915
		Vocational School of Health Services	**2.58039(*)**	.47923	**.000**
EmotionalQuestion: 5, 9, 11, 26, 27, 29, 31, 34, 35, 36, 38, 39, 40, 42, 44	**Educational Sciences**	Faculty of Technical Education	.82618	.61476	.535
		Vocational School of Health Services	119.724	.51629	.094
		Vocational School of Technical Sciences	-.33680	.50137	.908
	Technical Sciences	Faculty of Education	-.82618	.61476	.535
		Vocational School of Health Services	.37106	.54766	.906
		Vocational School of Technical Sciences	-116.298	.53362	.130
	Health Sciences (Associate degree)	Faculty of Education	-119.724	.51629	.094
		Faculty of Technical Education	-.37106	.54766	.906
		Vocational School of Technical Sciences	**-1.53404(*)**	.41639	**.001**
	Technical Sciences (Associate degree)	Faculty of Education	.33680	.50137	.908
		Faculty of Technical Education	116.298	.53362	.130
		Vocational School of Health Services	**1.53404(*)**	.41639	**.001**
Total	**Educational Sciences**	Faculty of Technical Education	190.160	156.527	.617
		Vocational School of Health Services	**5.87949(*)**	131.455	**.000**
		Vocational School of Technical Sciences	-.68205	127.656	.951
	Technical Sciences	Faculty of Education	-190.160	156.527	.617
		Vocational School of Health Services	**3.97788(*)**	139.443	**.023**
		Vocational School of Technical Sciences	-258.365	135.868	.228
	Health Sciences (Associate degree)	Faculty of Education	**-5.87949(*)**	131.455	**.000**
		Faculty of Technical Education	**-3.97788(*)**	139.443	**.023**
		Vocational School of	**-6.56154(*)**	106.019	**.000**

		Technical Sciences			
	Technical Sciences (Associate degree)	Faculty of Education	.68205	127.656	.951
		Faculty of Technical Education	258.365	135.868	.228
		Vocational School of Health Services	**6.56154(*)**	106.019	**.000**

As shown in Table 4 and 5, with the students Average Distribution by Gender values, the comparison of the distribution of communication skills (mental, emotional, behavioral) by sex was analyzed with T-test. Accordingly, a significant difference was found between Communication Skill Inventory Score Average ($p < 0.05$). The H0 hypothesis has been rejected. Differences according to sex were found to be due to male student group. This result shows a difference with the results of Bulut Bozkurt, Korkut and Toy, [27], [28], [26]. It is thought that the determination of the causes of this difference may be the subject of another research.

Table 4. Mean Distribution of Students by Gender

Communication Skills Inventory / Question No.	Gender	n	Mean	Standard Deviation
Behavioral	Male	710	37.6028	5.93785
	Female	405	38.9827	5.29545
Mental	Male	710	43.6000	6.52179
	Female	405	44.3901	6.98165
Emotional	Male	710	33.2342	5.34515
	Female	405	34.3827	6.37711
Total	Male	710	114.437	14.65457
	Female	405	117.7556	15.00864

Table 5. Comparison of Distribution of Communication Skills by Gender (T-test)

Communication Skills Inventory / Question No.	T-Test	Degree of Freedom	P Value
Behavioral	**-3.879**	1113	**.000**
	-4.002	921.287	**.000**
Mental	**-1.896**	1113	**.058**
	-1.861	794.161	**.063**
Emotional	**-3.212**	1113	**.001**
	-3.062	726.226	**.002**
Total	**-3.605**	1113	**.000**
	-3.581	824.027	**.000**

As shown in Table 6, there is no significant difference between the socioeconomic status of the students in the study and the mean scores of Communication Skills Inventory (mental, emotional, behavioral) ($p > 0.05$). H0 hypothesis has been accepted. According to this, no significant relationship was found between the total scores of behavioral, mental and emotional points in the socio-economic level and communication skills inventory of vocational education students. This result is similar to Toy's survey, [26].

Table 6. Determination of Source of Difference by Socio Economic Level (Multiple Comparison Analysis Post Hoc Tests) Tukey Test

Communication Skills Inventory / Question No.+H2:M26	Socio-economic Level	Socio-economic Level	Mean Difference	Standard Error	P Value
Behavioral Question: 2, 4, 7, 8, 10, 13, 14, 16, 19, 21, 22, 23, 25, 32, 41	Lower	Mid	-.14948	.48676	.949
		Upper	-1.26417	.82755	.278
	Mid	Lower	.14948	.48676	.949
		Upper	-1.11469	.72371	.273
	Upper	Lower	1.26417	.82755	.278
		Mid	1.11469	.72371	.273
Mental Question: 1, 3, 6, 12, 15, 17, 18, 20, 24, 28, 30, 33, 37, 43, 45	Lower	Mid	.28178	.56550	.872
		Upper	.80900	.96140	.677
	Mid	Lower	-.28178	.56550	.872
		Upper	.52722	.84076	.805
	Upper	Lower	-.80900	.96140	.677
		Mid	-.52722	.84076	.805
Emotional Question: 5, 9, 11, 26, 27, 29, 31, 34, 35, 36, 38, 39, 40, 42, 44	Lower	Mid	.19066	.48731	.919
		Upper	-.29376	.82848	.933
	Mid	Lower	-.19066	.48731	.919
		Upper	-.48443	.72452	.782
	Upper	Lower	.29376	.82848	.933
		Mid	.48443	.72452	.782
Total	Lower	Mid	.32296	1.25650	.964
		Upper	-.74894	2.13617	.934
	Mid	Lower	-.32296	1.25650	.964
		Upper	-1.07190	1.86813	.834
	Upper	Lower	.74894	2.13617	.934
		Mid	1.07190	1.86813	.834

4 Conclusions and recommendations

In general, communication skills such as self-expression and correct understanding of the other side are needed for success and satisfaction at the basic level. However, occupations differ in terms of the level of communication skills they need. For jobs that do not rely on human relations, communication skills are not expected to be high. Communication skills at a high level are of utmost importance if the social relations are in the forefront.

People who are technically trained will encounter in their business life during the production process for reasons arising from the necessities of the business environment - ensuring accurate and complete information flow (the smallest error resulting from lack of communication in mass production enterprises leads to quality, time, labor, price costs), monitoring and exploitation of the technology- as well as in their private life to have a balanced personality characteristics it is thought that they should have effective communication skills.

According to the data obtained within the scope of the research, it is seen that the communication skills of the students studying in the departments providing health education are higher. It is thought that the staff working or will work in the field of health care have to communicate well with a sensitive audience such as patients and their relatives as well as with other health personnel, and that the lessons they took during vocational education in the university have positive effects on improving their communication skills. As a result of our research, the average scores of the communication skills of the students who are studying in technical field were low. In real life, as a result of accurate (without obstacles) information flow in technical field it is possible to create quality products (output).

In the technical field where the technology is used at a high level, the human and communication factor plays an important role. From this point of view, it is thought that the persons who works or will work in vocational fields (health, social, technical, education, etc.) should have effective communication skills and should be able to use these skills effectively in daily and business life.

For individuals, especially for professionals who will take part in professional business life, for effective communication skills both in business environment and daily life;

- clear and accurate message delivery,
- provide a sense of respect and trust
- eye contact setup,
- attention to body language,
- feedback,
- being a good listener and learning to listen,
- building empathy,
- communication with the right person at the right time,
- accurate communication of information,
- being polite and flexible,
- to be practical,
- qualities such as being gum-faced and optimistic

are among the expected values.

In addition, it is suggested that all branches that provide vocational education in different fields should take in courses related to effective communication skills in the curriculum, and the relevant sector should carry out works to develop these skills both through education programs after graduation or periodical in-service trainings.

References

1. S. Tevrüz, İ. Artan ve T. Bozkurt, Davranışlarımızdan Seçmeler (Örgütsel Yaklaşım), Beta Yayınevi, İstanbul, (1999)
2. S. Tevrüz, Endüstri ve Örgüt Psikolojisi, Türk Psikologlar Derneği-Kalder Kalite Derneği Ortak Yayını, 2. Baskı, (1997)
3. E. Eren, Yönetim ve Organizasyon (Çağdaş ve Küresel Yaklaşımlar), Beta Yayınları, 6. Baskı, İstanbul, (2003)
4. M. Paksoy, Çalışma Ortamında İnsan ve Toplam Kalite Yönetimi, Cantay Kitabevi, İstanbul, (2002)
5. T. Koçel, İşletme Yöneticiliği, Beta Yayınları, 9. Baskı, İstanbul, (2003)
6. C. E. Shannon, "A Mathematical Theory of Communication", Reprinted with corrections from The Bell System Technical Journal, Vol. **27**, pp.379–423, 623–656, July, October, (1948)
7. G. M. Siegel, , April W.Gregora, "Communication Skills of Elderly Adults", Journal of communication Disorders, v**18** n6 p.485–94, (1985)
8. J. K. Burgoon, D. B. Buller & W. G. Woodall, Nonverbal Communication: The Unspoken Dialoge, New York: Harper & Row, (1989)
9. D. Alper, Psikolojik Danışmanlar ve Sınıf Öğretmenlerinin Duygusal Zeka Düzeyleri - İletişim ve Empati Becerilerinin Karşılaştırılması, Yüksek Lisans Tezi, Eğitim Bilimleri Enstitüsü, Dokuz Eylül Üniversitesi, (2007)
10. Z. Bozdoğan, Etkili Öğretmen Olabilmek, www.e-kutuphane.egitimsen.org.tr/331.pdf, (Erişim Tarihi: 15 Mart 2009)
11. R. M. Hodgetts, Yönetim-Teori, Süreç ve Uygulama, (Çev: Canan Çetin, Esin Can Mutlu), Der Yayınları, İstanbul, (1997)
12. F. Korkut, İletişim Becerileri Değerlendirme Ölçeğinin Geliştirilmesi: Güvenirlik ve Geçerlik Çalışmaları, Türk Psikolojik Danışma ve Rehberlik Dergisi, [S.l.], v. **2**, n. 7, p. 18-23, (1996)
13. B. Yılmaz, Üniversite Öğrencilerinin Kişilerarası İletişim Becerileri ve Bağlanma Stilleri Arasındaki İlişki, Yüksek Lisans Tezi, Sosyal Bilimler Enstitüsü, Muğla Üniversitesi, (2007)
14. F. Korkut, İfade Edici Saldırganlık Ölçeğinin Türkçe'ye uyarlanması üzerine bir ön çalışma, Çukurova Üniversitesi, Eğitim Fakültesi Dergisi, **2**(23); 48-53, (2002)
15. E. Bozkurt, Bireylerin İletişim Sorunları Ve İletişim Becerilerinin Geliştirilmesi, http://yayim.meb.gov.tr/dergiler/medergi/16.html, (Erişim tarihi: 15 Mart 2009)
16. Z. Sabuncuoğlu ve M. Tüz, Örgütsel Psikoloji, Alfa Yayınları, 3. Baskı, Bursa, (1998)
17. K. Ersanlı, S. Balcı, İletişim Becerileri Envanterinin Geliştirilmesi: Geçerlik ve Güvenirlik Çalışması, Türk Psikolojik Danışma ve Rehberlik Dergisi, [S.l.], v. **2**, n. 10, p. 7-12, (1998)
18. A. Ural, İ. Kılıç, Bilimsel Araştırma Süreci ve SPSS ile Veri Analizi, Detay Yayıncılık, Ankara, (2005)
19. Y. Yazıcıoğlu, S. Erdoğan, SPSS Uygulamalı Bilimsel Araştırma Yöntemleri, Detay Yayıncılık, Ankara, (2005)
20. R. Altunışık, R. Coşkun, S. Bayraktaroğlu ve E. Yıldırım, Sosyal Bilimlerde Araştırma Yöntemleri, SPSS Uygulamalı, Sakarya Kitabevi, Sakarya, (2005)
21. A. Akgül, O. Çevik, İstatiksel Analiz Teknikleri SPSS'te İşletme Yönetimi Uygulamaları, Emek Ofset Ltd. Şti., Ankara, 2005
22. Nural Bekiroğlu, Açıklamalı Bioistatistik Terimleri Sözlüğü, Nobel Tıp Kitapevleri, s. 44, İstanbul, 1998
23. R. Yiğit, F. G. Esenay, E. Derebent, Türkiye'de Hemşirelik Son Sınıf Öğrencilerinin Profili, Cumhuriyet Üniversitesi HYO Dergisi, Sayı:**11**, Cilt:3, (2007)

24. G. Başer, Hemşirelik Yüksekokullarında Öğrenim Gören Öğrencilerin Sosyal Özellikleri, Okulu Tercih Sıralamaları ve Seçme Nedenleri, Hacettepe Üniversitesi Hemşirelik Yüksekokulu Dergisi, Sayı:**2**(1), (1995)
25. G. S. Razı, A. Kuzu, A. N. Yıldız, A. F. Ocakçı, B. Ç. Arifoğlu, Çalışan Gençlerde Benlik Saygısı, İletişim Becerileri ve Stresle Baş Etme, TAF Preventive Medicine Bulletin, Sayı:**8**(1), (2009)
26. S. Toy, Mühendislik ve Hukuk Fakültesi Öğrencilerinin İletişim Becerileri Açısından Karşılaştırılması ve İletişim Becerileriyle Bazı Değişenler Arasındaki İlişkiler, Yüksek Lisans Tezi, Sosyal Bilimler Enstitüsü, Ankara Üniversitesi, (2007)
27. N. Bulut Bozkurt, İlköğretim Sınıf Öğretmenlerinin İletişim Becerilerine İlişkin Algılarının Çeşitli Değişkenler Açısından İncelenmesi, Türk Eğitim Bilimleri Dergisi, Sayı:**2**(4), (2004)
28. F. Korkut, Yetişkinlere Yönelik İletişim Becerileri Eğitimi, Hacettepe Üniversitesi Eğitim Fakültesi Dergisi, Sayı:**28**, (2005)

An Investigation on the Digital Addiction of the Students of Faculty of Sports of Kocaeli University

Elif Karagün[1*], *Zekiye Dilay* Ekiz[2], and *Müge* Sarper Kahveci[2]

[1] Faculty of Sports Sciences, Kocaeli University, Umuttepe-Kocaeli, Turkey
[2] Sports Sciences, Institute of Health Sciences, Kocaeli University, Umuttepe-Kocaeli, Turkey

Abstract. The purpose of this study is to investigate the digital addiction levels of the students studying at the Faculty of Sports of Kocaeli University in terms of variables such as their gender, age, school type, parental education level, income status, class level and success level. To this end, following the permission from the faculty administration, the Digital Addiction Scale, developed by Arslan, Kırık, Karaman and Çetinkaya (2015), was administered to a random sample of voluntary students. Data was analyzed by using the SPSS version 25.0. The results showed that digital addiction levels of the students in terms of their gender, age, school type, income level, parental education level, class level and success level were not significant; however, significant differences were found in favor of those who played sports only in class regarding playing sports, and those who attended the evening education regarding type of education programs.

1 Introduction

Today technological developments are evolving rapidly. The recent developments on artificial intelligence, in particular, have increased the number of new digital devices, and provided them for the needs of humans. Human needs comprise several fields of service including having fun time in sociocultural terms. It is stated that these developments in technology, along with the use of devices such as computers in the fields of entertainment, education etc., have increased the likelihood of the creation of digital usage habit, even the creation of digital addiction [1].

Addiction is defined as a state of people's giving harm to their psycho-physiological health or social life, and a state of irresistible desire to do something over and over again. It is said to be seen in various fields. It is defined as an illness regarding psychological health in the fifth edition of DSM, which stands for Diagnostic and Statistical Manuel of Mental Disorders [2]. Addiction is considered to begin with a constant desire to have a certain object and continue with a constant thought of that object, that is, a constant state of wanting. It is explained that if people cannot get what they want, they believe life will be unbearable. As for addiction in the digital field, it is also pointed out that loss of control

* Corresponding author: elif.karagun@gmail.com

over the use of technology, and excessive and unlimited use of technology cause very serious harm. Internet and technology addiction is defined as a state of deprivation when a person is not able to reach a technological product he is addicted to. When the consequences of technological addiction are considered, it is also stated that it causes attention deficit disorder, hyperactivity, obesity, depression, and sense of loneliness [3]. It is seen that children and young people experience several physical and psychological problems due to their inactive life styles and that they are advised to do activities based on cultural and, in particular, sports activities to cope with these problems. A heavy responsibility lies in the hands of sports trainers, sports managers, physical education and sports teachers and recreation specialists as the ones to take an action against digital addiction and make a habit out of it. Sports is considered to be important to deal with the problems that may be faced due to technology use such as obesity and digital addiction in the future [4-5-6]. It has been an issue of concern to the researchers to determine the addiction levels of the students studying at various departments of the faculties of sports which aim to train them with management, leadership and coaching skills as the future professionals of the sports activities. In this context, it was aimed to carry out a study to determine that. With reference to the question "Do people who study in the fields of profession considered important in coping with digital addiction which is believed to be on the increase today and in the future have digital addiction?", It was aimed to determine the digital addiction levels of the students studying at the Faculty of Sports Sciences of Kocaeli University. It was investigated whether there was a significant difference between the specified addiction levels and the variables such as age, gender, class level, type of education program, income level, parental education level, where they stay, academic success, whether they play sports or not, whether they have a sportsman's license if they do, how long they have been playing that sport, their branch of sports, whether they participate in any activities other than sports, frequency of social media use.

2 Method

2.1 Population and sampling

This study was carried out as Scanning model, and its population consists of students who are studying Recreation, Coaching Training, Sports Management, Physical Education and Sports Teaching at the Sports Sciences Faculty, Kocaeli University, during the spring term in the Academic year 2017-2018. The sampling of the study consists of 237 volunteering students, who were randomly chosen either in classrooms or training areas or at the canteen, dining hall and several resting areas via ''simple random sampling'' method after the formal written permission for our study was taken from the school management. Those students were explained the aim of the study first and then they were asked to fill in survey forms.

2.2 Data collecting tools

''The Digital Addiction Scale'', a 16-item questionnaire developed by [7], was applied to a random sample of voluntary students. This scale was applied to determine the Sports Sciences Faculty students' socio-demographic features such as gender, age, department, grade, education type, economic income, parental education level, the place where their parents have been staying for the last five years, their accommodation as a student, whether they have an access to the internet, whether they do regular sports outside school, their sports branch, and whether they are licenced to do that sport. The Digital Addiction Scale has three factors with 29 items. In the scale, which was developed by [7], 4 sub dimensions that are 'gaming', 'social media', 'its effect on the social life', and 'digital addiction' were evaluated [7]. The reliability coefficient of the scale was found as r= 0,92. The scale reliability Cronbach Alpha coefficient was calculated as 0,847 for our study and this shows that this study is reliable.

2.3 The analysis of the data

The data was analysed with SPSS 21.0 package program after the scale applications to the students at Sports Sciences Faculty. Because the data shows a normal dispersion, t test, one of the parametric measurements, was used for the binary clut comparison and ANOVA, another parametric measurement, was used for comparisons more than two clusters. The significance value was taken as 0,05.

3 Findings

Table 1. Frequency and Percentages of the Participants according to their Socio-economic features:

Variables		N	%
	Female	50	21,1
Gender	male	187	78,9
	Aged 16- 18	7	3,0
	Aged 19-21	157	66,2
Age	Aged 22-24	56	23,6
	Aged 25-27	12	5,1
	Aged 28 and over	5	2,1
	2000₺and less	80	33,8
Income Level	2001-2500₺	66	27,8
	2501-3000₺	46	19,4
	3001-3500₺	43	18,1
	State dorm.	107	45,1
Accommodation type	Private dorm.	18	7,6
	Flat with friends	66	27,8
	With family	46	19,4
	Literate	43	18,1
Mother's education	Primary school	137	57,8
	Secondary school	43	18,1
	University	14	5,9
	Literate	28	11,8
Father's education	Primary school	113	47,7
	Secondary school	70	29,5
	University	26	11,0

As seen in the Table 1, the experimental group, which consists of 237 students, is made up of 50 women (21.1 %), and 187 men (78, 9 %). Those aged between 16 and 18 are 7 (3,0 %) ; those aged between 19 and 21 are 157 (66,2%); those aged between 22 and 24 are 56 (23,6%) ; those aged between 25 and 27 are 12 (5,1%); and the ones at the age of 28 and over are 5 (2,1%). These people whose income is 2000 tl or less are 80 (33,8%); those who get between 2001 tl and 2500tl are 66 (27,8 %); those who get between 2501 and 3000tl are 46 (19,4 %); and those whose income is 3001tl and 3500 and over are 43 people (18,1%). As for the accommodation types; the answers are as the follows: those who stay at the State dormitory are 107 students (45, 1 %); the number of students staying at private dormitories is 18 (7,6%); Those who share a flat with friends are 66 (27,8); and finally the students who live with their parents are 46 (19, 4 %). Parental education level results were determined to be as the following: the number of students whose mothers are literate is 43 (18,1%); primary school graduates are 137 (57,8 %); secondary school graduates are 43 (18,1%); and the number of university graduate mothers is 14 (5,9%). As for the fathers' education levels; literate ones are 28 (11,8%); primary school graduates are 113 (47,7%); secondary school graduates are 70 (29,5%); and the number of fathers who are university graduates is 26 (11%).

Table 2. Frequency and Percentages of the Participants according to their education and sports

Variables		N	%
Education type	Formal Education	131	55,3
	Evening Classes	105	45,3
Department	Physical Education and Sport Teaching	60	25,3
	Coaching	77	32,5
	Recreation	30	12,7
	Sports Management	70	29,5
Grade	1st grade	112	47,3
	2nd grade	71	30
	3rd grade	22	9,3
	4th grade	32	13,5
Doing sports	Only at school, in classes	50	21,1
	Outside school, non-professionally	140	59,1
	Outside school, professionally (licenced)	46	19,4
How often s/he uses social media	Less than 1 hour	11	4,6
	1-2 hours	75	31,6
	3-4 hours	81	34,2
	5-6 hours	32	13,5
	More than 6 hours	38	16
Whether s/he has a hobby except for sport	Yes	125	52,7
	No	107	45,1

When Table 2 was examined, the dispersion of frequency and percentage according to Education type variables is 55,3 % for the formal education and the number for evening classes is 105 (45,3%). 25,3 % of those students are at Physical Education and Sport Teaching; 32,5% of them are at Coaching; 12,7% of them are at Recreation; and 25,3% of them are at Sport Management. As for their grades variable; 1st grade students are 47,3%; 2nd grade students are 30%; 3rd graders are 9,5%; and 4th graders are 13,5%.

For the variable 'whether they do any sport or not', the results were determined as the follows: non-professionally sport doers are 59,1%; sport doers only in classes are 21,1%; and professional and licenced sport doers are 19,4%. For the variable 'how often they use the social media', the results were like this: those who spend 3 or 4 hours on the social media are 34,'%; 1 or 2-hour users are 31,6%; more than 6-hour users are 16%; the ones who spend 5 or 6 hours on the social media are 13,5%; and 4,6% is the result for those who spend less than 1 hour on the social media. For the variable 'participation in any non-sportive activity', 52,7% of those admitted that they take part in activities. However, 45,1 % of them stated that they haven't participated in any other activities.

T test results of the digital addiction levels of the participants regarding their socio-demographic features were given in Table 3. Any significant difference was not found between their average scores in these findings except for gender, a non-sportive activity, education type and game dimensions. There was only a significant difference in education type dimension. ($p=0,028$, $p<0,05$).

Table 3. T test results of the digital addiction levels of the participants regarding their socio-demographic features

Variables		Gaming Dimension		Social media dimension		Effect on social life dimension		Digital Addiction	
		Me.+St.d.	P	Me.+St.d.	P	Me.+St.d.	P	Me.+St.d.	P
Gender	Female	2,67±,97	,827	3,19±0,81	,792	2,48±0,88	0,134	2,82±,66	,400
	Male	2,71±,89		3,23±1,01		2,73±1,11		2,92±,79	
Education type	Formal educat.	2,50,89	,028	3,22±1,03	,963	2,59±1,1	,161	2,84±,69	,163
	Evening classes	2,8±,89		3,23±,88		2,79±1,1		2,98±,68	
Non-sportive activity	Yes	2,68±,98	,875	3,27±,76	,659	3,05±1,1	,584	2,99±,69	,807

Table 4. ANOVA results of the digital addiction levels of the participants regarding their educational status:

Variables		Gaming Dimension		Social media dimension		Effect on social life dimension		Digital Addiction on	
		Me.+St.D.	P	Me.+St.D.	P	Me.+St.D.	P	Me.+St.D.	P
Depart.	Teaching	2.66±,93	,142	3.17±0,95	,792	2.64±1,04	,398	2.87±,96	,301
	Coaching	2.56±,83		3.17±0,93		2.54±1,07		2.80±,84	
	Recreation	2.64±1,15		3.18±1,34		2.80±1,15		2.88±,18	
	Management	2.90±,83		3.32±0,84		2.82±1,07		3.04±,85	
Grade	1st grade	2.69±,91	,952	3.08±1,02	,087	2.71±1,06	,770	2.86±,78	,641
	2nd grade	2.70±,90		3.46±,85		2.70±1,13		3.00±,70	
	3rd grade	2.62±,98		3.22±,96		2.69±1,0		2.87±,81	
	4th grade	2.76±,87		3.16±,98		2.49±1,26		2.85±,82	

When the Table 4 was examined, no significant difference was found in the sub dimension 'Digital Addiction' according to the department and grade variables.

Table 5. ANOVA results of the digital addiction levels of the participants regarding their use of social

Variables		**Gaming Dimension**		**Social media Dimension**		**The effect on sociallife Dimension**		**Digital Addiction**	
		Me.+St.d.	P	Me.+St.d.	P	Me.+St.d.	P	Me.+St.d.	P
Whether s/he does sports	Only in classes	2.68±,98	,179	3.27±,76	,441	3.05±1,1	**,017**	2.99±0,69	,23
	Non-prof. outside school	2.76±,85		3.19±,97		2.65±1,0		2.91±0,77	
	Prof., Licenced	2.58±0,97		3.27±1,13		2.36±1,0		2.80±0,81	
How often do you use social media?	Less than one hour	2,34±,87	,416	3,50±1,87	**,003**	2,59±1,0	,347	2,85±1,10	,09
	1-2 hours	2,74±,99		2,94±,77		2,50±1,1		2,76±,837	
	3-4 hours	2,61±,95		3,22±,96		2,75±1,0		2,88±,71	
	5-6 hours	2,78±,78		3,23±,92		2,66±1,0		2,94±,69	
	More than 6 hours	2,84±,75		3,68±,84		2,92±,98		3,19±,63	

ANOVA test results in Table 5 were evaluated according to the participants' sport-doing situations and social media variables. Significant differences were only observed in 'effect on social life 'dimension ((p=,017, p<0,05); 'how often he uses social media' dimension and 'social media' dimension (p=,003, p<0,05)

Table 6. ANOVA results of the digital addiction levels of the participants regarding their socio-demographic features

Variables		Gaming Dimension		Social media Dimension		The effect on social life Dimension		Digital Addiction	
		Me.+St. D	P	Me.+St.D .	P	Me.+St.d	P	Me.+St.d	P
Age	16- 18	2,63±,79	,588	2,53±,97	,436	2,4±1,16	,058	2,53±,91	,286
	19-21	2,71±,93		3,25±,91		2,73±1,0		2,94±,73	
	22-24	2,590,87		3,20±,90		2,39±1,0		2,78±,79	
	25-27	3,06±,62		3,32±1,6 8		3,23±1,3		3,19±,91	
	over 28	2,7±,90		3,21±1,1		3,16±1,2		2,95±,96	
Inc. level	Less than 2000₺	2.63±,88	,490	3.23±1,1	,968	2.73±1,1	,744	2.89±,85	,905
	2001-2500₺	2.69±,97		3.15±,82		2.67±0,95		2.87±,69	
	2501-3000₺	2.64±,90		3.26±,82		2.65±0,9		2.89±,67	
	3001-3500₺	2.92±,87		3.26±,96		2.67±1,2		2.99±,82	

Table 7. ANOVA results of the digital addiction levels of the participants regarding their socio-demographic features

Variables		Gaming Dimension		Social media Dimension		The effect on social life Dimension		Digital Addiction	
		Me.+St.d	P	Me.+St.d	P	Me.+St.d	P	Me.+St.d	P
Mother's education	Literate	2.59±,90	,620	3.28±1,02	,477	2.87±1,1	,257	2.93±,82	,531
	Primary school	2.77±,95		3.27±1,01		2.67±1,08		2.94±,80	
	Sec. school	2.620,84		3.02±0,83		2.67±1,05		2.78±,66	
	Uni.	2.64±,63		3.12±0,65		2.21±,84		2.73±,53	
Father's education	Literate	2.63±,94	,209	3.06±0,94	,121	2.89±1,11	,687	2.86±,87	,185
	Primary school	2.77±,93		3.35±1,07		2.68±1,15		2.98±,79	
	Sec. school	2.53±,83		3.03±0,81		2.60±,94		2.74±,64	
	Uni.	2.90±,94		3.30±0,85		2.64±1,06		3.01±,80	

As seen in table 7, the findings for digital addiction level were found insignificant when the variable, parental education level, was evaluated with ANOVA.

4 Discussion, result and suggestions

When the digital addiction scores were studied according to socio-demographic variables, no significant difference was found in any of the sub dimensions of Digital Addiction Scale in terms of gender variable. However, male scores for all sub dimensions were observed to be high. Although no significant differences were found in other studies done in this area,

there are studies that support our study [8]. Yet, it was observed in some studies that male students' scores were high in 'Gaming Addiction' dimension whereas female students' scores were high in 'Social Media Addiction' dimension. No significant difference was found in 'Negative Effect on Social Life' dimension between girls and boys [9]
It was also found that male students are significantly more addicted to gaming than female students. However, girls are much more addicted to 'Social Media' than boys [10].

When the Literature was examined, it can be said that there are studies which do not match with our study results, showing that women use the internet more intensively compared to men, social stress affects addiction to smart phone usage, men experience less social stress than women and therefore men use their smart phones for social media less than women. These findings can be said not to match with our study results [11].

When the education type was examined, the evening class students' scores for Gaming' dimension of 'Digital Addiction Scale' were found to be significantly higher than those who are at Formal education. This result made us think that studying in evening classes is a factor that increases the addiction to digital platform such as computers, the internet, and smart phones. As there are not studies aiming to find out digital addiction according to Education type, it is advisable to do more detailed studies in this area to obtain more accurate results [11].

When the results of the Digital Addiction Scale were examined in terms of participation in an activity other than sports, no significant findings were found. When literature studies were examined, it is seen that internet usage is negatively affecting the social and psychological development of young people [5]. In addition, it is also seen that not being able to socialise causes social anxiety and this leads to an excessive internet usage [11]. When those comments were taken into consideration, it can be said that every activity, either sportive or non-sportive, done in social environment can eliminate digital addiction and it is the key element for decreasing social anxiety.

It was determined that the Digital Addiction scores of the students at Sports Faculty created no significant difference neither in their departments nor in their grades. The reason why there was no difference is considered that these departments are social and active departments that require practice. When these results were examined, there were no other studies in the Literature examining the Digital Addiction in terms of departments.

When the answers to whether the students' do a sport or not were examined, significant results were obtained in favour of those who participate in any sport only in classes in the 'Effect on Social Media' dimension. Yet, when the Literature was examined, it was considered that social stress leads people to digital platform [11] doing a sportive activity has a great effect on decreasing social anxiety. All this information is taken into consideration, it can be said that social anxiety decreases as a result of doing a sport and therefore self-esteem level increases. Thus, it has a positive effect on social life. When the answers given to the question 'How often do you use social media?' were examined, quite significant results were obtained in favour of those who said more than 6 hours in the 'Social Media' dimension. What is interesting is that the digital addiction scores of those who use less than 1 hour comes the second after 6 hours' social media users. In the third line comes the ones who spend 4 or 5 hours on the social media, and then comes those spending 2 or 3 hours on the social media. Digital Addiction scores were ranked from high to low and these results were found significant. As for the Age, digital addiction scale scores were not found significant. When the studies on this issue in the Literature were examined, the incidence of internet addiction in adolescents was estimated as approximately 11% in China, 8% in Greece, and 18,4 in Korea [12].

When the studies on the internet addiction of high school students in Turkey were evaluated, it was found that the prevalence of the internet addiction changes between 6,6% and 15% [13-14].It was stated that social stress gets lower as the person gets older, it makes a positive effect on self-regulation, and the rate of digital addiction in the elderly such as the use of smart phones decreases [11].Our study results for Digital Addiction scores for income level do not show any significant difference. When the studies done before were examined, the income level is effective on socialising [6].

However, unlike this information, no change in the digital addiction level and income level was observed in our study. This can be explained in a way that the participants are studying at Social departments and that sport has an effect on socialising. That's why; this result was obtained. When the students at Sport Faculty were examined according to their accommodation types; no significant difference was found in the digital addiction scores for staying at dormitories, flats, sharing a house with a friend, staying at a relative's house or living with family. Again, there was no significant difference in Digital Addiction Scale scores in terms of mothers' education level and fathers' education levels.

References

1. R. Gökler, R. Koçak, Uyuşturucu ve Madde Bağımlılığı. Gaziosmanpaşa Üniversitesi Sosyal Bilimler Araştırmaları Dergisi, **3(1),** 89-104, (2008)
2. E. Köroğlu, *DSM V Tani Ölçütleri Basvuru Elkitabı.* HYB Publishing. Ankara (2014)
3. A.Gurcan, S.Ozhan and R. Uslu Digital Games and Children. Accessed via http://ailetoplum.aile.gov.tr/data/5429366a369dc32358ee2a92/ (2008-November).
4. K.Choi, H.Son, M.Park, J.Han, K.Kim, B.Lee, H.Gwak, Internet overuse and excessive daytime sleepiness in adolescents. Psychiatry and Clinical Neurosciences. **63(4),** 455-462, (2009)
5. J.Sung, J. Lee, H.M. No, Y.S.Park, E.J. Ahn Associations between the risk of Internet addiction and problem behaviours among Korean adolescents. Korean Journal of Family Medicine. **34(2):** 115-122. (2013)
6. H. Şahan, *The Role of Sport Activities in Socialising Process on University Students Selçuk University.* Social Sciences Institute Public Relations and Introduction unpublished thesis of Doctorate, (2007)
7. A.Arslan., A.Kınık, M.Karaman, A.Çetinkaya. Digital Dependence in High School and University Students. International Symposium on Communication and Literature Research July / August / September - Summer Issue: **8.** (2015)
8. M.B. Horzum, T.Ayas, Ö.Çakırbalta, Computer Game Addiction Scale for Children. Turkish Psychological Councelling and Guidance Journal, **3(30),** 76-88. (2008)
9. S. Balcı,, B.Gülnar. Proficiency of Internet addiction and Internet Addiction Among University Students., Selçuk University Press. **6 (1),** p. 5-22. (2009)
10. H.H.Çam, N. Nur, An Examination on the relationship between Internet Addiction Prevalence in Adolescents and Psycho-pathological Symptoms and Obesity, TAF Preventive Medicine Bulletin, TAF Prev Med Bull, **14 (3)**, 181-188, (2015)
11. J.A.M.Alexander, V.Deursen, C.L.Bolle, S.M.Hegner, P.A.M. Kommers, Modeling Habitual and Addictive Smartphone Behaviour: The role of smartphone usage types, emotional intelligence, social stress, self-regulation, age, and gender. Computers in Human Behavior, **45,** 411-420.(2015)
12. Y. Kim, J.Y. Park, S.B.Kim, I.K.Jung, Y.S.Lim, J.H.Kim, The effects of Internet addiction on the lifestyle and dietary behaviour of Korean adolescents. Nutrition Research and Practice, **4**, 51-57, (2010)

13. F.O. Öztürk, M. Ekinci, O. Öztürk, F. Canan.. The relationship of affective temperament and emotional-behavioral difficulties to internet addiction in Turkish teenagers. ISRN Psychiatry. **961734**,1-6. 7. (2013)
14. T. Şaşmaz, S. Öner,A.O. Kurt, G. Yapıcı, A.E.Yazıcı, R. Buğdaycı, M.Sis, Prevalence and risk factors of Internet addiction in high school students. European Journal of Public Health. **24(1),** 15-20, (2014)

Metaphors Used by the Students at Kocaeli University Sports Sciences Faculty Regarding E-sports Concept

Elif Karagün[1*], *Müge* Sarper Kahveci[2], *Inanc* Kahveci[2] and *Zekiye Dilay* Ekiz[2]

[1] Faculty of Sports Sciences, Kocaeli University, Umuttepe-Kocaeli, Turkey
[2]Kocaeli Üniversitesi, student at Institute of Health Sciences, Turkey

Abstract. This study aims to determine what the students at KOU Sport Sciences Faculty think about e-sports via using metaphors. In accordance with this aim, 293 volunteering students were given a questionnaire which evaluates their opinions about e-sports via metaphors. According to the results, which was applied by descriptive analysis, 47,4% of the students at Sport Sciences Faculty admitted that they hadn't heard of e-sports before. 56,9 % of the female students and 51,3% of the male students stated they had heard of this concept. The most frequently used metaphors by all the students were found to be ''digital technological environment'' (9,2%); ''basic need'' (7,5%); and ''entertainment-games'' (6,8%). The results for female students were as follows: The rate for ''basic need'' 9,2% ; ''positive feeling'' 6,2 %; and ''entertainment-games'' 4,2%. As for the male students; 11% of them used metaphors for ''digital technological environment''; 7,5% ''entertainment-games'' and 7% "basic need"

Keywords: Sports Sciences Faculty, Student, Metaphor, e-sports.

1 Introduction

E-sport history although it is accepted that it started between 1980 and 1990, the first real e – sport struggle started with the "Quake" tournament organized by 2,000 participants in 1997[1]. We see that young people are interested in the internet for social, academic, cultural and entertainment purposes, and nowadays they spend hours on the computer for competing games. in 2010, 37.6% of the internet usage in our country has reached today [2,3], these rates increase with increasing still time at the computer; obesity, post-inflammatory disorders, psychological problems and social loneliness such as [4,5] in order to cope with the negative, it is recommended that children and young people be directed to free-time activities, such as sports[6]. We know that families are trying to get their children to live in motion. On the one hand, while it is said that the use of the internet increases the still life and creates health risks, on the other hand, contradictions such as the increase in sports and games played in digital environment instead of moving sports on the other hand make it necessary to consider "e-sport" [7], which has become increasingly widespread in

* Corresponding author: elif.karagun@gmail.com

the virtual world. In particular, he chose sports as a profession and was put into academic life in order to receive education in this field, and he was wondering whether the students who continue to the Faculty of Sports Sciences, a place where sports-related information is gained, are aware of these changes in the field of sports. For this purpose, young people who were educated in a sports field were asked where they heard "e-sport" and where they heard it. In addition, the idea of "e-sport" was also tried to be learned through metaphor. Metaphor is to express directly or indirectly through metaphors to reinforce expression by comparing it to an object [8]. It is defined as a tool for explaining how an individual sees objects, abstract, complex situations, or the environment, life, and events through simulations using other situations and objects [9]. In our research, the students of the Faculty of Sports Sciences of Kocaeli University tried to determine the concept of "e-sport" by using metaphor. In addition, the comparison of whether these metaphors have created a change in gender or not has constituted another purpose.

2 Materials and methods

This research carried out in the descriptive scanning model [10] is composed of students studying in recreation, coaching, Sports Management, Physical Education and sports teaching departments of Kocaeli University, Faculty of Sports Sciences, spring 2017-2018 academic year. The research sample consists of a total of 293 students who studied at the Faculty of Sports Sciences, selected by "simple random sampling" method and completed the questionnaires after the purpose of the research has been explained.

2.1 Data collection tools

Students studying in sports Sciences; gender, age, read, chapter, class, type of instruction, economic income, parents ' educational status, place of residence of the family property for the last 5 years as a student where they are hosted, whether it is the internet where people are staying, whether or not regular exercise outside of school, such as whether insurance is licensed and socio-demographic characteristics to determine the survey with 13 questions created by the researchers and the students appended to the end of "E-sports" they have heard the term, if they heard, metaphor was used to measure sports related information. To determine students ' thoughts about e-sport through metaphors; "e-Sport........because, ..." a sentence with written spaces was added to the end of the questionnaire and students were asked to produce metaphors related to "e-sport" and write the first analogy that comes to their mind in a blank place. The relationship between the source and the content of the metaphor is determined by the word "similar". Because through the conjunctiva, the meaning of the metaphor produced and the reason for this meaning was tried to be revealed by filling gaps.

2.2 Statistical data analysis

The data obtained from the answers given to the questions about the socio-demographic characteristics of the students of the Faculty of sports sciences are summarized in SPSS 21.0 package program by removing the frequency and the percentages. Then, when the students studied at the Faculty of Sports Sciences expressed feelings about the concept of e-sport and their thoughts were examined and the answers they gave to the questionnaires filled with 293 students in total, it was observed that there were not any metaphors on the concept of e-sport in 164 questionnaires. These non-metaphorical forms were interpreted by analyzing the metaphors written in the other 129 questionnaires when they were excluded from the evaluation. Analysis of metaphors: a five-step process of classification, re-organization and compilation, category development and quantitative data analysis has been implemented in order to transfer data to the computer [11]. All the information contained in the questionnaires is processed in individual Excel files, and the metaphors that students fill in gaps are conceptualized and defined. A separate column is created and metaphors are written and sorted from A to Z. In the classification phase: "metaphor analysis" and "content analysis" [12], they were analyzed in terms of their similarities or common characteristics with other metaphors. Metaphor responses were eliminated from the questionnaires and evaluations were made with the remaining 129 Metaphoruses. After these operations, metaphors were re-examined by sorting them from A to Z. Personal information about who produced a metaphor image is encoded in parentheses just behind that metaphor statement. Category development stage: at this stage, the metaphor images produced by the students are examined in terms of the common characteristics of the concept of "e-sport". Student expressions representing each metaphor were chosen as a sample metaphor. Thus, a "sample metaphor list" was created for each of the 129 metaphors with the collection of the default student metaphor images represented by each of them. During this process, especially .... based on the "example metaphor list" about metaphor, how each metaphor image conceptualizes the concept of "e-sport". Then, a total of 9 different conceptual categories were created by associating each metaphor image with a specific theme from the perspective of the concept of "e-sports". In order to ensure the reliability of the research, the expert opinion was consulted to verify whether the metaphor images given under 9 conceptual categories in the research represent that conceptual category. For this purpose, two lists were given to students, a list of 129 sample metaphor images in alphabetical order, and a list of names and characteristics of 9 conceptual categories. By using these two lists, the instructor was asked to match the sample metaphor images in the first list with the 9 conceptual categories in the second list (not excluding any metaphor images). Then, the mappings made by the faculty member were compared to the researcher's own categories. The reliability of the research was calculated using miles and Huberman's (1994) Formula (reliability = unity of opinion / [consensus of opinion] *100) by determining the number of differences of opinion and opinion in the comparisons. More than 70% of the reliability accounts are considered reliable for research [13]. The faculty member metaphor (Digital technological environment and irrational), which is referenced in his / her opinion within the scope of reliability study, is associated with a different category than the researcher's. reability in this case = 110 /110 +19*100=0,85 as calculated. Aall data were transferred to SPSS statistical program for quantitative data analysis. After this process, the number of students and percentage representing each metaphor and category were calculated according to the grade level.

3 Results

In this section, data were analyzed and interpreted in accordance with the aim and sub-objectives of the research and supported by the relevant research results. When we look at the comparison of metaphors with variables (table 1), it was observed that the most preferred metaphor Digital technological Media metaphor with 9,2%. The distribution of E-Sport according to the situation of having heard before was 47.4% (139 people) of the group who said "no" was observed.

Table 1. Students 'knowledge about the concept of "e-sport" and the frequency and percentage distributions of categorized metaphors

Characteristics		**N**	**%**
Metaphor	Negative situation - Emotion	13	4,4
	Fun Game	20	6,8
	Basic requirement	22	7,5
	Positive emotion	9	3,1
	Mental activity	9	3,1
	Empty - Inability To Make Sense	10	3,4
	Addiction-Bad Habits	9	3,1
	Irrational	10	3,4
	Digital - Technological Media	27	9,2
	Those who can't answer	163	56,0
Has He ever heard of E-Sports?	Yes	154	52,7
	No	139	47,4
Where Did You Hear First?	Television	19	12,4
	School	32	20,7
	İnternet	101	65,5
	Newspaper	2	1,3

When the socio-demographic distributions of the students included in Table 2 are examined, it is seen that the majority (77,8) of the students are male, 18-20 years of age (48,8%), the Physical Education and sports teaching 36.9%, the incomes are 1500tl and below 20.5%, 49,8% of the 1.st class, using the internet 74.1%, of them are at the dormitory 60.9%.

Table 2 Frequency and percentile distributions of students ' demographic characteristics

Demographic characteristics		**N**	**%**
Gender	Female	65	22,2
	Male	228	77,8
Age	18-20 age	143	48,8
	21-23 age	107	36,5
	24-26 age	28	9,6
	27 and above	15	5,1
Department of faculty	Physical Education and sports teaching	108	36,9
	Coaching Training	31	10,6
	Recreation Department	86	29,4
	Sports management	68	23,2
class	1st class	146	49,8
	2nd class	62	21,2
	3rd class	34	11,6
	4th class	51	17,4
Type of Education	1st instruction	178	60,8
	2nd instruction	115	39,2
Using the internet	Yes	217	74,1
	No	76	25,9
Income status	1500tl and below	60	20,5
	1501-2000tl	57	19,5
	2001-2500	49	16,7
	2501-3000	31	10,6
	3001-3500	28	9,6
	3501-4000	19	6,5
	4001tl and above	48	16,4

When the socio-demographic distributions of the students included in Table 3 are examined, it is seen that the majority 65.9% (193 people) did not play sports, without license 70.4% (206 people), football, 32,4% (35people).

Table 3 Frequency and percentage distributions of students showing their family status and sportive status

Demographic characteristics		**N**	**%**
Fitness status	Doing	193	65,9
	Not doing	100	34,1
License Status	With license	87	29,7
	Without license	206	70,4
sports branch	Football	35	32,4
	Basketball	32	10,9
	Volleyball	28	9,6
	Track	10	3,4
	Swim	16	5,5
	Gymnastics	7	2,4
	Others	92	31,4

Table 4. Percentage distribution of metaphor categories chosen according to the socio-demographic characteristics of the participants

Variable		**Negative emotion/status**	**entertainment/ game**	**Basic requirement life**	**Positive emotion**	**Mental activity Positive status**	**Inability To Make Sense**	**Addiction-Bad** Habits	**Irrational**	**Digital - Technological Media**
		N (%)	N (%)	N (%)	N(%)	N (%)	N (%)	N (%)	N (%)	N (%)
Gender	**Female**	2(3,1)	3(4,6)	6(9,2)	4(6,2)	2(3,1)	1(1,5)	1(1,5)	4(6,2)	2(3,1)
	Male	11(4,8)	17(7,5)	16(7,0)	5(2,2)	0(3,1)	9(3,9)	8(3,5)	6(2,6)	25(11,0)
Income	**1500tl and above**	1(1,7)	3(5,0)	5(8,3)	1(1,7)	-	2(3,3)	2(3,3)	-	6(10,0)
	1501-2000tl	3(5,3)	5(8,8)	1(1,8)	2(3,5)	1(1,8)	2(3,5)	2(3,5)	3(5,3)	8(14,0)
	2001-2500tl	4(8,2)	3(6,1)	1(2,0)	1(2,0)	1(2,0)	1(2,0)	1(2,0)	1(2,0)	6(12,2)
	2501-3000tl	1(3,2)	1(3,2)	1(3,2)	1(3,2)	4(12,9)	1(3,2)	2(6,5)	1(3,2)	2(6,2)
	3001-3500tl	2(7,1)	2(7,1)	3(10,7)	2(7,1)	1(3,6)	1(3,6)	2(7,1)	1(3,6)	1(3,6)
	3501-4000tl	-	1(5,3)	3(15,8)	-	-	-	-	1(5,3)	2(10,5)
	4000tl and above	2(4,2)	4(8,3)	8(16,7)	2(4,2)	2(4,2)	3(6,3)	-	3(6,3)	2(4,2)
Type of instruction	**1th instr**	6(3,4)	13(7,3)	15(8,4)	3(1,7)	-	-	-	4(2,2)	14(7,9)
	2nd instr	7(6,1)	7(6,1)	7(6,1)	6(5,2)	9(7,8)	10(8,7	9(7,8)	6(5,2)	13(11,3)
Department	**Coaching**	3(9,7)	8(25,8)	5(16,1)	-	-	-	-	-	-
	Teaching	-	1(0,9)	2(1,9)	3(2,8)	-	-	-	4(3,7)	14(13,0)
	Recreation	9(10,5)	3(3,5)	11(12,8)	6(7,0)	9(10,5)	10(11,6)	9(10,5	6(7,0)	1(1,2)
	Management	1(1,5)	8(11,8)	4(5,9)	-	-	-	-	-	12(17,6)
Class	**1st class**	1(1,4)	4(2,7)	8(5,5)	3(2,1)	-	-	-	4(2,7)	23(15,8)
	2nd class	2(3,2)	3(4,8)	4(6,5)	-	5(8,1)	8(12,9	4(6,5)	5(8,1)	1(1,6)
	3rd class	4(11,8)	5(14,7)	6(17,6)	-	-	1(2,9)	5(14,7	1(2,9)	-
	4th class	5(9,8)	8(15,7)	4(7,8)	6(11,8	4(7,8)	1(1,8)	-	-	4(7,8)
access interne	**yes**	10(4,6)	18(8,3	18(8,3)	4(1,8)	7(3,2)	10(4,6	7(3,2)	5(2,3)	19(8,8)
	no	3(3,9)	2(2,6)	4(5,3)	5(6,6)	2(2,6)	-	2(2,6)	5(6,6)	8(10,5)

When we look at the comparison of metaphors with variables (Table 4.), it was observed that the most preferred metaphor in women is life with 9.2% and the interpretation for Digital technological Media metaphor with 11.0% for men. According to the

 https://doi.org/10.1051/shsconf/20184801058

distribution of income, digital technological media metaphor and basic life metaphor. Based on the variable of the Department, it was observed that the coaching department was the entertainment game metaphor with 25.8% maximum, the teaching program with 13.0% Maximum, the recreation program with 12.8% Maximum, the essential life metaphor with 12.8% maximum, and the management program with 17.6% maximum.

In the groups of the participants according to the sport making variable, it was observed that the students who performed sports had a 7.8% digital technological environment metaphor and a 12.2% interpretation of the same metaphor. According to the undergraduate status variable, students are grouped with 12.6% of the students who have a license and 8.7% of the students who have no license have been able to comment on the digital technological Media metaphor. According to the sports branch variable, students who are interested in football branch have a digital technological environment metaphor with a maximum of 10.5%, students who are interested in basketball branch have a digital environment with 9.4% and students who are interested in volleyball Branch have a maximum of 10.7% and students who are interested in sports branch have a maximum of 20.0%., Students who are interested in swimming have a positive mood metaphor of 12.5% and 9.8% of students who are interested in other disciplines.

The tables showing the most preferred metaphors according to the source in the sub-headings of the metaphors categories are presented below.

As a source of basic needs

Table 6 Metaphorical categories and percentage distributions selected according to participants ' sports status

Variable		**Negative emotion**	**Fun/ game**	**Basic requirement**	**Positive emotion**	**Mental activity**	**Inability To Make Sense**	**Addiction-Bad Habits**	**Irrational**	**Digital - Technological Media**
		N (%)	**N (%)**	**N (%)**	**N (%)**	**N (%)**	**N (%)**	**N (%)**	**N (%)**	**N (%)**
Fitness status	**Doing**	10(5,2)	14(7,3	16(8,3)	6(3,1)	4(2,1)	9(4,7)	7(3,6)	9(4,7)	15(7,8)
	Not doing	3(3,0)	6(6,0)	6(6,0)	3(3,0)	5(5,0)	1(1,0)	2(2,0)	1(1,0)	12(12,0
License Status	**With license**	4(4,6)	3(3,4)	11(12,6)	-	2(2,3)	5(5,7)	4(4,6)	1(1,1)	6(6,9)
	Without license	9(4,6)	16(8,2	10(5,1)	9(4,6)	6(3,1)	5(2,6)	4(2,1)	9(4,6)	17(8,7)
Sport branches	**Football**	5(5,3)	5(5,3)	7(7,4)	3(3,2)	1(1,1)	2(2,1)	5(5,3)	3(3,2)	10(10,5
	Basketball	-	2(6,3)	2(6,3)	1(3,1)	1(3,1)	3(9,4)	-	1(3,1)	3(9,4)
	Volleyball	1(3,6)	-	3(10,7)	1(3,6)	1(3,6)	1(3,6)	1(3,6)	-	3(10,7)
	Tracking	-	1(10,0	-	1(10,0	-	-	-	-	2(20,0
	Swimming	1(6,3)	1(6,3)	-	2(12,5	1(6,3)	-	1(6,3)	-	1(6,3)
	Gymnastics	-	2(28,6	-	-	-	-	-	1(14,3	-
	Other	6(6,5)	8(8,7)	9(9,8)	1(1,1)	4(4,3)	4(4,3)	1(1,1)	5(5,4)	4(4,3)

This category represents 22 students (7.5%) and 9 metaphors (see Table 1). In this category, metaphor was developed as the dominant source of basic needs in the group, respectively e-sport, (9) life (40.9%). (1) Life (4.5%), Beşiktaş (4.5%), (2) Water (9%), (2) Basic Requirement (9%), (1) Life Itself (4.5%), (1) Tree (4.5%), (1) Useful (4.5%), (1) Food (4.5%), (1) Ability to Move (4.5%), (1) Global Seed (4.5%), (1) Health (4.5%) it's likened. The metaphors that form this category are:

- e-sport is likened to eating something (water, Life, Tree, food).
- As a source of addiction

According to Table 3, The number of students representing the category "e-sports addictive substance" is 3.1 students 11 (%). The dominant metaphors of this category are as follows: e-sports, (4) addiction (44.4%), (1) antisocial (11.1%), (1) cigarette (11.1%), (1) heroin (11.1%), (1) drink (11.1%), (1) alcohol (11.1%), (1) alcohol (11.1%). An addiction metaphor has been expressed in common by all participants.

The metaphors that form this category are: 1. e-sports are likened to addictive substances (heroin, smoking, alcohol, etc.)

"e-sport is similar to addiction because there were times when I was busy for hours every day

4 Discussion

The aim of this study was to determine the level of knowledge and metaphors of the students of the Faculty of Sports Sciences of Kocaeli University about "e-sport". In our literature survey, it is important not to find any research that determines the level of information through metaphor in the field of "E-sports" in terms of the originality of our study. The findings of our research are divided into 9 categories by the definition of "e-sports" through metaphor. When these categories were evaluated in terms of gender variables, it was observed that women were more oriented towards the metaphors of "tree and life" related to nature, and their subsequent sentences were described as "e – sport is not life without an e-sport". The reason for turning women into such metaphors is that women may have used these metaphors [14] because they are more emotional than women because of their gender learning and because women are more emotional as well as because women are more emotional than men in a large study conducted in 37 countries [14,15,16]. It has been observed that men prefer metaphors in the category of "digital technological environment", "virtual sport, online Sport, Internet sport" and later sentences like "internet is common, Electronic and virtual environment". The reason for this is more technological toys than girls (Atari, etc.) until the age of men when they grow up.) their play is thought to be effective in making a comment in this way. E-sports metaphors created categories are examined according to the sections read; Physical Education and sports teacher and sports management departments tend to "digital technological Media metaphors" category because of the fact that in terms of the content of the courses in which the laws and laws are processed mainly because of the fact that they are included in the programs rather than it is thought that they can be directed to the meaning of a dictionary. Coaching training program, as a course content, is more about the physical and physiological effects of sports lessons and applications are intense and e-sport is not involved in movement because they are directed to the category that includes entertainment game metaphor. Finally, it was thought that the reasons for associating e-sport with the "basic requirement – life metaphor" were reflected in the interpretation of the course content as a source of similar recreational activities that will be constantly intertwined with their profession in the future. When the literature was scanned, no relevant source was found. According to the income distribution variables, the ratio of use of the Internet to use of the Internet has increased as the income increases compared to the situation of use of the Internet has been observed. As a result of the literature survey conducted in the light of this result, it was found that the rate of participation of the students in leisure activities differs significantly from the study conducted in the year 2012 [17]. Our results also coincided with the literature. Metaphor category 1 negative emotion and situation; students who prefer to describe e-sport through this metaphor have interpreted it as clumsy, does not involve physical activity, and does not run the cardiovascular system. It is estimated that the games collected under the roof of e-sport have been carried out in order to express that they have taken people away from the social environment and lead them to a still life. A typical player plays only one hour or two a day, and in China there are more than 6 million people who spend at least 22 hours a week, which is the equivalent of part-time work. In the United Kingdom, France and Germany, more than 10 million "hard core" players play at least 20 hours a week, and more than 5 million "extreme" players in the United States at the front of this growth curve play an average of 45 hours a week [18]. When interpreted in the light of this information, the long-term stationary time of the athletes on the computer coincided with the metaphors interpreted by the students. Category 2 entertainment and play; students who prefer to describe e-sport through this metaphor preferred to explain it by expressing their enjoyment of the time spent with e-sport as "enjoyable, fun and fun for hobby purposes". The study was carried out by the students of the age group 11-13 to use the "happiness "metaphor most of the positive metaphorical perceptions of the sport and the reason for this, the sport is connected not only to physical development, but also to the psychological development of the sport [19]. Category 3 basic needs life; students who prefer to explain e-sport through this metaphor have found e-sport suitable to simulate life, basic needs, food and water as they are included in the "people who spend more time in games" group. The study of the literature found that the students of digital games were likened to the metaphor bird and cloud about traditional game and digital game perceptions [20]. E-sports has been shown to be associated with natural life by a different age group, considering that it covers all of the digital games. Category 4 positive emotion: students who choose to explain e-sport through this metaphor prefer to define expressions such as school, love and music that make up the positive feelings of the time spent with e-sport. Category 5, mental activity; students who prefer to explain e-sport through this metaphor have applied to concepts such as chess, brain gymnastics and mental training. E-sports is thought to be caused by the influence of the strategy feature which is the basic in many games. Category 6 cannot give meaning; students who prefer to explain e-sport through this metaphor, often include empty, unnecessary and non-purposeful words. The reason for this is that it is thought to be composed mostly of people who do not know more about e-sports and do not like to play such games. Primary school 7. it has been determined that 6.93% of the class students have negative perception about sport and that they think that sport is not a necessary activity [21]. In other words, it is understood from the literature that there is a metaphor for negative interpretations of e-sports, and it has shown that people can feed negative thoughts even for a healthy study that improves our quality of life. Category 7 addiction - bad habit; students who choose to explain e-sport through this metaphor are often likened to addictive substances such as drugs, heroin and cigarettes. The reason for this is thought to be due to the fact that such games, which are mentioned in general information, are made up of people who "excessively spare time". In another study, "digital gaming culture is strong in a geography of young people living until the age of 21 playing about 10000 hours of online games," he said. In a country like the United States, this situation is important in terms of equal to 10800 hours a student takes from fifth grade to high school graduation. In the light of this information, it is stated that the situation of young people not being able to separate themselves from the computer can be described as a kind of dependency [22].

Category 8 senseless; students who prefer to explain e-sport through this metaphor have often described it as useless, unnecessary and absurd. In the explanation section, it is thought that they have defined this metaphor as it is a branch that does not contain any movement because it is mostly composed of active sports individuals. Category 9 digital technological medium; e-sport this metaphor of the explanation of the students, virtual sport, online sports and Internet sports, such as the words more dictionary is seen. As a result, it has been determined that the students have more positive perceptions of e-sport in the metaphors they have produced about e-sport. In addition, "e-sport", which is increasingly demanded by both commercial and young people's interests, has been thought to produce solutions to today's still life, to be programmed to include exercise and activity taking into account the interest of children and young people, and to be designed for games and sports scientists and to produce projects on this subject.

References

1. Dijital Sporlar, Accessed via http://dijitalsporlar.com/makaleler/dunyada-espor
2. A. Kolburan Geçer, Determination of the Computer Self-Efficacy Perception of Students and Metaphors Related to "Computer Ownership". Turkish Online Journal of Educational Technology - TOJET, **12 (3)**, 51-71 (2013)
3. A. Kolburan Geçer, A. Deveci Topal, Evaluation of Administrator, Teacher and Parent Opinions about the Project of a Computer to Each Student, Educational Administration: Theory and Practice. **19 (3),** 391-417. (2013)
4. K. Choi, H. Son, M. Park, J. Han, K., Kim, B.Lee, H.Gwak, Internet overuse and excessive daytime sleepiness in adolescents. Psychiatry and Clinical Neurosciences. **63(4)**, 455-462, (2009)
5. J. Sung, J. Lee, H. M. Noh, Y.S. Park, E. J. Ahn. Associations between the risk of Internet addiction and problem behaviors among Korean adolescents. Korean Journal of Family Medicine, **34(2),** 115-122. (2013)
6. H. Şahan, Üniversite Öğrencilerinin Sosyalleşme Sürecinde Spor Aktivitelerinin Rolü Selçuk Üniversitesi, sosyal bilimler enstitüsü halkla ilişkiler ve tanıtım anabilim dalı araştırma yöntemleri bilim dalı, Unpublished doctoral thesis, Konya (2007)
7. T. L. Taylor, Raising the Stakes: E-Sports and the Professionalization of Computer Gaming, Accessed via https://books.google.com.tr/books?hl=tr&lr=&id=CiL8aPrSeKcC&oi=fnd&pg=PR5&dq=ESPOR+&ots=dDCkRE7wgI&sig=VLr5iZPqFBo4FighHIUzUyg2XE&redir_esc=y#v=onepage&q&f=false Cambridge: The MIT Press. (2012)
8. D. Aksan "Anadili Eğitimi", VII. Dilbilim Kurultayı Bildirileri, 13-14 Mayıs, Ankara, DTCF, 201-202. (1993)
9. Y. Cerit, Öğretmen Kavramı İle İlgili Metaforlara İlişkin Öğrenci, Öğretmen ve Yöneticilerin Görüşleri. Türk Eğitim Bilimleri Dergisi, sayı **6 (4),** 693-712. (2008)
10. S. Kaptan, *Bilimsel Arastirma ve İstatistik Teknikleri.* Ankara: Tekışık Yayıncılık. (1995)
11. A.Saban, Öğretmen Adaylarinin Öğrenci Kavramina İlişkin Sahip Olduklari Zihinsel İmgeler, Türk Eğitim Bilimleri Dergisi, Bahar, **7(2),** 281-326, (2009)
12. A. Yıldırım, ve H. Şimşek, *Sosyal Bilimlerde Nitel Araştırma Yöntemleri.* Ankara: Seçkin Yayınları, (2005)
13. M.B Miles, & Huberman, *Qualitative Data Analysis: An Expanded Sourcebook.* London: Sage. (1994)
14. Z. Dökmen, Kendi Cinsiyetindekilere ve Diğer Cinsiyettekilere İlişkin Algı, Cinsiyet Rolleri Ve Depresyon İlişkileri. Kriz Dergisi **9(1)** 9-19. (1997)
15. A. H. Fischer, Rodriguez Mosquera, A. E Van Vianen., & A. S. Manstead, Gender and culture differences in emotion. Emotion, **4(1),** 87. (2004).
16. S. A. Shields, *Speaking From The Heart: Gender And The Social Meaning Of Emotion*. Cambridge, England: Cambridge University Press. (2002).
17. M. Özşaker, Gençlerin Serbest Zaman Aktivitelerine Katılamama Nedenleri Üzerine Bir Inceleme. Selçuk Üniversitesi Beden Eğitimi ve Spor Bilim Dergisi, **14(1),** 126-131. (2012).

18. J. McGonigal, Reality *is Broken: Why Games Make Us Better and How They Can Change the World*. Penguin Books. (2011).
19. E.D., Karakaya, O. Salıcı. Isparta'da Öğrenim Gören 11-13 Yaş Gurubu Öğrencilerin Popüler Spor Branşları Hakkındaki Metaforik Algılarının Belirlenmesi. International Journal of Social Sciences and Education Research, **2 (3),** 855-869. (2016)
20. Z. Hazar, Z. G. Tekkurşun Demir, ve H.Dalkıran, Ortaokul Öğrencilerinin Geleneksel Oyun Ve Dijital Oyun Algılarının İncelenmesi: Karşılaştırmalı Metafor Çalışması. SPORMETRE, 2017, **15 (4),** 179-190. (2017)
21. M. Koç, F. Murathan, Ü. Yetiş ve T. Murathan, İlköğretim 7. Sınıf Öğrencilerinin Spor Kavramına Ilişkin Algıları. Akademik Sosyal Araştırmalar Dergisi, **3(9)**, 294-303. (2015)
22. J. McGonigal, Gaming can make a better World. TED TALKS Accessed via http://www.ted.com/talks/jane_mcgonigal_gaming_can_make_a_better_world.ht ml. (2010)

Analysis of Science Teacher Candidates' Relation between Scientific Creative Thinking Skills, Creative Problem Solving and Project Development Skills

Sibel Demir Kaçan[1,*], and *Fatma* Şahin[2]

[1]Ondokuz Mayıs University Sciences, Education Faculty Science Education Department, Türkiye
[2]Marmara University Sciences, Education Faculty Science Education Department, Türkiye

Abstract. The research aims to determine the "relationship between the scientific creative thinking skills and creative problem solving and project development skills of candidate science teachers." The research was performed with 24 teacher candidates in the control group and 24 teacher candidates in the experimental group in the second class of the Department of Science Teaching in a university in Istanbul Province. In the experimental group of the research, the laboratory program to be designed by the researchers on the basis of scientific discussion and research; and in the control group, the conventionally designed laboratory program were applied for 14 weeks. The research data was gained through "Self-Assessment for Creativity Questionnaire" to be developed by Raudsepp [28] and adapted by Sungur [30] into Turkish with the reliability value by Gülel [11]; two projects which were "the kite project", "bridge project from spaghetti macaroni" and "personal interviews". The conclusions to be reached by the research are in favour of the experimental group and the last application. While it was found that the project development processes of the candidate teachers in the experiment group had an important impact on their scientific creativity, the positive opinions of the candidate teachers were also found.

Keywords: Fen eğitimi, bilimsel yaratıcılık becerisi, yaratıcılık, öğretmen adayı eğitimi, proje, STEM

1 Introduction

The creative thinking is seen as a quite equipped, high level thinking skill providing various thinking skills to bring together. The experts state that the students can be gained the thinking skills at all the stages of the education along with the intelligence and talents of them [25].

---

* Corresponding author: sibelfe@hotmail.com; this article is part of the first author's doctoral thesis.

In addition to that, the basic thinking form of creative thinking is generated by divergent and convergent thinking. The convergent thinking is the calm, careful, planned thinking by being clear and exact with positive judgements with reference to the aim [26]; the divergent thinking is the thinking permitting the imagination to be used for reaching more than one outcome without judging the thoughts for many alternatives as a result of a brainstorming in favour of new and different thoughts, pushing the individual borders more for producing ideas, providing time for idea formation, unification of the ideas [26]. The divergent thinking is generally seen as the way of thinking ensuring the creative thinking and problem solving with many right or wrong answers to be produced [13]. When the creative problem solving model to be developed by Lin and Cho [19] is examined, it is seen that the convergent thinking, divergent thinking, motivation and environment have relations with each other and this four situations form the general knowledge and skills in the life; however, only the divergent thinking can alone develop the creative problem solving, other three have firstly to enable the success and then bring a creative solution, if any. This is clearly indicate that the divergent thinking is quite a lot for a creative problem solving.

According to Meyer and Lederman [22], the creativity is the foundation of the scientific knowledge. The creativity is an enormous fact. Despite its basic consideration of many, various and original production, there are differences for the creativity in literature, art, social sciences and natural sciences. The human needs are firstly considered in scientific creativity and it is generally required to adapt current knowledge into new situations [Can, 2007; quoted by 15].

Park [27] states the scientific creativity with three dimensions which are creative thinking, scientific knowledge and scientific research and inquiry skills. On the other hand, Zhang, Liu and Lin [36] stated the existence of some requirements like internal motivation, autonomy and initiation, but these are also not sufficient. The problem solving, formation of hypothesis, test design, technical innovation require a certain form of creativity unique to the science [20].

The scientific creativity model of Hu and Adey [13] consists of three dimensions which are the process, characteristic (feature) and product. Thus, according to Demir [7], "The scientific creative thinking skill: *It can be defined as a skill of thinking providing the formation of numerous original ideas in various fields for the solution of a problem for which the solution is required by the individual, with an innovative and interdisciplinary approach including the science, technology and art (aesthetics). With reference to this definition, the scientific creativity is considered as a multi-dimensional and equipped field ensuring either uniqueness to the field or the aesthetic approaches of various disciplines to bring together under the same roof.*"

If it is known how humans learn and how configure the knowledge, an appropriate learning environment can be formed [8]. This approach generates the essence of the learning and teaching experiences in the science education as the teaching on the basis of research and inquiry in the science education and special approach for the learning on the basis of research and inquiry in science teaching and learning [9]. The scientific research inquiry contains the way of thinking of scientists while they are searching the real world and the perception of how they work to develop the knowledge [24]. This approach is the process of problem solving with indoor and outdoor activities of the students [31] and there are numerous studies emphasizing its importance in various educational discipline in recent years [24].

On the point, the projects which can be used efficiently as a creative problem solving process are so important. The project is a model promoting research, developing creativity, containing indoor and outdoor activities focusing on the students with various disciplines and problem solving skills from the real life, the cognitive process, technology and team working [35]. In other words, the project enables to search the problem in depth; to decide independently, gaining scientific research skill [6] and existence of the creativity [2]. Since, the STEM activities which can also be performed as a project work can also be beneficial in that sense. STEM is an interdisciplinary look consisting of science, technology, engineering and mathematics. STEM enables individuals a way to reach the required resources by using the creativity in social life [29]. There are studies on STEM and its effects. For instance, in one of such studies, Wai, Lubinski, Benhow and Steiger [34] analyse the relationship between the success in science, technology, engineering, mathematics (STEM) and the real life; the study of Tyson, Lee, Borman and Hanson [33] analyse the relationship between the demographical characteristics of the students and STEM. As it is seen in these researches, the science, technology, engineering, mathematics education provides an interdisciplinary look to understand the life and this vision is seen as a perception promoting the flexibility and fluency criteria which are effective to reveal the creative potential of the individual. With reference to this point, the problem of the research to determine the "relationship between the scientific creative thinking skills and creative problem solving and project development skills of candidate science teachers."

2 Methodology

It is research model (pattern) that is the research plan to be developed deliberately by the researcher to control the variance in order to test the hypothesis or to answer the research questions [3; 4]. The mixed model is a dominant model that provides the qualitative and quantitative methods to distinguish, define and unite [23]. This mixed model is used for the research.

The universe of this research is the 1st and 2nd education programs students in the Department of Science Teaching in a university in Istanbul. The working group of the research consists of 2nd grade of the Department of Science Teaching of the same university. The students selecting this course among candidate teachers in the 1st education program formed the control group and the candidate teachers from the 2nd education program formed the experimental group. Thus, this research was conducted with 24 candidate teachers in the control group and 24 candidate teachers in the experimental group in the Department of Science Teaching.

The program to be developed by the researchers was designed with reference to the conventional laboratory program for the control group and 5E model on the basis of scientific discussion and research for the experimental group. This program was developed along with the pilot applications and it was developed and selected according to the opinions of candidate teachers within the framework of the pilot application and 2 expert researchers, from the pool containing various activities to be tried on working groups in order to ensure the validation and it was finalised.

The questionnaire "How creative are you?" to be developed by Raudsepp [28] was adapted by Sungur [30] into Turkish and after all the articles (50 articles) were reviewed by Gülel [11] in terms of Turkish language and literature with the linguists, the reliability value was determined as 0.761 Cronbach alpha. The Cronbach alpha value of this value for the research was found as 0,82 and the "Self-Assessment for Creativity Questionnaire" was applied to the candidate teachers in the control and experiment groups as the pre- and post-application.

The research to be supervised for the process with the pilot application; in the research to be finalised with an exhibition, the spaghetti bridge project exhibition and kite project fest were performed by the candidate teachers in the experiment group. The similar studies of Gonzalez, Morsch and Masuero [10], and Karweit [14] were benefited for the spaghetti (macaroni) bridge project in the research.

In the analysis of the qualitative data to be extracted from the research, the usual distribution was firstly considered and the Self-Assessment for Creativity Questionnaire was normal for all four groups. Therefore, the t-test analysis was performed for the measuring tool.

The analysis of the qualitative data to be gained from the research was made with the rubric to be formed by the researchers. The rubric criteria to be used for the teaching process and stages; "*quite sufficient*" means "all given answers are accepted as appropriate ideas"; "*sufficient*" means "despite some omission/mistake/contradiction… in given answers, appropriate ideas are more"; "*insufficient*" means "despite the appropriateness of ideas in given answers, more omission/mistake/contradiction"; ""*quite insufficient*" means "omission/mistake/contradiction in given answers completely" and "*no answer*" means "no answer was given.

3 Findings

Findings from this study are presented in tables (table 3.1., table 3.2., table3.3) below.

Table 3.1. The Findings on "Self-Assessment for Creativity Questionnaire" of Candidate Teachers

	N	Ort.	t	P
Control pre	24	140,96	2,542	0,835
Experiment pre	24	140,46		
Control post	24	152,33	2,542	0,014
Experiment post	24	159,33		
Control pre-post	24	140,96-152,33	4,059	0,000
Experiment pre-post	24	140,46-159,33	6,935	0,000

As it is seen on the t-test results in Table 3.1, no meaningful difference was seen in pre-test distributions of control and experiment groups. This means that both groups were at equal level for this questionnaire. In the post-test results of the control and experiment groups, there is a meaningful difference in favour of the experiment group. This situation indicate that there is a change in favour of the experiment group in this last test.

Table3.2. Findings on Kite Project

	Imagination	Thinking	Fluency	Flexibility	Uniqueness	Scientific knowledge	Scientific problem	Scientific event	Technical production
Group1	5	5	5	5	5	3	4	4	4
Group2	4	5	4	5	5	5	5	5	5
Group3	5	5	5	5	5	5	5	5	5
Group4	5	5	5	5	5	5	5	5	5
Group5	3	4	3	3	3	4	3	3	4

As it is seen on Table 3.2, the groups developed successful projects in general. However, the kite to be made in a group was found insufficient in terms of its dimensions.

As it is seen on Table 3.3, the findings to be gained from the final projects of the groups for the spaghetti bridge exhibitions are found sufficient in general for their dimensions

Table 3.3. Findings on Spaghetti Bridge Project

	Imagination	Thinking	Fluency	Flexibility	Uniqueness	Scientific knowledge	Scientific problem	Scientific event	Technical production
Group1	5	5	5	5	4	4	4	5	4
Group2	5	5	5	5	5	5	5	5	5
Group3	4	5	5	4	3	5	5	5	5
Group4	5	5	5	5	5	5	5	5	5
Group5	5	5	5	5	5	5	5	5	5

4 Discussion and Conclusion

The conclusions to be reached by the research are in favour of the experimental group and the last application. While it was found that the project development processes of the candidate teachers in the experiment group had an important impact on their scientific creativity, the positive opinions of the candidate teachers were also found.

Despite low number of researches on scientific creativity, the number has been increasing in recent years. Liang [18] states that many researchers focus on the creative thinking, products and processes of the scientists in the researches on the scientific creativity, few researchers focus on the creativity of the students. The actions to be taken in the creative thinking may vary according to the structure of the problem to be worked on, it is considered as noticing and limiting the problem, forming hypothesis for the solutions, testing the hypothesis, finding the result, accepting or rejecting or changing [Sönmez, 1993, quoted by 1].

According to Chairman [5], in order to increase the quality of the education in the science and creativity program, the classes in which the teachers and the students involve in discussions; learning with doing and investigating; use of alternative teaching approaches including the use of computers, project works, simulation exercises and so on were mentioned. Especially in recent years, the students in the science education have been expected to have the skills starting from scientific process skills to research, questioning, problem solving, project development and indicating their creativity [32]. The neurobiological, psychological and cultural works generally indicate the creativity as a dialectical process between the configuration and non-configuration, the order and the chaos. The benefits of the interdisciplinary reflection in the creativity works in terms of the completion of special findings to be formed one by one in the fields of science are emphasized [12]. Therefore, the students in the research were especially promoted to express their opinions with reference to interdisciplinary thinking and this approach was tried to be applied in both the program contents and the projects.

The innovative perspective requires some uniqueness and interdisciplinary approach to the matters. The science is one of the best content fields to establish the interdisciplinary connections. Besides, the science courses give opportunities to reinforce the languages of the art and mathematics [16]. For the sake of the formation of the creative ideas, it is an important component to think with different dimensions through an interdisciplinary consideration. National research Centre (NRC) and AAAS strongly emphasize the provision of the science, technology, engineering and mathematics as a whole to the students [37].

References

1. Aktamış, H., & Ergin, Ö. Fen eğitimi ve yaratıcılık. *Dokuz Eylül Üniversitesi Buca Eğitim Fakültesi Dergisi*, ***20***, 77-83, (2006).
2. Aykaç, N. Öğrenme-öğretme sürecinde öğretim stratejileri, yöntem ve teknikleri. N. Aykaç, & H. A. (Eds.) içinde, Öğrenme-öğretme sürecinde planlama ve uygulama (s. 173-242). Ankara: Naturel Kitap Yayın Dağıtım, (2006).
3. Balcı, A. (2004). *Sosyal bilimlerde araştırma yöntem, teknik ve ilkeler*. Ankara: Pegem A Yayıncılık. 4. Baskı, (2004).
4. Büyüköztürk, Ş. *Deneysel desenler öntest-sontest kontrol grubu desen ve veri analizi*. Ankara: Pegem A Yayıncılık. 1.Baskı, (2001).
5. Chairman, B. P. (1994). www.teindia.nic.in/mhrd/50yrsedu/q/6J/BJ/6JBJ0101.htm adresinden 2 Aralık 2013 tarihinde edinilmiştir.
6. Çubukçu, A. Probleme dayalı öğrenme. B. Oral (Ed.) içinde, Öğrenme-öğretme kuram ve yaklaşımları (s. 527-540). Ankara: Pagem A Yayıncılık, (2012).
7. Demir, S. Bilimsel tartışma ve araştırmaya dayalı tasarlanan laboratuvar programının, fen bilgisi öğretmen adaylarının bilimsel yaratıcılıklarına etkisi. Yayınlanmamış Doktora Tezi, Marmara Üniversitesi, İstanbul, (2014).
8. Duban, N. İlköğretim fen ve teknoloji dersinin sorgulamaya dayalı öğrenme yaklaşımına göre işlenmesi: Bir eylem araştırması. Yayınlanmamış doktora tezi, Anadolu Üniversitesi, Eğitim Bilimleri Enstitüsü, Eskişehir, (2008).
9. Dunne, J., Mahdi, A., & O'Reilly, J. Investigating the potential of irish primary school textbooks in supporting inquiry-based science education(ıbse). International Journal of Science Education, **35**(9), 1513-1532, (2013).
10. Gonzalez, L. A. S., Morsch, I. B., & Masuero, J. R. Didactic games in engineering teaching-case: Spaghetti Bridges design and building contest. 18th International Congress of Mechanical Engineering. Ouro Preto, MG., (2005).
11. Gülel, G. Sınıf öğretmeni adaylarının yaratıcılık düzeylerinin çeşitli değişkenler açısından incelenmesi. Yayınlanmamış yüksek lisans tezi, Pamukkale Üniversitesi, Sosyal Bilimler Enstitüsü, (2006).
12. Holm-Hadulla, R. The dialectic of creativity: A synthesis of neurobiological, psychological, cultural and practical aspects of the creative process. Creativity Research Journal, **25**(3), 293-299, (2013).
13. Hu, W., & Adey, P. A scientific creativity test for secondary school students. *International Journal of Science Education, **24(4)***, 389-403, (2002).
14. Karweit, M. What is engineering? Spaghetti bridge. (no date). http://web.archive.org/web/20080517124842/http://www.jhu.edu/virtlab/spaghetti-bridge/ adresinden 7 Ocak 2009 tarihinde edinilmiştir.
15. Kılıç, B. İlköğretim sekizinci sınıf öğrencilerinin bilimsel yaratıcılık ve bilimsel tutum düzeylerinin belirlenmesi. Yayınlanmamış yüksek lisans tezi, Eskişehir Osmangazi Üniversitesi, Eğitim Bilimleri Enstitüsü, Eskişehir, (2011).
16. Klentschy, M., & Thompson, L. Scaffolding science ınquiry through lesson design. Portsmouth, NH: Heinemann, (2008).
17. Levy, B. M., Thomas, E., Drago, K., & Rex, L. Examining Studies of Inquiry-Based Learning in Three Fields of Education: Sparking Generative Conversation. Journal of Teacher Education, **64**(5), 387–408, (2013).

18. Liang, J. Exploring scientific creativity of eleventh grade students in Taiwan. Unpublished doctoral dissertation, The University of Texas at Austin, Texas, (2002).
19. Lin, C., & Cho, S. Predicting creative problem-solving in math from a dynamic system model of creative problem solving ability. Creatıvıty Research Journal, **23**(3), 255–261, (2011).
20. Lin, C., Hu, W., Adey, P., & Shen, J. The influence of case on scientific creativity. *Research in Science Education*, *33*, 143-162, (2003).
21. Lin, H., Hong, Z., Yang, K., & Lee, S. The impact of collaborative reflections on teachers' inquiry teaching. International Journal of Science, **35**(18), 3095-3116, (2013).
22. Meyer, A. A., & Lederman, N. G. Inventing creativity: an exploration of the pedagogy of ıngenuity in science classroom. School Science and Mathematics, **113**(8), 400-409, (2013).
23. Moghaddam, F. M., Walker, B. R., & Harre, R. Cultural distance, levels of abstraction and the advantages of mixed methods. A. Tashakkori, & C. Teddlie (Eds.) içinde, *Handbook of mixed methods in social & behavioral research* (s. 111-134). California: Sage Publication, (2003).
24. National Research Council (NRC). National science education standards. Washington, DC: National Academy Press., (2008).
25. Özden, Y. Öğrenme ve öğretme. Ankara: Pegem A Akademi. 11. Baskı, (2011).
26. Öznacar, M. D., & Bildiren, A. Üstün zekalı öğrencilerin eğitimi ve eğitsel bilim etkinlikleri. Ankara: Anı Yayıncılık., (2012).
27. Park, J. Scientific creativity in science education. *Journal of Baltic Science Education, 10(3),* 144-145, (2011).
28. Raudsepp, E. How Creative Are You? (1979). http://everything2.com/title/How+Creative+Are+You adresinden 10 Kasım 2013 tarihinde edinilmiştir.
29. Roth, W., & Van Eıjck, M. Fullness of life as minimal unit: Science, technology, engineering, and mathematics (STEM) learning across the life span. Science Education, **94**, 1027-1048, (2010).
30. Sungur, N. Yaratıcı düşünce. İstanbul: Evrim, (1997).
31. Şahan, H. H., Uyangör, N., & Işıtan, S. Öğretim stratejileri. B. Oral içinde, Öğrenme-öğretme kuram ve yaklaşımları (s. 283-324). Ankara: Pegem A Yayıncılık, (2012).
32. Şahin, F., & Benzer, E. The effect of the project practices improved with four question strategy to science process skills. *Necatibey Eğitim Fakültesi Elektronik Fen ve Matematik Eğitimi Dergisi (EFMED), 6(1),* 306-337, (2012).
33. Tyson, W., Lee, R., Borman, K., & Hanson, M. A. Science, technology, engineering, and mathematics (stem) pathways: high school science and math coursework and postsecondary degree attainment. Journal of Education for Students Placed at Risk (JESPAR), **12**(3), 243-270, (2007).
34. Wai, J., Lubinski, D., Benbow, C., & Steiger, J. Accomplishment in science, technology, engineering, and mathematics (STEM) and its relation to Stem educational dose: A 25-year longitudinal study. Journal of Educational Psychology, **102**(4), 860-871, (2010).
35. Yavuz, S. Proje tabanlı öğrenme modelinin kimya eğitimi öğrencilerinin çevre bilgisi ile çevreye karşı tutumlarına olan etkisinin değerlendirilmesi. Yayınlanmamış doktora tezi, Hacettepe Üniversitesi, Fen Bilimleri Enstitüsü, Ankara, (2006).

36. Zhang, J., Liu, G., & Lin, C. An action-oriented approach to gifted education: Evidence from the field of scientific creativity. *High Ability Studies*, ***23(1)***, 123-125, (2012).

37. Zubrowski, B. Integrating science into design technology projects: Using a standard model in the design process. Journal of Technology Education, 13(2), (2002). http://scholar.lib.vt.edu/ejournals/JTE/v13n2/zubrowski.html adresinden 11 Aralık 2013 tarihinde edinilmiştir.

The Impact of Scientific Creative Thinking Skills on Scientific Process Skills

Sibel Demir Kaçan[1,*], and *Fatma* Şahin[2]

[1]Ondokuz Mayıs University Sciences, Education Faculty Science Education Department, Türkiye
[2]Marmara University Sciences, Education Faculty Science Education Department, Türkiye

Abstract. The research aims to determine "the Impact of Scientific Creative Thinking Skills on Scientific Process Skills". Thus, the research was performed with 24 teacher candidates in the control group and 24 teacher candidates in the experimental group in the second class of the Department of Science Teaching in a university in Istanbul Province. In the experimental group of the research, the laboratory program to be designed by the researchers on the basis of scientific discussion and research; and in the control group, the conventionally designed laboratory program were applied for an academic semester. The research data was gained through "Scientific Creativity Test" to be developed by Hu and Adey [14] and adapted by Kadayıfçı [16]; "Scientific Process Skills Test" to be developed by Okey, Wise and Burns, and adapted by Geban, Aşkar and Özkan into Turkish. The conclusions to be reached by the research are in favour of the experimental group and the last application, and it has positive impact on the opinions of the teacher candidates related with the development of the scientific creativity skills.

Keywords: Science education, scientific creativity skill, scientific process skill

1 Introduction

According to the "Global Competitiveness Report 2012" that is annually published by the World Economic Forum, Turkey is ranked as 59th among 142 countries and it is lower than the average [3]. The indicators referring to the innovation and entrepreneurship are defined with the levels of creativity. In order to develop a new and important product for the innovation, the creativity skill is required. The formation of a "new" product means that its use should be "something different" from previous usages. On the other hand, it complies with the "benefit" or "value" feature of the creativity in terms of the innovation. For the innovation, in the theoretical meaning, there at least should be the solution to a problem (like non-existence of a certain product in the market) [31]. All the innovative approaches start with a creative idea [10]. The creativity and the innovation are the effective method of teaching providing a constructivist learning environment that is required for the active

* Corresponding author: sibelfe@hotmail.com; this article is part of the first author's doctoral thesis.

participation and integration of new information with previous learnings for the students to use their cognitive processes and skills [32]. The development of creative and innovative skills are in central importance in the education and these skills ensure a strong relationship between the information and the learning, so the innovative teaching is required for the creative learning [13]. The creativity contains the science and daily life [12]. Since, the problem solving, formation of a hypothesis, test design, technical innovations need certain form of the creativity [15]. According to Kocabas [19], the scientific creativity means the motivation for scientific researches, formulation of the research problems through the information, forming a comprehensive general field for the solution of a scientific problem, the skill of searching complying with the causes and similarities, and detailed search patience with the strength. Park [26] states the scientific creativity on three dimensions which are creative thinking, scientific information and scientific research and inquiry skills. On the other hand, Zhang, Liu and Lin [33] mention the crucial existence of some basic features like internal motivation, autonomy and initiative for the scientific creativity, together with their insufficiency, alone. Alexander (1992) and Amabile (1987) stated that all the creativities have their certain field of impact and components, so it is necessary to distinguish the scientific creativity from general creativity [quoted by 15]. Likewise, Hu and Adey [14] also mentioned that the scientific creativity is a special need other than usual creativity tests, so they developed "the scientific creativity model" unique to the field. The scientific creativity model to be formed by Hu and Adey [14] on the other hand, consists of three dimensions which are the process, characteristic and product. According to Demir [9], "*The scientific creative thinking skill: It can be defined as a skill of thinking providing the formation of numerous original ideas in various fields for the solution of a problem for which the solution is required by the individual, with an innovative and interdisciplinary approach including the science, technology and art (aesthetics). With reference to this definition, the scientific creativity is considered as a multi-dimensional and equipped field ensuring either uniqueness to the field or the aesthetic approaches of various disciplines to bring together under the same roof.*"

When the research based learning is considered for the development of the scientific process skills, the interaction of them will be quite effective on the science education [28]. Likewise, the study of Ünal Çoban [30] indicated that the scientific process skills of the science teaching candidates dramatically changed with the laboratory activities on the basis of research and inquiry which are reinforced with the argumentation. The scientific process skills are necessary for the scientific creativity and creative thinking [23]. Meador [22] emphasizes that thinking and discussing like a scientist are necessary for the scientific process skills and creativity, and the creative thinking and the science process skill are one in another, so the scientific creativity skills of the individuals who use the scientific process skills are better. Aktamış and Ergin [2] define the scientific process skills as the requirement for all people in the society to be a scientific reader and the people having these skills use them to solve the problems in their daily lives. They also state that the creative thinking is again important to notice the problems in the daily lives and the scientific process skills and scientific creativity interact with each other in creative thinking models. Liang [21] states that many researchers focus on the creative thinking, products and processes of the scientists in the researches on the scientific creativity, few researchers focus on the creativity of the students. Therefore, it is considered that the number of the researches on the scientific creativity of the students, teachers and candidate teachers should be increased. With reference to this point, the problem of the research to determine "The Impact of Scientific Creative Thinking Skills on Scientific Process Skills".

2 Methodology

It is research model (pattern) that is the research plan to be developed by the researcher to control the variance in order to test the hypothesis or to answer the research questions [4; 5]. The mixed model is a dominant model that provides the qualitative and quantitative methods to distinguish, define and unite [24]. This mixed model is used for the research. The universe of this research is the 1st and 2nd education programs students in the Department of Science Teaching in a university in Istanbul. The working group of the research consists of 2nd grade of the Department of Science Teaching of the same university. The students selecting this course among candidate teachers in the 1st education program formed the control group and the candidate teachers from the 2nd education program formed the experimental group. Thus, this research was conducted with 24 candidate teachers in the control group and 24 candidate teachers in the experimental group in the Department of Science Teaching. The program to be developed by the researchers was designed with reference to the conventional laboratory program for the control group and 5E model on the basis of scientific discussion and research for the experimental group.

The scientific process skills test was developed by Okey, Wise and Burns in 1985 with 36 questions with 5 alternative answers for each question; it was translated and adapted by Geban, Aşkar and Özkan in 1992, and the test with 0,85 scale reliability was reached by [29] and [6]. The reliability factor of this test for present research was 0,76 Cronbach alpha and this value is considered as an acceptable value, so the test was applied to the candidate teachers in the control and experiment groups as the pre- and post-application. In the study, the reliability factor of the scientific creativity test to be developed originally by Hu and Adey [14] with validated 7 open-ended questions was calculated as 0,89 and the reliability factor of the test to be adapted by Kadayıfçı [16] was calculated as 0,73. Besides, the Cronbach alpha value of the scientific creativity test for the present study was defined as 0,74 and the test was applied to the control and experiment groups as the pre- and post-application. In the analysis of the qualitative data to be extracted from the research, the usual distribution was firstly considered and "the Scientific Process Skills Test" was normal for all four groups. Therefore, the t-test analysis was performed for the measuring tool. In addition to all these analysis, the "quantified" qualitative data coming from the pre- and post-applications was statistically analysed; first of all, it was determined if the groups indicated normal distribution for each measuring tool. Since the data had to be $p>0{,}05$, the "Quantified" Scientific Creativity Questions were normally distributed for all four groups. Since the "quantified" qualitative data for each group was distributed normally, this data to be gained was applied t-test. In the research, the scientific creativity test consisting of 7 open-ended questions and was developed by Hu and Adey [14] was presented as pre- and post-application in both control and experiment groups. The data to be taken from all the candidate teachers personally was assessed by the researcher with content analysis in terms of the qualifications with reference to the fluency, flexibility and uniqueness features of the scientific creativity. For the assurance of the reliability of the assessment form of the researcher, the assessments of 2 different experts were taken and the compatibility of the researcher with the experts were checked as percentage. As a result of the consideration of the data to be gained, it was found that the compatibility rates change between 81,63% to 96,55%, the reliability and the validity of the assessment of the researcher was provided. For the test to be applied to indicate the scientific creativity, the assessment criteria to be developed by Hu and Adey to assess all three dimensions of the scientific creativity in pre- and post-applications in the control and experiment groups were followed.

3 Findings

Findings from this study are presented in tables and figures (table 3.1.; table 3.2.; table3.3; table3.4; table3.5.; figure3.1; figure3.2) below.

The fluency points to be gained through first six articles of the scientific creativity test from the candidate teachers are given in below table. There is not any data from the 7th question on apple picking machine having no fluency criteria, so no data from this question.

Table 3.1. Fluency Points of the Candidate Teachers from the Scientific Creativity Test

	Question1		**Question2**		**Question3**		**Question4**		**Question5**		**Question6**	
	Pre	**Post**	**Pre**	**Post**	**Pre**	**Post**	**Pre**	**Post**	**Pre**	**Post**	**Pre**	**Post**
Control	146	180	136	161	89	85	99	89	79	78	69	55
Experiment	134	222	124	189	79	111	101	147	78	88	43	68

As it is seen on Table 3.1., the fluency grades of 6 questions on the scientific creativity, there are findings in favour of the experimental group and the post-application.

The flexibility points to be gained through five articles of the scientific creativity test from the candidate teachers are given in below table. There is no flexibility criteria in the question 5, there is no data from this question.

Table 3.2. Flexibility Points of the Candidate Teachers from the Scientific Creativity Test

	Question1		**Question2**		**Question3**		**Question4**		**Question5**		**Question7**	
	Pre	**Post**	**Pre**	**Post**	**Pre**	**Post**	**Pre**	**Post**	**Pre**	**Post**	**Pre**	**Post**
Control	62	70	70	57	40	43	47	43	129	117	153	138
Experiment	56	100	60	103	43	71	58	98	99	183	171	237

As it is seen on Table 3.2, the flexibility grades of five questions on the scientific creativity, there are findings in favour of the experimental group and the post-application.

The uniqueness points to be gained through the scientific creativity test from the candidate teachers are given in below table.

Table 3.3. Uniqueness Points of the Candidate Teachers from the Scientific Creativity Test

	Question1		**Question2**		**Question3**		**Question4**		**Question5**		**Question7**		**Question1**	
	Pre	**Post**	**Pre**	**Post**	**Pre**	**Post**	**Pre**	**Post**	**Pre**	**Post**	**Pre**	**Post**	**Pre**	**Post**
Control	120	129	137	108	71	81	85	78	26	22	96	80	67	55
Experiment	103	199	116	205	78	118	111	190	26	31	72	122	75	97

As it is seen on Table 3.3, the uniqueness grades of all questions on the scientific creativity, there are findings in favour of the experimental group and the post-application.

Thus, in order to support these "quantified" qualitative data quantitatively, t-test of the scientific creativity test was also performed inside and among the groups.

Table 3.4. Pre- and Post-Application Findings for Control and Experiment Groups

	N	**Ort.**	**t**	**p**
Experiment pre	24	99,67	5,315	0,000
Experiment post	24	137,54		
Control pre	24	99,17	0,077	0,939
Control post	24	99,50		

As it is seen on Table 3.4, the t-test results inside the groups are in favour of the experimental group and the post-application, and there is not any difference between the pre- and post-application of the control group.

The below tables present the qualitative findings in relation with the Question 1 "*Please write the scientific use of a piece of glass as much as possible. For instance, 'a test tube can be made'*" for control and experiment groups.

Table 3.5. Categories to be Generated with reference to the "Piece of Glass Question" in the Scientific Creativity Test of Candidate Teachers

Category no	Category name
E1	Use for storing
E2	Use for making tests
E3	Use for innovation
E4	General use
E5	Use for physics
E6	Use for chemistry
E7	Use for biology
E8	Use for health / medicine
E9	Interdisciplinary use
E10	Use as a device
E11	Use for research
E12	Other

The answers of the candidate teachers were categorized here. As it is seen on the Table 3.5, there are 12 categories for this question in total. One of the categories is the "other" and the answers which are not considered in other categories with similar characteristics are taken into this category. These categories were defined for each answer to be given and the category of related answer was indicated next to the answers in the part of the annexes.

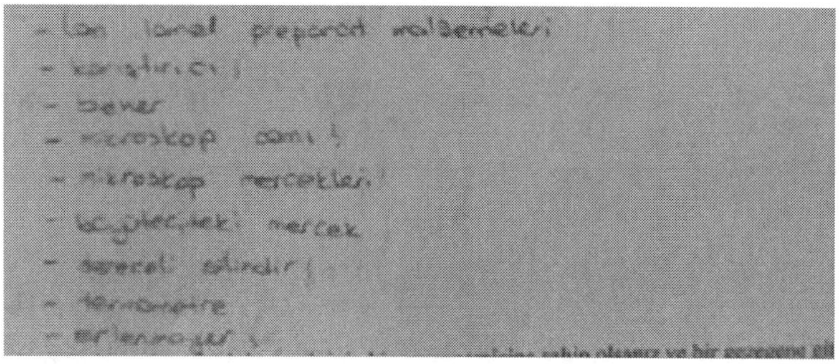

Figure 3. 1. Sample of Candidate Teacher having the code of dö14

For the 7th question the scientific creativity test, the categories to be formed by Hu and Adey [14] were used. There are 7 categories for this question in total. These categories were determined for each given drawing. For each function to be drawn in relation with the apple picking machine in the scientific creativity test, 3 point is given. There are 3 examples from pre- and post-applications of the candidate students either in control group or in experiment group.

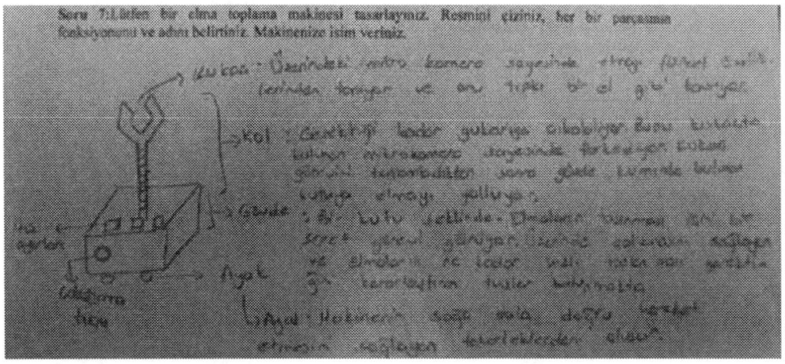

Figure 3.2. Drawing of Candidate Teacher having the Code of "dö24"

The candidate teacher having the code of dö24 performed the functions of reaching to the apple, finding the apple, picking the apple and placing into the carrying vehicle in this figure.

4 Discussion and conclusion

The conclusions to be reached by the research are in favour of the experimental group and the last application, and it has positive impact on the opinions of the teacher candidates related with the development of the scientific creativity skills. According to Kaptan and Korkmaz [17], the scientific process required more than organising the observable information and if the science is taught with these processes, the students acquire these skills and use in daily life, and they have more positive attitudes towards the science and their creativity skills develop. The scientific process skills is an approach focusing on the arrangement of skills which are the reflection of scientific behaviour, appropriate for different science disciplines and transferrable [18]. Likewise, Ewers [11] defines the scientific process skills as observation, classification, deduction, estimation, measuring and communication; however, he states that these skills provide a ground to scientific information, on the other hand, the scientific process skills are not included in science courses formally and many science curriculum focus on the content by ignoring how the information is developed.

According to Ferreira [2004], the researchers have defined three main aspects as the requirement and complementary component of the scientific education for the development of the scientific literacy, being a good tool for understanding the scientific information by catching up the changing speed of the information in relation with the mission of the scientific process skills in the science education [quoted by 20]. Therefore, it is so important for the science education to gain these skills. Likewise, Ongowo and Indoshi [25] mention that the aim of every science teacher is to promote the development of the scientific process skills and the use of these skills provide the students to search the important matters in the world and their close environment. One of the basic aims of the science education is to develop the scientific thinking and research skills. The scientific process skills are generally considered as an approach to be applied in a laboratory, so it is a laboratory approach [7]. In addition to the central role of the scientific process skills for the "meaningful learning", it is also the complementary for a scientific education [20]. The scientific process skills can also be described as the "learning to learn" determining how the learning is formed by using the critical thinking and creative information; learning with observation; organising the concepts, truths; assessing the results with reference to certain causes and commenting on the results; deduction by estimating the thing to be able to be changed [Martin et al., 2001; quoted by 27]. The creative thinking has a complementary role for the scientific process for the works in relation with the science and technology [1].

Therefore, the scientific creativity (creativity in science) education is considered to be one of the most crucial targets of the science curriculum and the content, structure and teacher approach of the course should be cared a lot. The creativity is an important aspect of human development. The technological developments and the globalisation trends require the productive and innovative people for all parts of the life. The education organisations have an important place for the development of the creativity skills and capabilities of the students and on that point the science education has the largest share for the improvement of the creative thinking quality [8].

References

1. Akçam, M. *İlköğretim fen bilgisi derslerinde yaratıcı etkinliklerin öğrencilerin tutum ve başarılarına etkisi.* Yayınlanmamış yüksek lisans tezi, Balıkesir Üniversitesi, Fen Bilimleri Enstitüsü, Balıkesir, (2007).
2. Aktamış, H., & Ergin, Ö. Fen eğitimi ve yaratıcılık. *Dokuz Eylül Üniversitesi Buca Eğitim Fakültesi Dergisi, **20**,* 77-83, (2006).
3. Ansal, H. bt haber, (2012). http://www.btnet.com.tr/54504-turk-egitim-sistemi-yaraticiligin-onundeki-en-buyuk engel.html adresinden 10 Aralık 2013 tarihinde edinilmiştir.
4. Balcı, A. *Sosyal bilimlerde araştırma yöntem, teknik ve ilkeler.* Ankara: Pegem A Yayıncılık. 4. Baskı, (2004).
5. Büyüköztürk, Ş. *Deneysel desenler öntest-sontest kontrol grubu desen ve veri analizi.* Ankara: Pegem A Yayıncılık. 1.Baskı, (2001).
6. Ceylan, E. *Effect of instruction using conceptual change strategies on students' conceptions of chemical reactions and energy.* Unpublished master thesis, Middle East Technical University, (2004).
7. Çepni, S., Ayas, A., Johnson, D., & Turgut, M. *Fizik öğretimi.* Ankara: YÖK/Dünya Bankası, (1997).
8. Daud, A. M., Omar, J., Turiman, P., & Osman, K.. Creativity in science education. *Procedia - Social and Behavioral Sciences, **59**,* 467-474, (2012).
9. Demir, S. Bilimsel tartışma ve araştırmaya dayalı tasarlanan laboratuvar programının, fen bilgisi öğretmen adaylarının bilimsel yaratıcılıklarına etkisi. Yayınlanmamış Doktora Tezi, Marmara Üniversitesi, İstanbul, (2014).
10. El Bassiti, L., & Ajhoun, R. (2013). Toward an innovation management framework: A life-cycle model with an idea management focus. *International Journal of Innovation, Management and Technology, **4(6)**,* 551-559, (2013).
11. Ewers, T. G. *Teacher-directed versus learning cycles methods: Effects on science process skills mastery and teacher efficacy among elementary education students.* Unpublished Ph. D. dissertation, University of Idaho, (2001).
12. Farooq, U. *Supporting creativity: Investigating the role of awareness in distributed collaboration.* The Pennsylvania State University, (2008).
13. Ferrari, A., Cachia, R., & Punie, Y. *Innovation and creativity in education and training in the eu member states: fostering creative learning and supporting ınnovative teaching.* Luxembourg: Office for Official Publications of the European Communities, (2009).
14. Hu, W., & Adey, P. A scientific creativity test for secondary school students. *International Journal of Science Education, **24(4)**,* 389-403, (2002).
15. Lin, C., Hu, W., Adey, P., & Shen, J. The influence of case on scientific creativity. *Research in Science Education, **33**,* 143-162, (2003).

16. Kadayıfçı, H. *Yaratıcı düşünmeye dayalı öğretim modelinin öğrencilerin maddelerin ayrılması ile ilgili kavramları anlamasına.* Yayınlanmamış doktora tezi, Gazi Üniversitesi, Eğitim Bilimleri Enstitüsü, Ankara, (2008).
17. Kaptan, F., & Korkmaz, H. *İlköğretimde etkili öğretme ve öğrenme öğretmen el kitabı ilköğretimde fen bilgisi öğretimi modül,* (1999). 7. 09. 08. 2013 tarihinde http://sakarya63.sa.funpic.de/ilkogretimde_fenbilgisi_01.pdf adresinden alındı
18. Karamustafaoğlu, O., & Yaman, S.. *Fen eğitiminde özel öğretim yöntemleri I-II.* Ankara: Anı Yayıncılık, (2006).
19. Kocabas, S. *Elements of scientific creativity.* AAAI Technical Report SS-93-01, (1993).
20. Kurtuluş, N. *Yaratıcı düşünmeye dayalı öğretim uygulamalarının bilimsel yaratıcılık bilimsel süreç becerileri ve akademik başarıya etkisi.* Yayınlanmamış yüksek lisans tezi, Karadeniz Teknik Üniversitesi, Eğitim Bilimleri Enstitüsü, Trabzon, (2012).
21. Liang, J.. *Exploring scientific creativity of eleventh grade students in Taiwan.* Unpublished doctoral dissertation, The University of Texas at Austin, Texas, (2002).
22. Meador, K. S. Thinking creatively about science suggestions for primary teachers. *Gıfted Child Today*, ***26****(25),* 25-29, (2003).
23. Miles, E. *In-servıce elementary teachers' familiarity, interest, conceptual knowledge, and performance on science process skills.* Unpublished master thesis, B.S. Southern Illinois University Carbondale, (2008).
24. Moghaddam, F. M., Walker, B. R., & Harre, R. Cultural distance, levels of abstraction and the advantages of mixed methods. A. Tashakkori, & C. Teddlie (Eds.) içinde, *Handbook of mixed methods in social & behavioral research* (s. 111-134). California: Sage Publication, (2003).
25. Ongowo, R. O., & Indoshi, F. C. Science process skills in the Kenya certificate of secondary education biology practical examinations. *Creative Education*, ***4****(11),* 713-717, (2013).
26. Park, J. Scientific creativity in science education. *Journal of Baltic Science Education,* ***10****(3),* 144-145, (2011).
27. Rauf, R. A., Rasul, M. S., Mansor, A. N., Othman, Z., & Lyndon, N. Inculcation of science process skills in a science classroom. *Asian Social Science*, *9(8),* 47-57, (2013).
28. Şahin, F., & Benzer, E. The effect of the project practices improved with four question strategy to science process skills. *Necatibey Eğitim Fakültesi Elektronik Fen ve Matematik Eğitimi Dergisi (EFMED)*, ***6****(1),* 306-337, (2012).
29. Şakir, T. *The effect of multiple intelligences based instructiion on students' achievement in basic compounds of living organisms concepts and attitude toward biology.* Unpublished doctoral dissertation, Middle East Technical University, (2013).
30. Ünal Çoban, G. The effects of inquiry supported by argument maps on science process skills and epistemological views of prospective science teachers. *Journal of Baltic Science Education*, ***12****(3),* 271-288, (2013).
31. Villalba, E. *On creativity; towards an understanding of creativity and its measurements.* İtaly Luxembourg: Office for Official Publications of the European Communities, (2008).
32. Wyke, R. M. *Teaching creativity and innovation in higher education.* Unpublished doctoral dissertation, University of Pennsylvania, (2013).
33. Zhang, J., Liu, G., & Lin, C. An action-oriented approach to gifted education: Evidence from the field of scientific creativity. *High Ability Studies*, ***23****(1),* 123-125, (2012).

SHS Web of Conferences **48**, 01061 (2018) https://doi.org/10.1051/shsconf/20184801061
ERPA 2018

Examples in Design Education: Inspiration or Fixation?

Serkan Can Hatıpoğlu[1*] and *Dilek* Yıldız[2]

[1]Eskişehir Technical University, Department of Architecture, 26000 Eskişehir, Turkey
[2]İstanbul Technical University, Department of Architecture, 34437 İstanbul, Turkey

Abstract. Inspiration has an important role in design education. Searching existing design examples is a widely-used practice for inspiration. There are two different approaches regarding exposure of examples in design process. Some researchers claim that examples can inspire designers and increase the originality of outcomes, while other researchers highlight that examples cause fixedness to their features as a negative effect for creativity. The aim of the study is to analyse different modalities of examples, such as text, photograph, diagram, object as stimulation and to examine the impact of quantity, abstraction, proximity and method on each modality in design education. The paper reviews empirical studies of idea exposure from the existing literature and summarizes results relevant to understanding the effects of the design examples. Overall, to avoid the potential negative effect of using examples in different modalities, designers could pay attention quantity, abstraction, and proximity of examples for each modality.

1 Introduction

Designers search for inspiration in diverse sources. Inspiration triggers the memory search and creativity. Searching existing design examples is a widely-used practice for inspiration since it has been assumed that idea exposure by existing examples stimulate designers. Some researchers found proves for the assumption that examples can inspire designers and increase the creativity of outcomes [1-5], while other researches claimed that examples cause fixedness to the features of existing examples [6-10]. Thus, there are two different approaches regarding to the exposure of examples in design process. It seems that this is an ongoing contradictory discussion in the literature. Being a crucial issue for comprehending the nature of a design problem, this dilemma has been searched by researchers extensively in the field of design education; and still needs further research evidence and attention.

The aim of this paper is to summarize and discuss the overall research findings which reveal the impacts of example exposure during design process from the literature. Thus, depending on the different modalities of examples such as text, photograph, diagram, object as stimulation, the paper is a systematic review of existing research findings which prove exposing examples cause inspiration or fixedness in design education. Each modality has

* Corresponding author: serkanch@anadolu.edu.tr

been examined according to the parameters of fidelity, quantity and proximity. The tested hypotheses based on these parameters are listed below:

- Fidelity (abstract or concrete) (H1); whether abstract or concrete example exposure create a difference or not.
- Quantity (one or more) (H2); whether one or more example exposure create a difference or not.
- Proximity (within-subject or between-subject) (H3); whether examples which are related or unrelated to the subject of the design problem create a difference or not.

The detailed and systematic review of this study can contribute to the future researchers to understand the whole picture of the issue and accordingly help to position their hypothesis in a more accurate way.

2 Background

The design task is ill-structured. There is initially no definite criterion to test a proposed solution [11]. Thus, design problem has ambiguity through problem and solution space (as a nature of ill-defined problem [12]. Memory search is prevalent practice to solve problems. Therefore, experience have a significant role to deal with new design problems. Schön [13] claim that actions of designers are affected by what they are seeing. Each new experience enables them to face the next design problem. Searching design examples is effective in establishing relationships with experiences. Acquired information is processed in ill-structured character of a design problem.

Designers often search some information or images related to design problem. Petre, Sharp and Johnson [14] claimed that designers tend to select and adapt a related source to generate indirect or unexpected ideas. Therefore, related source triggers designers as inspiration. Inspiration sources can be defined as any stimulus retrieved from one's memory or from the outside world, during a design process, that affects the framing of the problem [15].

In contrast, some researchers highlight that examples cause fixedness to their features which is called "fixation". Design fixation in creative problem solving describes a negative transfer of knowledge between a source (perceived stimuli) and target (solution idea/concept) [16]. In design contexts, this happens when one's adherence to the elements of previously seen examples in the current context [6]. Furthermore, it is generally an unconscious behaviour [7].

Examples can be exhibited in many ways, such as words, photographs, diagrams and objects. Likewise, those representations may be at different levels of abstraction. Number of examples can be another parameter as well as whether it is in the same or different problem domain. All of these parameters may explain the uncertainty of the impacts of example exposure in the literature.

3 Method

The paper reviews empirical studies of idea exposure and summarizes the results relevant to understanding the effects of the design examples. To do that, thirty-nine articles are analysed with respect to quantity, abstraction, proximity of examples and methods. We improve Vasconcelos and Crilly's [17] review and analysed them in terms of positive and negative resulted approaches.

Some studies do not explicitly mention the detailed features of examples. However, they can be understood from the figures illustrating examples which are shown to designers. Following that, the features of examples are compared with different modalities.

Two different approaches are examined depending on these variables in order to understand the reasons of opposite claims.

4 Results

The results gathered from literature review on textual, photographic, diagrammatic and physical object example exposure during design process have been analysed and presented based on the parameters of fidelity, quantity and proximity in the following section.

4.1 Results of textual examples

Figure 1 presents the results on the effects of textual examples from the literature. There are sixteen articles with positive implication and ten articles with negative implication. Positive outcomes result from seeing more examples rather than one. Although there are similar results as using abstract examples, concrete examples are used more in positive resulted articles comparing negative outcomes. Researchers who highlight that examples are kind of inspiration utilized more example as between-subject than within-subject

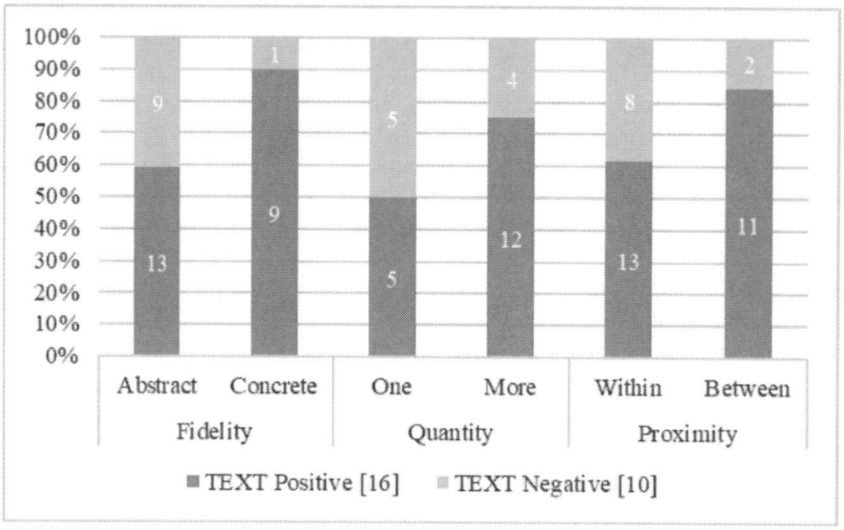

Fig. 1. Differences in fidelity, quantity and proximity of examples for textual examples.

4.2 Results of photographic examples

Figure 2 presents the results on the effects of photographic examples from the literature. Sixteen researches claim that examples inspire designers, ten researches claim that examples cause fixation. More example exposure than one is preferred from former researches. Positive resulted articles which were used concrete examples are more than negative resulted articles, while they have similar usage in abstract examples. Although within-subject examples have similar results, between-subject examples have an important role in positive outcomes.

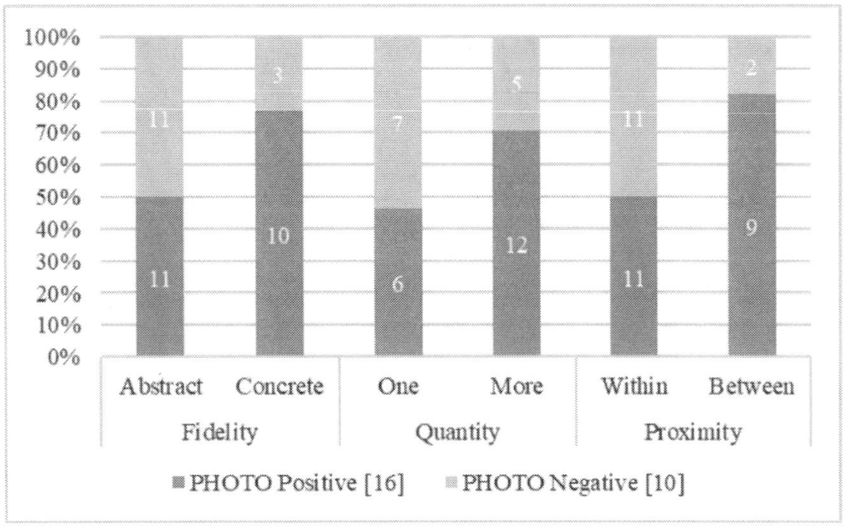

Fig. 2. Differences in fidelity, quantity and proximity of examples for photographic examples.

4.3.Results of diagrammatic examples

Figure 3 presents the results on the effects of diagrammatic examples from the literature. There are three articles with positive implication and one article with a negative implication. Positive outcomes result from seeing more examples rather than one. Abstract examples are used more in positive resulted articles comparing negative outcome. Researches who highlight that examples are kind of inspiration utilized more example as between-subject than within-subject.

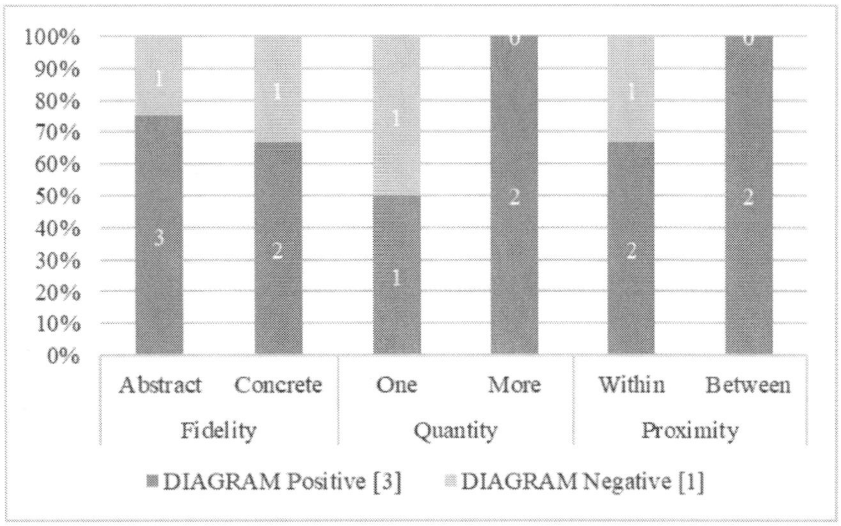

Fig. 3. Differences in fidelity, quantity and proximity of examples for diagrammatic examples.

4.4 Results of physical object examples

Figure 4 presents the results on the effects of physical examples from the literature. Three researches claim that examples inspire designers, two researches claim that examples cause fixation. More example exposure than one is preferred from former researches. Positive resulted articles which were used concrete examples are more than negative resulted articles, while they have similar usage in abstract examples. Although between-subject examples have similar results, within-subject examples have an important role in positive outcomes. It is a different result from all other modalities.

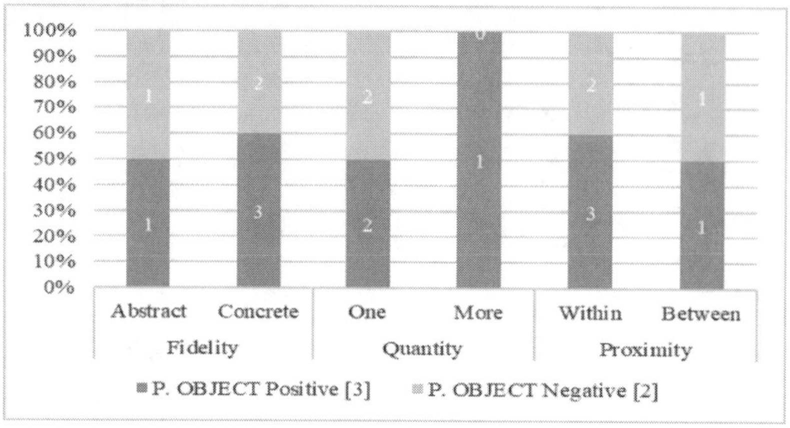

Fig. 3. Differences in fidelity, quantity and proximity of examples for physical object examples.

4.5 Overall results

Analysis of the literature allows us to draw inferences from the parameters of existing design examples which is shown in Table 1 and Table 2. When we compare two opposite approaches with the contribution of these tables, it is seen that the researches found more positive impacts of example exposure than negative ones. Besides, there are more research findings on the effects of texts and pictures than diagrams and physical objects both in positive and negative resulted researches.

Table 1. The review of the researches which highlighted that examples are a kind of inspiration.

	Author_Year	Modality of Representation				Fidelity		Quantity		Proximity	
		Text	Picture	Diagram	P. Object	Abstract	Concrete	One	More	Within	Between
POSITIVE OUTCOME	[1]										
	[34]										
	[2]										
	[3]										
	[4]										
	[5]										
	[31]										
	[30]										
	[15]										
	[32]										
	[35]										
	[36]										
	[37]										
	[20]										
	[38]										
	[39]										
	[21]										
	[23]										
	[24]										
	[33]										
	[25]										
	[27]										
	[28]										
	[29]										

Table 2. The review of researches which highlighted that examples caused fixation.

	Author_Year	Modality of Representation				Fidelity		Quantity		Proximity	
		Text	Picture	Diagram	P. Object	Abstract	Concrete	One	More	Within	Between
NEGATIVE OUTCOME	[44]										
	[42]										
	[6]										
	[7]										
	[18]										
	[8]										
	[19]										
	[10]										
	[22]										
	[9]										
	[16]										
	[41]										
	[26]										
	[43]										

As figure 5 shown, exposure to more than one example, concrete example, between-subject example and qualitative research tend to show positive impact in design process. Impacts of other parameters seem not clear from the overview. Therefore, a detailed review is required for drawing inferences.

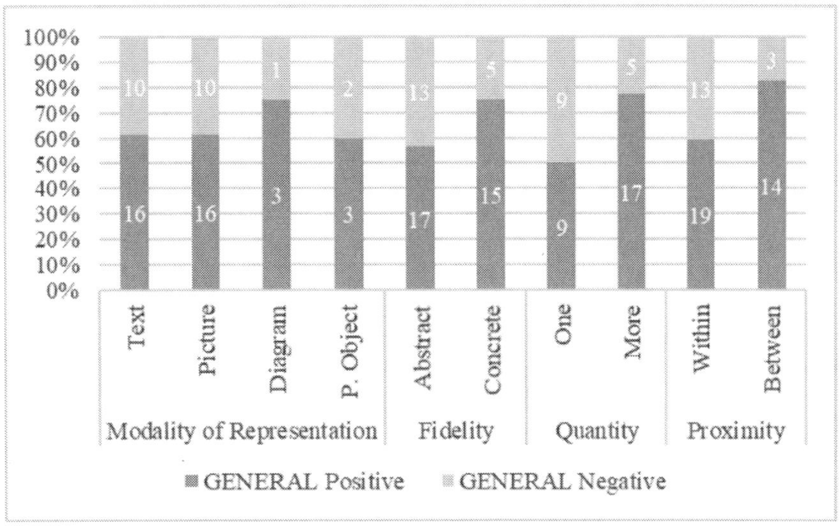

Fig. 5. Overall results of the literature review.

5. Discussion and conclusion

As conclusion, parallels and comparisons of outcomes between the results are drawn in the study. Then some issues are identified, such as more than one example exposure seems to reduce fixation. It suggests that alternative examples may help to hinder to fixate features of one example. A number of studies which include concrete examples differ between positive and negative resulted articles for textual, photographic and physical object examples. However, the abstractness of examples seems to have an important role for diagrammatic representation, in order to build relationships between examples and solution which designers proposed.

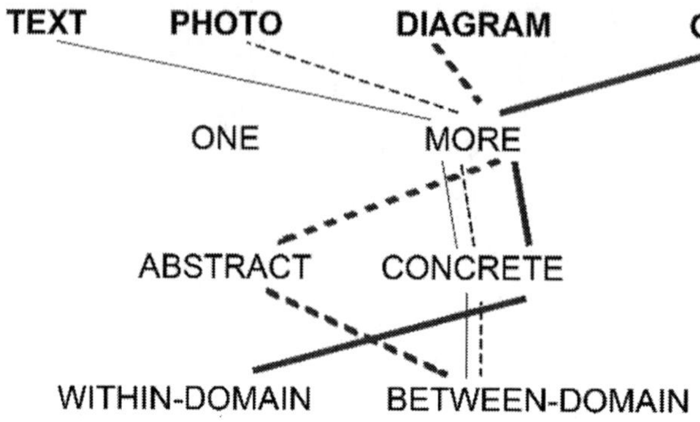

Fig. 6. Overall results of the literature review.

Most of the modalities in positive resulted articles have shown differences from negative resulted articles as between-subject examples. Different ideas which are out of the problem may stimulate designers to combine them into their design process. However, within-subject examples as physical object representation may have a positive effect on design education. To explain this result, we suggest that designers have a tendency to focus on mechanisms and functions of design when observing to physical objects. Overall, to avoid the potential negative effect of using examples in different modalities, designers could pay attention quantity, abstraction, and proximity of example for each modality.

As a limitation of the study, number of articles which is used examples of diagram and object can be found insufficient to infer to results clearly. Therefore, more studies with these modalities of representation need to study in detailed in order to extend existing literature and to analyse characteristics of diagrammatic and object examples.

References

1. C. Cardoso, P. Badke-Schaub and A. Luz, presented at the ASME 2009 International Design Engineering Technical Conferences and Computers and Information in Engineering Conference, 2009 (unpublished).
2. P. Cheng, R. Mugge and J. P. Schoormans, Design Studies **35** (4), 374-391 (2014).
3. D. W. Dahl and P. Moreau, Journal of Marketing Research **39** (1), 47-60 (2002).
4. K. Figl and J. Recker, Information & Management **53** (6), 767-786 (2016).
5. K. Fu, J. Chan, J. Cagan, K. Kotovsky, C. Schunn and K. Wood, Journal of Mechanical Design **135** (2), 021007 (2013).

6. E. G. Chrysikou and R. W. Weisberg, Journal of Experimental Psychology: Learning, Memory, and Cognition **31** (5), 1134 (2005).
7. D. G. Jansson and S. M. Smith, Design studies **12** (1), 3-11 (1991).
8. J. S. Linsey, I. Tseng, K. Fu, J. Cagan, K. L. Wood and C. Schunn, Journal of Mechanical Design **132** (4), 041003 (2010).
9. A. T. Purcell and J. S. Gero, Design studies **17** (4), 363-383 (1996).
10. M. K. Perttula and L. A. Liikkanen, Development Process: From Idea to the World's First Bionic Prosthetic Foot (2006).
11. H. A. Simon, Artificial intelligence **4** (3-4), 181-201 (1973).
12. C. M. Eastman, presented at the Proceedings of the International Joint Conference on Artificial Intelligence: IJCAI, 1969 (unpublished).
13. D. A. Schön, Educating the reflective practitioner: Toward a new design for teaching and learning in the professions. (Jossey-Bass, 1987).
14. M. Petre, H. Sharp and J. Johnson, Design studies **27** (2), 183-222 (2006).
15. M. Gonçalves, C. Cardoso and P. Badke-Schaub, Design Science 2 (2016).
16. S. M. Smith, T. B. Ward and J. S. Schumacher, Memory & cognition **21** (6), 837-845 (1993).
17. L. A. Vasconcelos and N. Crilly, Design Studies **42**, 1-32 (2016).
18. L. A. Liikkanen and M. Perttula, Journal of Engineering Design **21** (5), 545-560 (2010).
19. Z. Lujun, presented at the Computing, Control and Industrial Engineering (CCIE), 2011 IEEE 2nd International Conference on, 2011 (unpublished).
20. D. P. Moreno, A. A. Hernandez, M. C. Yang, K. N. Otto, K. Hölttä-Otto, J. S. Linsey, K. L. Wood and A. Linden, Design Studies **35** (3), 232-272 (2014).
21. B. A. Nijstad, W. Stroebe and H. F. Lodewijkx, Journal of experimental social psychology **38** (6), 535-544 (2002).
22. M. Perttula and P. Sipilä, Journal of Engineering Design **18** (1), 93-102 (2007).
23. P. Sarkar and A. Chakrabarti, Ai Edam **22** (2), 101-116 (2008).
24. P. Siangliulue, J. Chan, K. Z. Gajos and S. P. Dow, presented at the Proceedings of the 2015 ACM SIGCHI Conference on Creativity and Cognition, 2015 (unpublished).
25. I. Tseng, J. Moss, J. Cagan and K. Kotovsky, Design Studies **29** (3), 203-221 (2008).
26. V. Viswanathan, O. Atilola, N. Esposito and J. Linsey, Journal of Engineering Design **25** (1-3), 25-43 (2014).
27. S. Yilmaz, C. M. Seifert and R. Gonzalez, AI EDAM **24** (3), 335-355 (2010).
28. R. J. Youmans, The Journal of Creative Behavior **45** (2), 101-107 (2011).
29. R. J. Youmans, Design Studies **32** (2), 115-138 (2011).
30. G. Goldschmidt and M. Smolkov, Design Studies **27** (5), 549-569 (2006).
31. G. Goldschmidt and A. L. Sever, Design Studies **32** (2), 139-155 (2011).
32. M. Gonçalves, C. Cardoso and P. Badke-Schaub, presented at the DS 70: Proceedings of DESIGN 2012, the 12th International Design Conference, Dubrovnik, Croatia, 2012 (unpublished).
33. C. A. Toh and S. R. Miller, Journal of Mechanical Design **136** (9), 091004 (2014).

34. C. Cardoso, M. Gonçalves and P. Badke-Schaub, presented at the DS 70: Proceedings of DESIGN 2012, the 12th International Design Conference, Dubrovnik, Croatia, 2012 (unpublished).
35. S. Jang, Archives of Design Research **27** (4), 59-72 (2014).
36. J. S. Linsey, E. Clauss, T. Kurtoglu, J. Murphy, K. Wood and A. Markman, Journal of Mechanical Design **133** (3), 031008 (2011).
37. B. Lopez-Mesa, E. Mulet, R. Vidal and G. Thompson, Journal of Engineering Design **22** (1), 31-54 (2011).
38. C. Mougenot, J.-J. Aucouturier, T. Yamanaka and K. Watanabe, presented at the Proceedings of The Third International Workshop on Kansei, 2010 (unpublished).
39. C. Mougenot and K. Watanabe, presented at the DS 73-2 Proceedings of the 2nd International conference on Design Creativity Volume 2, 2012 (unpublished).
40. L. Sun, W. Xiang, C. Chai, C. Wang and Z. Liu, International Journal of Technology and Design Education **23** (4), 1047-1062 (2013).
41. L. A. Vasconcelos, C. C. Cardoso, M. Sääksjärvi, C.-C. Chen and N. Crilly, Journal of Mechanical Design **139** (3), 031101 (2017).
42. P.-J. Cheng, Bulletin of Japanese Society for the Science of Design **62** (3), 3_85-83_94 (2015).
43. V. Viswanathan, M. Tomko and J. Linsey, AI EDAM **30** (2), 171-184 (2016).
44. C. Cardoso and P. Badke-Schaub, The Journal of Creative Behavior **45** (2), 130-146 (2011).

An analysis of values in children's picture books in Turkish for 5-6 year-old children

Mine Kazancı Gül[1,*], *Mesude* Atay[2]

[1]Vocational School, Child Development Department, Fatih Sultan Mehmet Vakıf University, 34445, Beyoğlu, Istanbul, Turkey

[2] Elementary Education Department, Faculty of Education, Okan University, 34959, Tuzla, Istanbul, Turkey

Abstract. This study aims to examine the values of wisdom, tolerance, benevolence, happiness, courtesy, respect, love and responsibility in the children's books published in the years between 2000 and 2007 and in 2014 written in Turkish for 5-6 year old children. It is designed in content analysis pattern of qualitative research. A descriptive model of quantitative research methods was used to determine the frequency of values in picture books. The sample of the study consists of 40 children's picture books which are translated into Turkish and written in Turkish for the 5-6 age group determined by the criterion sampling strategy. The researcher developed a checklist as a data collection tool which is values checklist. As a result of the research, there are 46.80% values in the children's picture books published between 2000 and 2007; 53.20% values published in 2014, in analyzed picture books. It is found that children's picture books, those translated into Turkish and those written in Turkish differ in terms of inclusion of values. Regarding results of the study, it is necessary to give more importance to the value of wisdom and tolerance in the children's picture books and to transfer the values through positive examples toward proper behavior.

Keywords: Pre-school Education, Children's Picture Books, Values, Values Education, Children's Literature.

1 Introduction

Value is defined as the totality of material and spiritual elements that encompass the social, cultural, economic and scientific values of a nation [1].Values are moral principles that are abstract. Behaviors are the things that make values concrete. Values are not only universal, but also show a change between societies. The meaning of value is not the same in all the societies. For instance, behaviors that are considered to be indicator of value of respect vary from one country to another [2].

Value transfer can be expressed as a process of involving the entirety of life through culture, education, children's literature and parents [3, 4, and 5]. Values education includes

*Corresponding author: kzncmn@hotmail.com *Note: This study is transcribed by master thesis of Mine Kazancı Gül*

all education degrees from pre-school to high school and from primary school to university.

Pre-school education, defined as pre-school education, is as important as the food consumed by children and is seen as one of the educational features of developed societies [6]. It is important to add values to children in the preschool period, which is an important place in the life of the individual. Preschool children should be given values of responsibility, sharing, patience, happiness, honesty, respect, love, peace and cooperation [7].Children's literature positively influences the transfer of values with favorable examples [8]. Values are transmitted to children through children's books. It is thought that the products of a nation's children's literature are related to how the nation wants a future and a generation [9].

In this context; it was necessary to examine the pictures of children's books in terms of values. In the children's picture books for children ages 5 to 6, the main problem of this research is which values are tried to be given to children and whether these values are appropriate for children's age and developmental needs.

This research was conducted in order to determine whether children's books written in Turkish for 5-6 year old children are different in terms of friendship, success, wisdom, tolerance, benevolence, happiness, courtesy, respect, love and responsibility. This research will shed light on the role of valuing children's books and the values mentioned in children's books to academics, authors, writers and publishers interested in pre-school education and children's picture books, teachers and parents.

2 Methods

This research which is designed in the content analysis pattern of the qualitative research aims to examine the values of friendship, success, wisdom, tolerance, benevolence, happiness, courtesy, respect, love and responsibility in the children's picture books written between 2000-2007 in Turkish and published in 2014 for 5-6 age years. A descriptive model of quantitative research methods was used to determine the proportion of values in books.

The sample of the research consists of 40 children's books written in Turkish between the years 2000-2007 and in 2014, for the 5-6 age group determined by criterion sampling strategy. The division of the children's picture books by category and book type feature is shown in Table 1:

Table 1. Division of the children's picture books reviewed according to book type feature

Picture Books	**Turkish**	**Translated**	**Total**	**%**
2000-2007	10	10	20	50
2014	10	10	20	50
Total	20	20	**40**	**100**

According to Table 1, the distribution of the children's picture books according to the years they have been published and according to the book's type are as follows: A total of 40 picture children books (n = 10) and translated (n = 10) were included in the books published between 2000-2007, including Turkish books (n = 10) and translated books (n = 10) in the books published in 2014.

The researcher has developed the "Values Checklist" by reading the field text to examine the children's picture books. The "Values Checklist" has been reviewed by 1 specialist, 1 academician and 1 teacher on the field. The necessary corrections are made and the encoder reliability is calculated. Encoder reliability was found as 72%.In the initial phase of the study, the coding reliability is 70% and the results above this are reliable [10].Accordingly, it can be said that the values determined correspond to a great extent. The checklist consists of two parts. The first part contains general information about the book, and the second part contains the values in the book. Children's picture books included in the scope of the study were read. Each value in the books is noted in the list. "Value Checklist" contains 10 basic values which are friendship, success, wisdom, tolerance, benevolence, happiness, courtesy, respect, love and responsibility. The data were collected by document collection and review technique.

The values in the children's picture books were evaluated according to the "Value Checklist" developed by the researcher. Findings related to the values in children's picture books have been given the meaning and interpreted with the support of the area literature. Children's picture books were analyzed by content analysis. Different categories (codes) have been created according to the value of the examined value in the books. The value of friendship is coded in three different ways: peer friendship, imaginary friendship and both. Value of wisdom is categorized in two different ways: criticism and self-criticism. Value of benevolence is coded in two different ways: shared and assisted. Value of respect is coded is coded in two different ways: respect for elders and respect for differences. Value of love; human love, environment love and nature love, animal love, book love and art love are categorized in five different ways. In the quantitative dimension of the study, a percentage-frequency analysis was used to determine the frequency with which the values were included.

3 Results and Discussion

Some of the raw data for the values examined in the children's picture books are given below.

"In the end, Ibo, who could not be separated from the ball, also joined the children and started playing the ball with their friends until late hours."(Peer friendship, Ak, 2014, Book of Balls, p.16)

"After that day the daylights did never stop. They always worked. "(Sedulity, Cengiz, 2014, From the Book of Hardworking Day Lights, p.12).

"I've been watching you for weeks. What you do is not nice. And you have not grown. You were alone. Give up this feeling. "(Criticism, Freelance, 2007, from the book of Resentful Sunflower, p.14).

"Her mother was very sad when she heard this. But still she was not angry with her little beast. "(Tolerance, Callier, 2014, No, No, No, Me What!, p.14) .

"Finally, Daisy had to climb the trees and help them get out. "(Aid, Lindenbaum, 2006, from the book of Daisies and Wolves, p.22).

"They played games together in joy, laughed and giggled." (Happiness, Ercan Bilgic, 2014, From the Book of When Itır the Run, p.21).

"Please welcome," he said. They entered the house together. "(Courtesy, Fırat, 2005, from the book of the magical book, p.3).

"It's good that they are all different, or how would I distinguish my brother from the others?" (Respect for differences, Akal, 2014, From the Book of Stranger Friends of My Brother, p.36).

"After a while, they used to come to a river with forests. 'I have no trees left to climb.' said orangutan to the ones on the boat. The forest is disappearing. "(Environment and nature love, Preston Gannon, 2014, Book of Journey to Home, p.15).

"The responsibility for dealing with animals that want to be loved will be our sweet friend, Lea's!"(Responsibility, Kay, 2014, from the book of Sweet Friends, p.5).

Findings regarding the ratio of the number of sentences related to "Values" in the children's picture books to the total number of sentences are as follows:

Table 2. Percentage of number of sentences related to "values" in children's picture books to total number of sentences (N = 2698, Total sentence count)

Values	**2000-2007**				**2014**				**Book Type**				**Total**	
	Turkish		Translated		Turkish		Translated		Turkish		Translated			
	N	%	N	%	N	%	N	%	N	%	N	%	N	%
Friendship	15	0.55	15	0.55	18	0.66	10	0.38	33	1.22	25	0.92	58	**2.14**
Success	17	0.64	4	0.14	15	0.55	10	0.38	32	1.19	14	0.52	46	**1.71**
Wisdom	14	0.51	6	0.22	1	0.03	0	0.00	15	0.55	6	0.22	21	**0.77**
Tolerance	0	0.00	1	0.03	0	0.00	2	0.07	0	0.00	3	0.11	3	**0.11**
Benevolence	4	0.14	11	0.40	12	0.45	10	0.38	16	0.59	21	0.78	37	**1.37**
Happiness	16	0.60	0	0.00	21	0.78	5	0.18	37	1.38	5	0.18	42	**1.56**
Courtesy	30	1.12	9	0.33	6	0.22	29	1.08	36	1.34	38	1.41	74	**2.75**
Respect	10	0.38	0	0.00	5	0.19	4	0.14	15	0.57	4	0.14	19	**0.71**
Love	46	1.70	44	1.63	57	2.11	76	2.82	103	3.82	120	4.44	223	**8.26**
Responsibility	20	0.75	1	0.03	2	0.07	16	0.59	22	0.81	17	0.63	39	**1.44**
Total	**172**	**6.37**	**91**	**3.37**	**137**	**5.07**	**162**	**6.01**	**309**	**11.46**	**253**	**9.37**	**2698**	**20.83**

Compared to the total number of sentences (N = 2698) in the children's picture books according to Table 2, the total sentence rate for the "values" is 20.83%.Findings related to the ratio of the number of sentences related to "Values" in the children's picture books to each value are as follows:

Table 3. Division of number of sentences related to "values" in picture children's picture books by each "value" (N = 562, number of sentences related to total "values")

Values	**2000-2007**				**2014**				**Book Type**				**Total**	
	Turkish		Translated		Turkish		Translated		Turkish		Translated			
	N	%	N	%	N	%	N	%	N	%	N	%	N	%
Friendship	15	25.87	15	25.87	18	31.03	10	17.23	33	56.90	25	43.10	58	**100.0**
Success	17	36.96	4	8.69	15	32.61	10	21.74	32	69.57	14	30.43	46	**100.0**
Wisdom	14	66.67	6	28.57	1	4.76	0	0.00	15	71.42	6	28.58	21	**100.0**
Tolerance	0	0.00	1	33.33	0	0.00	2	66.67	0	0.00	3	100.00	3	**100.0**
Benevolence	4	10.82	11	29.73	12	32.43	10	27.02	16	43.24	21	56.76	37	**100.0**
Happiness	16	38.09	0	0.00	21	50.00	5	11.91	37	88.09	5	11.91	42	**100.0**
Courtesy	30	40.55	9	12.16	6	8.10	29	39.19	36	48.65	38	51.35	74	**100.0**
Respect	10	52.64	0	0.00	5	26.31	4	21.05	15	78.95	4	21.05	19	**100.0**
Love	46	20.63	44	19.73	57	25.56	76	34.08	103	46.18	120	53.82	223	**100.0**
Responsibility	20	51.29	1	2.57	2	5.12	16	41.02	22	56.41	17	43.59	39	**100.0**
Total	**172**	**30.61**	**91**	**16.19**	**137**	**24.37**	**162**	**28.83**	**309**	**54.99**	**253**	**45.01**	**562**	**100.0**

According to Table 3, in the children's books with pictures, there are more places in the Turkish books (54.99%); "Books" published between 2000 and 2007 included more "values" (30.61%); It is seen that in the books published in 2014, "values" were given more space in the translated books (28.83%).

https://doi.org/10.1051/shsconf/20184801062

Table 4. Friendship value in children's picture books

Friendship	Turkish	Translated
	Interpersonal bonds that break and reinforce.	Friendly behavior and tips for making friends.
	Resentful and touchy characters	The characters who know the value of the relationship
	Understanding the value of friendship by making mistakes	Having good time, invite-be invited.

In Table 4, there are cases which the friendship value is included the children's picture books.

Table 5. Success value in children's picture books

Success	Turkish	Translated
	Working non-stop, performing daily tasks	Production, working, getting tired, having rest, collaborate
	Artistic designs and associations with productions	Association with self-confidence
	Frequent repetition of work	Emphasis on effort and struggle

In Table 5, there are examples of the value of success in children's picture books.

Table 6. Wisdom value in children's picture books

Wisdom	Turkish	Translated
	Using thinking skills with the help of others	Demonstrate the ability to ask questions
	Self-criticism, being aware of her/his mistakes, inner settlement	Questioning

Table 6 shows the wisdom value of children's picture books.

Table 7. Tolerance value in children's picture books

Tolerance	Turkish	Translated
	-	Patience
	-	Acceptance
	-	Respect for different likes

In Table 7, there are cases where the children's picture books include tolerance value.

Table 8. Benevolence value in children's picture books

Benevolence	Turkish	Translated
	Helping	Asking Help
	Sharing	Helping animals
	Helping People	Helping People

Table 8 shows the benevolence value of children's picture books.

Tablo 9. The Happiness value in children's picture books

Happiness	Turkish	Translated
	Verbal expression of happiness	Reflection of happiness in behaviors
	Emotional awareness	Tips for happiness

Table 9 shows the happiness value of children's picture books.

Table 10. The courtesy value of children's picture books

Courtesy	Turkish	Translated
	Words of greeting and farewell	Expressing liking

Table 10 shows the courtesy value of children's picture books.

Table 11. Respect value in children's picture books

Respect	Turkish	Translated
	Refuse difference and regret	Respect, listen to the adult promises
	To see difference as a threat.	Embracing difference, emphasizing the positive aspects of difference.

In Table 11, there are cases where the children's picture books have the respect value.

Table 12. Love value in children's picture books

Love	Turkish	Translated
	Be aware of natural beauties and not to harm	Environmental problems, resources which are running out, protecting environment and saving
	Love words for animals	Damages to animals and animals' habitats
	Feeding cat, fish and bird	Feeding cat and dog
	Asking for reading, liking artists and works of art	Love of mother and sibling.

Table 12 shows the love value of children's picture books.

Table 13. Responsibility value in children's picture books

Responsibility	Turkish	Translated
	Division of labor	Division of labor
	Division of duties within the family	Reminding the tasks to the heroes
	Complaint from duty	Undertaking the consequence of behavior, regretting, trying to make up for the mistake

In Table 13, there are cases where the children's picture books have the responsibility value.

Wright [11] examined the books of moral education which were published in the recent years of 19th century and the beginning of 20th century. Within the scope of the research, moral texts, moral books, programs supporting moral education and bedside books used in moral education were examined. Ethical education is discussed from the values of obedience, patriotism and tolerance. The contents of the lessons were examined in the primary education programs and values tried to be given to children were stated as obedience, patriotism and tolerance values. The same values are mentioned in moral books. Although value of obedience is a common theme of ethical values, it is stated that there is no inclusive education for young people and children. It is stated that the value of tolerance is not included in the examined books; the value of patriotism is handled by many writers; tolerance value is frequently mentioned in the books. However, it was stated that only two authors included titles to cope with differences, differences and different thoughts. The results of the research are similar in terms of respect to differences with Wright's work. It is divided in terms of tolerance. This study also examined the value of respect for differences as a subcategory of respect value. In this study, there was less place for tolerance in books published between 2000-2007; it was found that domestic books did not include tolerance value. There are more places in the books published between 2000-2007 and in the domestic books for the respect for the differences; in translated books, and in books published in 2014, there was less place for respect for differences.

Gönen and Güler [12] studied 80 stories of story books published between 1995 and 2010, prepared for children between 2 and 12 years, in the research called as Environment and the Place of Environment in the picture storybooks. According to the results of the research, 80% of the books are the main theme for the environmental theme. The books contain 22.5% of the concepts related to environment and the terms of environment. The concepts related to the environment and the terms of environment have been found to be included in children's picture books over 6 years of age. Gönen and Güler have found that 80% is the main theme for the concept of environment. In this study, it was found that 81.33% of books in the sub-categories of environment and nature love were printed in 2014.he results of the research are similar with the study of Gönen and Güler in terms of the love of environment and nature which are subcategory of love value.

Akyol [13] examined the value contained in domestic and foreign children's picture books which are written in Turkish for pre-school children in Turkey. In the research which consists of a total of 250 children's books both Turkish and foreign, a check list developed by the researcher was used. In the control list, 24 values belonging to the categories of personal, interpersonal and social values are included. In the study it was found that the values of happiness, kindness, sensitivity, love, friendship, cooperation in the categories of personal and interpersonal values in children's picture books are high; the values of humility, sincerity, honesty, freedom, respect and harmony are low. The research results are similar in terms of love which has been mentioned the most to respect which has been mentioned the least. It differs in terms of the values of wisdom and tolerance the ones that in mentioned least. In this research, the values that are at least involved are the values of wisdom and tolerance.

Dirican [14] reviewed the picture story books published for children in the age group of 3-6 in terms of some basic values. In the study of 135 children's books written by Turkish authors by content analysis, it was found that the texts of the books had a value of 28.69% and the picture parts had a value of 53.04%.It is seen that in the text part, love, sharing, friendship, happiness and courtesy are the most common values; courage, leadership and peace are least mentioned values. It was found that in the division of values in picture books sharing, love, happiness, friendship and helpfulness are included most; respect, cleanliness, courtesy, empathy and diligence are included as in a middle level. In the text part, it is determined that love value is mentioned the most, in the picture part value of sharing is mentioned and value of peace is mentioned the least in both parts. When the results of the research are compared, it is mentioned that there is one-to-one correspondence in terms of value of love. In this study, love value was found to be mentioned the most. In this study, sharing, friendship, courtesy and happiness have been mentioned as well. The happiness value has been mostly included in domestic books published in 2014.Dirican has found that courage, peace and leadership values are mentioned at least. In this study, the values mentioned the least are the values of wisdom, tolerance and respect. In this study, The 28.69% value ratio found in the texts is similar to the 25.46% value published in books published in 2014. Another aspect of this study that distinguishes Dirican's work is in the books published between 2000-2007, the value ratio is 17.25%; the value ratio in domestic books is 54.99%.

Calışkan [15] studied the literary works of world literature on the list of 100 Basic Works selected by the Ministry of Education for primary school students in terms of value education. Respect for friendship, family, love, perseverance, diligence, personal development, compassion, benevolence, sacrifice, honesty, freedom, responsibility, justice, social ethics, solidarity, peace, equality, being against to injustice, missing, neighborliness, tolerance, apology, goodness, foresighted, austerity were found in works. The "love of nature" is mentioned as sub value of love in the determinations made. Within the value of friendship, non-identical species emphasize the strong bond between each other; it is stated that the family is described as an institution that continuously supports each other on the good and bad days that are supported in difficult times. The research results are similar in terms of friendship, love, diligence, helpfulness, responsibility, tolerance and goodness. Another similar aspect is that as a subcategory of love value, in this work, the value of environment and nature love has been determined as a value included in the books. Another similar aspect is the way in which friendship and family values are transferred. Family value was associated with the value of human love, which is the subcontract of love value in this study. In this study, it is seen that friendship is included as an imaginary friendship and the value of human love is included in translated books in terms of mother and sister love, and father love is not included. In the first years of life, mother's love may have been included in children's picture books because the children's basic needs are often met by their mother.

Gilmore and Howard [16] examined children's books in terms of supporting of diversity and disability. As a result of the research, 50 children's books are proposed to guide children from different ages and to develop respect and empathy for differences in children. In the study, the messages given in books are mentioned with examples. Some of these messages were stated as everyone is unique, some of them are weak spots and strong spots, and we do not need to compare ourselves with others. The research results are similar in terms of respect to differences through the work of Gilmore and Howard. This study also examined the value of respect for differences as a subcategory of respect value. It has been found that respect for differences was mentioned more in the books published between 2000-2007, and the domestic books. Studies that are similar in terms of mentioning about respect for differences however differs mentioning about the same value. In this study it has been determined that there are examples in the domestic books which may damage the value of respect for differences. The differences are not based on respect for differences attitudes, but on people who are aware of their mistake(s).

4 Conclusions

In children's picture books, values were mentioned less in books published between 2000-2007 (46.80%) and it was mentioned more in books published in 2014 (53.20%).In the children's picture books, the values were mentioned more in Turkish books (54.99%) and in translated books they were mentioned less (45.01%). Compared to the total number of sentences in the children's picture books published between 2000-2007, he total sentence rate of the value expressing sentences is 21.55%.Tolerance values are not included in the children's picture books published between 2000-2007.In the pictures of domestic children's books printed between the years of 2000-2007, the value of love was included in the sub-category of art love in maximum; at least in the category of animal love subcategory; it was found that the human love subcategory was not included. In the pictures of domestic children's books published between 2000-2007, there is no sub-category of sharing value of benevolence; was found to be included in the subcategory of helping.

Compared to the total number of sentences in the children’s picture books published between 2000-2007, the total sentence rate of the expressing values is 12.53%.Translated children's picture books published between 2000 and 2007 the love value was mentioned most and tolerance and responsibility values are mentioned at least. Values of happiness and respect were not included in the children's picture books published between 2000-2007.In the children's picture books published between 2000 and 2007, the value of love was included in the category of animal love in the sub category; there is a little space for the sub-category of human love; environment and nature love, book love and art love subcategories were not included.

Compared to the total number of sentences in the children's picture books published between 2000-2007. the total sentence rate of the expressing values is 17.25%. Children’s picture books published between the years 2000-2007 included the love value most land at least the value of tolerance. In the children's picture books published between 2000-2007, the value of love was included most in the category of animal love in the sub category of love; at least in the sub-category of human love was found. Compared to the total number of sentences in the books in the pictures of domestic children's books published in 2014, the total sentence rate of the expressing values is 20.78%.In the Turkish children's picture books published in 2014, the most mentioned value is love, the least value is wisdom, and the value of tolerance were not included. In the domestic children's picture books published in 2014, the value of love was mostly included in the sub-categories of environment and nature love; book love sub-category has been given little space; human love and art love subcategories were not included. In the children's picture books published in 2014, the value of wisdom was included in the sub-category self-criticism; criticism was not included in the sub-category; it was not included in sub-category of criticism.

Compared to the total number of sentences in the books in the translated children's picture books published in 2014, the total sentence rate of the expressing statements is 31.45%.In the children's picture books published in 2014, the value of love was mentioned at least and the value of tolerance and wisdom was not included. In the translated children's picture books published in 2014, the value of love was included most in animal love in the sub category; the value of love was mentioned at least in the sub-category of human love; book love and art love were not included in the subcategories.

Compared to the total number of sentences in books in children 's picture books published in 2014, the total sentence rate of the expressing values is 25.46%.In children's picture books published in the year 2014, the most mentioned value was love and at least the value of wisdom was included. In the children's picture books published in 2014, the value of love was included in the categories of animal love and environment and nature love subcategories; it has been determined that the love value was mentioned at least as a sub-category of human love. It has been determined that in domestic and translated children's picture books, there is a need to relate values in terms of availability. While the value of friendship is conveyed through negative examples in domestic books, there are positive examples of friendship in translated books. While the value of success is associated with division of tasks, artistic design and productivity in domestic books, translated books are associated with the value of effort, struggle and self-confidence. Tolerance in the translated books is conveyed with patience, acceptance and respect for different tastes and it is seen that the value of tolerance is not included in the domestic books. The value of benevolence is associated with sharing in domestic books, while translated books are associated with reluctantly help.

While the happiness value is conveyed through the acts and behaviors of the heroes in the translated books, it is conveyed in domestic children's books by expressing that heroes are happy. The value of courtesy is conveyed in domestic children's books mostly through words used during greetings and farewells, and in the translated children's books is conveyed by expressing likeness. Respect for differences, which are subcategories of respect, are conveyed through characters that embrace differences entirely in translated books and in the domestic books, conveyed through the characters that are disturbed by difference beforehand, and who recognize and regret the mistake afterwards.

Tolerance value should be included in children's picture books. It is thought that in the children's picture books, values of benevolence, respect and animal love should be mentioned more. The value of wisdom should be described in a way that includes the value of criticism. Children should see the heroes who question, not the heroes who obey unconditionally in books. The establishment of an independent committee or commission dedicated to the study of children's picture books can contribute to the achievement of children's books that are qualified and appropriate for their development. It is thought that it is better to explain about heroes in children's picture books in ways that do not damage their values, and to convey values through positive examples and with an idea of correct behavior.

References

1. TDK, (2018). Değer. http://www.tdk.gov.tr/index.php?option=com_yanlis&view=yanlis&kelimez=101 (23.07.2018)
2. Sapsağlam, Ö. (2016). Okul Öncesi Dönemde Karakter ve Değerler Eğitimi. Esra Ömeroğlu (Ed.), Ankara: Pegem Akademi.
3. Alpöge, G. (2011). *Okulöncesinde Değer Eğitimi* (4. Basım). Ankara: Bilgi Yayınevi.
4. Mills, C. (2016). Ethics and Children Literature. Claudia Mills (Ed.), *Ethics and Children Literature*. (p. 1-41). New York: Routledge.
5. Akbaş, O. (2008). Değerler Eğitimi Akımlarına Genel Bir Bakış. *Değerler Eğitimi Dergisi,* **6(16)**, 69-91.
6. Oktay, A. (1983). Türkiye'de Okul Öncesi Eğitimin Dünü ve Bugünü. *http://egitimvebilim.ted.org.tr/index.php/EB/article/view/5743 (Date of Access: 18.11.2017)*
7. Uyanık Balat, G. (2012). Okul Öncesinde Değerler Eğitimi. Gülden Uyanık Balat (Ed.), *Okul Öncesinde Değerler Eğitimi ve Etkinlik Örnekleri* (p. 2-33). Ankara: Pegem Akademi.
8. Kimmel, E. A. (1970). Can Children's Books Change Children's Values?. *Research In Review*. www.ascd.org/ASCD/pdf/journals/ed_lead/el_197011_kimmel.pdf can children's books change children's values (09.08.2017).
9. Erdal, K. (2009). Eğitim Değerleri Açısından Çocuk Kitapları. *Akademik Bakış*, **17**, 1-18.ISSN:1694-528X
10. Miles, M. B., Huberman, A. M. (2015). *Nitel Veri Analizi*. Ankara: Pegem Akademi.
11. Wright, S. (2009). Our Future Citizens: Values in Late Nineteenth And Early Twentieth Century Moral Instruction Books. His. of Edu. & Chil. Lit, **IV(1)**, 157-177.
12. Gönen, M., Güler, T. (2011). The Environment and Its Place in Children's Picture Story Books. Procedia Social and Behavioral Sciences, **15**(2011), 3633-3639.

13. Akyol, T. (2012). *Resimli çocuk kitaplarında yer alan değerlerin incelenmesi.* Yayınlanmış Yüksek Lisans Tezi, Hacettepe Üniversitesi Sosyal Bilimler Enstitüsü, Ankara.
14. Dirican, R. (2013). *3-6 Yaş Grubu Çocuklarına Yönelik Yayımlanan Resimli Hikâye Kitaplarının Bazı Temel Değerler Açısından İncelenmesi.* Yayınlanmış Yüksek Lisans Tezi, Gazi Üniversitesi, Ankara.
15. Çalışkan, A. (2016). *İlköğretim 100 Temel Eser İçerisinde Yer Alan Dünya Edebiyatına Ait Eserlerin Değerler Eğitimi Açısından İncelenmesi.* Yayınlanmış Yüksek Lisans Tezi. Necmettin Erbakan Üniversitesi Eğitim Bilimleri Enstitüsü, Konya.
16. Gilmore, L., Howard, G. (2016). Children's Books that Promote Understanding of Difference, Diversity and Disability. J. of Psych. and Coun. in Sch. **26(2)**, (218-251). doi 10.1017/jgc.2016.26

Research on the Fundamentals of Architectural Restoration Associate Degree Program

Ozlem Atalan[1,*]

[1]Manisa Celal Bayar University, Architectural Restoration Program, Kula Vocational School, Manisa, Turkey

Abstract. Today, the effects of globalization can be easily seen in many areas in the world. In the changing process, both Architectural education and side branches need various updates. The "Architectural Restoration Program", which is one of these branches of Architectural education, aims to provide to the sector "Technicians" and educates "Architect Candidates". The "Architectural Restoration Associate Degree Program" is a two year degree. In this context, the importance of this program's course curriculums is great. The Program is aimed to train qualified technical personnel for cultural assets that are common heritage of mankind which must be transferred to future generations. Program's graduates work in the laboratories, on the construction site and office, in the archaeological excavation, as a technical staff with architects. In this study, the relationship between "Architectural Education" and the basic objectives of the "Architectural Restoration Program" is examined. In this study, various Turkish and American universities' "Architectural Restoration Program" module details will be subject for a further examination and evaluation

1 Introduction

In the field of architecture and urbanization, the effects of globalization are affecting our historic cities [3]. Different courses and information are needed in both architectural education and education of side branches. The "Architectural Restoration Program", guiding the future of the historic cities, is an important program in the field of architecture sciences. This program educates architect candidates as well as bringing in technical engineers with two years of education. In this context, the importance of the curriculum that will be included in this program is great.

In Turkey, Architectural Restoration Program is located in the Vocational School. "Architecture and Urban Planning Departments" also provides training as an associate degree program. At the end of the Architectural Restoration program, students graduate with the title of "technician". In general, the aim of the Architectural Restoration Program is to educate qualified technical personnel for cultural assets that are a common heritage of mankind and must be passed on to future generations. Our aim is that after graduating from

* Corresponding author: oatalan@hotmail.com; ozlem.atalan@cbu.edu.tr

this program students will be able to work in the laboratories, on the construction sites, in the archaeological excavation teams, as a technical staff. Over the two years of training, the student will learn a large number of different field lessons.

Scope of research;

- Four situations (Associate Degree Programs Architectural Restoration) were examined in the Turkey and Worldwide.
- Basics of Architectural Undergraduate Education and Architectural Restoration Associate Education have been researched.
- Objectives to be achieved in the training of Architectural Restoration Programs are discussed.

2 Fundamental Points of Architectural Restoration Program

Architectural restoration programs offer academic curriculum that ranges from restoration methods and conservation theory to courses designed to allow students to learn various trades used in preserving historical heritage. Techniques learned in the class and the field labs are then practiced on real preservation projects.

These programs are aimed to teach students the basic professional acquisitions that are used to preserve and restore historic heritages. Architectural Restoration Program's outcomes are to have a thorough understanding of historic preservation theory and be able to apply that theory in real life situations. Moreover, at the end of the program students will be able to understand the materials and the basic concepts behind the techniques used in the conservation of historic buildings and will be able to carry out those methods when necessary. Graduates of this program will be capable to work successfully in the business environment, develop an effective work ethic and make quality workmanship.

The title of Architectural Restoration Technician requires some technical skills. Graduated students can draw in both modern and traditional architecture. Graduated students can take part in the restoration and restitution projects and applications. They will be able to support the architect and engineer in need. In other words, they will contribute to the field of architecture.

Architecture; Due to its close relationship with technology, engineering, science and art, and because it has many disciplines, it needs a common language. In architecture this language is drawings. It is necessary to know this language both in the field of architecture and in the Architectural Restoration Associate Degree Program. The most important courses that develop the language of drawing in Architecture, Interior Architecture, Planning and Design fields are the courses called "Technical Drawing, Perspective, Space Geometry and Design Geometry. The architectural restoration associate degree program consists of four semesters.

Two-year architectural restoration programs are similar in terms of course content and programs. However, in some universities, the "workplace practice internship", which has become widespread in recent years, has entered the curriculum. There are about six fields in the program.

(1) Construction Courses (Theoretical and Practical): Traditional Construction Technique, Structure, Building Material and Details, etc.

(2) Drawing Courses (Theoretical and Practical): Technical Drawing and Computer Aided Design, etc.

(3) Conservation and Restoration (Theoretical): Historical Sites, Cultural Heritages, Restoration and Conservation, etc.

(4) History Courses (Theoretical): Art, Architecture and Civilization History, etc.

(5) Conservation and Restoration (Theoretical and Practical) Courses: Building Conservation Technique, etc.

(6) Others Courses: Mathematics, Chemistry, Language, etc.

2.1 Construction courses (theoretical and practical): Traditional construction technique, structure, building material and details, etc.

Explanation of building techniques in Turkish Architecture has been made by examining and drawing civil and monumental constructions. Monumental and civil structures inform about historical and traditional construction systems and building elements. These structures are demonstrated to the students. Traditional wood, carcass and masonry construction systems, materials and structural systems are taught. Additionally, drawing of plans, sections, facades and details of these constructions is taught. Introductions of building materials and application information are taught to the students. Doors, windows, etc and their decorative details are introduced to the students. These building elements are taught drawing.

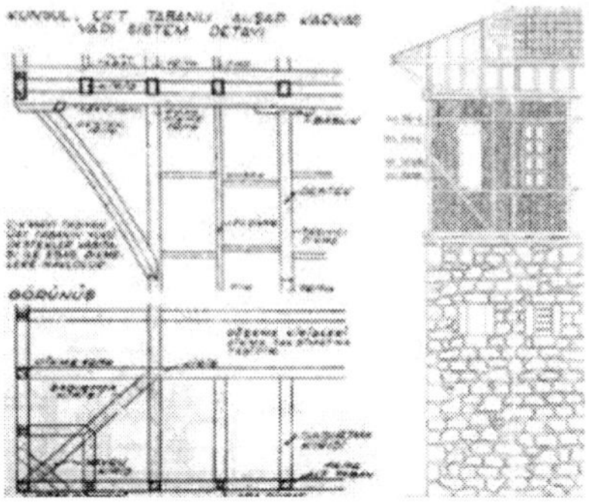

Fig. 1. Traditional Turkish House drawings, details and section [4, 5]

2.2 Drawing courses (theoretical and practical): Technical drawing and computer aided design, etc.

The technical drawing is a language using special lines and symbols. It provides a common language and a communication between architects, engineers and other technical staff.

In this respect, it is necessary that every technical person who will take part in the production has learned the technical drawing rules and methods. Nonetheless, technical drawings, facilitates mutual understanding and ensures regular production [2]. In these lectures, drawing tools, basic drawing techniques and architectural project drawings are taught theoretically and practically. Having said that, the program seeks to introduce the leading computer aided drawing programs and to teach computer usage during the architectural and restoration drawing.

2.3 Conservation and restoration (theoretical): Historical sites, cultural heritages, restoration and conservation, etc.

The importance of environmental protection in the word, its definition, development process and legislation of conservation are taught in these courses. By introducing rural heritage, traditional heritage and archaeological heritage, contemporary problems are evaluated. Cultural assets in national and international scale, factors causing deterioration in monuments, types of deterioration are taught. During the restoration work, before and after the completion of the work phases, the principles of intervention for protection are exemplified.

Measurement techniques are taught theoretically and practically in the courses. Students, separated into groups, are asked to measure the historical monuments or the heritages. Drawings were made in scale. That said, students are taught restitution and restoration projects and preparation techniques.

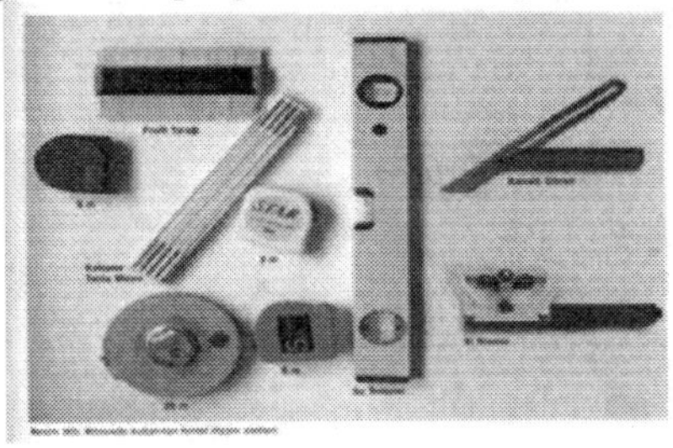

Fig. 2. Basic Measuring Tools [1]

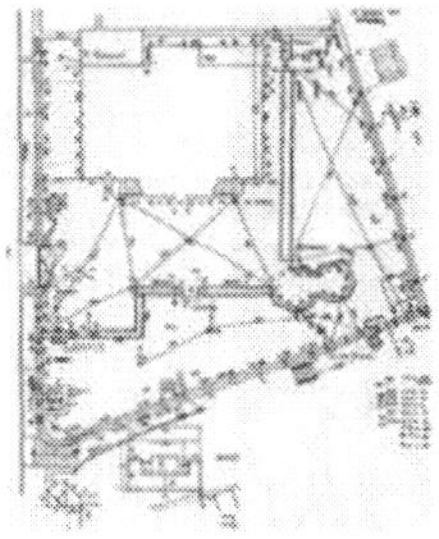

Fig. 3. Measurement Drawings [1].

2.4 History courses (theoretical): Art, architecture and civilization history, etc.

In these lectures, the developments of styles, architecture and urban planning related to Islam and later are explained from prehistoric times. European and Western civilization, architectural and urban planning progress is explained.

Monumental and civil architectural heritages; architectural plan and facades schemes, usage typology, material, construction technique are examined. Archaeological heritages, Ottoman architecture, European, World architecture, their development processes and features are explained.

2.5 Conservation and restoration (theoretical and practical): Building conservation technique, etc.

In these lessons, firstly the traditional production techniques are explained. Conservation methods, terracotta works, glass and metal works are taught. The principles and methods to be followed in conservation and restoration of cultural assets are informed. The program includes theoretical and practical courses such as "stone and metal technology", "mosaic construction techniques", architectural ornament and repair", "stone and facade cleaning", "conservation and restoration methods".

2.6 Others Courses

All courses in this area improve the professional competences of students and at the same time courses contribute to the general cultural knowledge of the student. All samples were evaluated using AKTS rate.

3 Architectural restoration programs examples in Turkey

3.1 Example 1: Yildiz Technical University, National Palaces and Historical Buildings Vocational School, Architectural Restoration Program, Istanbul, Turkey

The purpose of the Architectural Restoration Program is to provide vocational education on national and international criteria in Yildiz Technical University. The program trains technicians to work in architectural protection and renovation works of palace, pavilion and historical monuments [9].The lecture list of this program is given below.

Courses (AKTS):

1.st Semester: Ornamentation on Traditional Buildings (3), Materials of Traditional Buildings (3), Theory of Conservation (5), Technical Drawing, (5), History of Art and Civilization (4), Computer 1 (3)

2.nd Semester: Elective 1 (4), Elective 2 (4), Internship 1 (3), Computer (3), Documentation with Photography (2), Degradation Reasons and Conservation Methods on Traditional Buildings (2), History of Architecture 1 (2), Survey (4)

3. rd Semester: Elective 3 (3), Elective 4 (3), Elective 5 (4), Conservation 1 (3), Restoration Chemistry 1 (3), Metal Material on Traditional Building (2) , Research, Measuring and Documentation (2), History of Architecture 2 (2) , Restoration Project 1 (8)

4. th Semester: Elective 6 (4), Elective 7 (4), Elective 8 (4), Internship 2 (3) , Restoration Project 1 (9) , Conservation 2 (3) , Restoration Chemistry 2 (3)

Elective Courses 1 (4): Traditional Buildings and Interior Analysis, Traditional Buildings and Facade Analysis.

Elective Courses 2 (4 AKTS): Traditional Pattern Techniques, Materials of Traditional Buildings 2.

Elective Courses 3 (4 AKTS): Timber and Building Technology (4), Masonry and Building Technology, Wall, Floor and Ceiling Design of Traditional Building, Doors and Windows on Traditional Buildings.

Elective Courses 4 (4 AKTS):Degradation Reasons and Conservation Methods on Wooden Buildings, Degradation Reasons and Conservation Methods on Masonry Buildings, Degradation Reasons and Conservation Methods of Wall Surfaces.

Elective Courses 5 (4 AKTS): Wooden Ornamentation Techniques, Masonry Ornamentation Techniques, Degradation Reasons and Conservation Methods of Doors and Windows.

Elective Courses 6-7-8 (4 AKTS): Workshop of Timber, Workshop of Stone, Workshop of Furniture, Workshop of Metal, Workshop of Engraving, Workshop of Painting , Workshop of Textile [9].

3.2 Example 2: Mimar Sinan Fine Art University, Architectural Restoration Program, Vocational School, Istanbul, Turkey

Mimar Sinan Fine Art University, Vocational School educates technical staff to prepare the restoration, restitution and restoration projects of old buildings in the country. The Architectural Restoration Program, which was established to train qualified personnel who will take part in restoration workshops of the constructions, practice lessons as well as theoretical training [8].

Courses (AKTS):

1.st Semester: Cost Estimation (3), Technical Drawing 1 (4), Systems and Elements of Traditional Construction 1 (3), Measured Drawings 1 (4). Finishing Materials 1 (3), Technical Drawings 1 (4), Immovable Culture Monuments (3)

2.nd Semester: Systems and Elements of Traditional Construction 2 (3), Technical Drawing 1 (4), Internship (6), Finishing Materials 2 (3), Measured Drawings 2 (4)

3. rd Semester: Introduction To Restoration Techniques (3), Fine Arts I (3), Building Materials 1 (4), Computer Aided Design 1 (3), Techniques of Ornamentation and Restoration (3)

4. th Semester: Fine Arts 2 (3), Introduction To Restoration Projects (4), Building Materials 2 (3), Computer Aided Design 2 (3), Pattern Making in Turkish Ornaments (3).

Elective Courses (AKTS): Use of Metal and Conservation Methods (3), Use of Photography in Measured Drawings (3), Mosaics: Construction Techniques, Courses Of Deterioration, Methods Of Preservation Of Restoration (3), Reading in Ottoman Language (3), Model, Practices of Natural Stone and Conservation Methods (3) , Use of Photography in Measured Drawings (3), Glossary of Traditional Architecture (3), Late Period of Ottoman Architecture (3), Use of Wood and Conservation Methods (3), Late Period of Surface Painting Practices (3), Material Problems in Historical Buildings (3), Measured Drawings 3, Professional Practice (3), Use of Metal in Historical Buildings and Conservation Methods (3), Use of Photography in Measured Drawings (3), Mosaics: Construction Techniques (3), Courses Of Deterioration, Methods Of Preservation Of Restoration (3), Reading in Ottoman Language (3), Construction Details of Historical Buildings (3)

Table 1. Architectural restoration program's branches of courses (Example 1)

Architectural Restoration Program's Branches of Courses (Theoretical And Practical Education, AKTS)				
Construction Courses (Theoretical And Practical Education)	**Technical Graphic Drawing and Computer Aided Design Courses** (Theoretical And Practical Education)	**Historical Sites, Cultural Heritages, Building Conservation, Restoration Project, Survey, Courses** (Theoretical And Practical Education)	**History of Architecture/Art /Civilization** (Theoretical)	**Building Conservation and Traditional Construction Techniques, (Lab, Atelier, Workshops)** Theoretical And Practical Education)
(1)	**(2)**	**(3)**	**(4)**	**(5)**
Materials of Traditional Buildings (3), Materials Details (3), , Traditional Buildings and Interior Analysis (4), Traditional Buildings and Facade Analysis (4), Materials of Traditional Buildings 2 (4). Wall, Floor and Ceiling Design of Traditional Building (4), Doors and Windows on Traditional Buildings (4),	Technical Drawing, (5), Computer 1 (3) Computer 2 (3)	Theory of Conservation(5), Survey (4) Documentation with Photography (2), Degradation Reasons and Conservation Methods on Traditional Buildings (2), Research, Measuring and Documentation (2), Restoration Project 1 (8),	History of Art and Civilization (4) History of Architecture 1 (2), , History of Architecture 2 (2)	Ornamentation on Traditional Buildings (3), Internship 1 (3), Metal Material on Traditional Building (2) , Internship 2 (3) , Restoration Chemistry 2 (3) Conservation 1 (3) Conservation 2 (3) Timber and Building Technology (4), Masonry and Building Technology (4), Degradation Reasons and Conservation Methods on Wooden Buildings (wood) (4), Degradation Reasons and Conservation Methods on Masonry Buildings (Masonry) (4), Degradation Reasons and Conservation Methods of Wall Surfaces (4), Wooden Ornamentation Techniques), Masonry Ornamentation Techniques (4), Degradation Reasons and Conservation Methods of Doors and Windows (4), Workshop of Timber(4), Workshop of Stone(4), Workshop of Furniture(4), Workshop of Metal(4), Workshop of Engraving(4), Workshop of Painting(4), Workshop of Textile(4)

Table 2. Architectural restoration program's courses (Example 2)

Compulsory And Elective Courses (Theoretical And Practical Education, AKTS)				
(1) ↓	(2) ↓	(3) ↓	(4) ↓	(5) ↓
Estimation (3), Systems and Elements of Traditional Construction 1 (3), Finishing Materials 1 (3), Systems and Elements of Traditional Construction 2 (3), Finishing Materials 2 (3), Building Materials 1 (4), Building Materials 2 (4), Construction Details of Historical Buildings (3)	Technical Drawing 1 (4), Technical Drawings 2 (4), Computer Aided Design 1 (3), Computer Aided Design 2 (3),	Measured Drawings 1 (4), Immovable Culture Monuments (3) Measured Drawings 2 (4) Introduction To Restoration Techniques (3), Use of Photography in Measured Drawings (3), Mosaics: Construction Techniques, Courses Of Deterioration, Methods Of Preservation Of Restoration (3), Glossary of Traditional Architecture (3), Measured Drawings 3,	Fine Arts I (3), Reading in Ottoman Languag e (3), Late Period of Ottoman Architect ure (3	Internship (6), Pattern Making in Turkish Ornaments (3), Use of Metal and Conservation Methods (3), Mosaics: Construction Techniques, Courses Of Deterioration, Methods Of Preservation Of Restoration (3), Practices of Natural Stone and Conservation Methods (3) , Model (3), Use of Wood and Conservation Methods (3), Late Period of Surface Painting Practices (3), Material Problems in Historical Buildings (3), Professional Practice (3), Use of Metal in Historical Buildings and Conservation Methods (3), Mosaics: Construction Techniques (3), Courses Of Deterioration, Methods Of Preservation Of Restoration (3)

4 Architectural restoration programs examples in the World

The Architectural Restoration Program is located in many universities and colleges around the world. It takes 2 years (4 semesters). Graduates may tend towards various branches such as "*Architect, Blacksmith, Carpenter, Curator, Decorative Painter, Economic Development Specialist, Grant developer or Manager, Heritage Tourism Specialist, Historian, Historic Site Supervisor, Mason, Materials Conservator, Museum Administrator, National Park Service Specialist, Plasterer, Preservation Consultant, Preservation Contractor, Preservation Design Consultant, Restoration Artisan, Stained Glass Artisan, Compliance Specialist, State Historic Preservation Office Specialist*" and continue their education.

Architectural Restoration Associate Degrees are located in universities and colleges in America. Below is "Belmont College" and "Clatsop Community College"s "The Building Preservation /Restoration Program". It appears that the programs consist of 4 semesters.

These colleges provide an affordable way for students to transfer to a four-year college and a bachelor's degree. Many students complete the first two years of their bachelor's degree at these colleges and then transfer to a four-year-school to finish. A typical choice is to get an Associate of Arts or an Associate of Science degree [6,7].

4.1. Example 3: Belmount College The Building Preservation/Restoration Program, Cadiz, OH, USA (Associate of Applied Science Degree)

Education offers a foundation in preservation theory and history together with an in-depth technical analysis of why buildings and materials fail and explores traditional and modern approaches used to repair cultural heritages. Students have the chance to apply their theoretical course knowledge in though workshops in order to learn the fundamentals of restoration technique. Students also practice the techniques learned in the workshops on real-world preservation projects. Students work on the department's own historic field lab house and completing community based projects [6].

Picture 1. The Building Preservation/Restoration Program Education [6]

Courses (AKTS):

1.st Semester: Introduction to Historic Preservation (3), Architectural Drafting and Design (3), Materials and Methods of Construction (3), Composition 1, History of American Architecture 1

2.nd Semester: Historic Research and Documentation (2), History of American Architecture 2 (3), Restricted Elective(3), Material Science Elective(3), Math Elective(3)

Summer Term: Field Lab Community Service (1), Material Science Elective (3)

3. rd Semester: Building Pathology (4), Speech (3), Field Lab. (1), Material Science Elective (3), Social Science Elective (3)

4.th Semester: Construction Management and Estimating (3), Chemistry for Conservation(3), Field Lab. (1), Material Science Elective (3), Social Science Elective (3), Restricted Elective (3) Summer Term: Capstone (2)

Restricted Elective: Mechanical Systems (3), Windows and Doors (3), Roofing and Flooring (3), Specials Problems 1 (3), Directed Studies 1 (3)

Materials Science Electives: Decorative Finishes (3), Masonry and Ceramics (3), Plaster and Composition (3), Metals (3), Stained Glass (3)

4.2. Example 4: Clatsop Community College, Astoria, Oregon, USA (Associate of Applied Science Degree)

Students learn function and performance characteristics of historic building materials, methods and sequence. Both modern and historic materials are examined. Students study tools and techniques for sketching and drafting for architecture, and improve communication skills for construction and restoration projects. They improve skills to document historic heritages and survey measured drawings [7].

Courses (AKTS):

1.st Semester: Introduction to Historic Preservation (2), Construction Math (2), : Construction Safety for Historic Preservation (1), Printreading for Construction (3),

Computer Aided Design 1 (4), Workshop: Wood Window Replication (2), Beginning Stone Masonry (1), Plaster Repair (2)

2.nd Semester: Project Management (3), Historic Preservation 1 (3), Computer Aided Design 1 (4), Printreading for Construction (3). Workshops: Facade Restoration (2) , Fundamentals of Woodworking (2) , Faux Finish Techniques (1)

3.rd Semester: Residential Materials & Method (3), s, Construction Drawing (3), Computer Aided Design 2 (3), Computer Graphics (3), Workshop: Wood Window Restoration, Decorative Glass Glue Chipping, Plaster Repair

4.nd Semester: History of Pacific Northwest (3), Computer Aided Design 3 (4), Computer Graphics 2 (4), Historic Preservation Project (4), Workshops: Dry Stack Masonry (3), Monument Restoration (2)

Selected Work Shop Courses: Blacksmithing, Building Documentation, Column Restoration, Dry Stack Masonry, Deck Reconstruction, Documentation & Deconstruction, Door Analysis, Door Reconstruction, Facade Restoration, Faux Finish, Floor Framing, Historic Glass, Millwork, Ornamental Plaster, Plaster, Porch Restoration Roof Restoration, Stained Glass, Stair Layout, Window Restoration, Woodwork Restoration [7].

Picture 2. National Register Of Historic Places, 1984 [7]
Picture 3. Historic Glue Chipped Glass Sign [7].

Students work on historic Alderbrook Hall which is an early 20th Century Pacific-Northwest Bungalow Style fire station. Other building is Doughboy Monument which is National Register of Historic Places [7].

Table 3. Architectural restoration program's courses (Example 3)

Compulsory And Elective Courses (Theoretical And Practical Education, AKTS)				
(1) ↓	**(2)** ↓	**(3)** ↓	**(4)** ↓	**(5)** ↓
Materials and Methods of Construction (3), Construction Management and Estimating (3), Mechanical Systems (3), Windows and Doors (3), Roofing and Flooring (3), Specials Problems 1 (3), Decorative Finishes (3)	Architectural Drafting and Design (3), Composition 1,	Introduction to Historic Preservation (3), Historic Research and Documentation (2)	History of American Architecture 1 (3), History of American Architecture 2 (3)	Field Lab Community Service (1), Building Pathology (4), Field Lab. (1), Chemistry for Conservation(3), Field Lab. (1), Capstone (2) Directed Studies 1 (3) Masonry and Ceramics (3), Plaster and Composition (3), Metals (3), Stained Glass (3)

Table 4. Architectural restoration program's courses (Example 4)

Compulsory and Elective Courses (Theoretical And Practical Education, AKTS)				
1 ↓	2 ↓	3 ↓	4 ↓	5 ↓
Project Management (3), Residential Materials & Methods (3), Printreading for Construction (3).	Construction Drawing (3), Computer Aided Design 1 (4), Computer Graphics 1 (4), Computer Aided Design 2 (4), Computer Aided Design 3 (4), Computer Graphics II (3)	Introduction to Historic Preservation Historic Preservation 1 (3), Historic Preservation Project(4)	History of Pacific Northwest (3)	Dry Stack Masonry (3), Monument Restoration (2) , Fundamentals of Woodworking (2) , Faux Finish (1) Techniques, Facade Restoration (2), Wood Window Restoration (3), Decorative Glass Glue Chipping(2), Plaster Repair (2), Workshop: Dry Stack Masonry, Blacksmithing, Building Documentation, Column Restoration, Deck Reconstruction, Documentation & Deconstruction, Door Analysis, Door Reconstruction, Facade Restoration, Faux Finish, Floor Framing, Historic Glass, Millwork, Ornamental Plaster, Plaster, Porch Restoration Roof Restoration, Stained Glass, Stair Layout, Window Restoration, Woodwork Restoration

5 Conclusions

It is undeniable that today's constructions are produced with an understanding that does not match the structural and spatial character of the traditional architecture of our country. At the same time, traditional building trades and crafts professions are disappearing. Technicians cannot be found in restoration construction. In this context, Architectural Restoration Associate Degree schools are important for the protection of our Cultural Heritages.

Since the graduates of this program work as technicians with the architects and the civil engineers, courses and internships given within this program are very important. In addition, learning to apply from local building masters will contribute to the maintenance of the disappearing professions. Traditional building craftsmen will be educated. At the same time, courses and the scope of the program are important because students who want to continue their academic career can pass to the Architecture or Interior Architecture (etc.) departments of their university.

Within the scope of the study, courses of the architectural restoration program have been researched. Courses required for the development of the "Architectural Restoration Associate Degree Program" have been examined. It is observed that curriculum includes "*Drawing Courses, Building Constructions Courses, Conservation Technique Courses, History of Civilization- Art- Architecture Courses And Historical Heritages Courses*" in the curriculum. Notwithstanding, in some universities, the internship lasts for one semester, while in some universities it is done as a summer internship. It is observed that the courses in *"Preservation, Restoration, Technical Conservation and Methods"* often take place in the curriculum in the Architectural Restoration Associate Degree Programs. However, it seems that the number of courses related to the *"History of Architecture", "History of Art", and "History of Civilization*" should be increased in the curriculums of the programs.

It is important to understand the value of Cultural Heritages in order to develop conservation methods. Students studying in the Architectural Restoration Programs of the universities will guide the future of the architecture. In order to protect the Cultural

Heritage and to deliver it to the future generations, this education should be given to the students in a comprehensive way. Architectural Restoration Programs vary from different models and traditions. All programs are designed to have a similar infrastructure for the education of the students. However, one must not forget the difference of local cultures. For this reason, information on preservation of Cultural Heritage and knowledge on Architecture, Art and Civilization history is important in Architectural Restoration Associate education. In addition, with detailed drawing, theoretical and practical courses, workshops to be given in Architectural Restoration Programs, students will be successful "*technical staff*" in the historic buildings restorations or etc.

References

1. B. Uluengin, Rölöve. Yem Kitabevi, (2005).
2. D.E. Bilgiç, N. Konak, *Tasarı Geometri, Teknik Resim Ve Perspektif Derslerinin Mimarlık Eğitimi Ve Düşünsel Altyapısına Etkisi Ve Prof. Dr. Yılmaz MORÇÖL*, Mimarlık ve Yaşam Dergisi, Cilt:1 No:1, 2016(1-12).
3. D.Kuban, Tarihi Çevre Korumanın Mimarlık Boyutu. Yem Kitabevi, İstanbul, (2000)
4. M. Soygeniş, Yapı 2-3-4, Birsen yayınevi, İstanbul, (2000, 2002, 2003)
5. S. H. Eldem, Yapı 1, Birsen yayınevi, İstanbul, (2000)
6. URL. http://www.belmontcollege.edu/current-students/programs-of-study/building-preservationrestoration/
7. URL. https://www.clatsopcc.edu/preservation
8. URL. http://www.msgsu.edu.tr/tr-TR/mimari-restorasyon-programi/419/Page.aspx
9. URL . http://www.mst.yildiz.edu.tr/

The Analysis of Pre-service Math Teachers' Level of Understanding the Derivative Concept within the Context of APOS Theory

Selin Urhan[1,*], and *Şenol* Dost[2]

[1]Hacettepe University, Department of Mathematics and Science Education, Ankara, Türkiye
[2]Hacettepe University, Department of Mathematics and Science Education, Ankara, Türkiye

Abstract. APOS (Action-Process-Object-Schema) learning theory is the result of the studies of a mathematics education research group named Research in Undergraduate Mathematics Education Community (RUMEC), whose aim is to examine students' level of comprehending university mathematics subjects. This study aimed to investigate how secondary mathematics education pre-service teachers in a public university structured the geometric dimension of the concept of derivative in their minds in the context of the components of the APOS theory. As data collection tools, questions developed by Çekmez [1] based on the genetic decomposition of Asiala, Dubinsky, Cottrill and Schwingendorf [2] for the geometric dimension of derivatives were used. The study revealed that secondary mathematics education pre-service teachers did not have the mental structures related to this topic and could not learn it at the desired level.

Keywords: APOS theory, derivative concept, preservice math teachers.

1 Introduction

Among the topics of analysis, the richest concept in terms of geometric and graphical representations is the concept of derivative. Researchers have reported that students have difficulty relating the geometric dimension to the algebraic dimension of the concept of derivative [1, 2], and insufficient at analyzing the graphs and understanding the conceptual basis of the slope of the tangent line [3, 4]. In order for students to comprehend the concept of derivative at the desired level, it is first necessary for them to establish a good level understanding of the geometric dimension of the derivative [1, 5, 6].

The APOS theory developed based on understanding the concepts in mathematics is a theory Dubinsky put forward drawing on Jean Piaget's theory of reflective abstraction [7, 8]. The APOS theory analyzes the mental structures of an individual when a mathematical concept is being learned. In this way, it is possible to analyze the level of conceptual understanding of students about a concept [9, 10, 11].

* Corresponding author: selin.urhan@hacettepe.edu.tr

The APOS theory is composed of action, process, object and schema mental structures, and mental mechanisms such as interiorization, encapsulation, de-encapsulation, and thematization. Action is the external transformation of a concept. At this stage, the individual needs to think in each step of transformation and to be guided by an external stimulus. By repeating the actions over time, the individual starts not needing the external stimuli and has internal control over the actions (interiorization). This means that the individual does not have to think about every single step and can skip some steps, which shows that he is in the process stage of understanding a concept [12].

If the individual is aware of the process as a whole, he comprehends that transformations can affect a whole and that transformations can be structured. In this case, the individual encapsulates the process and turns it into a mental object. When a process is encapsulated into an object, it can be de-encapsulated as needed and it would be possible to return to the process. The schema is the structure involving the definitions, organization, and examples of mental structures that an individual builds on mathematical concepts. In the APOS theory, genetic decomposition is a hypothetical model for describing these mental structures and mechanisms that a student may need to learn mathematical concepts [7].

In his doctorate study, Çekmez [1] examined the effect of using dynamic mathematics software on comprehension level of the elementary mathematics pre-service teachers of the geometric dimension of derivative using the APOS theory. Genetic decomposition put forward for the geometric dimension of the derivative concept by Asiala et al. [2], was used to determine the structures students will constitute about the geometric dimension of the derivative concept in their minds.

This study aims to examine how secondary mathematics education pre-service teachers structured the geometric dimension of the concept of derivative in their minds within the framework of the APOS theory.

2 Method

This study was carried out with 33 fifth grade students who were studying in the department of secondary mathematics education of a public university during the 2015-2016 spring term.

Of the questions about the geometric dimension of the derivative concept developed by Çekmez [1] based on the genetic decomposition of Asiala et al. [2], two questions that are appropriate to the mental structures of action, process, and object were used to collect data. The schema is evaluated within the context of the results given to the questions at the level of action, process and object, since it is a mental map involving the definitions and organization of all the mental structures that the individual builds on a mathematical concept.

The questions were applied in a single session in a quiet classroom environment on a day and at a time when all participants could attend. Unlimited time was given to the participants. They were asked to explain their thinking process and the steps they have taken in the documents in which they conveyed the solution process.

The solution processes participants produced for the questions were evaluated according to the rubrics prepared by Çekmez [1] as seen in Table 1.

Table 1. Coding table

0 (Incorrect)	1 (Partially Correct)	2 (Correct)
Giving the wrong answer or not answering the question.	Doing some of the steps the question requires, or not being able to reach the exact answer.	Doing the question correctly.

In addition to the solution processes, the written discourses of students through which they conveyed their thinking processes were included in the analysis and these discourses were used to clarify the analysis results of the solution processes. Expert opinion was obtained during the analysis of the data and the evaluation of the results.

3 Findings and discussion

Of the two questions prepared in accordance with the mental structures of action, process and object, a question providing rich data appropriate to the purpose of study was selected. In this section, findings and results related to this question are presented.

3.1 Findings regarding the question at the action level

Figure 1 depicts the question prepared at the level of action to understand the geometric dimension of the derivative.

The graph of $y = f(x)$ function was given in the figure.
Order the $f'(1), f'(2), f'(3), f'(4), f'(5), f'(6), f'(7)$ values in descending order.

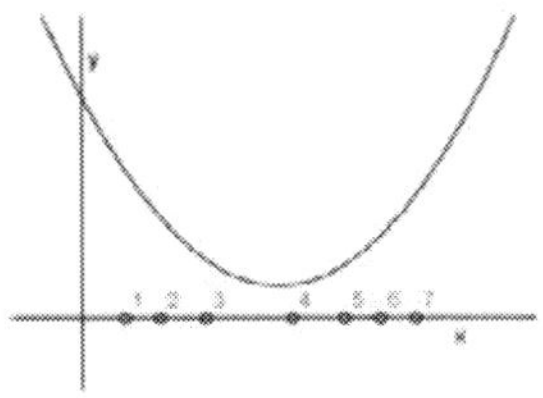

Fig. 1. The question at the level of action

The distribution of the scores students received from this question is given in Table 2.

Table 2. The distribution of scores for the question at the action level

	0	1	2
Frequency Values	4	6	23
Percentage Values	12	18	70

Twenty-eight students did not need an algebraic expression of the function; they were able to see the derivative value of a function at a point as the slope of the tangent line plotted on its graph on that point. An example of this situation is given in Figure 2. It is seen that the student solved the question correctly and conveyed his thinking process in accordance with the communication norms in mathematics.

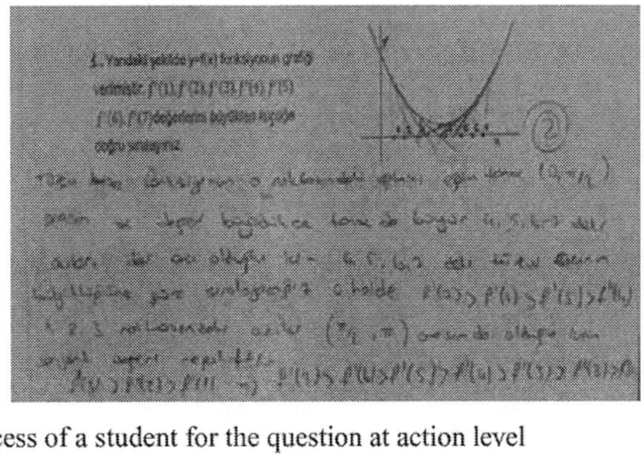

Fig. 2. The solution process of a student for the question at action level

It was observed that some of the students had some deficiencies in the preliminary knowledge they should have before forming a scheme for the derivative concept. For example, some students had difficulty making a "graphical representation of the line to include the concept of slope". An example of this situation is given in Figure 3.

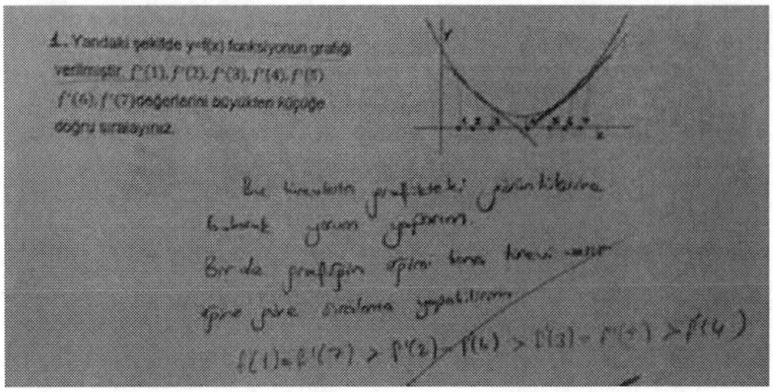

Fig. 3. The solution process of a student for the question at action level

It is seen that the student who uses a mathematically insignificant expression of "The slope of the graph gives me the derivative; I can make an order based on slope" evaluates the derivative value of the function at the given points as an image at those points. The inability of students to form the relation between the derivative value of a function at a point and the slope of the tangent curve drawn on a graph of function at that point was also revealed by Ubuz [13].

3.2 Findings regarding the question at the process level

The question prepared at the process level is given in Figure 4 to comprehend the geometric dimension of the derivative.

In the figures, the graphs of the first $y = f'(x)$ and second $y = f''(x)$ order derivative functions of the function $y = f(x)$ were given. Based on these two graphs, which of the function graphs below represent the $y = f(x)$ function best? Put a tick (√) in the parenthesis ( ) above the graph you choose.

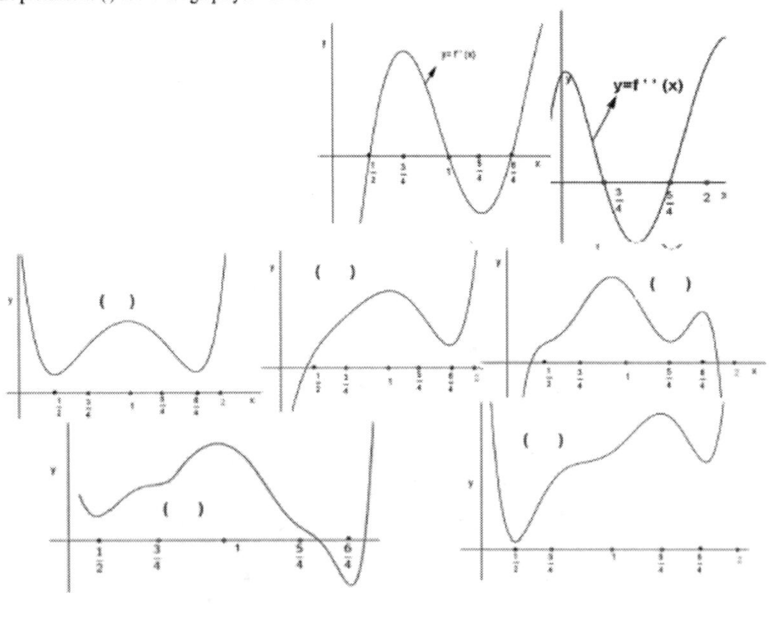

Fig. 4. The question at the process level

The distribution of the scores students received from this question is given in Table 3.

Table 3. The score distribution for the question at the process level

	0	1	2
Frequency values	8	0	25
Percentage values	25	0	75

It was seen that students who answered the question correctly could relate the graph of the first derivative and the second derivative of the function to its own graph. An example of this situation is given in Figure 5.

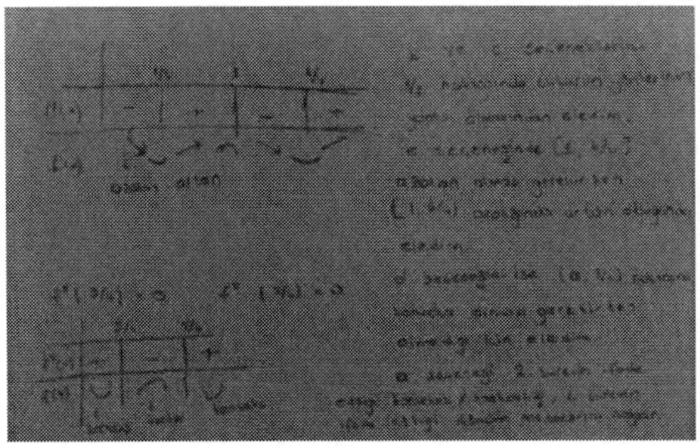

Fig. 5. The solution process of a student for the question at process level

The student who finds out that the function is increasing and decreasing using the points where first derivative graph of the function intersects the x-axis and sign diagram also determines the intervals where the function is convex and concave using the points where the second derivative graph intersects the x-axis and sign diagram.

It was noted that some students had incomplete knowledge about the relationship between the first and second derivative function of a function and itself. Figure 6 shows an example of this situation.

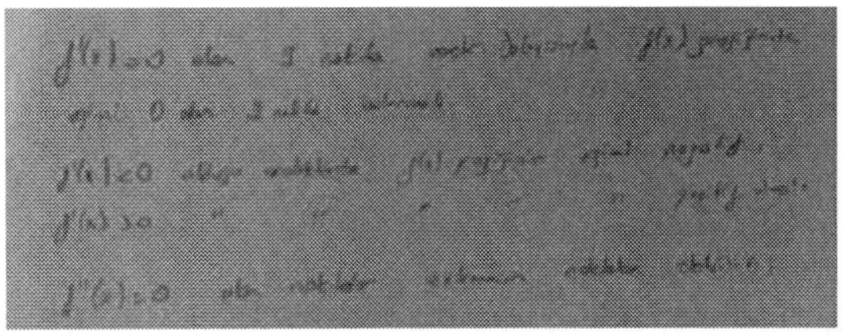

Fig. 6. The solution process of a student for the question at process level

This student only finds the x values that are the zeros of the first derivative and second derivative function of a function and does not make a sign table for derivative functions. This suggests that the student had a lack of knowledge about determining the ranges in which a function is increasing-decreasing and convex-concave. Similar to this finding, Çetin [14] also found that university students could not establish the relationship between a function and the derivation of this function.

Another student went through an invalid solution process as a result of his incorrect knowledge. The solution process of this student is shown in Figure 7.

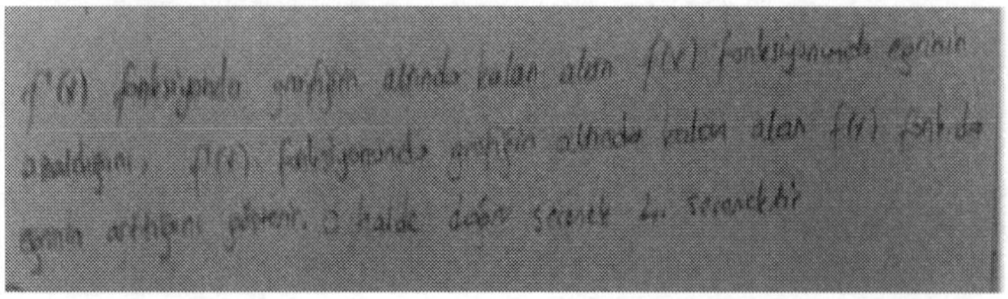

Fig. 7. The solution process of the student

The student's association of the increasing-decreasing state of the function with the area under the graph of the first derivative function indicates that he had incorrect knowledge. The expressions written by the student with incorrect and incomplete knowledge are invalid.

3.3 Findings regarding the question at the object level

Figure 8 depicts the question prepared at the object level to comprehend the geometric dimension of the derivative.

It is known that $y = f(x)$ is a function and $\lim_{x\to1}\frac{f(x)-f(1)}{x-1} = 3$. When $\varepsilon = \frac{1}{2}$ within the definition of limit, what is the biggest δ value that corresponds to this ε variable?

Which of the following is the statement above equivalent to? Put a tick (√) next to the item or items you believe is/are equivalent.

i) How far the variable x could be to the value 1 so that the distance of the slope of the line passing through the $(x, f(x))$ and $(1, f(1))$ points to value 3 is smaller than ½.

ii) How far the variable x could be to the value 3 so that the distance of the slope of the line passing through the $(x, f(3))$ and $(x, f(1))$ points to value 1 is bigger than ½.

iii) How close the variable x could be to the value 1 so that the distance of the slope of the line passing through the $(1, f(3))$ and $(x, f(3))$ points to 3 is smaller than ½.

iv) How close the variable x could be to the value 3 so that the distance of the slope of the line passing through the $(x, f(x))$ and $(x, f(1))$ points to 1 is minimum½.

Fig. 8. The question at the object level

The distribution of the scores received by students for this question is given in Table 4.

Table 4. The distribution of scores for the question at the object level

	0	1	2
Frequency values	7	5	21
Percentage values	21	15	64

It was observed that students who gave the correct response generally made a drawing or used the formal definition of the limit. Figure 9 shows the solution process of a student who answered the question correctly using the formal definition of the limit.

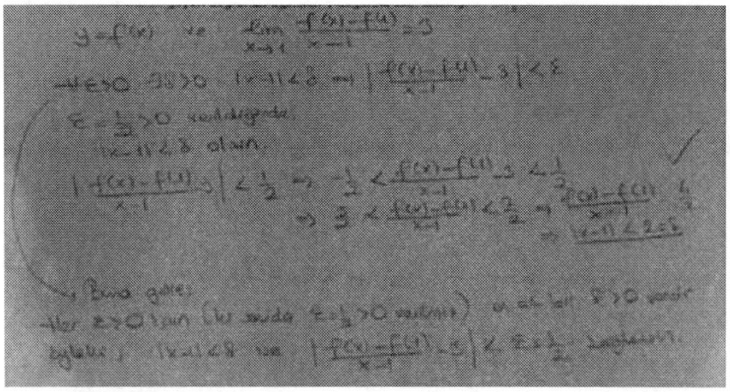

Fig, 9. The solution process of the student

As seen in Figure 9, the students who answered the question correctly mostly provided a detailed explanation and used the symbolic language of the mathematics correctly and carefully.

Some students chose the expression given in (iii) as the equivalent of the expression given in the question, indicating that these students had difficulty making "the graphical interpretation of the ordered pair (x, y) when y is defined by $f(x)$". This suggests that some students lack the preliminary knowledge about the concept of the derivative.

On the other hand, some students seem to have thought that the use of the word "far" is wrong in the explanations regarding the concept of limit. Figure 10 exemplifies this situation.

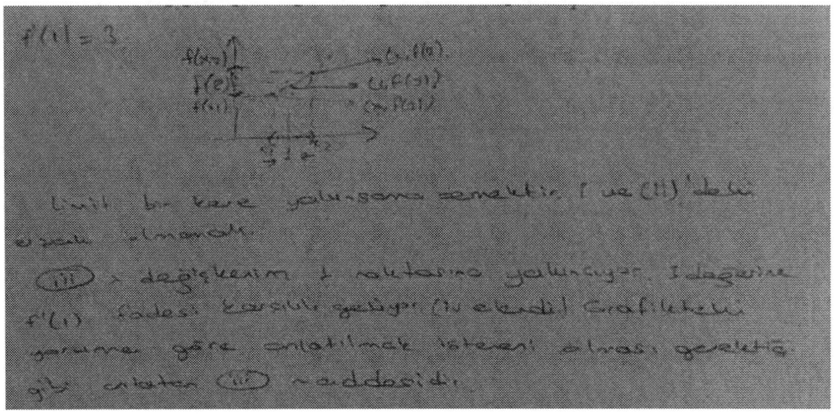

Fig. 10. The solution process of the student.

It is understood from the statements of the student that he reaches the conclusion that the word "far" should not be used in the definition of the limit concept. It is seen that the student could not understand the formal definition of limit, and thus eliminated the correct answer. This result coincides with the findings of Barak's [15] study conducted to reveal the misconceptions of pre-service teachers regarding the limit concept.

4 Conclusions and suggestions

This study investigated how secondary mathematics education pre-service teachers structure the geometric dimension of the concept of derivative in their minds within the framework of the APOS theory. The results show that the pre-service teachers have some deficiencies in their preliminary knowledge or incorrect knowledge about this topic. This means that the pre-service teachers do not have the mental structures about this topic and could not learn the topic at the desired level, and thus the derivative scheme they have did not develop adequately. This situation should be taken into consideration by the instructors and the teaching environments for the concept of the derivative should be arranged in this context; and measures aiming at eliminating the deficiencies of students should be taken.

On the graphs of one variable functions, either a tangent line cannot be drawn or if and only if one can be drawn at a point. However, as Çekmez [1] maintained, more than one tangent can be drawn at one point on the graphs of parametric functions. In this context, it would also be useful to conduct research that explores students' understanding level of parametric functions.

A study can be conducted with secondary school students on their level of understanding the concept of derivative. Within the framework of the results of this study, learning environments should be arranged in a way to reduce the difficulties experienced by students.

References

1. E. Çekmez, *Dinamik matematik yazılımı kullanımının öğrencilerin türev kavramının geometrik boyutuna ilişkin anlamalarına etkisi.* Doktora tezi. Karadeniz Teknik Üniversitesi, Eğitim Bilimleri Enstitüsü (2013).
2. M. Asiala, E. Dubinsky, J. Cottrill, E. K. Schwingendorf, Journal of Mathematical Behavior, **16**, 4 399-431. (1997).
3. I. Biza, *Is the Tangent Line Tangible? Students' Intuitive Ideas About Tangent Lines,* 6-11. (2007).
4. J. Isaacson, *The effects of static graphic, animated graphic, and interactive animated graphic presentations on acquisition of the tangent concept.* Unpublished doctoral dissertation. University of Florida. (1999).
5. M. Artigue, *Analysis,* 167-198. (1991).
6. B. Hartter, *Concept image and concept definition for the topic of derivative.* Unpublished doctoral dissertation. Illinois State University. (1995).
7. E. Dubinsky, *Reflective abstraction in advanced mathematical thinking,* 95–123. (1991).
8. E. Dubinsky, *Towards a theory of learning advanced mathematical concepts,* 121-123. (2000).
9. I. Arnon, J. Cottrill, E. Dubinsky, A. Oktaç, S. Roa Fuentes, M. Trigueros, K. Weller, *APOS theory: A framework for research and curriculum development in mathematics education.* (2014).
10. E. Dubinsky, G. Harel, *The nature of the process conception of function,* 85-106. (1992).
11. Ö. Şefik, *Öğrencilerin iki değişkenli fonksiyon kavramını anlamalarının APOS teorisi ile analizi.* Yüksek lisans tezi. Hacettepe Üniversitesi, Eğitim Bilimleri Enstitüsü. (2017).
12. E. Dubinsky, K. Weller, M. McDonald, A. Brown, Educational Studies in Mathematics, **58** 335–359. (2005).
13. B. Ubuz, International Journal of Mathematical Education in Science and Technology, **38**, 5 609–637. (2007).
14. İ. Çetin, *Students' understandig of limit concept: An APOS perspective.* Doctoral dissertation. Orta Doğu Teknik Üniversitesi, Fen Bilimleri Enstitüsü. (2009).
15. B. Barak, *Limit konusundaki kavram yanılgılarının belirlenmesi.* Yüksek lisans tezi. Balıkesir Üniversitesi. (2007).

Sample Activities in Teaching Functions through ICT Support

Selin Urhan[1,*], *Gizem* Kuh[2] , *Irem* Günal[3] and *Selay* Arkün Kocadere[4]

[1]Hacettepe University, Department of Mathematics and Science Education, Ankara, Türkiye
[2]Reyhanlı Şahika College, Hatay, Türkiye
[3]Aydin Bahçeşehir College Anatolian High School, Aydın, Türkiye
[4]Hacettepe University, Department of Computer Education and Instructional Technology, Ankara, Türkiye

Abstract. Functions are one of the most important topics of algebra in which the success rate of students is quite low and many misconceptions are commonly encountered. Studies argue that by means of technological support, mathematics teaching in general and functions in particular will be facilitated. On the other hand, the rapid development in technology and digital natives necessitate the integration of technology into the field of education. The aim of this study is to present sample activities with regard to the integration of information and communication technologies into the teaching and learning process of functions by using readily available e-contents; Autograph, one of the softwares used for mathematics teaching; and other basic tools.

Keywords: Teaching mathematics, instructional technologies, function, ICT, ICT integration.

1 Introduction

Function is one of the most important topics of mathematics as it involves basic concepts of algebra and helps understand and associate other mathematical topics in algebra [1, 2]. However, as it has a complex and abstract nature, students have difficulty understanding the functions and cannot learn the function concept in mathematics at the desired level [1, 3, 4, 5].

One of the main reasons why students have difficulty in functions is that they make some wrong generalizations about the topic, especially about the definition of function [6, 7, 8]. Many students see functions only as a matching, a formula, an equation, or a rule [4]. Some students believe that what makes a function is the concept of variable, and that when there is no variable, a given expression, i.e. the constant function, does not signify a function [9]. Furthermore, there are students who think that every function expression they encounter must be injective and surjective [6, 8, 9]. Some students consider the relations that match one element in the domain with more than one element in the range as a function [10]. On the other hand, it was also found that while writing ordered pairs, students believe

* Corresponding author: selin.urhan@hacettepe.edu.tr

that the first component represents the range and the second component represents the domain [10].

Ozmantar, Bingölbali, and Akkoç [10] report that although the x-axis shows the domain, and the y-axis shows the range, students are generally confused about this. Güveli [11] found that most students are unable to reflect the algebraic expression of the function on the graph of function, or they have difficulty in doing so. Carlson and Oehrtman [12] revealed that students have difficulty in algebraic and graphical representation of particularly the partially defined functions. It has been found most students believe that function can be defined by a single algebraic formula, and thus, their graphs cannot have a disconnection.

Polat and Şahiner [8] state that students do not associate function with everyday life situations and they consider it as a product of a disconnected and a totally abstract world. Thus, students fail when they are asked to give examples of functions from everyday life or to explain a situation with algebraic or graphical representations of functions.

According to Carlson and Oehrtman [12], students also have difficulty with inverse functions. It has been observed that students do not know why they follow some certain steps to find the inverse of an algebraic function algebraically or based on graph, and also they forget these steps in a short time as they apply them without making sense of them.

In order to reduce the difficulties faced by students in learning functions, researchers have made various suggestions. In this context, Ural [13] emphasized the importance of the teaching method and teaching materials. Dikici and İşleyen [14] and Carlson and Oehrtman [12] stated that functions should be taught by visualizing them with graphs and diagrams. Akkoç [15] stated that examples for descriptive characteristics should be increased.

According to Kabael [4], especially the first parts of the function topic should be taught to the students through visualization and concretization as much as possible. In this context, it would be quite effective to associate function with a machine that produces output values depending on a specific rule for some input values, and even to use a machine model made from a cardboard to teach the subject. Polat and Şahiner [8] stated that the use of technological tools will be effective in the teaching of the function. Kabael [4] argues that the use of appropriate computer programs in the following sections of the topic will be useful for effective teaching of function graphs. According to Kabael [4], as computer programs draw function graphs quickly and effectively, students have time to think and comment on the graphs and thus they can relate the algebraic and graphical representations of functions. Tüzün, Arkün, Bayırtepe, Kurt and Yermeydan Uğur [16] found that the educational computer game they developed can be used as an effective tool to teach the function concept and its types. Kutluca and Baki [17] reported that the computer-assisted worksheets they developed with the help of electronic spreadsheets and computer algebra systems to teach second-order functions have saved teaching from monotony and enabled students to become more motivated by attracting their attention. Brown [18] found that students in the technology-supported learning environments constructed by computers and TI 83/83 + calculators for effective teaching of functions performed better than students who worked on functions only manually. Lagrange [19] revealed that the exploration and modeling of a concept with the aid of a technological tool helps students understand the related concept better. In their study, Mwangi, Waweru and Mwathi [20] designed a computer game to teach functions and they reported that the students found the process very fast and they understood the difference between relations and function better.

Studies frequently point to the contribution and necessity of technology integration in the learning and teaching process of mathematics in general and functions in particular. On the other hand, the habits of new generation defined as digital natives and the human power needed in the age of knowledge necessitate the use of technology in education as well as in many other areas.

2 Aim of the study

The aim of this study is to present a series of sample activities aimed at integrating information and communication technologies with the teaching-learning process using the infrastructure that FATİH project, which is the most extensive work aiming at the integration of technology into the teaching process in Turkey offers; ready-to-use e-content like EBA and Vitamin; Autograph, which is one of the special software for mathematics teaching, and simple tools that do not require high technical skills and knowledge. For this purpose, activities aiming at achieving the outcomes of the functions topic with technology support have been selected or developed. In this way, it is aimed to create an awareness of the effective use of the opportunities offered and to set an effective example to prepare instructional environments for the integration of technology into the teaching process with the aid of simple tools.

3 Activities for teaching functions

A story was written by the researchers reflecting the daily life situation of the learning outcome of "Students explain the concept of function" and it was visualized using the Prezi presentation tool. In this story, the student, Arda, is elected the class president. The teacher wants Arda to place his classmates in one of the activities in the school. It is imperative that each student in the class participate in an activity. However, it is not possible to participate in more than one activity since all activity club meetings are held on the same day at the same time. Through this story, it is aimed that students will define function as "the relation that matches each element of one set (domain) to one and only one element of another set (range)". It is also aimed to reduce the misconceptions of students such as not accepting the relations that match more than one element in the domain with the same element in the range as a function, and accepting the relations that match one element in the domain with more than one element in the range as a function. Besides, it is aimed to prevent problems such as not being able to relate function to everyday life situations and considering function as a product of a disconnected, completely abstract world.

In the following parts of the lesson, the idea that "The function is a machine that produces y output values for x input values" is shown to students through an application in EBA at http://f.eba.gov.tr/MatematikAraclariUygulamasi/ as seen in Figure 1.

Fig. 1. Function machine application (EBA)

In the application "Function Machine", there is a machine programmed to produce output values ($f(x)$) for some input values (x) based on a certain rule. In this application, students are asked to assign the input value for a given function to the machine and to calculate the output value corresponding to the input value. When students push the "Control" key, the machine gives feedback to students' answers as correct or incorrect. In the top left corner, the domain and range of the function and the matching of the input values with the appropriate output values are given. In this way, it is aimed to enable students to learn the function concept with its multiple representations, and to prevent students from considering functions only as a match, a formula, an equation or a rule, and from thinking that every function expression must be injective and surjective. Besides, it is aimed to reduce the difficulties such as not being able to make enough sense of domain and range and confusing them, and not being able to convert a function given with one representation into another representation.

The Autograph software was used to achieve the learning outcome of "Students make the graphical representation of functions". With Autograph, students can see the graph drawn from different perspectives, and reach the coordinates of the points on the graph or the slope of the graph. Students are asked to enter the function expression into the window that opens from the "Equation" button in the Autograph coordinate plane and to determine the domain and range of the function looking at the graph. In this way, it will be possible to obtain the images of some elements in the domain as well as reverse images of some elements in the range. Thus, the outcomes of "The domain and range are shown on the graph of the function" and "The image of some elements in the domain of a given function and the reverse images of some elements in the range are determined" will be reached in an effective way. With such activities structured through Autograph, it is aimed to reduce difficulties like not being able to transform the function given with algebraic expression into graphical representation, seeing the graph of function as a constant object, not being able to determine the domain and range of the function based on the graph, confusing that the x-axis represents the domain and the y-axis represents the range.

The outcome "In the graph of a function, the line drawn parallel to the y-axis from a point where the function is defined on the x-axis cuts the graph at only one point (vertical/perpendicular line test)" is planned to be achieved with an Autograph activity as seen in Figure 2. In this activity, algebraic expressions will be presented to the students. Students will be asked to draw graphs of algebraic expressions using Autograph and to draw vertical lines passing through the x coordinate of any point on the graph. The result to be reached is that when any of the drawn lines cut the graph at more than one point, the graph will not represent a function, and when the drawn lines cut the graph at only one point, the graph will show a function. With this activity, it is aimed to eliminate the misconception of accepting the relations matching one element in the domain with more than one element in the range as function.

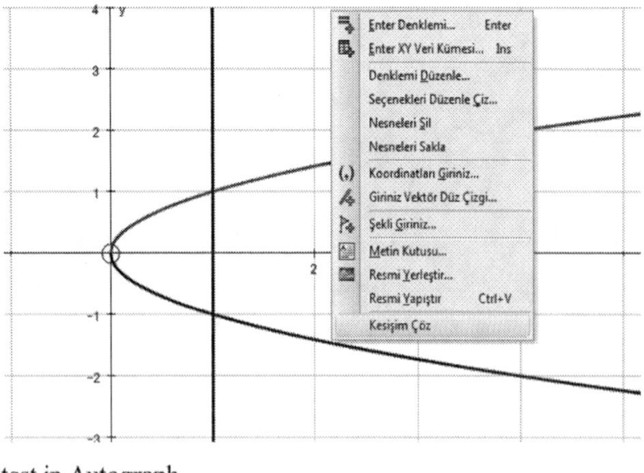

Fig. 2. Vertical line test in Autograph

To achieve the objective of "The graphs of partially defined functions are drawn and the related operations are performed. In this context, the absolute value function is also given as an example of a partially defined function", the EBA activity (http://f.eba.gov.tr/MatematikAraclariUygulamasi/) was used as seen in Figure 3. In this application, how the graph will change by changing the discontinuity point in partially defined functions is observed. Also, the function of absolute value is addressed. In the activity, students are asked to change the discontinuity value of x and the coefficients of the functions. In this way, students are expected to examine the formation of partially defined functions according to the critical value of x (discontinuity value). Through multiple representations (algebraic and graphical) of the partially defined functions, it is aimed to reduce the difficulties students experience in both algebraic and graphical representations.

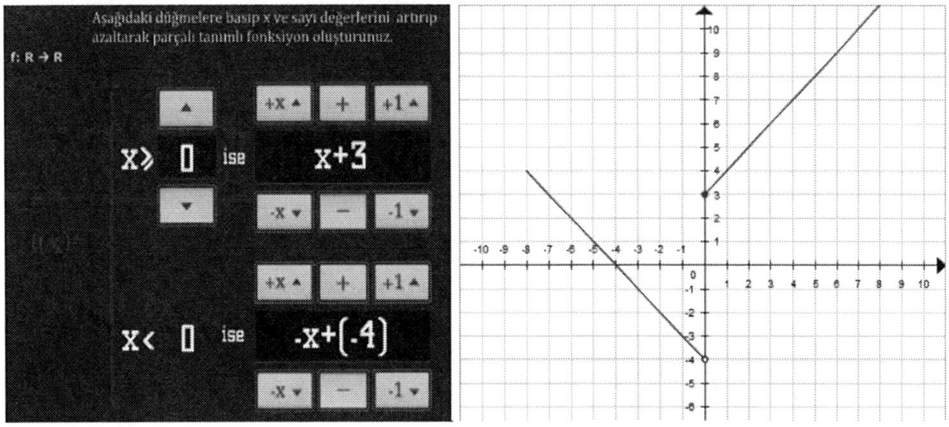

Fig. 3. An application for the graph of partially defined functions (EBA)

To reach the objectives of "Activities about the graphs of the functions in the form of $f\ (x) = ax + b$ are carried out" and "The relationship between the rate of change and the slope of the line is addressed", the activity under the "first-degree functions" category in the "function graphics" section in EBA (http://f.eba.gov.tr/MatematikAraclariUygulamasi/) was utilized. In this application, it is aimed to help students discover how the graph of the function changes as a result of the change in the a value, which is the coefficient of x, in a linear function expression given as $f\ (x) = ax + b$. Students are asked to change the a value in the function expression and interpret how the graph changes; they are also asked to identify the domain and range of the function at each change. Here, it is aimed to avoid the difficulties experienced by students like seeing the graph of the function as a fixed object, not being able to define the domain and range of function on the graph, and not being able to reflect the algebraic expression of the function on the graph of the function. In this process, it is also possible for students to see that the function is a constant function when a value is 0. It is also aimed to eliminate the misconceptions of students that when there is no variable, a given expression cannot specify a function and a function graph should cut both the x and y axes.

To achieve the objective of "It is emphasized that the points at which the f function intersects the x-axis are the solution set of the $f\ (x) = 0$ equation at real numbers", an application in the Vitamin Lisego was utilized (http://www.vitaminegitim.com/proxy/HSStudentPlayerv0.0.228/index.html#lessonplayer). In the application, the aim is to find the zeros (roots) of the functions and to determine the points where the functions are equal to each other using the intersection points of the two function graphs. With this activity, students are expected to generate solutions by developing higher-order thinking skills instead of trying to find the roots of the functions through many algebraic operations.

Another Vitamin Lisego applicaton was chosen to achieve the objective of "The image of some elements in the domain of a function whose graph was given and the reverse images of some elements in the range are determined" http://www.vitaminegitim.com/proxy/HSStudentPlayer_v0.0.228/index.html#lessonplayer. In this activity, students are expected to find the images of some elements in the domain of functions and the reverse images of some elements in the range using function graphs. With this activity, it is aimed to eliminate misconceptions like not being able to make sense of domain and range and having confusion about the fact that the x-axis represents domain, and the y-axis represents range. In this activity, students are also asked to express the elements in the domain with the elements they match in the range as ordered pairs. In this way, it is aimed to avoid conceptual misconceptions such as thinking that the first component represents the range, while the second component represents the domain while expressing the ordered pairs.

The aim of another Vitamin Lisego activity is to find the domain and range of a function on the coordinate plane using the graph of the function as seen in Figure 4. With this activity, it is aimed to achieve the objective of "The domain and the range are shown on the graph of the function". It is thought that in this way, the conceptual misconceptions such as not being able to make sense of domain and range and having confusion about the fact that the x-axis represents domain and the y-axis represents range may be eliminated.

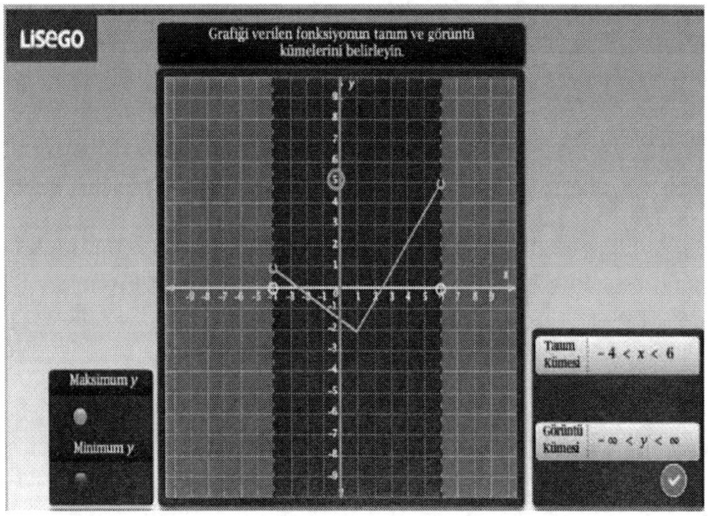

Fig. 4. Identifying the domain and range of the function using the graph of the function http://www.vitaminegitim.com/proxy/HSStudentPlayer_v0.0.228/index.html#lessonplayer

An activity involving the use of Autograph was prepared to achieve the objective of "Students draw the graphs of functions in the form of $(x) = x^n, (n \in Z)$" as seen in Figure 5. In the first stage of this activity, students are asked to draw the graphs of functions in the form of $f: R \rightarrow R, f(x) = x^n$ for $n = 3,5,7$ on the coordinate plane in the Autograph, and to interpret the change in the graphs as the n value increases. In the second stage, students are expected to draw the graphs of functions of the same form for $n = 2, 4, 6$ and to interpret the change in the graphs while the n value increases. In the third stage, students are asked to compare the graphs and interpret the change in graphs for negative and even n values and for the negative and odd n values. With this activity, it is aimed to make it easier for students to understand the parabola and curve concepts, the differences between them, and which concept is formed when. It is also believed that some advanced mathematical skills of students can be improved by giving students the opportunity to interpret the results obtained by drawing a graph with software instead of by drawing a graph manually after complex and long algebraic operations.

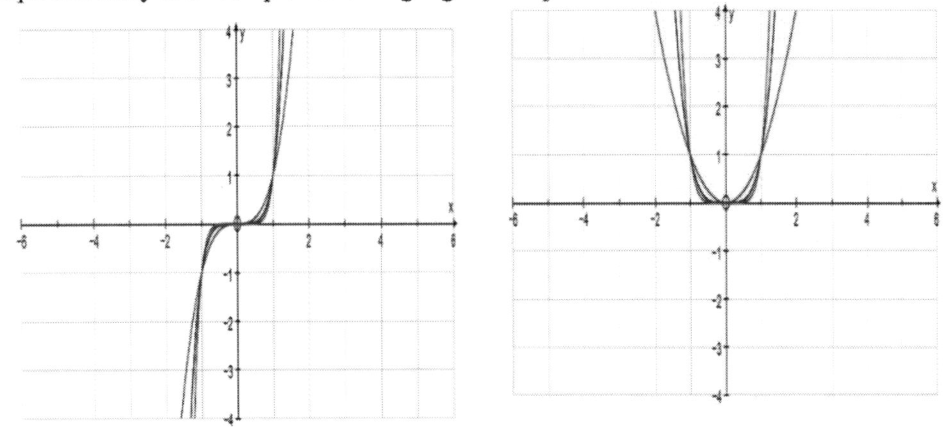

Fig. 5. Graphs for $f: R \rightarrow R, f(x) = x^n$ for $n = 2, 4, 6$ and $n = 3, 5, 7$

A drag-and-drop activity was developed by the researchers for the objective of "Students explain the injective and surjective functions". It is also aimed to present examples from daily life for functions. In the first part of the activity, students are asked to match the primary players in a school basketball team with the jerseys they will wear in the match using the scheme method, and then to determine which type of function this matching exemplifies. In the second part of the activity, it is stated that Arda, İlayda, Aslıhan and Onur bought tickets for seats $19, 20, 21$ and 22 for a theater play and students are asked to match these people with the seats using the scheme method and to find out what type of function this matching represents. In the last part of the activity, it is stated in an experiment in the biology class that Belgin's blood group is A, while Ergin's, Ceren's, Ilgin's, and Selen's blood groups are $0, B, B,$ and AB, respectively. Students are asked to match these people with their blood groups using the scheme method. Students are also expected to determine which type of function their matching corresponds to. The activity aims to eliminate the misconception that every function has to be an injective and surjective function.

4 Conclusions and suggestions

It is stated in the literature that students have difficulty in making sense of functions, associating them with daily life, comprehending the definition of function, drawing function graphs, identifying the domain and range of function from its graph or algebraic expression, and understanding constant function, inverse function, composite function, and partially defined function. Studies aimed at minimizing these difficulties show that ICT integration may make important contributions to the teaching and learning process of functions. Studies by Brown [18], Kutluca and Baki [17], Lagrange [19], Mwangi and colleagues [20], and Tüzün and colleagues [16] are the examples of such studies. In these studies, teachers are particularly recommended to concretize the subject by giving examples from daily life and through visualizing, and to enrich the teaching process in the sections related to graphs and sub-concepts of the subject with computer programs, graphical calculators and other applications.

In this study, a series of activities related to the teaching of functions topic with the integration of ICT was presented. These activities are believed to raise awareness as to the effective use of tablets distributed within the scope of FATIH project and the e-content presented in EBA and Vitamin. Various teaching materials developed using simple tools that do not require high technical knowledge and skills and readily available software for mathematics were also included in the study.

The habits of the new generation defined as digital natives and the human power needed in the age of information necessitate the use of technology in education as in other fields. On the other hand, studies point to the contribution and necessity of technology integration in the teaching and learning process. Many investments are made in instructional technology all over the world, including Turkey. The improvement in education and raising individuals who meet the requirements of the present age depend on making good use of these investments. In this context, both educational researchers and teachers have a great responsibility. The increase in the number of studies like this, the production of high quality e-content, and effective in-service training sessions for teachers are the suggestions that could be put forward in this respect.

References

1. İ. Bayazıt, *Matematiksel kavram yanılgıları ve çözüm önerileri*, 91- 117. (2013).
2. National Council of Teachers of Mathematics, *Principles and standards for school mathematics.* (2000).
3. T. Dreyfus, *Mathematics and cognition, ICMI study series,* 113-134. (1990).
4. U.T. Kabael, Tübav Bilim Dergisi, **3**, 1 128-136. (2010).
5. E. J. Knuth, Journal for Research in Mathematics Education, **31**, 4 500-508. (2000).
6. E. Dubinsky, G. Harel, *The concept of function: aspects of epistemology and pedagogy,* 85-106. (1992).
7. R. Even, Educational Studies in Mathematic, **21**, 6 521–554. (1990).
8. Z. S. Polat, Y. Şahiner, Eğitim ve Bilim, **32** 89-94. (2007).
9. D. Tall, M. Bakar, International Journal of Mathematical Education in Science and Technology, **23**, 1 39-50. (1992).
10. M. F. Özmantar, E. Bingölbali, H. Akkoç, *Matematiksel kavram yanılgıları ve çözüm öneriler.* (2010).
11. E. Güveli, *Lise-1 fonksiyonlar konusunun web tabanlı öğretim tasarımı, uygulaması ve değerlendirilmesi.* Doctoral dissertation. Karadeniz Teknik Üniversitesi, Fen Bilimleri Enstitüsü. (2004).
12. M. Carlson, M. Oehrtman, *Key aspects of knowing and learning the concept of function.* (2005).
13. A. Ural, Ege Eğitim Dergisi, **7**, 2 75–94. (2006).
14. R. Dikici, T. İşleyen, Kastamonu Eğitim Dergisi, **11**, 2 105-116. (2003).
15. H. Akkoç, Lise 3 öğrencilerinin çekirdek fonksiyon kavramını anlamaları. *VI. Ulusal Fen Bilimleri ve Matematik Eğitimi Kongresi.* (2004).
16. H. Tüzün, S. Arkün, E. Bayırtepe, F. Kurt, B. Yermeydan Uğur, Fonksiyonlar Konusunun Oyun Ortamında Öğretilmesi. *5. Matematik Sempozyumu.* (2006).
17. T. Kutluca, A. Baki, Hacettepe Üniversitesi Eğitim Fakültesi Dergisi, **28**, 3 319-331. (2013).
18. J. Brown, *Proceedings of the 30th annual conference of the mathematics research group of Australasia (MERGA),* 153 – 162. (2007).
19. J. B. Lagrange, International Journal for Technology in Mathematics Education, **21,** 1. 3-10. (2014).
20. R. W. Mwangi, R. Waweru, C. W. Mwathi, Journal of Theoretical and Applied Information Technology, **26,** 1 394-404. (2011).

The determination of the pain beliefs of the students at Akdeniz University Vocational School of Health Services

Hatice Gül[1, a] and *Suat* Erel[2]

[1]*Akdeniz University Vocational School of Health Services, Antalya, Turkey*
[2]*Pamukkale University School of Physiotherapy and Rehabilitation, Denizli, Turkey*

Abstract. The purpose of this study is to determine the pain beliefs of Akdeniz University Vocational School of Health Services (AUVSHS) students. Fifty Physiotherapy Assistants students, 54 Paramedic students and 37 Elderly Care students who take pain education in their curriculum and 50 Child Development and Care students who do not take pain education were included in this study. The pain beliefs of the students were evaluated with Pain Beliefs Questionnaire. There was no statistically significant difference between organic (OBS) and psychological pain belief scores (PBS) of programs with and without pain education (p>0,05). There was statistically significant difference between OBS and PBS in favor of PBS in all programs (p<0,05). In conclusion, it was determined that pain beliefs in AUVSHS were similar in all programs. It is important to balance between organic and psychological pain beliefs. So we plan to develop new training strategies to balance student's pain beliefs.
Keywords: Pain; organic pain beliefs; psycholological pain beliefs; students

1 Introduction

"Pain is a subjective, unpleasant sensory and an emotional experience that can reflect a real or potential physical injury" [1]. Acute pain is defined as a type of pain that lasts less than 3 months or the pain that is related to tissue damage. Chronic pain can be defined as pain that persists beyond normal tissue healing time and lasts more than 3 months [2,3]. Chronic pain is influenced by physical, cognitive, behavioral and psychological factors.

There are studies in the literature evaluating pain related beliefs in individuals with chronic pain [4-6]. Several studies have demonstrated that beliefs of the patients about the cause of their pain affect treatment compliance and outcome of treatment [7,8]. It was found that organic pain beliefs were approved by chronic pain patient more frequently than healthy persons [9]. It was determined that pain beliefs based on organic nature of pain lead to increase patient's physical dysfunction and decrease coping strategies [10-12].

We educate the student who serves in medical facilities in future. Thinking that only patient's beliefs are a problem for treatment would be wrong. Beliefs of healthcare

[a] Corresponding author: haticegul@akdeniz.edu.tr

professionals could also affect the treatment outcome and cause to conflicts with patients [13,14]. Traditional pain education model in medical school associate the health of tissue to pain generally. This pain explanation model called as biomedical model may be helpful to clarify the pathoanatomic cause of injury in acute, subacute or perioperative conditions, but do not be helpful to clarify the cause of the chronic condition [15]. Because the health of tissue does not correlate with pain in chronic condition [16,17].

The beliefs of the patient and healthcare professional get together during therapetic approaches. This meeting defined as therapeutic encounter described as a complex process of negotiations. The collaboration develops between patient and healthcare professional after negotiation. The healthcare professional who have a good knowledge and appropriate belief about pain process will be successful in collaboration with the patient [18].

In our study we want to investigate the beliefs of our student regarding organic and psychological nature of pain. Also we want to compare the pain beliefs of different programs which received and did not receive education about pain.

2 Method

The present study is a descriptive study that evaluates pain beliefs of the students at Akdeniz University Vocational School of Health Services. The Akdeniz University Clinical Research Ethics Committee gave approval for the present study (272/11.04.2018).

2.1 Participant

191 students were included in this study. Fifty Physiotherapy Assistants students, 54 Paramedic students and 37 Elderly Care students who took pain education in their curriculum and 50 Child Development and Care students who did not take pain education were participated in this study.

2.2 Procedure

Socio-demographic characteristics of students such as age, sex, past pain experience were saved. The pain beliefs of students were evaluated with Pain Beliefs Questionnaire (PBQ). The PBQ was developed as 20 items questionnaire and then reduced to 12 items. The questionnaire includes two scales, the Organic Beliefs Scale (8 items), and Psychological Beliefs Scale (4 items). Organic Beliefs Scale addresses organic nature of pain and deals with perceived cause of the pain. Psychological Beliefs Scale addresses the effect of psychological factors such as anxiety, depression and relaxation on pain. Each item is scored with 6 point ("always" to "never") scale. The PBQ organic and psychological sub-scales scores were obtained with calculation of the items score for each scale [4]. This questionnaire has been used successfully with chronic back pain [5,9,19]. But it is not necessary for a respondent to be in pain. This questionnaire could applied to healthy persons. It was determined that the Turkish version of PBQ is valid and reliable [20].

2.3 Statistical Analysis

SPSS for Windows 21.00 computer package program was used for all statistical analyses. Descriptive statistics were shown as the mean and standard deviation (X±SS) in the table. Mann Whitney-U test was used to compare organic and psychological pain beliefs between groups. Wilcoxon-signed test was used to compare organic and psychological pain beliefs within group.

3 Findings

191 students were participated in this study. The mean age of the students was 20,30±2,25 years. Also 150 students (%78,5) were female and 41 students (%21,5) were male in this study. One hundred fifty-five (%81,2) students did not have past pain experience and 34 students (%18,8) had past pain experience in this study. A large number of the students who had past pain experience were from the Child Development and Care program. The mean pain duration of the participants was 11,52±13,96 months.

The mean organic belief score of Physiotherapy Assistants students was 4,29±0,62 and the mean psychological belief score of Physiotherapy Assistants students was 4,85±0,74. The mean organic belief score of Paramedic students was 4,00±0,72 and the mean psychological belief score of Paramedic students was 4,56±0,89. The mean organic belief score of Elderly Care students was 4,20±0,64 and the mean psychological belief score of Elderly Care students was 4,75±0,77. The mean organic beliefs score of Child Development and Care students was 4,01±0,67 and the mean psychological beliefs score of Child Development and Care students was 4,47±0,93. According to results, there was a statistically significant difference between Organic Beliefs Scale and Psychological Beliefs Scale in favor of Psychological Beliefs Scale in all programs (p<0,05) (Table 1).

Table 1. Organic and psychological pain belief scores within groups comparison

Groups	Organic Pain Beliefs Score X±SS	Pscychological Pain Beliefs Score X±SS	z	p*
Physiotherapy Asistant Students (n=50)	4,29±0,62	4,85±0,74	-4,377	**0,000***
Paramedic students (n=54)	4,00±0,72	4,56±0,89	-4,233	**0,000***
Elderly Care Student (n=37)	4,20±0,64	4,75±0,77	-3,489	**0,000***
Child Development and Care students (n=50)	4,01±0,67	4,47±0,93	-2,831	**0,005***

*p<0,05

There was no statistically significant difference between organic and psychological pain belief scores of the students who took pain education and did not take pain education (p>0,05). (Table 2).

Table 2. Organic and psychological pain beliefs score between groups which took pain education and did not take pain education.

Pain Beilefs Questionnaire	Took pain education (n=141)	Did not take pain education (n=50)	z	p*
Organic Pain Beliefs Score X±SS	4,15±0,67	4,01±0,67	-1,194	0,232
Pscychological Pain Beliefs Score X±SS	4,71±0,81	4,47±0,93	-1,503	0,133

*p<0,05

There was no statistically significant difference between Organic Beliefs Scale and Psychological Belief Scale of the students who had past pain experience and did not have past pain experience (p>0,05) (Table 3).

Table 3. Organic and psychological pain beliefs score between groups which had past pain experience and did not have past pain experience.

Pain Beilefs Questionnaire	Past Pain Experience		z	p*
	Yes (n=34)	No (n=155)		
Organic Beliefs Score X±SS	4,06±0,73	4,13±0,66	-0,615	0,539
Pscychological Beliefs Score X±SS	4,67±0,80	4,64±0,86	-0,047	0,962

There was no statistically significant difference between Organic Beliefs Scale and Psychological Belief Scale of the male and female students (p>0,05) (Table 4).

Table 4. Organic and psychosocial pain beliefs score between female and male students.

Pain Beilefs Questionnaire	Gender		z	p*
	Female (n=150)	Male (n=41)		
Organic Beliefs Score X±SS	4,08±0,69	4,24±0,59	-1,328	0,184
Pscychological Beliefs Score X±SS	4,65±0,87	4,63±0,78	-0,498	0,618

*p<0,05

4 Discussions and Conclusions

In the present study, we searched pain beliefs of the students at Akdeniz University Vocational School of Health Services. For this purpose, we applied the Pain Beliefs Questionnaire to 191 students.

There were a few studies in the literature which use PBQ to examine pain beliefs of patients with chronic pain and students at university. It was determined that organic pain beliefs of chronic pain patient were stronger than their psychological belief [5,19,21]. There was no study which compare organic and psychological pain beliefs of students. But there was a study which correlate organic pain beliefs and psychological pain beliefs of the student. In this study it was found that there was a negative and weak correlation between organic and psychological pain beliefs of students [22]. In the present study we compared organic and psychological pain beliefs of our student. According to our results, it was determined that psychological beliefs of our students were stronger than their organic beliefs. In the study which determined that psychological beliefs of nonclinical sample is stronger than their organic beliefs was found same result with us [5]. We think that this result cannot be relevant to our education strategies. Even so this is an important finding because beliefs related organic nature of pain cause to use fearful terminology to patient during medical application of healthcare professional. This fearful terminology could increase patient's fear. On the other hand, it is important to provide the balance between organic and psychological pain beliefs of students. Because organic beliefs come to prominence during acute care, psychological beliefs come to prominence during chronic pain treatment. Physiotherapy assistant students, Paramedic students and Elderly Care students serve both in acute and chronic care period.

It was determined that pain beliefs in Akdeniz University Vocational School of Health Services were similar in all programs regardless of pain education situation. We couldn't decide whether the education of pain affect or does not affect the pain beliefs of our students. Because we didn't evaluate pain knowledge and past pain education model of our students. There is a questionnaire in literature which evaluate pain knowledge and is named as Neurophysiology of Pain Questionnaire. But we could not use this questionnaire because the Turkish version of this questionnaire haven't been validated yet.

It is recommended that professionals should receive education based on the biopsychosocial model and should know how to integrate it to care of patients [23]. Five studies assessed the effect of educational interventions that aimed to change pain beliefs of rehabilitation professionals and beliefs of students toward pain [24-28]. So we are planning to balance organic and psychological pain beliefs of students by developing new education strategies which based on pain neurophysiology education. Pain Neurophysiology Education program increase knowledge and beliefs about pain's biopsychosocial nature.

In the literature, it was determined that organic beliefs of female students were stronger than male students in nonclinical sample [22]. In our study it was determined that pain beliefs of students did not change in relation to gender. In a study it was found that organic beliefs of individuals who had past pain experience stronger than individuals who did not have past pain experience [5]. In our study we did not find any difference between the groups which had past pain experience and who did not. We think that this findings related to our young sample and unequal sample size.

In conclusion, the findings of this study show that psychological pain beliefs of our students stronger than organic pain beliefs. The level of pain knowledge of the students should be determined in future. We believe that beliefs affect from knowledge. Therefore, education of the students should consist of knowledge about pain based on biopsychosocial perspective. Also this education model should support organic and psychological pain beliefs of students. We believe that this perspective improves the efficacy of treatment.

References

1. International Association for the Study of Pain. IASP Taxonomy 2014 Available from: http://www.iasp-pain.org. [2016].
2. H. Merksey, N. Bogduk.. Classification of chronic pain (2nd ed.) [Seattle: IASP Press 1994].
3. P.S. Wall, R Melzack. Textbook of Pain (5th edn ed.) [London:Elsevier 2005].
4. D.A Walsh, J.C Radcliffe. Pain beliefs and perceived physical disability of patients with chronic low back pain. Pain, 97, 23–31 [2002].
5. A.J.Baird, R.A. Haslam. Exploring differences in pain beliefs within and between a large nonclinical (workplace) population and a clinical (chronic low back pain) population using the pain beliefs questionnaire. Phys. Ther, 12,1615–1624 [2013].
6. A. Baird, D. Sheffield. The Relationship between Pain Beliefs and Physical and Mental Health Outcome Measures in Chronic Low Back Pain: Direct and Indirect Effects Healthcare, 4,58 [2016].
7. D.P Schwartz, DE DeGood, MS Shutty. Direct assessment of beliefs and attitudes of chronic pain patients. Arch Phys Med Rehabil, 66: 806–809 [1985]..
8. M.J. Simmonds, S. Kumar, E. Lechelt. Psychological factors in disabling low back pain: causes or consequences? Disabil Rehabil, 18:161–168 [1996].
9. L.C. Edwards, S.A. Pearce, L. Turner-Stokes, A. Jones. The Pain Beliefs Questionnaire: an investigation of beliefs in the causes and consequences of pain. Pain, 51: 267–272 [1992].
10. D.A. Williams, M.E. Robinson, M.E. Geisser. Pain beliefs: assessment and utility. Pain, 59:71–78 [1994].
11. P. Arnstein, M. Caudill, C.L. Mandle, A. Norris, R. Beasley. Self efficacy as a mediator of the relationship between pain intensity, disability and depression in chronic pain patients. Pain, 80:483–491 [1999].
12. J.A. Turner, M.P. Jensen, J.M. Romano. Do beliefs, coping, and catastrophizing independently predict functioning in patients with chronic pain? Pain, 85:115–125 [2000].
13. S.J. Linton, J. Vlaeyen, R. Ostelo. The back pain beliefs of health care providers: are we fear-avoidant? J Occup Rehabil, 12:223–232 [2002].
14. J.E. Jeffrey, N.E. Foster. A qualitative investigation of physical therapists' experiences and feelings of managing patients with nonspecific low back pain. Phys Ther, 92:266–278 [2012].
15. G.L. Moseley. Reconceptualising pain acording to modern pain sciences. Physical Therapy Reviews, 12: 169–178 [2007].

16. S. Haldeman. Presidential address, North American Spine Society: Failure of the pathology model to predict back pain. Spine, 15: 718–724 [1990].
17. P. Kjaer, C. Leboeuf-Yde, L. Korsholm, J.S. Sorensen, T. Bendix. Magnetic resonance imaging and low back pain in adults: A diagnostic imaging study of 40-year-old men and women. Spine, 30: 1173–1180 [2005].
18. A.M. Øien, S. Steihaug, S. Iversen, M. Råheim Communication as negotiation processes in long-term physiotherapy: a qualitative study. Scand J Caring Sci, 25: 53-61 [2011].
19. T. Sloan, R. Gupta, W. Zhang, D, Walsh. Beliefs about the causes and consequences of pain in patients with chronic inflammatory or non-inflammatory low back pain and in pain-free individuals. Spine, 33, 966–972 [2008].
20. Ö. Sertel-Berk Kronik ağrı yaşantısı ve ağrı inançları: Ağrı İnançları Ölçeği' nin Türkçe geçerlik ve güvenirlik çalışması. (Doktora tezi). [İstanbul Üniversitesi Sosyal Bilimler Enstitüsü, İstanbul 2006].
21. A.Ö. Birge, M. Mollaoğlu, Pain beliefs of patients and the nonpharmacological methods they use to manage the pain. Agri, 30(2):84-92 [2018].
22. B. Babadağ, G.B. Alparslan. Hemşirelik Öğrencilerinin Ağrı İnançları. Sted, 26(6):244-250 [2017].
23. P. Van Wilgen, A. Beetsma, H. Neels, N. Roussel, J. Nijs. Physical therapists should integrate illness perceptions in their assessment in patients with chronic musculoskeletal pain; a qualitative analysis. Man Ther, 19:229-34 [2014].
24. R.W. Ostelo, S.G. Stomp-van den Berg, J.W. Vlaeyen, et al. Health care provider' attitudes and beliefs towards chronic low back pain: the development of a questionnaire. Man Ther, 8: 214-22 [2003].
25. J. Latimer, C. Maher and K. Refshauge. The attitudes and beliefs of physiotherapy students to chronic back pain. Clin J Pain, 20: 45-50 [2004].
26. D. Jones, J. Ravey and W. Steedman. Developing a measure of beliefs and attitudes about chronic non-malignant pain: A pilot study of occupational therapists. Occup Ther Int, 7: 232-45 [2000].
27. T. Overmeer, K. Boersma, C.J. Main, S.J. Linton. Do physical therapists change their beliefs, attitudes, knowledge, skills and behaviour after a biopsychosocial orientated university course? J Eval Clin Pract, 15: 724-32 [2009].
28. D.L. Rochman, M.J. Sheehan and R.J. Kulich. Evaluation of a pain curriculum for occupational therapists: experiences from a master's-level graduate program over six years. Disabil Rehabil, 35: 1933-40 [2013].

A research on the basic psychological needs of swimmers in Kocaeli province in terms of any variances (İzmit district case)

Hakan Akdeniz[1*], *Özlem* Keskin[1], *Fatma Yeşim* Körmükçü[1] and *Burak* Varol[1]

[1]Kocaeli University Sports Sciences Faculty Recreation Department

Abstract. This study was conducted with the aim of investigating the basic psychological requirements of swimmers who perform individual sports in Kocaeli province with respect to certain variables. The sample of the study consisted of 80 swimmers who perform individual sports in Kocaeli province, İzmit district between the years of 2016 – 2017, 32 of whom were male and 42 of whom were female. In collecting data, the Basic Psychological Needs Scale which was developed by [4] was used in order to determine the psychological needs of individuals. Basic Psychological Needs Scale was adapted into Turkish by [9] A personal information form that was developed by the researcher was used. No significant difference was observed when basic psychological need scores were compared according to gender ($P<0,05$). In consequence of comparing the results of basic psychological need scale by means of age variable, a significant difference was observed by means of the need for relatedness between the 14 – 16 and 20 – 22 age groups ($P<0,05$). When basic psychological need scores were compared with respect to educational background, a significant difference was found in terms of the need for autonomy, need for competence and need for relatedness while a significant difference was observed by means of all scores ($p<0,05$). With respect to need for autonomy and need for competence; a significant difference was observed between Secondary Education and High School while the need for relatedness and total scores created a significant difference between Secondary Education and University ($p<0,05$). As a consequence of the comparison between the results of basic psychological need scale according to family attitudes, a significant difference was only observed by means of the need for competence between the variables ($p<0,05$). With respect to the sub-dimension of the need for competence, a significant difference was found between democratic family structure and authoritarian family structure ($P<0,05$). As a result of a comparison between basic psychological needs considering the educational background of female parents, there was a significant difference between the variants by means of the need for competence and the need for relatedness. With respect to need for competence and relatedness, a significant difference was observed for both, between the educational levels of primary school and high school ($P<0,05$).

* Corresponding author: hakanakdeniz@gmail.com

1 Introduction

Human has in need of several requirements since the birth till the death. Those needs can be accepted as physiological or psychological necessities. [5] expressed that the human has needs that guide specific inborn attitudes of the human.

Imbalance and inadequacy emerge in individuals whose mental needs are not satisfied. This imbalance and inefficacy stress the person out. The organism activates the homeostasis mechanism to normalize this stress stressful situation.

Another dimension within the scope of meeting the human need is the necessities such as the psychological protection.

The reactions in person become positive when the physical and mental needs of him. [2] pointed out that the person can actualize the personality development, bliss and the well-being in case of meeting the requirements. In a similar manner, [7] mentioned that growing, surviving and reaching personal maturity take an important place in satisfying the needs. With reference to [5], the human has necessities such as surviving, love, belonging, power and freedom; satisfying the needs of love and belonging eliminates the problems.

Some of the situations like apathy, boredom, discouragement, lack of sense of humor, alienation, selfishness, grudge, anhedonia, joylessness, uneasiness, hopelessness can develop as somatic complaints in human when the physiological and psychological needs are not satisfied [10].

The importance of the surveys and their necessity to be used can be seen in the light of the investigations. It is argued that psychology needs to be used correctly in the sports concept.

Need is the high impulses such as motive, wish, requirement, desire, hope and desire to achieve. The need is explained as a pressure, driving power or necessity that emerge in the brain by an effect from inside or outside. All the psycho-social needs are called as the basic needs [9]. Psychological needs are the center of interest because of being one of the determinants of the human behaviors. [6] who discussed the needs through a hierarchical approach mentioned that other needs emerge from meeting other physiological needs which are the most powerful ones. These newly emerging needs domineer the organism as well as the human needs to become organized in a relative dominance hierarchy.

Murray defined 20 different needs such adaptation, self-determination, submission, success, fun, kinship, tidiness [3]. Glasser who is a theoretician deals with the needs aligned five basic needs that all the people have. These are; surviving, belonging, power, love, freedom, and fun [13].

With reference to the self-determination theory that discusses the psychological needs, people have three main psychological needs as autonomy, competence, and relatedness that are essential for personal development, integrity and psychological health [4]. Autonomy (self-determination) means dealing with the activities which are decided by the person himself; competence means the desire to affect the circle; sense of competence means the capacity to effectively interact with the environment; relatedness means the sense of belonging, namely, a real loyalty to others [4] These needs result from the combination of personal experiences and the environmental factor [11].

2 Methodology

2.1 Research Group

The population was composed of 80 licensed swimmers whose 37 of them were in 14-16 (46,3%) age group; 21 of them were in 17-19 (26,3%) age group; 22 (27,5%) of them were in 20-22 age group. The sample of the study was composed of randomized 80 people whose 42 was female and 38 was males from the swimmers of Yıldızlar Swimming Club, Kocaeli Swimming Club, Akademi Swimming Club and Çınarlı Swimming Clubs.

2.2 Data Collection Tools

Basic Psychological Needs scale that was developed by [4] to determine the psychological needs of people was used to collect the data. Besides, personal information form that was developed by the investigator was utilized. Basic psychological needs scale (BPNS) was adapted into Turkish by [9] this scale is a five points Likert scale that consists of 21 items that change between "Absolutely Right (5) Right (4) A bit right (3) Wrong (2) and absolutely wrong (1). The scale is composed of three sub-scales as the autonomy need, competence need and relationship need. As the points of participants increase, it is accepted that the person feels that need more in comparison with other needs.

2.3 Data Collection

The survey was applied to participants from Yıldızlar Swimming club, Akademi Swimming club, Kocaeli Swimming club, Çınarlı Swimming Club, Kocaeli Indoor Pool by face to face meeting. Conducting the surveys took 5 days.

2.4 Analysis of Data

SPSS 21 (Statistical Package For Social Sciences) packaged software analyzed the data. First of all, the average, standard deviation, frequency and percentage values relating to the variables with descriptive statistics were found. Unpaired t-test was used for the difference between the two groups in data analysis. ANOVA test was used for the difference between more than two groups; Tukey test specified the group created the difference. Significance level was determined as 0,05 ($p<0,05$).

3 Findings

Table 1. Frequency analysis distribution of basic psychological needs of swimmers in Kocaeli district based on the ages

	n	%
14-16	37	46,3
17-19	21	26,3
20-22	22	27,5
Total	80	100,0

46,3% of the participants were in the 14-16 age range; 26,3% of the participants were in the 17-19 age range; 27,5% of the participants were in the 20-22 age range.

Table 2. Frequency analysis distribution of basic psychological needs of swimmers in Kocaeli district based on the gender

	n	%
Male	38	47,5
Female	42	52,5
Total	80	100,0

47,5% of the participants were males; 52,5% of the participants were the females.

Table 3. Frequency analysis distribution of basic psychological needs of swimmers in Kocaeli district based on the educational background

	n	%
Secondary education	30	37,5
High school	27	33,8
University	23	28,8
Total	80	100,0

37,5% of the participants graduated from the secondary education; 33,8% of the participants graduated from the high school; 28,8% of the participants were the bachelors.

Table 4. Comparing the basic psychological needs of swimmers in Kocaeli district based on the gender; Distribution by T-test

	Gender	n	x	ss	t	p	Significance
Autonomy need	Male	38	23,3947	2,56314	,267	,790	P>0,05
	Female	42	23,2381	2,66696			
Competence need	Male	38	19,9211	2,12300	-,831	,408	P>0,05
	Female	42	20,3095	2,05400			
Relationship need	Male	38	26,7368	2,40140	-,498	,620	P>0,05
	Female	42	27,0238	2,71839			
Total	Male	38	70,0526	4,36167	-,480	,633	P>0,05
	Female	42	70,5714	5,21322			

There was not found a significant difference between the variables at the end of comparing the basic psychological needs scores of the swimmers who participated in the research (P<0,05)

Table 5. Comparing the basic psychological needs of swimmers in Kocaeli district based on the age; Distribution by one way ANOVA analysis

		n	x	ss	f	p	Significance
Autonomy need	14-16	37	23,7568	2,94774	3,011	,055	P>0,05
	17-19	21	23,7143	2,43193			
	20-22	22	22,1818	1,76302			
	Total	80	23,3125	2,60279			
Competence need	14-16	37	20,0270	1,72380	1,757	,179	P>0,05
	17-19	21	19,6190	2,83683			
	20-22	22	20,7727	1,68839			
	Total	80	20,1250	2,08293			
Relationship need	14-16	37	27,5676	2,69300	3,432	,037	14-16 yaş – 20-22 yaş.
	17-19	21	26,8095	2,22753			
	20-22	22	25,8182	2,34290			
	Total	80	26,8875	2,56063			
Total	14-16	37	71,3514	5,07836	2,062	,134	P>0,05
	17-19	21	70,1429	4,79881			
	20-22	22	68,7727	4,03475			
	Total	80	70,3250	4,80447			

There was an observed difference in a relationship needs dimension at the end of comparing the basic psychological needs based on the age. There was no significance in terms of self-determination need, competence need and total scores. A significant difference was observed between 14-16 and 20-22 age groups in a relationship need dimension (P<0,05).

Table 6. Comparing the basic psychological needs of swimmers in Kocaeli district based on educational background; Distribution by one way ANOVA analysis

		n	x	ss	f	p	Significance
Autonomy need	Secondary education	30	24,0000	3,19482	3,786	,027	Secondary education-High school
	High school	27	23,5556	2,18972			
	University	23	22,1304	1,74002			
	Total	80	23,3125	2,60279			
Competence need	Secondary education	30	20,2333	1,73570	3,489	,035	Secondary education-High school
	High school	27	19,3704	2,49843			
	University	23	20,8696	1,71370			
	Total	80	20,1250	2,08293			
Relationship need	Secondary education	30	27,8333	2,81723	4,419	,015	Secondary education-University
	High school	27	26,7407	2,14104			
	University	23	25,8261	2,28935			
	Total	80	26,8875	2,56063			
Total	Secondary education	30	72,0667	5,22549	3,561	,033	Secondary education-University
	High school	27	69,6667	4,53194			
	University	23	68,8261	3,95028			
	Total	80	70,3250	4,80447			

There was found a difference in self-determination need, competence need, relationship dimension and total scores at the end of comparing the basic psychological need scores based on the eduction. A significant difference (P<0,05) was observed between secondary education and university in self-determination need and competence need dimension.

Table 7. Comparing the basic psychological needs of swimmers in Kocaeli district based on family attributes; Distribution by one way ANOVA analysis

		n	x	ss	f	p	Significance
Autonomy need	Democratic	4	26,2500	2,98608	2,347	,079	P>0,05
	Authoritarian	21	23,3333	3,56838			
	Protector	35	22,8000	1,74558			
	Careless	20	23,6000	2,34857			
	Total	80	23,3125	2,60279			
Competence need	Democratic	4	17,5000	3,69685	3,033	**,034**	Democratic-Authoritarian
	Authoritarian	21	19,7619	2,11907			
	Protector	35	20,5143	1,78838			
	Careless	20	20,3500	1,87153			
	Total	80	20,1250	2,08293			
Relationship need	Democratic	4	25,7500	2,06155	,946	,423	P>0,05
	Authoritarian	21	27,0476	2,69214			
	Protector	35	26,5429	2,39292			
	Careless	20	27,5500	2,78104			
	Total	80	26,8875	2,56063			
Total	Democratic	4	69,5000	4,04145	,549	,650	P>0,05
	Authoritarian	21	70,1429	5,74705			
	Protector	35	69,8571	4,78443			
	Careless	20	71,5000	3,95368			
	Total	80	70,3250	4,80447			

There was observed a difference just in the competence dimension between the variables at the end of comparing the basic psychological need scores based on the family attitudes. There was no significant difference in autonomy need, relationship needs and total scores (P<0,05). In the competence need dimension, there was observed the difference between democratic family structure and authoritarian family structure (P<0,05).

4 Discussions

This research contains research findings, comparisons, and evaluations of statistical analyses on the data about age, gender, educational background and family attitude variables that may be effective in meeting the basic psychological needs of the students study in secondary education, high school and university in Izmit district of Kocaeli province in Turkey.

There was no significant difference (P<0,05) between the variables when looking at the comparison of basic psychological needs based on the gender. With reference to this finding, there was no significant difference in comparison of the self-determination, relationship and competence needs of the students based on the gender need.

[8] conducted a study called 'Reviewing the Basic Psychological Needs and Satisfaction Levels of Academicians by Various Variables'. He found a significant difference between self-determination, competence and relationship variables of the academicians based on the gender variable. There is not a parallelism between these two surveys.

There was found a difference between the variables in a relationship need dimension as the result of comparing basic psychological needs based on the age. A significant difference was observed between 14-16 yaş and 20-22 age groups in a relationship need dimension (P<0,05).

[12] performed a research and found that the self-determination needs significantly varies by the ages of the students. There is seen a parallelism between these two surveys.

A difference was determined between self-determination need, relationship needs, and total scores as the result of comparing the basic psychological need scores based on the educational background. Also, there can be seen a significant difference (P<0,05) between secondary education and university in relationship need and total scores dimensions. This difference can also be seen between secondary education and high school in self-determination need and competence need dimensions.

About this issue, [1] conducted a study and did not found a significant difference between self-determination, competence, and relationship need based on the educational background of volleyball referees. There is not a parallelism in these two surveys.

There was observed a difference just in the competence need between the variables as the result of comparing basic psychological needs based on the family attitudes. A significant difference was observed between democratic family structure and authoritarian family structure in the competence need dimension (P<0,05).

In other words, the competence needs of the students who have nurturing family attitude are met more in comparison with the same need of the students who have a democratic family attitude.

It is pointed out with reference to these findings that the family attitude is important in decreasing or increasing the competence needs.

5 Conclusion

In other words, the competence needs of the students who have nurturing family attitude are met more in comparison with the same need of the students who have a democratic family attitude.

It is pointed out with reference to these findings that the family attitude is important in decreasing or increasing the competence needs.

References

1. Arslanoğlu E, Tekin M, Arslanoğlu C, Özmutlu İ. (2010). Voleybol hakemlerinin çeşitli değişkenlere göre kaygı ve temel psikolojik ihtiyaç düzeylerinin incelenmesi (Ankara ili örneği). Uluslararası İnsan Bilimleri Dergisi, **7**(2):985-995.
2. Baard, P. P., Deci, E. L. and Ryan, R. M. (2004). Intrinsic need satisfaction: A motivational basis of performance and well-being in two work settings Journal of Applied Social Psychology, **34**, 2045-2068.
3. Çivitçi, A. (2012). Üniversite Öğrencilerinde Genel Yaşam Doyum ve Psikolojik İhtiyaçlar Arasındaki İlişkiler. Çukurova Üniversitesi Sosyal Bilimler Enstitüsü Dergisi, **21**(2), :321-336.
4. Deci, E. ve Ryan, R. (2000). The "What" And "Why" of Goal Pursuits: Human Needs and The Self- Determination of Behaviour. Psychological Inquiry, **11** (4), 227-269.
5. Glasser, W. (1965). Reality therapy. New York: Harper & Row Publisher.
6. Maslow, A. H. (1970) Motivation and Personality, Harper & Row Publishers Second Edition, USA.
7. Ryan, R. M., Sheldon, K. M., Kasser, T. ve Deci, E. L. (1996). All goals are not created equal: An organismic perspective on the nature of goals and their regulation. In P.M. Gollwitzer ve J. A. Bargh (Eds.), The psychology of action: Linking cognition and motivation to behavior (pp. 7-26). New York: Guilford.
8. Türk, S. (2013). "Akademisyenlerin temel psikolojik ihtiyaçlarının ve ihtiyaç doyum düzeylerinin çeşitli değişkenler açısından incelenmesi", Marmara Üniversitesi / Sağlık Bilimleri Enstitüsü / Psikiyatri Hemşireliği Anabilim Dalı, İstanbul.
9. Kesici, Ş., Üre Ö., Bozgeyikli, H., Sünbül, A., M. (2003) Temel Psikolojik İhtiyaçlar Ölçeğinin Geçerlik ve Güvenirliği". *VII. Ulusal PDR Kongresi Bildiri Özetleri Kitabı*, İnönü Ün., Malatya.
10. Özaydın N. (2011). Mesleki Müzik Eğitimi Alan Öğrencilerin Psikolojik İhtiyaçlarının ve Yaşam Doyumlarının İncelenmesi. S.Ü. Eğitim Bilimlerim Enstitüsü, Yüksek Lisans Tezi, Konya.
11. Yavuzer, Y., Gündoğdu, R. (2012). Eğitim Fakültesi Öğrencilerinin Öznel İyi Oluş ve Psikolojik İhtiyaçlarının Demografik Değişkenlere Göre İncelenmesi. Mehmet Akif Ersoy Üniversitesi Eğitim Fakültesi Dergisi, **12**(23), 115-131.
12. Yiğit R. (2012). Konya ilinde öğrenim gören yabancı uyruklu üniversite Öğrencilerinin temel psikolojik ihtiyaçlarının bir kısım değişkenler bakımından incelenmesi. Selçuk Üniversitesi Sosyal Bilimler Enstitüsü Dergisi, **27**, 317-326.
13. Rapport, N., Abbink, J., Canfield, R. L., Denby, D., Keane, W., Neveu, C., ... & Rapport, N. (2007). An outline for cosmopolitan study: Reclaiming the human through introspection. *Current Anthropology*, **48**(2), 257-283

Reviewing sports sciences students' perceived freedom levels in leisure in terms of any variables (Kocaeli university case)

Hakan Akdeniz[1] Yeşim Körmükçü[1,*] Gülşah Sekban[2] and İrem Bostan[1]

[1]Kocaeli University Sports Sciences Faculty Recreation Department
[2]Kocaeli University Sports Sciences Faculty Physical Education and Sports Teaching Department

Abstract. This study was executed with the aim of investigating whether the perceived freedom levels of students who study in the Faculty of Physical Education and Sports Sciences vary by any variables. The target population of the study composed of 240 voluntary students who study at Kocaeli University, the Faculty of Physical Education and Sports Sciences, 132 (55%) of whom was female and 108 (45%) of whom were male. Perceived Freedom in Leisure Scale, which was developed by Witt and Ellis (1985) and adopted into Turkish by [21] was used as the data collection tool of the study. Kolmogrov-Smirnof test analyzed whether the data showed normal distribution and it was observed that data do not display a normal distribution. As a result of this, Mann Whitney U and Kruskal Wallis H tests were applied. The significance level was considered as 0,05. No significant difference was identified between perceived freedom levels in leisure by means of certain variables such as gender, department, participation in social activities, approximate participation in recreation activities and frequency of leisure participation ($p>0,05$). A significant difference was found between knowledge and skill – excitement and joy by means of participation in sportive activities, participation in cultural and artistic activities and competence in recreation areas ($p<0,05$). Consequently, when knowledge and skill – excitement and joy sub-dimensions of students who use their recreational areas, attend to sportive and artistic activities were evaluated, it was seen that individuals who actively participate in any activity may perceive him or herself freer when he or she is compared to the individuals who participate in an activity in a passive way. Therefore, a further activity participation sense may be created.

1. INTRODUCTION

People in modern societies need activities in leisure time besides to blow off steam beside relaxation. Leisure time is the time that person gets rid of all challenges or connections and makes an activity that he desires [2].. Moreover, leisure time is the period that is left from the things that the person is obliged to make to meet the needs (eating, sleeping, physical needs) and sustain the life [10,19]. In the light of all these expressions, the leisure time is

* Corresponding author: ysmkormukcu@gmail.com

accepted as the time period that has satisfactory experiences, free of charge, exciting the sense of happiness and gladness. Personal control is provided independently from the external pressures [9, 13, 14]. mentioned that the activities that people attend to value this period are the recreative activities or leisure time activities which individuals participate in to value this period. Even though the leisure time activities or recreative activities concepts mean valuing the leisure times, they also mean restful and funny activities that individual voluntarily participate in to enjoy or develop physical, social and affective behaviors [5, 6]. People want to value the leisure time by actively or passively participating in leisure time activities in open and confined spaces in urban and rural areas because of several different reason and expectations [5].

There are various dimension and reasons for people to prefer and participate in the recreative activities. Desiring a repetition of an activity after performing it is the conclusion of positive experiences and perceiving that activity process as positive. Participating in the recreative activities is important because of creating freedom perception [1].

There are several studies show that active participation constitutes positive emotions on the individuals [3, 12, 24]. The freedom concept that is perceived as one of those feelings has emerged as a significant dimension to measure the leisure time behavior. It is assumed that the perceived freedom concept provides a causative relationship between the actor and the behavior as well as underlies the behavior of the actor himself [4].

Optimal effects of participating in the leisure time activities are associated with the freedom perception and controlling the leisure time optionally. Perceived freedom is a significant dimension to understand the leisure time activities. According to Heider's definition, perceived freedom is a tool that is used to estimate the human behaviors. It is the expression of the sense of perceived freedom of a person against the acts of another person. Besides, the perceived freedom is closely related to the responsibility and intent [1].

Since perceiving the freedom in leisure time is a voluntary behavior [17] and the individuals need to have skills such as competence, controlling the experiences and participating in the activities by internal expectations[20], perceiving the freedom is a concept that is needed for attention in measuring the leisure time behavior.

The main focus of the freedom concept that is perceived in leisure time is based on Neulinger's theory (1974) called 'leisure time as a mood' [22]. Perceived freedom is expressed as a cognitive-motivational structure by [20]. It is pointed out within this scope that one of the components that leisure time behavior depends is the depth of the participation.

This research aimed to review the perceived freedom based on gender, department, participation to social, sportive, cultural and artistic activities, leisure time and recreation area adequacy variables in terms of measuring the behaviors of students towards the leisure time activities.

2 Methodology

2.1 Research Group

The population was composed of 967 students of Sports Sciences Faculty in Kocaeli University. Those students chose one of the lessons from among basketball, football, volleyball, mountaineering, handball, fitness, swimming, chess, tennis, and table-tennis in the 2016-2017 academic year. This randomized sample group consisted of 240 students whose 132 (55%) of them were male and 108 (45%) of them were females.

2.2 Data Collection Tools:

In the first stage, the personal information form that has 10 questions on age, gender, university and department, leisure time, type of leisure time activities was used. In the second stage 'Perceived Freedom Leisure Scale' that was developed by [20] to measure the competencies, perceived control and perceived internal motivation was used. This same scale was adapted to Turkish by [26]; they also performed reliability and validity works of the scale. The original form of the scale is composed of 25 items; however, there was reached 17 items at the end of the factor analysis conducted. The scale consists of 2 sub-dimensions as (1) Knowledge and skill, (2) Excitement and Entertainment. Internal consistency coefficient of the scale was found as .94 as the result of the reliability and validity studies of [26]. Internal consistency coefficient was computed as .85 for knowledge and skill sub-dimension; .83 for excitement and entertainment sub-dimension. The scale mentioned is a five-point Likert scale; the questions are answered as 1 "Strongly Disagree", 5 "Strongly Agree" [26]. Knowledge and skill sub-dimension has 1st, 2nd, 3rd, 4th, 5th, 8th, 9th, 10th, 15th; excitement and entertainment sub-dimension has 6th, 7th, 11th, 12th, 13rd, 14th, 16th, 17th.

2.3 Data Collection

Data collection process for students of Sports Sciences Faculty of Kocaeli University was actualized in the spring terms of the 2016-2017 academic year. Students were informed about the qualification before the data collection; it was also provided to be counted the volunteer participants in the research. It was asked them to deliver the surveys within the same day to avoid the data loss in survey collecting. Missing answered questionnaires were not included in the study.

2.4 Data Analysis

Data were organized in Microsoft Excel 2013 program and analyzed by using SPSS 21.0 packaged software. Percentage and frequency methods were used to determine the distribution of the personal information of participants. Kolmogrov-Smirnof test was applied to specify whether the sub-dimensions of both scales show a normal distribution. With reference to the test results, all the sub-dimension of Perceived Freedom in Leisure Scale do not show normal distribution. Mann Whitney U test was utilized for bivariant data; Kruskal Wallis test was applied for more than two variables. The significance level was accepted as p<,05.

3 Findings

Table1. Gender distribution of participants

Gender	n	%
Male	132	55,0
Female	108	45,0

Table2. Department distribution of participants

Department	n	%
Coaching	48	20,0
Physical Education and Sports Teaching	46	19,2
Recreation	97	40,4
Sports Management	49	20,4
Total	240	100,0

Table 3. Weekly leisure time of participants

Weekly Leisure Time	n	%
1-5 hours	27	11,2
6-10 hours	78	32,5
11-15 hours	64	26,7
16 hours and above	71	29,6
Total	240	100,0

Table 4. Types of participating in sportive activities as leisure time activity distribution of participants

Activity	Type of Participation	n	%
Sportive Activity	Aktive	208	86,7
	Pasive	32	13,3
Total		240	100,0

Table 5. Types of participating in sportive activities as leisure time activity distribution of participants

Activity	Type of Participation	n	%
Social Activity	Active	186	77,5
	Passive	54	22,5
Total		240	100,0

Table 6. Types of participating in cultural and artistic activities as leisure time activity distribution of participants

Activity	Type of Participation	n	%
Cultural and Artistic Activity	Active	69	28,7
	Passive	171	71,3
Total		240	100,0

Table 7. Recreative area adequacy of university to participants' mind

Recreative Area	n	%
Absolutely Adequate	10	4,2
Adequate	90	37,5
Partly	84	35,0
Inadequate	43	17,9
Absolutely Inadequate	13	5,4
Total	240	100,0

Table 8. Relationship of perceived freedom in leisure sub-dimension based on gender variable

	Gender	N	Rank Value Average	z	p
Knowledge and Skill sub-dimension	Male	132	121,98	-,368	,713
	Female	108	118,69		
Excitement and Entertainment sub-dimension	Male	132	121,26	-,188	,851
	Female	108	119,57		

Table 9. Relationship of perceived freedom in leisure sub-dimension based on department

	Department	n	Rank Value Average	df	p
Knowledge and Skill sub-dimension	Coaching	48	120,79	3	,950
	Physical Education and Sports Teaching	46	125,65		
	Recreation	97	118,59		
	Sports Management	49	119,16		
Excitement and Entertainment sub-dimension	Coaching	48	133,22	3	,370
	Physical Education and Sports Teaching	46	118,13		
	Recreation	97	112,85		
	Sports Management	49	125,42		
	Total	240			

Table 10. Relationship of perceived freedom in leisure sub-dimension based on leisure time period variable

	Leisure Time Period	n	Rank Value Average	df	p
Knowledge and Skill sub-dimension	1-5 hours	26	136,19	3	,474
	6-10 hours	78	123,85		
	11-15 hours	64	114,24		
	16 hours and above	71	115,03		
	Total	239			
Excitement and Entertainment sub-dimension	1-5 hours	26	131,15	3	,605
	6-10 hours	78	123,09		
	11-15 hours	64	120,70		
	16 hours and above	71	111,89		
	Total	239			

Table 11. Relationship of perceived freedom in leisure sub-dimension based on participating in social activities variable

	Participating in social activities	n	Rank value average	Average	z	p
Knowledge and Skill sub-dimension	Active	186	120,12	22343,00	-,157	,875
	Passive	54	121,80	6577,00		
	Total	240				
Excitement and Skill sub-dimension	Active	186	124,88	23228,00	-1,830	,067
	Passive	54	105,41	5692,00		
	Total	240				

Table 12. Relationship of perceived freedom in leisure sub-dimension based on participating in cultural and artistic activities variable

	Participating in Cultural and Artistic Activities	n	Rank Value Average	Average	z	p
Knowledge and Skill sub-dimension	Active	68	140,38	9546,00		
	Passive	172	112,64	19374,00	-2,813	,005
	Total	240				
Excitement and Entertainment sub-dimension	Active	68	138,11	9391,00		
	Passive	172	113,54	19528,00	-2,485	,013
	Total	240				

Table 13. Relationship of Perceived Freedom in Leisure Sub-Dimension Based on Participating in Sportive Activities Variable

	Participating in Sportive Activities	n	Sıra Değer Ortalama	Ortalama	z	p
Information and Skill sub-dimension	Active	208	128,57	26742,00	-4,615	,000
	Passive	32	68,06	2178,00		
Excitement and Entertainment sub-dimension	Active	208	125,56	26115,50		
	Passive	32	87,64	2804,50	-2,900	,004
	Total	240				

Table 14. Relationship of perceived freedom in leisure sub-dimension based on recreational areas adequacy variable

	Recreational Areas Adequacy	n	Rank Value Average	df	p
Information and Skill sub-dimension	Absolutely Adequate	10	120,05	4	,026
	Adequate	90	132,94		
	Partly	84	100,67		
	Inadequate	43	131,43		
	Absolutely Inadequate	13	126,65		
	Total	240			
Excitement and Entertainment sub-dimension	Absolutely Adequate	10	89,60	4	,004
	Adequate	90	119,69		
	Partly	84	106,31		
	Inadequate	43	145,57		
	Absolutely Inadequate	13	158,65		
	Total	240			

There was a significant relationship ($p<0,05$) between sub-dimensions perceived in leisure time and participating in cultural, artistic, sportive activities and recreation areas variables

4 Discussions

This research aimed to review the perceived freedom of students study in Sports Sciences Faculty of Kocaeli University based on gender, department, participation to social, sportive, cultural and artistic activities, leisure time and recreation area adequacy variables in terms of measuring the behaviors of students towards the leisure time activities.

There was not found a significant difference between the sample group's perceived freedom levels based on gender, department, participation in social activities and leisure time. However, significant differences were observed between recreational area adequacy and participation to sportive, cultural and artistic activities.

According to another finding, there was no significant difference in 'Knowledge and Skill' (,713) and 'Excitement and Entertainment' (,851) sub-dimensions based on gender variable. Lapa and Ağyar [23] conducted a study to determine the perceived freedom levels of university students based on leisure time participation. They pointed out that the gender is not a significant factor in specifying the perceived freedom level. [27]; performed a survey towards the perceived freedom in leisure time and leisure time satisfaction levels of the employees work in catering food-drink sector. With reference to their research findings, there are significant differences in 'Knowledge and Skill' sub-dimension. It can be seen when viewed from this aspect that our research finding shows parallelism with their research in terms of 'Knowledge and Skill' sub-dimension.

There was not found a significant difference in 'Knowledge and Skill' (,950) and 'Excitement and Entertainment' (,370) sub-dimensions in terms of the perceived freedom levels based on the department. According to this outcome, even though the students study in different departments, they approach to the leisure time activities by the similar attitudes. While the students of Recreation department get excited more in comparison with the students study in Physical Education and Sports Teaching, the participants sho study in Coaching and Sports Management department accept themselves as well-versed on this activity.

There was not found a significant difference in 'Knowledge and Skill' (,474) and 'Excitement and Entertainment' (,605) sub-dimensions in terms of the freedom levels perceived in leisure time.

It was observed that the participants actively participate in the sportive and social activities; they passively participate in the cultural and artistic activities. We can easily see that active participants participate to leisure time activities at a higher rate in comparison with the participants who passively attend in the same activities based on the types of participation in knowledge and skill sub-dimension. The research that was performed by [23] shows parallelism with our research findings. Moreover, our research findings have parallelism with the study that was conducted by [16] as well.

This research reviewed whether being the participation active or passive create the difference in perceived leisure times. It is seen that the perceived freedom levels of active participants are higher than the passive participants in all of the social activities. Besides, there were mostly the passive participants who attend in the cultural and artistic activities.

There was seen a significant difference in 'Knowledge and Skill' (,0,12) and 'Excitement and Entertainment' (,0,06) sub-dimensions in terms of perceived freedom levels in leisure time based on participation to the cultural and artistic activities.

[22] conducted a study and modeled the structural relationship of perceived freedom and leisure time participation; this relationship revealed a compatible model. Finding the perceived freedom is high is normal when the previous studies [3, [12], [24] on the positive feelings of the active participation to the leisure time activities on the people are considered.

There was found a significant difference in 'Knowledge and Skill' (,026) and 'Excitement and Entertainment' (,004) sub-dimensions in terms of the perceived freedom in leisure time based on the recreational area adequacy. It was observed with regard to this finding that the general run of the students finds the recreational areas as adequate. Also, the ratio of students who answered as 'partly' is close to the ratio of students who find those areas as adequate.

In some of the situations, the perceived freedom in leisure time has an improver effect on the leisure time participation. [11] performed a study for the high school students and emphasized that the leisure time participation is significantly higher in students with high freedom levels. [25] expressed that the perceived freedom in leisure time is a mechanism that affects the satisfaction for leisure time needs, competence, depth of the participation and leisure time outputs in children (10-13 ages) with developmental coordination disorder.

References

1. Ardahan, F. Turgut, T. Kalkan, K. (2016). *Her Yönüyle Rekreasyon* Ankara: Detay yayıncılık.
2. Bakır M. (1990). Rekreasyon ve Turizm İlişkisinin Turizm Politikalarının Oluşturulmasındaki Önemi. Basılmamış Doktora Tezi. İstanbul Üniversitesi. Sosyal Bilimler Enstitüsü.
3. Caldwell L, Smith E, Weissenger E. (1992). The relationship of leisure activities and perceived health of college students. *Society and Leisure*, **15**(2), 545–556.
4. Kane TR, Joseph JM, Tedeschi JT. (1977). Perceived freedom, aggression and responsibility, and the assignment of punishment. *The Journal of Social Psychology,* **103**, 257-263.
5. Karaküçük S. (2005). *Rekreasyon*. Ankara: Gazi Kitabevi.
6. Kılbaş Ş. (2001). *Rekreasyon: Boş Zamanı Değerlendirme.* Adana: Anaca Yayınları.
7. Lapa TY, Ağyar E. (2011). Cross-cultural adaptation of perceived freedom in leisure scale. World Applied Sciences Journal, **14**(7), 980-986.
8. Lapa, T. Y., Ağyar, E. (2012). Üniversite Öğrencilerinin Serbest Zaman Katılımlarına Göre Algılanan Özgürlük. *Spor Bilimleri Dergisi, 23*(1), 24-33.
9. Mieczkowski Z. (1990). *World Trend in Tourism and Recreation.* New York: Peter Lang Publishing
10. Mull RF, Bayless KG, Ross CM, Jamieson LM. (1997). Recreational Sport Management. (3th Edition) USA: Human Kinetics.
11. Munson WW. (1993). Perceived freedom in leisure and career salience in adolescence. Journal of Leisure Research, **5**(3), 305-314
12. Murphy H. (2003). Exploring leisure and psychological health and wellbeing: Some problematic issues in the case of Northern ireland. *Leisure Studies,* **22**(1), 37–50.
13. Önder S. (2003). Selçuk üniversitesi öğrencilerinin rekreasyonel eğilim ve taleplerinin belirlenmesi üzerine bir araştırma. *S.Ü. Ziraat Fakültesi Dergisi,* **17**(32), 31-38.
14. Ragheb MG, Tate RL. (1993). A behavioral model of leisure participation based on leisure attitude, motivation and satisfaction. *Leisure Studies,* **12**, 61-70.
15. Serdar E. Ay SM. (2016) Üniversite Öğrencilerinin Katıldıkları Serbest Zaman Etkinliklerinden Tatmin Olma ve Algılanan Özgürlük Düzeylerinin İncelenmesi. Sobider Sosyal Bilimleri Dergisi. **3**(9), 365-374
16. Serdar E. (2016). Üniversite Öğrencilerinin Katıldıkları Serbest Zaman Etkinliklerinden Tatmin Olma ve Algılanan Özgürlük Düzeylerinin İncelenmesi. Yayınlanmış Yüksek Lisans Tezi, Marmara Üniversitesi. Sağlık Bilimleri Enstitüsü.
17. Siegenthaler KL, O'Dell I. (2000). Leisure attitude, leisure satisfaction and perceived freedom in leisure within family dyads. *Leisure Sciences,* **22**, 281-296.
18. Şener A. (2009). Yaşlılık, yaşam doyumu ve boş zaman faaliyetleri. *Çağın Polisi Dergisi.* **93**, 04 Nisan 2012, http://www.sdergi.hacettepe.edu.tr/yasamdoyumu.pdf.
19. Torkildsen G. (2005). *Recreation and Leisure Management* (5th Edition). London and New York: Routledge, Taylor and Francis Group.
20. Witt PA, Ellis GD. (1985). Development of a short form to assess perceived freedom in leisure. *Journal of Leisure Research,* **17**(3), 225-233.
21. Yerlisu Lapa, T., & Agyar, E. (2011). Cross-cultural adaptation of perceived freedom in leisure scale. *World Applied Sciences Journal, 14*(7), 980-986.
22. Wu HC, Liu A, Wang CH. (2010). Taiwanese university students' perceived freedom and participation in leisure. Annals of Leisure Research, **13**(4), 679-700.

23. Yerlisu Lapa, T., Ağyar, E., & Bahadır, Z. (2012). Yaşam tatmini, serbest zaman motivasyonu, serbest zaman katılımı: beden eğitimi ve spor öğretmenleri üzerine bir inceleme (Kayseri ili örneği). *Spormetre Beden Eğitimi ve Spor Bilimleri Dergisi, **X** (2)*, 53-59.
24. Şener A. (2009). Yaşlılık, yaşam doyumu ve boş zaman faaliyetleri. Çağın Polisi Dergisi. 93, 04 Nisan 2012, http://www.sdergi.hacettepe.edu.tr/yasamdoyumu.pdf.
25.Poulsen AA, Ziviani JM, Cuskelly M. (2007). Perceived freedom in leisure and physical co-ordination ability: Impact on out-of-school activity participation and life satisfaction. Child: Care, Health and Development, **33**(4), 432-440.
26. Yerlisu Lapa, T., & Agyar, E. (2011). Cross-cultural adaptation of perceived freedom in leisure scale. *World Applied Sciences Journal, **14***(7), 980-986.
27. Kodaş, D., Kodaş B., Arıca, R. (2015) Yiyecek içecek Çalışanlarının Serbest Zaman tatmin Düzeyleri ile Serbest Zaman Algılanan Özgürlüklerinin İncelenmesi 3. Rekreasyon Araştırmaları Kongresi, Eskişehir Anadolu Üniversitesi.

Health education and teaching innovation at the university: Experience with students of social sciences

Encarnación Pedrero-García[a]

[a]Facultad de Ciencias Sociales, Universidad Pablo de Olavide, Crta. De Utrera, Km.1 Seville, ES-41013, Spain

Abstract. The objective of this paper is to show how health education can be introduced transversally in the university to improve the quality of life of students. Through a teaching innovation project, we have incorporated a meeting point to educate and inform about health education, involving 180 students from the social education degree at the Pablo de Olavide University (Seville, Spain). The methodology followed is quantitative using an ex professo script and analyzing the data with the SPSS software in order to measure the satisfaction degree of student with respect to 5 variables: usefulness, methodology, organization and resources, teaching staff and general satisfaction. The results show that the majority of students are satisfied with the inclusion of health education related topics.

1 Introduction

The teaching team of this project has consolidated, through a decade of continuous work in the field, a strategic line on Education and Health Promotion (developed by the WHO in the Ottawa Charter, 1986), within the Pablo de Olavide University of Seville. This work has been carried out in four main areas:

-Teaching and training in undergraduate, master's, expert and university extension courses, as well as conferences and seminars such as: Education for Health and Quality of Life, Prevention of Drug Addiction and Addiction, Educational Action in Children and Youth, Sociocultural Animation and Community Development, Youth Mediators in Health Education, Prevention of psychosocial risks in adolescents and young people....

-Research: through different projects and studies on the prevalence, attitudes, patterns and motivations of the university population in relation to drug use, etc., from which a good number of papers have been published in indexed journals as well as books.

-Dissemination: through information and training activities on prevention and awareness campaigns aimed at the whole of the University Community, held on the commemorative days most closely related to healthy habits.

-Collaboration with other public and private bodies and institutions: Regional Ministries of Education, Health and Social Welfare of the Regional Government of Andalusia, Seville City Council, Dos Hermanas City Council, Proyecto Hombre, Fundación de Ayuda contra

[a]Corresponding author: epedgar@upo.es

la Drogadicción, Reina Sofía Centre, ISTAS Foundation, National Institute for Health and Safety at Work...), in the establishment of agreements and projects for the dissemination and advancement of Health Education/Promotion.

In this same line of work, we consider it essential that at the Pablo de Olavide University of Seville, which is already part of the Spanish Network of Healthy Universities (www.unisaludables.es), as well as the Andalusian Network of Healthy Universities, a Youth Form point is created, which will contribute to our centre becoming a healthy space where young people can receive information and attention to help them decide on the healthiest answers (http://www.formajoven.org/).

The Forma Joven is a Youth Information and Training Program for adolescents and young people. It is constituted as a health strategy aimed at promoting healthy environments and behaviours among young people in Andalusia. The strategy consists of bringing health promotion and health risk prevention activities closer to the environments where young people live and give them an active and central role in these activities. It is based on intersectoral action and its development involves several Departments of the Andalusian Regional Government, as well as other institutions and social agents such as town halls, associations, etc. Thousands of students have participated in it since its development.

Forma Joven aims to train boys and girls to make the healthiest choices in terms of their lifestyles: nutrition, physical activity, sexuality, etc. and their psychological and social well-being, as well as in the prevention of accidents, smoking and other addictions. It takes place in the Youth Form Points, located in the various spaces frequented by the youth population, including the universities.

The creation of this point Forma Joven and its full integration into the University is carried out by involving students in three subjects of the Faculty of Social Sciences through the methodology of collaborative learning.

2 Methodology

We start from a methodology based on collaborative learning, which implies that students actively participate in a motivated and committed way in their own teaching-learning process, while developing basic professional skills.

For the development of the project we started by establishing the work teams, and within them, small groups in each of the subjects involved in the project. The small working groups are made up of a maximum of 4 people, promoting diversity within them and, if possible, a balance between the number of boys and girls in the group. The more talents, visions and different sensibilities we integrate into the project, the more enriching the experience will be.

The functioning of the groups is based on rules of dialogue as well as on the assignment of roles based on their motivations and abilities, which are given to them in writing in advance at the beginning of the semester. The philosophy of collaborative work implies that students must take responsibility for their own learning as well as the learning of the rest of the small group. This makes it easier for both the assignment of roles and the commitment and fulfilment of tasks to be managed by the students themselves. The number of participants in the project is approximately 200 students.

The task of the project's teaching staff is to guide them through each of the phases, but to allow them to assume maximum responsibility gradually, so that they can plan, organize and develop their own ideas.

The reason for choosing the methodology of collaborative learning is the flexibility it offers us as it allows us to work through project-based learning, webquests, flipped classroom, etc....

The students have the necessary time to generate ideas, discuss and contrast them, both in small groups and in the large group, encouraging them to participate in the decision-making process of the project in a group setting.

The project has been developed in 4 phases:

1) Creation of the point Forma Joven in the University.

2) Management and dissemination of the Youth Information Point among the university community.

3) Planning and execution of activities to be developed from the point of Youth Form based on the five areas of intervention: Emotional education, healthy lifestyles, sexuality and egalitarian relationships, positive use of ICT, consumption prevention.

4) Project Evaluation.

The actions and milestones developed in each phase are detailed below:

The first phase in which the Forma Joven point was created took place in September, with the beginning of the course.

During the month of October, the physical space and website of the Forma Joven was managed and disseminated through the social networks and posters distributed throughout the university.

During the months of November and December we worked with the group of the subject "Educational action in childhood and youth" (3rd double degree Social Education-Social Work) in the planning of the activities to be developed from the Youth Form. The large group was divided into 15 small groups of 4 people. These groups chose the theme to work on within the 5 priority areas of Forma Joven: Emotional education, Healthy lifestyles, Sexuality and egalitarian relationships, Positive use of ICT, Consumption prevention. At the same time, actions were planned for December 1 (World AIDS Day) to spread and prevent the disease.

With the beginning of the second semester, we involved two new groups, students from the subjects "Sociocultural Animation" (4th of the double degree ES-TS) and "Health Education" (3rd ES). Following the methodology developed in the first semester of collaborative learning, the students were distributed in small groups and we began to carry out training for the university community. Workshops were held in February, March, April and May, as well as on 7 April (World Health Day) and 30 May (World No Tobacco Day).

3 Research result

The project will be evaluated in a processual way with the achievement of milestones that we establish in each of its 4 phases. In turn, the evaluation of students with respect to their participation in the project will be carried out through rubrics so that they can self-evaluate and evaluate the work done by their peers in the groups, in accordance with the methodology of collaborative learning. On the other hand, the teaching team will arrange individual and group interviews to follow up with the project participants. The interviews, together with the observation and the headings of the students will constitute the instruments of evaluation of the same one.

We believe that this teaching innovation project is a benefit for the entire University Pablo de Olavide, and not only for the participants in it, since by creating the youth information point we are influencing the improvement of the quality of life of the entire university community in the long term. The project aims to research, innovate, apply, train, and inform about healthy lifestyle habits using the collaborative learning methodology.

The innovation can be easily transferred, as the collaborative learning methodology can be replicated in any subject, subject or qualification. In addition, our priority objective is to provide an environment in which the students of the Faculty of Social Sciences can become professionals in the university, so we are promoting professional skills that they will need in the near future, while working collaboratively.

Results show that Forma Joven is a support tool for those promoting youth health and for the educational institution. Teachers coordinating the program are a crucial figure to promote health. Encouraging the participation and implication of students in the different activities is the key to the program success. The majority of students are satisfied with the inclusion of health education-related topics. The self-perception shown indicates that they find beneficial having knowledge and specific information about sexuality, addictions, emotional education and healthy habits, as they believe these are important topics for their personal and career development.

4 Conclusion

In conclusion, the program Forma Joven is an excellent strategy for the promotion of healthy contexts and behaviours among students and young people. It also encourages youth learning and the collaboration between the educational institution and healthcare community resources. Regarding the originality and value of the proposal, we think that teaching innovation projects where health education is integrated in order to improve the quality of life of students can hardly be found in our country.

The Forma Joven programme is a health strategy for adolescents and young people launched in 2001 by different Departments of the Regional Government of Andalusia, in who also collaborate with other institutions and agents social as city councils and/or mothers' associations and parents, who consider it objectives:

- Bringing the promotion closer from health to the places they frequent usually the boys and girls.
- Contribute to providing them with resources and capacities to deal with the risks.
- Encourage the possibility of combining health and fun.
- Encourage the choice of healthier behaviors.

It takes place preferably in schools in Andalusia, although it also takes place in other places frequented.

by this population as associations, leisure spaces or NGOs, among others.

By virtue of the pedagogical, organisational and managerial autonomy of educational establishments, they may choose to register for "Forma Joven" on a voluntary basis, making the application for participation. The development of the program responds to a project of action planned, carried out and evaluated by the Forma Joven Team. In this cooperation, professionals from the education, health and other sectors, such as education, health and of drug prevention.

For the Forma Joven Team to be constituted, it will always be a necessary condition for coordination between the centre and the health center. Almost 85% of the educational centres

states that there is a coordinated working relationship between the coordinating faculty and staff of the programme health professional, the telephone being the way of communication used by these professionals.

At the same time, communication and coordination with the persons involved in programme activities take place at the meetings of the Forma Joven Team. The usefulness of these meetings is rated with a score of average of more than 7 on a scale of 0 to 10. The teaching staff coordinating the programme is a key figure in promoting health at this age by enabling a greater rapprochement with boys and girls. In this sense, all the agents surveyed assess the continuity of the programme in educational establishments with a score of "remarkable". In general, the areas of "Healthy Lifestyles" and "Sexuality and Relationships" are the most frequently addressed by young people. The activities corresponding to "Drug prevention and other addictions" are preferred. The Evaluation Study of the Youth Form Programme concludes that it is an excellent strategy for the promotion of contexts and healthy behaviors among young people, while also encouraging the learning of young people.

References

1. Bisquerra, A. R. (coord.). *Educación emocional. Propuestas para educadores y familias.* Bilbao: Desclée de Brower, (2011).
2. Bisquerra, A. R. Educación emocional y competencias básicas para la vida. *Revista de Investigación Educativa, 21*(1), 7-43, (2003).
3. Cobo Romaní, R. El concepto de tecnologías de la información. Benchmarking sobre las definiciones de las TIC en la sociedad del conocimiento. *ZER: Revista de Estudios de Comunicación, Volumen 14 – Número 27*, (2009).
4. O.M.S. *Carta de Ottawa para la promoción de la salud. Conferencia internacional para la promoción de la salud.* Ottawa: Asociación Canadiense de Salud Pública, (1986).
5. Martínez, A., Muñoz, M.C., Cobos, D. "Intervención educativa en socioadicciones y adicciones sin sustancia". En *Educación para la salud y prevención de riesgos psicosociales en adolescentes y jóvenes"* (181-198). Madrid: Narcea, (2017).
6. Morón, J.A, Pérez, I. y Pedrero, E. *Educación para la Salud y prevención de los riesgos psicosociales: En adolescentes y jóvenes*. Madrid: Narcea, (2017).
7. Morón, J.A. (2015). *Investigar e intervenir en Educación para la Salud.* Madrid: Narcea.
8. Pedrero, E. El Ámbito Preventivo en Drogodependencias: Revisando Programas de Promoción y Educación para la Salud. Actas del Congrés Internacional Virtual d'Educació CIVE 2010. Palma de Mallorca: Escola de formació en Mitjans Didàctics (STEI-i), (2010).
9. Pedrero, E. "Los modelos de educación afectivo-sexual en adolescentes y jóvenes". En *Investigar e intervenir en Educación para la Salud (*133-146). Madrid: Narcea, (2015).

The study of form structuring through musical rhythm analogies for architecture students

Andrei Racolța[1,*] and *Diana* Giurea[2]

[1]Faculty of Architecture and Urbanism, Politehnica University of Timisoara, Traian Lalescu 2/A, 300223, Timisoara, Romania

Abstract. The aim of the study is to facilitate the rhythmic management of shape by understanding the basics of the sonorous rhythm.The method used is based on an examplification using musical instruments, audio tools and a specific/ intuitive rhythmical semiography.This theoretical part is applied in the discipline called "The study of form",conducted at the Faculty of Architecture in Timisoara, in the 2nd year of the bachelor programme using an exercise entitled rhytmical volumetric frieze. The method and results are presented in the illustrative part of the paper. Understanding musical rhythm is a fertile base for those working in the field of architecture, design and visual arts in general. The formal diversity obtained exhibites the polyrhythmics and the variation specific to musical rhythm, contrary to monorhythm and isorhythm.

1 Introduction

The full association of the idea of rhythm with repetition and, especially, with the equal and identical repetition of a single element is the main cause for rhythmic scarcity of architecture because it reduces the potential of a highly fecund language element to its most trivial and primitive version. The phenomenon is due to the confusion that most [1,2] make between rhythm and measure, between rhythmics – the living component of musical rhythm – and metrics – the virtual component represented by bars and metric accents repeated, indeed, at equal intervals, but whose voicing is not mandatory, a confusion sometimes made by musicians, too. In other words, musical rhythm can occur unevenly on equal measures without disturbing the order and symmetry imposed by metrics. The only period in which rhythmic emphasis (ictus) overlaps with the metric one (thesis) is represented by the functional tonal music, generally known as "classical music" (18th – 19th century) where periodic and equal repetition of the rhythmic emphasis was valued aesthetically as the main means of expression, with synchronous or slightly offset correspondences in the period's architecture.

Music theory tells us that the idea of monorhythm, that is a rhythm consisting of a single element repeated endlessly and similar to the natural isorhythm, does not make sense in music [3]. The monorhythm makes no sense in nature either, because, if we were to consider the ebb and flow as equal in duration, they still do not resemble each other, being

[*] Corresponding author: diana.giurea@upt.ro

even antagonistic, and that is why they make up a couple, so a rhythm of 2, i.e. binary. The same goes for systole and diastole, which are not even equal. In the case of the rhythmic formula based on equal note values, rhythmic emphasis will fall on the note to be decided by the other component of rhythm – intensity. If we were to consider the equal repetition of a single sound with the same intensity, note and timbre, where nothing would suggest an emphasis of any kind, we would not obtain a musical rhythm, because in the absence of emphasis musical rhythm has no meaning. The so-called "rhythm of 1" [2] exists in the visual field, where it manifests by the same element repeated at equal intervals, but it is actually a "rhythm of 2" [4]. The rhythm of 1 of a classical colonnade might be translated into a repeating binary rhythmical formula consisting of two beats in which one was replaced by a rest, in which case we would have the simple example of developing rhythm by means of rests, and thus obtain a reconciliation with music theory.

2 Theoretical basis

2.1 Musical definitions

To formulate a definition, it is necessary to treat rhythm at two levels: macrostructural and microstructural. At a macro scale, starting from the etymology of the Greek word reo meaning "to flow, to move, to pass", rhythm represents movement, a succession over time of world phenomena and processes. Movement is the basic principle of the whole world; all processes in the universe known to man are based on dynamic principles. In music, "rhythm means the entire process of movement of all elements of sound" [5], i.e., the succession of all musical parameters (length, frequency, timbre, dynamics, tempo) in their full flow. In other words, at a macrostructural level, rhythm is not only the distribution and succession over time of sound elements perceived as beats, because it also includes melodic movement.

However, at a microstructural level, the definition of rhythm considers only the relationships over time from the sound movement, i.e., "the distribution over time of sounds under the notion of length" [5], musical rhythm being thus considered as an independent and concrete parameter, sounds and rests forming a body which then determines the existence of other movements: melodic, harmonic, polyphonic, dynamic. According to musicologist Constantin Rîpă, "the full definition of rhythm would be: rhythm means lengths, intensities and tempo." [5]

2.2 General definitions

To have an artistic rhythm, it is necessary to simultaneously fulfill some conditions: some component elements (audio or visual) need to exist; in order to have a succession, there must be at least two elements; there needs to be a development environment; this succession needs to have an organization rule, an order and a variation. In this context, a comprehensive definition of artistic rhythm would be: "the organized and varied succession of elements in space and time" [6].

In the composition of static visual arts, therefore in architecture, too, rhythm refers to the organization of the succession of lines, shapes, sizes and differences, and not to their identical repetition. Identical repetition of a linear, formal or dimensional element does not contradict the meaning of rhythm, but it does not represent a condition there of either.

3 Disabstractification by analogy

The disabstractification of the concept of visual rhythm can be made by sound analogies. The aim of the study is to facilitate the rhythmic management of form by understanding the basics of sonorous rhythm. The method used is based on the examples using musical instruments, audios and an own, intuitive rhythmic semiograhpy.

The raw material of music is sound, so the elements that will make up the musical rhythm will be the sounds with all their physiological characteristics: pitch (note), length (continuity over time), intensity (strength) and timbre. However, rhythm will manage the organization of sounds, intercorrelating their length and positioning on the time axis. The primary elements of artistic language are forms. Thus, in a purely analytical dissociation of the configurational constituents, forms can be distinguished from each other by: size, color, consistency and texture. As the sound's physiological characteristics (length, pitch, intensity, timbre) are contained entirely in a sound unit, similarly the form's physiological characteristics (size, color, consistency and texture) are found in a visual configuration.

To make a full analogy between sound and form starting from the correspondences found in physics of the physiological characteristics of sound is impossible, because, if for forms one can detect a rule for its structuring on the three dimensions of space, the situation is not the same for sounds. We can make analogies between length (continuity over time) and size (continuity in space), sound intensity (volume, amplitude) and visual intensity (poignancy, visibility, consistency), pitch (oscillation frequency of the sound wave) and color (frequency of the electromagnetic, light radiation) [7], between timbre (spectral form of vibrations, exterior characteristic given by the construction material of the sound transmitter and its production technique) and texture or, once again, color, but if a form can contain two or three dimensions simultaneously, sound can only have one length, because time is one-dimensional.

Rhythm has an exclusively linear development in music because of the existence of a single axis, that of time. In two-dimensional arts, it can be deployed linearly or on the surface, and, in three-dimensional arts, it can be deployed on all three dimensions of space, organizing it at spatial volumetric level. From the point of view of the systematics of musical rhythm, notes are organized into simple rhythmic formulas that can be binary or ternary, while heterogeneous rhythms (made of 5, 7, 8 notes, etc.) will be the many possible combinations of binary with ternary. In the bimodular sense of the rhythmic formula in which notes may have two different values, the emphasis will be the long note of the formula. In the case of the rhythmic formula based on equal values (in the unimodular sense), the note on which the rhythmic accent (ictus) will fall will be decided by the other internal component of rhythm – intensity.

Measure in music can be treated as a macromodular system based on a single equal module, represented by the note value of the fraction's denominator (quarter, eighth, sixteenth) and on a number that designates in how many such equal modules is the mensural frame divided. If for the measure in music this module is very suggestively called "beat" and has actually a purely temporal connotation, in the visual field it belongs to size, distance in the physical space. The part of musical theory presented to students does not include the development procedures of musical rhythm (classical, harmonic and rhythmic, melodic and rhythmic) because they belong to the superior theory of rhythm, which is unfortunately accessible only to students from music high schools or faculties.

4 The experiment

This theoretical part is applied to the discipline titled 'The Study of Form' from the Faculty of Architecture in Timisoara, Furniture and Interior Design specialization, conducted with 2nd year students by two exercises titled: "Modular Spatial Composition" and "The Rhythmic Frieze".

4.1 Modular spatial composition

This exercise is based on the analogy between a visual modular system and the divisional system of musical values (Fig. 1a), an analogy on the dimensional growth by addition and doubling in one direction, as in music, in two directions, as in the two-dimensional arts (Fig. 1b), or in volume, as in spatial arts (Fig. 1c).

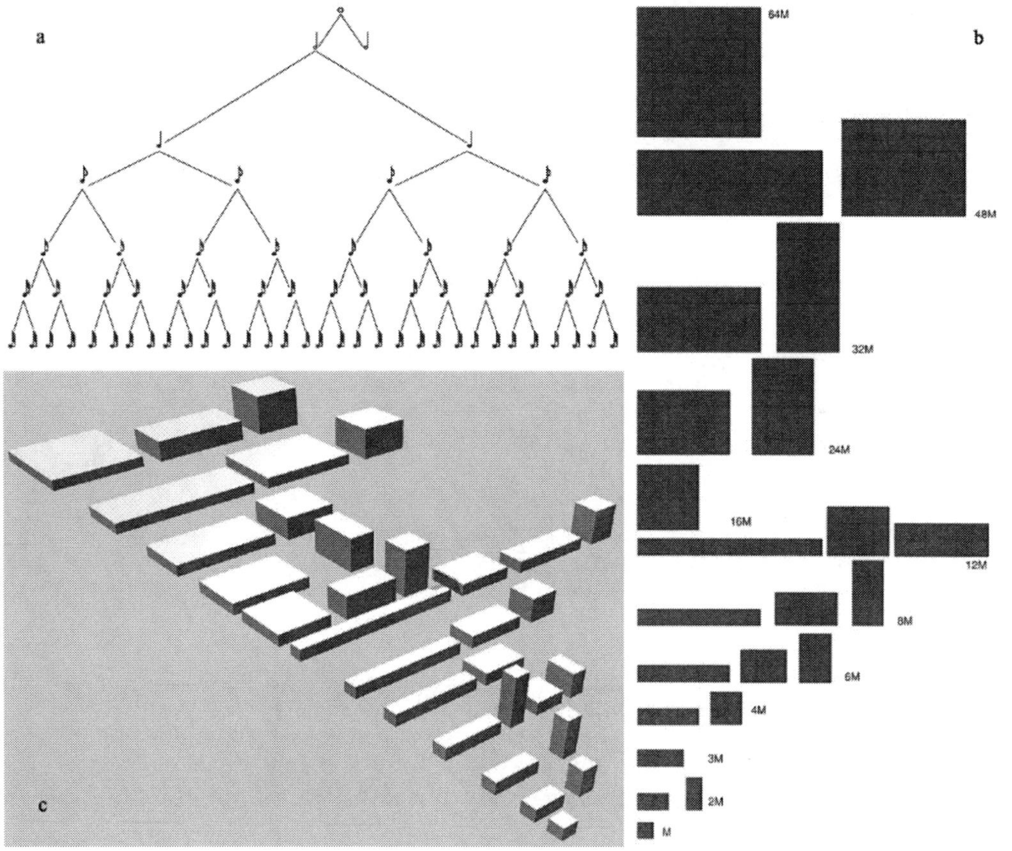

Fig. 1. (a) The divisional system of musical values; (b) bidimensional analogy; (c) threedimensional analogy

The task: develop a spatial composition in a 32-cm cube, modulated according to a spatial scale relative to divisional proportioning system – similar to the divisional system of music values. The module – the basic unit that divides all volumes – is a 2-cm cube. This cube-module represents the "point". By adding (or "moving") in one direction, it describes the "line". Moving the "line" in one direction perpendicular to it defines the "plan" . Moving the "plan" in a direction perpendicular to it generates the "volume". The spatial composition shall use all four modalities of expressing form: volume, plans, lines and points. Working materials: colored cardboard paper (any color), glue. A "point" shall have one color. A "line" shall consist of points of the same color, resulting, in fact, in a square section tubular volume (2x2cm), continuous but divisible by 2 cm; it will not be a succession of little cubes. Identically, a "plan" will be a monochromatic prism with a height of 2 cm, divisible the other two sides by 2 cm, while a "volume" will also be monochromatic. The colors of "volumes", "plans", "lines" and "points" shall be different. The underlying grid shall remain virtual; it should not be expressed physically (no support cube, wires, etc. need to be built), but composition must have the statics secured on either side of the virtual cube framing it.

As a preparatory exercise for the ultimate purpose of the experiment, students received the visual examples given in Fig. 1 and Fig.2, plus other similar ones. For this reason, the results were somewhat similar.

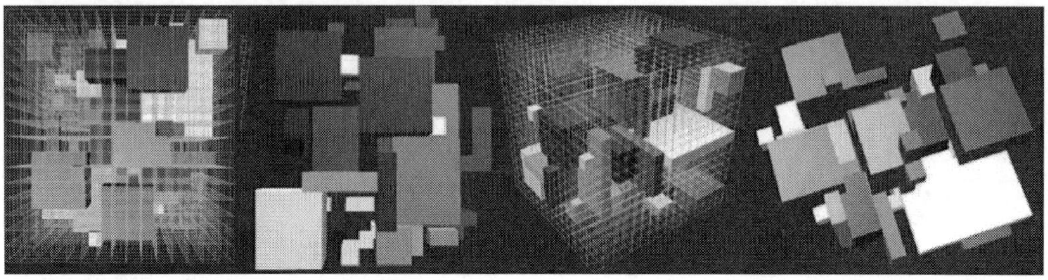

Fig. 2. Visual examples

Fig. 3. Student work

4.2 The rhythmic frieze

The task: choose four measures from a favourite song, and translate them into the visual field on a cardboard paper support, showing the movements of the instruments involved in the sound fragment. The students were helped by us to detect the beginning and end of a measure, the beats in the bar and their number, thus observing the difference between the time values voiced in the actual rhythm and the virtual, voiceless beats. Previously, using a drum machine and an electric guitar, we exemplified how on the same percussion rhythm the guitar can perform extremely varied rhythms, and vice versa. Being a rather intuitive exercise, the results were very different, although the measure was identical in all cases, 4/4. They reveal in most cases the time values and dynamic accents of each participant in the song initially overlaid on the divisional metro-rhythmical structure, and then overlaid in different combinations, resulting in the abstract acoustic friezes characteristic to each variant. It is the perception of rhythm at a microstructural level. The similarity with the frieze type is evident due to the predominantly unidirectional horizontal development.

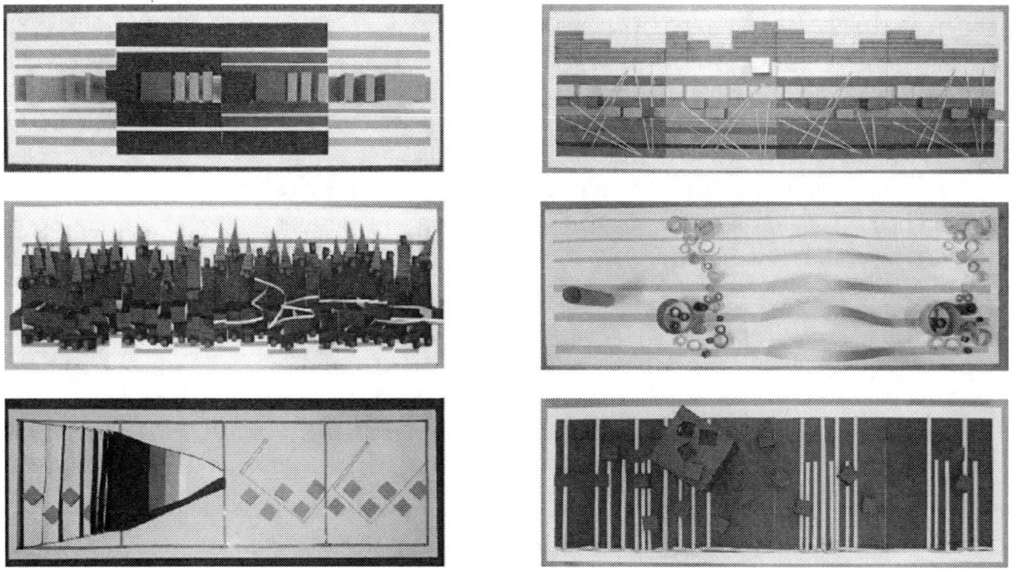

Fig. 4. Student work

However, in other cases, the examples capture rhythm at a macrostructural level, the overall movement of the sound complex, the overall dynamic of sound. In these situations, students have used graphic simulations associated with software used to listen to music on PCs, imitating them in a more or less creative manner. (Fig. 5)

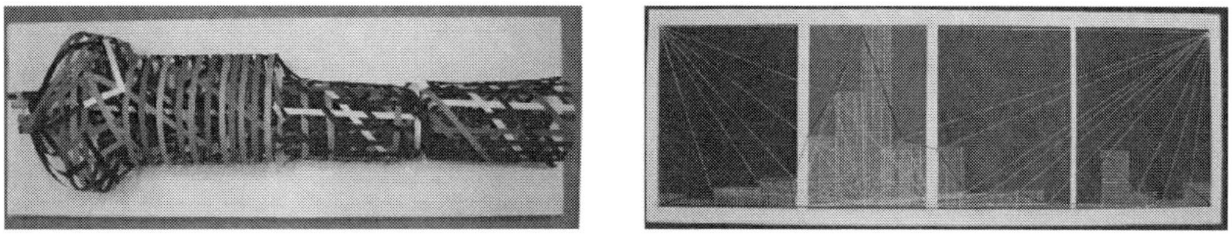

Fig. 5. Student work

The results also confirm notes by Richard Wallaschek (1860-1917), known for his contributions in the fields of comparative musicology and music psychology; he noticed that people perceive music in different ways: some appreciate the musical ensemble of a performance, even if it contains errors; others tend to notice only certain musical elements, beats or chords, while the whole eludes them. Transposing Wallaschek's theory in the visual field, we see an obvious similarity.

5 Conclusions

It is wrong to believe that a rhythm is strictly what is performed by percussion, because each instrument contributes to the interpretation of a musical segment that has its own movement, its own sound dynamics. Similar to music, in architecture and fine arts, in general, we can detect overlaps of multiple rhythms in the same work.

In a multiple instrument or voice composition, the melody of each of these is seconded by its own rhythmic line, except where they would all play in unison, i.e., the same notes using the same rhythm. Polyphony has managed the overlay of different melodies, and polyrhythmy dealt with their rhythms in the art of counterpoint which organically connected them without cancelling their individual meanings. Contemporary electronic music, acoustic and electro-acoustic runs on the same principles, without denying (most times) the real function of measure.

The fact that the students discovered intuitively polyrhythmy by analogy with music is a step forward for the recovery of rhythm as morphological and syntactic language element to its true potential, unfortunately manifested only in the field of sound.

Understanding musical rhythm represents a fertile base for those working in architecture, design and visual arts, in general. The diversity of results obtained illustrates the polyrhythmy and variation specific to musical rhythm, contrary to monorhythmy and isorhythmy.

References

1. P.A. Michelis,. *Estetica arhitecturii (The Aesthetics of Architecture).* Bucureşti, (1982)
2. Y. Hasan, *Paul Klee şi pictura modernă, studiu despre textele lui teoretice (Paul Klee and Modern Painting. Study on His Theoretical Texts).* Bucureşti, (1999).
3. V. Giuleanu, *Principii fundamentale în teoria muzicii (Fundamentals of Music Theory*). Bucureşti, (1975)
4. A. Racolța., *Sincretism vizual şi sonor în ritmurile arhitecturale (Visual and Sound Syncretism in Architectural Rhythms)* Timişoara, (2014)
5. C. Rîpă, *Teoria superioara a muzicii, volumul II – Ritmul (The Superior Theory of Music, Volume II – The Rhythm*) Bucuresti, (2002)
6. A. Racolța, *Rolul ritmului in generarea formei arhitecturale (The Role of Rhythm in Creating Architectural Form).* Forma-Formare-Sens. 281-295. Timisoara, (2013).
7. W. Kandinski, *Spiritualul în artă (The Spiritual in Art).* Bucureşti, (1994).

Shaping the quality of second language learning: Students' perspective

Irina M. Solodkova[1,*], *Elena V.* Grigorieva[1], and *Liliya R.* Ismagilova[1]

[1]Kazan Federal University, 18, Kremlevskaya St., Kazan, 420012, Russia

Abstract. The paper dwells on the problem of identifying the most crucial factors affecting the quality of foreign language learning from the students' perspective. Quality foreign language education is a disputable issue in 21 century due to the increased global workforce competition. Human capital has a great impact on education as an important factor in shaping a new quality of country's economy and well-being of society. Foreign language skill is an integral component of highly qualified professionals as the global economic processes make them participate in cross-border business communication. In these conditions the aim of higher education establishments is to provide quality of language learning and teaching that allows future specialists not to distort the meaning in written and oral communication within their professional framework. The two-phase survey conducted among 67 students of the Institute of Management, Economics and Finance of the Kazan Federal University provided with quantitative data. The respondents ranked differently the factors determining the quality of language learning and teaching responses after two years of completing their foreign language education and were generally satisfied with the quality of service rendered. The obtained results give optimistic forecasts regarding the improvement of foreign language education and help reconsider the way of teaching a foreign language basing on the chosen factors.

Keywords: foreign language, learning, quality foreign language education, communicative competence, facilities and teaching materials, education infrastructure

1 Introduction

Intellectual potential is proclaimed to be the main source of welfare in the 21st century. The potential of human capital could be determined by the extent to which fundamental science is developed, by the overall level of education people of the particular country have, as well as by the accessibility of education to the broad layers of population.

The influential role of human capital has a great impact on education as an important factor in shaping a new quality of country's economy and well-being of society in general. Education is a source of formation of qualified human resources and a key driver in country's competitiveness, its economic growth, its future stability and prosperity [1, 2].

* Corresponding author: imsold@mail.ru

In this regard, the system of higher education is to be modernized, first of all, improving the quality of services rendered. The new quality of education should not be oriented only at assimilation a certain amount of knowledge needed for successful accomplishment of professional duties, but also at the development of future specialists' personality, their cognitive and creative abilities, vital competencies and skills.

In the context of our research we discuss the factors that affect the quality of foreign language education in particular. Authors would like to investigate students' perspective on the discussed issue as they act as the ordering consumers of the educational service. The analysis of students' answers would allow reconsider the way of teaching a foreign language basing on the chosen factors.

Foreign language skill is an integral component of highly qualified professionals as the global economic processes make them participate in cross-border business communication. English for specific purposes is defined as "a complex of linguistic means used by specialists of a certain field of knowledge with the aim to provide an unambiguous understanding" [3]. Following this definition, the aim of higher educational institution is to provide qualitative language proficiency level in their specialty. The one that would allow future specialists to communicate with colleagues worldwide successfully and to become international workforce. That means that the process of teaching a foreign language 'is supposed to be based on effective study strategies and established on the basis of sustainable development, with a high quality result as a final outcome'. High quality teaching is 'to train students to become effective and confident language users, to get involved into problem-solving easily and independently, to become cooperative and excellent workers and integrative thinkers' [4].

2 Theoretical background

It is obvious that the issue of quality in ESP teaching and learning is not a recent trend. The changes that occurred in socio-economic and political spheres in different periods influenced the changes in the requirements for language training. Since 1985, one of the distinctive features of public life in Russia has become an increased interest in a foreign language learning. It happened due to an open policy of the country towards the world community. That period is distinguished by an introduction of early learning of a foreign language in secondary schools, by the transfer of the subject to the category of educational disciplines of federal significance, by an increased number of people (including some narrow specialists) involved into foreign language studying. Thus, the ongoing socio-economic and political processes determine the social requirements of the society to the level and quality of a foreign language. Social order acts as a "strategic benchmark for foreign language teaching policy" [5]. Society requires specialists who are able to communicate with foreigners on topics within their professional framework as well as in everyday informal settings. The same aims are set by the Federal Standard. It indicates the importance of the four language skills (listening, speaking, reading, writing) which have to be acquired to the extent that allows not to distort the meaning in written and oral communication in the professional sphere. So, using English in professional surroundings does not mean using clichés, memorized cues, speech blocks and texts, but the ability to freely combine linguistic units to express their thoughts in any situation.

The English language Syllabus implies the formation of such skills as:

- the ability to use information of a linguistic nature and to master the basics of everyday communication;
- the opportunity to conduct business contacts with foreign partners (including presentations, negotiations, including telephone calls);
- the ability to improve their activities, drawing on the data of foreign sources;

- the ability to process texts in various types of business documents: reports, letters, memos, orders, etc.

Following these points we may assume that to get high quality of language education there should be strict auditing of target that is to develop learners' communicative competence [6, 7, 8]. W. M. Rivers [7] emphasizes the importance of students' ability to interact freely in order to bridge the gap between what they say and what others share. To reach communicative competence language tasks and activities must make students take part in different communicative practices such as 'exchanging information, negotiation of meaning, and interaction' [9]. Lessons structured on communicative method involve language learners in the 'pragmatic, authentic, functional use of language for meaningful purposes, fluency and accuracy are seen as complementary principles underlying communicative techniques, students ultimately have to use the language, productively and receptively, in unrehearsed contexts' [9, 8].

Having defined the aim of language education, it is crucial to detect the factors which help to form and to later maintain and develop high quality of language teaching and learning. I.M. Krsmanović, V. M. Petrović [4] point out four factors affecting quality language teaching, among them: teacher's skills and qualifications; teaching process; working conditions; evaluation and monitoring'.

Hong Thi Nguyen , W. Warren & H. Fehring [8] identified such problems as: the teachers' teaching styles and methods; teachers' classroom management; teachers' investment for teaching; and students' abilities and attitudes.

We agree with S. Hubackova [10] who insists that 'the factors influencing success or failure may be various with each student'. This helps to conclude that particular students' groups have to be tested to later exploit the findings in designing foreign language lessons which could fit the needs on the quality teaching.

Researchers of the quality teaching are convinced that it is no longer possible to take into consideration only traditional factors, connected exclusively with the contents of study, school devices and teaching styles. The aspects like motivation, support at home, prior linguistic knowledge, student personality and even age are said to matter in a foreign language teaching and learning as well [11].

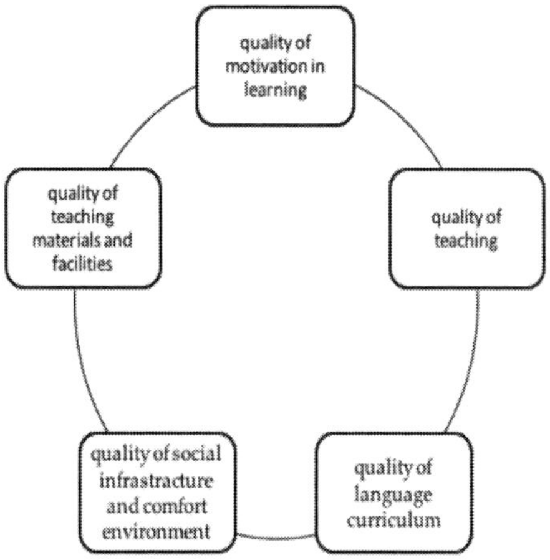

Fig. 1. Factors affecting quality of foreign language learning and teaching.

Literature review and personal pedagogical experience allowed to determine a group of factors which influence the process of foreign language acquisition, bringing it to the desired level of quality. (Fig 1.)

Though, each factor is important by itself only a combination of interdependent and related aspects could help achieve a goal of foreign language teaching. For instance, students may assume that their motivational level is enough to guarantee high quality learning, however they might lose it in case there is no rapport in the classroom or if a teacher uses outdate information for discussion. Clearly, some factors from students' perspective would be given more importance than others but it is this what could provide us with the evidence what to pay attention to while working with particular groups.

Let us consider each factor in details. Motivation in learning. Motivation, according to Harmer [12] is an internal drive which pushes someone to do things in order to achieve something. Penny Ur [13] thinks that it is better to articulate this term from the point of view of ' a motivated student'. This is the one who is willing or even eager to invest effort in learning activities and to progress.

R.C. Gardner [14] provides 3 main characteristics of a motivated learner, he is the one who is (a) eager to learn the language, (b) willing to expend effort on the learning activity, and (c) willing to sustain the learning activity".

Motivation and success in education are interconnected. Success in a foreign language acquisition is linked to motivation in particular. As well as R.C. Gardner [14], Z. Dornyei [15], R. L. Oxford & J. Shearin [16] we believe that attitude and motivation play a major role in a foreign language acquisition.

Foreign language is a subject that requires constant motivational level especially if is acquired in simulated, unreal conditions lacking the communication with native speakers. Motivation in second language is an eclectic, multifaceted construct, hence it needs to include different levels to integrate the various components [17]. If there is a real life application of a foreign language it would be learnt faster and more successfully. Students would have high level of motivation if they are encouraged a certain goal to achieve - to be able to travel, to find new friends, to be employed. Intrinsic motives can be fostered by 'theme-based curriculum' [11], by positive atmosphere in the classroom, by enthusiastic teacher and his/her teaching style and the way of communication with learners. Students could have de-motivating factors: 'lack of confidence in their English proficiency, crowded classes with unequal students' English levels' [8].

As motivation depends on quality teacher, here we turn to the second factor quality teaching, by which we mean teachers' skills and qualifications, teaching style and methods, approaches used as well as their personal characteristics.

The first and foremost aspect is teaching approach. We agree with M. Lochana & G. Deb [18], J. C. Richards [9], G.M. Jacobs & S. Hall [19] who consider the importance of student-centered collaborative approach, which in modern foreign language education paradigm is regarded to be the most effective. Following the definition of collaborative teaching and learning that is a 'variety of educational approaches involving joint intellectual effort by students, or students and teachers together' [20] we could point out its advantages over the traditional teacher-centered approach, as it:

- 'stands against the competitive system followed in a traditional classroom' [21];
- 'allows to obtain greater resources, recognition and reward when facing competition for finite resources' [22];
- treats 'teachers and students as equal partners, they can 'actively interact by sharing experiences and take on asymmetry roles' [23];
- helps teachers and students 'capitalize on one another's resources and skills (asking one another for information, evaluating one another's ideas, monitoring one another's work, etc.)' [24, 25];
- 'aims to provide learners with interactive tasks that can help them develop communicative competence [9].

The forms of interaction vary but all of them create atmosphere for productive foreign language communication. In a group work students work in small groups on tasks that entail interaction: conveying information, for example, or group decision-making, while a teacher walks around, listening, intervenes little if at all. In a question and answer form students answer teacher's questions, make their own questions to peers; a teacher is an expert and observer. When working individually, students work on tasks independently, and a teacher gives a task or a set of tasks, walks around monitoring and assisting where necessary. If we consider a collaboration form, students do the same sort of tasks as in 'individual work', but work together, usually in pairs; a teacher may or may not intervene (consulting). If a student happens to act as a teacher, students create tasks for quizzes and games, and the teacher consults on preparatory stage and participates in doing the tasks. In full-class interaction students debate a topic or do a language task as a class; a teacher may intervene occasionally to stimulate participation or to monitor [26].

Fulfilling the ideas of student-centered education teachers imply many roles. Ability to perform several tasks at ones appeals to English language teachers. They facilitate the process of learning, assist and navigate, provide guidance, solve disagreements. To provide high quality teaching teachers have to be engaged in constant development and take part in research. I. M. Krsmanović, V. M. Petrović [4] in their research distinguish six core components of teacher knowledge: a) practical knowledge: the teacher's repertoire of classroom techniques and strategies; b) content knowledge: the teacher's competence of grammar, phonology, second language acquisition, teaching theories; c) contextual knowledge: familiarity with the school context, norms, cultural and other relevant information; d) pedagogical knowledge: ability to restructure content knowledge for teaching purposes and to plan, adapt, improvise; e) personal knowledge: the teacher's personal beliefs and principles, and his/her individual approach to teaching; f) reflective knowledge: the teacher's capacity to reflect on and access his/ her own practice.

It is said that expert teacher could 'compensate for deficiencies in the curriculum or the resources' [4]. It is true if the teacher is experienced and enthusiastic enough, sooner or later it would be problematic to deliver high quality teaching if there is a lack of modern facilities and studying materials. Quality of teaching materials and facilities have a great impact on language learning and teaching, as well as, the quality of language curriculum on the basis of which materials are chosen [27]. Their findings prove that both students and teachers agree with an idea of an important role of facilities and quality textbooks play in efficient language education.

The choice of facilities and teaching materials is determined by the curriculum. The main aim of a quality curriculum is 'to enable students to acquire and develop the knowledge, skills and values, and the associated capabilities and competencies, to lead meaningful and productive lives'. The curriculum is considered to be successful if the students demonstrate stable progresses and implement that knowledge for their 'personal, social, physical, cognitive, moral, psychological and emotional development' [28]. English language curriculum should opt for relevance, be up-to-date, provide solid knowledge of the studied subject, guarantee flexibility and set clear aims.

High quality teaching and learning cannot be delivered without satisfactory education infrastructure. Overcrowded classes with old, sometimes broken furniture, absence of modern devices as computers, overhead projectors, white boards and labs hinder efficient and productive studying. Otherwise, comfortable studying conditions could enhance students' progress and increase motivation. That why, when we speak about language education we refer to infrastructure, which together with highly qualified teaching staff, effective teaching materials and facilities ensure quality foreign language acquisition.

3 Methods

To obtain both qualitative and quantitative data the following collection methods were used: theoretical (analysis, generalization); diagnostic (questionnaire, interview), empirical (students observation); methods of statistics and graphic results.

The survey was conducted during the period from 2015 to 2017 at the Department of Foreign Languages in Economics, Business and Finance of the Institute of Management, Economics and Finance of the KFU. 67 first and second-year students of the same focus group of different cognitive abilities, score results, language proficiency and both genders were involved as the participants in this research. Participants' responses were confident and for research purpose only.

The focus group was interviewed twice: at the beginning of the first-year course and at the end of the second-year one. The aim of the survey was to find out what factors affect the quality of foreign language learning and teaching from students' perspective. The questionnaire comprised 3 types of questions specifically suited to the aim of the research: rank order scaling question requiring the students to rank the given factors according to their importance, closed question which supposed students to circle 'yes' or 'no' answer, open-ended question involving respondents' own answers. Q1 was designed to find out to what extent each factor has importance for the students. Q2 was aimed to define if students are satisfied or not with the quality of foreign language learning and teaching (for 2'd year students only). Q3 was devoted to clarify what influences the quality of foreign language learning and teaching from students' perspective.

4 Findings

The results obtained from the responses on the questionnaire (Q1) conducted among the first-year students revealed that the respondents ranked the factors from the most to the least essential (from 1 to 5) as follows:

1. quality of teaching
2. quality of teaching materials and facilities
3. quality of motivation in learning
4. quality of language curriculum
5. quality of social infrastructure and comfort environment (Fig.2).

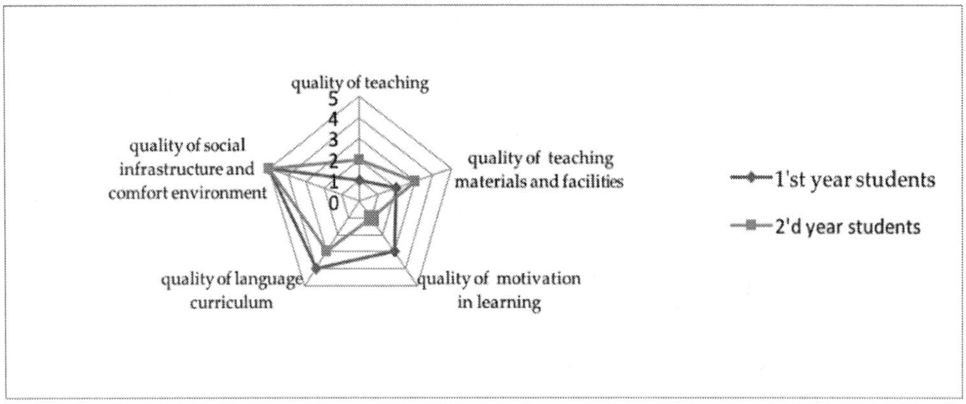

Fig. 2. Rank order of factors.

The factor "quality of teaching" was prioritized by almost a half of students (48%) while no one ranked "quality of social infrastructure and comfort environment" as the most important by ranging it as number 4 or 5. The "quality of teaching materials and facilities" received mostly ranks 2, 3 and 1, "quality of motivation in learning" – 2 and 3 though 4.5% of respondents found this factor as dominating; "quality of language curriculum" was ranked 3, 4 and 5.

After the two years of study the ranking of factors showed the next scale:

1. quality of motivation in learning
2. quality of teaching
3. quality of teaching materials and facilities
4. quality of language curriculum
5. quality of social infrastructure and comfort environment (Fig.2)

The 2'd year students pleaded the "quality of motivation in learning" factors determining. The "quality of teaching" was prioritized by 28% and gathered the ranks from 1 to 3. Meanwhile the "quality of teaching materials and facilities" and "quality of language curriculum" scored the equal ranks of 3 and 4. The factor "social infrastructure and comfort environment" has not changed its rank 5.

The answers to the Q2 demonstrated that the students were mostly satisfied with quality of the language learning and teaching: 73% responded positively, 22% responded negatively, 4.5% didn't indicate their attitude.

The responses to the Q3 gave evidence that students mostly admitted that time management, appealing to the future profession; contemporaneity of language curriculum affected their quality of learning. Some pointed out personal attitude of a teacher toward them, and the system of monitoring and progress-checking as influential aspects.

5 Discussion

The comparative analysis showed that students recentralized the learning from teacher instructing to personal acquisition of language. To shape the students' willingness to study it was necessary to develop motivation stimulating the full realization of cognitive potential; to form the skills and abilities of effective learning; to target at the sustainable achieving of the results; to enhance students' confidence. The constant aspiration of students to improve their language competence was developed by student-centered approach; the creation of achievable perspectives in mastering foreign language; stimulating initiative, activity and perseverance; formation of "competitive personality" environment.

It was noted that increase in skills and competence took place when individual work was organized and effective methodological assistance to the student was provided; the hours for self-education were increased; interactive forms and techniques of teaching were implemented; individual creative assignments and the active involvement of students in research and development were carried out. Thus role of teacher shifted from the leading to assisting but was still vital.

Moreover, the quality of teaching encouraged personal motivation of students and their level of knowledge. Personal interest of teachers in obtaining a high result of their students defined the quality of motivation in learning. The most successful approach is to organize and implement the search process, to initiate the class activity, to motivate and aim students at revealing their potential for competitiveness.

The fact that factors 'quality of teaching materials and facilities' and 'quality of language curriculum' were reconsidered to be equally important constitutes that means of transmitting information and applicability of knowledge are vital for contemporary students. Furthermore, the quality is measured not in numbers, but by the timeliness and suitability for the learning of modern specialists. These will allow not only to diversify the learning process of ESP but significantly improve foreign language acquisition.

However, the factor 'quality of social infrastructure and comfort environment' reached the least popularity among young generation which demonstrates that decorations of premises, number of students in one class, existence of advanced equipment was not found to be a priority when discussing the issue of quality education.

The created atmosphere of cooperation and collaboration, proper teaching process, updated methods and materials developed prospects for the success of each student and facilitated their confidence, which made the majority of students be satisfied with the quality of learning and teaching.

6 Conclusion

Research carried out and the results gained allowed the authors to conclude that students recognize quality education, have their own understanding of this phenomena and factors affecting it. A combination of 5 quality factors could provide students with adequate learning environment to acquire communicative competence. The acknowledgment of student's opinions is substantial for optimization and facilitating educational process in order to form qualified human resources. The results received give optimistic forecasts regarding the improvement of the quality education.

References

1. E.V. Grigoryeva & I.M Solodkova, *Foreign language skill as a component of self-development procedure: undergraduate and graduate levels.* Social Sciences and Interdisciplinary Behavior - Proceedings, 99, (2016)
2. A. Pulverness., I.I. Klimova, O.A. Kalugina, D.G. Vasbieva, L.R. Ismagilova, *The formation of students' intercultural communicative competence in an English language learning environment at a non-linguistic higher school.* XLinguae, **10**, (4), 381, (2017)
3. S.V. Kolyadko, *Problems of selecting a productive lexical minimum for teaching foreign language communication in a non-linguistic university. Linguistic education in the university: A methodical manual for teachers of higher education, postgraduate students, students.*- SPb .: KARO, **4**, 113, (2005)
4. I.M. Krsmanović & V.M. Petrović, *Factors affecting quality in teaching English (as a second language).* 6th Research/Expert Conference with International Participations "Quality 2009", Neum, B&H, 702, (2009)
5. N. Galskova, *Modern Methods of Foreign Languages: A Handbook for Teachers.* 2nd ed., Moscow: ARCTI, 15, (2003)
6. L.A. Liu, *New Perspective on the Goals of TEFL in China.* Internet TESL J., **IX,** (11), (2003)
7. W.A. Rivers, *A practical guide to the teaching of English as a second or foreign language.* New York: Oxford University Press, (1978)
8. H.T. Nguyen, W. Warren & H. Fehring, *Factors Affecting English Language Teaching and Learning in Higher Education.* Engl. Lang. Teach., **7**, (8), 97, (2014)
9. J.C. Richards, *Approaches and methods in language teaching* (2nd ed.). Cambridge, U.K., (2001)
10. S. Hubackova, *Factors influencing the quality of teaching and the foreign language knowledge.* 7th World Conference on Educational Sciences, (WCES-2015), Novotel Athens Convention Center, Athens, Greece. Procedia - PROCD SOC BEHV, **197**, 1952, (2015)

11. A. Miller, *9 factors that influence language learning.* Retrieved from https://www.whitbyschool.org/passionforlearning/9-factors-that-influence-language-learning,(n.d.)
12. J. Harmer, *The Practice of English Language Teaching* // Essex: Longman Press, 51, (2001)
13. Penny Ur, *A course in Language Teaching. Practice and Theory,* Cambridge University Press, (1996)
14. R.C. Gardner, *Social psychology and second language learning: The role of attitudes and motivation.* London: Edward Arnold, (1985)
15. Z. Dornyei, *Motivation in second and foreign language learning.* ET: Int. Ab. J. for Lang. Teach., **31**, (3), 117, (1990)
16. R. Oxford & J. Shearin, *Language Learning Motivation: Expanding the Theoretical Framework.* Mod. Lang. J., **78**, 12, (1994)
17. Z. Dornyei, *Motivation and motivating in the language foreign language classroom.* Mod. Lang. J., **78**, (3), 273, (1994)
18. M. Lochana & G. Deb, *Task-based teaching: Learning English without tears.* Asian EFL J., **8**, (3), 140, (2006)
19. G.M. Jacobs & S. Hall, *Implementing cooperative learning.* In J. C. Richards, & A. W. Renandya (Eds.), *Methodology in language teaching: An anthology of current practice.* New York: Cambridge University Press, 52, (2002)
20. B.L. Smith & J.T. MacGregor, *"What is Collaborative Learning?"* in Goodsell, Maher, Tinto, Smith & MacGregor's. *Collaborative Learning: A Sourcebook for Higher Education*; National Center on Postsecondary Teaching, Learning and Assessment; Pennsylvania State University, (1992)
21. Dr. K. B. Ranee, edited by: N. Gunnell *A Definition of Collaborative Learning.* Retrieved from http://www.brighthubeducation.com/teaching-methods-tips/69801-definition-of-collaborative-learning/, (2012)
22. C.S. Wagner, & L. Leydesdorff, *Globalisation in the network of science in 2005: The diffusion of international collaboration and the formation of a core group*, (2005)
23. R. Mitnik, M. Recabarren, M. Nussbaum, & A. Soto, *Collaborative Robotic Instruction: A Graph Teaching Experience.* Comp. & Ed., **53,** (2), 330, (2009)
24. M.M. Chiu, *Group problem solving processes: Social interactions and individual actions.* Theory Soc. Behv., **30**, (1), 600, (2000)
25. M.M. Chiu, *Flowing toward correct contributions during groups' mathematics problem solving: A statistical discourse analysis.* J. Learn. Sci., **17**, (3), 415, (2008)
26. E.O. Zalyaeva, I.M. Solodkova, *Teacher-student collaboration: Institute of economics and finance Kazan federal university approach.* Procedia - PROCD SOC BEHV, **152**, 1039, (2014)
27. T.T. Abebe, & L.M. Davidson, *Assessing the role of visual teaching materials in teaching English vocabulary (Report).* Lang. In India, **12**, (3), 524, (2012)
28. P. Stabback, *What Makes a Quality Curriculum? Current and Critical Issues in Curriculum and Learning*, **2**, IBE/2016/WP/CD/02, (2016)

Font games in typography education: Typewar

Hatice Öz Pektaş[1]*

[1]Nişantaşı Universitesi, Commonication Design Departmnent, 34398 Istanbul, Turkey

Abstract. Typography is an area of expertise that focuses on artistic and design-based features and production technologies of all printed scripts. Although typography is an important element of many design branches, it is primarily one of the basic courses of Communication Design, Visual Communication Design, and Graphic Design departments. Current education methods are outdated and boring for the young target audience who got used to a lifestyle full of computers and mobile devices. Digital games are important means used in educational environments thanks to computer technologies. In 2017-2018 Academic Year's Fall Semester, 20 students from Graphic Design and Communication Design Departments who took Typography I course was made to play "typewar" game and the results of the games were recorded and the success of the students in recognizing the writing types in this game was measured. The typewar game was preferred in order to teach students "the anatomical structures of the whole alphabet by introducing serif and non-serif fonts" as a purpose of the course. In the research, it was observed that there was a difference in the number of the font types that students can remember and distinguish between classical methods and typewar game. In the survey made after the game, students' opinion on the use of games in typography education was taken.

1 Introduction

To recognize the serif and non-serif fonts and to learn the whole anatomical structure of alphabet.

1.1 Quoted fonts

Quoted fonts are still widely used in books and encyclopedias. While we encounter with them rarely, they are frequently used in blog posts and they continue to make the digital world more beautiful both for readability and stylish designs.

The greatest benefit that they provide is that they are understandable and not eye-straining. The dentations that are added to the letter ends make them clearer and the eyes spend much less time to see a letter and deliver it to the brain and the brain gets tired much latter accordingly [6, 7].

* Corresponding author: hatice.pektas@nisantasi.edu.tr

1.2 Sans serif fonts

Their main feature is that they do not have any quote, cedilla, notch and dentation and they provide top level aesthetics. For the considerably long letters, the reader feels that the letters converge as it concentrates and the eyes becomes tired swiftly. Such fonts are mostly used for short materials such as signs, titles, short children's books and places with aesthetic concerns [3, 4].

1.3 Problem

The term "typography" was first used to describe Johan Gutenberg's metal letters. Today, it is regarded as a field of expertise dealing with the artistic and design-based features and production technologies of all printed scripts. Typography is the visual and functional editing made on a page specified by the elements needed for letters, words, and spacing. Although typography is an important element of many design branches, it is primarily one of the basic courses of Communication Design, Visual Communication Design, and Graphic Design departments. At the undergraduate level, typography education requires a theoretical and practical curriculum. [3, 4, 6, 7].

1.4 Purpose

The objective of this research is to emphasize that learning through game contributes to university education. It further aims to observe and evaluate the impact of the different games in the typography lectures in the department of graphic design on the learning.

1.5 Importance of research

The content of Typography I course includes: The development of alphabet; face types; right typeface selection; spacing, punctuation marks and problems in text editing and solutions; rules of script use.

Students who took the class are expected to be able to these: 1. To have a good grasp of Basic Typography concepts and to express them. 2. To recognize the serif and non-serif fonts and to learn the whole anatomical structure of alphabet. 3. To be able to distinguish the readability of texts after spacing. 4. To keep the script readable and to use it properly. 5. To be able to recognize the fonts and their families quickly with experimental studies. 6. To be able to see the result of right font selection in design.

Typewar game was preferred in order to teach students "the anatomical structures of the whole alphabet by introducing serif and non-serif fonts" as a purpose of the course. It is very crucial for a communication designer to distinguish between font types. For this reason, Typewar is a fun game of font identification and learning for both beginners and experienced designers. Typewar was developed by the Massive Overrated company and it is available both on mobile and web. In the game, two different font type is shown on the screen and you are expected to name them. After selecting the font type regarding your guess, right answer and the score screen is shown [8, 9, 10, 11, 12].

While playing, you can see your accumulated score on the bottom of the screen. If you guess right your score goes up and if guess wrong it goes down. As you level up, new font types are shown. The longer you play Typewar, the more font types are unlocked and difficulty increases. Although the game gets more difficult as new font types are added, there are many ways to choose the right answer. In Typewar, if you choose the right font type, your score goes up and if you choose the wrong answer your score goes down. There is no time limit, beginning or ending in the game. [8, 9, 10, 11, 12].

2 Research methods

In 2017-2018 Academic Year's Fall Semester, 20 students from Graphic Design and Communication Design Departments who took Typography I course was made to play "typewar" game and the results of the games were recorded and the success of the students in recognizing the writing types in this game was measured..

In the research, students were first shown the names of different font types and were taught their distinguishing features with examples. Then, they were asked to tell the names of font types they remember and recognize some of the font types in the examples shown in the class.

2.1 Research group

We have selected the students of Department of Graphic Design, Faculty of Art and Design in Nisantasi University as a research group.

2.2 Sample group

Selected research group represents the university students at graphic design department, having an age range of 18-25.

2.3 Data gathering system

We have used the game screen of the students as a data collection tool. We have interpreted the views on the screenshots and asked for the students who play the game about their opinions.

2.4 Data Analysis

It was observed that the number of font types they can remember and distinguish after the classical method and after the typewar game was different. In the survey made after the game, students' opinion on the use of games in typography education was taken.

3 Findings

As a result of the research and survey, it can be said that the use of typewear game for educational purpose increases the students' interest in the course and contributes to the learning of typography.

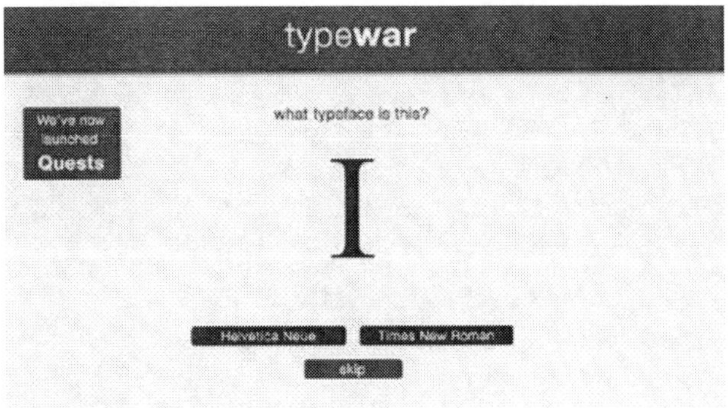

Fig. 1. "I" Times New Roman or Helvetica Neue

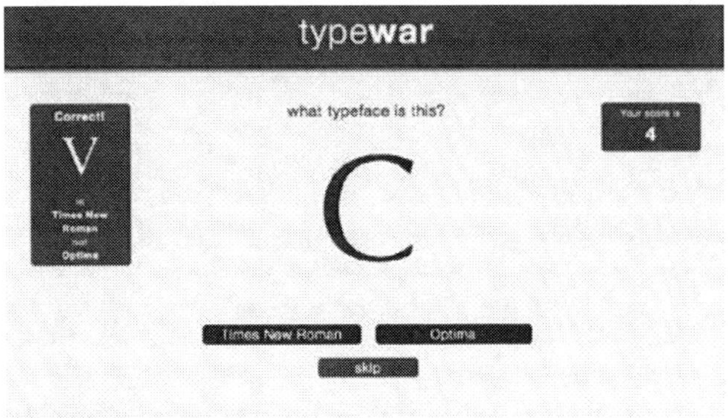

Fig. 2. "C" Times New Roman or Optima

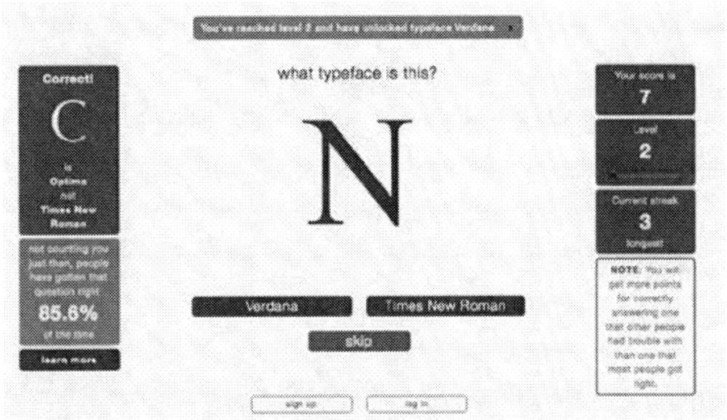

Fig. 3. "N" Times New Roman or Verdana

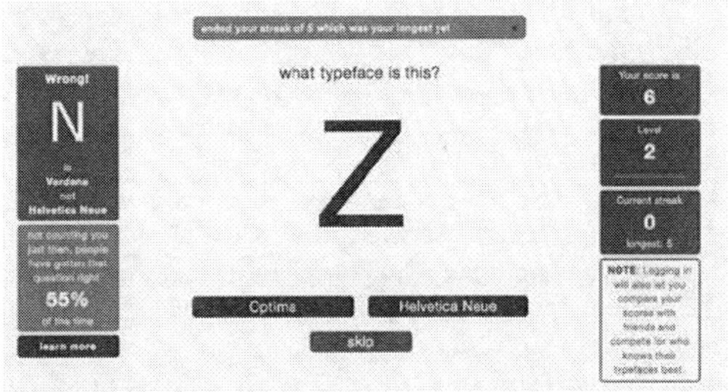

Fig. 4. "Z" Helvetica Neue or Optima

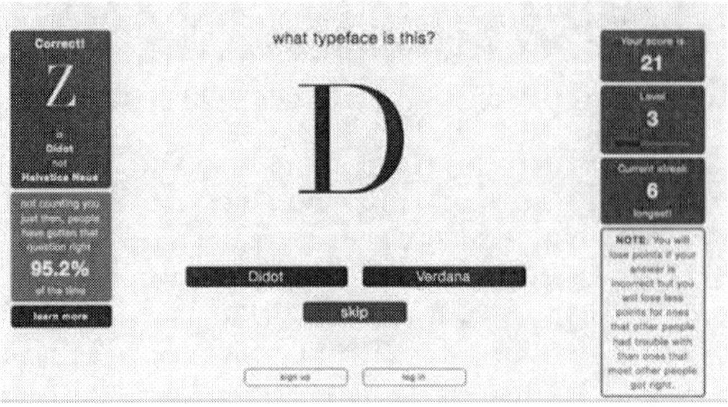

Fig. 5. "D" Didot or Verdana

4 Discussion

Digital game based learning aims to teach students through educational computer games. The characteristics of the digital game based learning is an intentional education by students. They can be any form of educational computer games like normal computer games: strategy, action and etc. For each content, students can be offered a wide range of different learning methods through many types of game. Educational computer games provide hidden learning. In other words, the student plays the computer game with a joy and realizes that he has learned when the game is over. Educational computer games can be combined with other learning methods and provide complete learning [1, 2, 5].

5 Appreciations

As a result of the research and survey, it can be said that the use of typewar game for educational purpose increases the students' interest in the course and contributes to the learning of typography.

References

1. Binark, M., Bayraktutan Sütçü, G., Barış Fidaner, Işık., Dijital Oyun Rehberi, Kalkedon Yayınları (2010)
2. Binark, M., Dijital Oyun, Kalkedon Yayınları (2008)
3. Harris, P., Ambrose, Görsel Tipografi Sözlüğü, Literatür Yayıncılık (2012)
4. Harris, P., Ambrose, G., Grafik Tasarımda Tipografi, Literatür Yayıncılık (2014)
5. Prensky, Marc *"Digital Natives, Digital Immigrants"* On the Horizon (MCB University Press, Vol. 9 No. 5, October 2001)
6. Sarıkavak, N., Tipografinin Temelleri, Doruk Yayınları (1997)
7. Sarıkavak, N., Çağdaş Tipografinin Temelleri, Seçkin Yayıncılık (2014)
8. www.typewar.com (01.07.2018)
9. *"Typewar and The Font Game for iPhone"* https://www.macworld.com/article/1150829/typewar_thefontgame.html (Date of acces: 01.07.2018)
10. *"Typeface Clustering Based on Typewar"* https://eldarion.com/blog/2010/02/02/typeface-clustering-based-typewar/ (Date of acces: 01.07.2018)

11. *"Typewar: Points and Levels"* https://eldarion.com/blog/2010/01/20/typewar-points-and-levels/ (Date of acces: 01.07.2018)
12. *"Best Typography Games for Designers"* https://medium.com/@order_group/best-type-games-for-designers-e51f17bbe464" (Date of acces: 01.07.2018)

AUTHOR INDEX

AUTHOR INDEX